# Oracle Enterprise Manager Cloud Control 12*c*: Managing Data Center Chaos

Get to grips with the latest innovative techniques for managing data center chaos including performance tuning, security compliance, patching, and more

**Porus Homi Havewala (OCM)**

[PACKT] PUBLISHING enterprise
professional expertise distilled

BIRMINGHAM - MUMBAI

# Oracle Enterprise Manager Cloud Control 12*c*: Managing Data Center Chaos



First published: December 2012

Production Reference: 1111212

Published by Packt Publishing Ltd.
Livery Place
35 Livery Street
Birmingham B3 2PB, UK.

ISBN 978-1-84968-478-1

www.packtpub.com

Cover Image by John M. Quick (john.m.quick@gmail.com)

# Credits

**Author**
Porus Homi Havewala

**Reviewers**
Kamran Agayev A.
Richard Ridge
Mark Fletcher

**Acquisition Editors**
Stephanie Moss
Robin de Jongh

**Lead Technical Editor**
Arun Nadar

**Technical Editors**
Charmaine Pereira
Prashant Salvi

**Copy Editors**
Brandt D'Mello
Insiya Morbiwala
Aditya Nair
Alfida Paiva

**Project Coordinator**
Joel Goveya

**Proofreader**
Kevin McGowan

**Indexer**
Tejal Soni

**Production Coordinator**
Nitesh Thakur

**Cover Work**
Nitesh Thakur

# About the Author

**Porus Homi Havewala** works as the Senior Manager (for database management) in the Enterprise Technology Program Office of Oracle Corporation, based in Singapore, and specializes in Oracle Enterprise Manager. He is a double **Oracle Certified Master (OCM)** in 10*g* and 11*g*, as well as the first Oracle employee ACE in the country. He was awarded the prestigious Oracle ACE Director title by Oracle HQ in 2008. There are less than 150 Oracle ACE Directors in the entire world and Porus was the very first Oracle ACE and ACE Director in Singapore – a recognition of his outstanding achievements in the Oracle world.

Porus has had extensive experience in Oracle technology since 1994; this includes him working as a Senior Production DBA, Principal Database Consultant, Database Architect, E-Business Technical DBA, Development DBA, and Database Designer and Modeler (using Oracle Designer). He has published numerous articles on Oracle Enterprise Manager on OTN, and has created `http://enterprise-manager.blogspot.com`, one of the world's first blogs dedicated to Enterprise Manager (with Oracle Press Credentials). Porus is also the author of the book, *Oracle Enterprise Manager Grid Control, Rampant TechPress* which was published in 2010.

He started in the IT industry in the mid-1980s as a Turbo-C programmer in India and then as a dBase/FoxPro Developer in Australia. In the early 1990s he wrote a book on Microsoft FoxPro, which was his first published technical work. He entered the heady world of Oracle technology from 1994 as an Oracle DBA/Developer (using Oracle Forms, Oracle Reports, and Oracle Designer).

In Telstra, the largest telecommunications company in Australia, Porus was the Senior Database Consultant in the central DBA team for a number of years and was responsible for database standards, database architecture, and the architecture, setup, and management of the first production Enterprise Manager Grid Control site in the world. He next worked in Oracle ACS India (Mumbai), and then with an Oracle Platinum Partner, S&I Systems in Singapore, before rejoining Oracle in the same city.

Porus is an enthusiast for Oracle technology, especially Oracle Enterprise Manager, on which he has conducted popular seminars and webinars for large MNCs, and implemented this powerful enterprise toolset. The following is a full list of his published technical articles and white papers on the **Oracle Technical Network (OTN)**. A couple of these articles were in the most popular OTN article list in 2009. The OTN is the world's largest community of developers, DBAs, and architects.

Published white papers on OTN include:

- *Advanced Uses of Oracle Enterprise Manager 11g*
- *Managing Oracle Applications with Oracle Enterprise Manager 11g*

Published technical articles on OTN include:

- *Using Grid Control with Filer Snapshotting*
- *Oracle Enterprise Manager Grid Control Architecture for Very Large Sites*
- *Oracle RMAN Backups: Pushing the Easy Button*
- *Patch a Thousand Databases, Using Oracle Enterprise Manager Grid Control*
- *Easy Disaster Proof Production with Grid Control*
- *Using Oracle GoldenGate for Real-Time Data Integration*
- *Mask Your Secrets Using Oracle Enterprise Manager*
- *Manage Mass Provisioning Using Oracle Enterprise Manager Grid Control*
- *Overview of Oracle EM Management Packs*
- *Provision Your Oracle RAC Systems Using Oracle Enterprise Manager*
- *Ease the Chaos with Automated Patching: Oracle Enterprise Manager Cloud Control 12c*

For the Internet links to the articles and white papers, please see the blog entry:

`http://enterprise-manager.blogspot.sg/2012/11/latest-list-of-published-white-papers.html`

In early 2009, Porus was also voted leader of the Oracle RAC **Special Interest Group (SIG)** in Singapore, a rotating position he held for 2 years.

# Acknowledgements

No book is complete without an initial dedication and a thanks to all. I would like to dedicate this book to Lord Shri Ganesha, who is India's favorite deity - the Lord of Beginnings (every Start is dedicated to Him) and the Remover of obstacles. I pray for His Blessings on this work of mine, may it be a Success.

I also dedicate this book to a great revered saint of my Zoroastrian religion, Sant Dasturji Jamshedji Sorabji Kukadaru Saheb, who worked various miracles in his lifetime and to whom all of my Parsi community prays, when they need divine help. I pray for His Blessings on this work of mine, may it be a Success.

I would also like to dedicate this book to my dear departed father, Shri Homi Maneckji Havewala, who was a great unpublished writer of the English language and who imparted his love of English, as well as all things spiritual, to me as his only son. I pray for his Blessings on this work of mine, may it be a Success.

I would like to thank everyone involved in the book, especially my readers who have stood by me on the internet, making my Enterprise Manager articles on OTN quite popular over the years. It is for the readers that a writer writes, even a technical writer, and I have been blessed with excellent readers who have appreciated my enthusiasm for the product.

Most importantly, I would like to thank Havovi, my beloved wife who has helped and supported me throughout the writing of this book.

As always, I would like to thank my ex-manager, David Russell, who lives and works in Australia. I was the Lead Database Architect for Enterprise Manager under his corporate database technologies team for many years, and it is there that I started working with Enterprise Manager Grid Control 10*g*. Our company was the first production site for this version of Enterprise Manager. It is indeed true that a good manager can actually make a person's career, and David has done this with his continual appreciation and encouragement, and I thank him for it.

I would like to thank all the editorial staff at Packt Publishing for helping out with the publication and editing of this book through all the versions and chapters.

Thanks are also due to my management at Oracle Corporation for their encouragement and support in writing the book, and to the Oracle Legal team for allowing the use of screenshots of the product from various sources.

Of course, the views and opinions expressed in this book are entirely my own, and do not represent the views and position of Oracle Corporation.

# About the Reviewers

**Kamran Agayev A.** is an Oracle ACE and Oracle Certified Professional DBA working at AzerCell Telecom. He's an author of the book, *Oracle Backup & Recovery*, published by *Rampant TechPress* , and also shares his experience with a lot of step-by-step articles and video tutorials in his blog, `http://kamranagayev.com`.

He also makes presentations at Oracle OpenWorld, TROUG, and local events.

**Richard Ridge** is currently the APAC Database Manager for First Data. Richard has spent more than 15 years working as a Database Administrator and leading database administration teams. Richard has worked for large global corporations in the finance and telecommunication industry in both Australia and the UK, and has a strong background in running large and complex database platforms. He is an ex-colleague of the author.

**Mark Fletcher** has over 22 years of experience in the computer industry, working his way up from a simple Operator, to Helpdesk Support, to Programmer, Analyst, and Consultant. After working for 13 years with Oracle, which involved engagements in a number of countries, he is now putting what he has learned through his many experiences to practice in a large Australian company. He is also an ex-colleague of the author.

# www.PacktPub.com

## Support files, eBooks, discount offers and more

You might want to visit www.PacktPub.com for support files and downloads related to your book.

Did you know that Packt offers eBook versions of every book published, with PDF and ePub files available? You can upgrade to the eBook version at www.PacktPub.com and as a print book customer, you are entitled to a discount on the eBook copy. Get in touch with us at service@packtpub.com for more details.

At www.PacktPub.com, you can also read a collection of free technical articles, sign up for a range of free newsletters and receive exclusive discounts and offers on Packt books and eBooks.

PACKTLIB®

http://PacktLib.PacktPub.com

Do you need instant solutions to your IT questions? PacktLib is Packt's online digital book library. Here, you can access, read and search across Packt's entire library of books.

## Why Subscribe?

- Fully searchable across every book published by Packt
- Copy and paste, print and bookmark content
- On demand and accessible via web browser

## Free Access for Packt account holders

If you have an account with Packt at www.PacktPub.com, you can use this to access PacktLib today and view nine entirely free books. Simply use your login credentials for immediate access.

## Instant Updates on New Packt Books

Get notified! Find out when new books are published by following @PacktEnterprise on Twitter, or the *Packt Enterprise* Facebook page.

# Table of Contents

# Preface

I would like to extend a warm welcome to all readers of this new book, *Oracle Enterprise Manager Cloud Control 12c: Managing Data Center Chaos*.

You are about to enter the exciting and wonderful world of Enterprise Manager, Oracle's premium product for management of the Oracle stack, right from the application layer down to disk level.

If you have used Enterprise Manager before and are aware of its capabilities, this will be a good primer for learning the brand new capabilities of the new version. For people who want to be introduced to Enterprise Manager for the first time, this will be a whole new world drawn from my professional experience of many years in the IT industry, written in easy-to-understand English.

I have included a number of advanced topics that demonstrate how Enterprise Manager Cloud Control 12*c* aids in database performance management, configuration management, security compliance, automated provisioning, automated patching, and database change management. You will also learn how Cloud Control 12*c* allows Exadata database machine monitoring and management, test data management for subsetting data of large databases, and sensitive data de-identification using data masking. This is followed by various real-life examples and case studies of actual Oracle customers to show how they have benefited from using Oracle Enterprise Manager.

Sit back and enjoy!

## What this book covers

*Chapter 1, Chaos at Data Centers*, introduces the reader to the typical chaos in data centers and discusses the way these common issues are normally resolved, by manual labor or manual scripting using extensive human resources.

*Chapter 2, Enter Oracle Cloud Control*, reveals Oracle Enterprise Manager Cloud Control 12*c* as the suggested solution for managing the typical data center. The chapter includes recommended installation techniques and best architecture practices for this latest version of Oracle Enterprise Manager.

Additional content about this chapter can be found in the online chapter [italics] Installation/Upgrade Tactics and Architecture for Large Sites [/italics] at: `http://www.packtpub.com/sites/default/files/downloads/4781EN_Installation_Upgrade_Tactics_and_Architecture_for_Large_Sites.pdf`

*Chapter 3, Ease the Chaos with Performance Management*, explains how Cloud Control 12*c* aids in database performance management by guaranteeing performance levels, proactively using various innovative techniques for diagnosis and tuning.

*Chapter 4, Ease the Chaos with Configuration Management and Security Compliance,* demonstrates how Cloud Control 12*c* aids in configuration management by automatically discovering components, collecting configuration information, and allowing configuration comparisons and historical searches of changes. Configuration compliance and security compliance is also explained.

*Chapter 5, Ease the Chaos with Automated Provisioning*, demonstrates how Cloud Control 12*c* performs automated provisioning of Oracle databases and software, enabling Provisioning Designers to use the new facility of profiles and locked-down procedures, which make it easier to provision a fully configured gold copy in the Oracle database and at the same time prevent Provisioning Operators from deviating from corporate standards.

*Chapter 6, Ease the Chaos with Automated Patching*, demonstrates how Cloud Control 12*c* allows automated patching of Oracle databases in the data center, thus making it possible to easily apply critical patch updates or patch set updates on a quarterly basis. The Patching Designer selects from a list of recommended patches, creates a patch plan template, and publishes it to the Patching Operator, who then creates a patch plan to apply the patch to target databases. After the initial selection, the download, validation and deployment of the patch (single or multiple) is fully automated, thus enabling mass deployment of patches to multiple database homes at prescheduled times. The new feature of out-of-place patching is explained in the chapter, as is the patch plan templates.

*Chapter 7, Ease the Chaos with Change Management*, explains how Cloud Control 12*c* allows  the capture of all database schema changes and comparison of databases or schemas to aid in propagation of changes across the development lifecycle, greatly assisting in the auditing process as a result. The new Change Plans and the capability of data comparisons for seed or configuration data are also covered in the chapter.

*Chapter 8, Ease the Chaos with Test Data Management,* explains how Cloud Control 12*c* simplifies test data management by allowing subsetting of data so smaller test databases can be created from a larger production database. This leads to considerable storage cost savings in test environments.

*Chapter 9, Ease the Chaos with Data Masking,* explains how Cloud Control 12*c* can be used to discover confidential data and set up a centralized masking template library that can achieve obfuscation (de-identification) of any confidential data when copying data from production to test databases.

*Chapter 10, Ease the Chaos with Exadata Management,* explains how Cloud Control 12*c* aids in monitoring and managing the powerful Oracle Exadata system as a whole, both the hardware and software components, as well as the network infrastructure.

*Chapter 11, Real-life Examples and Case Studies, and It's a Wrap – the Future is the Cloud,* includes various real-life examples and case studies of actual Oracle customers to show how they have benefited from using Oracle Enterprise Manager. The final chapter explores the future of Cloud Computing and Oracle's strong standing in the cloud game, now also strengthened by the new Enterprise Manager Cloud Control 12*c*.

# What you need for this book

This book is a practical step-by-step tutorial, with screenshots, for carrying out tasks and shows you how to manage and administer your data center with Oracle Enterprise Manager Cloud Control 12*c*.

It is packed with best practices and tips that will help you benefit from the author's extensive experience working with Oracle Enterprise Manager for over a decade, combined with his IT industry experience spanning more than 25 years.

To follow the steps in this book, you need access to an Enterprise Manager Cloud Control 12*c* installation. You can install your own environment by following the detailed steps in the online chapter *Installation/Upgrade Tactics and Architecture for Large Sites*, Even if you don't have access to an environment, you can still read the book to get an idea of the capabilities of Enterprise Manager.

# Who this book is for

If you are a data center, IT, or database team manager who wants to take advantage of the automation and compliance benefits of Enterprise Manager Cloud Control 12*c*, *Oracle Enterprise Manager Cloud Control 12c: Managing Data Center Chaos* is for you. CTOs will also find this book useful.

Experience with Enterprise Manager is not essential as the author's experience tells you all you need to know about getting started with Enterprise Manager. More experienced readers will learn about the brand new capabilities of the Cloud Control 12*c* release.

# Conventions

In this book, you will find a number of styles of text that distinguish between different kinds of information. Here are some examples of these styles, and an explanation of their meaning.

Code words in text are shown as follows: "Previously there were only two association types available, namely `depends on` and `hosted on`."

Any command-line input or output is written as follows:

```
sysctl -w kernel.shmmax=4294967295
```

**New terms** and **important words** are shown in bold. Words that you see on the screen, in menus or dialog boxes for example, appear in the text like this: "Clicking the **Next** button moves you to the next screen".

[ Warnings or important notes appear in a box like this. ]

[ Tips and tricks appear like this. ]

# Reader feedback

Feedback from our readers is always welcome. Let us know what you think about this book—what you liked or may have disliked. Reader feedback is important for us to develop titles that you really get the most out of.

To send us general feedback, simply send an e-mail to `feedback@packtpub.com`, and mention the book title in the subject of your message.

If there is a topic that you have expertise in, and you are interested in either writing or contributing to a book, see our author guide at `www.packtpub.com/authors`.

# Customer support

Now that you are the proud owner of a Packt book, we have a number of things to help you to get the most from your purchase.

## Errata

Although we have taken every care to ensure the accuracy of our content, mistakes do happen. If you find a mistake in one of our books—maybe a mistake in the text or the code—we would be grateful if you would report this to us. By doing so, you can save other readers from frustration and help us improve subsequent versions of this book. If you find any errata, please report them by visiting `http://www.packtpub.com/support`, selecting your book, clicking on the **errata submission form** link, and entering the details of your errata. Once your errata are verified, your submission will be accepted and the errata will be uploaded on our website, or added to any list of existing errata, under the Errata section of that title. Any existing errata can be viewed by selecting your title at `http://www.packtpub.com/support`.

## Piracy

Piracy of copyright material on the Internet is an ongoing problem across all media. At Packt, we take the protection of our copyright and licenses very seriously. If you come across any illegal copies of our works, in any form, on the Internet, please provide us with the location address or website name immediately so that we can pursue a remedy.

Please contact us at `copyright@packtpub.com` with a link to the suspected pirated material.

We appreciate your help in protecting our authors and our ability to bring you valuable content.

## Questions

You can contact us at `questions@packtpub.com` if you are having a problem with any aspect of the book, and we will do our best to address it.

# 1
# Chaos at Data Centers

Studies show that many corporations world wide expect their IT footprint to grow in the coming years. They expect more servers, more databases, more data, and more of everything.

They require more floor space in their data centers, and correspondingly a greater power footprint. Have you heard of a data center where no more servers can be added as the power supply has reached its limit, or the **uninterruptible power supply** (**UPS**) can no longer cope? This story is not new, it happened a few years ago.

The growth seems to be endless—and this is fuelled by today's information age, where larger and larger volumes of data need to be stored and distributed to satisfy an ever-growing demand. More applications are using those databases, on more and more application servers.

So, for an IT manager, this will mean more of everything in his/her data centre. There may be different hardware platforms, different operating systems, for example, Solaris, Linux, IBM AIX, or Microsoft Windows, and in each such case there may be different versions such as the different flavors of Linux supplied by different vendors, including Oracle Enterprise Linux, Red Hat, SUSE Linux, and so on.

In the database arena, if a company has no policy of standardization for one particular database vendor, there may be different databases, such as Oracle, IBM DB2, or Microsoft SQL Server, in use by different projects.

Even if the databases belong to only one vendor, for example Oracle, the databases may be of different versions, such as Oracle Database 9*i*, 10*g*, or 11*g*. In the real world, it is very difficult to standardize on one version, as all applications may not be certified to use on that one database version. You may have some application vendors that say they are certified on Oracle Database 10.2.0.3 and not 10.2.0.5, and some that say they only use a particular version of Oracle Database 11*g* Release 1 and no other version.

So multiple database versions need to be installed separately, managed, patched as required, and upgraded when required. Also, development as well as test, staging, and production environments need to be provisioned (created) for each such database version. This level of complexity is the ground reality in today's data centers.

# Team effort

The installation effort itself for each new project is huge.

First, a business project identifies the need for an application server and/or a database server. A formal request is made for these. The request is approved, and arrives at the doorstep (or mailbox) of the Unix/Windows team. Teams such as these are normally present in any reasonably sized IT department.

The Unix/Windows team then procures the necessary servers, gets access, and installs the operating system—frequently following manual checklists where they tick off each step. This team may also need to install additional packages/patches at the OS level, as requested by the project managers, and this information may or may not be available to the management at this stage. It may well be the case that any missing OS-level packages could cause delays and annoyances later down the track, but let us say this information is known, and the additional packages/patches are applied by the Unix/Windows team.

The hardware with the installed operating system is then forwarded to the database team in the IT department, where the DBAs get access to the server and install the database software, such as the Enterprise Edition of the Oracle database.

Certain options for the Oracle database may also need to be installed at this stage, such as the partitioning option or the advanced security option, depending on the requirements of the project and the licenses available with the company. Let us presume there is no standardization at this stage, so everything has to be decided manually, or guessed—if there are no clear instructions from the project side.

At this point, if certain OS packages/patches are missing, the DBAs may redirect the servers back to the Unix/Windows team for the missing components to be installed. Assuming this is done in a day or so, the DBAs then re-attempt the database software installation the next day (if they are lucky).

The database software thus installed may itself need to be patched, for example, if Oracle Database 10*g* Release 2 (10.2.0.1.0) had been installed as the base release on the Solaris Operating System (SPARC) (64-bit), it should be patched on to the ultimate release of Oracle Database 10.2 on this platform, such as 10.2.0.5. It is always recommended to do this for production databases. Not patching for the ultimate or penultimate release can lead to issues later on when applying regular security patches that are often provided only for the latest releases of any version.

After this, the actual database is created. If there are no company standards, it is possible that each database created by different DBAs even in the same team may be different, for example one database may have the Sample Schemas provided by Oracle installed but another database may not have these installed. This is normally done via a simple manual selection in **Database Configuration Assistant** (**DBCA**)—Oracle's standalone graphical utility for creating new databases. One DBA may decide to select this, the other DBA may not.

There are other examples of similar configuration drifts. One DBA may decide to use **Oracle Managed Files (OMF)** for the data files of the database, another may not. It may depend on each individual and his/her likes or dislikes. For example, I, personally, have never used Oracle Managed Files even though there is nothing wrong with using them.

Even if there are published company standards for database creation, they may not be followed 100% of the time as standards are difficult to enforce when manual methods of installation are used and no control is enforced when performing the installation.

There is no separation of roles in the manual installation, there is no DBA Designer (the Senior DBA) who designs the database to be installed, and there is no DBA Operator (the Junior DBA) who follows the design and installs the database. It just depends on who does the installation and who does a better job—the Senior DBA or the Junior DBA. And frequently, the Senior DBA does not even have the time for repetitive installations and just leaves it to the Junior DBA. The Junior DBA then decides to try out different things for educational purposes - possibly.

The same scenario may be applicable to the middleware team when they install the application server software, such as Oracle WebLogic Server or Oracle Application Server, or application servers belonging to other vendors. Manual methods will lead to major or minor differences in the setup and configuration, and if there are no automated methods of checking the configuration compliance, it may lead to a near-impossible situation and there would be no way to enforce company standards on the middleware servers and domains either during or after installation.

The DBAs install the database software, patch it to the required level, and then create the databases required by the applications. They repeat this process for development, test, staging, and production environments.

After a reasonably successful installation, the DBA team is also requested to set up the backup of each database and also to set up the standby databases for disaster recovery using some tool, for example, Oracle DataGuard.

The setup of each backup and standby database is reasonably complicated, especially the latter, and involves a number of detailed steps. Also, each backup and disaster recovery scenario needs to be tested to ensure that it works.

Where is the time to do all this if everything is done manually?

Once the databases are released to the production environment, either the same team of DBAs or a different production team looks into the day-to-day workings of each database, and attempts to ensure that the application is guaranteed a certain level of performance—and this is a difficult order without automated tools.

Every database sooner or later needs diagnosis and tuning—as databases are not static; they change, their data changes, their users change, and their application changes. More load is placed on the database. More data is used in queries. All these changes are inevitable and eventually lead to performance issues.

First of all, to gain an understanding of these issues, performance information from the database is collected, manually analyzed, and certain worst-performing SQL statements are identified.

Each such SQL statement is then painstakingly fixed, often by adding indexes, perhaps without understanding the effect of extra indexes placing a heavier strain on inserts and updates.

Such manual **performance diagnosis** (finding out the problem) and **tuning** (fixing the problem) is obviously a very lengthy and tedious process, and is compounded when there are many tens or even hundreds of databases. A team of DBAs would be needed just to look at and fix day-to-day performance issues.

What about patching these databases?

**My Oracle Support** (**MOS**) releases **Patch Set Updates** (**PSUs**) and **Critical Patch Updates** (**CPUs**) every three months, and recommends that all databases are patched regularly with either the CPU or the PSU.

The **CPU** is a collection of security patches, and the PSU includes the CPU as well as other patches that fix separate issues.

If a particular company is security conscious and wants to make sure that the latest security patches have been applied to all its databases, there will be a need for the DBAs to apply the CPUs or PSUs every calendar quarter, and this involves downloading the appropriate patch, FTPing or SCPing it to each server, and then going through a series of manual steps to apply the patch.

This is fine if there are few databases, but if there are hundreds compounded with several environments for development, testing, and production, then the patches must be painstakingly applied on each and every database home and database.

It is possible, but it takes a lot of time manually. The DBAs will never get their sleep in this case, when they stay behind to complete the manual patching of the numerous databases. Also, the manual repetitive tasks they follow for this patching will be more prone to mistakes—as the mind itself gets numbed by constant repetition of the same steps.

Let us say, on top of all this, there are development projects that constantly upgrade their applications and send database scripts to the DBAs to make schema changes corresponding to the new application release.

This may include new tables, new columns, a modification of existing columns, or new database structures as well as new/modified users and their privileges on the objects.

To implement these changes at the database level for the purpose of such application upgrades, they would use a collection of SQL or PL/SQL commands in a script that they supply to the DBA—to run in the test and then in the staging environments. Finally, the scripts would be run on the production database if the application is found to work well on the test and staging databases.

First of all, the scripts themselves need to be checked thoroughly by the DBA, and this takes time.

The DBA needs to ensure the script is doing the right thing, which he/she does with a manual check, then perhaps a dry run on a separate test database to work out script issues, for example, the creation of indexes on nonexistent columns, the granting of privileges before the table is created, errors in SQL syntax, and so on.

The script then has to be modified and re-run before it is finally ready to be executed in the test environment, and the DBA may send a few stern emails to the developer team to be more careful next time.

Once this is done, the project team commences testing the application on the test database. After a green signal is received, the DBA will be asked to run the script on the staging and production databases.

The DBA then rests easy, thinking that the job is over, but suddenly receives a shock—the developer tells him that the application is not working in production (although it is working in staging and testing).

The DBA calls his/her home to say that he/she will be coming home late today, then starts to investigate the issue by painstakingly comparing the staging and the production databases. Every table, user, and privilege in the two databases has to be compared until the DBA finds out that certain privileges are missing on the production database, whereas the user had higher privileges on the other databases.

This simple reason has taken hours to be discovered. The DBA fixes the script, creates a final version for the particular release, and runs the necessary part of granting the extra privileges (by a cut and paste from the final script), and the application finally works.

Also, the only way the history of all these changes can be preserved in this case is by retaining the script files on the database server, versioning them, and storing them in subdirectories. This is sometimes done instead on the DBA's Windows PC.

Trying to look into such files in this directory structure to find out a past change is normally a very manual, labour-intensive, and painstaking process. I have done this many times all by myself, so am well aware of the issues.

When manual effort is the norm, in such data centers, it is inevitable that the DBAs and other administrators spend much of their time being reactive. Junior and less-trained staff on night shift hours would compound the issue, as would offshore technicians working remotely without a proper understanding of the internal environment.

For example, if the OS maintenance is off sourced and, say, the admin is asked to apply an OS upgrade, and as a part of the process the admin decided to change some OS properties under the impression that it will improve the OS performance. However, the next day, the on-site DBA finds that the standby database has stopped working, and he/she has no way of knowing what has changed as there is no automatic capture or history of configuration changes in such a manual environment. All the DBA has is the general information that the OS was upgraded, and he/she has to then investigate further by comparing, bit-by-bit, the configuration of the server on which the database is still working and the server on which the database has had the problem.

You can guess how much time and effort this may take?

# Common solutions used in data centers

How do data centers attempt to address these issues? The short answer is simple: brute labor and/or an attempt at in-house automation using manually written scripts.

There is usually a team of Unix administrators and another team of Windows administrators who are responsible for manually preparing each and every piece of hardware by installing the operating system and patching it to the required level.

These administrators are also responsible for resolving issues with the systems they provision, such as missing pieces in the installation or performance issues that may be due to improper setup of the operating system (wrong values supplied for OS properties, for example, network buffer properties).

There is another team of **Database Administrators** (**DBAs**). These DBAs may specialize in Oracle or DB2 or SQL Server, and frequently in companies that seek to combine multiple roles, may dabble in all of these. (Indeed in the DBA world, it was once considered a plus point to know as many databases as possible, until the realization dawned that a real expert in one main database was more of a valuable asset than a DBA who knew multiple databases and their nuances, but only superficially.)

These teams of Unix, Windows, database and also the middleware administrators are put into action in their brute numbers, and this is normally seen in the highly-populated countries in the world today where there are a great number of administrators in the job market. The admin labor is available at a low cost in such markets, and consequently more administrators can be hired.

Such administrators, in an effort to be extremely competitive against their peers, and to appear extremely loyal to their work, proudly say "we never sleep" (sacrificing their family happiness in the process) and make themselves available for tackling all the issues mentioned—albeit in a manual, uncontrolled, haphazard manner that would be prone to multiple and deadly mistakes.

However, brute force, by throwing reams of administrators at the manual tasks, does work at fighting fires and keeping them under control. This technique is employed by a number of companies to handle their data centers. But then, they get used to fighting fires every other day.

The other scenario is the company that prides itself on the thousands of reams of scripts running its data center. These countless scripts are used in an attempt to automate the manual steps of managing the data center. They are used for provisioning, to collect the configuration, for patching, for applying the changes to the schemas, for backing up, and for creating and monitoring the standby disaster recovery databases.

However, these scripts are not a magic bullet—there needs to be an effort to write and maintain these scripts. As technology changes, more and more complicated scripts need to be written. The scripts may be layered unnecessarily and may become quickly outdated—for example, an Oracle RMAN script used to back up an Oracle 9*i* database may still be used to back up an Oracle 10*g* database, without using the new features such as Block Change Tracking and Fast Incremental Backups, present in the later releases of RMAN.

This is the very problem with scripts—they stay static.

The languages are not easy, and require expertise to write scripts—which is somewhat rare. The writers of such scripts soon establish a position for themselves in the company as heroes. They are available to script everything.

And when these heroes leave the organization, there is chaos.

# Summary

In this chapter, we have seen the common issues in data centers (albeit from the eyes of the administrators) and the chaos that can be seen in any such center if there is no controlled management and automation. We hope you have gained a good insight.

Brute manual force and multitudes of scripts are often used as the last bastion of defense against the chaos, but ultimately succumb. They cannot cope with rapid change.

Even the script heroes are eventually engulfed by the rising tide of continuous scripting and sooner or later quit the company.

In the next chapter, we will take our first look at powerful Enterprise-Management software from Oracle that can be used to reduce this chaos to a negligible extent, so that the data center can be managed efficiently from a central console, and with the barest minimum of scripts. Read on.

# 2
# Enter Oracle Cloud Control

What if we told you that there is an enterprise-class management product from Oracle, which, if used appropriately, would help in resolving the chaos of the data centers?

Yes, there indeed is such a product. Enter Oracle Enterprise Manager Cloud Control 12*c*, which is the latest version of Oracle's Enterprise Manager. This is installed centrally on a dedicated server and used for managing and monitoring the entire Oracle Technology Stack, with an Agent placed on each Target that Enterprise Manager is to manage or monitor.

In the previous versions of Enterprise Manager, 11*g* and 10*g*, the product could optionally be installed locally when the database software or application server software was installed on a server. In this cut-down form, it was known as Oracle Database Control or Oracle Application Server Control, respectively. This type of single Target Enterprise Manager is no longer available in the 12*c* version at the time of writing this book.

What we do have is Cloud Control 12*c*, which is the full, all-encompassing flavor of Oracle Enterprise Manager. Appropriately named, Cloud Control 12*c* can manage the 9*i*, 10*g*, and 11*g* versions of Oracle databases, and Oracle middleware, including Oracle Fusion, Oracle WebLogic Server, Oracle SOA Suite, and Oracle Application Server. Cloud Control 12*c* can also manage Oracle Applications such as Fusion Apps, Siebel, E-Business Suite, PeopleSoft, and JD Edwards Enterprise One. It also manages Oracle VM and Oracle Sun Servers and Storage in the form of Enterprise Manager Ops Center 12*c*.

Thus, it is apparent that Cloud Control 12*c* can do application-to-disk management, as it manages everything from the application down to the database, middleware, virtual machine, server, and storage (disk) level.

Cloud Control 12*c* even goes above, to the business layer, and is able to define and manage your business transactions on services across a service bus, and can be used to set up the entire infrastructure for the Cloud—whether the Cloud is **Infrastructure as a Service** (**IaaS**), **Database as a Service** (**DBaaS**), or **Platform as a Service** (**PaaS**).

It is also able to deliver the Cloud via self service, and manage the Cloud, including metering and chargeback services. As business transaction management capabilities are included, this means Enterprise Manager Cloud Control 12*c* is able to achieve business-driven Cloud Management.

The DbaaS Cloud capabilities of Enterprise Manager are based on the database lifecycle management features of the product. We will go through the database lifecycle management features in the coming chapters.

And besides the Oracle technology stack, Enterprise Manager Cloud Control 12*c* is able to monitor and perform configuration management of non-Oracle hardware and software, such as non-Oracle Hosts (for example, HP-UX, IBM AIX, and Windows), non-Oracle storage such as EMC and NetApp, as well as firewalls, load balancers, and network devices.

This is done via Enterprise Manager plugins written either by Oracle or third-party vendors. At the time of writing this book, a few of the plugins are being rewritten for Cloud Control and will be released in stages.

But is Cloud Control 12*c* a new product, or does it have a long history? The answer is yes to both. To understand this, we will have to go back in time.

Oracle Enterprise Manager Cloud Control 12*c* is certainly a long way from the days of Oracle Server Manager, the initial version that was released in the mid 1990s and was a simple and limited GUI interface used for some aspects of database administration only (along with a command-line interface, server manager line mode, or `svrmgrl`).

The DBAs at that time saw it as a novelty and used it very sparingly. They laughed at it. But it was the first attempt by Oracle at a GUI management tool.

This was followed by Oracle Enterprise Manager, called OEM initially. First OEM Version 1 was released, followed by OEM Version 2.2, which could be used with Oracle Database 8*i*. The next version, OEM 9*i* could be used with Oracle Database 9*i* and this was a much better-looking Java console that had to be installed on your Windows PC or workstation. Even though there were Java-related memory and performance issues with this version, it had increased acceptance among DBAs, who started using it in greater numbers.

The next version, **Enterprise Manager** (**EM**) 10*g* was introduced in the first decade of this century. It used the *N*-tier architecture, using Oracle Application Server as the backend application server for the actual Enterprise Manager Java application. This was an OC4J application, that is, **Oracle Containers For J2EE (OC4J)** 10*g*, which was compliant with **Java 2 Enterprise Edition (J2EE)** 1.4. The Enterprise Manager application was installed centrally as one or more Management Services using the same Central Repository, with Management Agents installed on multiple Targets that communicated with the Management Service. This type of centralized installation of Enterprise Manager was called **Grid Control**.

The backend application server OC4J application was replaced by Oracle WebLogic Server in Enterprise Manager 11*g*, released in April 2010. This version, for the first time, required the WebLogic Server software to be installed first, before the Enterprise Manager 11*g* Grid Control software was installed.

Enterprise Manager Grid Control 10*g* could manage 8*i*, 9*i*, 10*g*, as well as 11.1 databases, and other products such as Oracle Application Server. Enterprise Manager Grid Control 11*g* was able to manage 11.2 databases as well, although support for 8*i* databases was dropped.

And in October 2011, during Oracle OpenWorld, the latest Enterprise Manager 12*c*, renamed Cloud Control instead of Grid Control, was announced with great fanfare.

# The Grid – where the cloud came from

In 2003, Oracle Database 10*g* was released—where the "*g*" stood for **Grid**.

Oracle had previously released **Real Application Clusters** (**RAC**) in Oracle 9*i*, which was the first active/active database system (multiple nodes and instances accessing the same database).

This technology made it possible to cluster large numbers of smaller servers and place the application's database on the cluster as a whole. So, instead of placing the database on a larger and dedicated expensive server that had been sized suitably to accommodate the changes for the next two years of application life, it could be placed on a cluster of smaller servers, sized appropriately.

As the application's demand increased, it would be easy to just add an extra node to the database cluster and expand horizontally instead of vertically. The database services (applications) could also share any of the nodes in the cluster instead of having a dedicated server installed for each application. This intention to replace dedicated servers and expensive hardware from specialized vendors was the genesis of the Grid idea.

RAC technology was considerably enhanced in the 10*g* version. Oracle Clusterware software was now available in 10*g* for most platforms, thus negating the need for other clustering software. For example, using RAC 10*g* on SUN Solaris no longer meant having to preinstall the SUN Cluster, which was the case in RAC 9*i* for this platform.

It was now possible to have a Grid based on almost any platform where smaller servers could be clustered together with the clustering software from Oracle. This was applicable to the application servers as well, at that time using Oracle Application Server (please note, the current preferred cluster of application servers is Oracle WebLogic Server 12*c* Enterprise Edition).

Therefore, the versions of Oracle Database and Application Server from then on were named 10*g* and later 11*g*, emphasizing the importance Oracle was placing on the Grid.

For the management side of things, Oracle Enterprise Manager 10*g* and consequently 11*g* were released on an *N*-tier architecture. The powerful enterprise management product was named as Grid Control, due to its ability to manage the Grid based on Oracle Clustering technology. Multiple databases and application servers could be managed.

Provisioning capabilities were introduced from Enterprise Manager Grid Control 10*g* onwards, and this allowed the DBA to create gold copies of Oracle software and databases in a Software Library in Enterprise Manager, and then use the gold copy when seeking to provision the software or databases on new servers. Thus, provisioning of the Grid was now possible via an automated means. This helped with on-demand elasticity, or the ability to grow or shrink the Grid.

The Grid, as conceptualized by Oracle, was thus in place for a number of years. Then, a few years ago the idea of Cloud computing exploded on the IT scene. It seemed that almost every other hardware and software vendor was pushing Cloud computing.

But if you take a closer look, what is the Cloud? The **National Institute of Standards** (**NIST**) defines Cloud Computing as essentially being:

> *On-demand Access to a Shared Pool of Computing Resources.*

This is actually what the Grid is about. So how different is the Cloud to the Grid?

The Cloud as such is a superset of the Grid—but with a few more characteristics, such as self service by the user, metering, and chargeback.

The five essential characteristics of Cloud computing are defined as on-demand self-service, pooling of resources, elasticity (able to expand or scale down on notice), measured service (that is, metering of usage), and broad network access.

Oracle already had a deep technological foundation in the Grid, with technologies such as RAC Clustering, WebLogic Server Clustering, and Enterprise Manager management of the cluster with provisioning capabilities. Now, self-service, metering, and chargeback were added in Oracle Enterprise Manager on top of the Grid capabilities.

As a result, Oracle is now fully Cloud-capable. And its Enterprise Manager Cloud Control 12*c* is the management backbone of the entire Cloud.

# Overview of version 12*c*

We can now have a quick introductory look at the latest version of Enterprise Manager, which is Cloud Control 12*c*. The console login appears as follows:

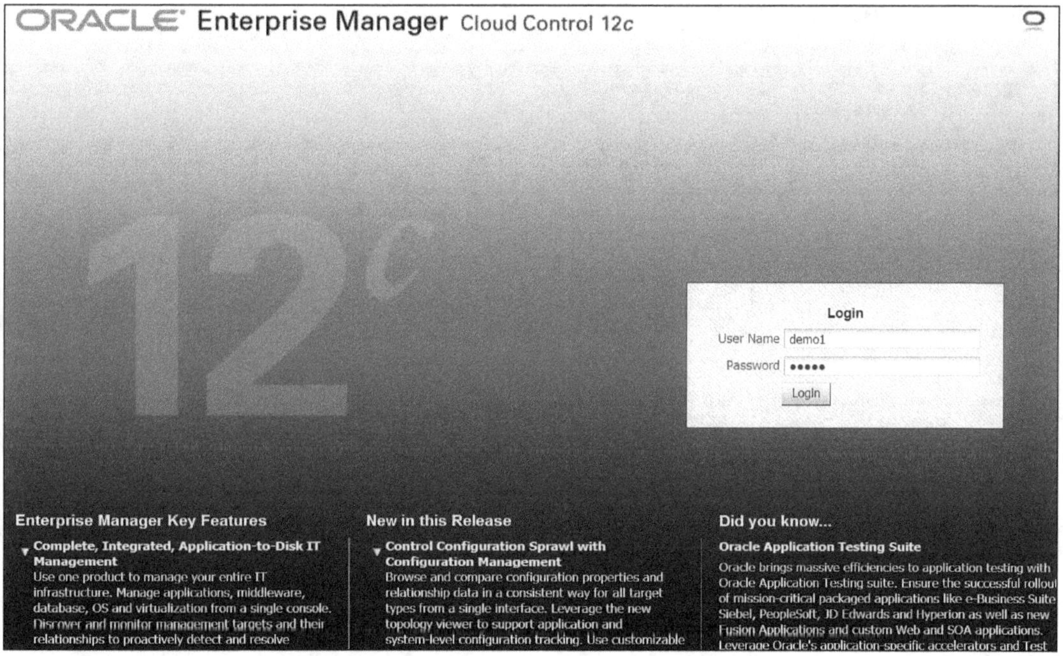


We can guess from this first splash screen that Cloud Control 12*c* has strong Oracle **Application Developer Framework** (**ADF**) looks and features, and we won't be far wrong. The new user interface in Enterprise Manager Cloud Control 12*c* was indeed developed using the ADF.

To make things interesting right at the outset, the splash screen of the console login also highlights some of the key features of Enterprise Manager - a section titled **New in this Release** and a **Did you know...** section. Every time you go to this console login, some new information is displayed. You can also expand any of the points to show more information.

In this new version, you can select your own home page—the page you see when you log in to Cloud Control. Suppose you have just installed Cloud Control and are logging in for the very first time, you will immediately be presented with a collection of home pages, one of which can be chosen as the preferred home page. This is seen in the following screenshot:

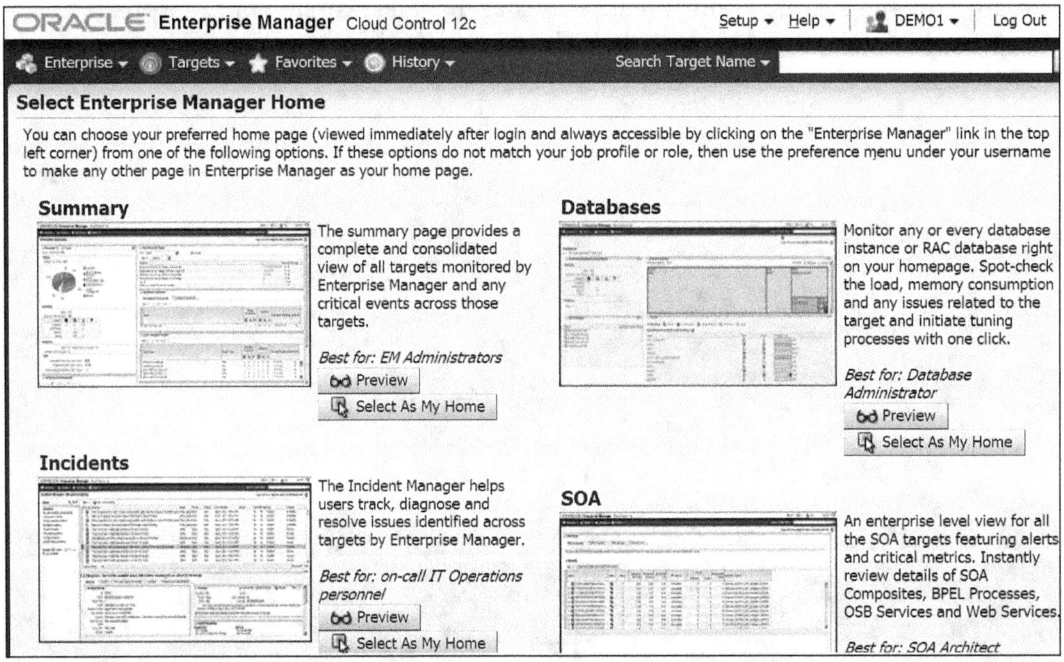


As we can see here, there are a number of home pages available for DBAs, middleware administrators, level 1 support staff and even Siebel administrators. There is a **Summary** page that **EM Administrators** can select; this is closest to the Enterprise Manager home page we used to see in versions 10*g* and 11*g*. This shows at a glance the availability and other details of all the Targets where there is an EM Agent talking to this Enterprise Manager system.

There is a **Databases** home page for DBAs. There are also **Middleware, Fusion Applications**, and **SOA** home pages, a **Service Dashboard** page, an **Incidents** page, and even a **Cloud Infrastructure** page for monitoring and managing the Cloud infrastructure. Any of these pages can be selected as the home page at this stage, when first logging on. In the future, it is possible to select any other page as the home page by going to **Setup | My preferences | Select My Home** from the Cloud Control menu.

Let's say we have selected the **Summary** page as the home page. The page that appears is shown in the next screenshot:

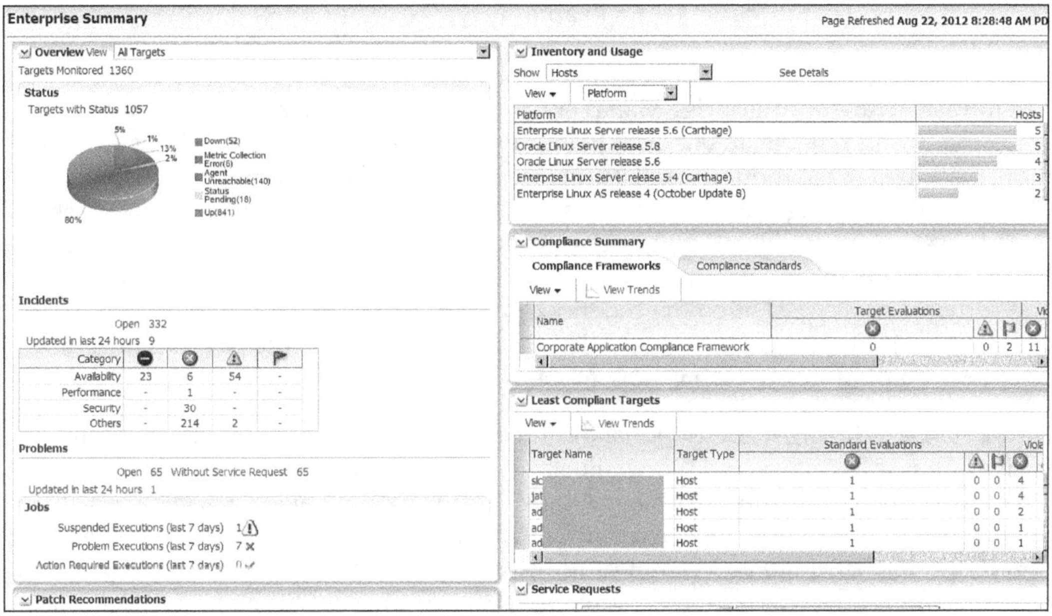


As we can see from this page, the Cloud Control **Summary** page displays the overall availability of all the Targets managed by the Enterprise Manager. You can see which Targets are down, and drill down immediately to find the issue. You can see the critical and warning **Incidents** that have been raised by the Targets, any **Problems**, or any **Jobs** that have failed. You can also drill down to the **Patch Recommendations** from here—Enterprise Manager Cloud Control 12*c* connects to **My Oracle Support** (**MOS**) and gets a list of all available patches for the Targets, and displays them here (more on this in a later chapter).

On the second half of the page we can see the inventory at a glance: what type of **Hosts**, what type of databases, and so on, are present in the enterprise. We can also see the **Compliance Summary** and the **Least Compliant Targets** sections, and finally the **Service Requests** section, which shows the service requests that have been opened. And all this just on the **Summary** page.

# Striking new features in 12*c*

Enterprise Manager Cloud Control 12*c* is a huge release with a plethora of new features. A few of the outstanding features are described shortly. If some of the terminology is new at this stage, no need to worry; we will go to the appropriate detail later on in most cases.

The infrastructure of Enterprise Manager Cloud Control 12*c* is now more scalable, performant, and reliable, to enable it to support millions of different Targets—much more than the tens of thousands of Targets you could scale up to in previous versions. The Enterprise Manager Framework has been enhanced to a pluggable framework that allows you to download and deploy any plugin via the new self-update feature. The plugins, which were primarily meant for non-Oracle databases, hardware, and software in the past, are now redefined so that even the Oracle Database or Middleware is managed via a plugin. This is quite a change to the basic architecture of Enterprise Manager, which is now more modular and extensible.

As we will see during the actual install process, there are some essential plugins, such as Oracle Database and Oracle Fusion Middleware, and some optional plugins, such as Oracle Virtualization, Oracle Cloud Application, Oracle Chargeback and Trending, Oracle Siebel, Microsoft SQL Server, Sybase, and IBM DB2. This demonstrates that there are Target plugins (for management of Oracle or non-Oracle Targets) and there are solution plugins (that give additional functionality, such as Cloud and virtualization).

Some plugins are dependent on one another; for example, the Oracle Cloud Application plugin is dependent on the Oracle Virtualization plugin, as can be seen in the following screenshot (this is from the installation process, which we will look into in detail in this chapter). The screenshot also demonstrates that the **Oracle Database** itself is listed in the available plugins:

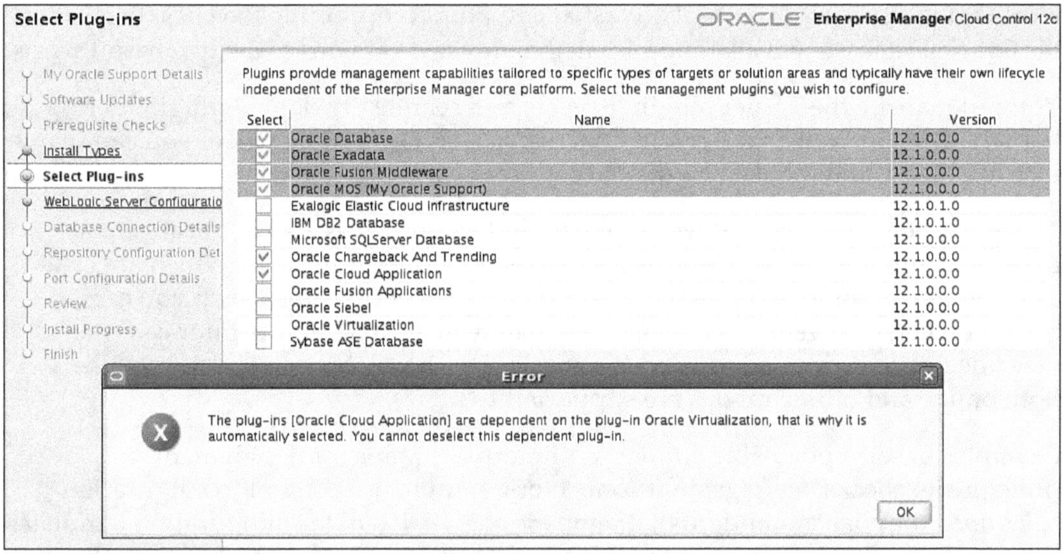


The advantage of this new pluggable framework is that Enterprise Manager Cloud Control 12*c* can be updated fast to manage a new technology, for example, if a new database version or a new WebLogic version is released tomorrow, your current installation of Cloud Control 12*c* should be able to manage it by simply updating the latest database or middleware plugin using the self-update feature.

In the past, you would have had to upgrade your entire Enterprise Manager Release in order to be able to manage a newer database or WebLogic version. As an example, Oracle 11.2 databases could be provisioned only with Enterprise Manager 11*g*, whereas 11.1 Databases were provisioned with Enterprise Manager 10*g*. If you had the latter installed and your company upgraded the database to 11.2, you would have to upgrade the entire Enterprise Manager system to fully manage the new release.

However, this is no longer the case. All you need to do now is to use the self-update feature for the plugin. As the plugin can now be revised separately from the core framework, it is possible for Oracle to release a new version of the plugin as soon as it is ready, even though the next Enterprise Manager Platform Release is some way off. So, you can get support for new features faster.

Note that the plugins are cumulative, that is, a plugin supporting the latest version of the Oracle Database will also support all the previous versions of the database Targets.

You can manage the Target plugin lifecycle and seamlessly deploy plugins across both the OMS as well as the Agent tiers, using a single console where you can search for, download, and manage all the Target plugins.

This self-update feature that we talked about for plugins, is also applicable to a number of other entities in Enterprise Manager Cloud Control 12*c*, which are called self-updateable entities. There are a number of such entities for which you can be notified when new versions are available, and you as an Administrator can then view, decide to download as needed, and deploy those new versions if you like. Both online and offline modes are supported.

Examples of self-updateable entities are Enterprise Manager deployment prerequisite checks, management connectors, compliance content (configuration rules and compliance standards), diagnostic checks, Exadata configuration templates, Agent software, (Agent core images), and of course the Target and solution plugins.

Such self-updateable entities also include provisioning bundles; so, for example, you can easily download the latest released and updated deployment procedures. Database provisioning profiles and gold images, middleware profiles and gold images, and virtualization templates and assemblies are also in the list of self-updateable entities.

Hopefully more entities will be made self-updateable in the near future. This truly enables the new version of Enterprise Manager Cloud Control 12*c* to be able to deliver new features and updates a lot faster, adding those updates outside of the main Enterprise Manager platform releases.

It is now easier to manage and diagnose issues with the Enterprise Manager Cloud Control 12*c* product itself. The Enterprise Manager console allows you to perform control operations such as starting, stopping, or restarting the OMS, as well as secure and resecure operations. You can update the OMS configuration properties, as well as the Agent properties—the latter can be done either individually or jointly for a group of Agents.

Using the Support Workbench for Enterprise Manager Cloud Control 12*c*, you can quickly diagnose any problems with the Enterprise Manager console, loader, and notification system. A **service request (SR)** can be opened easily with MOS and the diagnostic data pertaining to the enterprise manager issue can be collected automatically, packaged by the Workbench, and uploaded to the support site.

Security has also been enhanced. Integration with **Oracle Access Manager Single Sign-On** (**OAM SSO**) is now supported out of the box. There is also direct LDAP authentication support for Microsoft **Active Directory** (**AD**), as also for **Oracle Internet Directory** (**OID**). Kerberos authentication is also supported. The authentication module has been made pluggable, so if you like you can use your own customized authentication module or provider.

Strong authentication for host and database Targets is now supported, with SSH key pairs for host authentication. It is also possible to use Kerberos tickets for database authentication. These tickets can be used for both Cloud Control authentication as well as database authentication; in this case it is possible to seamlessly move between Cloud Control and database Targets without any prompting for database authentication because the same credential is used.

The new Enterprise Manager Cloud Control 12*c* release has a much more granular security model, with more than 100 fine-grained privileges. These can be used to control the access to enterprise manager resources such as Targets, templates, jobs, reports, and metric extensions, as well as enterprise manager functionalities such as buttons, pages, links, regions, and URLs. This release also supports Target-type, specific, fine-grained privileges.

You can group together any of these fine-grained privileges into roles, so that it becomes easier to manage your privileges across the enterprise. There are a few predefined out of the box roles that are meant to cater to certain types of enterprise manager users. Some examples are the Cloud Designer, Provisioning Designer, Patch Operator roles, and so on.

The roles in Cloud Control 12*c* are also integrated with enterprise roles. Suppose you have implemented an authorization management tool such as Oracle **Authorization Policy Manager (APM)**, and if you create a role in this tool for the Test DBA (as an example), then any users of that role will automatically inherit the relevant Cloud Control 12*c* roles and privileges.

Instead of a tab-driven interface, as in Enterprise Manager Grid Control 11*g* or 10*g*, there are drop-down menus in the new version, which help you to navigate easily through all the menu options. Another striking feature is excellent personalization in the 12*c* release. Your home pages can be customized in terms of layout and displayed data; extra regions from a catalog of predefined regions can be added or removed, and these changes are seen even when you log back in again. Target home pages can also be customized in this way. This is done using the ADF WebCenter technology.

This changes Enterprise Manager Cloud Control 12*c* from a more or less fixed page structure in the previous versions to a reasonably customizable interface, and that will help to increase its usage. A Web 2.0 user interface has been used throughout. Any page can now be your home page, and there are also predefined home pages, based on roles, you can select them as the home page.

There is also a new **Favorites** sub-menu where most pages can be added as **Favorites**. For example, in the following screenshot, the **Databases** page has been added as a favorite, and also the **Summary** page. This was an enhancement request many customers had made, to allow one to go directly to a certain page that was used most often.

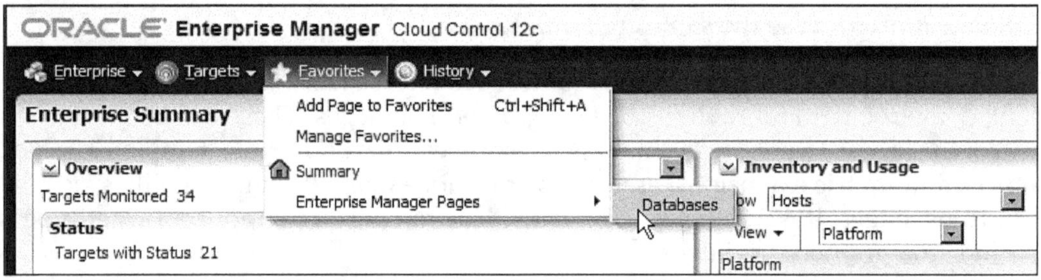


The **History** tab available alongside can be used to go to the recently visited Targets such as databases, listeners, and hosts. It is not a history of pages visited, as one would expect, but the Targets that have been visited. This is shown in the following screenshot:

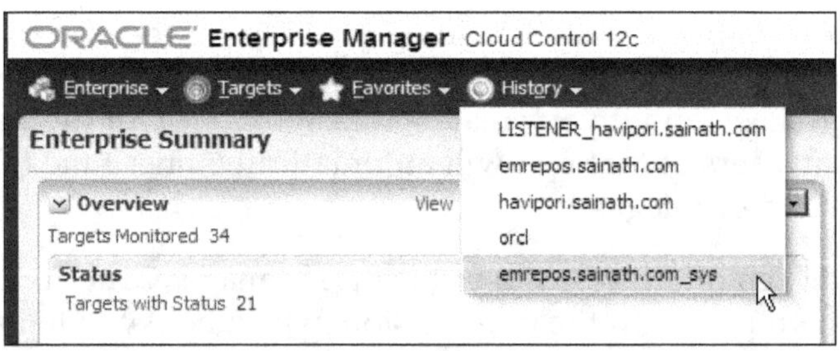


Enterprise Manager Cloud Control 12*c* is a powerful tool that executes a number of database and OS scripts, and performs a number of actions such as patching, cloning, and RMAN backups. To do all these things, a number of credentials are required for hosts, databases, and other Targets. To ease the difficulty in managing all these multiple credentials, the 12*c* version now boasts a central repository of credentials where all these credentials can be named and stored. These named credentials are another striking feature of the new version.

For these named credentials, passwordless and strong authentication credentials are also supported, for example, Kerberos tickets and SSH key pairs. It is possible to share the named credentials among many different users. Privileges for the access to these credentials can be granted by the owner of the credentials to different users, and the users can then re-use the credentials to gain access to the particular Target—and such users would not know the actual contents of the credentials. This access to the named credentials is controlled and protected by the privileges that are granted.

Global-named credentials can be associated with any Target, whereas Target-named credentials are associated only with a certain Target. You can create or modify named credentials by going to **Setup** | **Security** | **Named Credentials**:

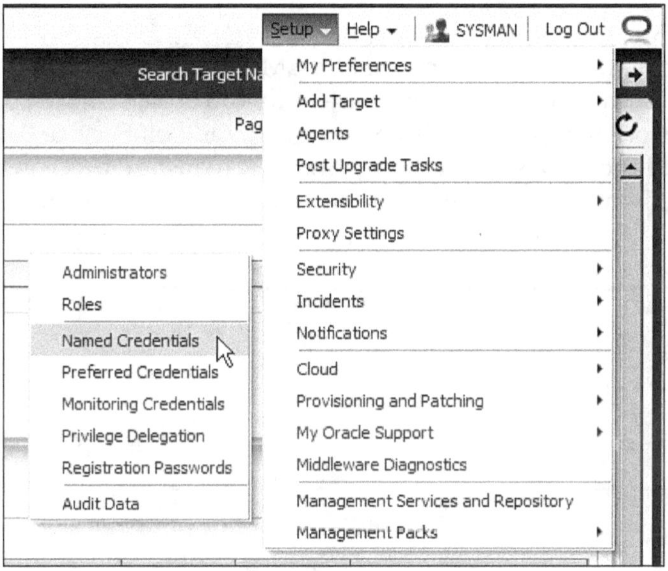


A credential can be simply referred to, instead of copying it. This has the advantage that the credential is stored in one location; the credential reference simply points to it so that when the actual credential is changed, this change will be automatically reflected in all the credential references. There is no longer any need to search through the whole enterprise manager system to find a particular credential stored along with a script or job, and change it, if it has changed. This simplifies credential management substantially. It is also possible to easily switch from one named credential to another.

In this version, all operations on credentials are audited and this can be easily reported on, so there is full accountability as well as traceability of any credential change. You can get a report of everyone who is using a named credential.

As far as enterprise manager reports go, there was always a limit as to what you could achieve. From now on, you can use Oracle **Business Intelligence** (**BI**) Publisher to design and schedule the delivery of Enterprise Manager Cloud Control 12*c* reports. Allowing the use of BI Publisher with Enterprise Manager is another great new feature. A Restricted Use License is included, allowing you to use this feature only to access the enterprise manager repository for the purpose of reports.

Reports can be created on the management repository views. These are fully documented in the *Oracle Enterprise Manager Cloud Control Extensibility Programmer's Reference 12c Release 2 (12.1.0.2)* document at the following URL:

`http://docs.oracle.com/cd/E24628_01/doc.121/e25161/views.htm#sthref1237`

To control access to the Targets and what an EM administrator can do, there are now more than 200 new privileges and out-of-the-box roles such as the Provisioning Designer, Provisioning Operator, Patch Designer, and Self Service Administrator. The available **Roles** can be seen in the following screenshot; this is when we are creating a new administrator by going to **Setup** | **Security** | **Administrators.**

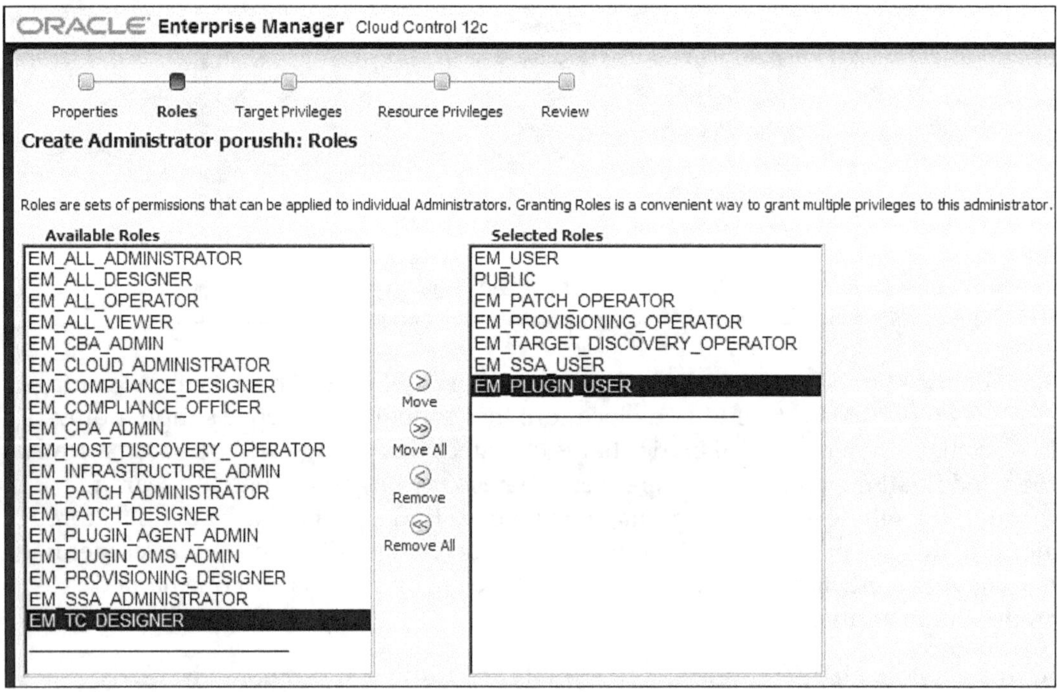

The **A**dministration Groups is another new feature in Enterprise Manager Cloud Control 12*c*. This is similar to a Target group that you could create in the earlier versions; however the administration group is a special type of group that has advanced functionalities as compared to a Target group.

In the case of the previously available Target groups, although you could create large groups and be able to monitor as well as manage the entire group, the disadvantage was that any new Target always had to be manually added to the Target group. At times, after creating new Targets in Enterprise Manager, manually adding them to the appropriate group was simply forgotten. This meant that the new Target would not be monitored and managed in an appropriate manner.

To resolve such issues, the new administration groups are defined based on certain Target properties, such as lifecycle status, location, line of business, and contact, in a predefined logical hierarchy of your organization. When a new Target is created, its properties can also be set, for example, it can be placed in the **Finance** line of business, and with the lifecycle status as `Test`. If there is an existing administration group hierarchy that has been set up with those properties, such as a **Finance-Test** administration group, the new Target will automatically be placed in the correct administration group without any DBA intervention.

Note that Targets cannot be assigned directly to such groups, they can only be automatically added based on the Target properties that are defined for the Target.

A related new feature called Template collection contains the management settings such as metric settings, compliance standards, and cloud policies. The Template collection can then be associated with a group. So, all the Targets that are automatically added to the group will have the same monitoring settings, compliance standards, and cloud policies propagated to them. Changes in the settings are also deployed automatically to all the members of the administration group.

Privileges are also propagated automatically to the new Target; so if an administrator had only read privileges on the other Targets in the administration group, he or she would have the same read privileges on the new Target. This simplifies management of privileges as well. Incident rules are also integrated with Administration Groups, in the sense that new incident creation, notification actions, and incident management can be defined for the group. These rules are also propagated to any new members.

There only needs to be an initial one-time setup of the administration group hierarchy and associated Template collections. This kind of multipronged automation would definitely be useful in the case of large data centers where new Targets are created and added continuously to the total IT Infrastructure. It would ease the administrative burden on DBAs who are responsible for ensuring that all new Targets are monitored in the same manner, using the corporate-approved monitoring settings and compliance rules. The only thing that needs to be done when adding a Target is to make sure that the Target properties are properly defined at the business or operational level. The screenshot that follows shows the creation of **Administration Groups**. This is done by going to **Targets** | **Groups** | **Create**.

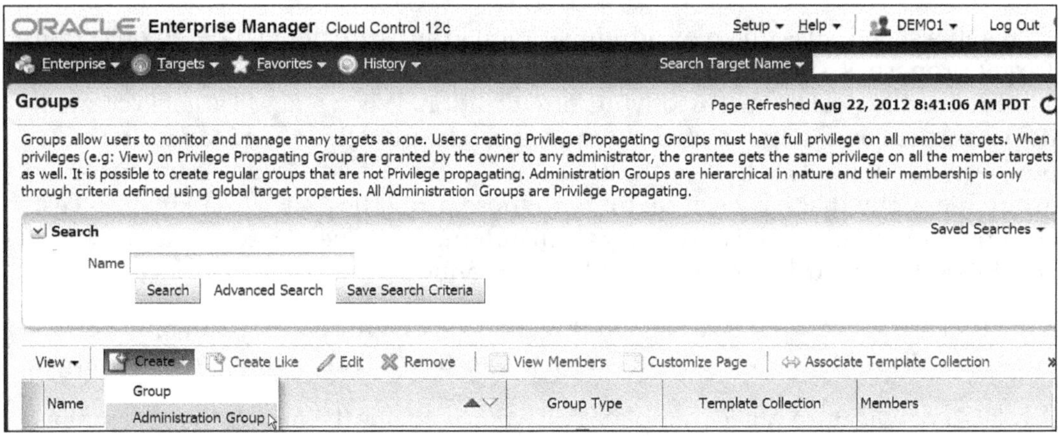


Systems in Enterprise Manager Cloud Control 12*c* are used to capture the dependency between Targets. Multiple dependent Targets can make up a system. In the new version, there are predefined out of the box systems for Oracle E-Business Suite, PeopleSoft, WebLogic Server, SOA, and also database Targets. As we will see in the following section, in which we will install Enterprise Manager, when a database Target will be discovered, there will also be a database system in the Target list.

You can create user-defined systems of your own, and in these systems there are more sophisticated association types that can be used; whereas previously there were only two association types available, namely `depends on` and `hosted on`. Now you can also use association types such as `authenticated by`, which helps you to specify the authentication system used by a Target. Other examples of the new types are `monitored by`, `hosted by`, `contains`, `uses`, and so on.

Availability for user-defined systems is now displayed. The home page and dashboard of any system can be customized with regards to customizable regions, and it is also possible to compare the configuration of a system with a gold image of a configuration stored in Enterprise Manager Cloud Control 12*c*.

You can now create a single instance or RAC database from Enterprise Manager Cloud Control 12*c*, using a supplied deployment procedure; you can also upgrade multiple databases in parallel for the first time from the central console of Enterprise Manager, using another such procedure. Previously, you could only upgrade a single database at a time using the traditional methods that were not supported by Enterprise Manager, such as the **Database Upgrade Assistant** (**DBUA**).

This upgrade capability supports database versions 10.2.0.4 and higher that are being upgraded to 11.2.0.x. Various advanced features are used to minimize the downtime of the database upgrade, such as out-of-place copies, a combination of software and database upgrade, preupgrade backup, preupgrade analysis, existing Oracle Home upgrade, and the ability to start or stop the execution of the upgrades. Any patches required before the database upgrade are also checked automatically by connecting to My Oracle Support.

There are also several database cloning enhancements, including the ability to include the Configuration Properties while cloning the database software.

Regarding the provisioning and patching capabilities of the Database Lifecycle Management Pack, one of the striking changes in Enterprise Manager Cloud Control 12*c* is that the Provisioning Designer and Provisioning Operator roles are now separated. The Provisioning Designer controls the logic of the provisioning flow and decides what is to be provisioned and how it will be provisioned. Provisioning profiles are now available, where you take any database environment and store it as a read-only snapshot. This can then be used for the purpose of provisioning. This will be explained in detail in a later chapter.

A number of deployment procedures are provided by Enterprise Manager out of the box, for example, database provisioning. The Provisioning Designer creates a provisioning profile from a reference database system, and then runs and saves a deployment procedure using the profile. The procedure can be locked down by him/her so as to limit and control the number of inputs by the Provisioning Operator.

For example, the Provisioning Designer may want every new database that is created by this procedure to use only **Oracle Managed Files** (**OMF**). This selection by the Provisioning Designer can be locked down so that it is unalterable by the Provisioning Operator, who will ultimately use this deployment procedure. The procedure is published to the Provisioning Operator. When the Provisioning Operator deploys this procedure, it will not be possible to change the database file's type from the OMF selection. The Provisioning Operators do not have to understand complex choices or make their own decisions, and this lessens the risk of human errors and also enforces a standard installation across the enterprise via the use of the officially authorized, locked-down procedures.

It is also possible to write a brand new deployment procedure from scratch, and this is known as a **User Defined Deployment Procedure** (**UDDP**). In previous versions, it was possible to copy an Oracle-supplied deployment procedure and then edit it by deleting or adding steps. But now, instead of doing that, you can define new and complex in-house deployment procedures of your own. This is helpful for custom software deployments.

This is done by going to **Enterprise** | **Provisioning and Patching** | **Procedure Library**, selecting **Create New** from the drop-down menu, and clicking on the **Go** button. This lets you create a new generic deployment procedure with any steps you yourself define, as in the following screenshot. You can integrate this functionality with other tools using either EM CLI or web service interfaces.

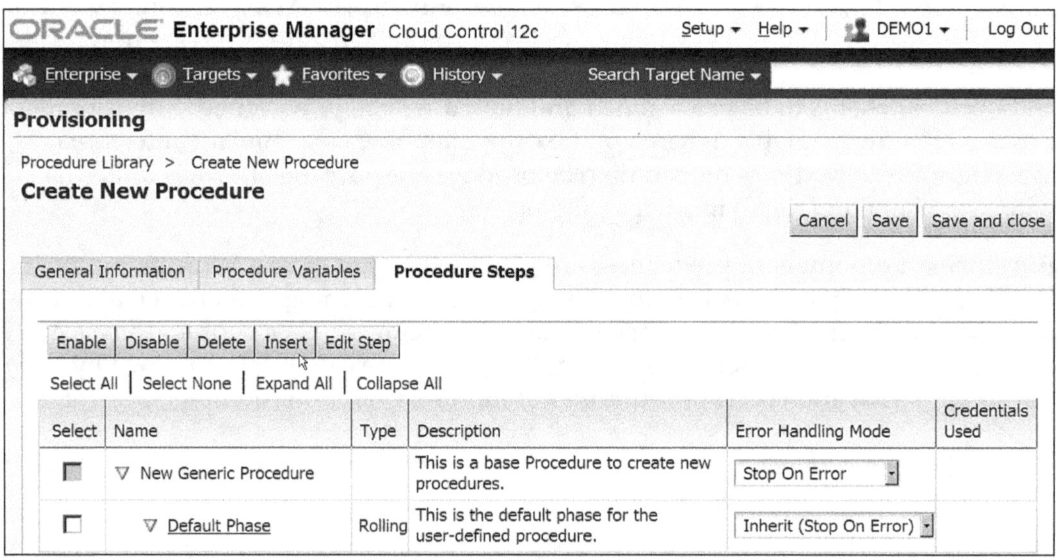

A powerful new feature in Enterprise Manager Cloud Control 12*c* is Real-Time **Automatic Database Diagnostic Monitor (ADDM)**. Complementary to the normal ADDM, the Real-Time ADDM is a boon in emergency situations. It allows you to access a hung or seemingly-hung and extremely slow database by accessing the SGA memory in the database server directly, bypassing the SQL layer (using the database preliminary connection capability). A fast non-locking analysis is performed by this tool to diagnose the database, and this aids troubleshooting considerably in such situations.

Real-Time ADDM will automatically detect problems like OS-level paging, database contention, a database hang, and storage subsystem I/O issues, in real time. Corrective actions will be implemented when possible, otherwise diagnostic data will be collected to aid in further analysis, when there is no way to fix the non-working database.

There is another new feature in relation to ADDM, and this is known as Compare Period ADDM. Rather than comparing two periods of AWR snapshots and just taking a statistical look at what's different, Compare Period ADDM goes one step further and executes the ADDM engine on top of the AWR snapshots. This will do a detailed analysis of the differences in performance between the two periods and the possible reasons why things are different. For example, if you feel the database is slower one day and faster on another, this new feature of Compare Period ADDM will help you understand why it is so.

DBAs will also be impressed by **Active Session History (ASH)** analytics in this version. This is a much more powerful and more flexible reimplementation of the Top Activity functionality from the previous versions of Enterprise Manager. The wait classes can now be viewed as a tree-map structure, and it is possible to analyze performance data by various dimensions such as top SQL, top sessions, active sessions, and wait classes. In the earlier versions, you could only have a limited view of metrics by the dimensions of top Sessions and top SQL.

For backup purposes, that very important aspect of the DBA's worklife, there is a brand new deployment procedure called system backup. This allows the DBA to back up multiple databases and files and directories from multiple servers at the same time. The procedure can back up the database using RMAN and, optionally, also back up the respective database's home—files and folders are backed up using Oracle Secure Backup.

The caveat is that the back up of multiple databases will only work with database versions 10.2 and above. Lower versions such as 10.1 and 9*g* can still be backed up from their database Target home pages, as was possible in the previous Enterprise Manager 11*g* or Enterprise Manager 10*g*.

There is a newly-combined Database Lifecycle Management Pack. This encompasses configuration management, provisioning, patch automation, and change management. These used to be separate packs in past releases.

In short, configuration management enables you to capture and centralize information about all the hardware and software resources, enables historical change tracking, and also includes security compliance plus configuration rules and violations.

Provisioning and patch automation allows deployment of Oracle software, applications and patches. You can provision the entire software stack, including the OS, middleware, and the database. You can patch the OS and the database. Beginning with Bundle Patch 1, which was released in February 2012, you can also patch your **WebLogic Server** (**WLS**) environments. Note that WLS provisioning and patching requires the separate license of the WebLogic Server Management Pack Enterprise Edition (EE).

Change management allows the capture and comparison of metadata (dictionary) definitions, which in real life keep changing across application releases. This includes schema objects, users, and privileges. You can track changes in a single database or compare multiple databases; you can reverse-engineer the database and schema definitions, capture and version baselines, compare databases and schemas or baselines, and propagate schema changes to multiple databases using synchronization.

We will learn about most of these features of the Database Lifecycle Management Pack in other chapters of this book. But coming back to the striking new features, I would like to mention at this point that the change management features have been enhanced with the addition of Change Plans that can be used by developers to capture their database's schema-level changes and send it to the DBA for approval and execution, either via Enterprise Manager or the free Oracle SQL Developer available on the **Oracle Technical Network** (**OTN**) website (`technet.oracle.com`).

This considerably automates the change management flow and is a welcome addition. In Enterprise Manager Cloud Control 12*c*, you can see this by going to the home page of the particular Target database, and then going to **Schema** | **Change Management** | **Schema Change Plans**. Here, you (or the developer) can create the Change Plan and populate it with change items, and this Change Plan can then be deployed.

Change management also includes, for the first time, a comparison of actual data in tables, and this is primarily intended for small tables such as seed data tables or configuration data tables. This makes it easier to compare such tables in different databases or schemas. This is done by selecting **Schema | Change Management | Data Comparisons** from the particular database's Target home page. Note that the caveat is that the reference database must be version 11*g* or later; this database is the one that will actually execute the comparison. The candidate database must be version 10*g* or later.

The configuration capabilities have been considerably improved in the new Enterprise Manager Cloud Control 12*c*. The previously separate **Application Change Console** (**ACC**), **Configuration Change Console** (**CCC**), and BEA Guardian tool have all been integrated into the main Enterprise Manager. This means there is only one Agent, console and repository for these tools, which were previously installed separately.

If there are any configuration exceptions, they will now appear in the incident console like any other alert. Previously, any violation of a configuration policy did not raise alerts, now it will do so. The configuration information from Enterprise Manager can also be pushed to any external **Configuration Management Database** (**CMDB**), if there is any. On the other hand, the external CMDB information can also be brought into Enterprise Manager and integrated with the configuration information there. There is also good integration of the configuration management capabilities of Enterprise Manager Cloud Control 12*c* with My Oracle Support. Custom configuration collections can also be created in this release.

With regards to the compliance capabilities of the Database Lifecycle Management Pack, there is now a new hierarchy of compliance in the Cloud Control 12*c* version. This replaces the compliance policies and policy groups that were there in the previous version.

At the bottom of the hierarchy, we now have compliance rules. These are checks or tests performed against a specific type of Target. One example is to check if a database or OS parameter is set as per best practices. On the second rung of the hierarchy, we have **compliance standards**, which are a collection of one or more rules for certain types of Target, and these standards can be associated with multiple Targets.

Compliance frameworks glue together all the various compliance standards for different types of Targets, and are at the highest rung of the hierarchy. These are conceptual folder-like structures that are used for the mapping of the configuration standards to the real-world frameworks such as PCI, CIS, and Exadata configuration. A good number of compliance rules and standards are shipped out of the box with Enterprise Manager and are mapped to these frameworks.

This is as per the industry standard model. Compliance frameworks assist DBAs, administrators, and IT managers in creating associated rules and standards, and after this is done, the auditors and security and compliance officers can utilize the frameworks to generate their compliance reports—of which there is a rich set.

It is also possible to define your own compliance standards in a vertical perspective for a system or application, or you can define compliance standards in a horizontal perspective for various industry frameworks such as HIPAA, COBIT, SOX, and so on.

Another striking new feature is the new Test Data Management Pack. This allows data subsetting via Enterprise Manager for the first time. This is done by going to **Schema** | **Data Subsetting** on the home page of the Target's database. As can be seen by the workflow in the following screenshot, first you define the application model by reverse-engineering the database, and then you define the subset tables or columns and also the subset conditions:

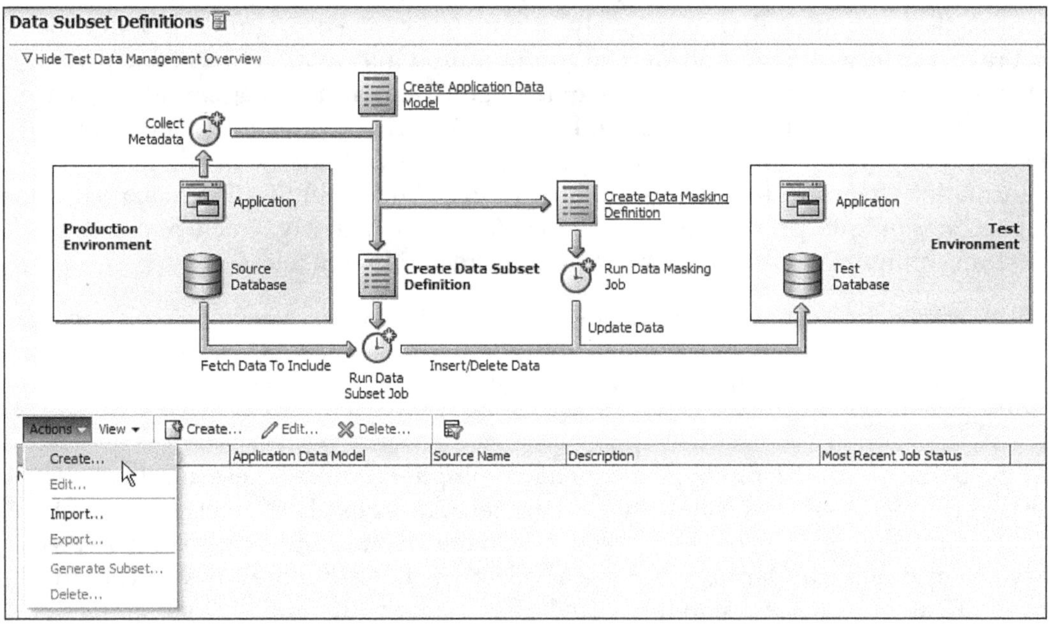

As a result, Enterprise Manager Cloud Control 12*c* automates the procedure of creating a smaller database for test or development, which is a subset of the database used for production. For example, you can create a test database with only 3 months of data in the invoice tables rather than the 3 years that is in the production database, provided there is an invoice date column to define the subset on.

For sensitive column discovery, Enterprise Manager has a new feature called **Data Discovery and Modeling (DDM)**, which lets you do sensitive data discovery. This is based on executing PL/SQL and regular expression pattern matching and, as such, is only possible on Oracle databases. This can be accessed by going to **Enterprise | Quality Management | Data Discovery and Modeling**. This is a part of the Data Masking Pack. You can also import from prebuilt data-masking templates for Oracle E-Business Suite and Oracle Fusion Applications, to get a list of all the sensitive columns in these applications.

Another feature in this new release is the integration of **Real Application Testing (RAT)** with Data Masking. If there is any sensitive data in the the files created by RAT and captured by the workload, or in the SQL tuning sets, it is also masked by the same masking templates that are used for the actual source data. This means a workload can be captured and executed on a test database that has similarly masked data. This protects the sensitive information while testing with RAT.

There is a new Auto Discovery capability using the IP scan (NMAP) functionality on single or multiple hosts, this is a true Agent-less discovery that scans your network and discovers the hosts on that network, along with some clever guesses about the software running on those hosts.

When this completes, Enterprise Manager Cloud Control 12*c* brings up a list of discovered unmanaged Targets that can then be selected by the DBA and promoted as managed Targets. This promotion then leads to the installation of the Enterprise Manager Cloud Control 12*c* Agent by pushing it to the Target.

The configuration information about the Target is then discovered in detail by the Agent. This makes it a lot easier to discover unmanaged assets throughout the enterprise, and manage them via Enterprise Manager Cloud Control 12*c*. The following screenshot demonstrates this:

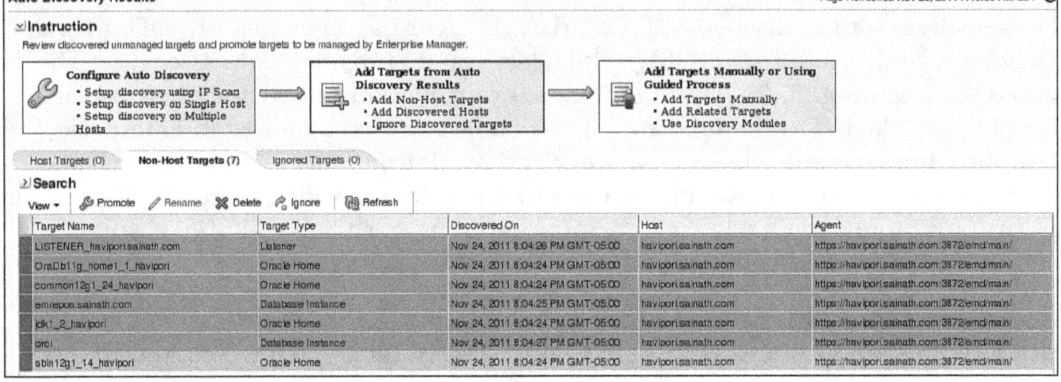


Metric extensions allow you to define your own metrics for any Target's type, for the first time. These replace the user-defined metrics in the previous releases, which were only applicable for certain Target types such as database, listener, and host.

This includes lifecycle support for metrics, including versioning of these extensions. It is also possible to migrate your previously created user-defined metrics to metric extensions.

There have been a lot of alerts and notification events coming from Enterprise Manager in the past, and with a large Target infrastructure, it has become more and more difficult for Administrators to manage so many detailed events. Experience has taught us that many events that have occurred may have had the same underlying root cause, so in the new release there is an incident manager system that manages the small number of incidents. Using this, you can identify, resolve, and remove the root causes of the underlying problems in a more efficient manner, and by business priority.

The **Incident Manager** (accessed via **Enterprise** | **Monitoring** | **Incident Manager**) is a centralized console to manage all the incidents across the enterprise from the entire Target subsystem. All incidents can be viewed, managed, diagnosed, and resolved. Lifecycle operations for incidents are supported. This includes assigning any incidents to other administrators who become the owners. You can acknowledge, prioritize, or suppress incidents and track their status. Escalation is also possible.

This new idea of incidents allows you to concentrate on the high-level incidents instead of individual events. An incident may be defined as a significant event by itself, or it can be defined as a combination of events which are all caused by the same root issue.

For example, when a Target is down, this can be defined as a significant event. Whereas, if there is a space issue in the system, there will be related events about the lack of space from various Targets such as the storage, server, as well as the database—and all these events can be grouped together as a "lack-of-space" incident. In Enterprise Manager Cloud Control 12*c*, it is possible to create your own incident rules, and in this way you can combine events together to form a new incident. Another example is the combining of various metric alerts to create a performance incident, and so on. Other events you can use in this way are job events, availability events, standards violation events, and so on.

The following screenshot shows the Incident Manager in action:

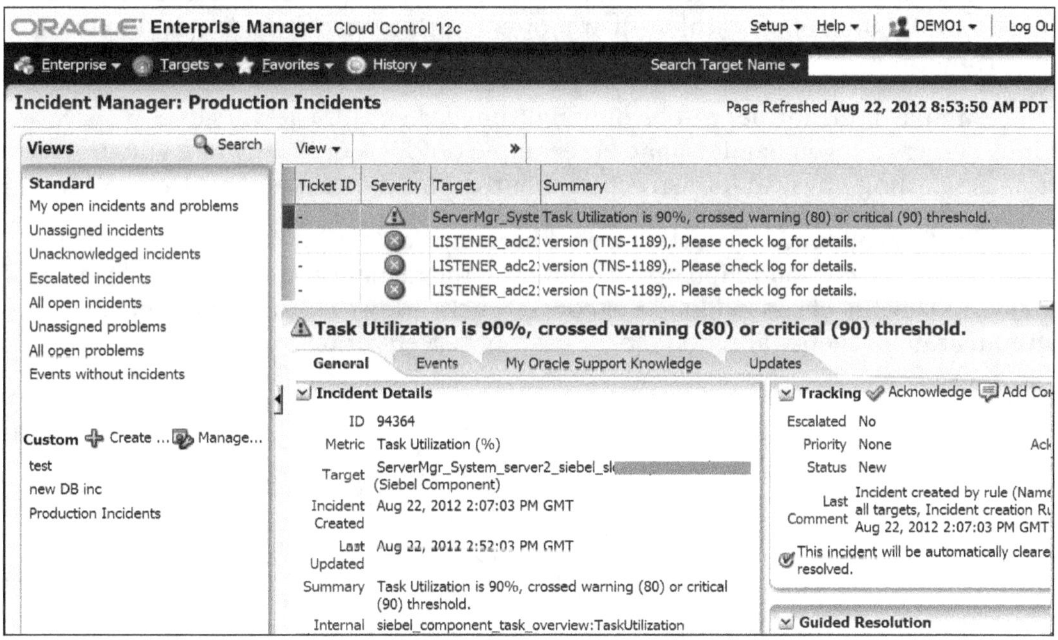

The Incident Manager is integrated with MOS to accelerate the diagnosis and resolution of these incidents. You can easily create service requests and examine knowledge articles related to the incident. It is also possible to integrate the incident management system with external ticketing systems such as Remedy helpdesk, so as to see the status of the help tickets raised for these Enterprise Manager incidents.

A Consolidation Planner is now available for the first time as part of the Base Enterprise Manager Cloud Control 12*c* release, this uses the historical metric data (CPU, memory, storage, and so on), collected by Cloud Control from the various Targets. The Consolidation Planner helps you decide which existing database and application servers can be consolidated, taking into consideration business and technical constraints. For example, a constraint may state that development and production databases should not be placed on the same consolidated server.

Based on all this information along with the constraints, the Consolidation Planner produces a recommended consolidation plan to assist in consolidation of underutilized servers to a lesser number of servers, that is, **Physical to Physical** (**P2P**), or migration of physical infrastructure to virtual machines, that is, **Physical to Virtual** (**P2V**).

One example of the former can be moving from current IBM servers to new SUN or Linux servers or even Exadata, and an example of P2V would be when you move from an existing physical infrastructure to virtual machines, namely Oracle VM.

Thus, the Consolidation Planner can enable an efficient use of the resources by the identification of consolidation opportunities in the manner just described. There are manifold benefits of consolidation of course, such as lower capital, maintenance, administration, energy and floor space costs of servers, and so on.

The following screenshot shows the Consolidation Planner in action. This is after a planning project has been set up by going to **Enterprise | Consolidation planner**, and analysis has been completed. The resource utilization of the various servers to be consolidated is displayed on a color coded basis, showing the underutilized and heavily-utilized data points. Again, a welcome addition to Enterprise Manager—but note that you still need to make your own consolidation decisions. The Consolidation Planner is to be treated as a mathematical advisor that is based on OS-level metrics:

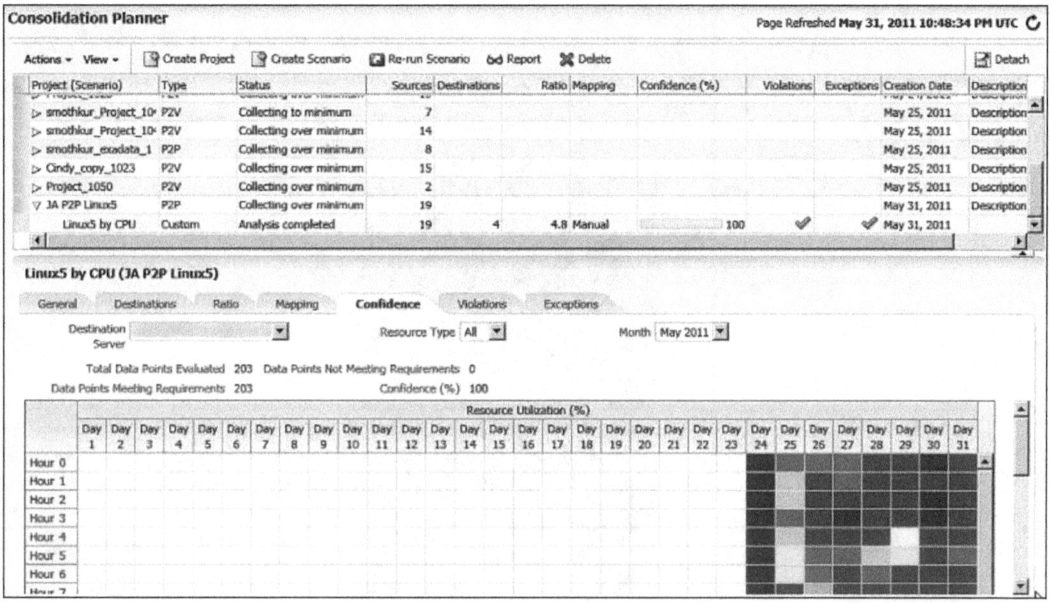

Installation of Enterprise Manager Cloud Control 12*c* has also been simplified, with the WebLogic Server (WLS) installation included as part of the Enterprise Manager install, instead of having to manually preinstall WLS before installing Enterprise Manager. We will go through a quick installation in the coming sections.

Managing Exadata- and Exalogic-engineered systems with Enterprise Manager Cloud Control 12*c* is also a lot more powerful, with the help of advanced lifecycle management capabilities. There are a number of enhancements in this area of engineered systems. For example, you are able to discover the Exadata storage cells and Infiniband network and switches out of the box, and see an integrated view of the hardware and software in Enterprise Manager.

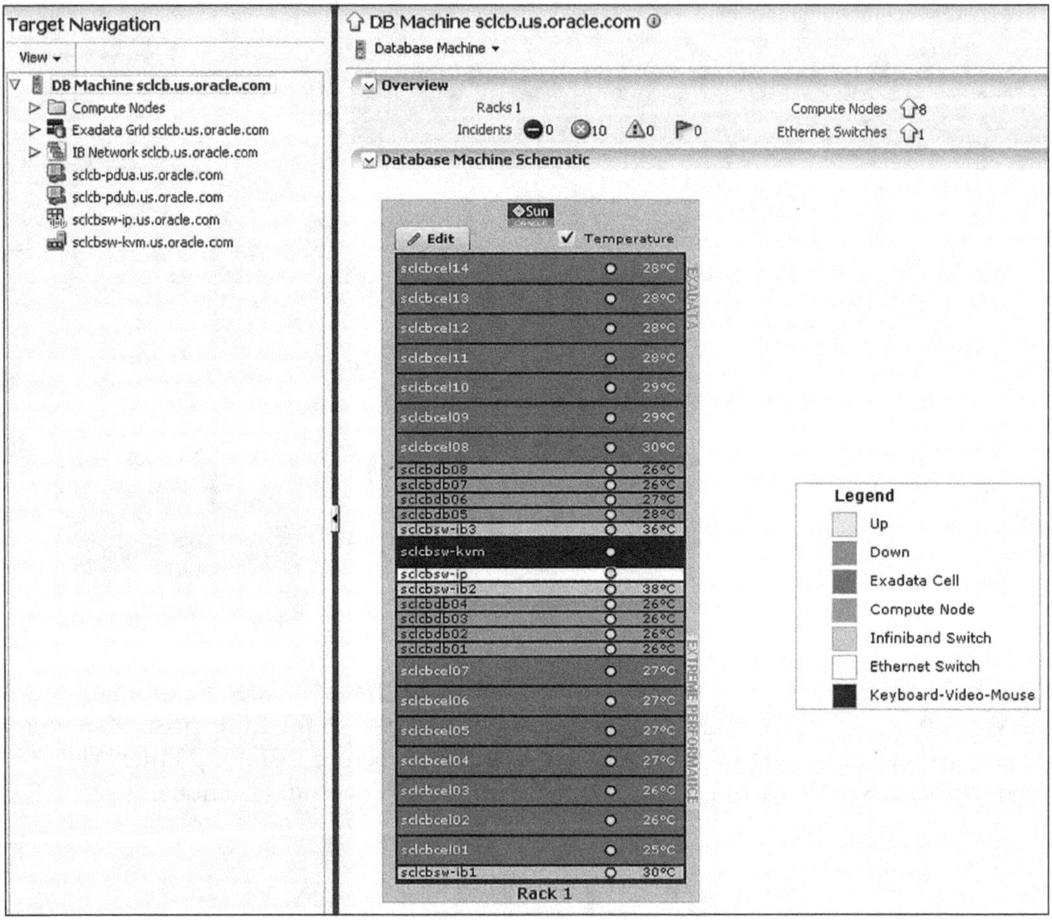


You can monitor and administer the storage cells and set up **I/O Resource Manager (IORM)** via Enterprise Manager to control the disk I/O utilization by any database.

You can manage the Infiniband network and monitor all the other components of the Exadata machine, such as the ILOM, Cisco Switch, KVM, and PDU. You can use the brand new Consolidation Planner in Enterprise Manager to get an idea of which of your existing servers can be consolidated with Exadata.

The SQL monitoring feature of the Tuning Pack and other performance pages in Enterprise Manager are now Exadata-aware, showing the Cell Offload Efficiency (the more the better) and the Cell Smart Table Scan. Full configuration management via Enterprise Manager is possible for Exadata, with the ability to compare configurations of the entire Exadata database machines, database servers, or storage cells. We will look at Exadata management in more detail in a later chapter.

And of course, we have the new Cloud management capabilities of the Cloud Management Pack as discussed earlier. These build on the foundation of the Database Lifecycle Management Pack or WebLogic Server Management Pack EE (either of these is required as a prerequisite, depending on the type of Cloud), and provide self service, metering, and chargeback facilities. You can set up, deliver, and manage the Cloud using Enterprise Manager in all these tasks, whether it be the IaaS, DBaaS, or PaaS type of Cloud infrastructure using Oracle VM pools, Oracle databases, or middleware.

Of course, you may or may not use Exadata- and/or Exalogic-engineered systems to achieve this level of Cloud management and lifecycle management of both your databases and middleware. Exadata and/or Exalogic is optional, but highly recommended.

In Enterprise Manager 11*g*, we had the combined **Application Management Suites** (**AMS**) that are integrated management solutions for managing sophisticated applications such as Oracle E-Business Suite, Siebel, PeopleSoft, and JD Edwards EnterpriseOne. There is a suite available for each of these.

Each of these suites combines capabilities for the respective application management, configuration management, end user management using **Real User Experience Insight** (**RUEI**), and the respective RUEI application accelerator into one single comprehensive product. In the case of the application management suite for Oracle E-Business Suite, in addition it also includes features of application change management for Oracle E-Business Suite, such as the ability to manage patches, customizations, and configuration data.

But what's new in Enterprise Manager Cloud Control 12*c* for the application management suites? First of all, an Applications Management Pack as well as an Applications Management Suite for Fusion applications has been released.

For all the applications, you can leverage the Enterprise Manager Cloud Control 12*c* enhancements, such as Metric Extensions (the ability to attach metrics to any Target type), Administration Groups, the use of BI Publisher, configuration management and compliance, for example, the latter capabilities are more robust in the 12*c* version with the ability to detect real-time changes via the Base EM Release itself, without installing separate software (as in the previous release). With this, you can have an automatic notification on a drift detection in any configuration aspect of your application.

A new feature called Oracle Site Guard is now available. This can be used to control the failover of the entire application, that is, for disaster-protection automation. Oracle Site Guard is licensed under the Database Lifecycle Management Pack for the database layer, and the Weblogic Server Management Pack Enterprise Edition (EE) for the WLS layer. This feature is documented at the following URL:

`http://docs.oracle.com/cd/E23943_01/doc.1111/e15250/site_guard.htm`

There are more new features in Fusion middleware management as well, such as the new Middleware Diagnostics Advisory. This is similar to the functionality of the database-side ADDM. It provides assistance in the diagnosis of performance issues in WebLogic servers, by looking at the metric data and configuration properties. Recommendations are then generated, which will help you to improve performance in the middleware tier.

There are other new application performance management and coherence-management features too. For a complete official list of new features, you can refer to the *New Features In Oracle Enterprise Manager Cloud Control 12c* chapter in the *Oracle Enterprise Manager Cloud Control Introduction* manual at `http://docs.oracle.com/cd/E24628_01/doc.121/e25353/whats_new.htm#CEGIFFGA`

# Bonus sections

The rest of the sections in this chapter deal with the steps of repository installation, OMS installation, Agent installation, post-installation steps, upgrade of existing Enterprise Manager installations, and also the recommended architecture for very large sites, along with disaster recovery tactics.

These sections can be downloaded from the Packt website from the location:

`http://www.packtpub.com/sites/default/files/downloads/4781EN_Installation_Upgrade_Tactics_and_Architecture_for_Large_Sites.pdf`

# 3

# Ease the Chaos with Performance Management

There are normally numerous applications running in a data center. These applications often impact the database in different ways at different times, and no application or database ever stays static; there is continuous change.

The data in the database changes as time goes by with more volumes of data being added or with continuous updates, deletions, and inserts. Application users also change in terms of more and more users and the application code itself changes with periodic application upgrades that add more functionality to the applications.

Consequently, with all these changes, the database performance is bound to deteriorate sooner or later and the DBA will always be forced to look into performance issues at the database layer.

As per the *IOUG Survey on Database Manageability* in 2011, 90 percent of DBAs mentioned that they had experienced unplanned downtime due to database changes not having been properly tested, and as a result over 50 percent of DBAs said that they avoid making changes to production because of these changes negatively impacting performance.

The question is, how do we guarantee the performance of the application? How do we make sure that what works today is going to work in the same way tomorrow? If performance can't be guaranteed, the data center degenerates to a day-to-day fire-fighting operation, where DBAs are even called up in the middle of the night if reports take longer than usual. This guaranteeing of the application performance is often the top concern in the minds of many IT managers and application managers.

The answer is Oracle Enterprise Manager. The new version of Cloud Control 12*c* has powerful features for diagnosis of database issues, complemented with tuning capabilities for most of the issues found. The diagnosis and tuning is a carry-on from the previous versions of Enterprise Manager; however, the capabilities have been considerably advanced, as we will see shortly.

# Laying the foundation

The foundation of the diagnostics capabilities is the built-in repository that is installed with every Oracle database (from version 10*g* onwards). This is known as the **Automatic Workload Repository** (**AWR**), and is stored in the `SYSAUX` Tablespace. Once every hour, by default, the database takes a snapshot of its workload and statistical information, and stores it in the AWR repository. This data is saved for 8 days by default.

Different classes of statistical data are stored: base statistics (such as physical reads), SQL statistics (such as reads per SQL statement), or different metrics (such as physical reads per second). Thus, historical information about the performance of the database is captured automatically, and the DBA does not have to set up any home-grown scripts or tables to do the capture, as in the past. The AWR is also self-managing and does not have to be micromanaged by the DBA. The space requirements are automatically managed; based on the retention interval, the old data is purged nightly.

Using the functionality of the AWR, accessing the views or running the `awrrpt.sql` script (used by DBAs to generate an AWR report) requires the license for the Enterprise Manager Diagnostics Pack.

AWR includes **Active Session History** (**ASH**) as one of its key components. ASH is responsible for sampling active sessions every second and storing their current state in memory. A v$ view can be used to access the data in memory, this is the `V$ACTIVE_SESSION_HISTORY` view. Every hour, some samples of the data are inserted into the AWR repository.

The main benefit of ASH is that you can now do performance analysis of very fast transient issues, which may occur for a few fleeting seconds, as ASH samples active sessions every second. Therefore, AWR and ASH form the basis of the diagnostics capabilities that can be accessed from Enterprise Manager, and lead to the tuning capabilities (since, after diagnosing a problem you will need to tune it). Both AWR and ASH are RAC database aware and include events such as cluster wait.

After logging in to the Cloud Control 12*c* console, go to **Targets** | **Databases** on the menu. This brings up a list of the database Targets being monitored by the Enterprise Manager system. Only the targets visible to the currently logged in administrator can be seen. In this case, we are logged in as `SYSMAN` to Cloud Control, so all database Targets can be seen.

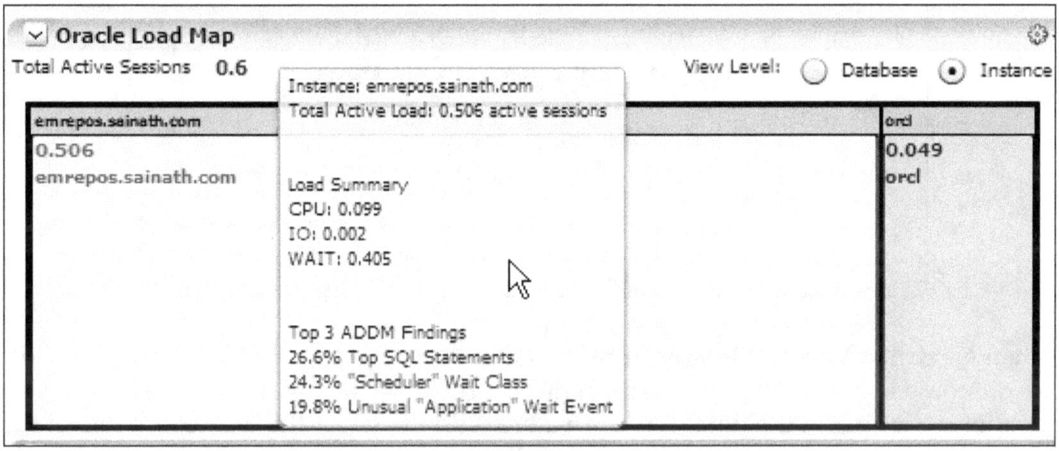


By default, the databases are seen in a Load Map (this can be changed to a Search List, if required). This is a fast, visually color-coded way of finding out the database that is placing the most load on a system (the total active load), or the database that has the most performance issues. Simply placing your mouse cursor on the largest box on the Load Map immediately shows more performance information about the database, such as the time consumed by database sessions in CPU, I/O, or WAIT (that is, waits in all other wait class categories), as well as the top three ADDM findings.

**Automatic Database Diagnostic Monitor** (**ADDM**) is like a doctor in the database, a self-diagnostic engine that is built into the Oracle database kernel. ADDM looks for performance issues and also supplies the recommendations and the fixes. This is part of the Diagnostics Pack license for Enterprise Manager.

Now, we can have a look at the performance home of the database. Log in to the database by clicking on it in the Load Map. In the initial login screen, shown in the following screenshot, we can create a named credential by simply checking the **Save As** checkbox and supplying a name for the credential. This named credential belongs to the current user and can be re-used by other users if they are granted the privileges for this credential:

When we drill down in this way from the Load Map, the performance home page of the database is displayed. The performance page shows over time the average active sessions occurring in the database, with a breakdown as per the wait class, which can be **Application**, **Concurrency**, **User I/O**, **CPU Wait**, among others. This is displayed in the following screenshot:

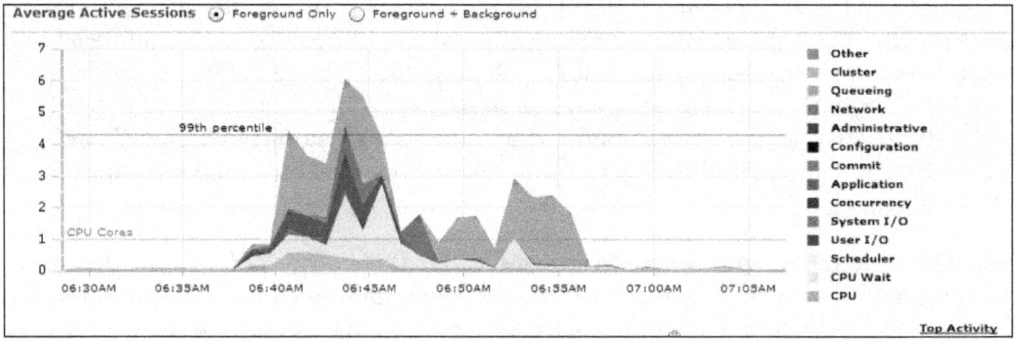

The data on this page comes from v$ views in the database, for example, `v$sysmetric`. Some of the information also comes from the operating system. The page also shows the host processes with or without the load average, as can be seen in the following screenshot, to give you an idea of the stress at the server level. It is important for the DBA to know if there is any other process outside the database that is impacting the database's performance:

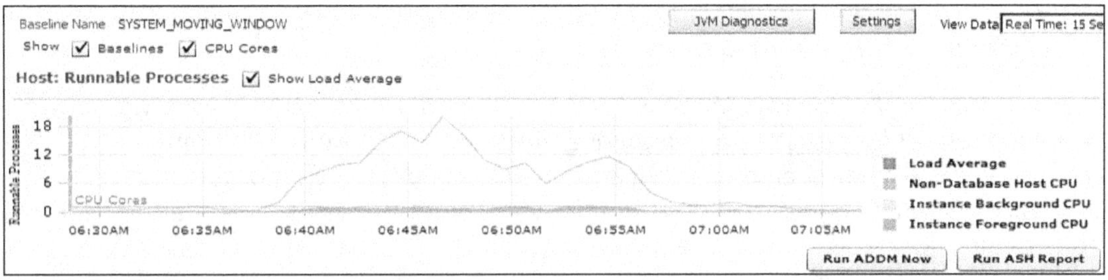


At the bottom of the performance home page, the instance throughput rate, including **Logons**, **Transactions**, **Physical Reads**, and **Redo Size** in KB per second is displayed in the **Throughput** tab:

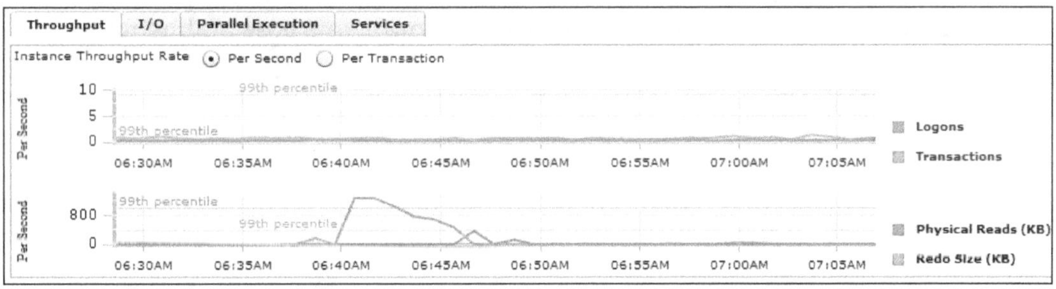


There is also a detailed **I/O** tab showing the I/O megabytes per second for each I/O function, and the I/O request per second. But the most interesting tab is the **Parallel Execution** tab, this shows an overview of the parallel activity happening in the database.

In this tab you can see a red line named **Parallel Max Servers**; this is as per the corresponding initialization parameter setting in the database. You can also see the active parallel sessions in the database, the parallel slaves that are being created. In the same tab, the DDL/DML/query statements that are being parallelized can be seen, as well as the amount of downgrading of the parallel operations, broken down into a percentage. This can quickly give the DBA an idea of how to tune the parallel operations in the database.

Finally, the **Services** tab on the screen gives you a breakdown of the service-level activity in the database, which is especially useful for multiple services in a RAC database.

You can change the performance page settings by clicking on the **Settings** button in the performance page. On the performance page settings screen, you can specify the **Throughput Chart Settings**, **I/O Chart Settings**, and the **Baseline Display** pages show the 99th percentile line using the system's moving-window baseline, or using a static baseline with computed statistics.

Coming back to the **Average Active Sessions** section on the performance home page, it is possible to ascertain at a glance the peaks of activities occurring in the database, and if you "click on the big stuff"—this is Oracle's way of putting it—you will find it is very easy to drill down to the wait event that is most severely affecting your database.

For example, if you click on the **CPU Wait** section in the graph, you will be shown the exact breakdown of the SQL statements and the sessions in the database that contributed towards that wait event. You can also move the shaded bar over the time period and the statements, and sessions displayed in the lower section will change accordingly. This is displayed in the following screenshot; due to the print size, the screenshot may not be readable, but it is included for the purpose of illustration:

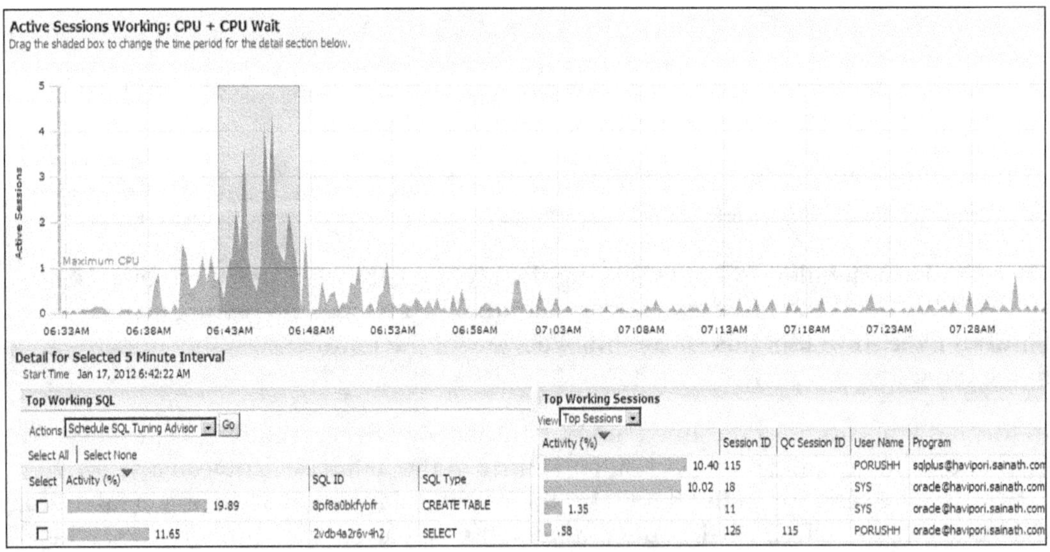

If you place your cursor on the SQL ID, the entire SQL statement is shown. It is possible to drill down further into any of the statements to see their execution plan details along with the plan control information for this statement, such as whether a SQL profile (auxiliary statistics that aid the optimizer) is associated with this statement, or whether a SQL plan baseline (a stored execution plan) has been enabled for this statement. Tuning history and SQL monitoring information for this statement may also be available. The following screenshot shows the execution plan for a particular statement. Either a graphical or a tabular view of the execution plan can be selected. This screenshot may not be readable, but is included for the purpose of illustration:

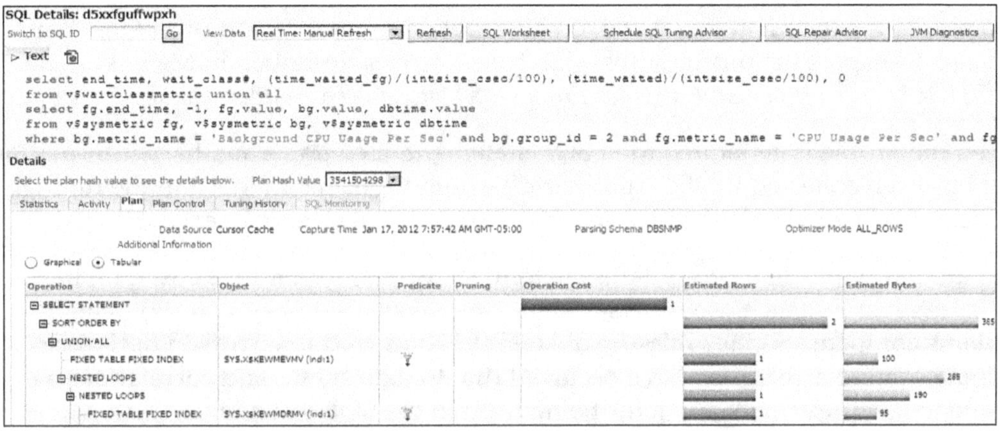

The **SQL Worksheet** button allows you to reexecute the SQL statement using bind variables, if present, and examine the results. There is an option in this to execute only the `SELECT` statements and ignore the DML part of the statement.

If your SQL statement is failing to execute properly, you can run the **SQL Repair Advisor** utility from this page; this will try to find alternate execution paths that allow the SQL statement to complete successfully. To fix this issue, a SQL patch may be recommended for this particular SQL statement, as a workaround.

If the SQL statement executes correctly but you are not happy with its performance, it is possible to simply click on the **Schedule SQL Tuning Advisor** button. This allows you to start a SQL tuning task for this statement that invokes the optimizer in tuning mode, and generates solutions for your SQL statement.

These solutions may be new indexes to speed up your queries, or a statistics update may be suggested for your tables or indexes if these statistics are missing or stale. Otherwise, SQL restructuring can be suggested if your SQL is improperly formed, for example, Cartesian joins where data from two tables is selected without a proper join clause. The most interesting and useful suggestion is of course the SQL profile.

The SQL profile offers auxiliary information to the optimizer, which aids in the efficient execution of a SQL statement without actually changing the statement. As such, it can tune SQL transparently, without changing the application code.

This makes it very useful for packaged application tuning; it has always been difficult to get vendors to change their application SQL when the DBA found certain statements were inefficient.

Now, there is no need to ask the vendor to change the SQL, as a SQL profile will simply make the SQL run better without changing it. This technology is only in the Enterprise Manager Tuning Pack.

The profile is persistent, it works even after database restarts and upgrades. You can also transport the profile across databases. This is described in MOS Note ID 457531.1: *How To Move SQL Profiles From One Database To Another Database.*

When the profile is generated for a SQL statement, it contains auxiliary information that has been collected by the **Automatic Tuning Optimizer** (**ATO**) in the tuning mode (it takes a longer time than in the case of normal optimizer execution).

This auxiliary information contains customized optimizer settings based on past execution history (such as whether `first_rows` was used or `all_rows`). It also contains compensation for missing or stale statistics, and for errors in optimizer estimates; these errors may have occurred due to data skews and correlations, or due to complex filters and joins being used in the SQL statement.

Once the SQL profile is accepted for a particular SQL statement, from then on whenever that statement is run in production, the optimizer in normal mode will use the SQL profile and its auxiliary information in deciding the best execution path possible. The result will be a well-tuned execution plan in which there has been no change to the actual SQL code.

Comprehensive analysis or limited analysis may be chosen for this task, limited analysis is faster but will not generate a SQL profile. The results of any task you have submitted can be seen by going to **Performance** | **Advisors Home** (also known as Advisor Central). The task completes and the SQL tuning advisor can recommend collecting optimizer statistics for a table (used in the SQL statement) and its indexes if it finds they are stale or missing, or creating a SQL plan baseline, and so on. Enterprise Manager further automates the tuning process by allowing you to fulfill these recommendations by simply clicking on the **Implement** button. In the case of table statistics, an Enterprise Manager task will be scheduled to gather the statistics, and this is done by using the `DBMS_STATS.GATHER_TABLE_STATS` database procedure.

You can also implement a new SQL plan baseline or a SQL profile in this manner. Clicking on the magnifying glass icon in the **Other Statistics** column allows you to select the plan (with the least elapsed time) that you can use to create the SQL plan baseline, as shown in the following screenshot:

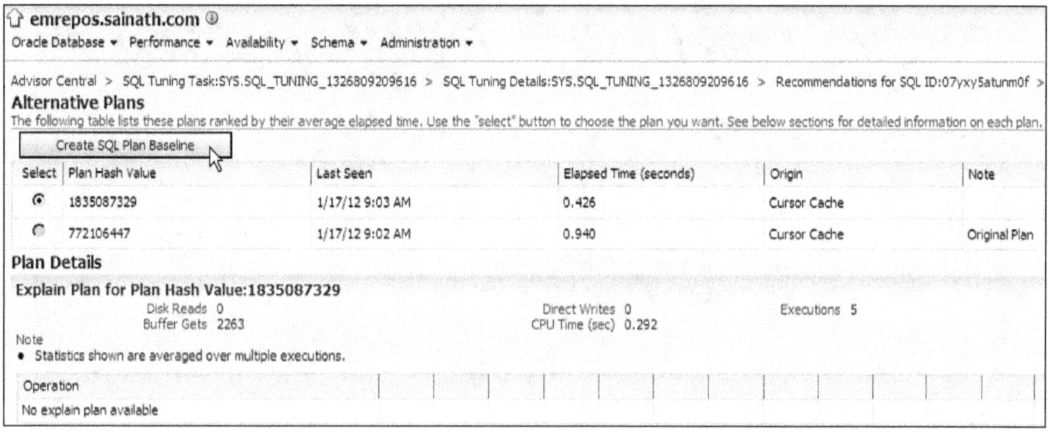


Automatic SQL tuning has been possible from Oracle Database 11*g* onwards. This feature can be set up to run automatically in the maintenance window and capture the highest-impact SQL. This SQL is then analyzed, SQL profiles are generated, and these profiles can be automatically implemented if they can substantially improve the execution plans. Thus, the application performance can be improved without changing the application.

The automatic implementation is optional and can be set up if needed, however, it is highly recommended. This is because a generated SQL profile can work very well one day and the same profile may not help a few days later, depending on the data that has changed in the tables. Thus, it is advisable to keep generating and implementing new SQL profiles every day for the highest-impact SQL statements, and this is best automated by automatic SQL tuning. The findings and actions taken by this process will be automatically reported to the DBA.

To set up automatic SQL tuning, on the database menu go to **Administration** | **Oracle Scheduler** | **Automated Maintenance Tasks**.

The automated maintenance tasks are enabled by default (in the case of the Enterprise Manager repository database, these tasks are disabled manually as a prerequisite before Enterprise Manager installation can start).

Click on the **Configure** button on the **Automated Maintenance Tasks** screen. This displays a page where you can enable or disable the maintenance tasks and also assign the daily maintenance windows to each task, as shown in the following screenshot:

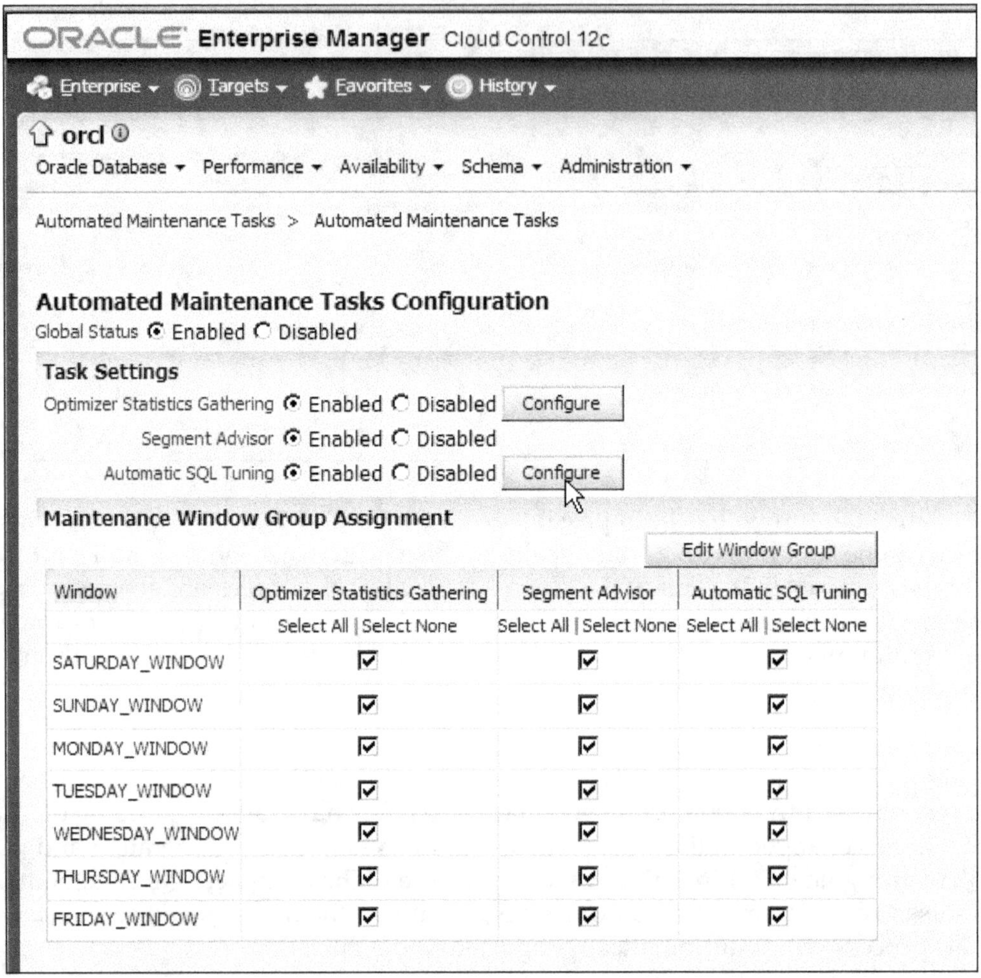


Click on the **Configure** button against **Automatic SQL Tuning**. This now allows you to confirm that SQL profiles should be automatically implemented. This is set to **No** by default. If you set this to **Yes**, you can also specify the maximum time spent per SQL during tuning (in seconds), the maximum number of SQL profiles implemented per execution of the automatic SQL tuning, and the maximum SQL profiles implemented (overall). The default values for these settings are 1200 seconds, 20, and 10,000 respectively.

# Top activity

At any point in time, it is possible to go to **Performance** | **Top Activity** and display a view of the top SQL statements as well as top sessions. You can drag the highlighted bar to select the particular time required.

This screen looks similar to the drilldown from the **Average Active Sessions** section on the performance home page. However, the difference is that all the wait events can be seen against the time in this graph, on the **Top Activity** page. This data is fully sourced from the ASH information in the database. The text in the following screenshot may not be fully readable, but it has been included for the purpose of illustration:

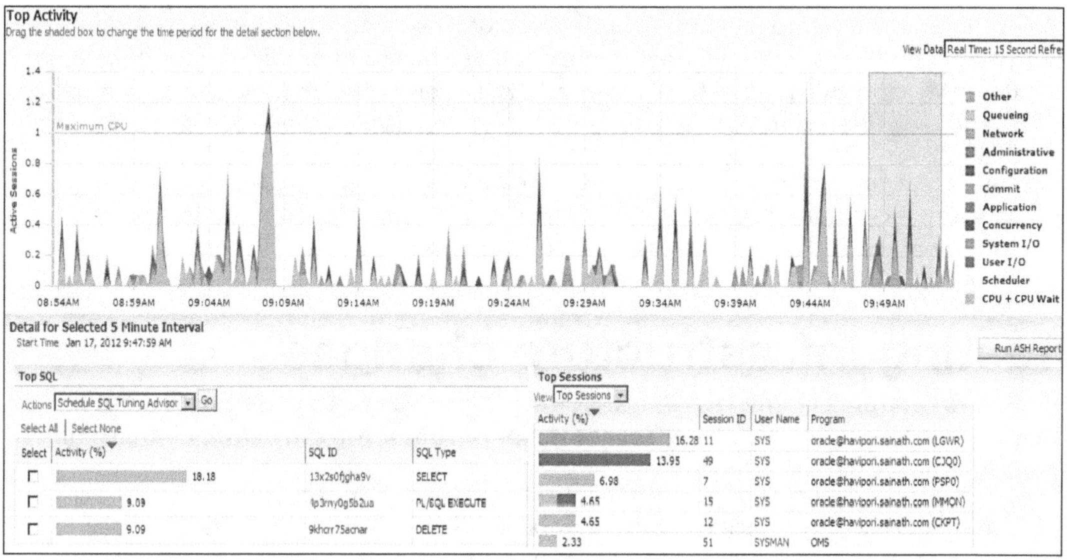


Another difference is the presence of the **Run ASH Report** button on this page. This allows you to generate an ASH report for a period as small as one minute. The beauty of ASH is that it allows you to examine database activity that happened in any small period of time you select.

Enterprise Manager Cloud Control 12*c* also allows you to examine the SQL statements issued by Enterprise Manager itself. This is accessed by going to **Performance** | **SQL** | **Cloud Control SQL History.** You can select the module as either administration, real-time monitoring, or repository to display the most recent 50 statements. You can also enable or disable SQL Trace on this page.

The **SQL Access Advisor** utility is another important part of the SQL tuning pack. This is accessed by going to **Performance** | **SQL** | **SQL Access Advisor**.

The SQL Access Advisor goes through SQL statements in the database cache or in a SQL tuning set (a collection of SQL statements), and will give you suggestions for creating new database objects or dropping existing objects to improve the performance of the workload.

These suggestions may include the creation of new B-tree indexes or Bitmap indexes, materialized views (for maximum query rewrite usage), materialized view logs (for fast refresh), or the creation of partitions (hash and interval only) for tables, indexes, or materialized views.

This advisor analyzes the entire workload, and not just independent SQL statements to arrive at its conclusions, plus it also considers the impact of the new access structures it recommends on DML operations. For example, a new index may speed up an existing query, but if there are a lot of insertions/updates/deletions happening on the same table, the Oracle database has to maintain the index to cater for the DML and this may actually degrade the overall performance; so this must be taken into consideration.

Storage, creation, and maintenance costs are all considered by the advisor before it gives any recommendations. New indexes or new materialized views are simultaneously considered, as well as a combination of both.

# Testing infrastructure changes

**Real Application Testing** (**RAT**) is an Oracle Database Enterprise Edition option that allows you to test out the effects of major or minor infrastructure changes on your database.

This may include any changes at the database layer or below, such as database upgrades from 9.2, 10.1, or 10.2 to 11*g*, moving from a single-instance database to a RAC database, migrating to a different OS, using a different storage subsystem, moving to Exadata, and so on. It may also include database patches, initialization parameter changes, optimizer setting changes, and so on.

RAT includes Database Replay as well as **SQL Performance Analyzer** (**SPA**). Both of these components of RAT can be fully executed via Enterprise Manager Cloud Control 12*c*.

Database Replay can be accessed by going to **Performance | Database Replay** on the database menu in Enterprise Manager. The screen appears as follows:

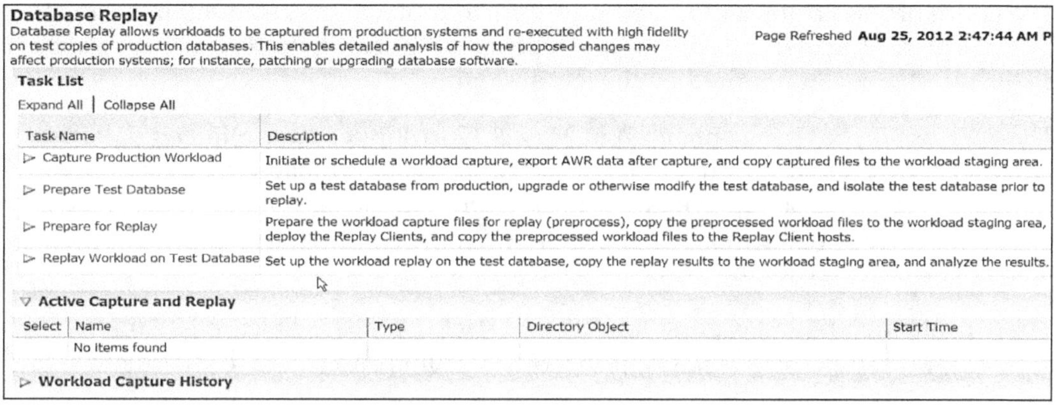


**Database Replay** is a unique feature available for Oracle databases. You can capture an entire workload from a production system, move it to a test system, and replay it there with exactly the same timing, concurrency, and transaction characteristics of the production database.

Database Replay then analyses the effect of the replay on the test system and reports extensively if any errors are encountered, if SQL statements have regressed in performance, or if there are new contention issues. These issues can then be fixed by using other tools such as the Enterprise Manager Tuning Pack.

Testing infrastructure changes in this way gives your company and your DBA greater confidence that the application database will have a guaranteed performance in production after the infrastructure change. For example, Oracle 9*i* databases upgrading to 10*g* in the past, without proper testing, were known to have performance regressions due to outdated parameter settings. Such upgrades from older databases will produce a higher degree of confidence if RAT has been used.

Any infrastructure changes from the database tier and below can be tested with this method. The performance impact to the production system during the capture phase has been estimated to be less than 5 percent, and you can start and stop the capture when you please.

The capture files are moved to the test system (where the infrastructure change has taken place). In the database there, they are preprocessed, and then replayed.

The entire process from capture to preprocess to replay is orchestrated in a workflow by Enterprise Manager. Multiple replay clients can be set up to replay the workload, so the mid-tier is not required by the test system.

The RAT option has been enhanced in May 2012 to support consolidated database replay. This allows two or more captured production workloads from the same or different systems to be replayed concurrently on a single test database. The idea is to assist in assessing the impact of consolidating the database workload of multiple databases on a single database.

The consolidated replay is possible only on Oracle Database Release 11.2.0.2 or higher. The multiple-workload captures can be from pre-11.2.0.2 database releases.

At the time of writing, the Enterprise Manager GUI interface could be used for the capture and replay of workloads on single databases as before, but could not be used for the replay of consolidated workloads from multiple databases onto a single database. Only the API can be used for this purpose. For the database patches required, and the actual procedure steps, please see the My Oracle Support note ID 1453789.1: *Real Application Testing: Consolidated Database Replay Feature*.

SQL Performance Analyzer, the other component of Real Application Testing, can be accessed by going to **Performance** | **SQL** | **SQL Performance Analyzer** on the database menu. The SPA screen appears as follows:

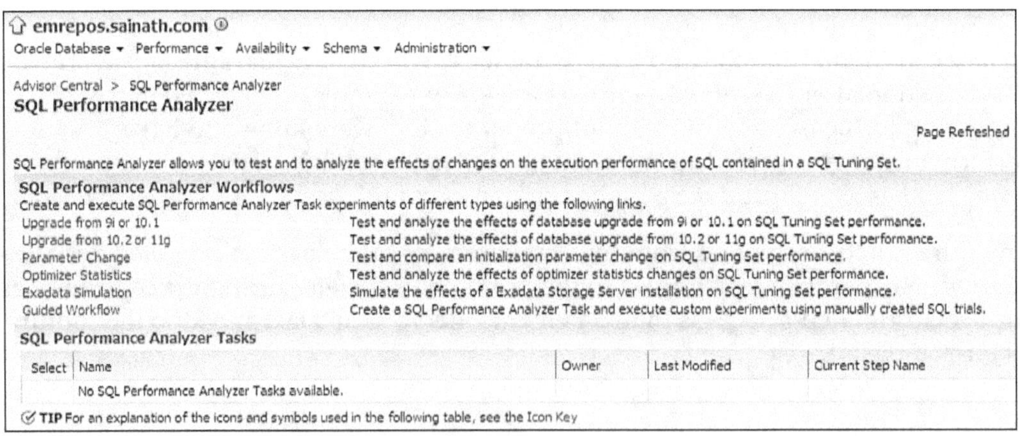


You can capture the SQL workload in production (in most cases done via a SQL tuning set), and the same SQL will be reexecuted serially (not concurrently like Database Replay) on the test database by SPA. The captured SQL output includes statistics and bind variables.

The analysis and report generated by SPA enables you to see if your SQL statements have improved or regressed in the new environment. Any regression can be fixed using other tools such as the SQL Tuning Advisor or SQL plan baselines, in a seamless flow from the SPA task-result screen.

The main difference between SPA and Database Replay (the two components of Real Application Testing) is that the latter captures the entire database workload in a specified time period and tests it out, whereas SPA can be used to test a limited set of SQL statements. While Database Replay runs the workload concurrently, SPA uses serial execution and tests each SQL statement one-by-one on its own.

SPA can also be used to test minor performance changes, such as the effects of optimizer statistics changes on SQL tuning set performance, or the effects of new indexes or other objects such as materialized views, as recommended by the tuning advisors. As such, SPA usage can go hand in hand with the Enterprise Manager diagnostics and tuning packs.

Interestingly, due to popular demand, RAT has been back ported to earlier releases of the Oracle database.

In the case of the Database Replay component of RAT, this back port is with respect to the capturing of the database workloads. Database Replay can capture workloads on 9.2 or 10.2 database versions, but the actual replay of the workload can only be done on 11*g* versions such as 11.1 (replay was first introduced in 11.1.0.6) and 11.2. Note that the replay cannot be done on 10*g* databases (for upgrades of 9*i* to 10*g*) because RAT is essentially an 11*g* product. Hence, there will be no back port for the replay.

On the other hand, the SPA component of RAT can use captured SQL from 9.2, 10.1, or 10.2 database releases and SQL can be tested by SPA in database versions 10.2 or 11*g* (11.1 and 11.2).

This means that SPA can be used to test an upgrade from 9.2 to 10.1 or 10.2, in case you want to do that, but this is not recommended as you should instead be upgrading to the latest 11.2 database version (to avoid the extra support costs for older versions, and to be able to use the new features of the most recent database version).

By the way, SQL Trace is used to capture the SQL statements for SPA in a 9.2 database since there is no SQL tuning set capability in this older version of the database.

For further details, you can refer to the MOS note ID 560977.1: *Real Application Testing for Earlier Releases*.

# SQL Monitoring

For managing and helping to tune long-running SQL statements, Enterprise Manager Cloud Control 12*c* provides a very useful utility called SQL Monitoring, which is enabled out of the box with no performance impact.

This will automatically monitor any long-running SQL statement that has gone beyond 5 seconds of either CPU or I/O time, as well as any parallel statements. However, in a very busy system with lots of such queries, SQL monitoring may not take place for all the queries. You can use the `/*+MONITOR*/` hint in your SQL statements to explicitly ask for SQL monitoring in this case.

You can access the SQL monitoring page by going to **Performance | SQL Monitoring**. Any SQL statements that are long-running or parallel will appear on this page. For example, the SQL executed by user **PORUSHH** has taken 36 seconds to execute so far, as shown in the following screenshot:

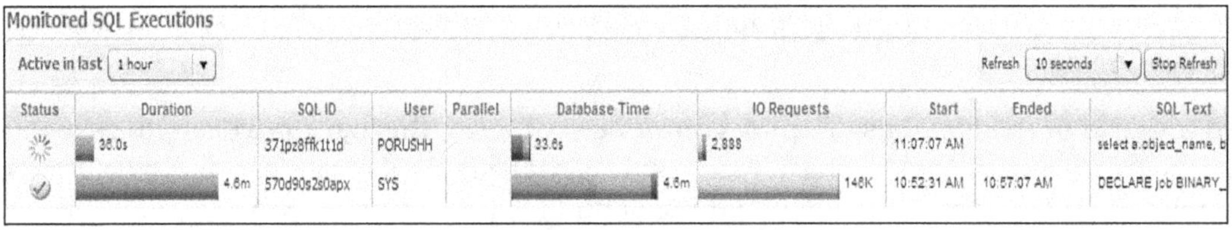


The completed SQL statements are shown with a tick mark. There is a rotating wheel shown against the statements that are still being processed at that point in time.

You can drill down on the long-running SQL and examine the actual execution steps it is working on. This is shown dynamically by Enterprise Manager in the following screenshot. The text in this screenshot may not be readable, but is shown for the purpose of illustration:

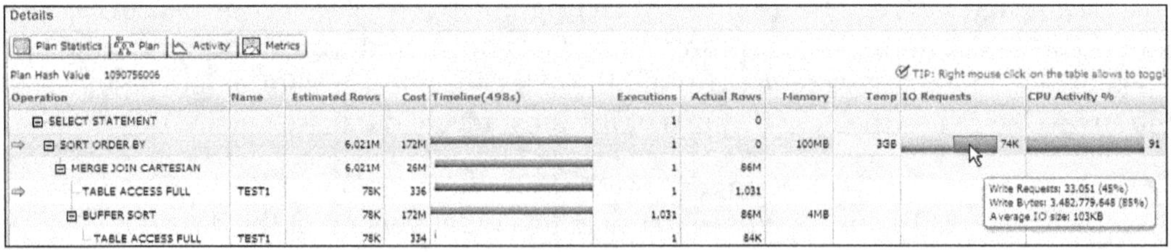

Under the **Plan Statistics** tab, green arrows instantly appear against the currently executing steps. Certain columns in this section such as **Actual Rows, Memory,** and **Temp** (this is the temporary space used) are refreshed with the latest data at every refresh interval—this is shown by the appearance of a green shading on the column data at the moment of refresh.

This makes it possible for the DBA to understand exactly the progress of the long-running SQL, and is very useful when it is required to find the status of a long-running major report or job working in the database. This feature is a part of the Database Tuning Pack.

One point to note in the preceding screenshot is that the red band in the **Wait Activity** column against the **SORT ORDER BY** operation signifies that the sort has spilled over to the disk. So this is an expensive operation.

From Oracle Database 11*g* Release 2 onwards, PL/SQL programs can also be monitored on the SQL monitoring page. You can drill down to the slow SQL statements in PL/SQL programs.

On navigating back to **Targets** | **Databases**, if the database list on this page had been changed to a search list instead of a Load Map, and you were to drill down to the database in that list, the database home page would appear instead as seen in the following screenshot for the Oracle database:

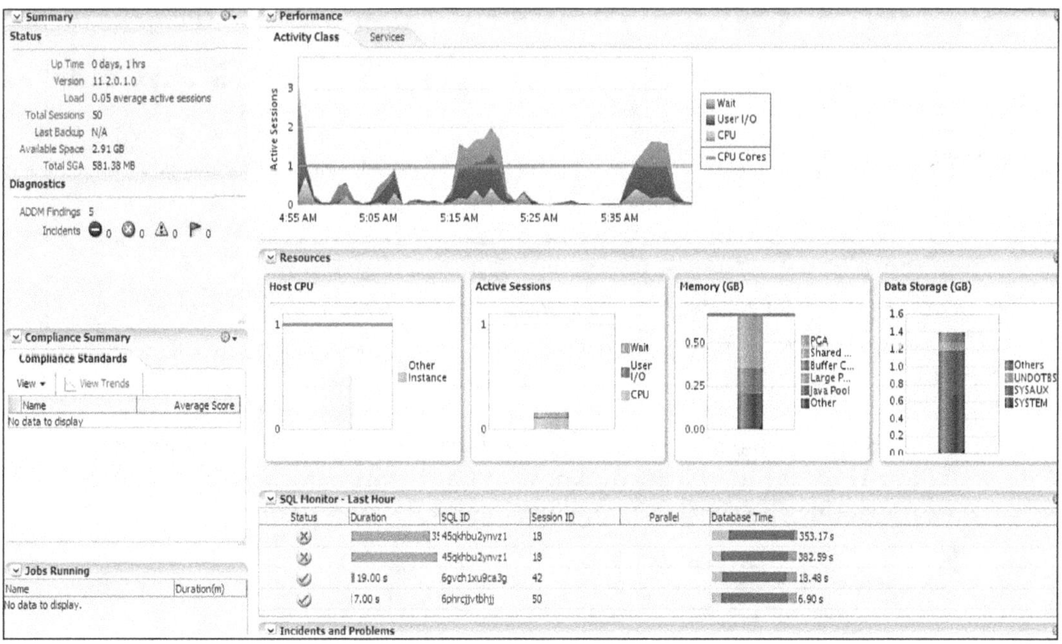

On this database home page, some summary information (such as **Up Time**, **Version**, **Total SGA**, and **Available Space**) about the database is displayed as well as some performance information (such as **Wait**, **Active Sessions**, **Host CPU**, and the long-running sessions shown by SQL Monitoring).

# Doctor in the database

What is also important is that the database home page shows the latest ADDM findings. This is a proactive diagnostics engine that runs every hour by default on the database, and generates a list of recommendations.

Clicking on the **ADDM Findings** button takes you to the last **ADDM Performance Analysis** page, which is displayed in the following screenshot:

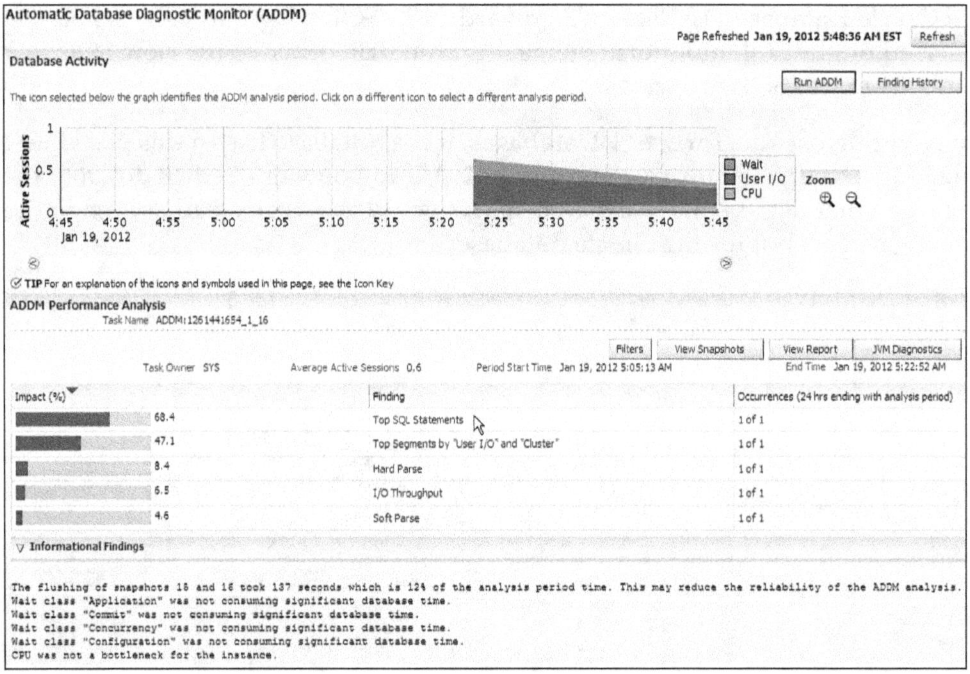


Informational findings are also shown. ADDM lets you know if the database is CPU-bound or I/O-bound, it lets you know of hard/soft parse issues, top SQL statements impacting the database, any locking issues, and so on.

ADDM is also RAC aware and informs you if there are any networking/interconnect or database configuration issues affecting the performance of the RAC database. For example, improper database sequence usage can have a severe performance impact on such active/active databases.

You can run ADDM at any time by going to **Performance** | **Advisors Home** on the menu and then selecting **ADDM** from the list of advisors available. When you run ADDM in this way, you can analyze the current database situation or use past performance data to tell you what went wrong in the past.

You can drill down further into any of the findings. For example, if you click on the **Soft Parse** finding on the previous page (shown in the preceding screenshot), ADDM displays the possible recommendations on how to fix this performance issue, such as by increasing the value of the `session_cached_cursors` parameter to increase the session cursor cache size and even allows you to action it on the spot by clicking on the **Implement** button:

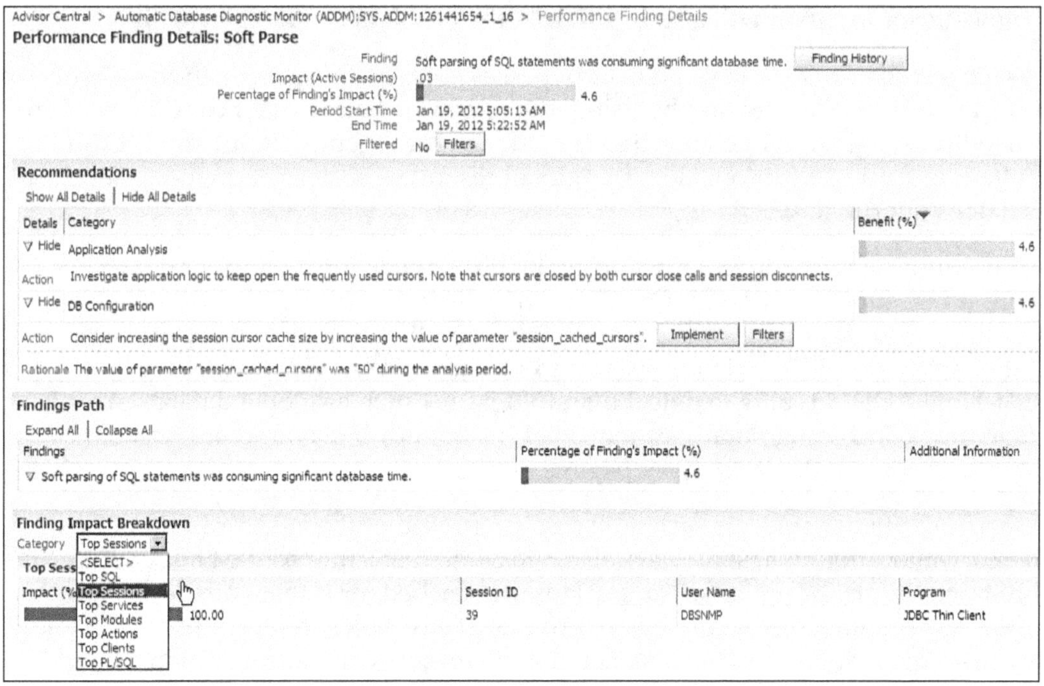

# Real-Time ADDM

ADDM is further enhanced in the new Enterprise Manager Cloud Control 12*c* version with a real-time feature. This is known as Real-Time ADDM (supported for any Oracle database Target of version 10.2.0.4 and higher) and is very useful for situations when the database has become very slow, or has hung and normal ADDM cannot work since it may not be possible to even log in to the database. Even if it is possible to log in to the database, taking an AWR snapshot or running an ADDM task may worsen the problem.

Sometimes it may be due to just one blocking session that the entire database arrives at this unresponsive state.

Often, not being able to find out the root cause of the problem, DBAs may resort to bouncing the database to fix the situation. But this is a very drastic step as all uncommitted transactions will be aborted and rolled back, and mid-tier connections and states will also be lost. The actual cause of the problem will not be found as all diagnostic information will also be lost and the problem can happen again.

In such a scenario, Real-Time ADDM bypasses the SQL layer through the Agent and directly accesses the database by using a special proprietary diagnostic connection capability. A lightweight connection is made via the Agent without any I/O and without acquiring additional locks or global resources such as enqueues or latches, as it does not run any SQL.

An attempt is also made to start a normal JDBC connection. Whatever data is returned by either of these connections can be used for analysis by Real-Time ADDM. It performs a non-locking analysis and will be able to detect problems and hangs. If it is a RAC database, a cluster-wide analysis will be provided. Real-Time ADDM is able to detect manifold issues such as global database-resource contentions, including databases that are CPU bound, I/O bound or interconnect bound, or with OS-level memory paging.

If there are memory issues, such as excessive growth of the PGA or library cache/memory allocation issues, they are also detected. Real-Time ADDM also warns you if resource limits for processes or sessions are reached, or if there are deadlocks affecting the database. Database hangs are detected, for example, if the ASM-storage system is not responding, the instance is in the process of shutting down, the memory pool is being flushed, and so on. Top-blocker analysis is performed.

The recommendations that are provided for single or RAC databases are precise and can be set into action immediately, and diagnostics data will be collected for further analysis if there is no fix available. In fact, there is no other tool like Real-Time ADDM available today, which can easily access a hung database and then recommend a solution by understanding and analyzing the problem in detail.

To access this feature of Real-Time ADDM, you need to go to **Performance | Real-Time ADDM** from the database menu. This brings up a screen where you need to enter the SYSDBA credentials that will be used to access the database in the diagnostic connection mode.

The **Real-Time ADDM** page now appears. Click on the **Start** button. This starts up both the normal JDBC connection as well as the diagnostics connection, and you can see the progress of each. The first time this is run, an error appears about a missing installation of some required PL/SQL packages. Click on the error to see the full error message in the box at the lower half of the screen, the text in the screenshot may not be readable but is included for the purpose of illustration:

You can click on the **PL/SQL Package Deployment** link, this allows you to deploy the package using either the **Simple Installation** method or the **Advanced Installation** method, as seen in the following screenshot. The difference is that in the latter, you can schedule a future time for deployment and you can also run on multiple databases.

In both methods, either a DBA credential is required or you can use the `DBSNMP` user (provided the `CONNECT`, `CREATE TYPE`, and `CREATE PROCEDURE` privileges have been granted to the `DBSNMP` user).

After this deployment completes, you can start the **Real-Time ADDM** utility again. This time there is no error and both the types of connections now report their full findings as shown in the following screenshot. There is one finding:

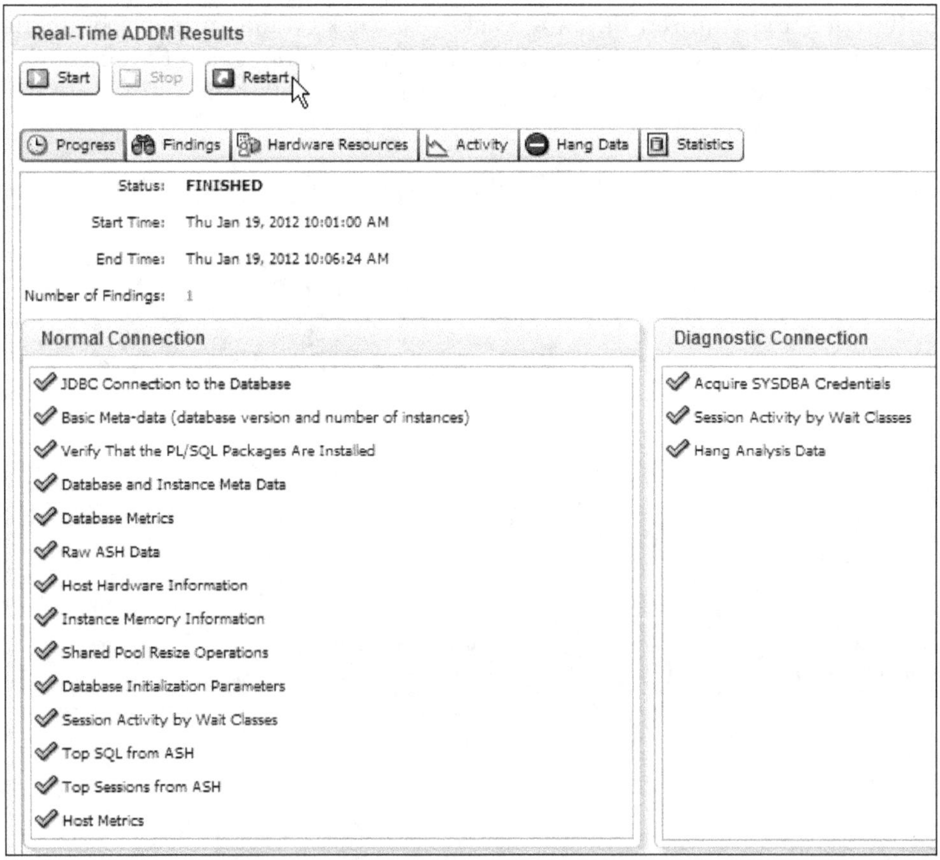

We move to the **Findings** tab and there the main finding is reported: a single SQL statement is taking up 75.29 percent of session activity in the database, which is a lot:

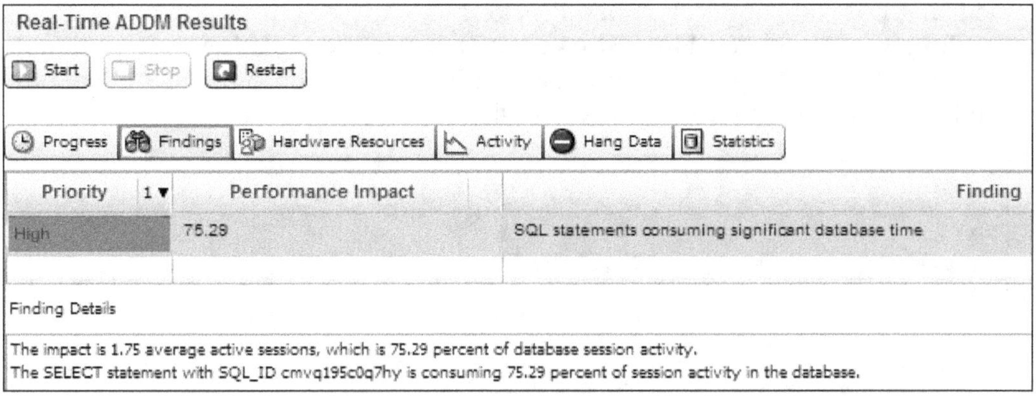


The **Hardware Resources** tab reports that the hosts are not CPU-bound, and graphically shows the average process load on the CPU including both Oracle and other processes. The Oracle databases have only taken up **30.2%** of the Run Queue. There are also other subtabs available, such as **Memory**, **I/O**, and **Interconnect**, which give the related information:

In the **Activity** tab, we can see the SQL IDs of the statements with the highest activity and also the user sessions with the highest activity.

In the **Hang Data** tab, under the **Final Blockers** subtab (seen in the following screenshot), we see the **Top Final Blockers by cumulative blocking time** section. **Session Ids 18** and **43** are waiting on Session ID 10 (the screenshot may not be fully readable but is included for the purpose of illustration):

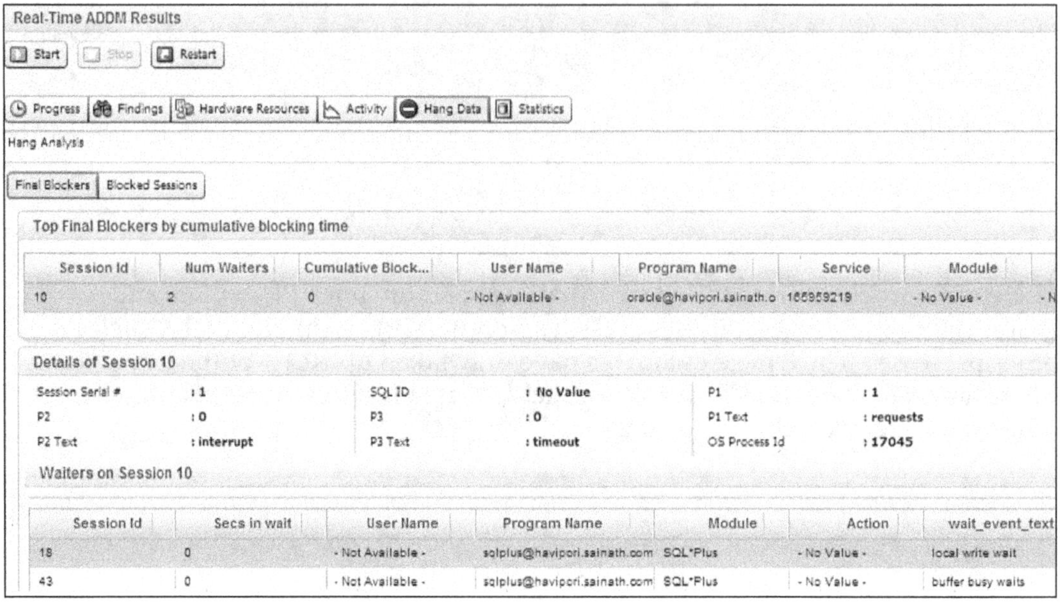


The **Blocked Sessions** subtab also shows more information about the top waits in the **Top Waiters by Wait Time** section (which in this case are **Session Ids 18** and **43**), **Immediate Blockers of Sessions 18** and **Blocker Chain above Session 18**, which could be useful in the case of a series of blocking sessions. In this case it is seen that **Session ID:10** is performing an I/O as shown by the text **db file async I/O**, whereas **Session ID:18** is waiting for a local-write wait. It turns out that there were two sessions doing a Cartesian join on tables along with a sort on the results, and this resulted in the blocking activity:

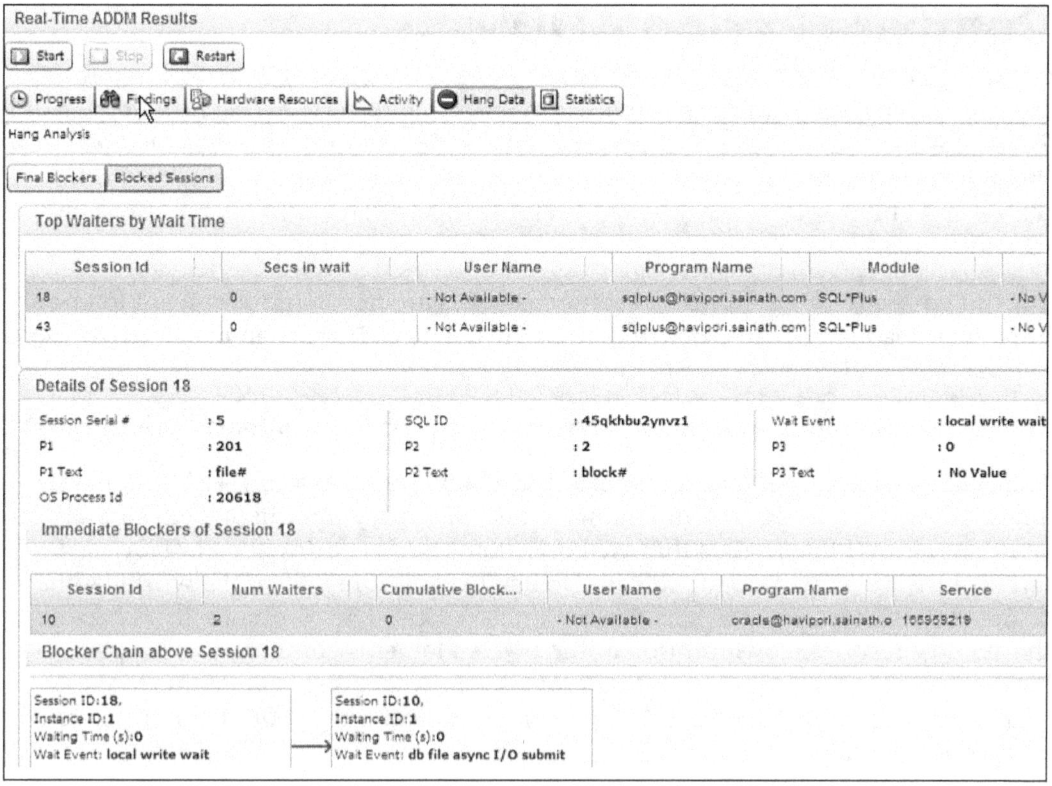


To have found this information via the standard ADDM would have been quite difficult, given the slow response of the database. And there can also be other cases when the database is actually so hung that a normal JDBC connection is not possible, in this case, the lightweight diagnostic connection of Real-Time ADDM would be a lifesaver for the DBA.

The last tab of **Statistics** on the **Real-Time ADDM** page shows database data and host data, including current OS load (number of processes), background CPU usage per second, database time per second, the average synchronous single block read latency, and so on.

# Compare Period ADDM

Compare Period ADDM (supported for any Oracle database Target of version 10.2.0.4 and higher) is another new feature related to ADDM in this new version. This helps in comparative performance analysis. For example, you may have noticed that the performance of your database is worse on some days and better on other days—and you want to know the reason for this. Are some other batch programs running on some days?

Or, you have a RAC database and some instances are faster and you want to know if the workload is unevenly distributed. If any changes have been made across those periods, that is also important to understand.

You access this feature by going to **Performance | AWR | Compare Period ADDM**.

This will take two AWR snapshot periods and will perform a full ADDM analysis across those periods. SQL commonality is also measured and displayed, so that you can get an idea if the periods that are being compared are roughly similar or not in terms of their SQL workload. This is also useful for finding out if the workload has changed in the case that the two periods are identical. The commonality is based on the average resource consumption of the SQL statements common to both periods. It examines the SQL that is executing and also the load of the statements that are executing. If the commonality is 100 percent, it indicates that both the periods have an identical workload signature.

During the analysis, causes for the differing performance are detected, such as workload changes or configuration changes, and the effects are measured, such as reaching the resource limits (either CPU, I/O, memory, interconnect, and so on) or if SQL has regressed.

Causes and effects are then correlated as per years of expert Oracle experience, and recommendations are given in the analysis report, which can be set into action on the spot. The impact of each of these recommendations is clearly quantified.

The first time you select Compare Period ADDM, it requests that certain PL/SQL packages be installed to handle this functionality. You have the choice to use either the simple install method or the advanced install method. This is similar to what we saw in the Real-Time ADDM.

The screen that appears allows us to select a base period and a comparison period as shown in the following screenshot. You can use an offset for the base period. The **Offset** option's value can be **One Day**, **One Week**, or the **Preceding Period** menu item. You can also select a **Baseline** option, such as the **SYSTEM_MOVING_WINDOW** menu item as the base period. Otherwise, you can use a customized period. Then press the **Run** button:

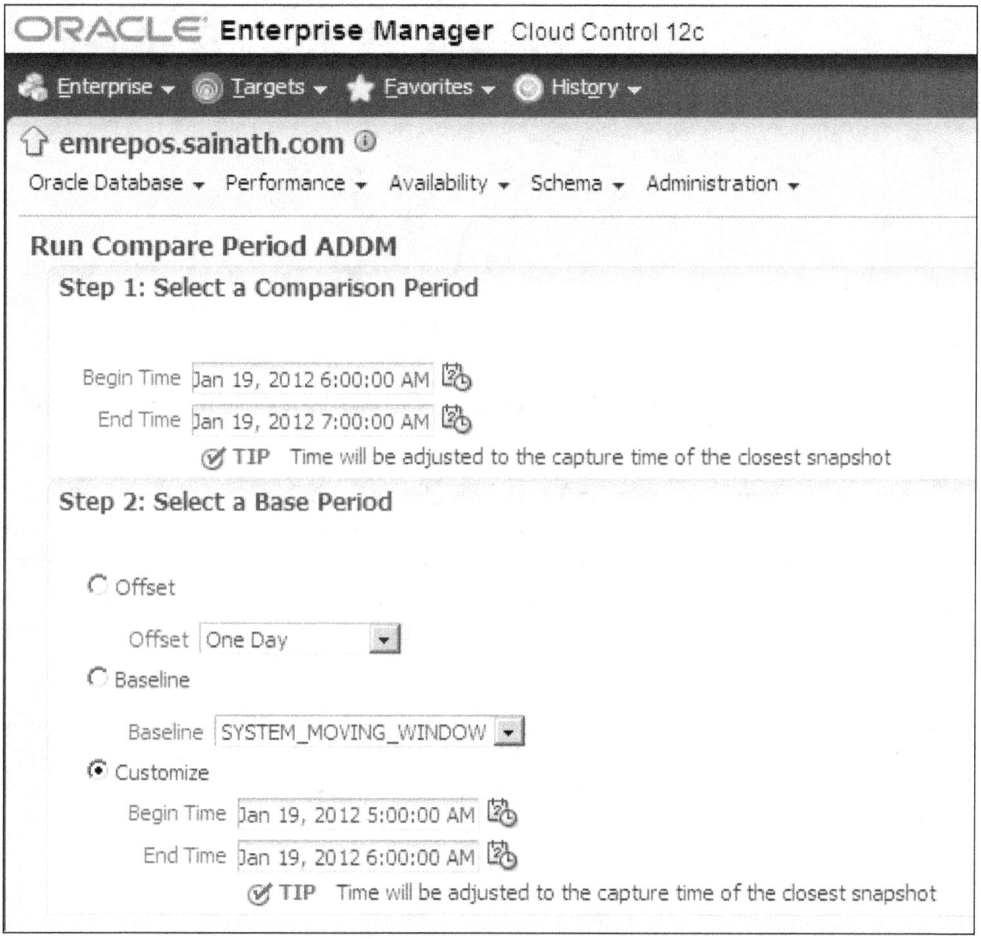

The **Compare Period ADDM Report** page appears at this point and displays the characteristics of the two periods side by side in a graphical format. The average active sessions of the **Base Period** section and the **Comparison Period** section are seen along with the **SQL Commonality** of 30 percent. This is a low commonality, and indicates that the workload signature is not identical in the two periods:

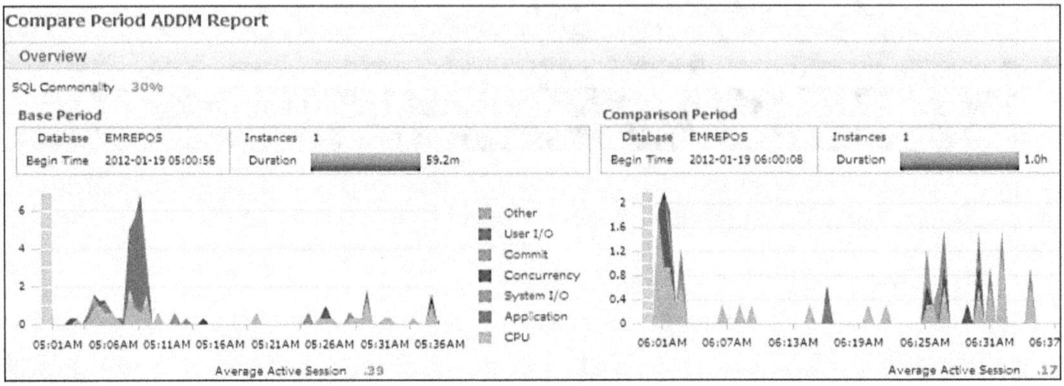


In the **Details** section, under the **Configuration** tab, we can select **Change Only** or **All**.

This allows you to examine any configuration changes to the host/instance across the two periods. Selecting **All** will display all the configuration properties regardless of whether they have changed or not. Selecting **Change Only** will show only the changed properties. Examples are initialization parameters at the database or instance level or host properties such as the number of CPUs, physical memory size, platform type, and so on.

In the **Findings** tab shown in the following screenshot, we can see the performance differences between the two periods and the impact of the change in percentage. In this case we can see that there are several improvements and no regressions across the periods:

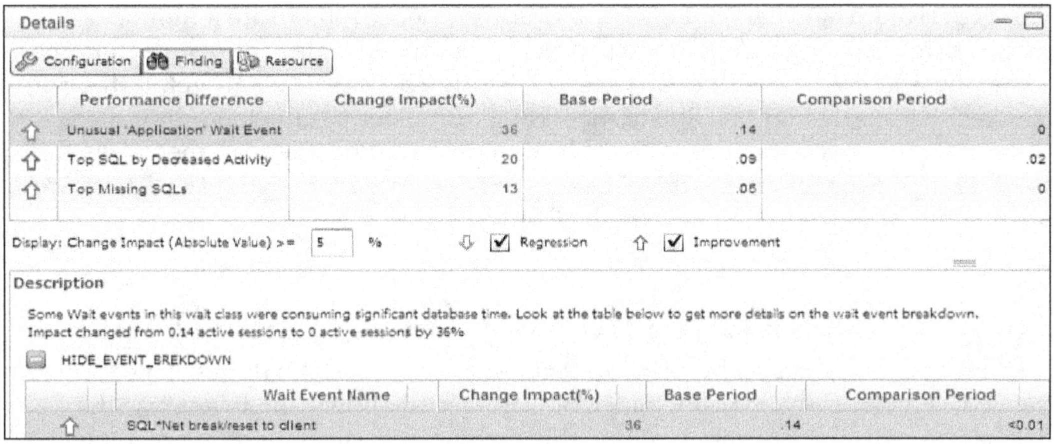


In the **Resource** tab, we can see the average processes on the CPU for the **Oracle Run Queue** and **Other Run Queue** utilities on the host as compared across the periods. The memory paging, I/O, and interconnect comparisons are also available for the two periods.

The method used by the Compare Period ADDM feature is as follows: first it finds out what has changed in the database configuration (for example, if the memory settings have changed) or if the database workload has changed (SQL commonality).

In the second step, it compares the two periods in terms of performance and finds out what the major changes are (for example, top SQL impact and I/O reads may have increased).

The third step by the Compare Period ADDM is to identify the root cause and correlate the performance decrease with the configuration changes, in the preceding case, the changes to the database-memory settings such as a reduction in the buffer size could cause I/O reads to increase.

This is derived from years of Oracle experts' experience—there are a number of preset correlation rules. For example, if the symptom is paging, the cause could be a low physical memory size or an excessively large SGA or PGA Target. If there are SQL regressions, it could be due to the wrong optimizer parameters. Or, if there is hard/soft parsing happening, it could be due to improperly set parameters such as `shared_pool_size`, `session_cached_cursors`, or `cursor_sharing`. There are many more rules like these used by the Compare Period ADDM.

# Active Session History (ASH) analytics

**ASH** analytics is accessed by going to **Performance** | **ASH Analytics**. This feature is new in Enterprise Manager Cloud Control 12*c* and allows you to analyze the database performance across multiple dimensions. It is supported for any Oracle database Target of Version 10.2.0.4 or higher.

The information on this page comes entirely from the in-memory ASH samples that are captured per second, or from the disk data, which is one sample in every ten seconds. These ASH samples are active session information, and the corresponding session attributes are also captured; these become the performance dimensions on this page.

Each second of DB time is stored as one row in each sample. Different dimensions can be selected on this page in a sort of user-defined hierarchy, for example, **Instance** | **Module** | **SQL ID**, and as such you are able to perform analysis on this performance data with the help of slicing and dicing.

The topmost graph on the **ASH Analytics** page can be seen in the following screenshot:

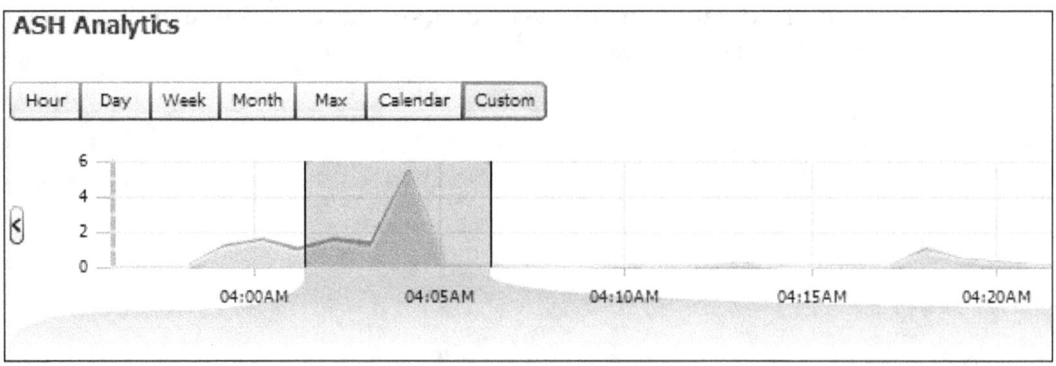

The graph can be based on an hour, day, week, month, and so on. We can select any period from this graph by moving the shaded area, and this is automatically reflected in the detail graph shown in the following screenshot. Here, we can either look at the **Activity** or the **Load Map** utility this screenshot may not be fully readable, but is included for the purpose of illustration:

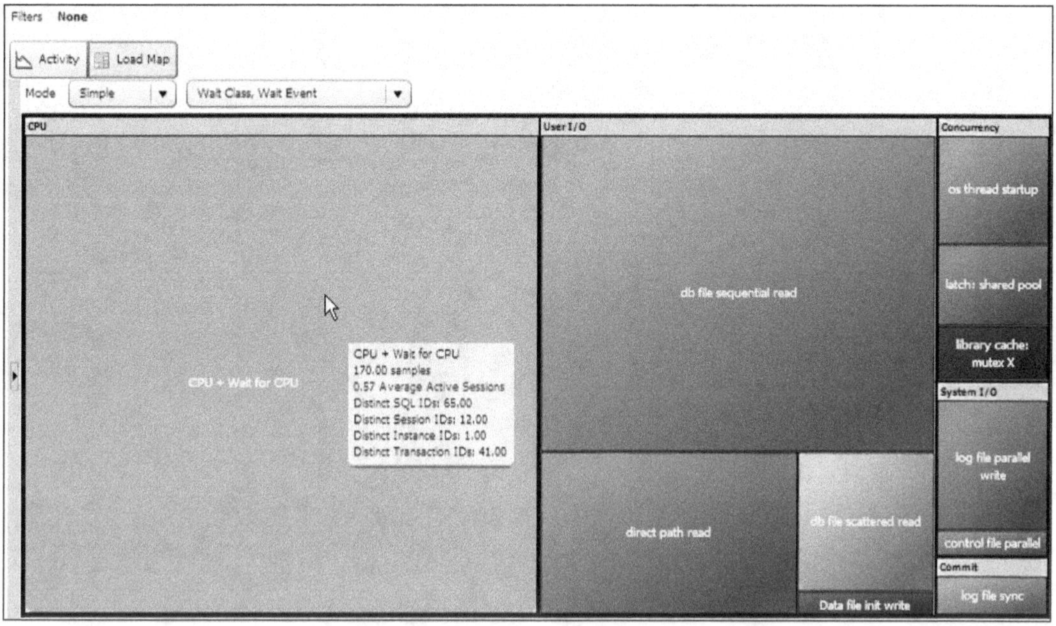


The **Load Map** has been selected, which shows the largest wait events in that period in a stacked-chart format. The color coding is as follows: blue stands for I/O, green for CPU, and orange is for all other waits. The ASH data has been rolled up into these three different categories.

Selecting the **Activity** button instead of **Load Map** shows the familiar-activity graph. You can then select a different dimension for the graph by clicking on the **Wait Class** drop-down menu, as shown in the following screenshot. The same thing can be done for the **SQL ID** and **User Session** drop-down boxes in the regions on the lower half of the page.

Many performance dimensions are collected by ASH and these have been logically grouped into five categories: **SQL**, **PL/SQL**, **Resources Consumption**, **Session Identifiers**, and **Session Attributes**. Examples of the performance dimensions are **SQL ID**, **Wait Event**, **User Session**, **Module**, **Object**, and so on:

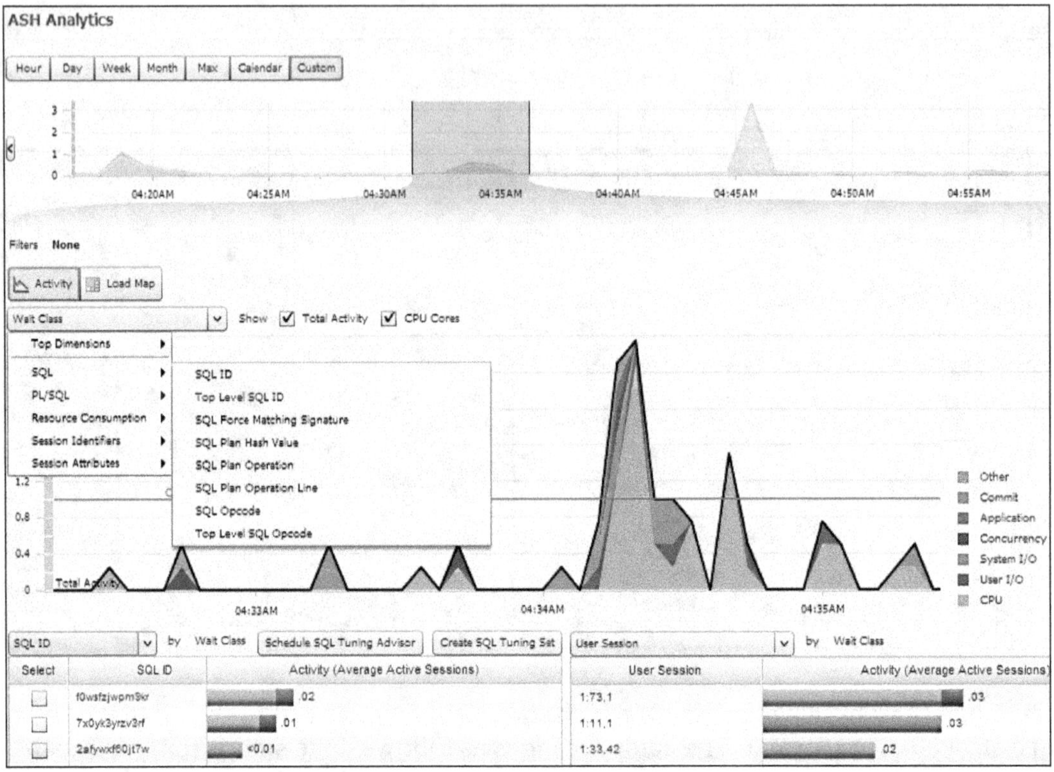


Also, clicking on any section in the graph creates a filter automatically, and you can drill down further into that filter. For example, if a filter is created on the CPU wait class by clicking on it, you can then select to drill down to all the instances of **SQL ID** in the main graph. This shows the actual SQL IDs that have contributed to the high CPU wait.

Then, in the two regions in the lower half, you choose to select to drill down further to the user ID in one of the regions and **Module** in the other. This shows the users that have caused the CPU wait and the main modules responsible for the wait. You can see this in the following screenshot (the screenshot may not be fully readable, but is included for the purpose of illustration):

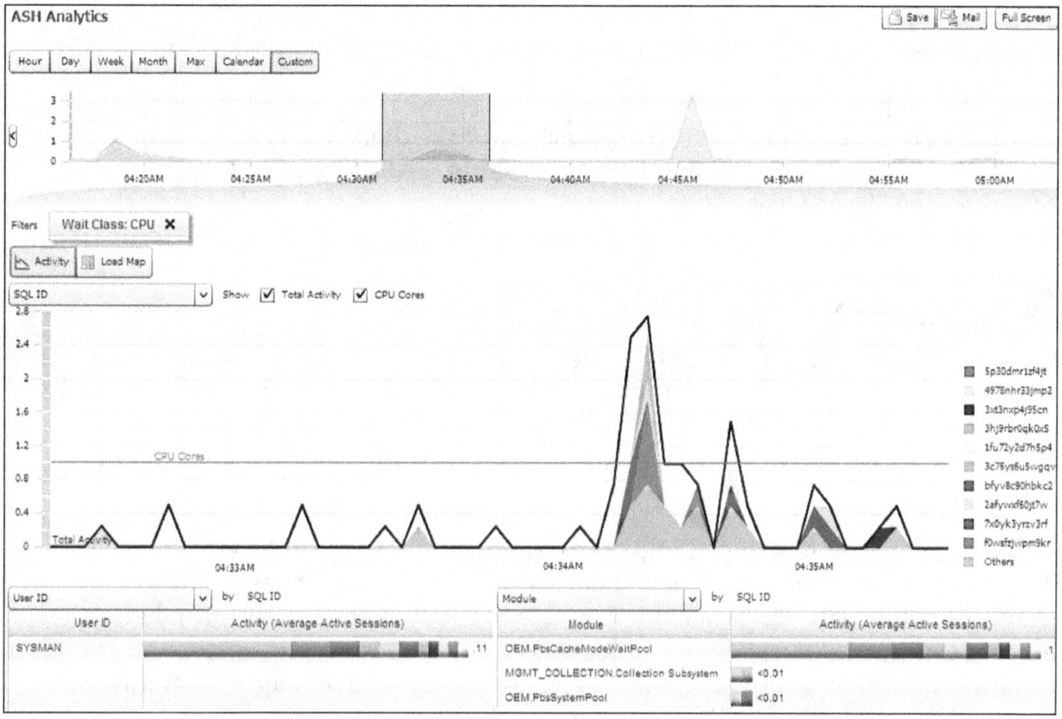


You can create a second filter by clicking further in the main graph, for example, you can select a particular SQL to look into. You can delete the filters any time you wish.

The **ASH Analytics** page therefore becomes highly customizable, and you can do advanced analysis of any performance situation on any time period.

Using the Active Reports feature, it is possible to save the **ASH Analytics** page as an active report and send it to collaborators for offline analysis—you do this by clicking on the **Save** button at the top of the page.

Only an internet connection is required at the recipient's end to perform rendering on the report. An Enterprise Manager installation is not required. However, note that Microsoft Internet Explorer 8 is not able to render the report, instead use the latest version of Mozilla Firefox or Google Chrome.

It is apparent that the Enterprise Manager Diagnostics and Tuning packs have many capabilities and they are enabled out of the box, as they are a part of the core database engine. However, if you do not want to use these packs due to your license obligations (you do not have a license) then, from Oracle database 11*g* onwards, you can use the initialization parameter `CONTROL_MANAGEMENT_PACK_ACCESS` to control the use of these packs.

This parameter can be set to either `DIAGNOSTIC+TUNING` (both packs' functionality is enabled in the database server), `DIAGNOSTIC`, or `NONE`.

You can also turn off any of the packs for any of the database Targets from Enterprise Manager itself, by navigating to **Setup** | **Management Packs** | **Management Pack Access**.

# Summary

Ensuring the performance of data-center applications is foremost in the minds of the IT manager. The database is a crucial part of the IT center, and if it is not properly managed, performance issues can easily get out of control—especially with the increasing data and users of today's applications. DBAs do not want to fight fires every day.

Oracle's Enterprise Manager Cloud Control 12*c* offers very strong performance-management capability for Oracle databases. Using the Enterprise Manager Diagnostics and Tuning packs, it is possible to easily diagnose performance issues by capturing workload statistics in the AWR and the per second session information captured by ASH for transient issues. There is the proactive diagnosis engine in the database—ADDM, which runs every hour out of the box and displays any outstanding issues.

You can then tune those issues seamlessly with the advanced tuning capabilities in the Tuning pack, such as the SQL profile, which offers auxiliary information to the optimizer for executing a SQL statement in the most efficient manner possible. This can tune SQL transparently without changing the application code, which makes it very useful for packaged application tuning. This technology is only in the Enterprise Manager Tuning Pack.

The SQL Tuning Advisor and SQL Access Advisor give other valuable advice for tuning, such as new indexes, materialized views, and partitions. SQL monitoring also makes it possible to monitor long-running SQL statements or PL/SQL programs to see the exact status of the execution.

This diagnosis and tuning of Oracle databases by Oracle Enterprise Manager is further enhanced in the new Cloud Control 12*c* version. There are several new performance features such as ASH Analytics, Real-Time ADDM for emergency situations, and Compare Period ADDM.

In short, Enterprise Manager Cloud Control 12*c* further builds on the solid performance capabilities of the previous Enterprise Manager versions and can definitely be considered to be a lot better in terms of performance management. Words directly from the mouth of a DBA who has been tuning Oracle for many years.

In the next chapter we will examine how Enterprise Manager Cloud Control 12*c* allows total configuration management of all the database servers, and the security-compliance capabilities of the product.

# 4

# Ease the Chaos with Configuration Management and Security Compliance

In a large data center, it is perfectly possible to have tens of thousands of Targets - servers, databases, listeners, application servers, web servers, and so on. So it is almost impossible to attempt to gather and maintain the configuration details manually—unless you have a veritable army of configuration clerks, which is not possible in any company.

So how do you find what's out there in the data center? In such situations, information gathering is very ad hoc, there are spreadsheets all over the place with little bits of information such as IP addresses and network details, or server details with CPU sizing. Some companies even use large white boards in their offices to deal with the configuration details—written by hand with markers and complete with the warning to others not to erase the white board!

Even when there are semi-automated tools to collect the configuration details, such efforts are sparse and disjointed, and they often fail to remain updated with the rapidly changing configuration details in such a large data center. Sooner or later such efforts become useless.

And when something stops working, how do you find out what has changed? Common sense dictates that unauthorized changes would be the main reason for things to stop working in the data center. However, when there are so many Targets, how do you get the hierarchy of related Targets? How would you check each Target manually to see what has changed?

With no configuration management system in place, a data center would degenerate in such a situation to a fire-fighting tale. A major issue would probably take hours or even days to investigate and resolve, and millions of dollars in business would be lost in downtime. All this would happen because the configurations of the thousands of data center components were not being collected and managed.

If one server was working and the other was not, there would be no way to compare the configurations of the two servers in a fast, seamless, and efficient manner. It would take a lot of time to collect the current configuration of the two servers and then to compare the two manually to find out what was different.

If you wanted to go back in time to find out which configuration had changed on which day on your thousands of Targets, such historical changes would be very difficult to track manually, if not downright impossible.

Security compliance is considered very important in today's world with several compliance standards such as SOX, HIPAA, and PCI DSS already existing. How would you check the security compliance in a large data center? Your auditors would need to be satisfied that your hosts, operating systems, databases, application servers, and applications were security compliant as per industry standards, and they would need regularly generated reports to that effect.

However, in most cases, only some rudimentary home-grown scripts are used to check the security compliance of a few Targets—and they are certainly not written or verified against industry standards. So, there would be no real security-compliance checking as such in these data centers and ultimately they would be open to all sorts of attacks.

And if everything to do with configuration is manual or running on a few scripts, you may as well forget about company standards or golden configuration standards, as every Target, even of the same type, can be configured differently when done manually, and there would be no way to check the configuration compliance, or the configuration drift.

Sounds like a nightmare? It really is, if you insist on doing everything manually in your data center.

## Lifecycle management

To resolve most of the issues just described, Oracle Enterprise Manager Cloud Control 12*c* offers excellent functionality for configuration management and security compliance as part of the Database Lifecycle Management Pack, in the case of database servers and the databases on these servers. For other targets such as application servers or applications, different packs may be required—for example, the WebLogic Server Management Pack Enterprise Edition is required for configuration management of WebLogic servers, and the Application Management Suite for Oracle **E-Business Suite** (**EBS**) is required for configuration management of EBS, and so on.

In general, this configuration management functionality includes the ability to automatically discover your servers, then do a deep discovery and collect the configuration of all the components on the servers. The configuration is stored inside the centralized Enterprise Manager repository, and it is possible to do comparisons between the configurations of hosts, databases, application servers, or applications.

You can go back in history and see the configuration changes over time. You can also check the security compliance and configuration compliance of your Targets as per various industry-standard compliance frameworks. There are out-of-the-box as well as user-defined compliance frameworks, standards, and rules in Enterprise Manager.

The end result is that the company will be able to reduce configuration management effort by 90 percent, as most of the manual steps to do with configuration collection, comparisons, historical tracking of changes, and compliance checking are now executed in an automated manner. You can easily meet compliance and audit requirements. You can maintain configuration consistency across the enterprise.

First of all, you can discover your assets efficiently. In this way you can ensure that all the critical assets in the company have been discovered and are being utilized, otherwise there may be cases where there is a lot of capital expenditure on assets and these assets are forgotten if they have not been used. So you can maximize the utilization of assets, and this could result in a reduction in further capital expenditure.

Secondly, due to the automated and continuous security and configuration compliance, you are able to reduce downtime (due to the prevention of configuration errors) and the business risk of security incursions. This also drastically reduces the effort you need to make in order to meet your compliance requirements. Configuration policy violations are now reported in the incident console of Enterprise Manager Cloud Control 12*c*, so you can take action immediately.

In the previous release of Enterprise Manager, there were separate configuration-control tools, such as the **Application Change Console** (**ACC**), **Configuration Change Console** (**CCC**), and BEA Guardian tools, that had to be installed separately from the Enterprise Manager OMS installation. These have all been combined in Enterprise Manager Cloud Control 12*c*. As a result there is now only one agent repository as well as console for configuration management in Enterprise Manager.

# Auto discovery

The new Auto Discovery feature in Enterprise Manager Cloud Control 12*c* uses IP Scan (NMAP) to discover host and non-host Targets without the need for an Agent, scanning your network and discovering all the hosts thereon. Certain information about which software is running on the hosts comes from smart guesses. This goes into a list of discovered unmanaged Targets in Enterprise Manager.

The DBA can then select any Target host from this list and promote it as a managed Target; this then pushes the Enterprise Manager Agent to the server. The Agent then performs deep discovery of all Targets on the server and collects the detailed configuration.

**Setup** | **Add Target** | **Configure Auto Discovery** brings up the screen shown in the following screenshot, where you can initially perform an **Agent-less Hosts and Virtual Server Discovery Using IP Scan**:

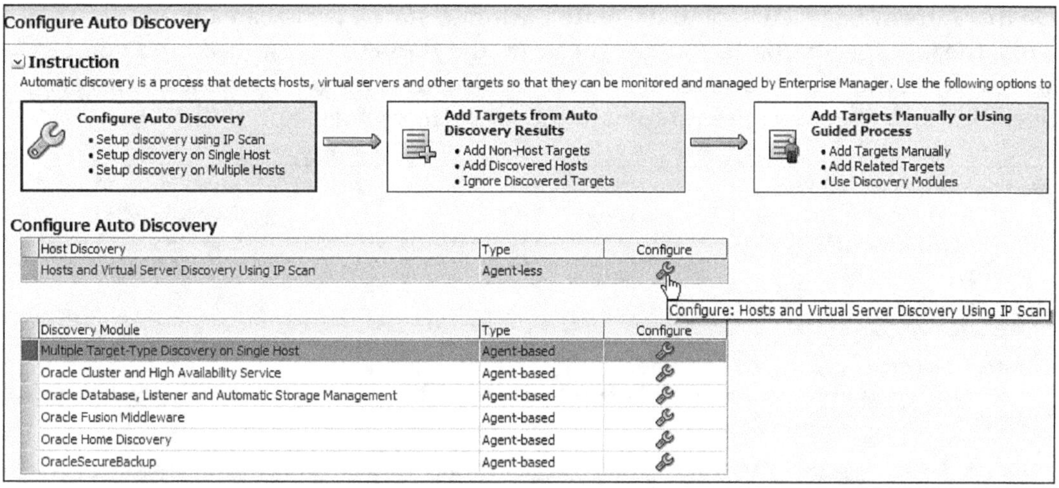


This page also allows different types of **Agent-based** discovery. A guided workflow is shown in the **Instruction** section for your reference.

The first step is to click on the spanner icon in the **Configure** column, against the **Agent-less** host discovery. This brings up the associated screen—**Host Discovery (Agentless)** as shown in the following screenshot:

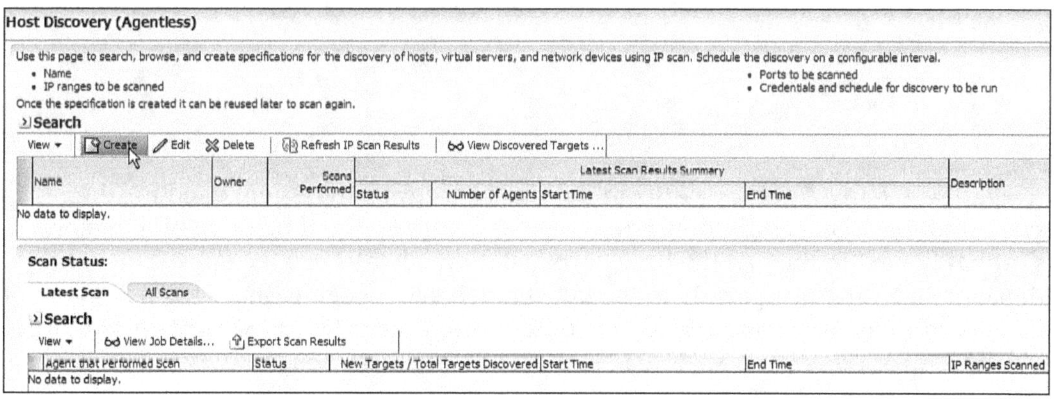

On this screen/page, click on the **Create** button to start a new scan job. You can name the job, specify the **IP Ranges for Scan**, the **Ports** to be scanned, and you can also perform the scan at a repeatable interval. This is done on the **Host Discovery Specification: Create** page as shown in the following screenshot:

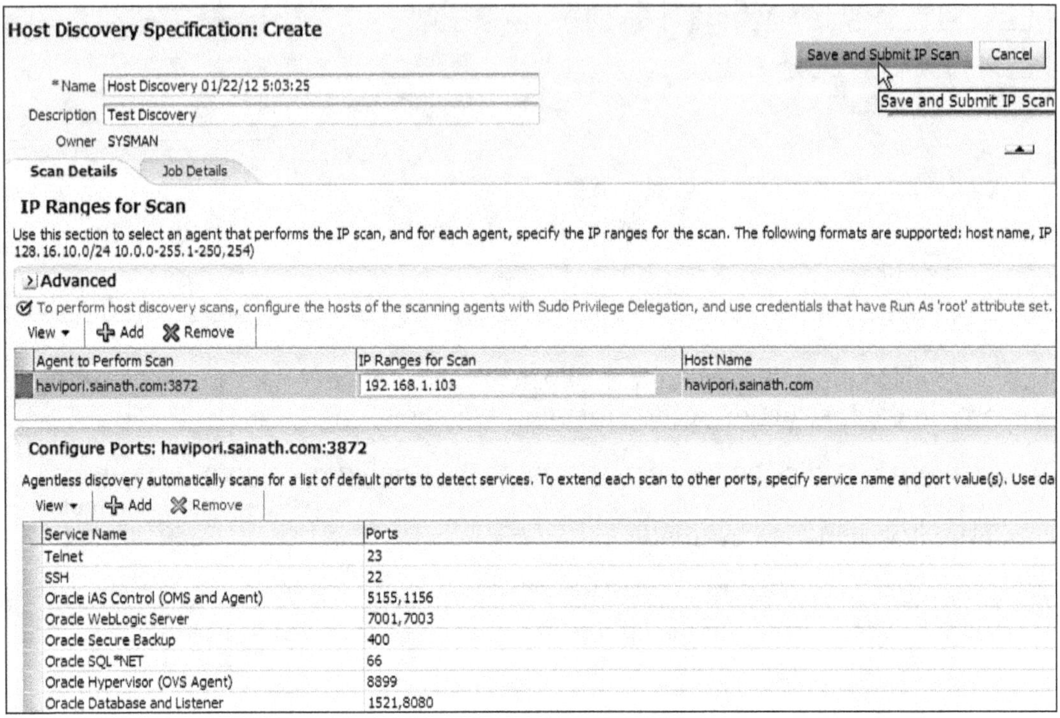


You can select any Agent to perform the scan, however, the Agent used for the scan can only be on certain platforms, such as Linux, at the time of writing. Solaris is probably next in line. At the time of installation, always use the latest Enterprise Manager software, or upgrade to the latest patch set once released. This will give you the maximum features and platforms for various capabilities of Enterprise Manager Cloud Control 12*c*.

You need to configure the host of the scanning Agent with Sudo Privilege Delegation. Normally, the scanning Agent will be the Agent on the Enterprise Manager OMS server, and this type of privilege will be set on that machine. (This is set up by going to **Setup** | **Security** | **Privilege Delegation**).

On the **Job Details** tab on this page, you can specify if the discovery job is to be run immediately or at a later time. You can also set the job to be repeatable every *N* hours, days, or weeks. Or you can run it on specific days of the week, month, or year.

This means that you can keep on discovering new targets via IP Scan auto discovery, as and when they get added in the future.

You also need to specify the credentials for the Target host. As the scan is run as root, you need to use privileged credentials or Sudo or PowerBroker.

Then click on the **Save and Submit IP Scan** button. The scan job runs successfully:

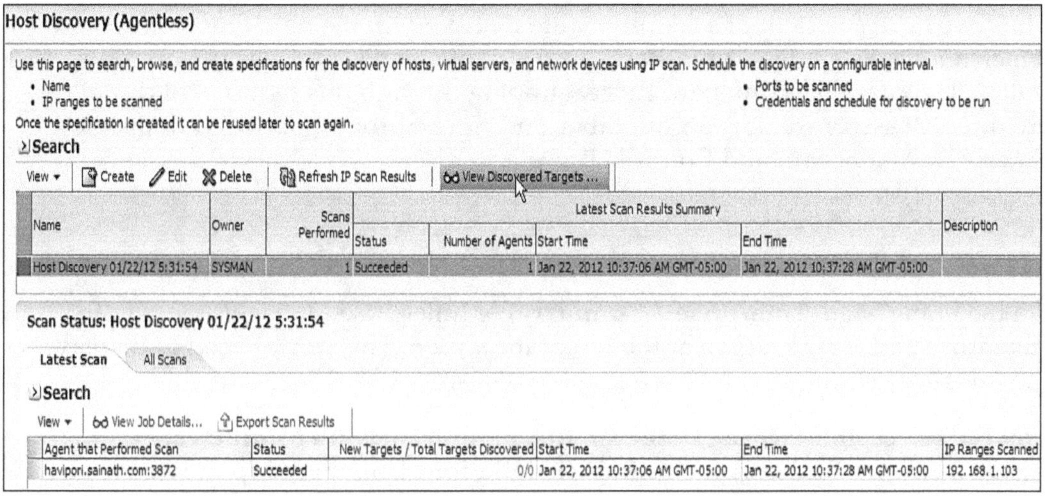


You can now click on the **View Discovered Targets** tab. This brings up the list of **Host Targets** and **Non-Host Targets** that have been discovered so far by the Auto Discovery jobs (any that have run successfully so far). The same list of targets can also be seen if you navigate to **Setup** | **Add Target** | **Auto Discovery Results** from the menu:

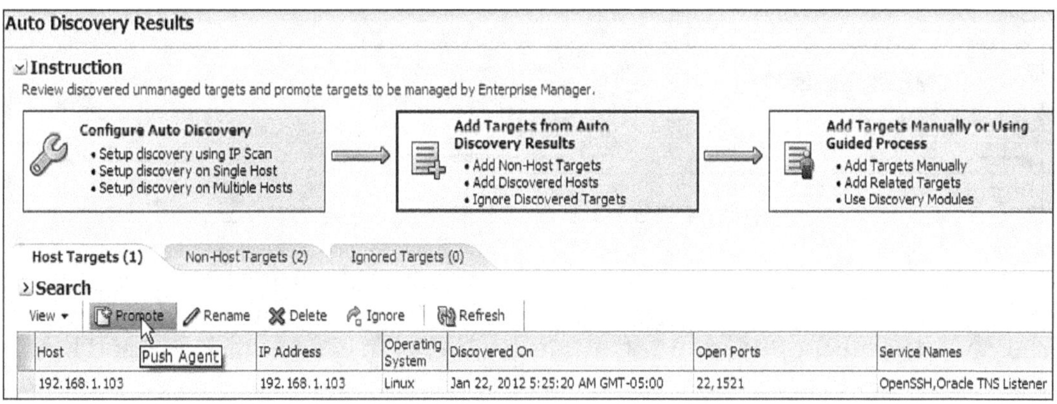

The next step is to click on the **Promote** button against the host Target, this will enable you to add your host Target as a managed Target, meaning that the Enterprise Manager Cloud Control 12*c* Agent will be pushed out to this Target.

After the Agent is pushed out in this manner, it will commence detailed configuration collection from the host. The configuration information will be stored in the central Enterprise Manager system as we will see now.

Thus, we have a system of scheduled auto discovery in the new Enterprise Manager, which allows a seamless Agent-less discovery of any new Targets in your data center. The chances of any new Target slipping through this tight net of discovery are rare. All assets are now accountable, and can be properly utilized thanks to Enterprise Manager Cloud Control 12*c*.

# Inventory

On the home page (**Enterprise** | **Summary**) of Enterprise Manager, there is an **Inventory and Usage** region at the top of the screen. This can be used to display the Inventory summary as shown in the screenshot we will soon see.

You can select either **Hosts**, **Database Installations**, **Fusion Middleware Installations**, or **Fusion Applications Installations** from the drop-down menu/drop-down box in this region. This then correspondingly displays the inventory summary in the table.

As an example, if you select **Hosts**, it will display all the different types of hosts installed. Everything in your Enterprise will be seen, provided Agents have been placed on every host and the administrator who has logged into Enterprise Manager has the right to see these hosts. This is shown in the following screenshot:

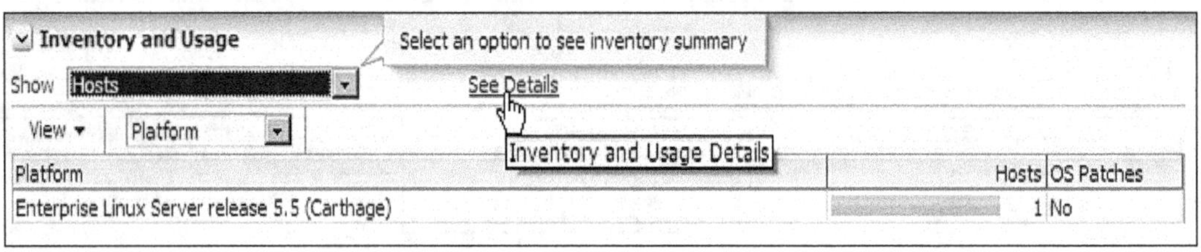


Click on the **See Details** link to drill down further to examine an elaborate listing of the inventory and usage details. By default, the details are rolled up on **Platform**. You can select other options for roll up, such as version, vendor, lifecycle, and line of business.

Note that some of these attributes are not set by default for the Targets, and you may have to add them manually for each Target. For example, we can specify the host **havipori.sainath.com** as a test server (specifying the lifecycle as either development, test, or production).

Host attributes can be changed by going to **Host** | **Target Setup** | **Properties**. When you select any row and click on the **View Details** button, the detailed information about the host appears in the lower section. This is seen in the following screenshot:

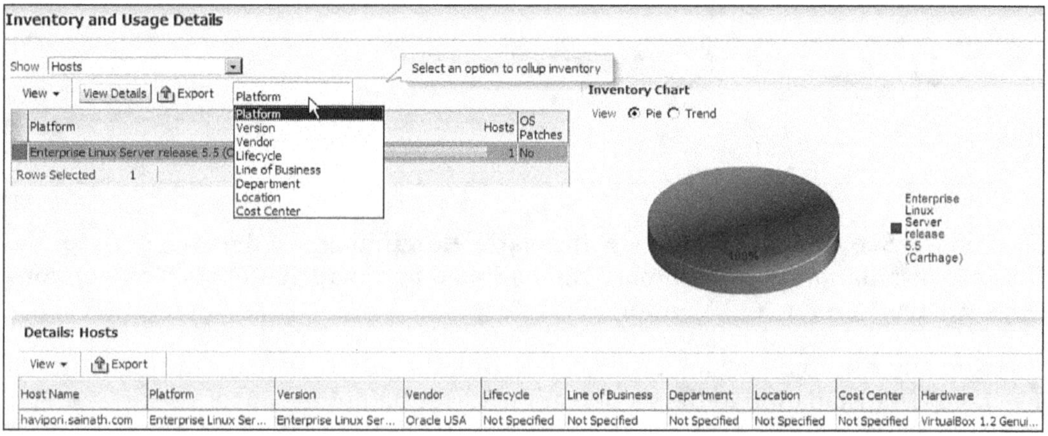


There is also an inventory chart on this page that shows the breakdown of the details in graphical format. For example, if you have rolled up on **Platform**, the graph will attempt to show the distribution of platforms. In the same manner, you can show the different versions or vendors, and so on.

An interesting aspect is that if you select the **Trend** radio button instead of the **Pie** button, a trend chart will appear showing the different values of the attribute over time. This is the population trend, which indicates the growth of assets or can indicate a possible configuration sprawl that may need to be controlled:

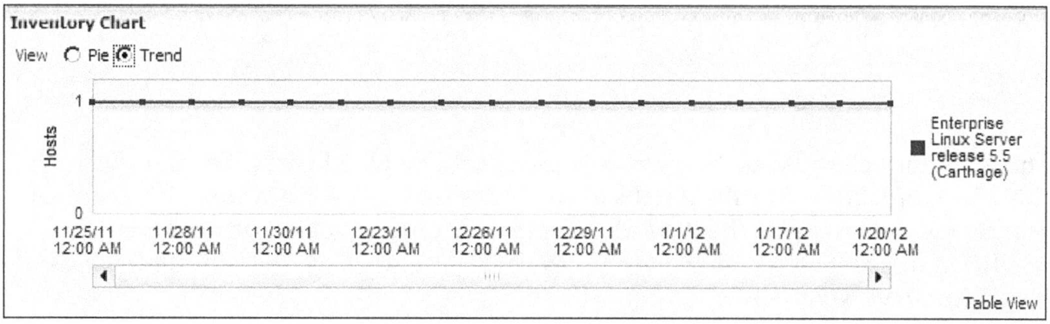

The **Export** button on this page allows you to create a Microsoft Excel spreadsheet with this configuration information, so you can use it externally.

Coming back to the Summary page via **Enterprise** | **Summary**, if we select **Database Installations** in the **Inventory and Usage** section, you can see a list of all the Oracle database versions installed in the enterprise—with the same caveat that Agents should be installed on every server, and you as an Enterprise Manager administrator should have rights to see all the database Targets. Right now, as `SYSMAN`, we can see everything:

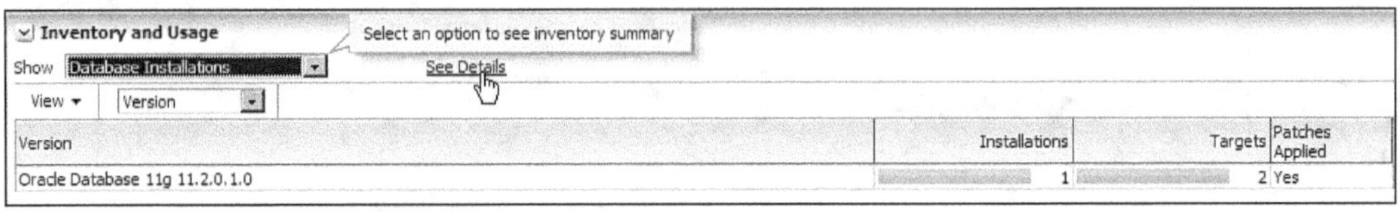


Click on the **See Details** link to view the elaborate summary of the inventory for the database installations. The summary can be rolled up on attributes such as **Version**, **Platform**, **OS Version**, **OS Vendor**, and **Lifecycle**.

Selecting any row and clicking on the **View Details** button displays the attributes of this database installation in the section at the lower half of the page:

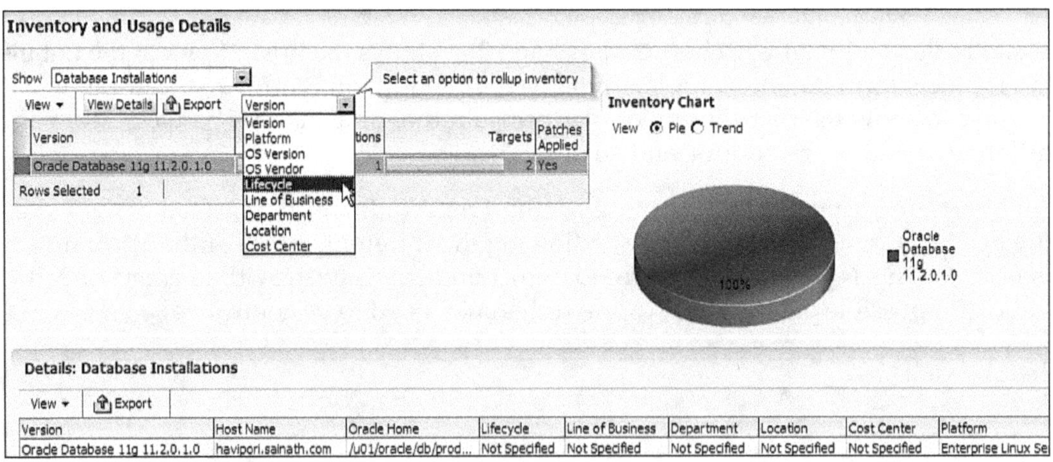


The inventory chart, as before, can be a pie chart or a trend chart. The pie chart shows the breakdown of the database attributes selected, for example, if version is selected as the roll up in the drop-down menu/drop-down box, the chart will show the different database versions. In the case of the trend chart, the different values of the database version will be displayed over time.

# Detailed configuration

From the main Enterprise Manager Cloud Control 12*c* console menu, go to **Targets | Hosts**. This brings up a list of hosts. When you select the host you want, it brings up the host's home page as shown in the following screenshot:

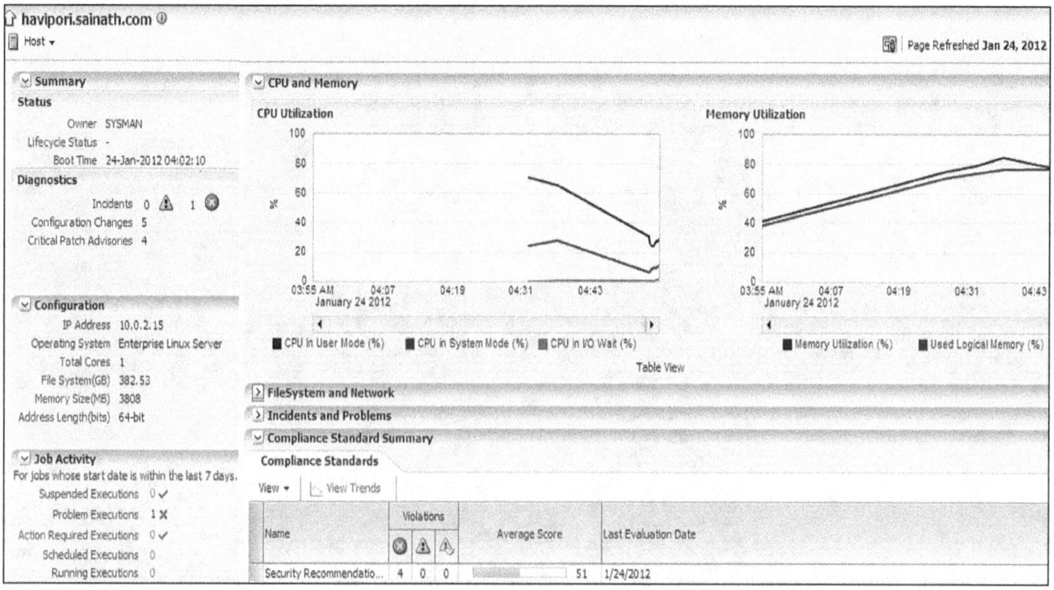


Right on the host's home page itself, there is a **Configuration** section, which shows certain basic information collected about the host. This includes **IP Address**, **Operating System** version, CPU Cores, **File System** size, **Memory Size**, and so on.

Under the **Compliance Standard Summary** section on the same page, it also tells you if there are any security or compliance violations for this Target.

Note that some of the sections on this page have been collapsed to give you a better view; in this version of Enterprise Manager Cloud Control 12*c* it is possible to collapse or expand sections at will or move them around on the page.

To view the detailed configuration of this host, go to **Host** | **Configuration** | **Last Collected** in the **Host** menu (not the **Enterprise** menu). This displays the **Latest Configuration** page as shown in the following screenshot:

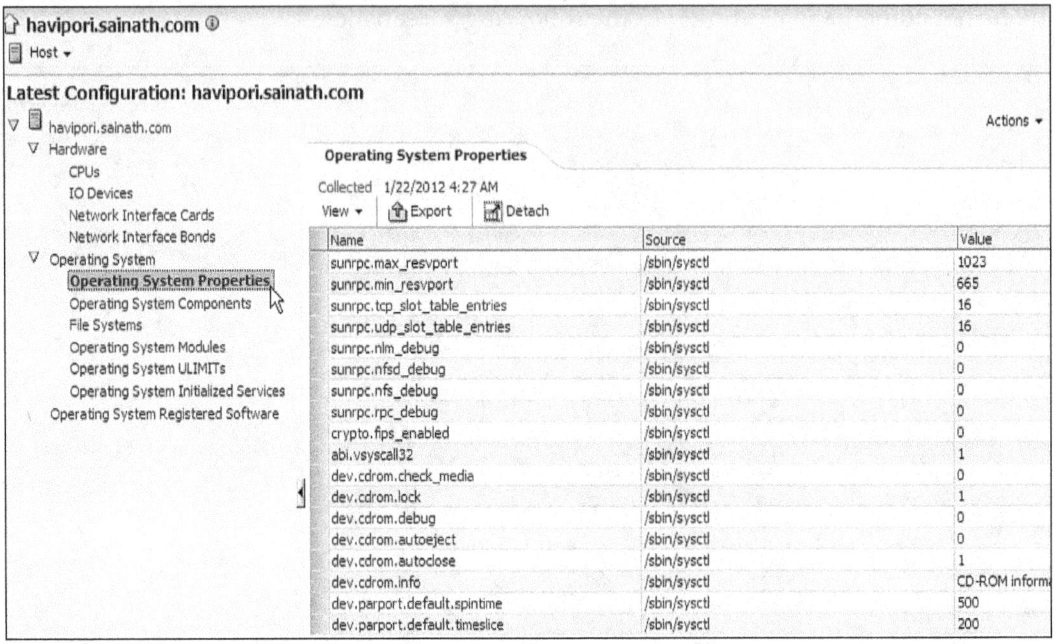

As is apparent, Enterprise Manager Cloud Control 12*c* has captured a lot of detailed configuration information about this host. This includes hardware information such as the CPUs, network interfaces, IO devices, as well as software information such as the operating system properties, components (for example, packages), modules, ULIMITs, installed services, registered software (including the installation time), as well as the filesystems in use. In this case, we have selected **Operating System Properties** on the left-hand side pane.

This information can also be exported to a Microsoft Excel spreadsheet by clicking on the **Export** button. You can also view any of the information in a detached table for easy viewing, by selecting the **Detach** button.

Notice the **Actions** drop-down menu/drop-down box in the middle of the page. This has two important options—**Search** and **History**. These options are visible regardless of any item being selected in the left-hand side pane. However, when we select the host name, more options are visible in the **Actions** drop-down menu/drop-down box, such as **Export**, **Topology**, and **Compare**. Let us first look at the **Search** option.

# Search capability

Suppose you want to find out which Oracle software is installed on this host. If you have to do this manually, it will be a lengthy process as you have to search through the whole box using Unix commands such as `find`, and have root privileges, since Oracle software can be installed under different Unix usernames. Even if the `/etc/oratab` file is present, it may not have been maintained by the DBA and may not contain all the Oracle homes. And in many cases this file is not even present.

But you are now using Enterprise Manager and the Agent has already collected this information and put it in the repository. All you need to do is to invoke the configuration search capabilities, which you can do from the latest configuration page:

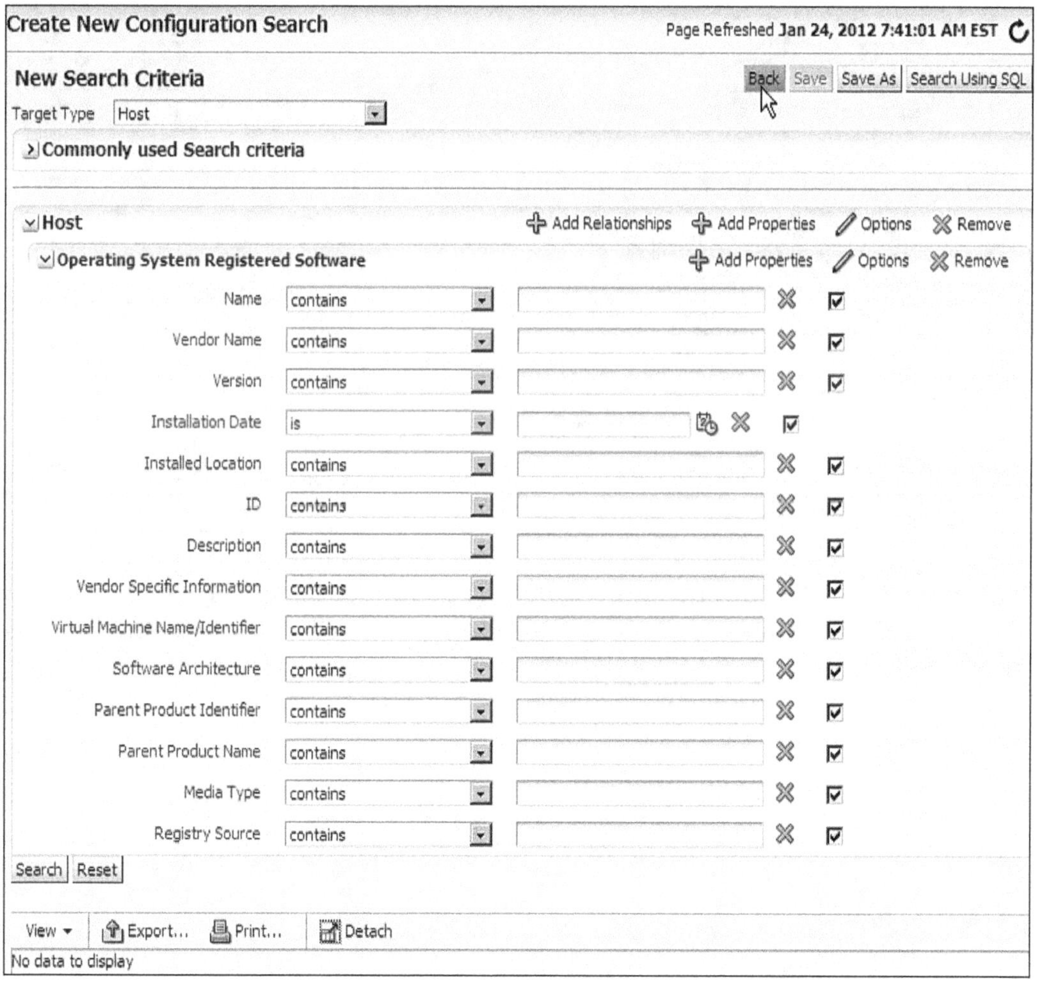

If the **Search** button is not visible on this page, remember to drag the regions apart.

Instead of filling in anything on this page, click on the **Back** button at the top. This moves us to the **Configuration Search Library** page as shown in the following screenshot:

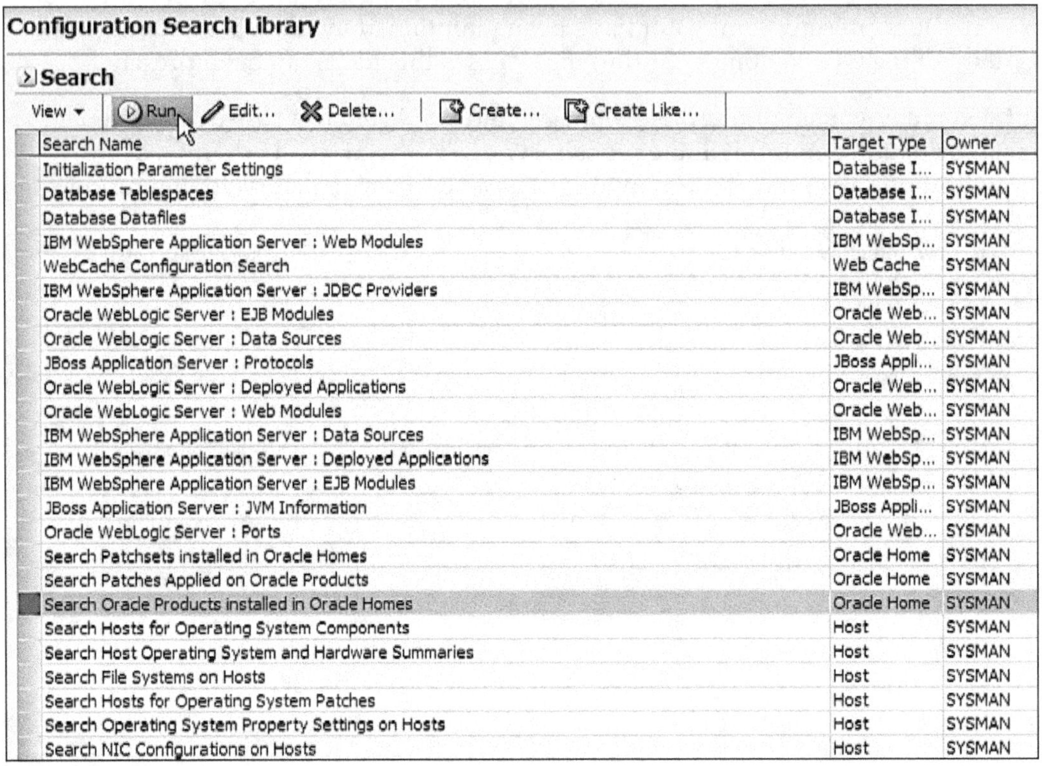


These are out-of-the-box search procedures supplied by Oracle. You can use these or create your own procedures, or make a copy of these by selecting the procedure and then clicking on the **Create Like...** button.

In our case, we simply select the supplied **Search Oracle Products installed in Oracle Homes** configuration and click on the **Run** button. This starts the search and the results are displayed on the **Edit/Run Search** page, as shown in the following screenshot:

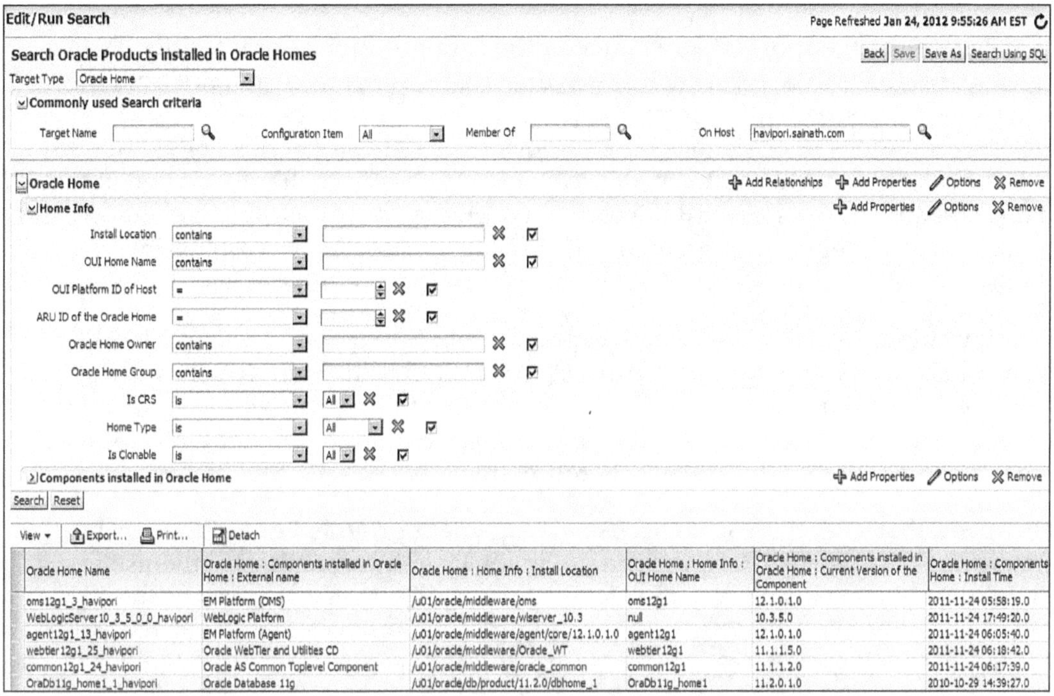

The list of Oracle software installed on this host is displayed, including the install location, install time, component external name, component version, and so on.

Note that it is possible to hide or display columns in this list, or change the order of the columns by going to **View | Columns | Show More Columns** or **View | Reorder Columns**.

You can also refine the search criteria by using the fields on the page and then clicking on the **Search** button again. In this case, we have entered `havipori.sainath.com` as the host to be searched, in the **Commonly used Search Criteria** section. However, we can leave the field blank and this will conduct the search on all the hosts managed by Enterprise Manager Agents.

This reiterates an important advantage of the configuration search facility. We can use this to verify the Oracle licenses that are in use in the company. In large enterprises, it is frequently difficult to keep track of Oracle licenses. Even in the early 2000s, when Enterprise Manager Grid Control 10*g* Release 1 was installed in such enterprises, this was found to be an excellent way to collect all information about all databases and all versions of databases in use in the entire company throughout the branches (provided Agents were installed on all servers). So it was possible to easily report this information back to Oracle for the licensing requirements.

Configuration collection and search capabilities in Enterprise Manager Cloud Control 12*c* are even better, with Auto Discovery using IP Scan, which was not available in the old versions. You can discover things that you didn't even know existed. Also, other licenses like Oracle WebLogic Server, and other Oracle software are now being discovered and are therefore trackable.

However, that said, there is no license management provided out of the box by Enterprise Manager. The clients have to do the license reconciliation themselves. Enterprise Manager can provide a detailed list of all Oracle software installed "everywhere in the enterprise" using configuration search capabilities. Enterprise Manager even knows how many cores are present in each host, and what the type of the host is—which is important for license calculations.

# History and compares

Back on the latest configurations page, select `havipori.sainath.com` in the left-hand side pane, and then go to **Actions** | **Refresh**. Enterprise Manager reports that the Target collection has succeeded and the refreshed configuration data is displayed. This is how you would manually refresh the configuration if you wanted to be sure that the information stored in the Enterprise Manager repository was up-to-date.

Now go to **Actions** | **History**. We want to see which operating system property has changed in the current state of the host.

Click on the **Clear** button next to **Configuration Item**, and then click on the magnifying glass icon and select **Operating System Properties** (from the **Type of Change** drop-down menu) to be used in the search. Then click on the **Search** button.

The results that come up, as shown in the following screenshot, tell us that one of the important operating system properties has changed recently—this is **fs.file-max**, and the exact change is also shown:

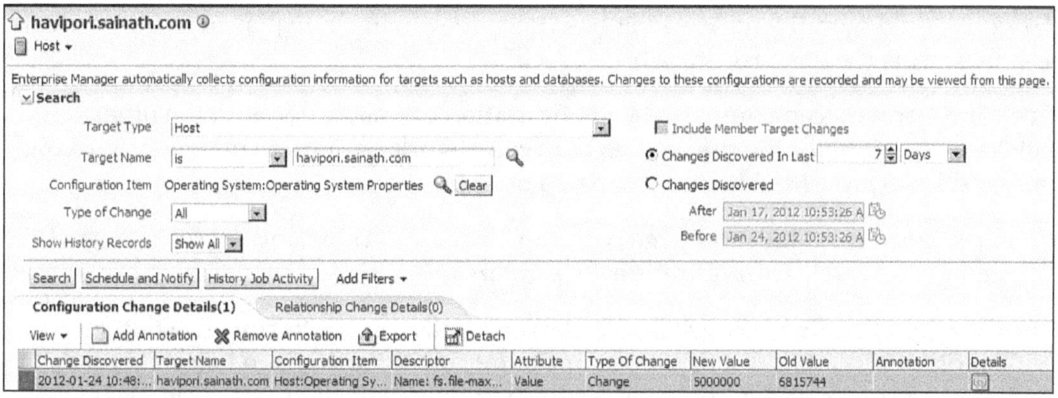


This demonstrates that Enterprise Manager Cloud Control 12*c* retains a history of all the configuration changes on the host, and it is easy to go back in time and see the exact nature of each change, including the values that have changed and the time the change was discovered. This is an important aspect of trouble shooting - if something has stopped working or is not working properly, the first thing to do is to find out what has changed. The configuration history facility of Enterprise Manager will help you to do this easily.

As an example, suppose there is an Oracle Data Guard set up with a primary and a standby database server. Logs are being shipped across and everything is working fine. Suddenly one day, out of the blue, the shipping of logs stops with an error that indicates the network is at fault. The DBAs wonder what has happened. They were aware that a Unix OS patch had been applied the day before, but they are not sure what it has to do with the problem. The DBAs request the Unix system administrators to send them a list of all operating system level changes that have anything to do with the network. They receive a reply that there have been no such changes.

Luckily, Enterprise Manager has been used to set up and monitor the standby database up to the point of this network error. Using Enterprise Manager is a much more efficient way of creating and managing Oracle Data Guard standby systems, as it is wizard-driven and automated, and consequently avoids the errors that may occur in the manual methods of creation.

As Enterprise Manager is already in place, with Agents on both the production and standby servers, it has already collected the configuration and the history of changes on both servers. It is a simple matter to go back in time in the configuration history and view what has changed at the OS level, on the standby server. If any OS property to do with the networking has changed, it will be displayed in a historical search such as the one just described.

Even simpler, you can compare the configuration of one server with the other. This helps you to pinpoint the differences between a working server and a non-working one, and Enterprise Manager is able to do this very easily.

From the latest configuration page, you can click on **Actions** and select **Compare**. Or you can go to **Host** | **Configuration** | **Compare**.

The **Compare Configurations** wizard starts and allows you to compare this server with another server's latest or saved configuration. A comparison template can be used in the process of this comparison, this is a new feature in Enterprise Manager Cloud Control 12*c*:

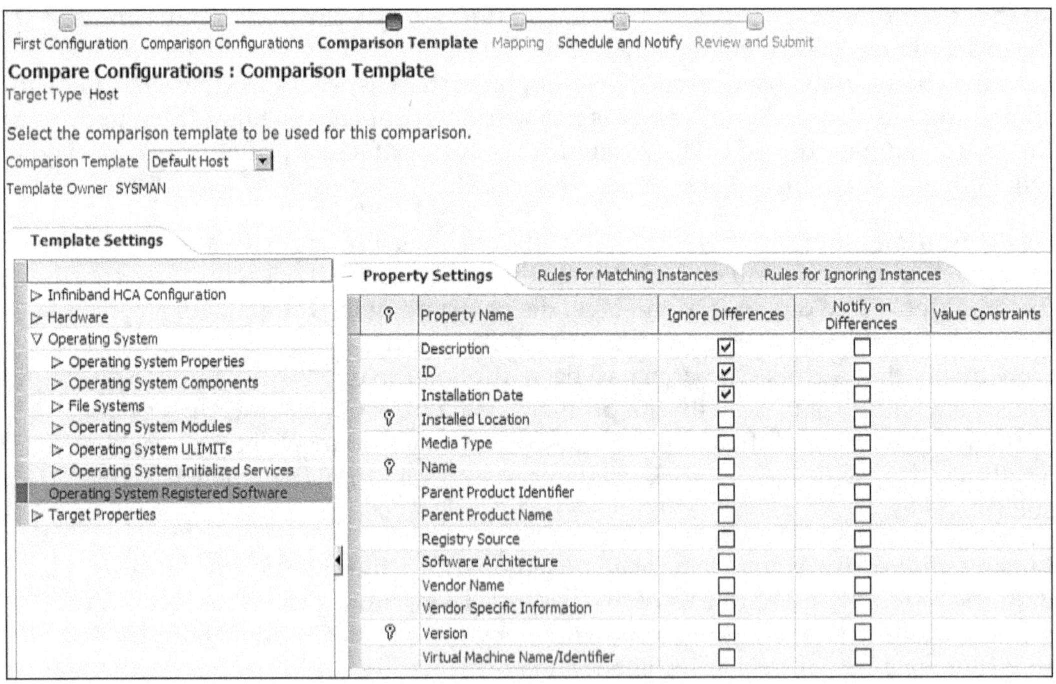

The **Comparison Template** page is used for fine tuning comparisons. It is a list of property settings that are being compared for a certain Target type, and also controls whether differences will be ignored or notified. However, you cannot change the comparison templates that are supplied out of the box, you need to copy an existing template and then change it.

You can manage comparison templates by going to **Enterprise** | **Configuration** | **Comparison Templates**, as shown in the following screenshot. Simply click on the **Create Like** button after selecting the template you want to copy:

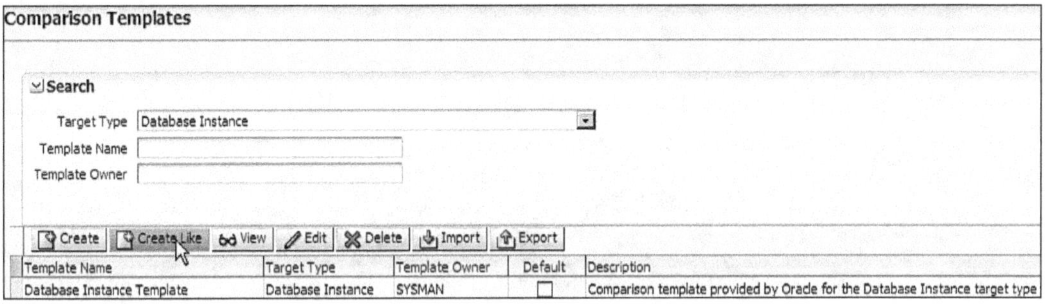


Inside the template, it is possible to use constraints to define correct values for any of the properties. If, during the comparison, a property doesn't obey the constraint, it will be counted as a difference.

In this way, it is very easy to compare two hosts, two databases, or a current configuration and a saved (historical) configuration, and simply see the differences in the properties. With the configuration templates, you can ignore the properties that you know would normally be different; for example, when you compare two hosts, the difference in the hostnames can be ignored.

Note that a much more powerful configuration comparison facility is available when you invoke **Enterprise** | **Configuration** | **Compare** from the main menu. This allows you to compare any type of Target, even a database system or aggregate service with another. Comparison templates are not provided out of the box for all Target types.

When systems are compared, the wizard will automatically map the components of one system to another and you can select which component you want to include or exclude from the comparison. The comparison completes and you can drill down into the differences for each component, for example, the databases have different properties as can be seen in the in the following screenshot showing the **Compare Result** page:

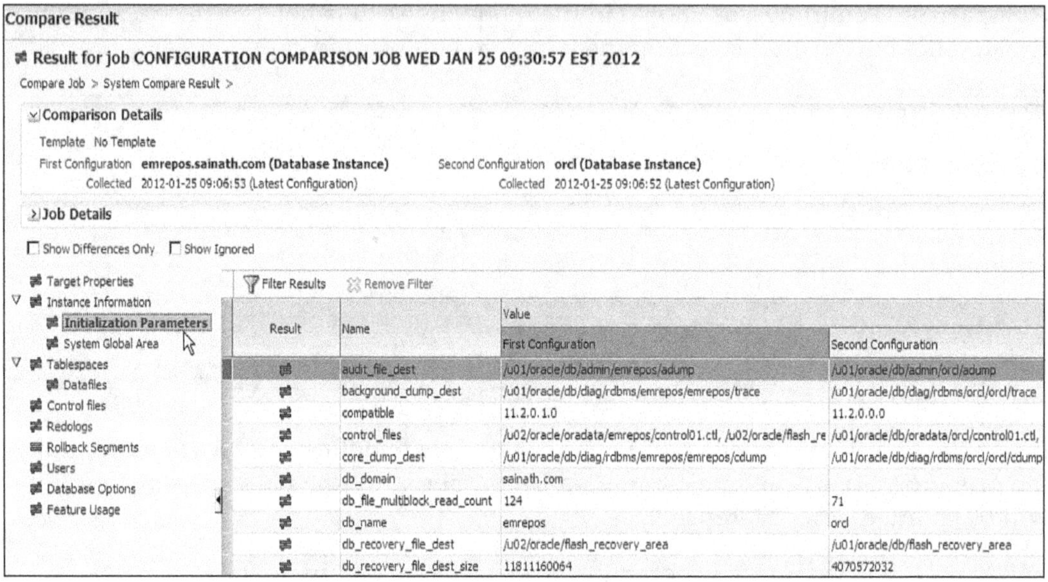


This shows the usefulness of comparing multicomponent systems. Other examples are Exadata database machines or storage cells, WebLogic systems, E-Business, Siebel, or Fusion application systems, and so on. The comparison can be done as per your preference, you can either compare individual components or the full system.

One-to-one or one-to-many comparisons are possible. You can compare the current existing configuration to a stored baseline configuration (that basically works as a gold image), different lifecycle environments such as a production system to a test system, or a development system to a test system.

The comparisons can be scheduled for a future date and time, run at repeated intervals, or run on the spot. You can also get an automatic notification if a configuration drift has been detected. In this way, you can ensure that configuration standards are followed throughout the IT infrastructure in your company.

# Topology

Topology mapping is also an important feature of configuration management in Enterprise Manager. You can best see this in a database system. A **system** is a collection of components that can be managed together, rather than managing each component separately.

Go to **Targets** | **Systems** and then select **emrepos.sainath.com_sys**, which is the name automatically given by Enterprise Manager to a system that has been created for this database. The system home page appears as shown in the following screenshot:

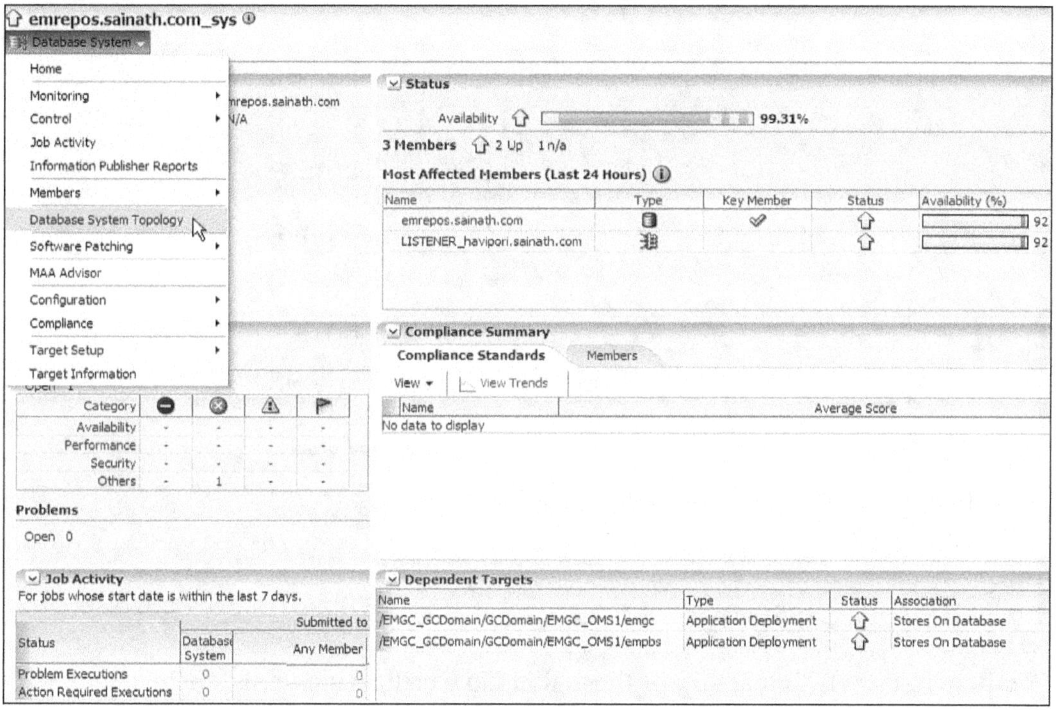

Now, go to **Database System** | **Database System Topology**. This displays all the interconnected components in a graphical format. Click on the components to expand them. The relationship between the components are shown.

In a complex system, such a map would be useful to find out the interdependencies. You can search for individual components and you can also change the annotations that appear on the topology view, such as the status, metrics (with names or values), and incidents:

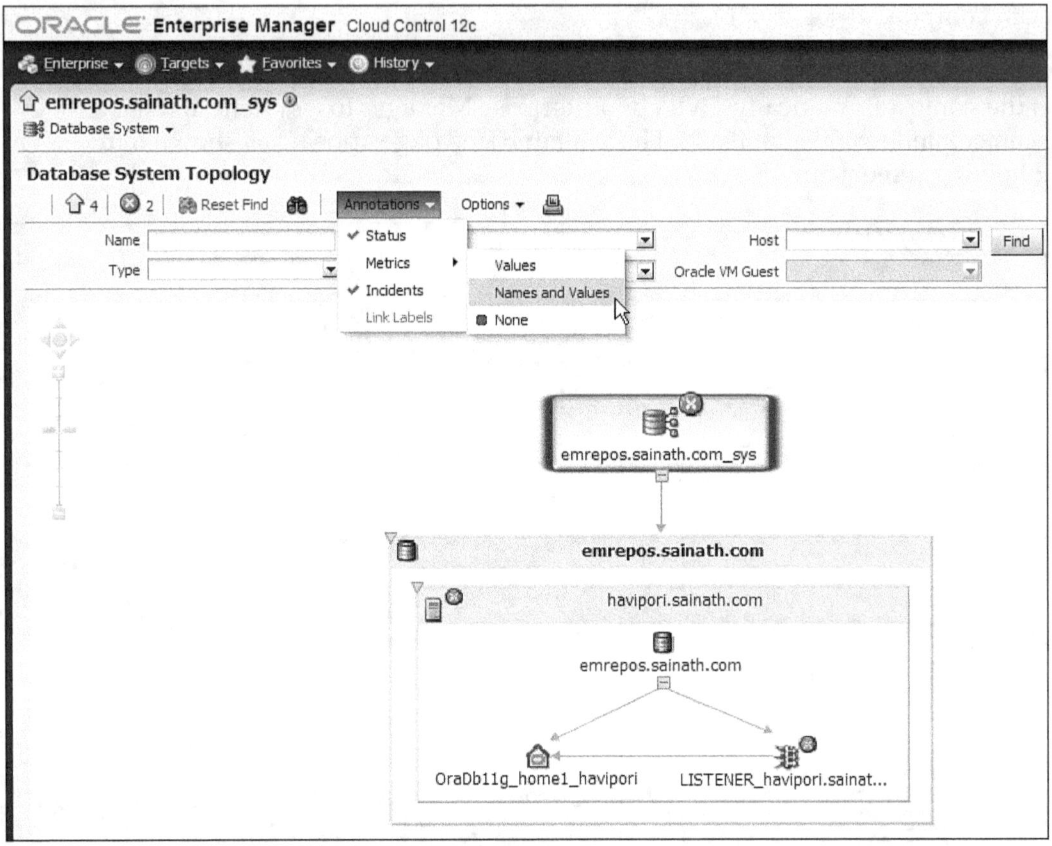


Component targets that are up or those that have critical incidents, such as the listener in the preceding screenshot, are pinpointed easily and quickly. This points out an interesting use of the topology viewer.

The root cause of the database system having a critical incident is traced to the host and then to the listener, this is known as **Root Cause Analysis** (**RCA**); Enterprise Manager Cloud Control 12*c* goes through all the components in the system one by one until it finds the root cause.

If the same task was to be done manually in a complex multicomponent system, every component would have to be checked manually and this is where the automation power of Enterprise Manager is most useful. For example, consider an application system with a number of databases, listeners, hosts, and application servers. If the system was reported as non-functional, the administrators would have to go through it and manually check every host, every database, every listener, and every application server to pinpoint the problem.

Suppose they were using Enterprise Manager, all they would have to do is to view the topology of the application system, and they would immediately know where the problem lay due to the RCA being performed.

The components in this database system use associations such as **Installed at** (an Oracle Home), **Exposed by** (a listener), or **Relies on key component**. These associations were autogenerated by Enterprise Manager. If you were to create your own system with more than one Target component, associations would again be autogenerated, but you would be able to add your own associations manually. You can use different associations such as **Hosted by** (a host), **Monitored by** (an Agent), and **Stores data on**. If you are associating two databases in a system, you are able to use either **Cloned from** or **Replicates to**.

Thus, the visual representation of system components and their associations in a topology diagram are very useful for impact analysis as well as dependency analysis. For example, a DBA may want to know what applications will be impacted if the database needs to be shut down for maintenance work.

# Custom configurations

Enterprise Manager collects a rich set of configuration information for different types of Targets, such as databases, hosts, middleware, and many Oracle applications: E-Business Suite, Siebel, PeopleSoft, JD Edwards, and Fusion Applications. The blueprints for collection are updated regularly by Oracle, and are downloadable using the self-update facility in Enterprise Manager Cloud Control 12*c*.

There is also a close integration with MOS. The Target configuration information that is collected by the Agent and stored in the **Configuration Management Database** (**CMDB**) within the repository is collated regularly by the Enterprise Manager Harvester process and pushed to MOS. The Harvester is actually a part of the Enterprise Manager's Base Framework, and replaces **Oracle Configuration Manager** (**OCM**) in the case of most Enterprise Manager Targets for this critical upload of configuration information to MOS. However, at the time of writing, except for Fusion Applications, Oracle applications such as EBS, Siebel, PeopleSoft, and JD Edwards are not harvested Targets, and still need a separate installation of OCM on the Target servers.

This detailed configuration information, once aggregated, is accessible from both MOS as well as Enterprise Manager. One big benefit is that it assists greatly with the solving of **service requests (SRs)**; it certainly helps the Support Engineers if the information they are seeking to resolve an issue is readily available.

The other humongous benefit is that, since MOS knows the detailed configuration of all the Targets at the customer site, it can easily and proactively offer advice on which component needs to have a critical security patch or update patch applied, and so on. This recommendation capability is now also present in the Enterprise Manager engine itself, even without the upload of configuration data taking place to MOS.

Consequently, the customer is able to download the patches directly, create or modify their SRs from within Enterprise Manager itself, and also browse the knowledge articles. We will see the patching capability in more detail in an upcoming chapter.

Regarding the configuration collections by the Agent, you can now ask the Agent to collect even more, and you do this by using custom configurations in this new release. You can now supplement whatever configuration information is being collected by Enterprise Manager. Custom configurations use special parsers and associated rules to transform the configuration data collected by the Agent.

A good number of parsers are supplied out of the box – such as parsers for Java policy files, LDAP's `.cfg` files, Oracle's `.ora` files, and `pam.conf` files. When custom configuration is created and deployed on a specific target, the Agent on that target immediately starts collecting the special configuration information, which is then parsed and stored in the repository.

Go to **Enterprise** | **Configuration** | **Custom**, this displays the **Custom Configurations Library** page where you can create, export, import, and deploy custom configurations. Selecting **Create** displays the page shown in the following screenshot:

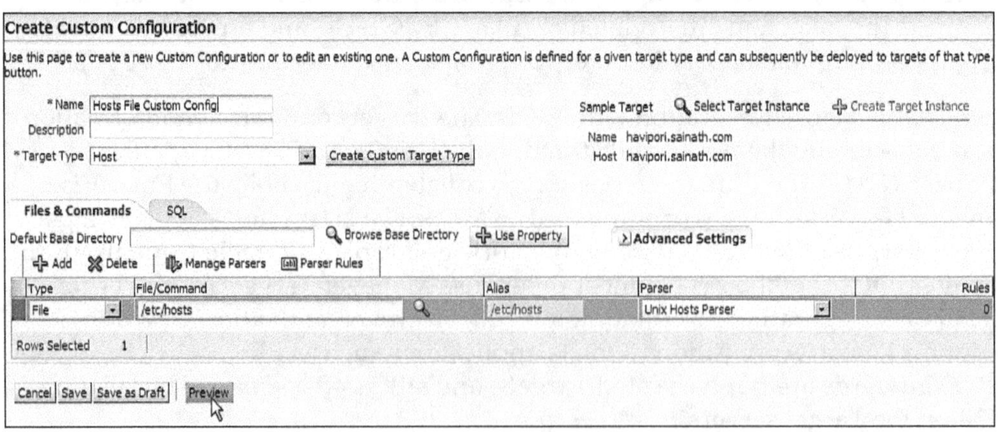

Here, you have created a new custom configuration called **Hosts File Custom Config**, which is responsible for collecting the configuration of the `/etc/hosts` files on any Target that is of type **Host**.

The parser used is the **Unix Hosts Parser** parser, which is one of the supplied out-of-the-box parsers. You have also selected **Sample Target** so that you can then click on the **Preview** button and see the type of configuration information that is collected. When you are satisfied, the custom configuration can be saved and it then appears in the **Custom Configurations** library, from where it can be deployed on any of the Targets of the same Target type:

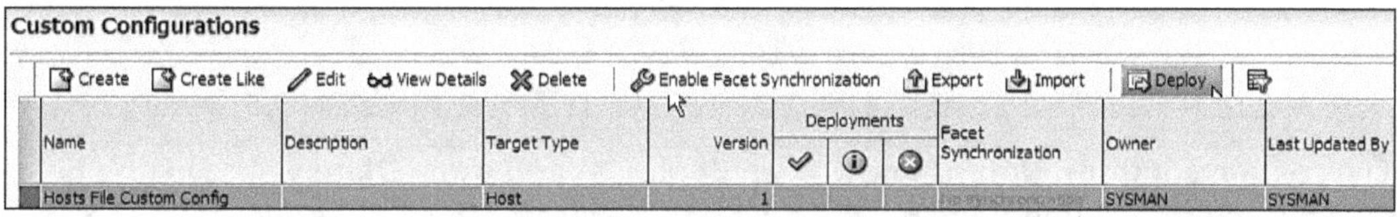


If you want to have a look at the parsers that are available out of the box, you can click on the **Manage Parsers** button on the **Create Custom Configuration** page. This brings up the list of **Parsers** as shown in the following screenshot:

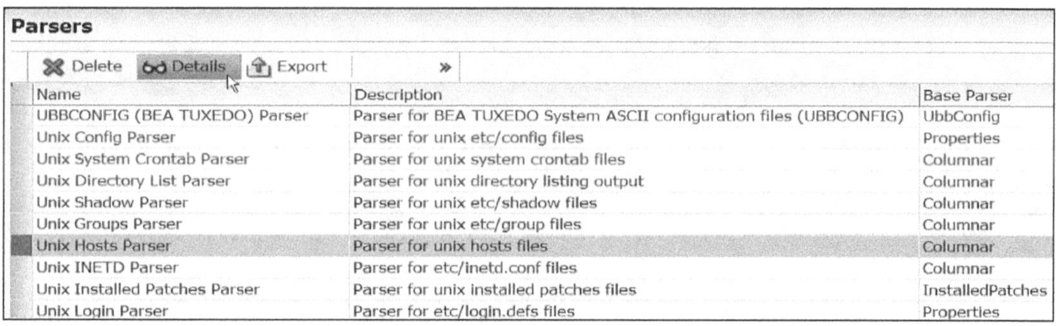

Select the **Unix Hosts Parser** parser that you used in your example and click on the **Details** button. The parser details are displayed as shown in the following screenshot:

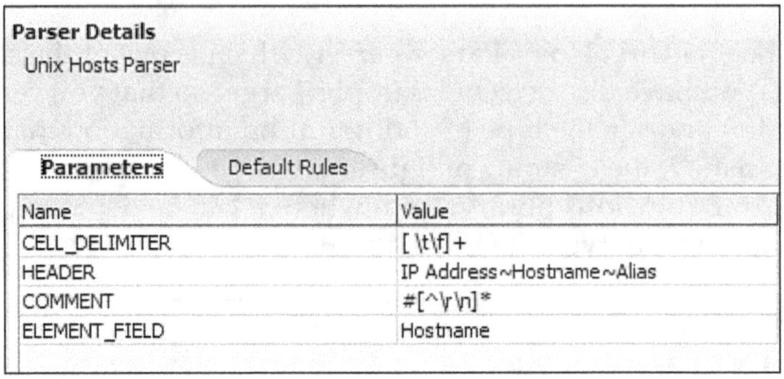


The custom configuration has now been deployed and immediately shows up on the latest configuration page for the host **havipori.sainath.com**, as shown in the following screenshot. The new information about the contents of the `/etc/hosts` file is displayed:

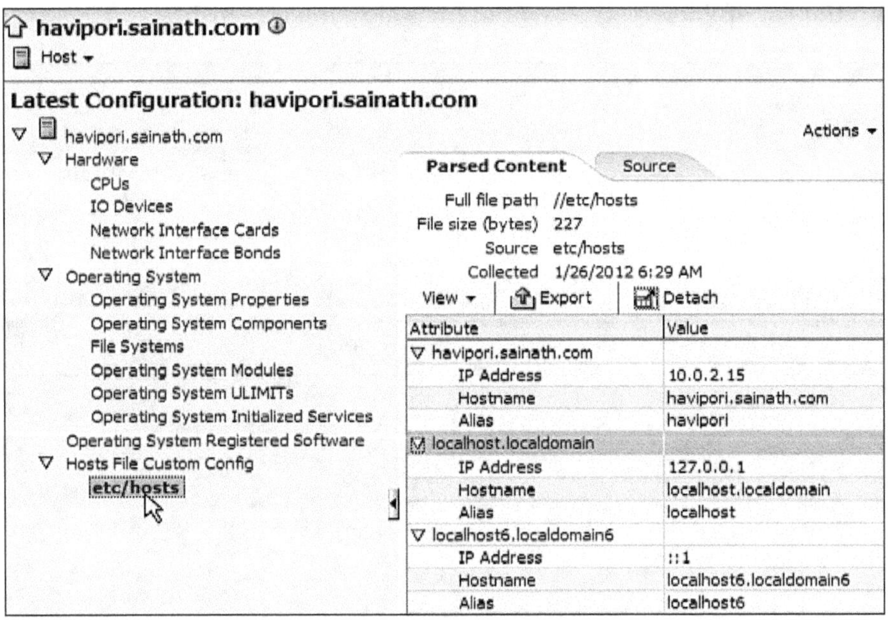


Note that any **Custom Configuration** created and deployed in this manner can be used in configuration comparisons and historical searches, just like any other configuration item. In the above case, we can easily search for a history of all changes to the `/etc/hosts` file, or we can compare the file in different hosts.

Besides capturing configuration information in this way from files, it is also possible to specify an OS-level command and capture the output, or a SQL command to a database and capture the query output. The database-query parser is used in the latter case.

# Client configurations

The latest version of Enterprise Manager Cloud Control 12*c* allows collection of client configurations. This is accessible when we navigate to **Enterprise** | **Configuration** | **Client Configurations**.

In this context, a client means an end-user system that is external to your company's IT systems. Configuration data can also be collected from such an end-user system.

The collection is performed by an application called **Client System Analyzer** (**CSA**). This application is preinstalled with Enterprise Manager Cloud Control 12*c* and can be accessed by going to **Enterprise** | **Configuration** | **Client System Analyzer**, which brings up the page shown in the following screenshot:

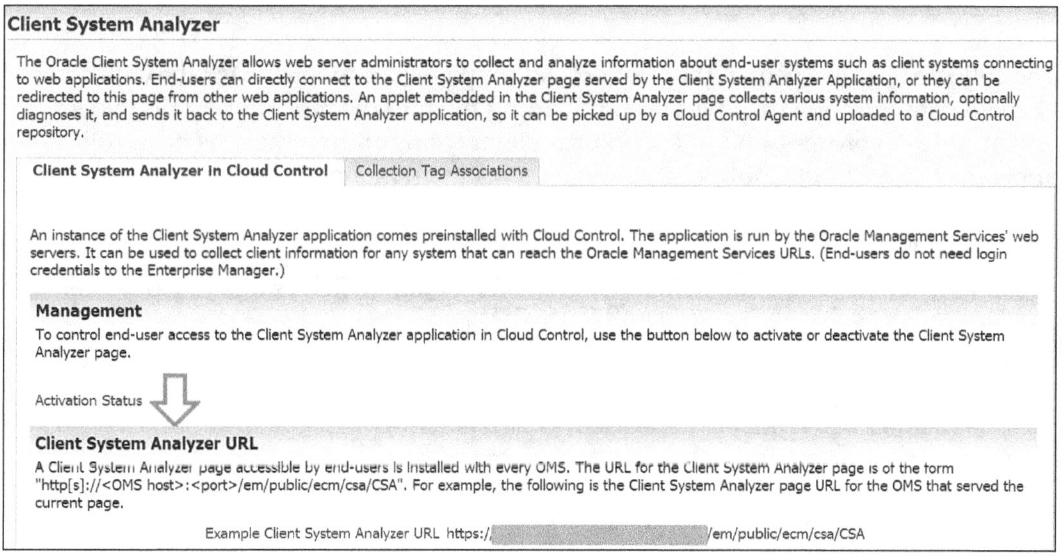


This allows you to activate or deactivate the CSA application page. If the end-user system can access the URL shown in the screenshot, which is on the OMS web servers, then it can use the CSA application to collect the client information. No login credentials to Enterprise Manager are needed.

If the OMS web servers cannot be reached, CSA can be deployed independently on the end-user web server, by the external administrator.

CSA works via an applet that is responsible for collecting client data, diagnosing it, and transferring it to the CSA application.

In our case, the client system-analyzer URL is

`https://havipori.sainath.com:7799/em/public/ecm/csa/CSA.`

When this URL is accessed from our browser on the host Windows PC, the applet is downloaded and the collection starts:

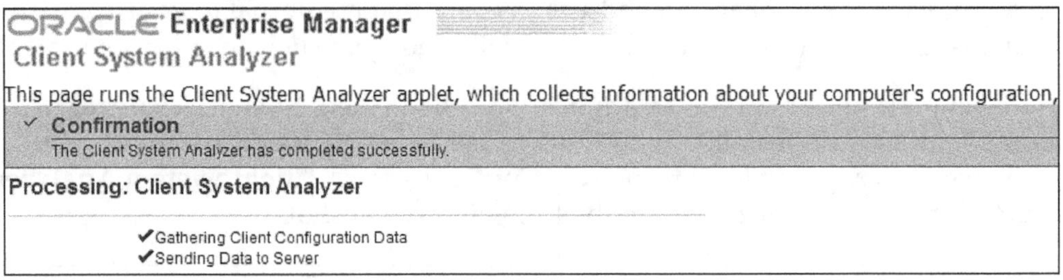


The collector Target seen on the CSA activation page is responsible for the collection of client configuration data files and uploading them to the repository. This takes a few minutes to process, and in the end the client configuration that has been collected appears on the **Client Configurations** page, as shown in the following screenshot:

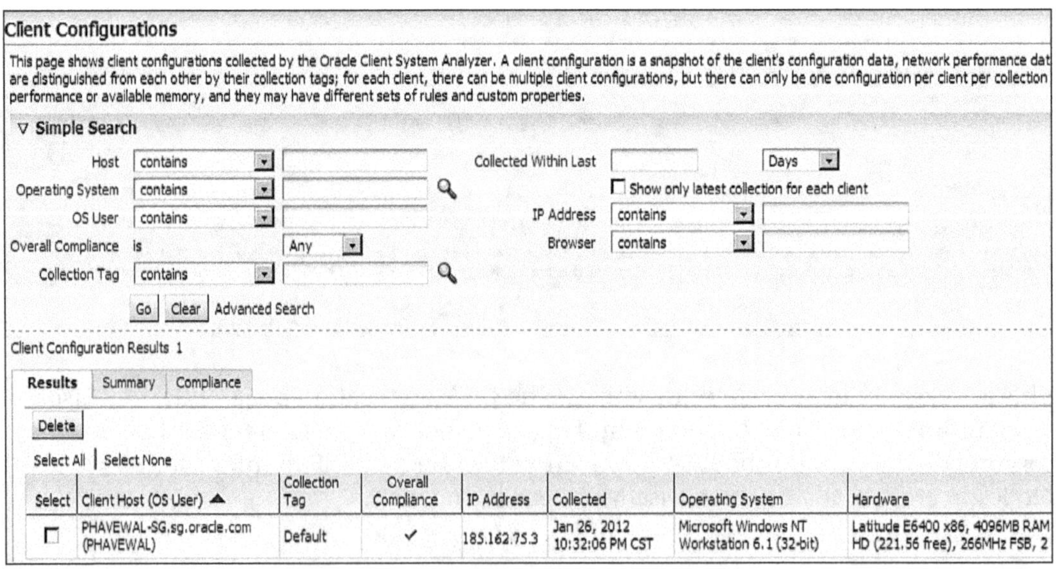

Drilling down deeper into the client configuration shows the details, including the **Hardware** details, **Operating System** details, and also the **OS-Registered Software** details on this client machine:

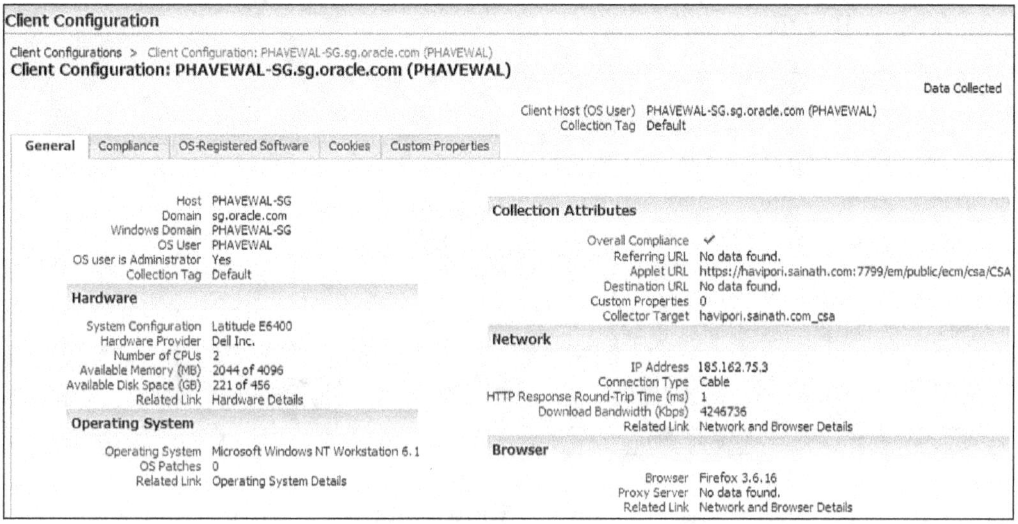

# Compliance

Configuration and security compliance is monitored by Enterprise Manager Cloud Control 12*c*. Right on the enterprise's summary page, Enterprise Manager displays the compliance information for each of the Targets. In our case, there are four critical violations for the **havipori.sainath.com** target:

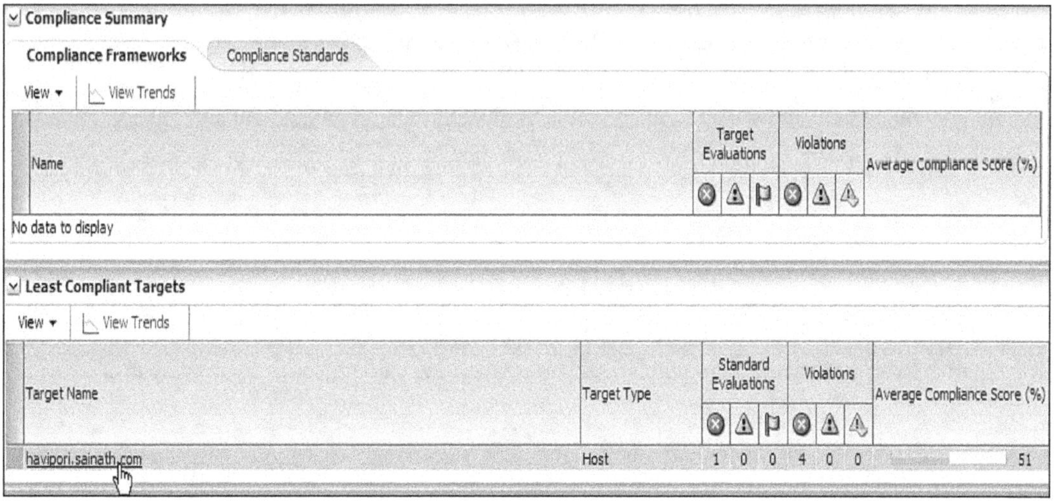

The average compliance score of this target has been calculated as **51** percent. To view the violations in detail, you have to drill down by clicking on the target name in this table. This brings up the **Compliance Results** page as shown in the following screenshot. This page can also be displayed by going to **Enterprise** | **Compliance** | **Results**:

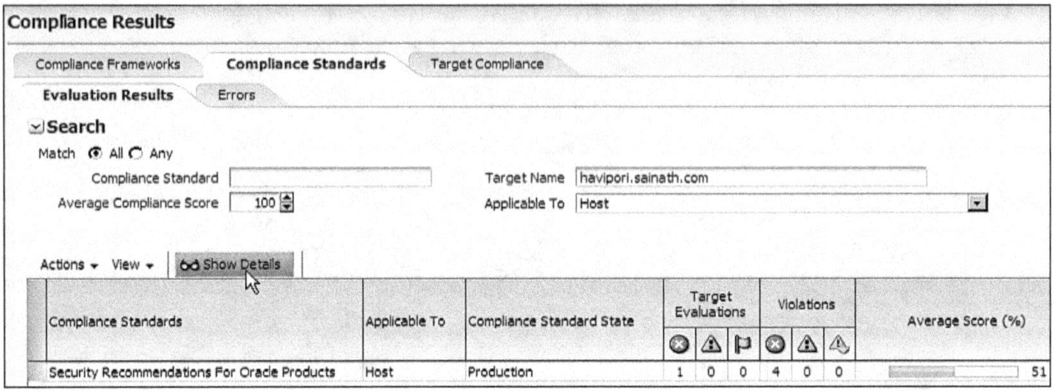


To view the actual violations, click on the **Show Details** button and then select **Security Recommendations** on the left-hand side pane. This brings up the list on the **Violation Events** tab. If you select any of the violations in this list, the detailed information will be displayed in the section that is underneath:

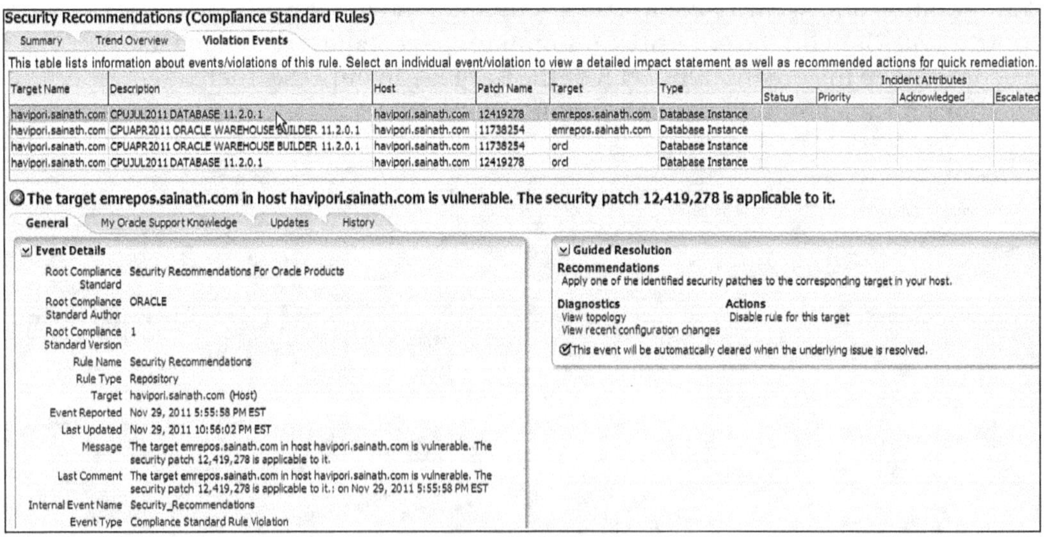

You may have noticed the **Incident Attributes** columns, such **Status**, **Priority**, **Acknowledged**, and **Escalated** in the violations table. This shows that each violation has contributed towards an Enterprise Manager incident.

Go to **Enterprise** | **Monitoring** | **Incident Manager**. Click on the **Search** button and select **Type** as **Events**. In the **Event Type** drop-down menu/drop-down box, select **Compliance Standard Rule Violation** as well as **Compliance Standard Score Violation**. Then click on the **Get Results** button. This brings up the list of violations as shown in the following screenshot. Select any of the violations to see the details. Note that the **Include members** field is irrelevant in this case:

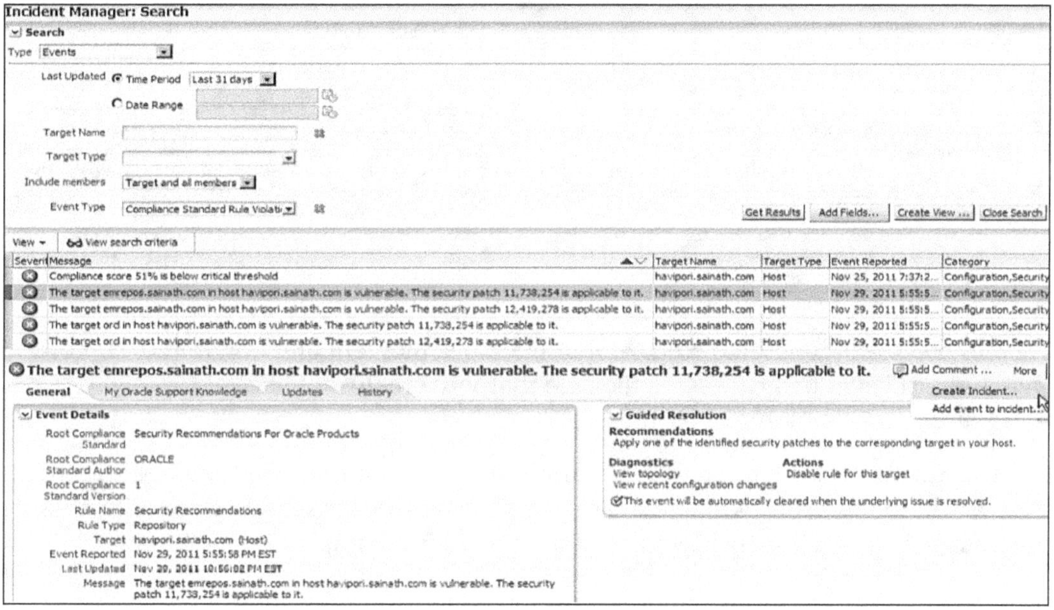

You can click on the **More** link to manually create an incident for this event, which is a **Compliance Standard Rule Violation** event.

However, in the case of the compliance standard score violation event, you do not need to create an incident manually because there is already an existing incident rule to create an incident from such an event. This can be seen in the **Incident Rules - All Enterprise Rules** page, which can be accessed by going to **Setup** | **Incidents** | **Incident Rules**:

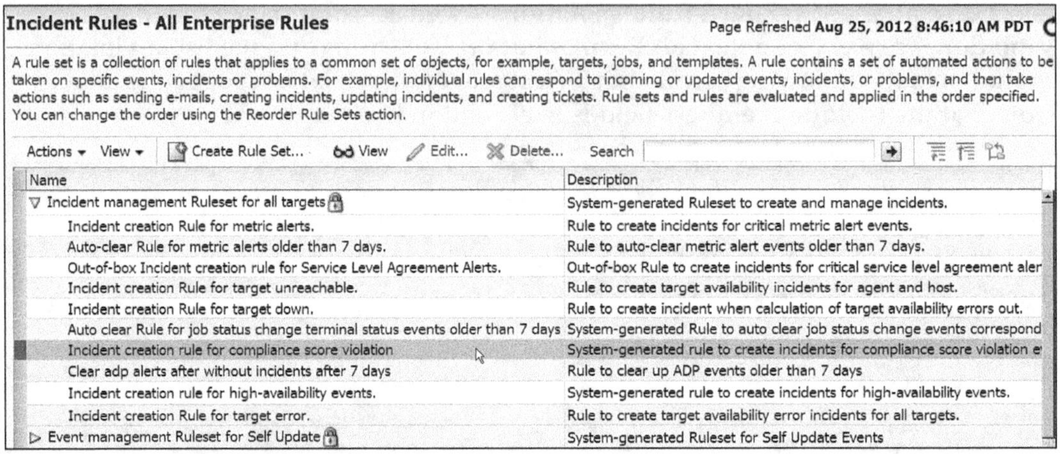


There is a system-generated rule set that manages incident creation for all Targets. One of the rules in this rule set is the rule that will create an incident for any compliance score violation event.

If you want an incident to be created automatically for any **Compliance Standard Rule Violation** event as well, you can create a new rule set on this page with a new rule that will create this incident every time there is a compliance violation.

The incident that was automatically created for the compliance score violation can be seen in the incident manager:

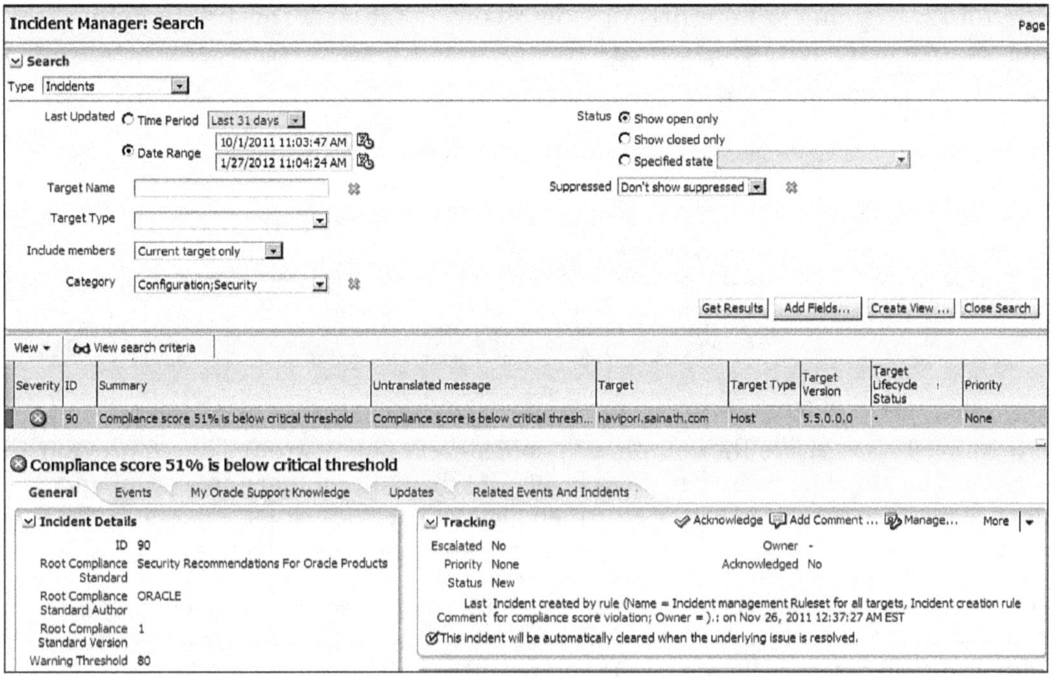

Here we have searched for incidents of a specified date range, and also used the **Add Fields...** button to add a new search field **Category**. In this field, we have searched for **Configuration** or **Security** as the values.

The generated incident is listed on clicking the **Get Results** button. Enterprise Manager Cloud Control 12*c* also makes it possible to add searches like this as a new view in the incident manager, if you wish. Simply click on the **Create View...**button.

# Compliance library

You can view the centralized compliance library in Enterprise Manager Cloud Control 12*c* by going to **Enterprise** | **Compliance** | **Library**. This brings up the view shown in the following screenshot:

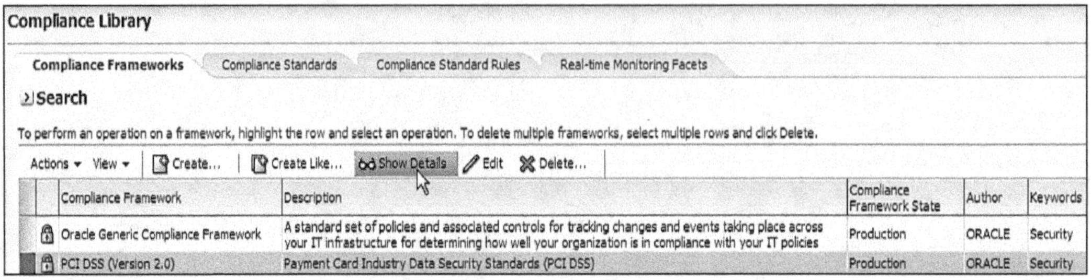


Enterprise Manager Cloud Control 12*c* now uses a new hierarchy for the compliance capability. This replaces the compliance policies and policy groups of the previous version. The new hierarchy has three levels – at the bottom, there are compliance rules, which are checks or tests performed against specific Target types, such as a check to see if a database or OS parameter is set as per best practices.

On the second level, we have compliance standards. These are a collection of one or more rules for a certain Target type. Compliance standards can be associated with multiple targets. When the various compliance standards for different Target types are combined together, they form compliance frameworks, which are at the topmost level.

The frameworks are conceptual folder-like structures that map the configuration standards to the real-world PCI, CIS, and such other frameworks. Many out-of-the-box compliance rules and standards are provided with Enterprise Manager Cloud Control 12*c*, which are mapped to these frameworks.

For example, click on the **Show Details** button on the **Compliance Frameworks** tab to see the information for the **PCI DSS (Version 2.0)** framework:

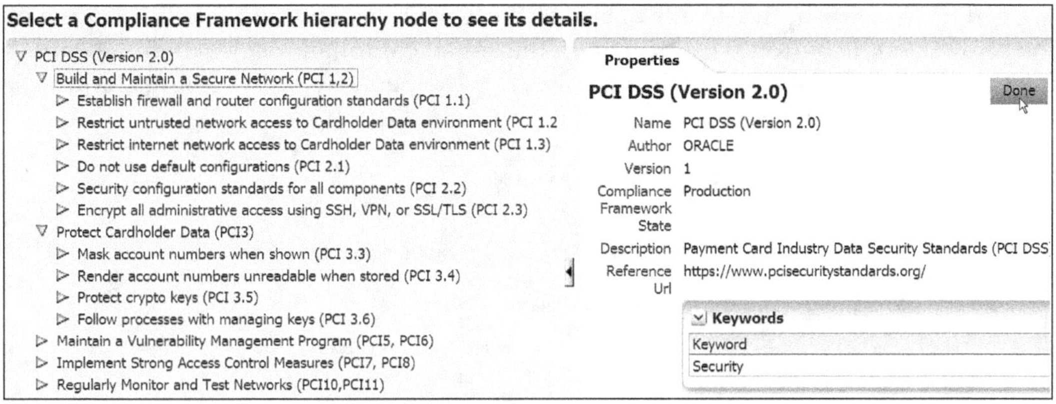

Note that the information shown is only a skeleton. Compliance frameworks are useful in assisting DBAs, administrators, and IT managers to create associated rules and standards, as a sort of a guideline. At the higher level, people like the auditors, security, and compliance officers can use the frameworks and generate the necessary compliance reports.

Move to the **Compliance Standards** tab to see the various out-of-the-box standards pertaining to different Targets, such as database instance, listener, Oracle WebLogic domain, cluster database, and Oracle WebLogic Server:

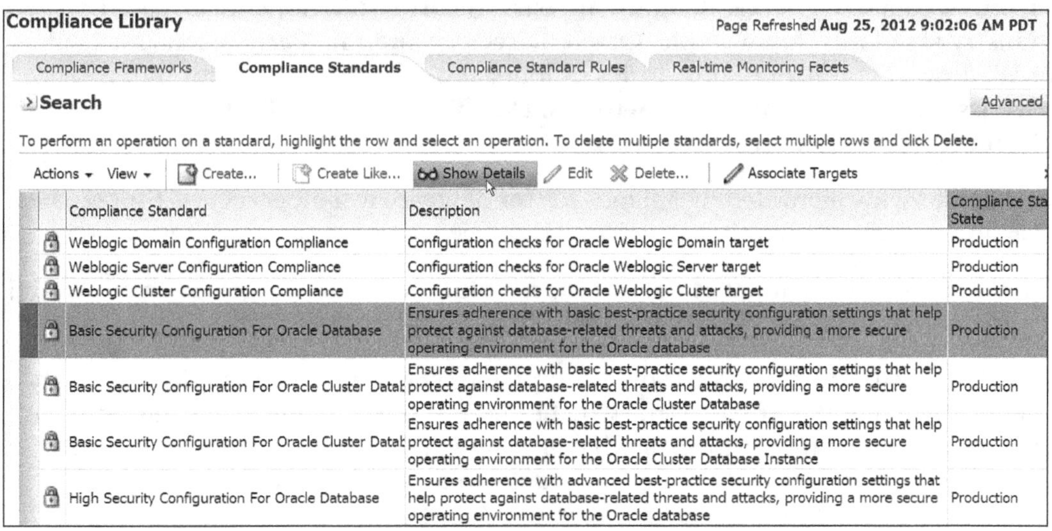

We can have a look at the details of any of these compliance standards by clicking on the **Show Details** button. This brings up the actual compliance rules that make up the standard we have selected. In this case, it is the **Basic Security Configuration For Oracle Database** page:

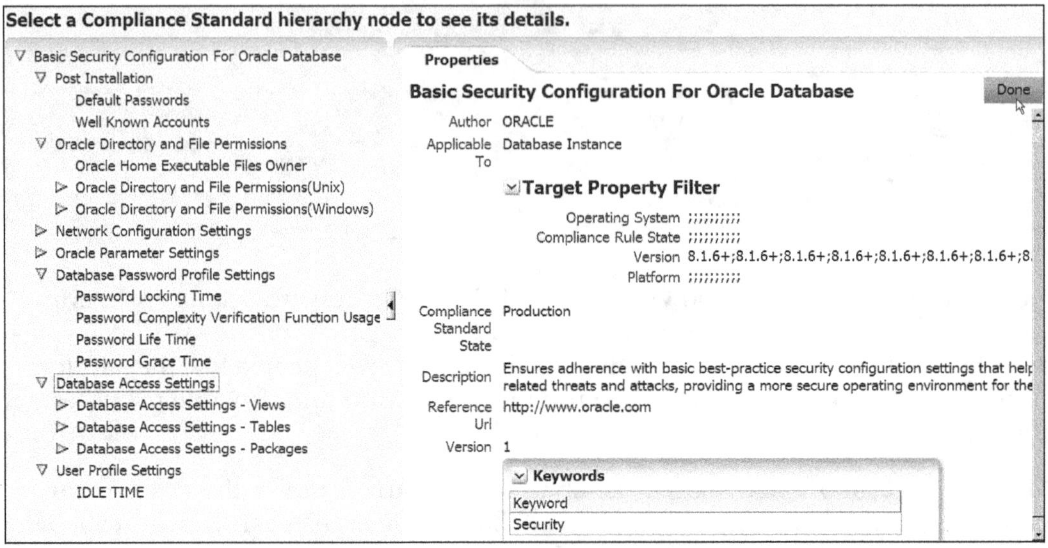


The rules contained in this standard are basic security rules for Oracle, based on industry standards, for example, **Oracle Directory and File Permissions** for Unix or Windows (a number of directories/folders and files are checked for the correct permissions), **Oracle Parameter Settings**, **Database Password Profile Settings**, **Database Access Settings**, and so on.

In a similar way, there are other standards for database instances such as **Storage Best Practices**, **Configuration Best Practices**, **High Security configuration**, and so on.

On the compliance standards page, it is possible to associate Targets with any of the standards. This is done via the **Associate Targets** button.

It is also possible to define your own compliance standards. You can do this by clicking on either the **Create** or the **Create Like...** button on this page. Suppose we create a new standard for the Sainath company via the **Create** button. You name it, specify the Target type to which it is applicable, and set the **Standard Type** – whether **Repository**, **WebLogic Server Signature** (previously BEA Guardian), or **Real-time Monitoring**. Then click on the **Continue** button:

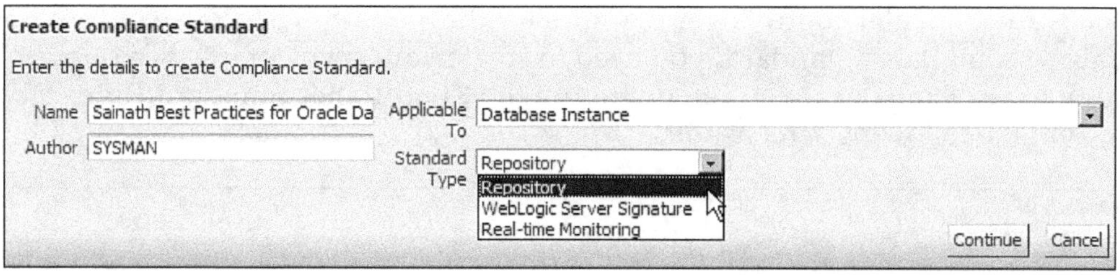


On this page, you are now able to create the new compliance standard in detail. You can add rules and/or standards, and create a rule folder if you wish. You can select Target filters that apply to the standard, and can also decide if this standard is for development or production. You can also add keywords such as **Configuration**, **Security**, **Storage**, **Capacity**, **Performance**, and so on (or create your own keyword):

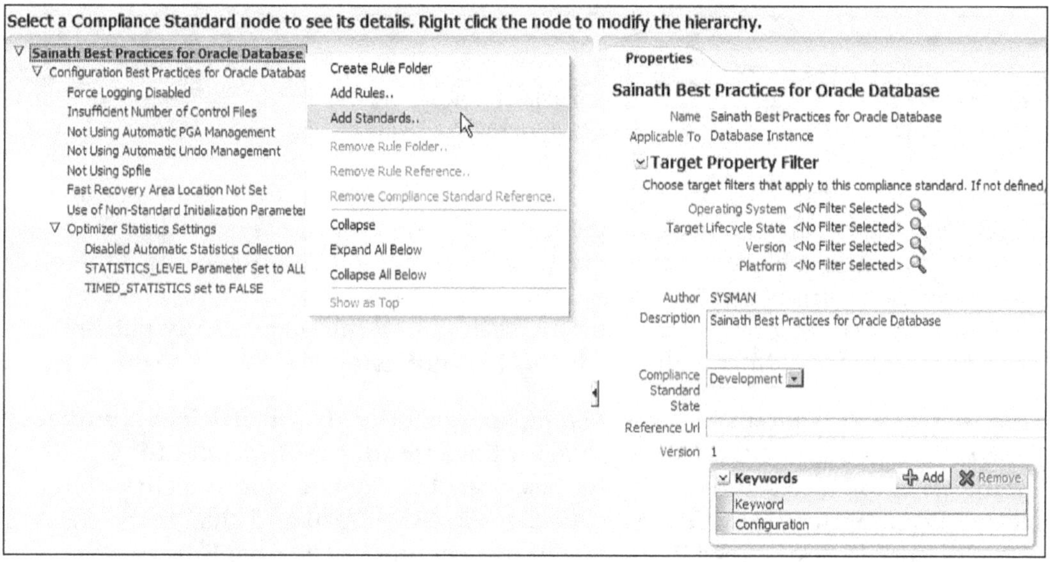


In this example, we have added a predefined standard to the **Sainath Best Practices for Oracle Database** compliance standard. The standard we have selected is **Configuration Best Practices for Oracle Database**. Once the standard is inserted, we cannot change the actual rules, all we can do is change the importance of any of the rules—**Low**, **Normal**, or **High**. By default the importance is **Normal**.

If you wanted greater control over the rules for the **Sainath Best Practices for Oracle Database** compliance standard, you need to create your own compliance rules or modify the existing ones. You can do this on the **Compliance Standard Rules** tab as shown in the following screenshot:

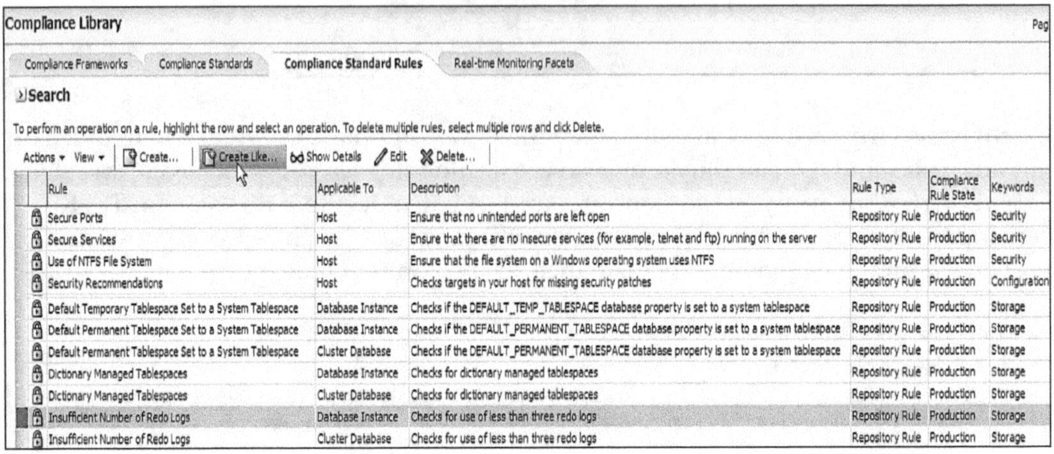


This page displays all the out-of-the-box compliance rules for different types of Targets. Examples are the checks to see if the `SYSTEM` Tablespace is used as the default temporary Tablespace or as the default permanent Tablespace, or if there is an insufficient number of redo logs or insufficient redo log size. Other checks make sure that all the ports on the host are secure, find missing security patches for Targets, or warn if Microsoft Windows OS is not using NTFS, and so on.

Suppose you wanted to modify an existing compliance rule, **Insufficient Number of Redo Logs**, and use the modified rule for the **Sainath Best Practices for Oracle Database** compliance standard. To do this, select the existing rule and click on the **Create Like...** button. Move through the steps in the wizard and change the check for `3` redo logs to `5` redo logs in the case of this company. The final **Review** screen for this new compliance rule, along with the actual SQL statement responsible for getting the redo log information from the repository is shown in the following screenshot:

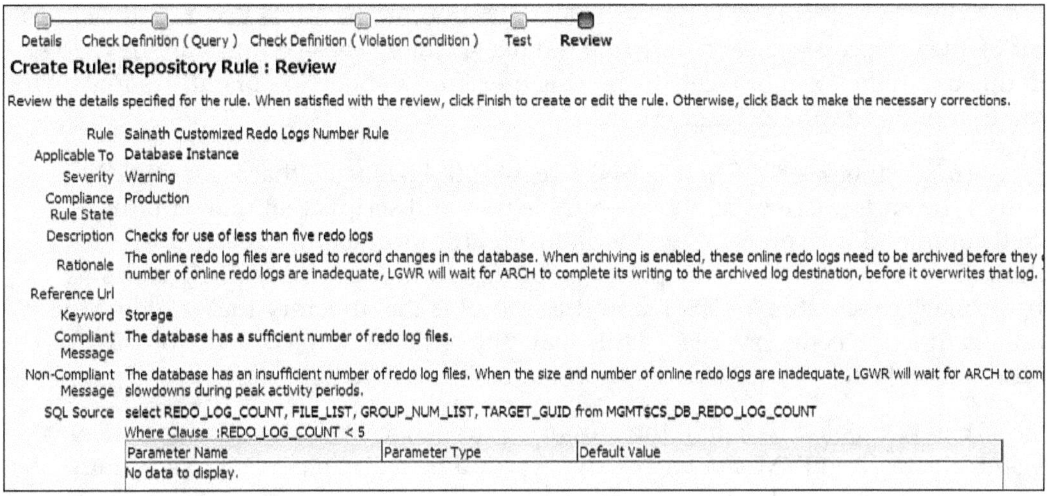

In this way you can create compliance rules and standards in a vertical perspective for a system or application in your company. You can also take the other approach and define compliance standards in a horizontal perspective for various industry frameworks such as HIPAA, COBIT, and SOX.

The last tab on the **Compliance Library** page is the **Real-time Monitoring Facets** tab, as shown in the following screenshot:

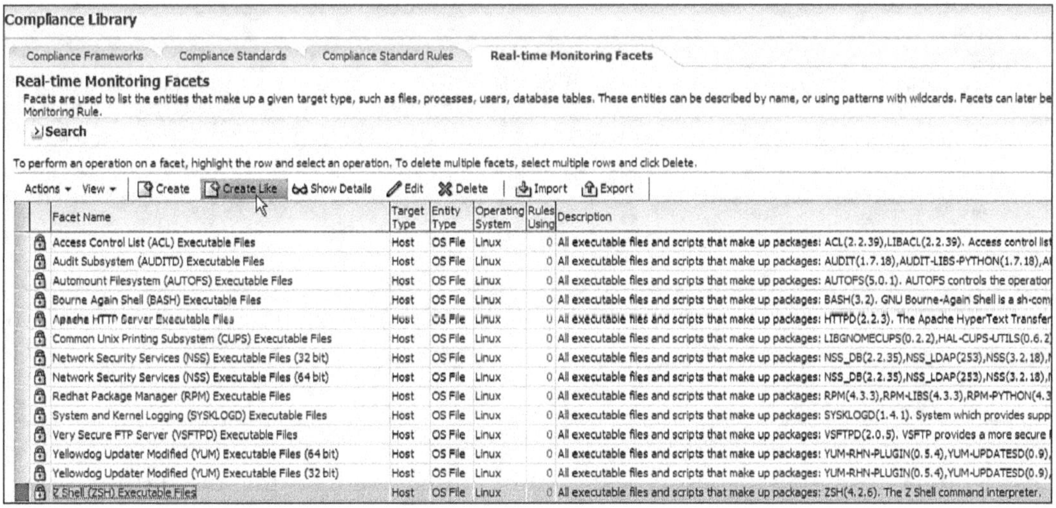

In real-time monitoring, a Target type is understood to be made up of entities; these can be files, processes, users, or actual database tables. These entities are described on this tab in the form of facets. A **facet** is therefore a collection of entities that enable you to monitor a certain Target type.

For example, there is a **Z Shell (ZSH) Executable Files** facet that is an **OS File** entity type and describes all the executable files and scripts that make up the Z Shell command interpreter. If you look inside this facet using **Create Like...** or **Show Details**, you will see the patterns **/bin/zsh** and **/usr/share/zsh**. The first is the primary executable for ZSH, and the second is the directory that contains the built-in function code for ZSH. In this way, the entities can be described using wildcard patterns, or explicitly by their names.

Facets can be created based on the Target type, such as host, database instance, Agent, cluster, and JVM. For each Target type, the facet can pertain to a certain entity type, such as database user, table, and view for a database instance Target type, or the facet can pertain to an OS file, OS user, OS process for a host Target type. It is recommended that each facet be created based on a specific purpose.

As an example, the Sainath company has created a new facet called `Sainath Facet for /etc/passwd`, which works on a **Host** Target type and **OS File** entity type. The pattern given is `/etc/passwd`. It is possible to browse files directly on the host to build your facet, and to do this you first need to select your host on this page:

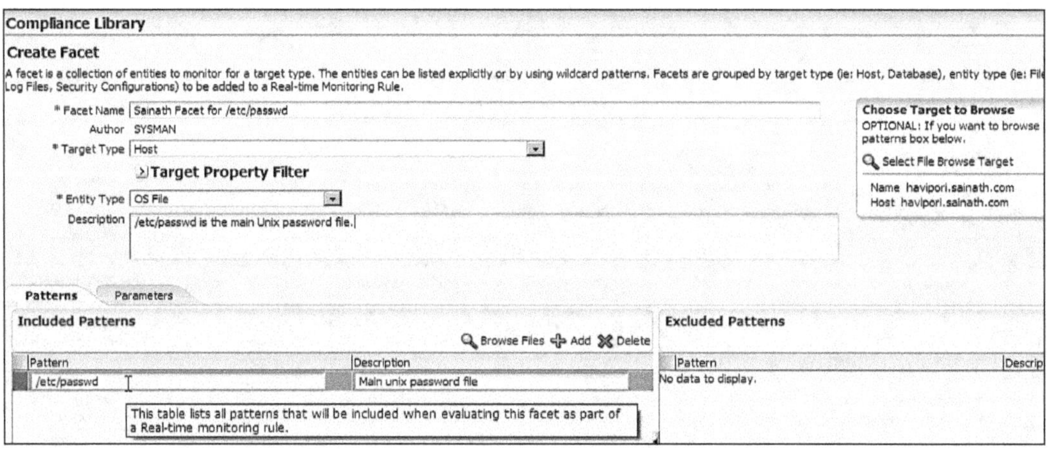


Once you have defined the facets, they can be added to a real-time monitoring rule during its creation. This is done in the **Compliance Standard Rules** tab.

When you create a rule, you are asked to specify if it is a **Repository Rule, WebLogic Server Signature Rule,** or **Real-time Monitoring Rule**. You proceed and create the `Sainath Real-time Monitoring Rule for /etc/passwd` rule, and include the `Sainath Facet for /etc/passwd` facet created previously.

The rule is applicable to a host, and uses the entity type of **OS File**. The **Review** screen appears as shown in the following screenshot:

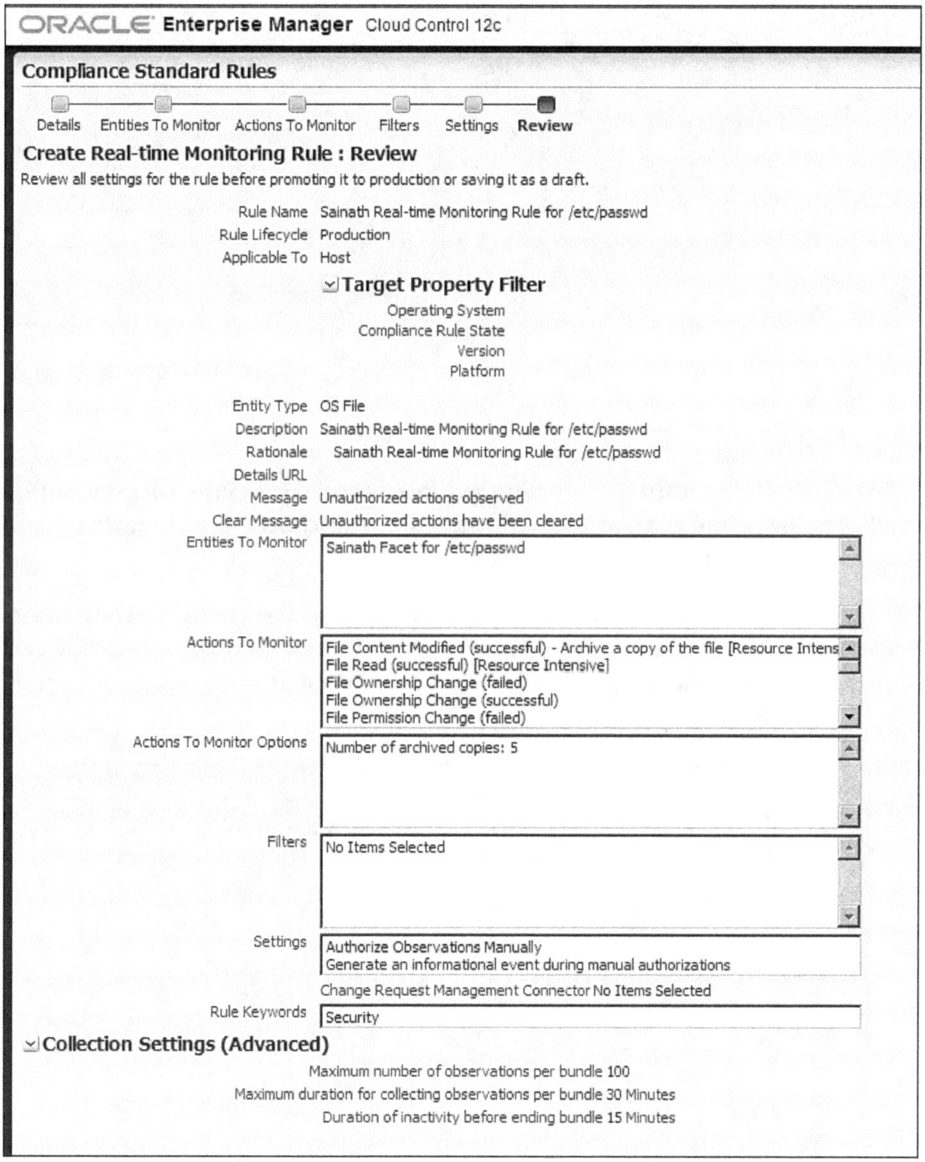

The final step is to go to the **Compliance Standards** tab, create a new compliance standard named `Sainath Real-time compliance standard for host files`, and select set **Applicable To** as **Host** (Target type) and **Standard Type** as **Real-time Monitoring**.

We now add the `Sainath Real-time Monitoring Rule for /etc/passwd` rule created previously, to this standard:

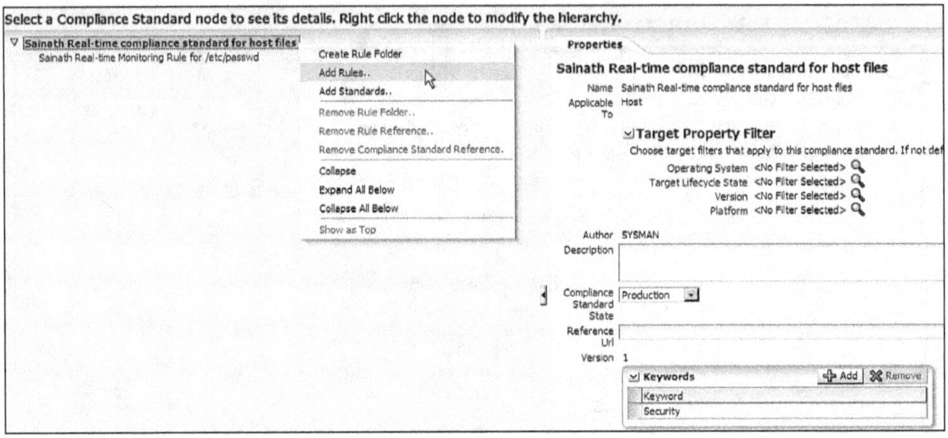


The next step, on the **Compliance Standard** tab, is the **Associate Targets** button, which helps to associate the Target with this new standard. Note that the **Association Count** column shows a value of zero until this is done.

When the real-time monitoring compliance standard is associated with the host Target, it is at that point that the real-time monitoring capabilities are deployed to the actual Agent on the Target. You are asked to confirm this, as shown in the following screenshot:

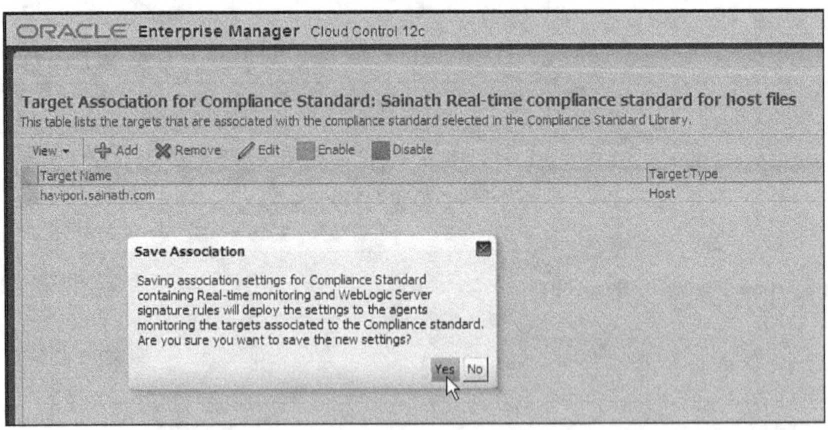

The compliance standard is submitted to the Target for processing.

After this is done, you can see the new compliance standard being monitored when you go to **Enterprise** | **Compliance** | **Results** (also shown via **Enterprise** | **Summary**, on the home page under the **Compliance Summary** section). Currently, the compliance score for this standard is seen to be **100** percent:

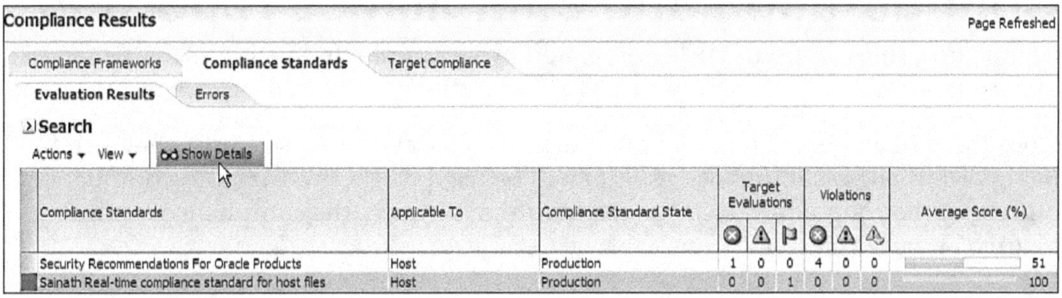


Some more steps need to be followed at the host end for the real-time compliance monitoring to be successful. There are different requirements for Linux, Windows, Solaris, or Oracle database monitoring. For the Linux portion, refer to the *Oracle Enterprise Manager Lifecycle Management Administrator's Guide* document at the following URL:

`http://docs.oracle.com/cd/E24628_01/em.121/e27046/install_realtime_ccc.htm#EMLCM11832`

These steps show you how to install a loadable kernel module on the Linux host, which is the file audit module. Note that the audit module is not a requirement for Linux Version 5 and higher. If the module is not present, information is still collected and, if present, only slightly more information is collected. So it is possible to go without the audit module in Linux Version 5 or higher and still have real-time monitoring.

Using OS-level kernel modules is a much more efficient way to perform real-time monitoring. Similarly, OS-level auditing is used in the case of Windows servers and Solaris servers, and the audit capability of the Oracle database is used in the case of Oracle database monitoring.

To view the real-time observations, navigate to **Enterprise** | **Compliance** | **Real-Time Observations**. These are the detected user actions that are being monitored by a real-time compliance rule. You can browse observations by compliance frameworks or via system Targets, and drill down in both cases. You can also search observations directly.

As we can see, by using this real-time change detection feature of Enterprise Manager Cloud Control 12*c* it is possible to pinpoint the user who triggered a change, and when exactly the change was made to OS-level files or database objects, as well as capture process and user-based activity such as login, su, and sudo.

# Configuration and compliance reporting

Compliance rules and standards are created by technical administrators, DBAs, and IT managers—and these would normally map to industry-wide compliance frameworks.

Once these have been set up and are working in a day-to-day scenario, they need to be reported. These compliance reports will be used by the security and compliance officers of the company, as well as the auditors. As such, the compliance reports assume an important role.

A number of these compliance reports are provided by Enterprise Manager Cloud Control 12*c*, which you can access by going to **Enterprise** | **Reports** | **Information Publisher Reports**. Search for `Compliance` as the title. You can also create your own reports by using the **Create Like** button on the page shown in the following screenshot:

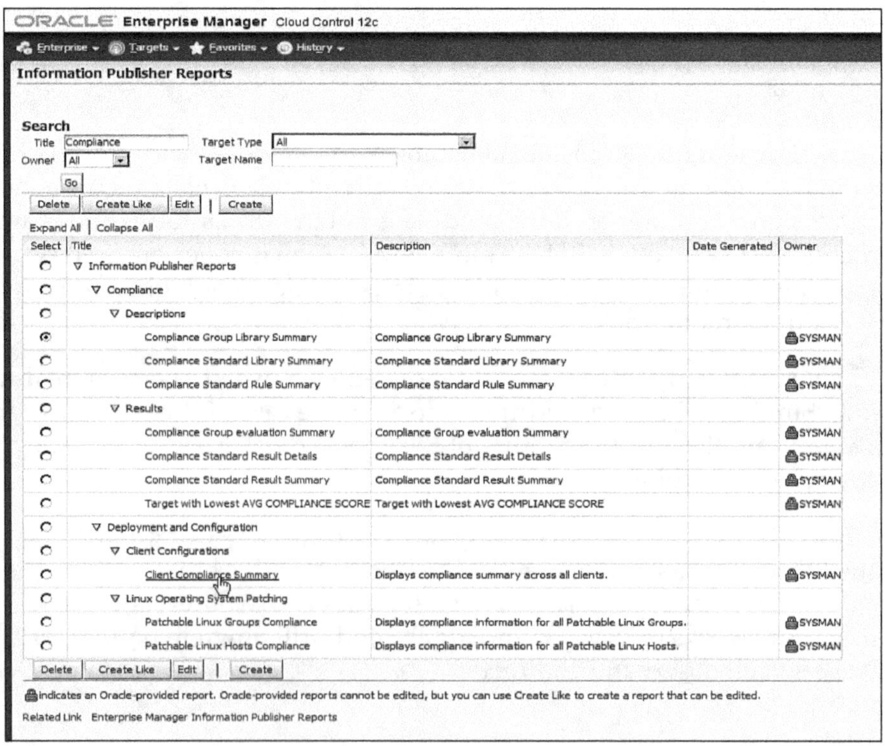

Configuration reports are available on the same page. Simply search for `Configuration` as the **Title** field's value. The following list appears:

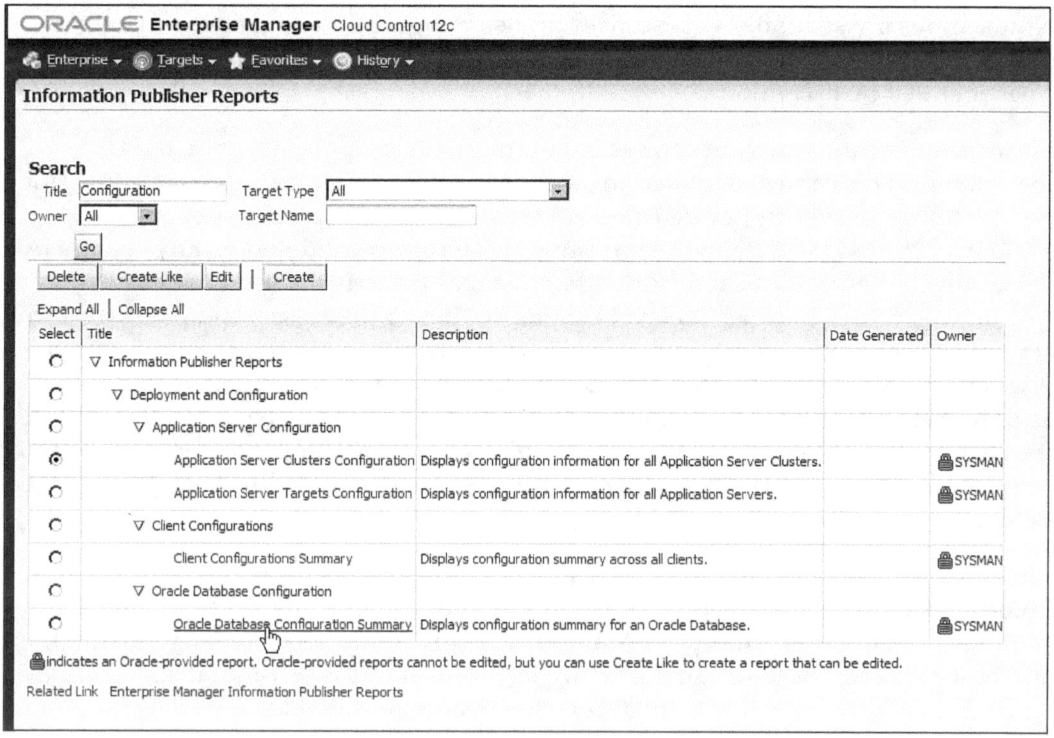


# Summary

In this chapter we have seen the configuration management and compliance capabilities of Enterprise Manager Cloud Control 12*c*, and how they combine together to enable your company to have standardized configurations throughout the IT infrastructure. Standardization enables ease of deployment and troubleshooting besides a number of other benefits.

You can have an automated configuration drift check between different systems, which may be across the lifecycle, for example, between staging and production, or between a primary site and a disaster-recovery (standby) site. Any configuration violations can be instantly reported in the incident console of Enterprise Manager.

In the new release, configuration management enjoys a scalability suitable for the largest IT environments. Only changed configuration data is loaded, and rules are evaluated at the point when a change has taken place in the related data. Notifications are sent only when a drift in the configuration data has been detected or when there is a change in a subscribed property. So this can truly be described as "management by exception".

The computer infrastructure can easily comply with the policies set by the IT department. This can be validated in various ways - repository rules, real-time rules, and WebLogic server signature rules. A repository rule is so named because it is evaluated against the data in the repository. The rule is validated on any change in the target configuration. On the other hand, a real-time rule is used to detect any real-time activities, such as OS-level actions on files or processes, and database-level actions on tables, views, or users. It is also possible to detect unauthorized changes if Enterprise Manager has been connected with change management systems, such as BMC Remedy Service Desk. In this way, real-time rules can be used to ensure that the change management process is being followed. Also, WebLogic server signature rules are for the use of WebLogic server Targets. These are health checks that will be executed by the Agent on the WLS Target.

There is a rich set of compliance rules and standards supplied out of the box by Enterprise Manager. There are more than 1,700 compliance rules, and about 30 compliance standards. Enterprise Manager also gives you security recommendations and best practices for your infrastructure targets. All this is self-updateable, with the latest coming down the line from MOS whenever it is available.

The compliance scores are kept up-to-date at all times, to give you an idea of the current compliance situation in your company. You can also see historical trends. If there are violations, detailed information is available with the reason for the violation, and the resolution that has been recommended.

So, we have seen how Enterprise Manager Cloud Control 12*c* is able to meet various challenges in the real world. As infrastructure servers increase in a growing sprawl, Enterprise Manager can track the inventory of the entire IT infrastructure, with its Agent-less Auto Discovery (using IP Scan) that can be run on an ongoing basis to discover new assets.

Elasticity is important for business, but will often result in sudden changes in topology. Enterprise Manager helps with its sophisticated topology mapping and impact/dependency analysis.

Changes may occur very rapidly in the real world. To capture and understand these changes and to ensure that they are authorized, Enterprise Manager can perform real-time monitoring. To handle drifts from established company standards, there are configuration baselines that can be stored in Enterprise Manager so that drift tracking can occur.

Finally, to handle all sorts of compliance requirements in the industry, there are compliance frameworks, standards, and rules available in Enterprise Manager Cloud Control 12*c*.

In the next chapter, we will look at the automated provisioning capabilities of Enterprise Manager Cloud Control 12*c*, and how it assists in the mass deployment of Oracle software and databases.

# 5

# Ease the Chaos with Automated Provisioning

Large corporates typically have tens of thousands of systems, including databases, database servers, and middleware application servers. In such a complex environment, the operating systems used may be different, and database versions may also vary considerably. For example, there may be a database firm using the Oracle Database **Enterprise Edition** (**EE**) 10*g* version on Linux servers, and another firm with Oracle 11*g* databases on Solaris. Middleware application servers may also vary considerably. You may have WebLogic servers or other application servers, and these may also use different Operating Systems with several versions.

Typically, manual methods would have been used to create the myriad of systems in such an environment. The various operating systems would be manually installed by a dedicated team of system administrators, who would need specialized knowledge of each operating system. So there would be a Linux team, a Solaris team, or a Windows team, all in the same company. The different database versions would also be installed using manual methods such as the **Database Configuration Assistant** (**DBCA**), either in the GUI mode, or silently using the silent install facility. This would be done by a specialized DBA team. The application servers such as WebLogic server and others would also be installed manually by the middleware team in the company.

While the manual methods are being used, how would you make sure that corporate standards (configuration and security) are being followed? Manual checklists would normally be used, with a person ticking off each step, but with no guarantee that the standards are being fully observed. And how do you make sure that the license obligations of the company are being met? Suppose the company does not have a license for Oracle **Advanced Security Option** (**ASO**), but the database team mistakenly enables this option on a few database servers, what then?

So, many different types of software are being installed manually by many different people. This would be fine in a small company, but as the numbers increase it becomes more and more difficult to keep on using manual tools, especially if there are many tens of thousands of Targets to provision in this way. The human effort required is tremendous.

# Lifecycle management

Oracle Enterprise Manager's DBLM Pack includes the powerful capability of provisioning and patch automation. This is in addition to the configuration management capabilities we looked at in the previous chapter. We will now discuss the provisioning features, and move to patch automation in the next chapter.

In a nutshell, the provisioning capabilities of Enterprise Manager allow you to create gold copies of different operating systems, different database versions, or middleware software. You can then use these gold copies to automate the deployment of the OS, database software, or middleware servers in a controlled and highly efficient manner. The actual work is performed out of the box or by customized deployment procedures in Enterprise Manager, which are a series of steps that automate the provisioning of the software. This allows the administrator's labor and effort to be drastically reduced, and quality of service to be increased.

Consider the example of a central database team which is using manual methods to install Oracle software and create databases. They normally allocate a DBA and about four hours to install the database software and create a new database as per the predefined company standards. If a project manager asks them to create five new databases by tomorrow, the chances are that the database team will decline, citing the short notice and the lack of manpower. So, the only way the team can deliver quality of service is by increasing the cost—by hiring a certain number of contract DBAs to create the five databases by the next day.

Now take the same example, and assume that the database team is using Enterprise Manager and its provisioning capabilities. In this case, the Enterprise Manager's Software Library would already have the gold copies of different database versions such as Oracle Database 10*g* or 11*g* on different operating systems (a different gold copy is required for each version on each operating system). When the request comes from the project manager to install and create a number of new databases on new servers by the next day, the database team can easily fulfill that request by simply starting the provisioning procedures of Enterprise Manager. The gold copies would be used to install the Oracle database software on each new host, and then to create a new or cloned database, and all this would happen in parallel. All company standards would be followed and all license agreements would be observed, as all these things would already be in the gold copy. The database team would have achieved full quality of service without increasing the cost. Administrator productivity is increased considerably, and there is a saving in the administrator's labor charges. The software images and provisioning processes have also been standardized as a result.

Using Enterprise Manager Cloud Control 12*c*, you can provision single-instance Oracle databases as well as RAC multi-instance databases or RAC One Node databases. You can also extend or delete existing RAC nodes. For the first time, the upgrade of single-instance databases is possible via Enterprise Manager. You can also create databases directly from the Cloud Control 12*c* console.

There is also a new concept of provisioning roles in the new version. The super administrator such as `SYSMAN` (who owns the Enterprise Manager repository) can create the Provisioning Designer and Provisioning Operator roles. Provisioning designers can then create deployment procedures with certain inputs preconfigured and locked down, and access is then granted to the provisioning operators who can no longer change the locked down inputs. This allows more control and standardization in the company and also reduces errors when the provisioning is executed by the operators (normally Junior DBAs).

The designer and operator roles for provisioning, as well as the other out-of-the-box roles in the new version of Enterprise Manager are integrated with enterprise roles. This means that if you use a tool like **Oracle Authorization Policy Manager** (**OAPM**) for authorization management in the enterprise, it is possible to create a role in OAPM such as a Senior or Junior DBA, and map it to the corresponding Cloud Control role such as Designer or Operator respectively. Any enterprise users who belong to the OAPM-defined role will also have the corresponding privileges inside Enterprise Manager because of this integration.

# First steps: Software Library

We decide to take a quick look at database provisioning. From the Enterprise Manager Cloud Control 12*c* menu, we go to **Enterprise** | **Provisioning and Patching** | **Database Provisioning**. The very first screen that comes up tells us that the Software Library setup is **Not Done**, as shown in the following screenshot:

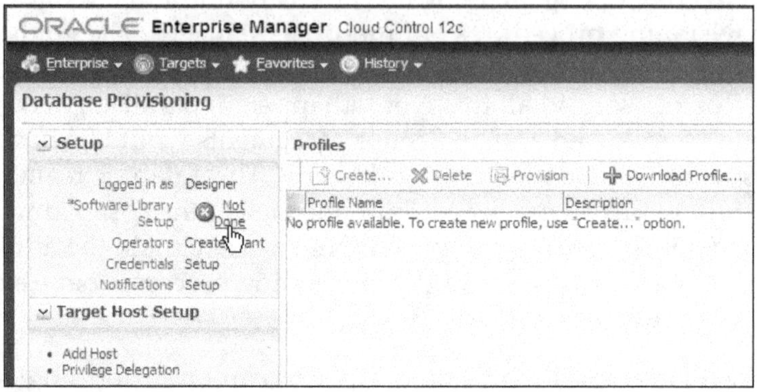


Click on the **Not Done** link. This takes us to the **Software Library: Administration** page (which can also be accessed by going to **Setup** | **Provisioning and Patching** | **Software Library**). This page displays a warning that the Software Library does not have an upload file location configured. This is one of the two options for file storage that can be used by the Software Library. The other option is **Referenced File Location**, which we will look into later on. Right now, specifying an upload file location is the very first step that needs to be done:

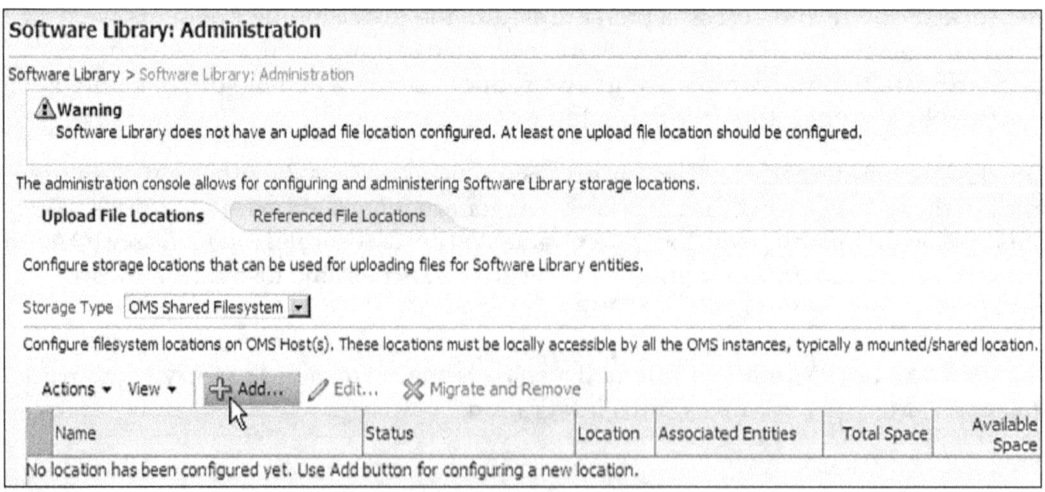

The **Upload File Locations** tab is used to upload the files that will go into the Software Library. The **Storage Type** attribute for these file locations can be set as either an **OMS Shared Filesystem** or an **OMS Agent Filesystem** menu item.

If you are using the OMS shared filesystem and you have a multi-OMS setup, make sure that normal preferred credentials are set up for all the OMS servers. You can set up the credentials by going to **Setup** | **Security** | **Preferred Credentials**. The shared filesystem must be accessible from all the OMS servers. In our case, there is only one OMS server.

Click on the **Add** button to add a new upload file location, name it `SainathUploadLocation`, and use the directory location `/u02/oracle/emsoftlib` as the **Location** field's value:

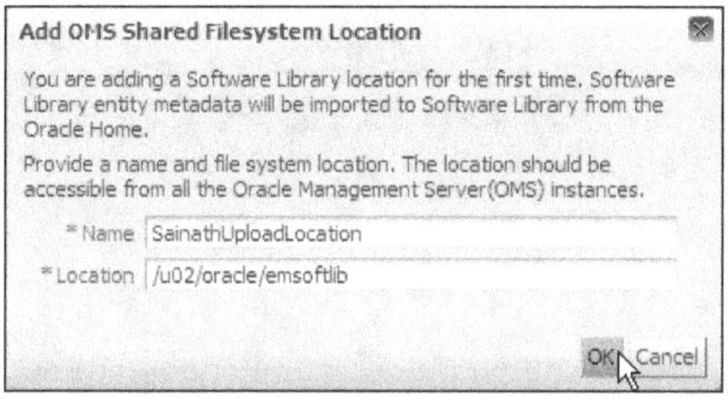


When you click on the **OK** button, the OMS shared filesystem location `SainathUploadLocation` is added and a job is submitted for importing Software Library metadata (including deployment procedures, other components, and directives that are provided out of the box) from Oracle Home.

This process will take a few minutes. At least 2 GB of free disk space will be required. Provisioning and patching activities should only be performed after the successful completion of the job, as shown in the following screenshot:

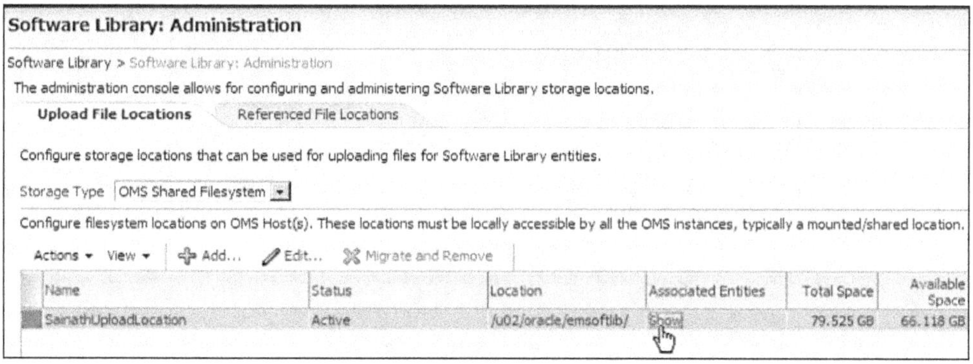

Click on the **Show** link to see the **Associated Entities** page for this upload location. You can see the **Directives** as well as the **Component** types. The directives are actual actions such as Create Directory, and Execute Root Script:

**Associated Entities - Oracle Enterprise Manager**

Search Name → Advanced

View ▾

| Name | Type | Subtype | Directory |
|---|---|---|---|
| Clean up stage area | Directives | | Application Server Provisioning Utilities/11.2.0.1.0/10.1.3/all_platforms/ |
| CVU Generic Prerequisite-Fixup component | Component | Generic Component | CVU Prerequisite-fixup components/all_platforms/ |
| CVU OSD Prerequisite-Fixup component | Component | Generic Component | CVU Prerequisite-fixup components/windows32/ |
| CVU OSD Prerequisite-Fixup component | Component | Generic Component | CVU Prerequisite-fixup components/linux32/ |
| CVU OSD Prerequisite-Fixup component | Component | Generic Component | CVU Prerequisite-fixup components/aix_ppc64/ |
| CVU OSD Prerequisite-Fixup component | Component | Generic Component | CVU Prerequisite-fixup components/hpux_parisc64/ |
| CVU OSD Prerequisite-Fixup component | Component | Generic Component | CVU Prerequisite-fixup components/windows64/ |
| CVU OSD Prerequisite-Fixup component | Component | Generic Component | CVU Prerequisite-fixup components/solaris_sparc64/ |
| CVU OSD Prerequisite-Fixup component | Component | Generic Component | CVU Prerequisite-fixup components/linux_x64/ |
| CVU OSD Prerequisite-Fixup component | Component | Generic Component | CVU Prerequisite-fixup components/hpux_ia64/ |
| System Config File | Component | Generic Component | DB Provisioning/11.2.0.1.0/unix/sysctl/ |
| SSHSetup component | Component | Generic Component | DB Provisioning/11.2.0.1.0/ |
| Create Directory | Directives | | DB Provisioning/11.2.0.1.0/unix/ |
| Prepare Clone Zipfile | Directives | | DB Provisioning/11.2.0.1.0/ |
| Stage CVU Prerequisite and Fixup Component 11201 | Directives | | DB Provisioning/11.2.0.1.0/ |
| Run Prereq and Fixups 11201 | Directives | | DB Provisioning/11.2.0.1.0/ |
| Set ASM Disk Permission | Directives | | DB Provisioning/11.2.0.1.0/unix/ |
| Deploy Single Instance High Availability | Directives | | DB Provisioning/11.2.0.1.0/ |
| RUN KFOD 11201 | Directives | | DB Provisioning/11.2.0.1.0/all_platforms/ |
| Execute Root Script | Directives | | DB Provisioning/11.2.0.1.0/unix/ |
| High Available Root Script | Directives | | DB Provisioning/11.2.0.1.0/ |
| Update Nodelist Script | Directives | | DB Provisioning/11.2.0.1.0/ |
| Run Network Configuration Assistant Tool | Directives | | DB Provisioning/11.2.0.1.0/ |

It is also possible to reimport metadata into the upload file location from the **Actions** menu, and to check the accessibility of the location.

In the Unix filesystem, we can see that a number of subdirectories have been created and a number of files are present in each subdirectory, as can be seen in the following screenshot. This is what normally happens in a file content management system:

```
[oracle@havipori emsoftlib]$
[oracle@havipori emsoftlib]$ pwd
/u02/oracle/emsoftlib
[oracle@havipori emsoftlib]$
[oracle@havipori emsoftlib]$
[oracle@havipori emsoftlib]$ ls
0   12  16  2   23  27  30  34  38  41  45  49  52  56  6   63  67  70  9
1   13  17  20  24  28  31  35  39  42  46  5   53  57  60  64  68  71
10  14  18  21  25  29  32  36  4   43  47  50  54  58  61  65  69  72
11  15  19  22  26  3   33  37  40  44  48  51  55  59  62  66  7   8
[oracle@havipori emsoftlib]$
[oracle@havipori emsoftlib]$
[oracle@havipori emsoftlib]$ cd 43
[oracle@havipori 43]$
[oracle@havipori 43]$ ls
B7BE6434DE65E4D4E040000A0F020E5C  B7BE6434E296E4D4E040000A0F020E5C
B7BE6434DEC3E4D4E040000A0F020E5C  B7BE6434E3F2E4D4E040000A0F020E5C
B7BE6434E066E4D4E040000A0F020E5C  B7BE6434E4F6E4D4E040000A0F020E5C
B7BE6434E25AE4D4E040000A0F020E5C
[oracle@havipori 43]$
[oracle@havipori 43]$
```

On the **Software Library: Administration** page, there is a second tab named **Referenced File Location**. This is a new facility in Enterprise Manager Cloud Control 12*c*. You can refer to files outside of the Software Library but required for deployment, and Enterprise Manager keeps a reference to that location. The storage type for such a reference file system can be HTTP, NFS, or Agent. This allows you to refer to files stored on an HTTP server or NFS-mounted directory, or any of the Enterprise Manager Agents can be used to access read-only files stored on the server where the Agent is running.

If you now go to **Enterprise** | **Provisioning and Patching** | **Software Library**, you can see a number of items on the **Software Library** console. The gold images we mentioned earlier are contained in this library, as are virtual machine images, assemblies, patches, application software, as well as associated directives. Any of these can then be referenced from a deployment procedure. Attachments and notes can be used with Software Library entities, for example, you may have attached a Readme file to a patch component:

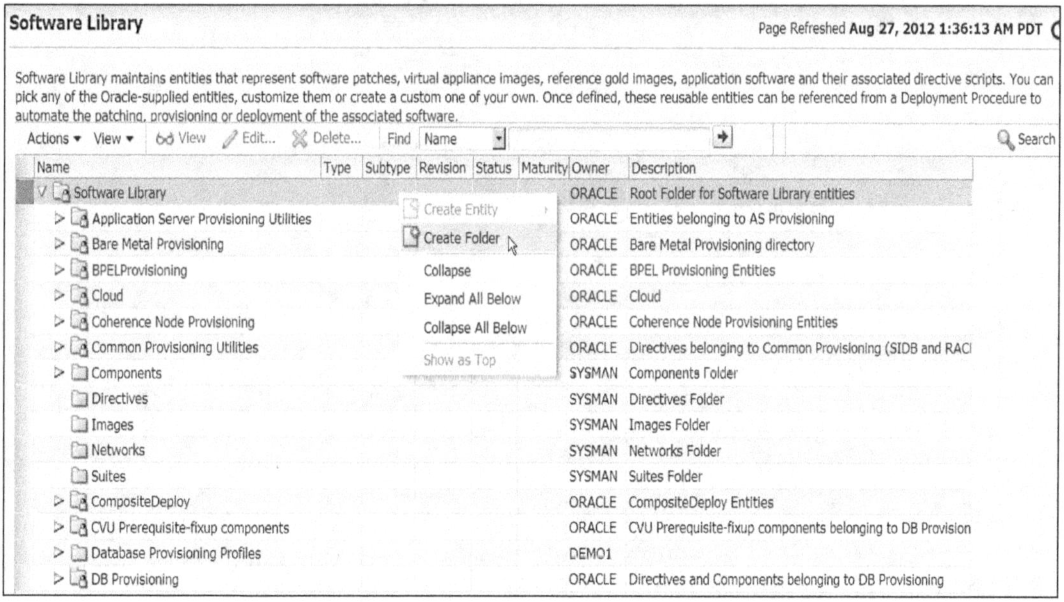

On this console, the out-of-the-box entities can be customized and it is also possible to create a totally new entity. You can create your own components and directives to use in your deployments. The first step is to right-click on **Software Library** in the tree, and select **Create Folder**. This allows you to create a new custom folder where you can add your own entities:

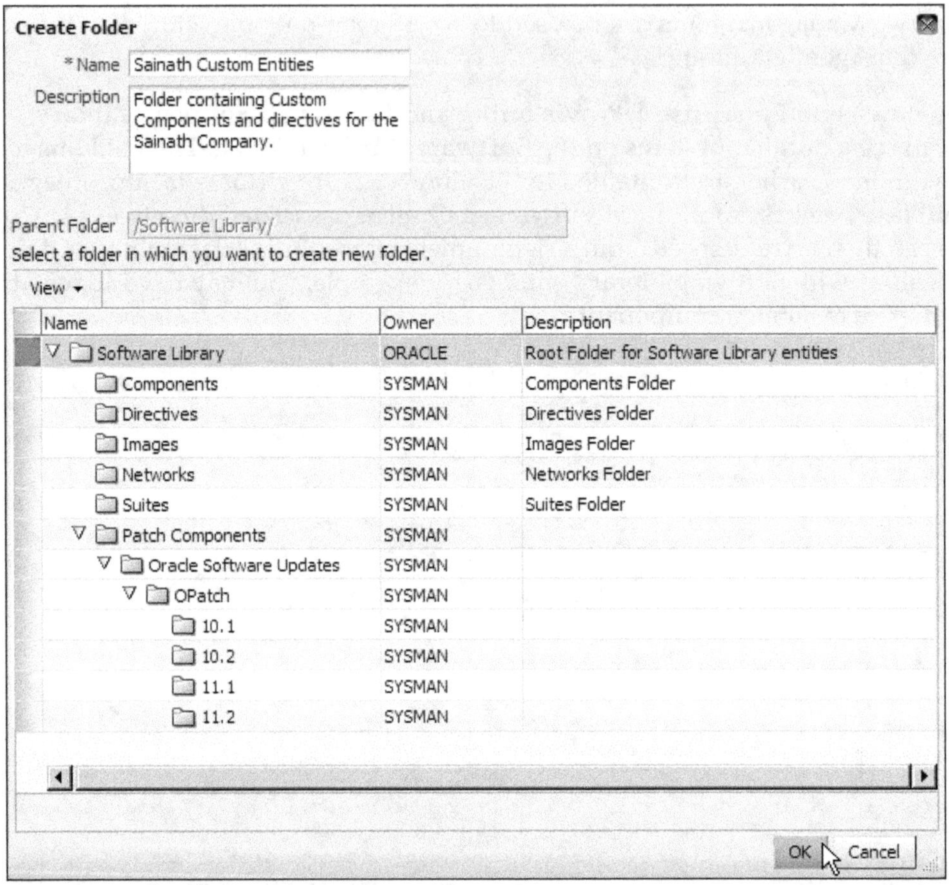


Suppose you want to add a component under this custom folder. Select the folder in the Software Library console, and on the **Actions** menu go to **Create Entity | Component**.

There are various types of component subtypes you can select, such as generic component (the default), database template, installation media, Oracle database software clone, and Oracle middleware home gold Image.

We are selecting **Oracle Database Software Clone** as the subtype. Click on the **Continue** button. You can now enter the component details as shown in the following screenshot:

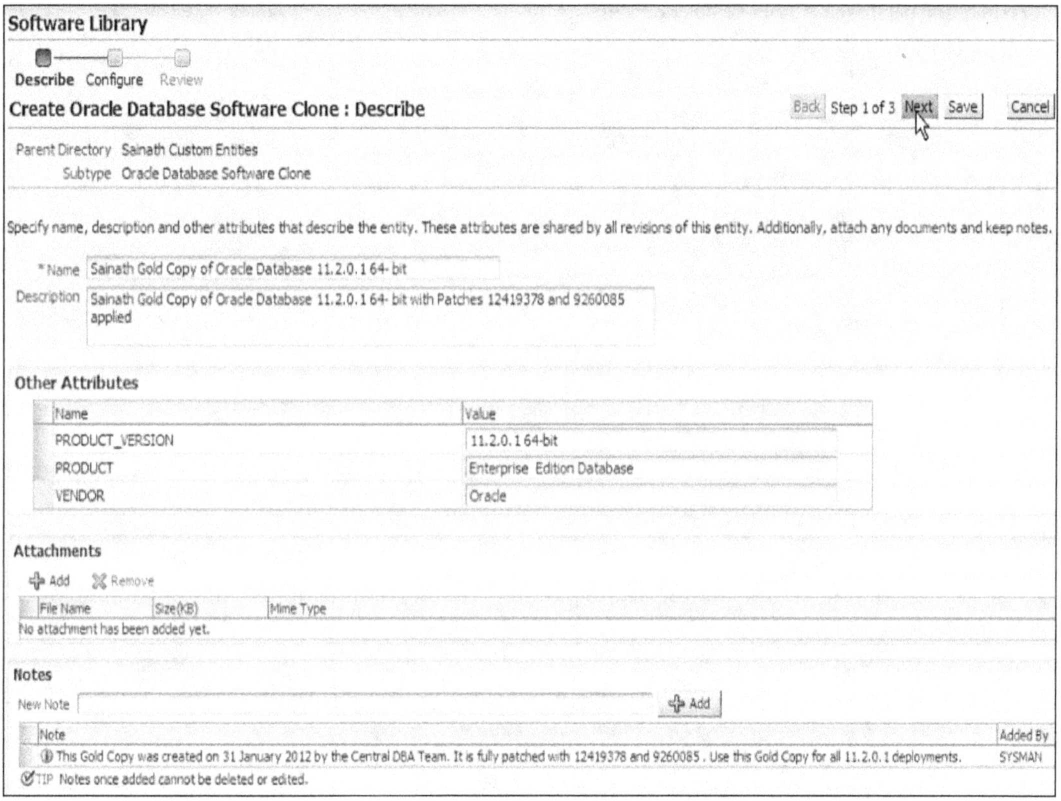

This component will be a clone of a fully patched Oracle database home of version 11.2.0.1 on the 64-bit Linux platform, with patches 12419378 and 9260085 applied.

You can also add files that are of relevance to the entity. These files should not be more than 2 MB in size. You can also add notes with any related information, for example, a list of the patches applied or the modification history of the entity. We have added a descriptive note. Click on the **Next** button to continue:

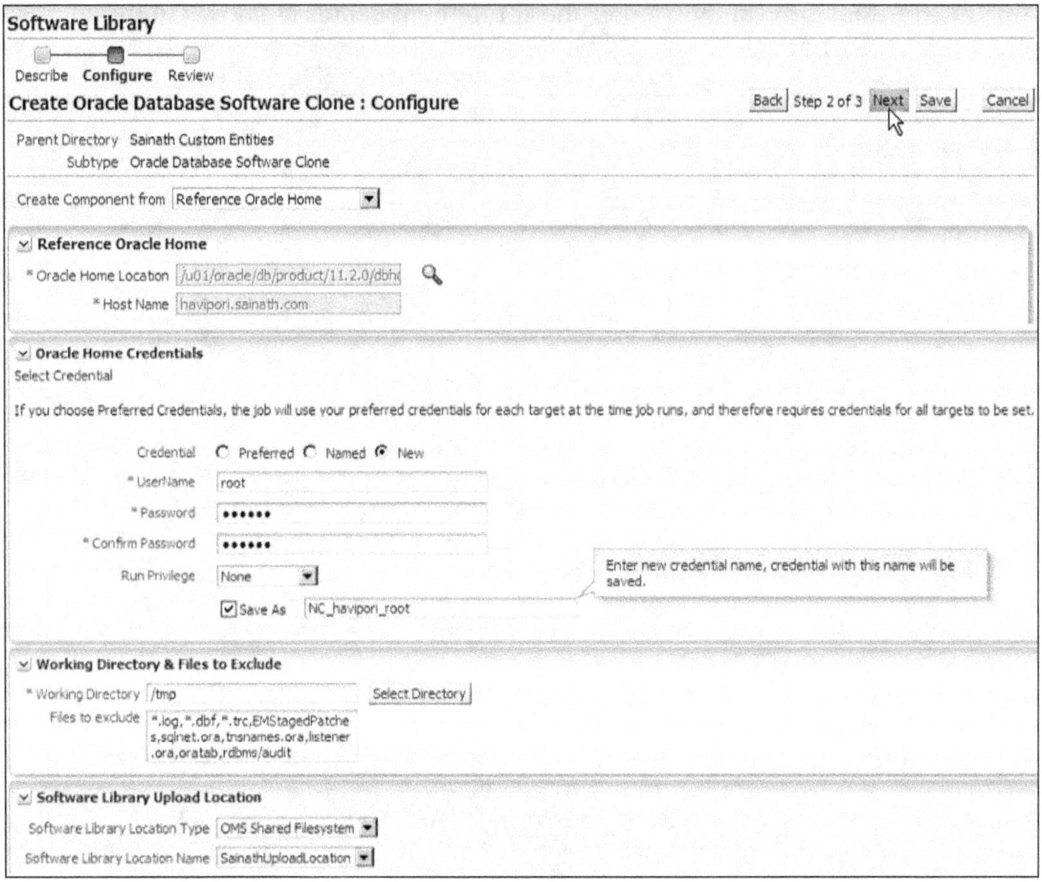


On the next page, you are asked to specify the source of the component. You can create the component either from the reference Oracle Home or an existing Oracle Home archive. We select the reference Oracle Home on the host **havipori.sainath.com** as an example. This home is being used by the `orcl` database as well as the `emrepos` database.

Also specify the **Oracle Home Credentials, Working Directory**, and **Files to exclude** fields (such as `.dbf` and `.lock` files). Finally, specify the upload location in the Software Library where the component will be uploaded. When you click on the **Next** button, the **Review** screen appears as shown in the following screenshot:

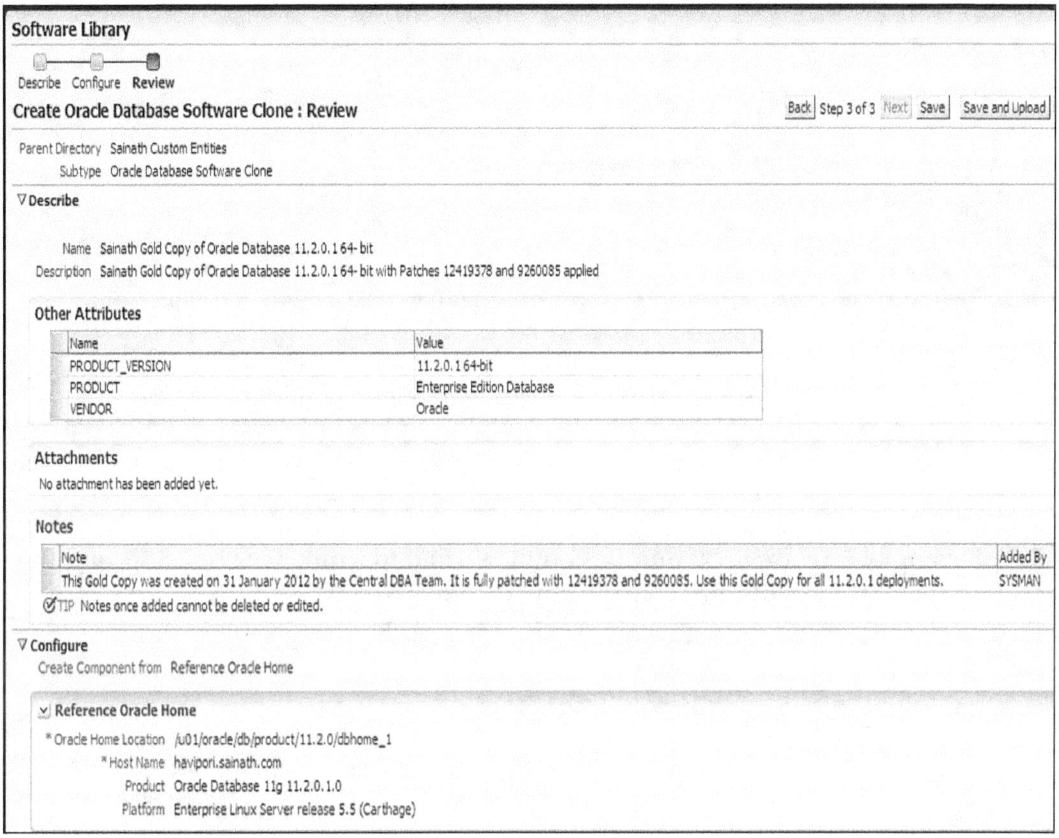


Click on the **Save and Upload** button, which will save all changes and start uploading the files using an Enterprise Manager job.

The new component has been created and appears in the **Software Library** console under the recently created custom folder. The status is marked as **Incomplete**, and the maturity is **Untested**. This is because a job (name displayed on the screen) has been submitted to upload the files associated with this component. You can see the job status by going to **Enterprise** | **Job** | **Activity**:

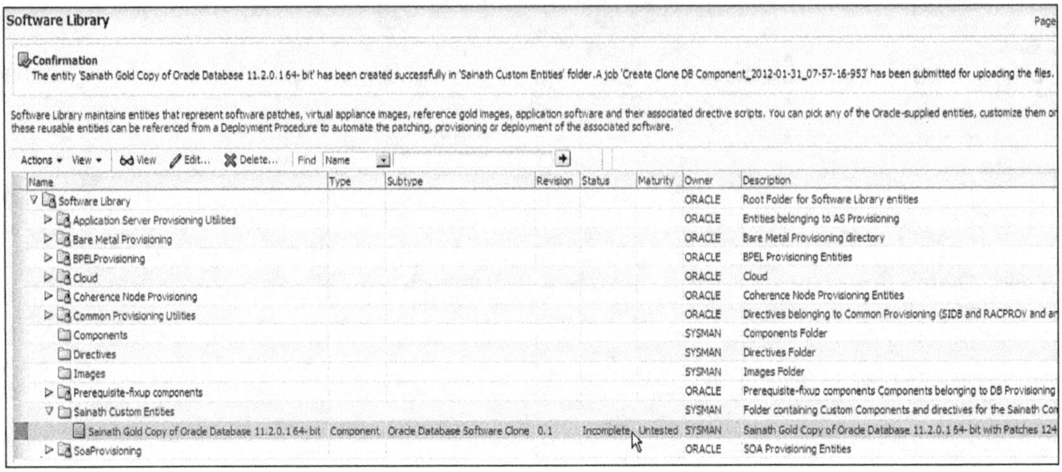

The job completes in about 30 minutes on the virtual machine we are using, and the status in the **Software Library** console now displays **Ready**:

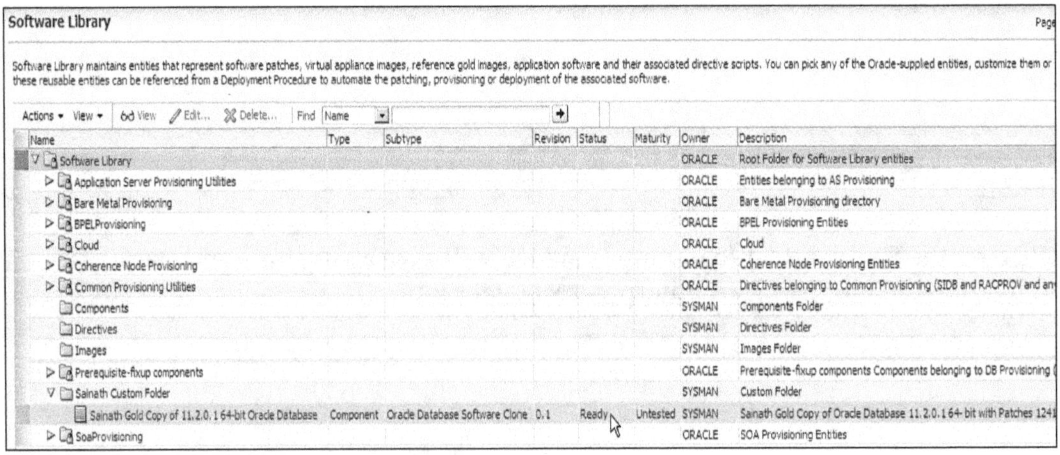

The gold image that we have created and stored in the Enterprise Manager's Software Library can now be used in the actual deployment on new Targets, as we will see shortly.

# Provisioning library

Navigate to **Enterprise** | **Provisioning and Patching** | **Procedure Library**. This opens the library of deployment procedures that are supplied out of the box with Enterprise Manager Cloud Control 12*c*. A **deployment procedure** is an advanced piece of automation that can be fully responsible for the entire process of provisioning or patching, and is also customizable. The library of deployment procedures is shown in the following screenshot:

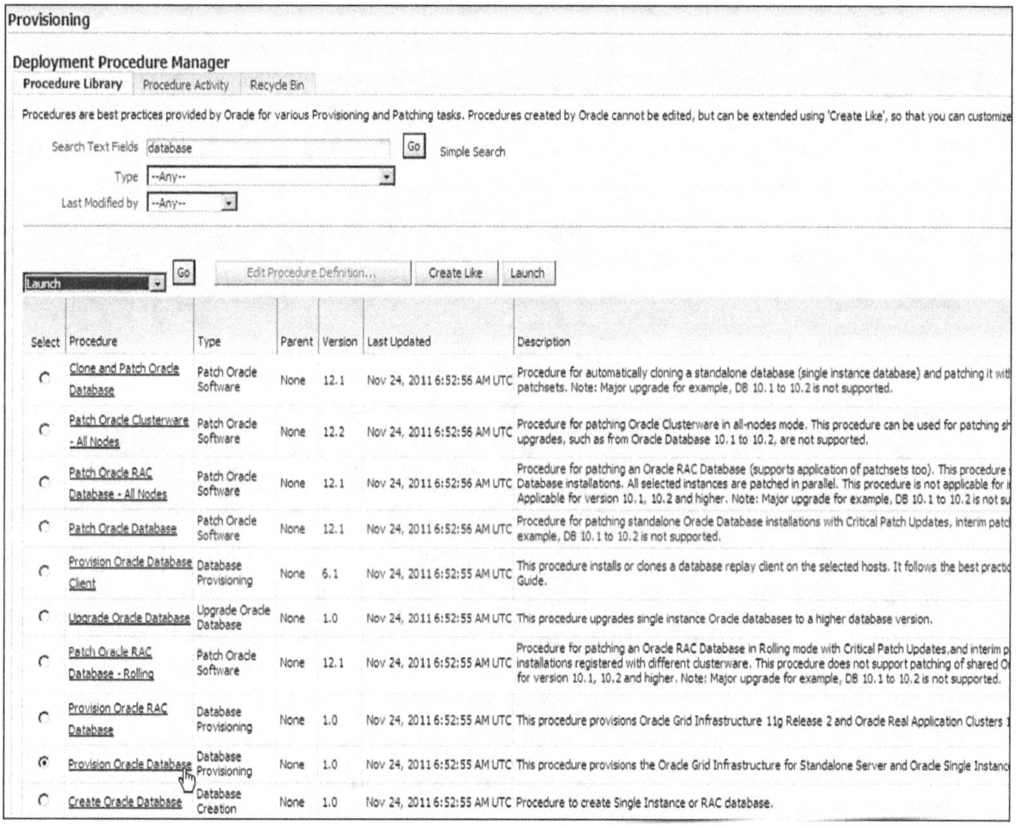


On this page, we have conducted an advanced search to display only the procedures with the word `database` in the text description. As we can see, there are a number of deployment procedures for provisioning as well as patching databases.

We can select the appropriate procedure to provision either single-instance or RAC databases, or procedures to scale-up or scale-down the RAC cluster (add or delete RAC nodes). There is also a new type of procedure to create an Oracle database (single-instance or RAC), or to upgrade an existing Oracle database. We also have different types of patching procedures, which we will discuss in the next chapter.

You can use the **Create Like** button to make a copy of an existing deployment procedure, and then customize it as per company requirements, such as adding or deleting procedure steps.

To have a quick look at the steps in the single database provisioning procedure, simply click on its name. This brings up the screen shown in the following screenshot:

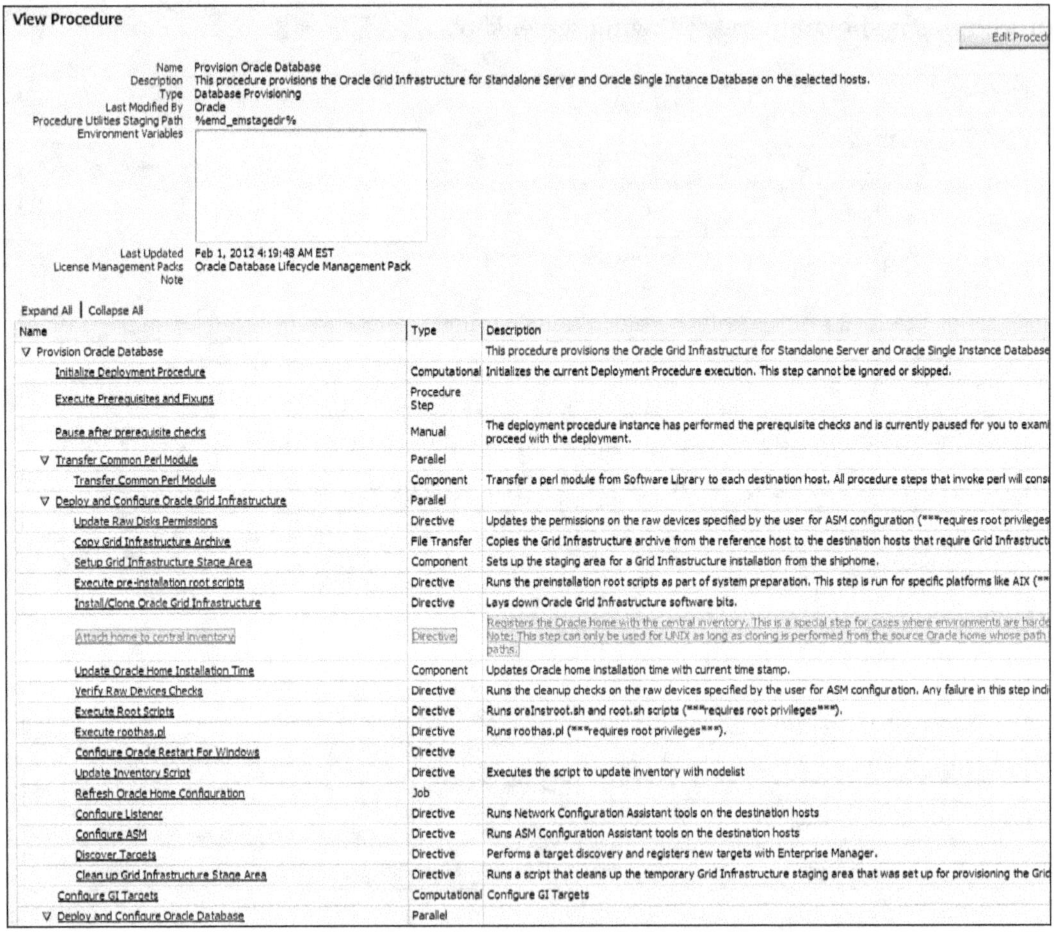


Examining the steps in this procedure, you can see that it first deploys the Oracle grid infrastructure (which is the new home in database version 11.2 onwards), configures the listener and ASM, followed by the deployment and configuration of the Oracle database.

This is interspaced with the nitty-gritty steps, such as running preinstallation and postinstallation scripts—all manual, labor-intensive tasks normally performed by the DBA. Configuration (compliance) standards are also associated automatically with the new database Targets at the end of the procedure.

The **Upgrade Oracle Database** procedure goes through a number of steps:

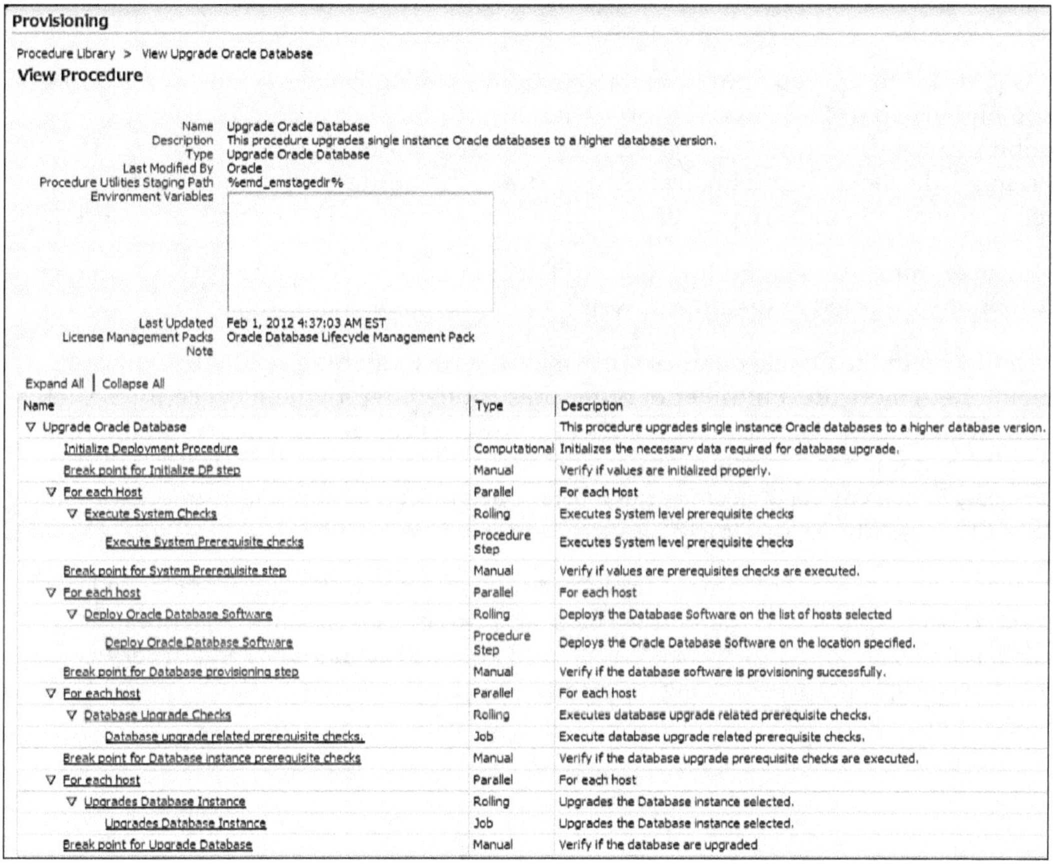


In this procedure, we can see that there is an iteration over the list of hosts on which you are upgrading the Oracle database.

First, the system prerequisite checks take place, then the Oracle database software (the new version) is deployed. Prerequisite checks related to the Oracle database then take place, followed by the actual upgrade.

This means that Enterprise Manager is now able to assist with mass automated upgrades of your single-instance Oracle databases, rather than a DBA performing each upgrade manually. The cost saving in administrator productivity itself can be immense.

It is possible to upgrade multiple databases in parallel. Database versions 10.2.0.4 and higher, up to 11.2.0.x, are supported. Out-of-place copies can be used to minimize the downtime for upgrade, or an existing Oracle Home can be used. Preupgrade backups and analysis can be done, including preupgrade patch requirements via MOS. Upgrade execution can be stopped or started as required.

However, mass automated upgrades of RAC databases using Enterprise Manager were not supported at the time of writing.

In addition to the Oracle database provisioning and patching procedures just mentioned, there are a number of other presupplied deployment procedures such as provisioning a Database Replay client for use with Database Replay in the RAT database option, or procedures to provision an Oracle application server, a BPEL process, SOA Artifacts/Composites, Coherence nodes, WebLogic Home/Domain, Java EE applications, or Oracle Service Bus resources.

There is also a new deployment procedure called System Backup, which can be used to back up multiple databases, files, and directories in one single operation. Also, there is another new procedure to add an additional management service to an existing Enterprise Manager system.

# Provisioning profiles

We can now test out the actual provisioning of databases. Go to **Enterprise | Provisioning and Patching | Database Provisioning**. This brings up the **Database Provisioning** screen as shown in the following screenshot:

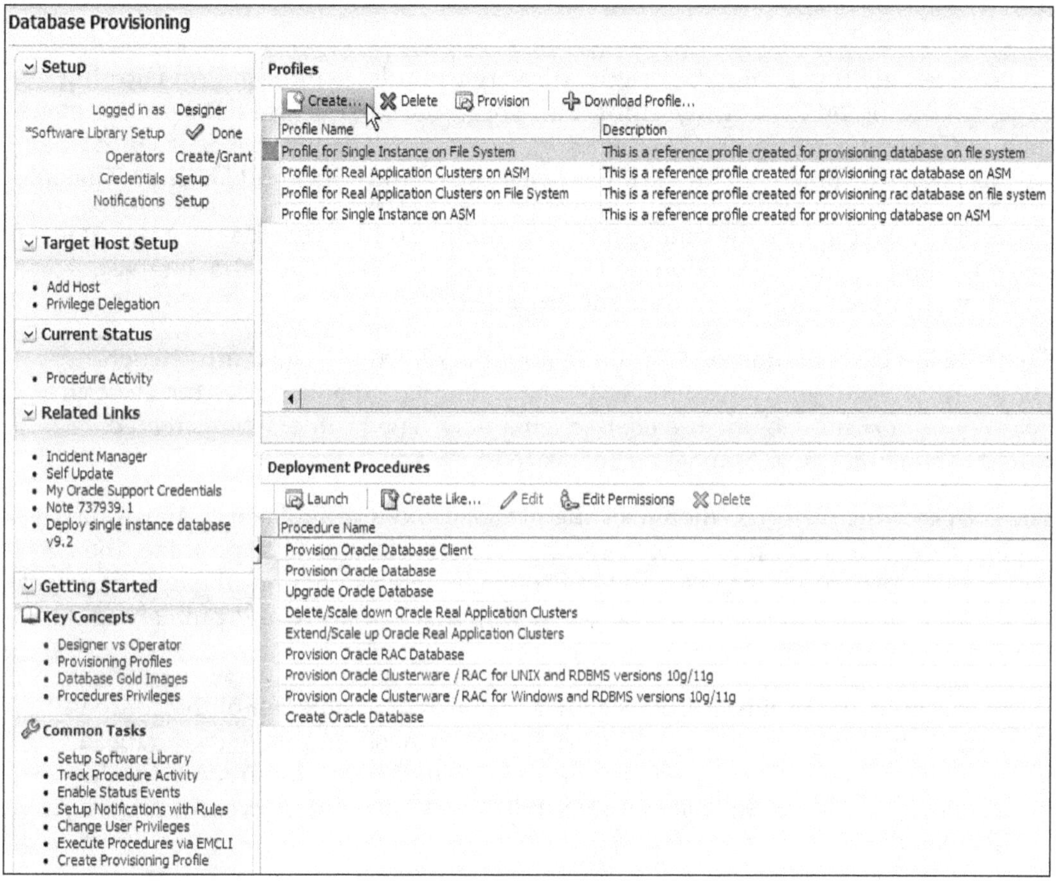

Notice that as you are logged in as `SYSMAN`, you have the rights of a designer. This is shown on the left-hand side corner of this page.

You can create new administrators and assign to them the rights of a Provisioning Designer or Provisioning Operator – this is done by allocating the Enterprise Manager administrator roles `EM_PROVISIONING_DESIGNER` and `EM_PROVISIONING_OPERATOR` respectively.

You can create Provisioning Operators directly from the **Database Provisioning** page by clicking on the **Create/Grant** link. There are other useful links on this page, such as **Credentials**, **Privilege Delegation**, **Incident Manager**, and **Self Update**, as well as links to online help on various topics (**Key Concepts** and **Common Tasks**).

The table at the top lists the database provisioning profiles (**Profiles**) – a new concept in the Cloud Control 12*c* version, whereas the table below it lists the database deployment procedures (**Deployment Procedures**).

A **profile** is a combination of a database home's gold copy, a grid infrastructure home's (if present) gold copy, and a database template that includes the structure but may or may not include the user-schema data. The profile, when created, is stored in the Enterprise Manager's Software Library.

The Provisioning Designer then uses the profile as an input to a customized database deployment procedure that he/she creates. The profile is used to populate the deployment procedure inputs, and the Provisioning Designer has the option to lock down some or most of the inputs before saving the procedure and publishing it to the Provisioning Operator.

As an example, the Provisioning Designer may decide (on behalf of the company) that any Oracle database to be deployed in the future should have its database files stored only on Oracle Automatic Storage Management and not on the Unix filesystem, and this can be locked down in the customized deployment procedure being created.

The Provisioning Designer grants privileges to execute the customized procedure to a Provisioning Operator (another Enterprise Manager administrator). This means the procedure is published. The Provisioning Operator will then be able to run the procedure and perform the provisioning process, but without changing the locked-down inputs. In the preceding scenario, the Provisioning Operator will not be able to select the filesystem for storage when deploying a database using the customized procedure.

Click on the **Create...** button to start creating a new database provisioning profile:

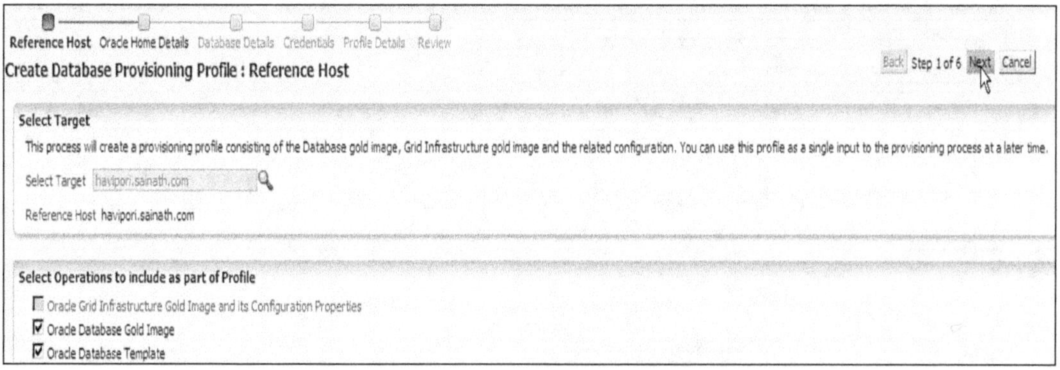


The first step is to select the reference host. This is the source of the database's gold image (and/or the grid infrastructure's gold image if it is present).

You can also include an Oracle database template in the profile. You have the option of including any of these components. At least one component must be selected as part of the profile creation. Click on the **Next** button:

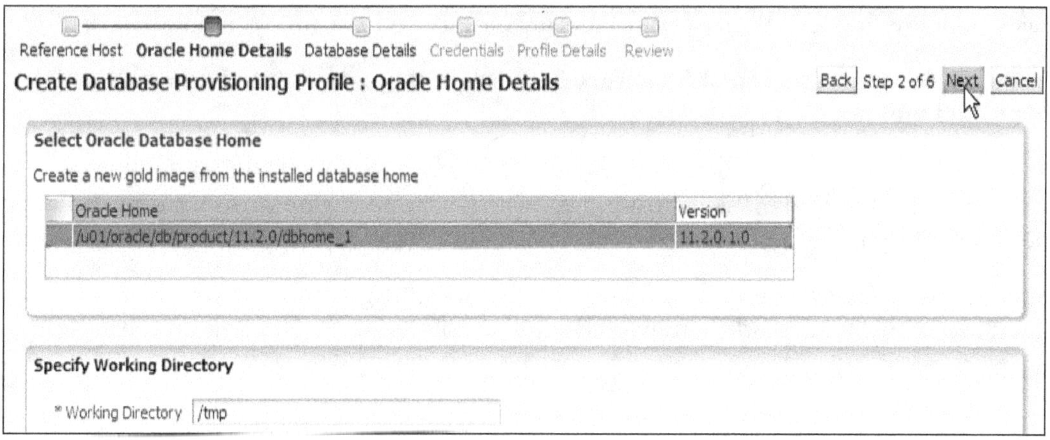

Select the Oracle database home that is to be used in the gold copy contained in the profile. Also select the **Working Directory** field, and click on the **Next** button:

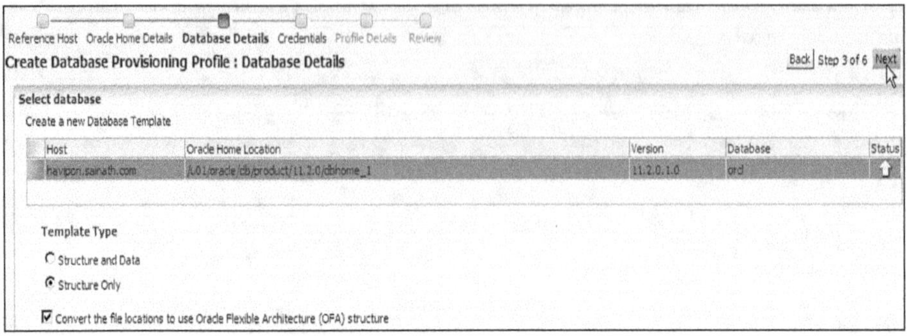

At this point, you need to select the database from which the profile is being made. As you have opted to include the template in the profile, you must select whether you want only the structure, or structure as well as data.

When you select **Structure and Data**, all user-defined schemas and their data will also be included; however, the database will be shut down during template creation. You can also choose to black out the database target during template creation in this case, which will prevent any critical alerts being raised because the database is down.

In the alternative case, if just **Structure** is selected, the user-defined schemas and their data will not be included.

You can also decide whether to convert the directory locations to **Oracle Flexible Architecture** (**OFA**). This is useful if a directory structure similar to the source is not present in the Target server where you will be doing the database provisioning.

Specify the credentials to be used both for the operating system as well as the database. You can also add a new credential at this stage by clicking on the **+** sign:

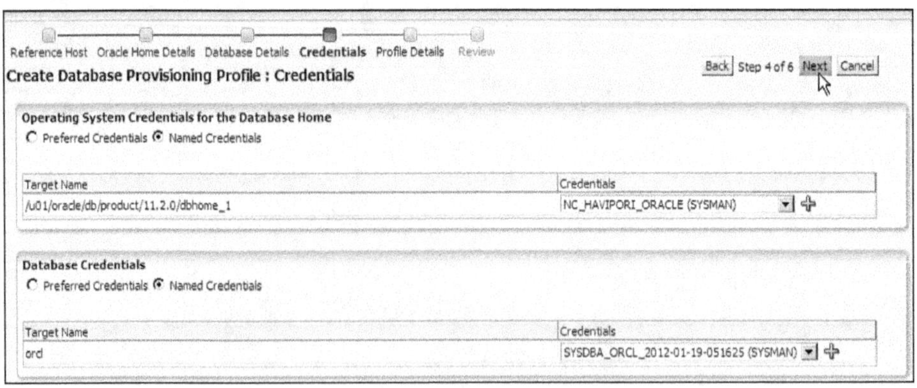

On this next screen, you can input the details about the database provisioning profile. The **Profile Location** field is prefilled for you based on the previous inputs. This location is in the Software Library. You can enter the name of the profile, a description, and other details. This screen also shows the components that will be included in the profile, in this case **Oracle Database Gold Image Component** and **Oracle Database Template Component**:

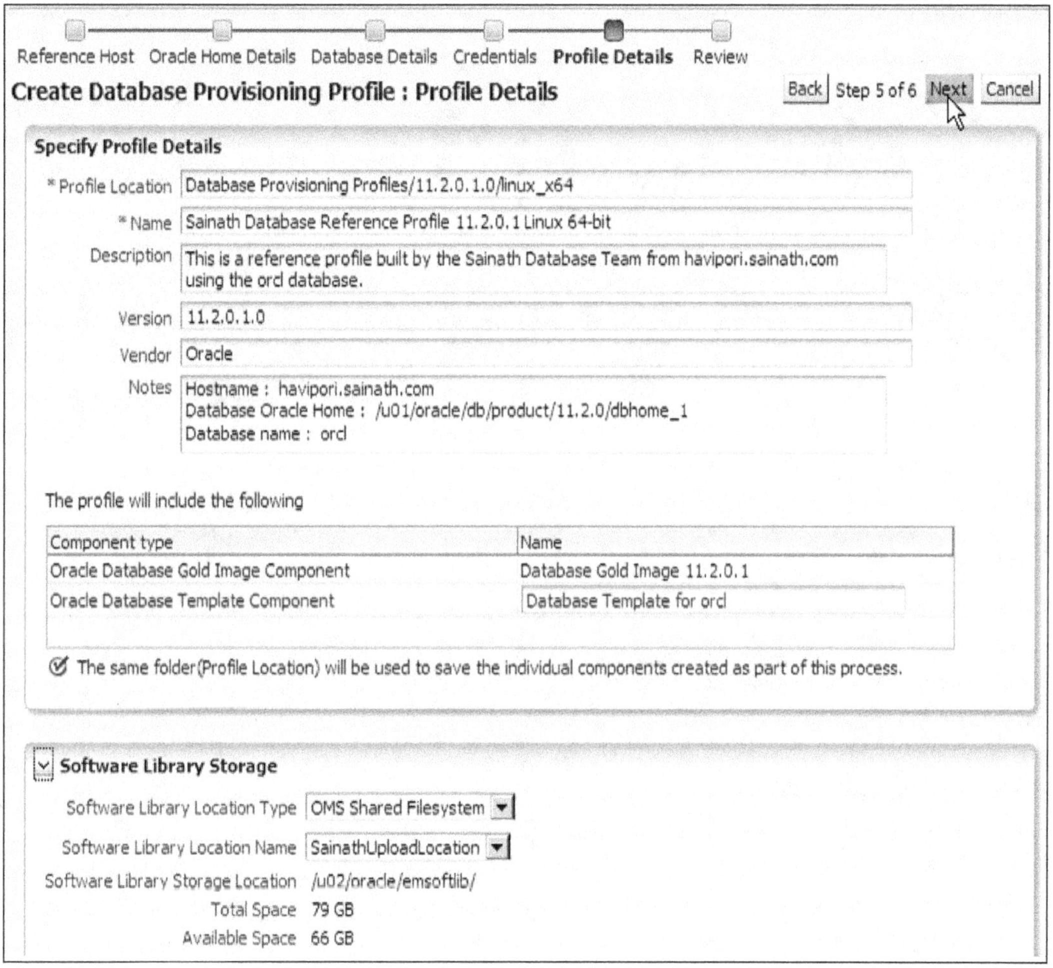

The **Review** screen shows all the inputs to the profile wizard so far. Double check all the details and click on the **Submit** button:

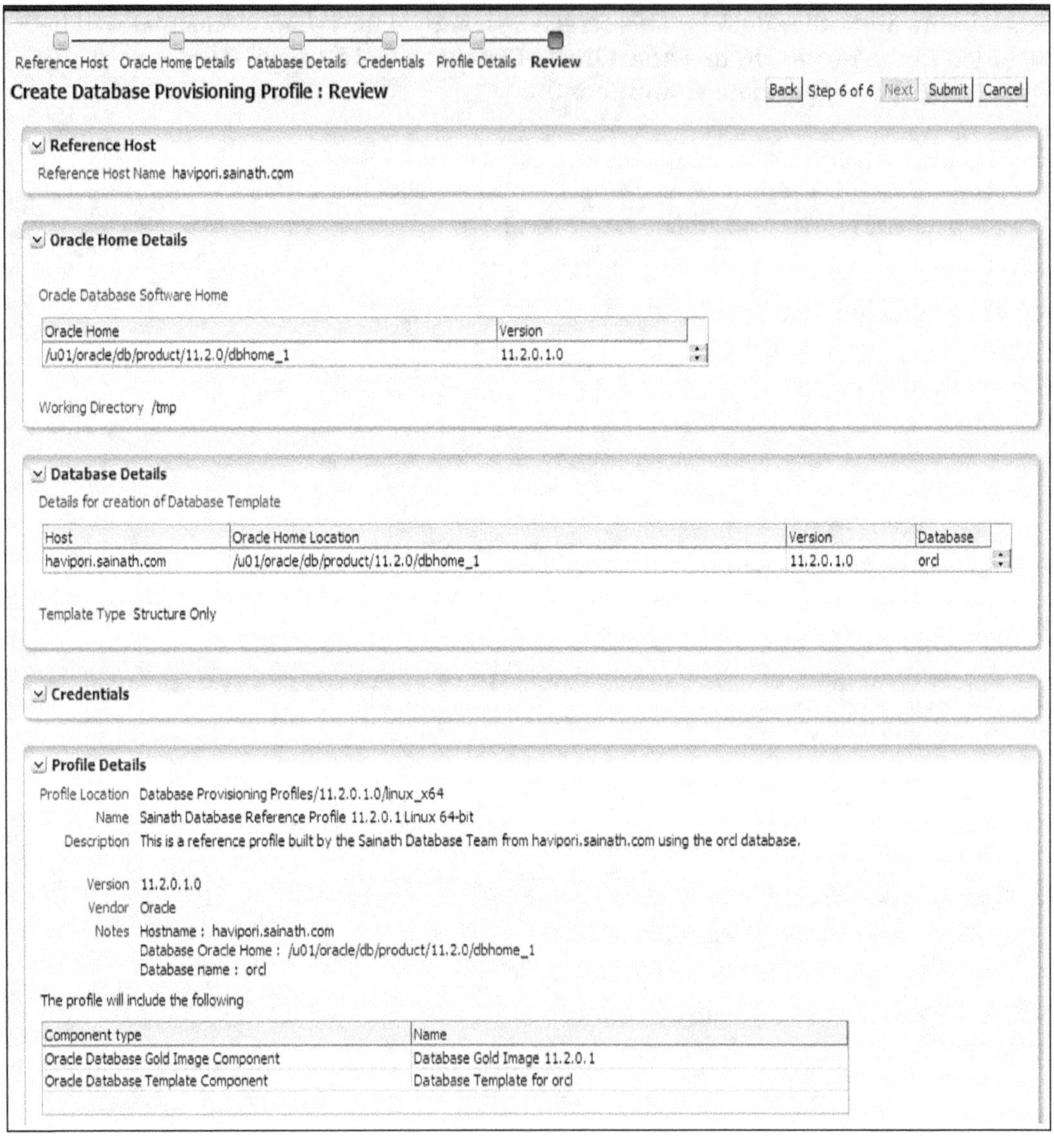

The job to create the profile executes and completes in around one hour on our virtual box VM. The final status of the job is shown as **Succeeded**:

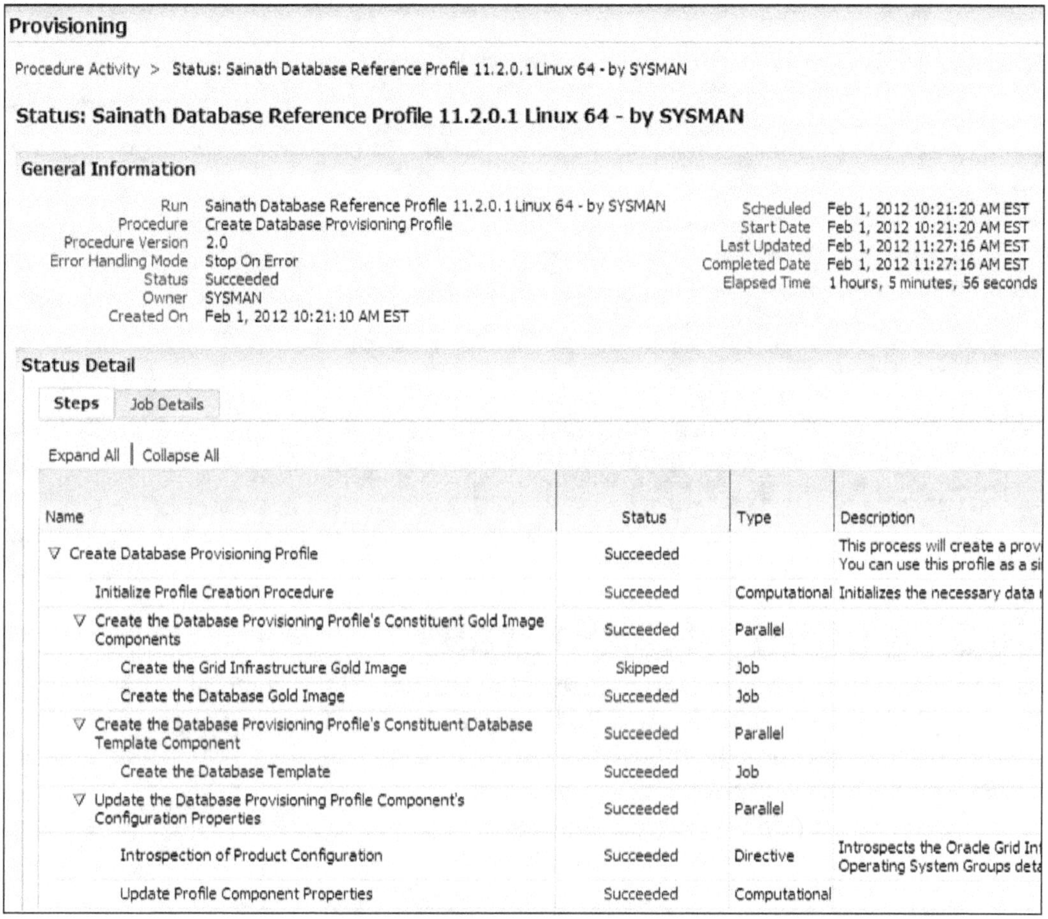

On the **Database Provisioning** page, the newly created profile is now visible:

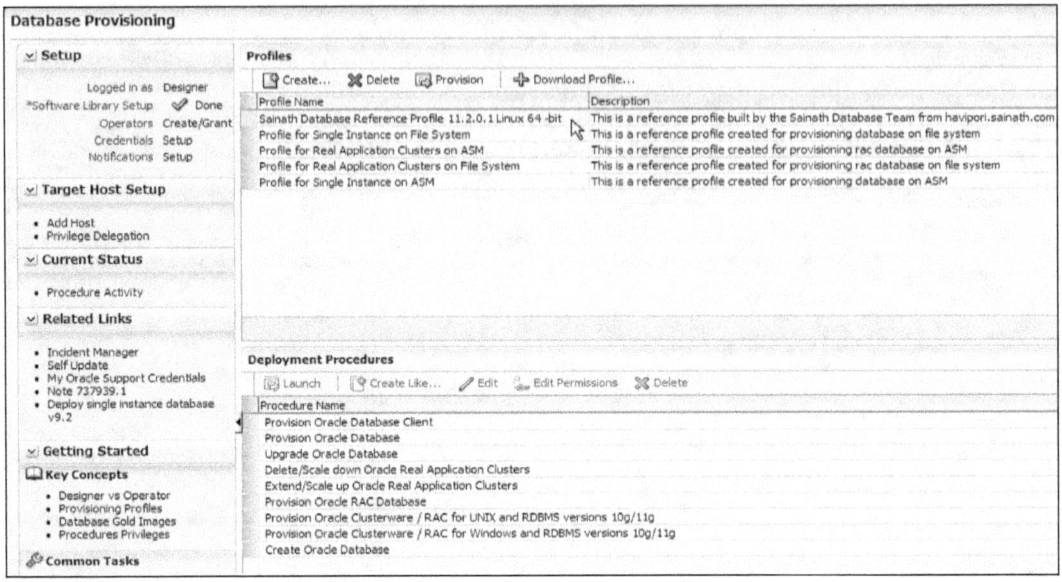

## Deployment procedures

We now proceed to the next step, which is the creation of the customized and locked-down deployment procedure. Move to the **Database Provisioning** page, select the existing **Provision Oracle Database** procedure and click on the **Create Like...** button, as shown in the following screenshot:

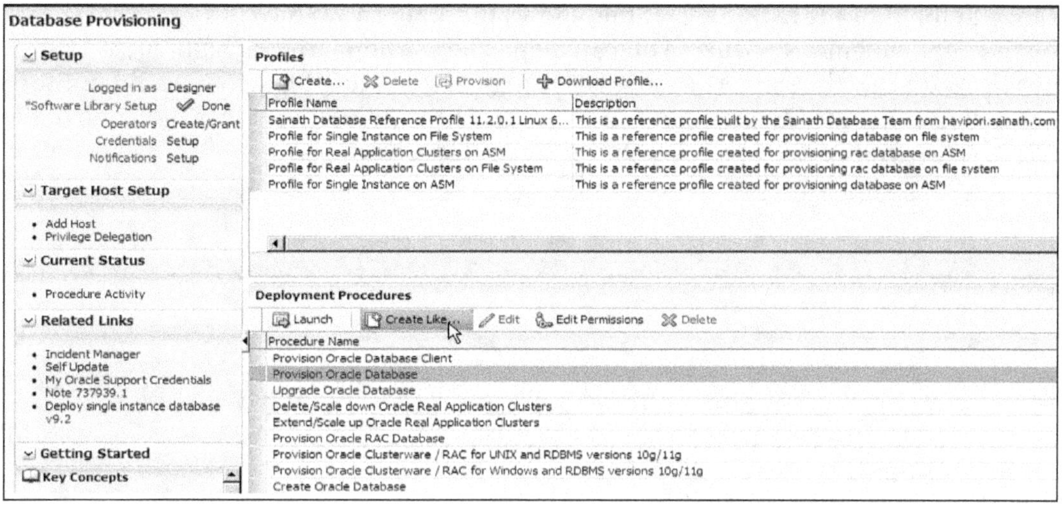


On the **Create Like Procedure** page, rename the new procedure as `Sainath Customized Procedure For Provisioning of Oracle Database` on the **General Information** tab, as shown in the following screenshot:

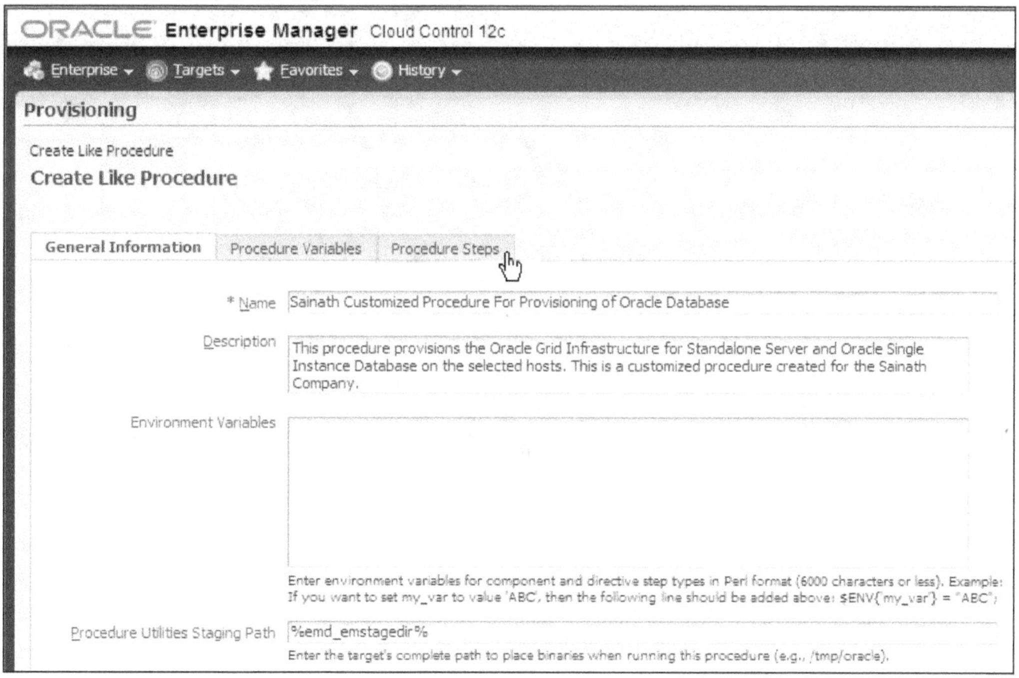

Move to the **Procedure Steps** tab, this shows the actual sequence of steps as executed by the deployment procedure. You can delete, insert, and edit any step, or you can enable or disable the step. You can also change **Error Handling Mode** to either **Stop On Error, Continue On Error**, or **Skip Target**. In the following screenshot, one of the steps has been successfully edited to **Continue On Error**:

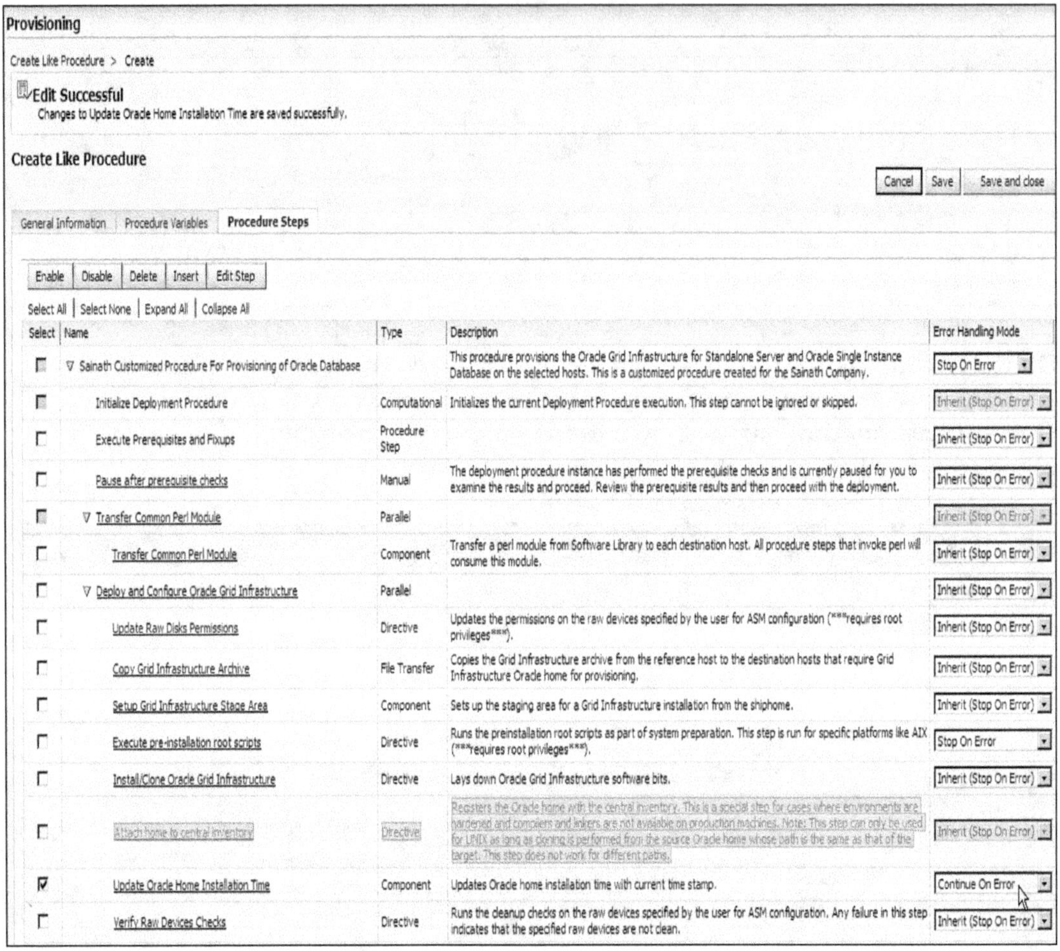

# Customization

This helps you to customize any deployment procedure as per your company's requirements. As a result, deployment procedures become a very powerful tool.

For example, you can add a step to send an e-mail notification in Unix before the actual provisioning starts, or call a procedure to insert information into another database in the company. Any company-specific procedure can be incorporated in this manner in the existing deployment procedures (customized), or a totally new deployment procedure can be created from scratch.

The latter is known as a **User Defined Deployment Procedure** (**UDDP**). You can define new and complex in-house deployment procedures of your own in this manner for automating custom software deployments. UDDPs can be created by selecting **Create New** by going to **Enterprise** | **Provisioning and Patching** | **Procedure Library**.

The UDDP can use any entity that has been uploaded to the Software Library, such as scripts or other components. Steps can be added that directly execute host commands or call other scripts, perform file transfer, and so on. For getting user inputs when the UDDP is executed, you can add global variables to the UDDP.

On the **Database Provisioning** page, we can now see our new **Sainath Customized Procedure For Provisioning of Oracle Database** deployment procedure. However, so far it only has a copy of the steps from the out-of-the-box deployment procedure that provisions a single database. There are no locked-down steps. If `SYSMAN` or the Provisioning Designer grants access to this procedure to a Provisioning Operator, the latter will be able to run the procedure with absolutely any input of his own choice.

# Lock down

To prevent this scenario, we need to lock down the procedure, which we can now do by using the **Launch** button as shown in the following screenshot:

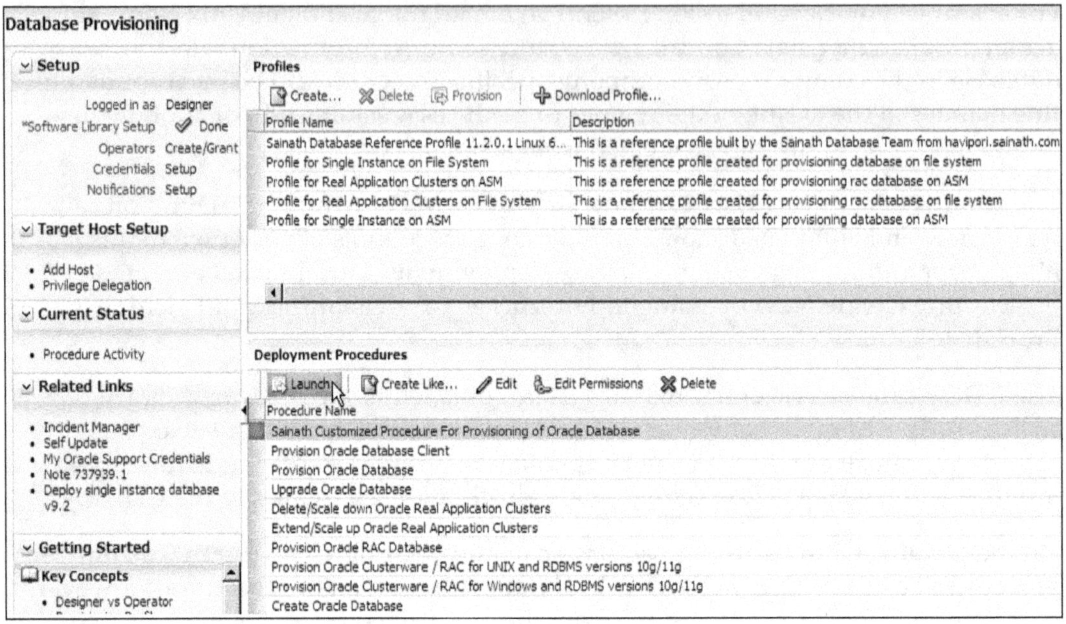

The procedure launches. Note that the aim is not to actually run the procedure, but lock it down and save it.

First, you choose the correct provisioning profile to be used. In our case it is **Sainath Database Reference Profile 11.2.0.1 Linux 64 - bit**. We also select the software to deploy and configure, as shown in the following screenshot:

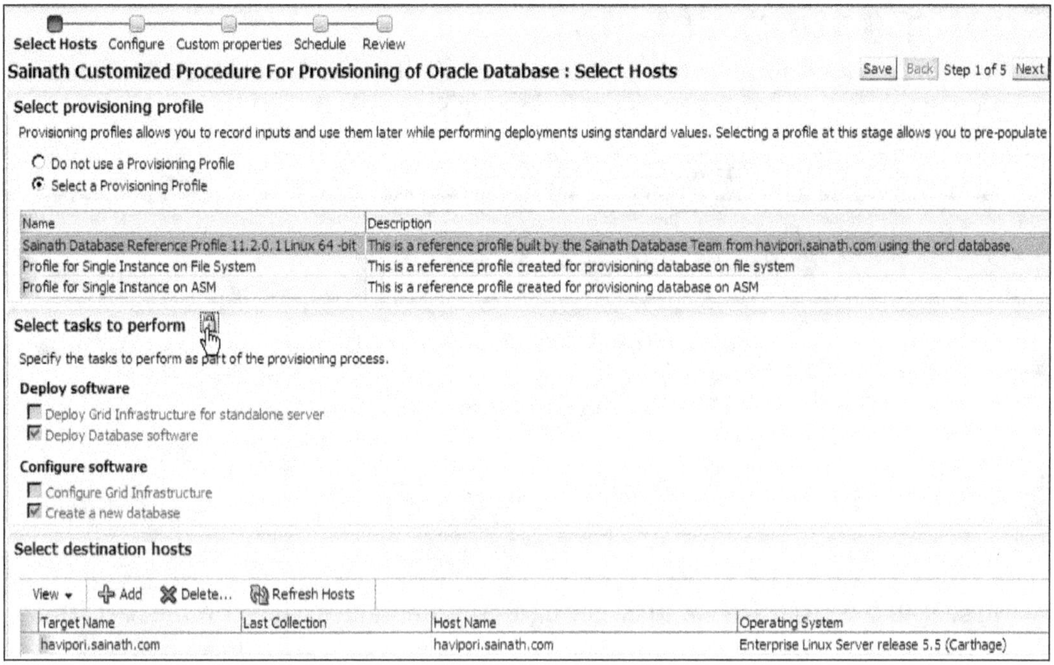


As we want only the database home, without the grid infrastructure home (there is no ASM or Clusterware to be used), de-select the grid Infrastructure checkboxes. Then, lock down these inputs by clicking on the lock icon. This prevents the Provisioning Operator from changing the inputs.

Finally, on this page, select the actual Target host, but note that the Provisioning Operator will be able to select a new host when he/she runs the procedure.

# Configuration details

The next page shows four sections where the configuration details are provided for the provisioning task, as shown in the following screenshot:

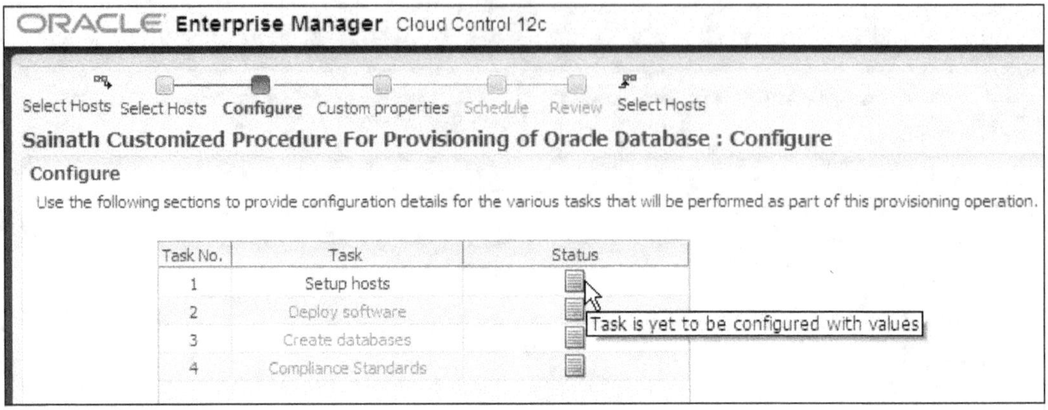


As we see, all the tasks are yet to be configured with values. Click on the first task, **Setup hosts**.

This page is used to specify the OS credentials required for the host. We have selected the named credentials that we had created previously and we have locked the input so that only these credentials can be used:

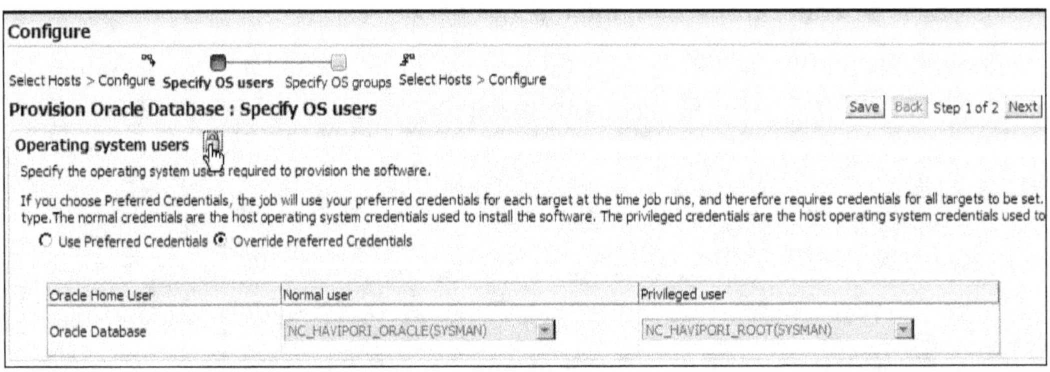

As these are named credentials, they must be granted to the appropriate user who is going to run this procedure, as we will see later.

Move to the next page:

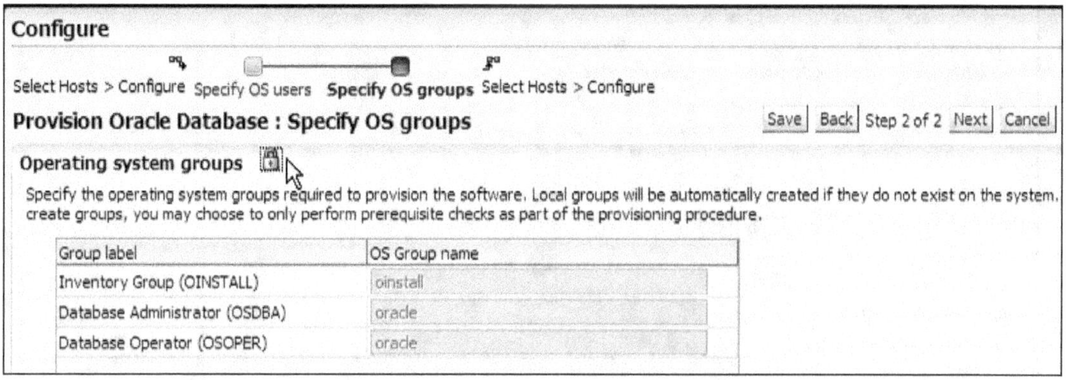


Here, we specify the OS groups to be used for the inventory, database administrator, and database operator. This is also locked down so that all future provisioning of databases will use these OS groups.

This completes the first task, **Setup hosts**. You are back to the list of four tasks:

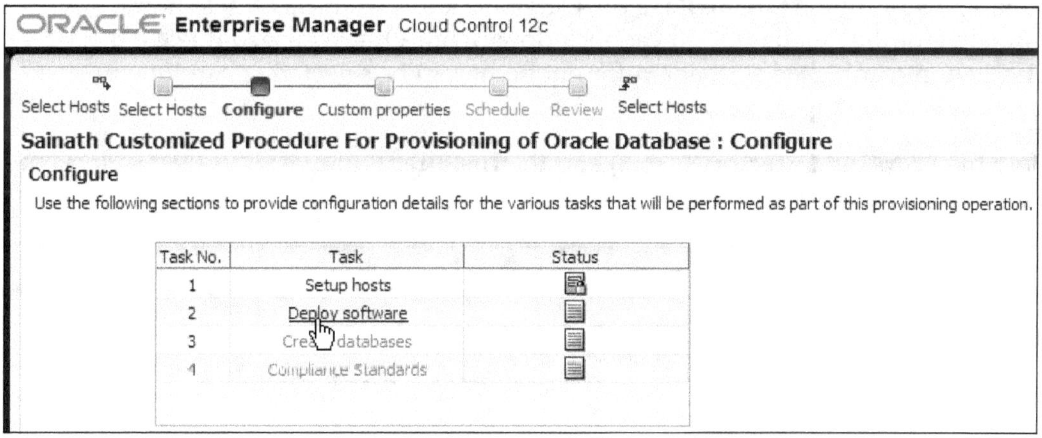

Click on **Deploy software**, which is the second task. This lets you specify how the database software will be deployed, as shown in the following screenshot:

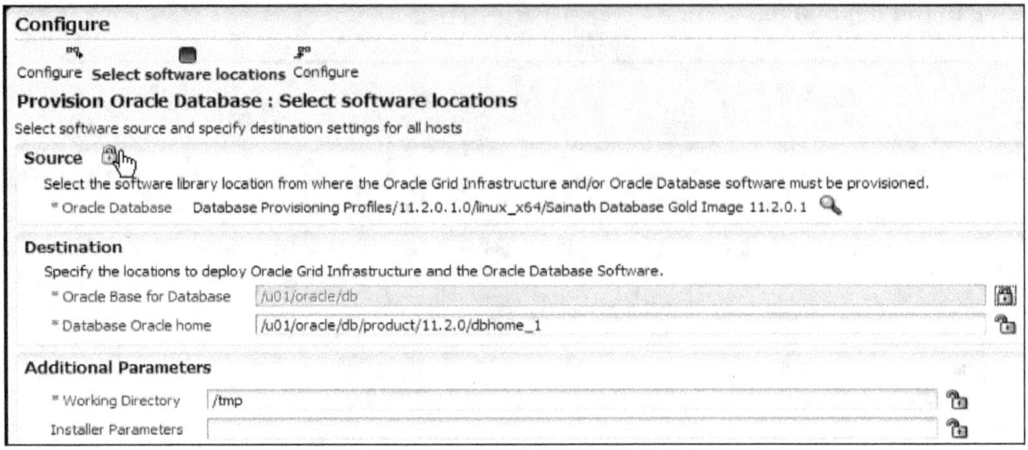

First you specify the source of the database software you are deploying. In this case, because you have selected the profile at the start, the **Sainath Database Gold Image 11.2.0.1** field appears as the default. This is now locked down, so no other image can be used.

Next you specify the **Oracle Base for Database** and **Database Oracle home** locations for the database. You can lock down your Oracle base, but leave the Oracle home unlocked so that a different home can be selected at run time by the Provisioning Operator.

Both the **Working Directory** (`/tmp`) and the **Installer Parameters** are left unlocked. Move to the next screen:

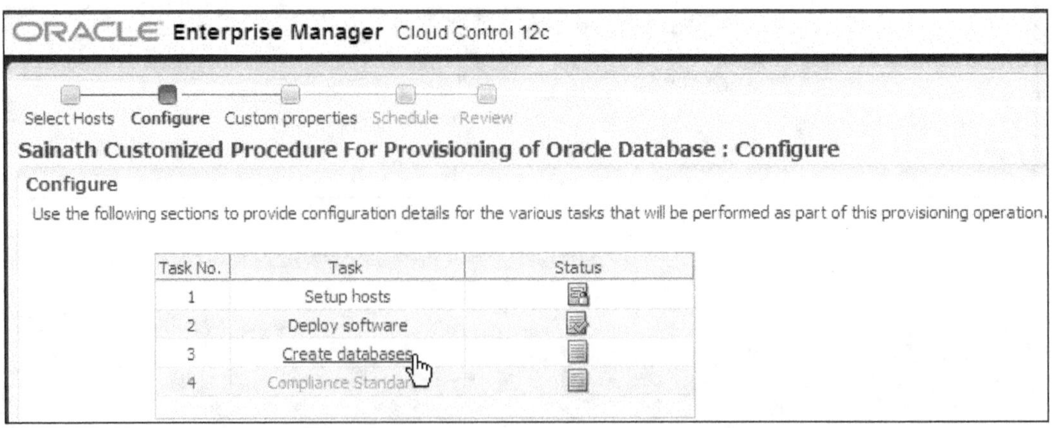

In the list of tasks, click on **Create Database**, which will allow you to specify configuration parameters for the database being deployed:

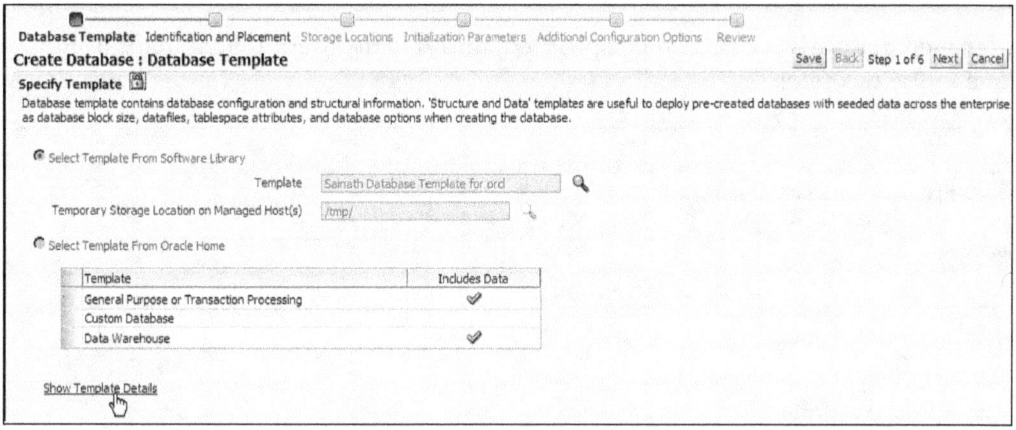


The first step in the **Create Database** task is to specify the database template to be used.

As we had selected a database profile at the start, this page has prefilled the value appropriately as **Sainath Database Template for orcl** from the Software Library. Alternatively, it is possible to select one of the standard Oracle database templates such as **General Purpose or Transaction Processing**, and **Data Warehousing**.

The template is locked down so it cannot be changed at runtime. To see the actual settings in the template, click on the **Show Template Details** link. After this, move to the next step:

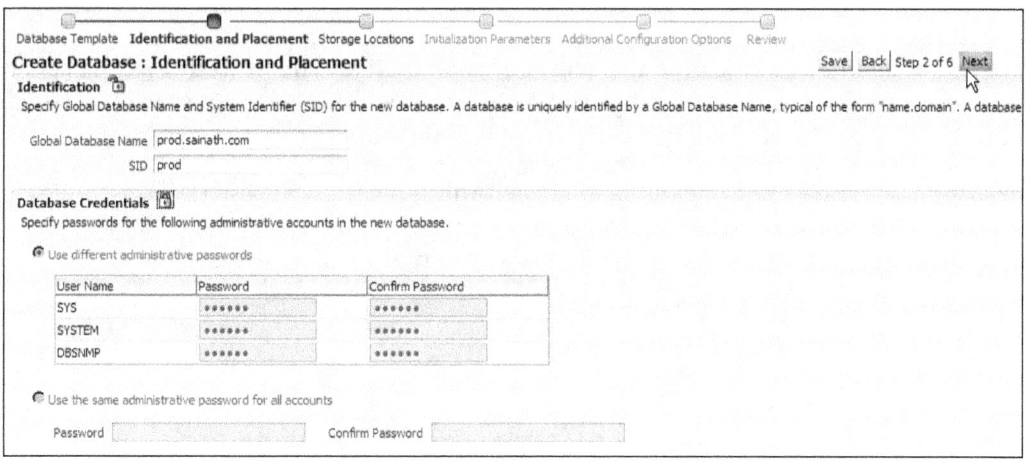

At this point you can specify the intended **Global Database Name** and the **SID** fields for the new database. These are not locked down, so the operator can choose a different name if it is required.

**Database Credentials** can also be specified, and it is decided to lock them down. Move to the next step:

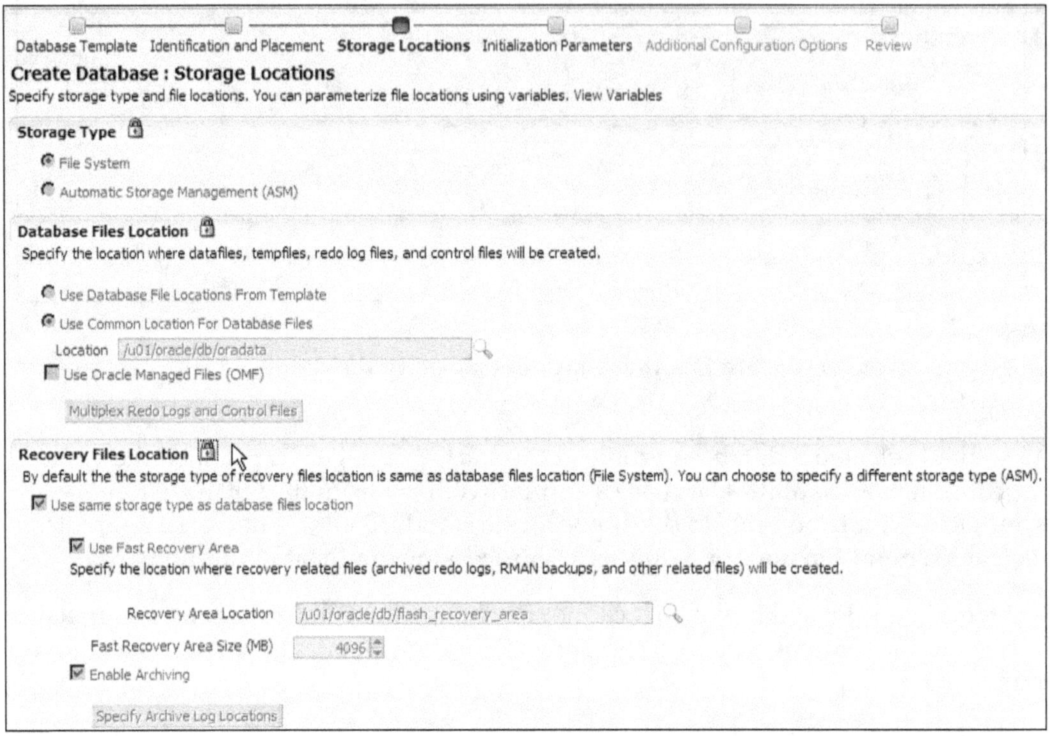


On this page, you locked down the **Storage Type** field as **File system**, as it has been decided in this particular company that **Automatic Storage Management (ASM)** is not to be used as the storage type for any new databases.

Specify `/u01/oracle/db/oradata` as the common location for the database file's location in the **Location** textbox, and this is also locked down. You could also use the database file's location from the database template at this stage.

As **Recovery Files Location**, you decide to use the same storage type as the database files, namely **File System**. You also specify a fast **Recovery Area Location** file, and set **Fast Recovery Area Size (MB)** as `4096` (the starting size).

Archiving is enabled for the new database, and all this is locked down. Click on the **Next** button to arrive at the following step:

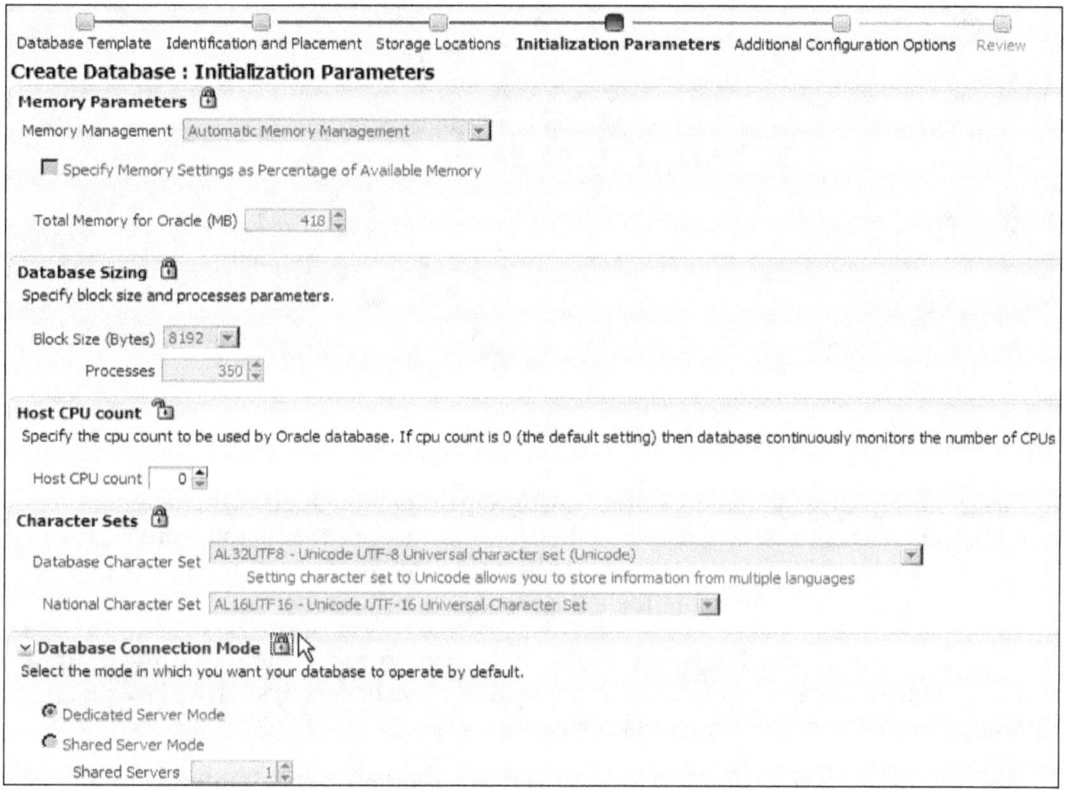


**Initialization Parameters** are now specified. You can decide whether to use the new **Automatic Memory Management** or the old **Automatic Shared Memory Management** option.

The total memory to be used, the block size, **Host CPU count**, the database's **Character Sets**, and **Database Connection Mode** can all be specified. All are locked down except the **Host CPU count**. Proceed to the next step:

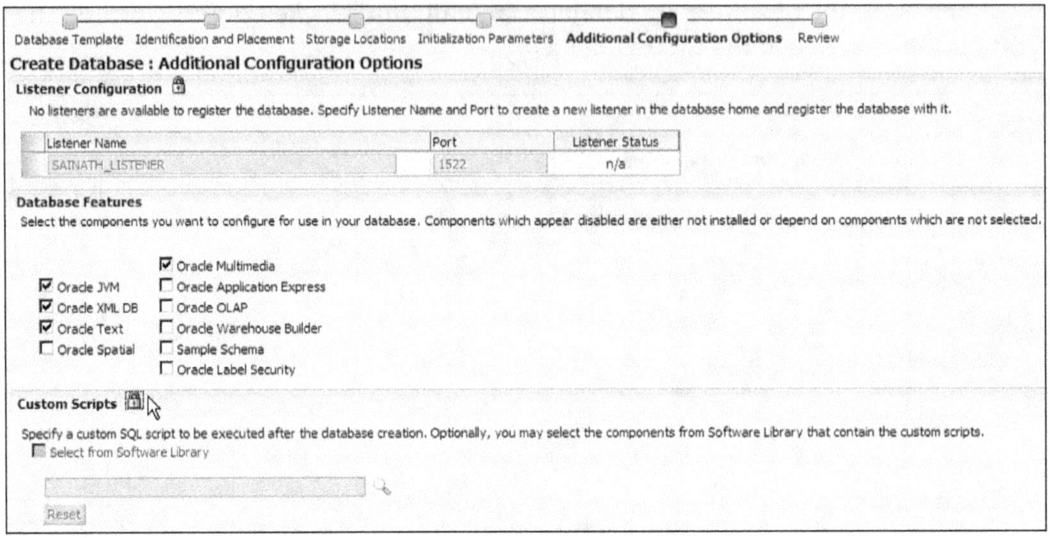


In this final step of **Advanced Configuration Options**, you specify the listener that the database is to be registered with, or a new listener that is to be created. It is decided to name all new listeners in the company as `SAINATH_LISTENER` and use the port `1522`. These are locked down.

You can also specify the database features to be configured. Note that some of these features require the appropriate database option to be licensed, such as **Oracle Spatial, Oracle OLAP**, or **Oracle Label Security**.

Allowing **Custom Scripts** (SQL scripts) to be executed after the database creation is also locked down so that custom scripts cannot be run. Move to the **Review** page:

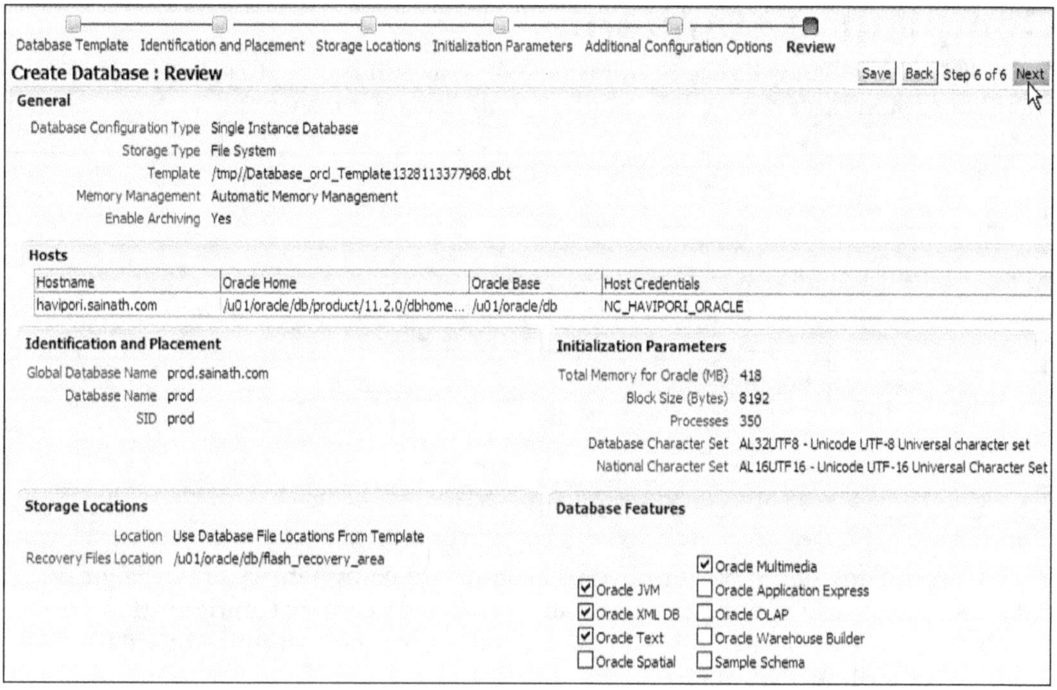

After checking that all the details on the **Review** page are correct, click on the **Next** button. This takes you back to the list of four tasks as shown in the following screenshot:

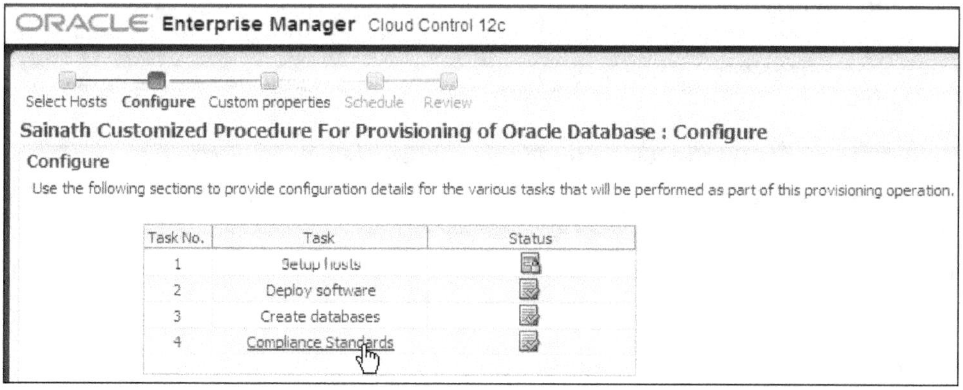

# Compliance standards

Now click on the **Compliance Standards** task. You will be able to select the compliance standards that will be applied to the new database:

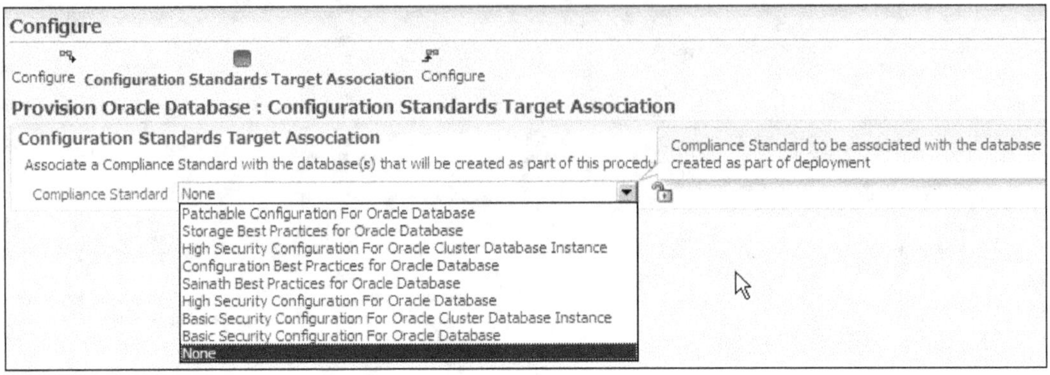


You can select any of the presupplied or customized compliance standards for the database. For example, you can choose to have **Basic Security Configuration For Oracle Database** associated with the new database, or the customized **Sainath Best Practices Compliance Standard**.

This shows the close integration of the configuration management/compliance capabilities with the provisioning capabilities of the DBLM Pack in Enterprise Manager.

Move to the next page:

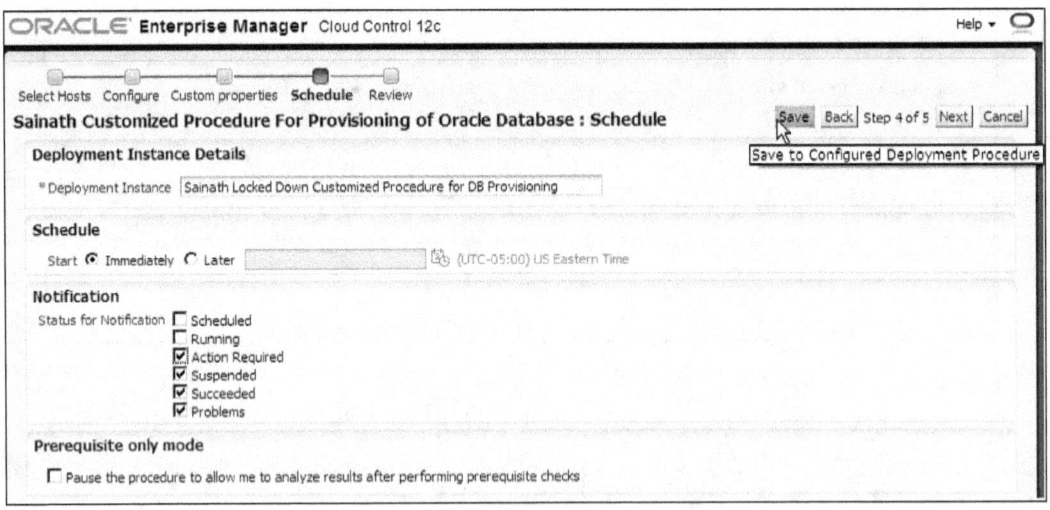

At this point, on the **Schedule** page, you can name the locked down procedure. The schedule can be ignored at this stage. We have used the name `Sainath Locked Down Customized Procedure for DB Provisioning`.

Click on the **Save** button, which will save all your inputs and lock-downs into a configured deployment procedure.

The locked-down procedure now appears in the list of deployment procedures on the **Database Provisioning** page. This is shown in the following screenshot:

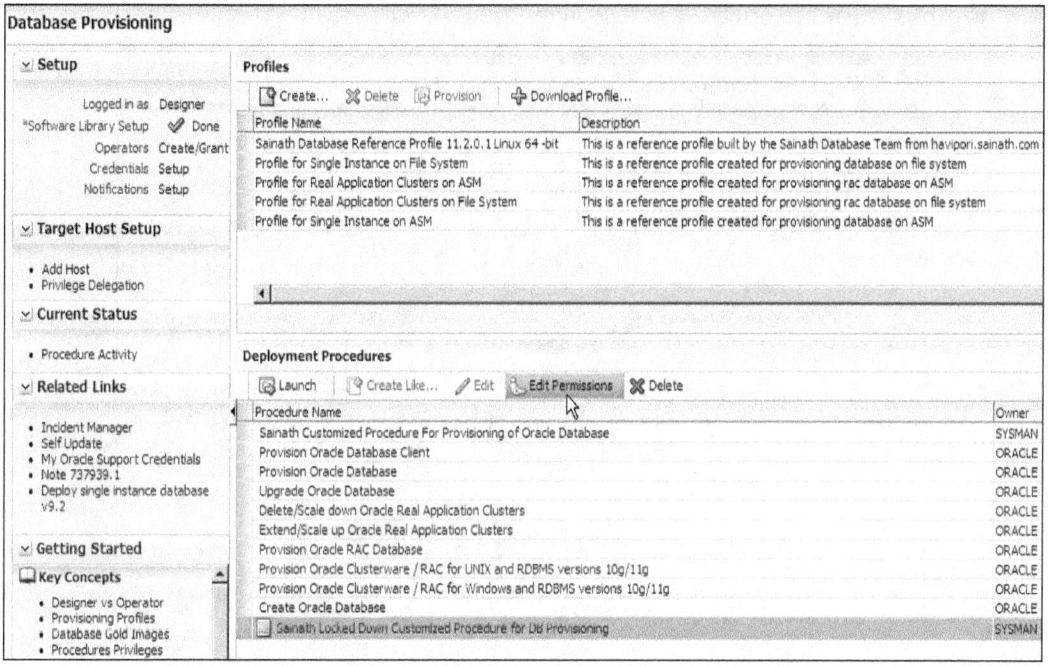

# Granting permissions to the Provisioning Operator

The next step is to grant permissions on this procedure to the Provisioning Operator. This can be done on the same page using the **Edit Permissions** button.

However, before this is done, you need to first create the Provisioning Operator. This is done by going to **Setup** | **Security** | **Administrators** on the Enterprise Manager Cloud Control 12*c* menu, and then clicking on the **Create** button. The details for the new administrator are entered as follows:

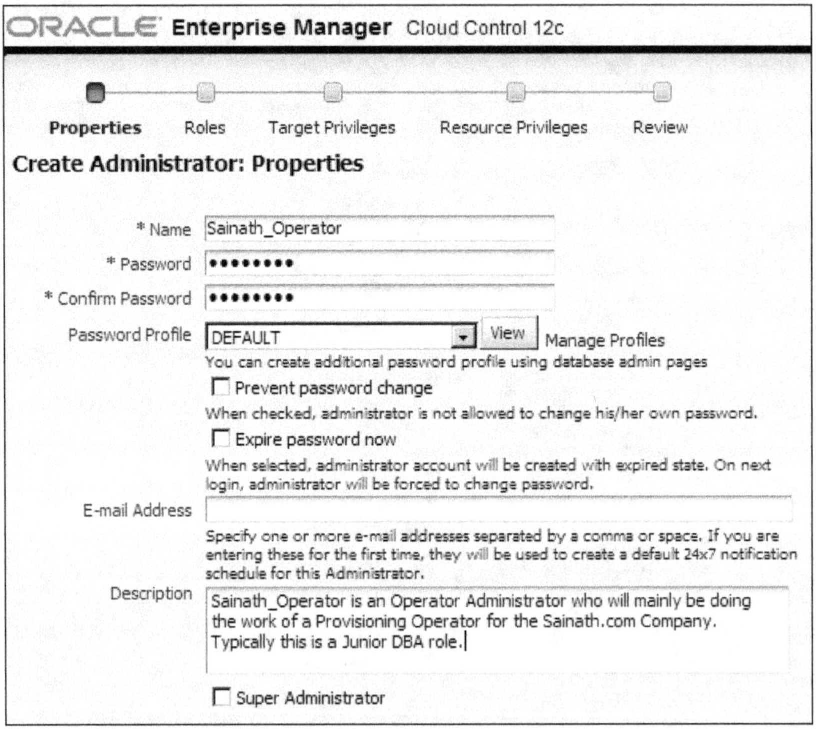

We are creating `SAINATH_OPERATOR` as a new Enterprise Manager administrator who will mainly be doing the work of a Provisioning Operator for the Sainath company. Typically, this is a Junior DBA role. Move to the next page to assign the roles to the new administrator.

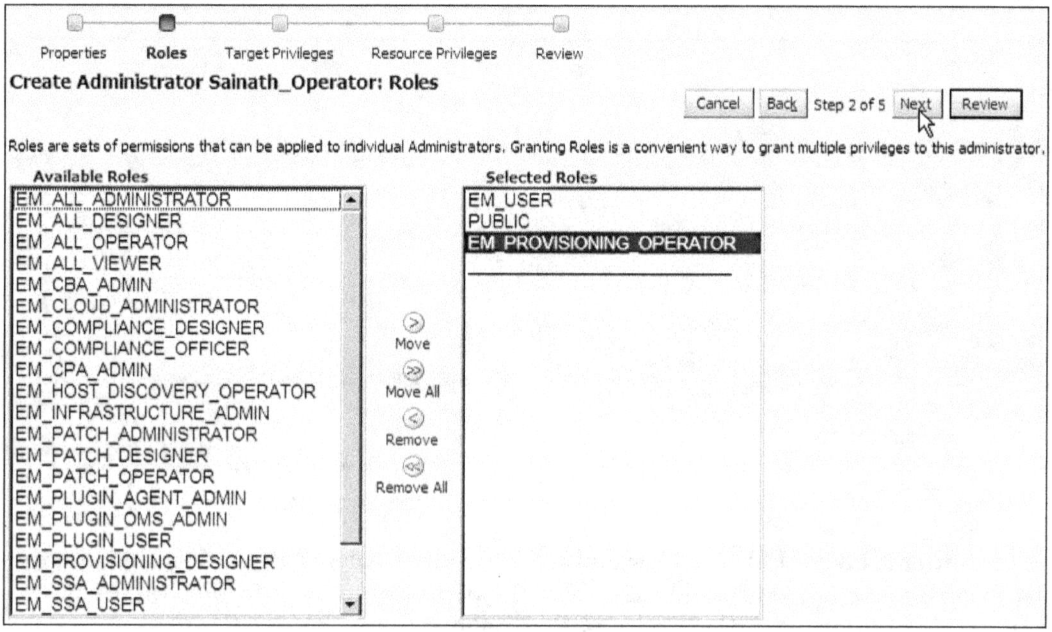


Select the role **EM_PROVISIONING_OPERATOR** from the left-hand side pane of available roles and move it to the right-hand side pane. This is the most important role for a Provisioning Operator. After this, you can complete creating the administrator.

Once `SAINATH_OPERATOR` has been created, this Provisioning Operator can be assigned the rights to the locked-down deployment procedure. This is done either by the steps described previously (the **Edit Permissions** button on the **Database Provisioning** page) or by going to **Enterprise** | **Provisioning and Patching** | **Procedure Library**.

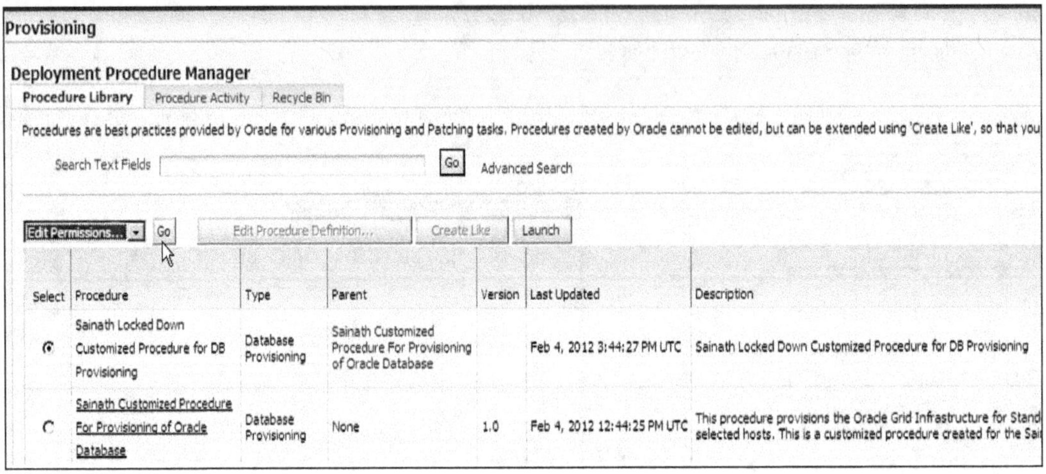


Select **Sainath Locked Down Customized Procedure for DB Provisioning** from the list. Then choose **Edit Permissions...** from the drop-down list and click on the **Go** button. This brings up the edit permissions page:

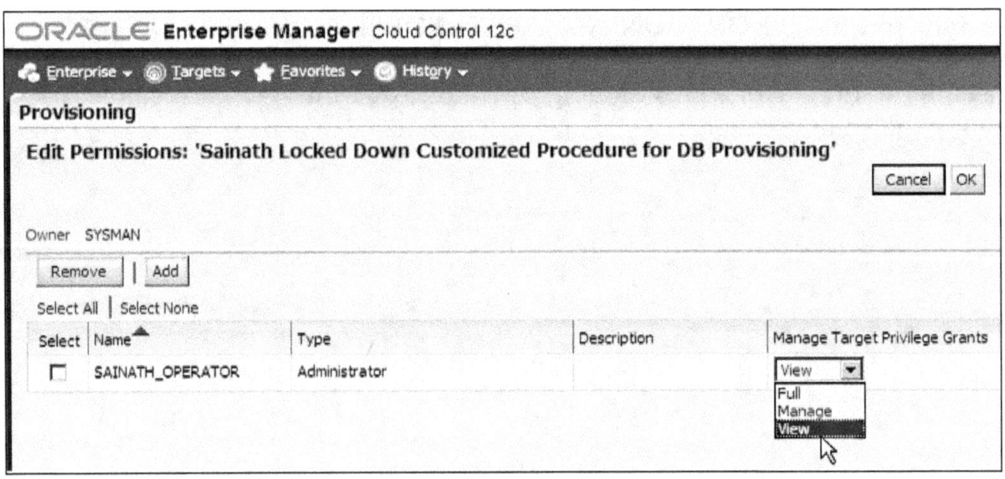

You can now add Enterprise Manager administrators to the list on the screen, and grant either **Full**, **Manage**, or **View** privileges on the procedure. In this case, the Provisioning Operator just needs to run the procedure and will not change it, so we have granted the **View** privilege.

In this way, you can grant the **View** privilege on the locked-down procedure to one or more Provisioning Operators who will be doing the actual provisioning. Click on the **OK** button to continue.

However, before **SAINATH_OPERATOR** can actually run the deployment procedure, there is one more thing that needs to be done. The Provisioning Operator needs to be granted appropriate privileges on the named credentials used in this procedure, otherwise these named credentials will not be visible to the Provisioning Operator.

To do this, go to **Setup** | **Security** | **Named Credentials** on the Enterprise Manager menu. This displays the **Named Credentials** page:

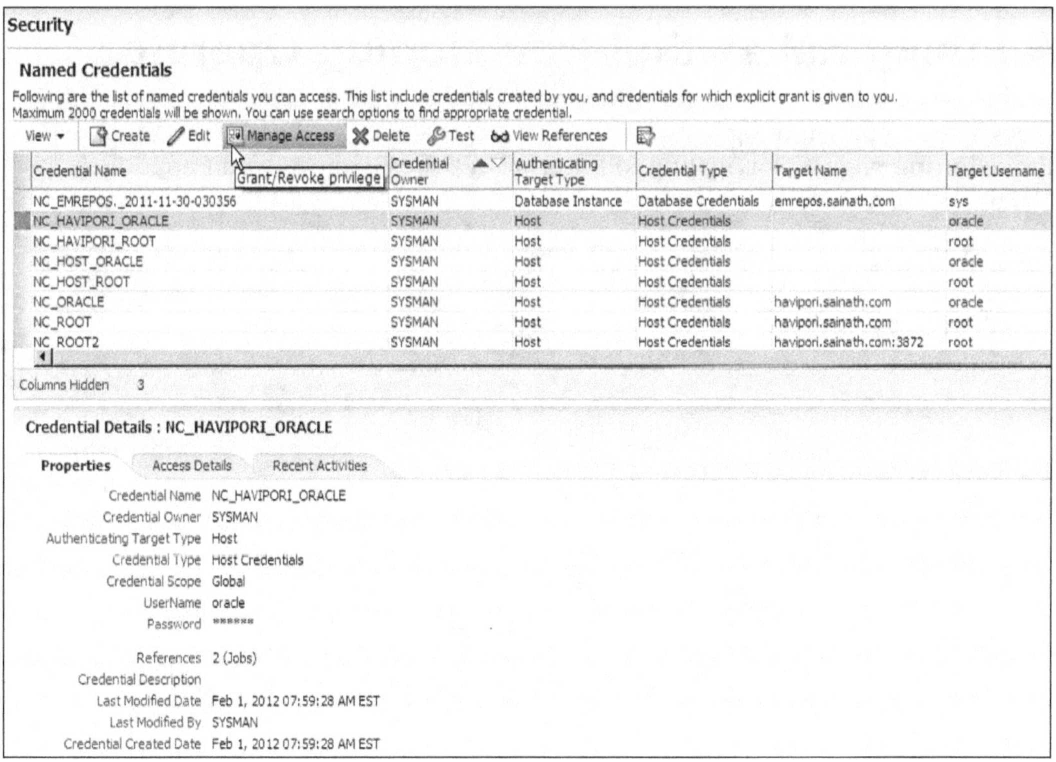

Select the named credential that was used in the locked-down procedure. This was **NC_HAVIPORI_ORACLE** and **NC_HAVIPORI_ROOT**. Select the credentials one by one, and click on the **Manage Access** button to grant or revoke privileges on that named credential:

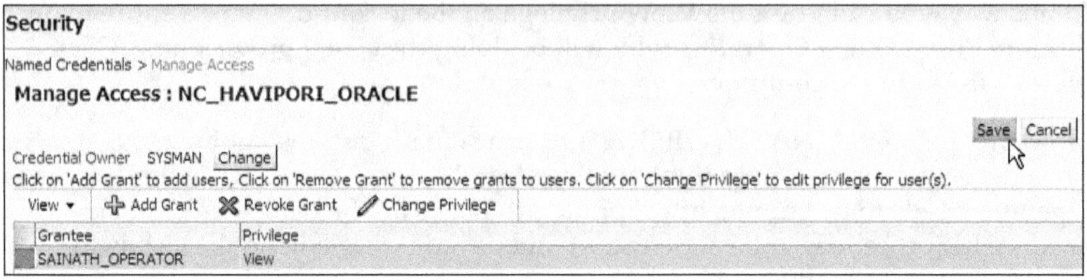


Use the **Add Grant** button to add the **View** privilege to **SAINATH_OPERATOR**. Multiple administrators can be added to the list. Click on the **Save** button to exit.

# Running EM as the Provisioning Operator

At this point, log out of Enterprise Manager Cloud Control 12*c* as the Provisioning Designer (`SYSMAN`) and log in again as `SAINATH_OPERATOR`. Move to the **Database Provisioning** page by navigating to **Enterprise** | **Provisioning and Patching** | **Database Provisioning**:

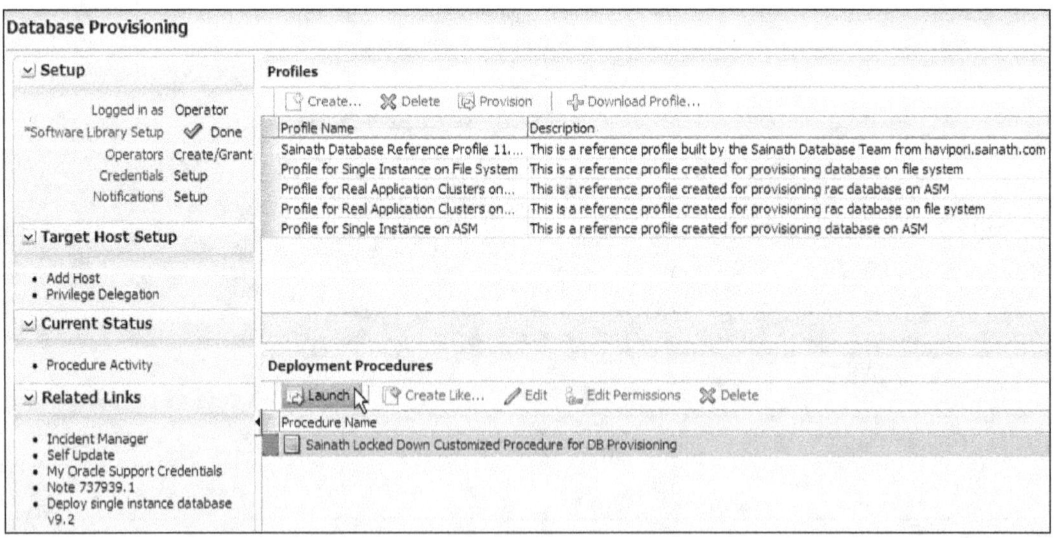

As you are logged in as `SAINATH_OPERATOR`, the upper-left corner of the page clearly shows your status as **Operator**.

You can see all the profiles under the **Profiles** section, but the **Deployment Procedures** section shows only the **Sainath Locked Down Customized Procedure for DB Provisioning** procedure, to which you have been granted access.

Select the procedure and click on the **Launch** button. This starts the provisioning process (usually done by the Provisioning Operator):

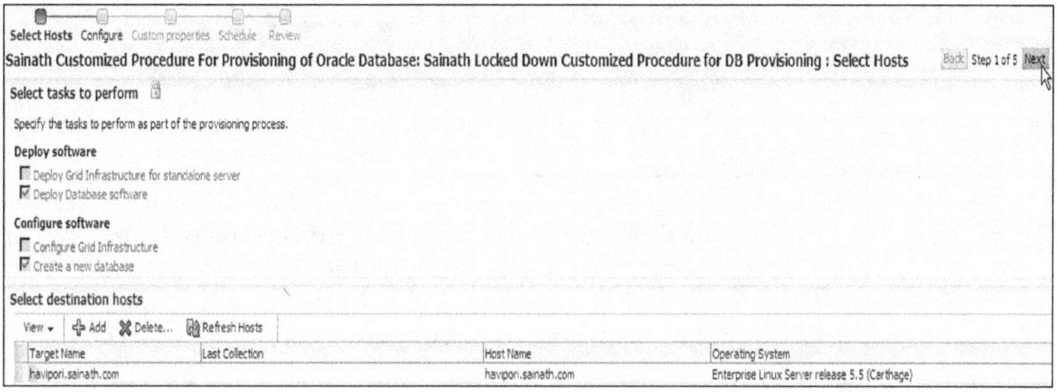


In the screens that now appear, we can note that the sections that were locked down by the Provisioning Designer appear grayed out, and it is not possible for the Provisioning Operator to change those sections. For example, in the preceding screenshot, the Provisioning Operator is forced to deploy only the database software and configure it, not the grid infrastructure software.

The Provisioning Operator is allowed to select the actual host on which the database software is to be deployed. In this case, as there is only one host on our virtual machine, we select the same host, that is **havipori.sainath.com**.

In this way, most of the pages in the procedure are unchangeable since they are locked down. Some pages allow input, as shown in the following screenshot:

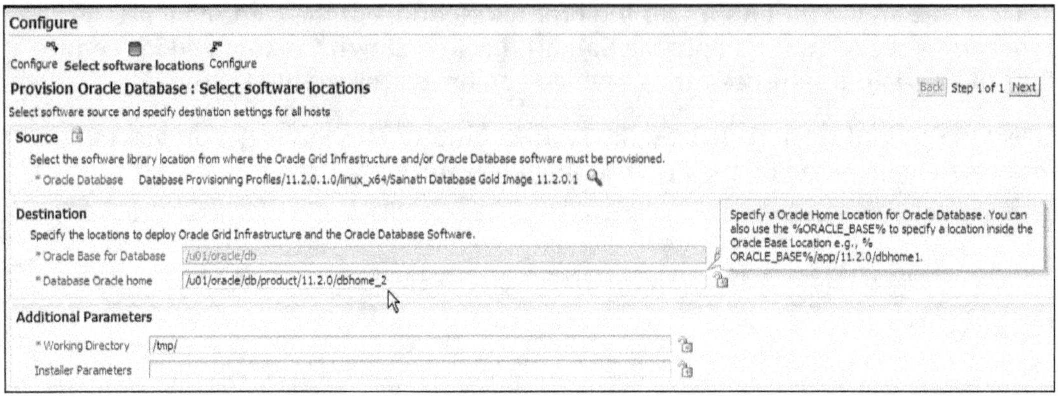


On this page, the Provisioning Operator has changed **Database Oracle Home** to `/u01/oracle/db/product/11.2.0/dbhome_2`. Leaving this unlocked has allowed the Provisioning Operator to install the database in a different Oracle home in case `/u01/oracle/db/product/11.2.0/dbhome_1` already exists on his/her server.

The following page also allows the Provisioning Operator to change the **SID** from the supplied name **prod** to a new name `saiprod`. Likewise, **Global Database Name** is also changed:

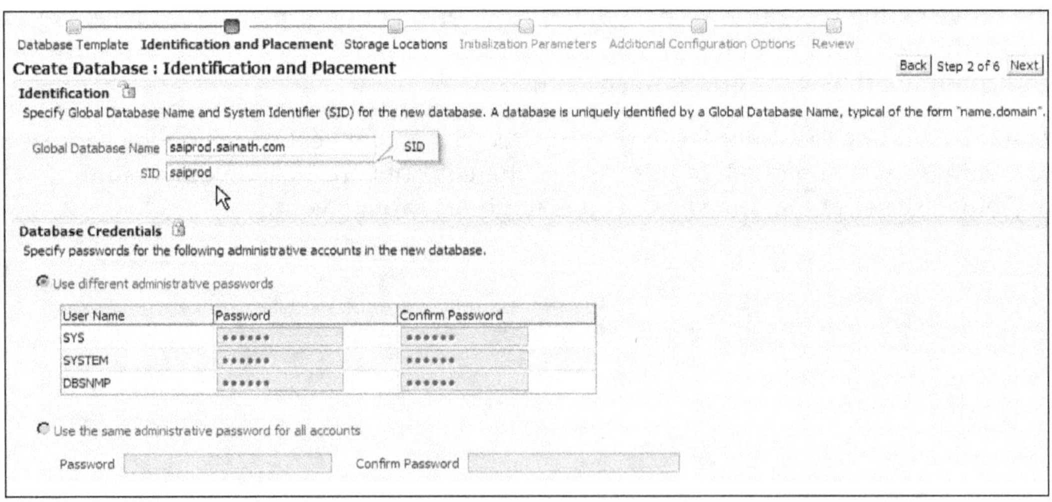

On the **Additional Configuration Options** page, the listener is locked down and cannot be changed:

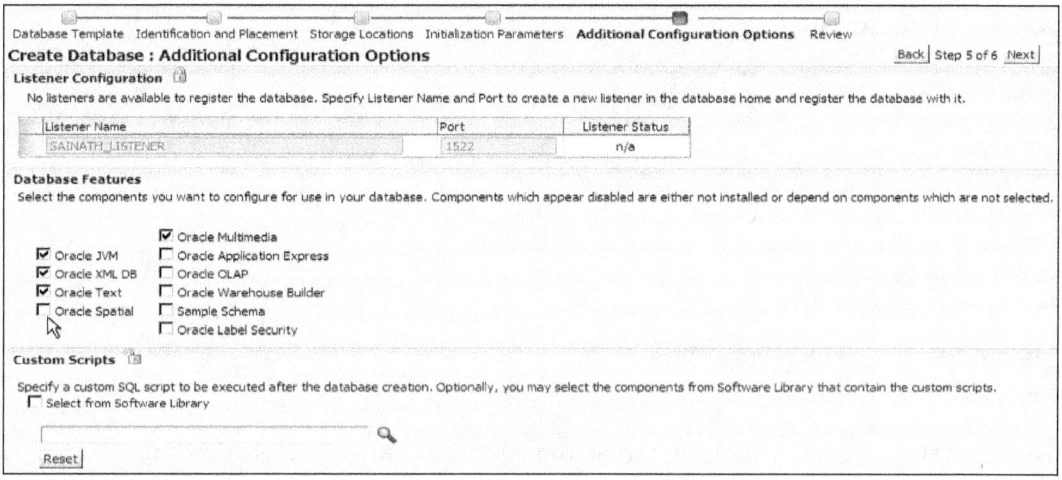

However, the database features can be modified as per your preference:

On the **Create Database: Review** page, the Provisioning Operator can check all the information about the database that is going to be created. This includes the template to be used, the **Oracle Home** location, **Database Name** and **SID**, **Initialization Parameters**, **Database Features**, and so on. Click on the **Next** button to continue.

At the very end of the locked down procedure, the Provisioning Operator can schedule the procedure to run immediately or at a later time. Notifications for certain types of status can also be set, for example, a notification can be sent if a procedure is waiting for an **Action Required** event or if it is **Suspended**, and so on:

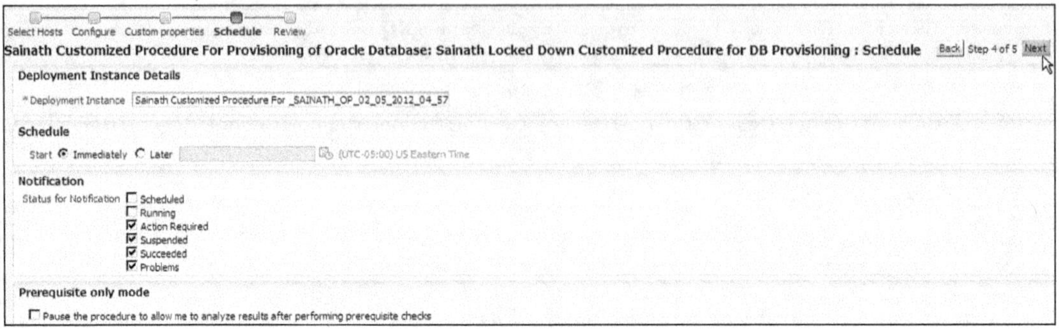


The Operator can also choose to pause the procedure after performing prerequisite checks. This allows you to fix any checks that may fail, for example, insufficient swap space. If this pause option is not set and a prerequisite check fails, the entire procedure will fail and have to be restarted from the beginning.

Now the final **Review** page appears. After a glance through the page, the Provisioning Operator decides to submit the procedure:

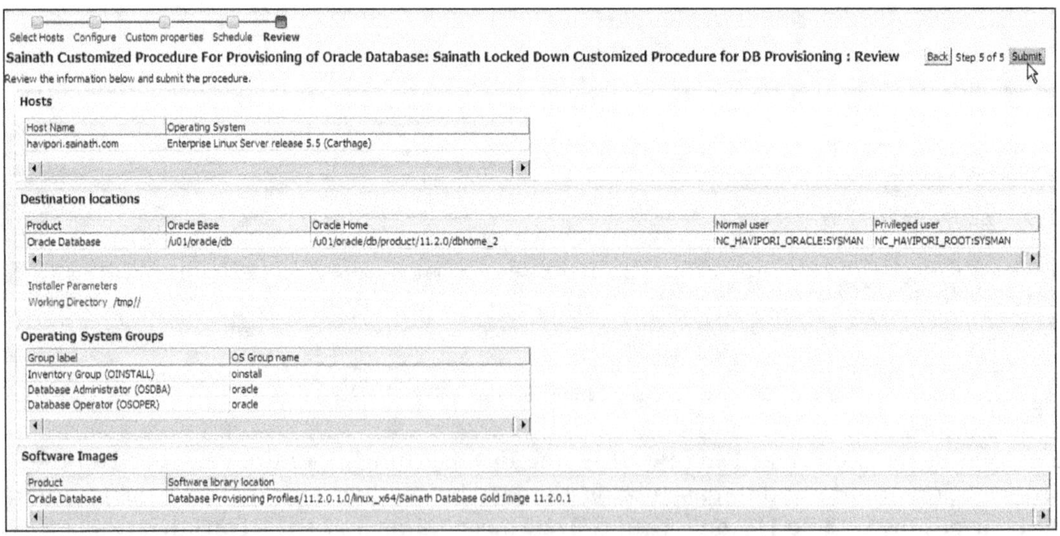

The Provisioning Procedure Activity page now appears, and it shows the status:

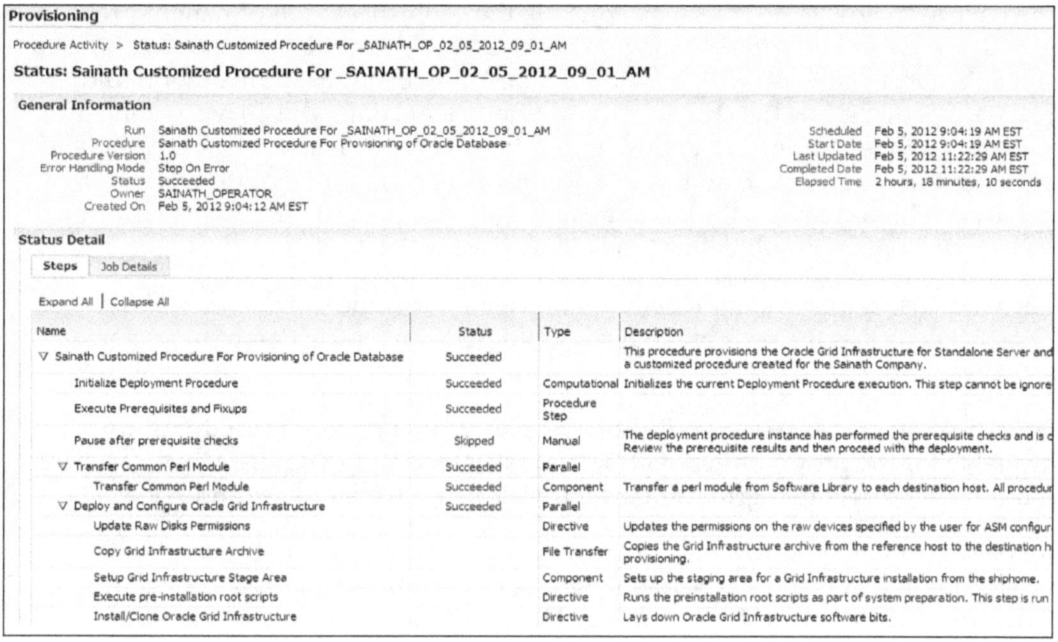


# Running the procedure

The procedure takes about two hours to complete on our virtual machine. As can be seen, it progresses through the steps of running the prerequisite checks, pausing if required, copying the grid infrastructure software (if required), followed by the database software.

Root scripts are run, the listener is configured, and ASM too again if required. This is followed by the discovery of a Target. After the software is set up, the database is created from the template and configured. Finally, the configuration standards you have chosen are automatically associated with the newly provisioned database Targets.

At the end of the deployment procedure, a brand new Oracle home `/u01/oracle/db/product/11.2.0/dbhome_2` has been created on the server, and a new listener `SAINATH_LISTENER` has been created to listen on port `1522`.

Most importantly, a new database **saiprod.sainath.com** is now provisioned on the server, and an entry in `/etc/oratab` has also been made. Also, if you issue the command `opatch lsinventory`, you will see that the same patches are present as were in the gold copy used in the provisioning profile.

# Other possibilities

We have seen how easily this was done via the sophisticated deployment procedures now available in Enterprise Manager Cloud Control 12*c*. This was the creation of a single-instance database with or without ASM, however, there are other deployment procedures that allow the creation of multinode RAC databases. This is done by installing all the grid infrastructure homes (for Oracle Clusterware and ASM) and database homes on all the nodes, followed by the creation of a multi-instance RAC database. This automates the software and database provisioning steps performed by the DBA when installing an Oracle RAC cluster.

There are also deployment procedures to scale up or scale down Oracle RAC clusters, as well as the new procedures to upgrade an Oracle database or create an Oracle database.

For older versions such as 10*g* and 11.1, separate deployment procedures are available for the provisioning of Oracle Clusterware and RAC since these versions did not have a separate grid infrastructure home for Clusterware and ASM.

In the same manner, Enterprise Manager Cloud Control 12*c* enables middleware provisioning. This can be accessed by going to **Enterprise** | **Provisioning and Patching** | **Middleware Provisioning**. The list of deployment procedures on this page is shown in the following screenshot:

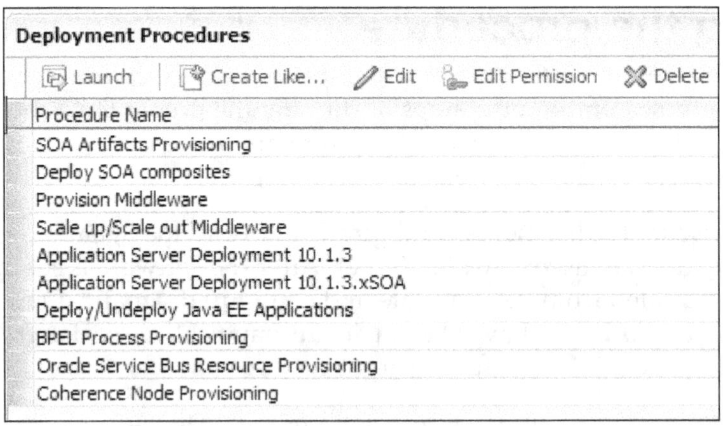

As can be seen, the middleware deployment procedures can be used for provisioning middleware (WebLogic Server), application server deployment, **Scale up/Scale out of Middleware** clusters, **SOA Artifacts Provisioning**, **BPEL Process Provisioning**, **Coherence Node Provisioning**, and so on. There is also a new deployment procedure that automates the deploying, redeploying, or undeploying of Java EE applications to or from domains.

Thus there are tremendous automation capabilities in the new version of Enterprise Manager Cloud Control 12*c* for scaling WLS and SOA domains, and there is also automation for mass deployment of Java EE applications.

# Summary

In large and complex environments, the provisioning process if performed manually can easily take up to 50 percent of an administrator's time. There are many disparate pieces of hardware and software that need to be provisioned using different procedures. During the course of this chapter, we have seen how a great deal of the provisioning process can be automated by Enterprise Manager Cloud Control 12*c*, using the powerful gold images, provisioning profiles, and deployment procedures. This will greatly reduce the provisioning effort and save the valuable time of the administrator.

A Provisioning Designer, normally a Senior DBA in the database engineering department, can create a locked-down procedure that can be published to the Provisioning Operator, who may be the Junior DBA. The Provisioning Operator can then seamlessly perform the actual action of provisioning without being able to change the locked-down inputs, and new databases can thus be provisioned as almost exact replicas of a gold copy.

Enterprise Manager can also be used to provision bare-metal boxes with Linux operating systems and Oracle VM servers. This is known as Bare Metal Provisioning, which can be accessed by going to **Enterprise** | **Provisioning and Patching** | **Bare Metal Provisioning**. This requires a stage server, boot server, and an RPM repository to be configured on the infrastructure page.

Note that the self-update mechanism in Enterprise Manager Cloud Control 12*c* now includes middleware provisioning and database provisioning profiles, gold images, virtualization templates and assemblies, as well as provisioning bundles. This makes it easier to get the up-to-date copies of the provisioning tidbits as described in this chapter.

The **Enterprise Manager Command Line Interface** (**EMCLI**) and web service interfaces are also available for integration of the provisioning facility in Enterprise Manager with other external tools.

The database provisioning capabilities lay the groundwork for the database cloud, that is **Database as a Service** (**DBaaS**). Likewise, middleware provisioning can take place via a similar mechanism and this is the base technology for the **Platform as a Service** (**PaaS**).

These types of clouds require the license for the Cloud Management Pack for Database, or Cloud Management Pack for Fusion Middleware respectively. The prerequisites are the Database Lifecycle Management Pack for the former, and the WebLogic Management Pack Enterprise Edition (EE) for the latter.

For further details on the lifecycle management aspects for both the database and middleware, as well as Bare Metal Provisioning, refer to the *Oracle Enterprise Manager Lifecycle Management Administrator's Guide* document at the following URL:

`http://docs.oracle.com/cd/E24628_01/em.121/e27046.pdf`

In the next chapter, we will look at the patch automation capability of the Enterprise Manager Database Lifecycle Management Pack, and see how it greatly assists with the repeated mass patching requirements of a large data center—easing the patching burden on the administrator and increasing productivity at every step.

# 6

# Ease the Chaos with Automated Patching

We have seen how the provisioning capabilities of the Oracle Enterprise Manager's **Database Lifecycle Management** (**DBLM**) Pack enable you to deploy fully patched Oracle Database homes and databases, as replicas of the gold copy in the Software Library of Enterprise Manager. However, nothing placed in production should be treated as static. Software changes in development cycles, enhancements take place, or security/functional issues are found. For almost anything in the IT world, new patches are bound to be released. These will also need to be applied to production, testing, reporting, staging, and development environments in the data center on an ongoing basis.

For the database side of things, Oracle releases quarterly a combination of security fixes known as the **Critical Patch Update** (**CPU**). Other patches are bundled together and released every quarter in the form of a **Patch Set Update** (**PSU**), and this also includes the CPU for that quarter.

Oracle strongly recommends applying either the PSU or the CPU every calendar quarter. If you prefer to apply the CPU, continue doing so. If you wish to move to the PSU, you can do so, but in that case continue only with the PSU.

The quarterly patching requirement, as a direct recommendation from Oracle, is followed by many companies that prefer to have their databases secured with the latest security fixes. This underscores the importance of patching.

However, if there are hundreds of development, testing, staging, and production databases in the data center to be patched, the situation quickly turns into a major manual exercise every three months. DBAs and their managers start planning for the patch exercise in advance, and a lot of resources are allocated to make it happen—with the administrators working on each database serially, at times overnight and at times over the weekend.

There are a number of steps involved in patching each database, such as locating the appropriate patch in **My Oracle Support** (**MOS**), downloading the patch, transferring it to each of the target servers, upgrading the `OPATCH` facility in each Oracle home, shutting down the databases and listeners running from that home, applying the patch, starting each of the databases in restricted mode, applying any supplied SQL scripts, restarting the databases in normal mode, and checking the patch inventory.

These steps have to be manually repeated on every database home on every server, and on every database in that home. Dull repetition of these steps in patching the hundreds of servers in a data center is a very monotonous task, and it can lead to an increase in human errors.

To avoid these issues inherent in manual patching, some companies decide not to apply the quarterly patches on their databases. They wait for a year, or a couple of years before they consider patching, and some even prefer to apply year-old patches instead of the latest patches. This is counter-productive and leads to their databases being insecure and vulnerable to attacks, since the latest recommended CPUs from Oracle have not been applied.

What then is the solution, to convince these companies to apply patches regularly? If the patching process can be mostly automated (but still under the control of the DBAs), it would reduce the quarterly patching effort to a great extent. Companies would then have the confidence that their existing team of DBAs would be able to manage the patching of hundreds of databases in a controlled and automated manner, keeping human error to a minimum.

The Database Lifecycle Management Pack of Enterprise Manager Cloud Control 12*c* is able to achieve this by using its Patch Automation capability. We will now look into Patch Automation and the close integration of Enterprise Manager with My Oracle Support.

# Recommended patches

By navigating to **Enterprise** | **Summary**, a **Patch Recommendations** section will be visible in the lower left-hand corner, as shown in the following screenshot:

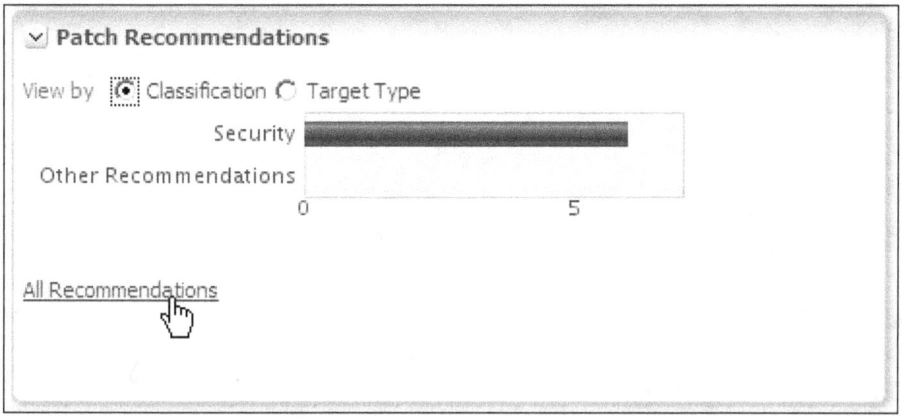


The graph displays either the **Classification** output of the recommended patches, or the **Target Type** output. Currently for this system, more than five security patches are recommended as can be seen in this graph. This recommendation has been derived via a connection to My Oracle Support (the OMS can be connected either directly to the Internet, or by using a proxy server). Target configuration information is collected by the Enterprise Manager Agent and is stored in the **Configuration Management Database (CMDB)** within the repository. This configuration information is collated regularly by the Enterprise Manager's Harvester process and pushed to My Oracle Support.

Thus, configuration information about your targets is known to My Oracle Support, and it is able to recommend appropriate patches as and when they are released. However, the recommended patch engine also runs within Enterprise Manager 12*c* at your site, working off the configuration data in the CMDB in Enterprise Manager, so recommendations can in fact be achieved without the configuration having been uploaded on MOS by the Harvester (this upload is more useful now for other purposes, such as attaching configuration details during SR creation).

It is also possible to get metadata about the latest available patches from My Oracle Support in offline mode, but more manual steps are involved in this case, so Internet connectivity is recommended to get the full benefits of Enterprise Manager's integration with My Oracle Support.

To view the details about the patches, click on the **All Recommendations** link or on the graph itself. This connects to My Oracle Support (you may be asked to log in to your company-specific MOS account) and brings up the list of the patches in the **Patch Recommendations** section.

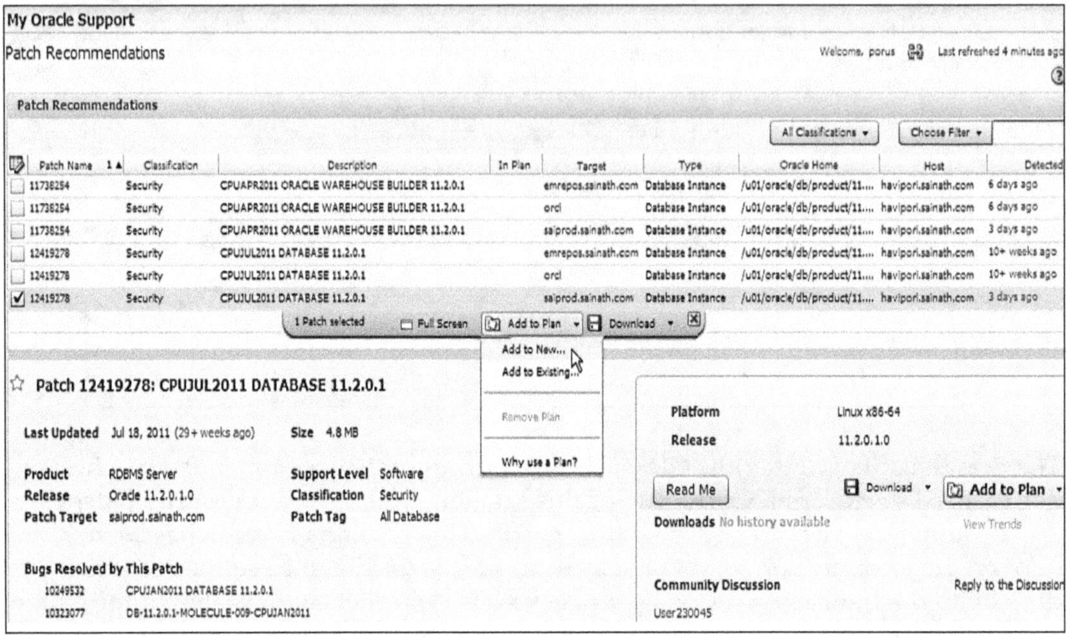

The database (and other types of) targets managed by the Enterprise Manager system are displayed on the screen, along with the recommended CPU (or other) patches. We select the **CPU July** patch for our `saiprod` database. This displays the details about the patch in the section in the lower part of the screen.

We can see the list **Bugs Resolved by This Patch**, the **Last Updated** date and **Size** of the patch and also **Read Me**—which has important information about the patch.

The number of total downloads for this patch is visible, as is the **Community Discussion** on this patch in the Oracle forums. You can add your own comment for this patch, if required, by selecting **Reply to the Discussion**.

Thus, at a glance, you can find out how popular the patch is (number of downloads) and any experience of other Oracle DBAs regarding this patch—whether positive or negative.

# Patch plan

You can view the information about the patch by clicking on the **Full Screen** button. You can download the patch either to the Software Library in Enterprise Manager or to your desktop. Finally, you can directly add this patch to a new or existing patch plan, which we will do next.

Go to **Add to Plan** | **Add to New**, and enter **Plan Name** as `Sainath_patchplan`. Then click on **Create Plan**. If you would like to add multiple patches to the plan, select both the patches first and then add to the plan. (You can also add patches later to the plan).

After the plan is created, click on **View Plan**. This brings up the following screen:

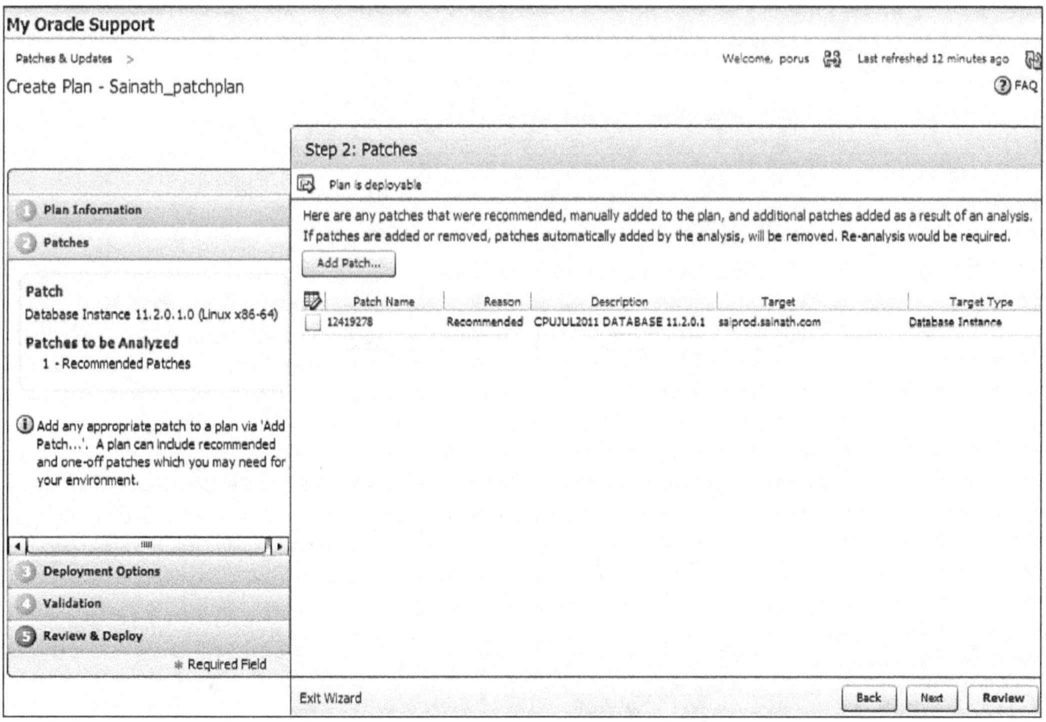

A patch plan is nothing but a collection of patches that can be applied as a group to one or more targets. On the **Create Plan** page that appears, there are five steps that can be seen in the left-hand pane. By default, the second step appears first. In this step, you can see all the patches that have been added to the plan.

It is possible to include more patches by clicking on the **Add Patch...** button. Besides the ability to manually add a patch to this list, the analysis process may also result in additional patches being added to the plan.

If you click on the first step, **Plan Information**, you can put in a description for this plan. You can also change the plan permissions, either **Full** or **View**, for various Enterprise Manager roles. Note that the **Full** permission allows the role to validate the plan, however, the **View** permission does not allow validation.

Move to step 3, **Deployment Options**. The following screen appears.

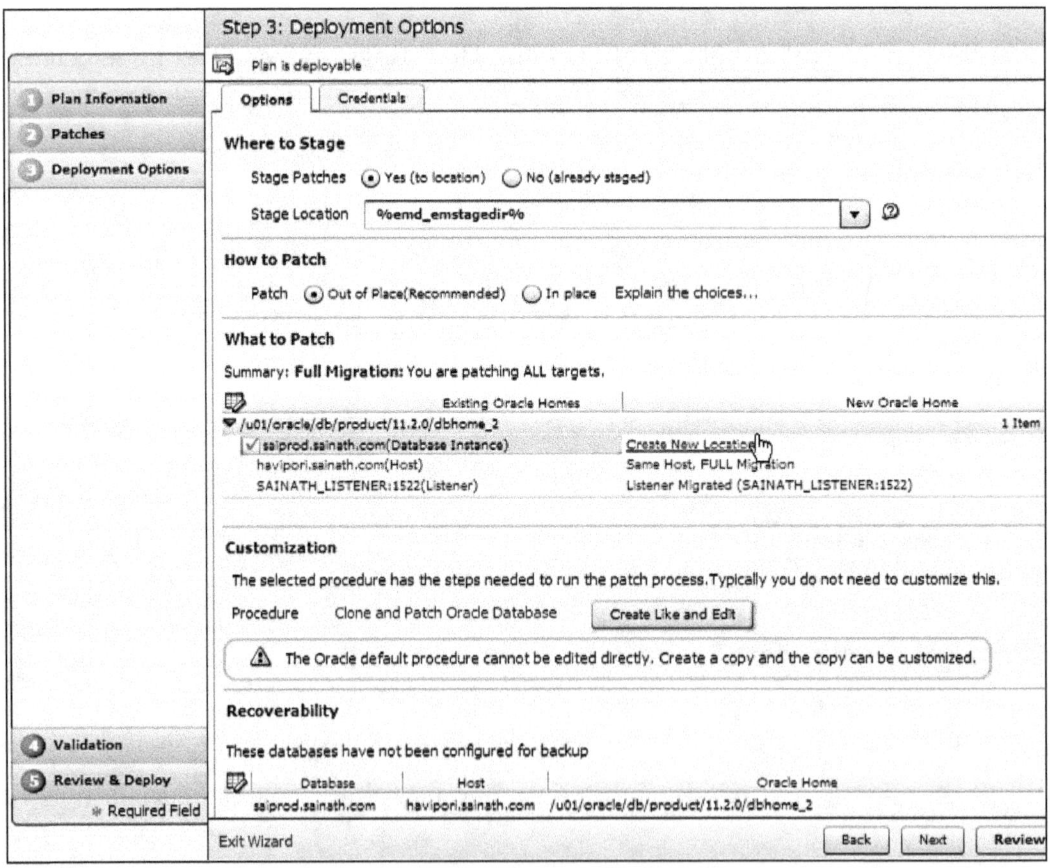

# Out-of-place patching

A new mechanism for patching has been provided in the Enterprise Manager Cloud Control 12*c* version, known as out-of-place patching. This is now the recommended method and creates a new Oracle home which is then patched while the previous home is still operational. All this is done using an out of the box deployment procedure in Enterprise Manager.

Using this mechanism means that the only downtime will take place when the databases from the previous home are switched to run from the new home. If there is any issue with the database patch, you can switch back to the previous unpatched home since it is still available. So, patch rollback is a lot faster.

Also, if there are multiple databases running in the previous home, you can decide which ones to switch to the new patched home. This is obviously an advantage, otherwise you would be forced to simultaneously patch all the databases in a home. A disadvantage of this method would be the space requirements for a duplicate home. Also, if proper housekeeping is not carried out later on, it can lead to a proliferation of Oracle homes on a server where patches are being applied regularly using this mechanism.

This kind of selective patching and minimal downtime is not possible if you use the previously available method of in-place patching, which uses a separate deployment procedure to shut down all databases running from an Oracle home before applying the patches on the same home. The databases can only be restarted normally after the patching process is over, and this obviously takes more downtime and affects all databases in a home.

Depending on the method you choose, the appropriate deployment procedure will be automatically selected and used.

We will now use the out-of-place method in this patch plan. On the **Step 3: Deployment Options** page, make sure the **Out of Place (Recommended)** option is selected. Then click on **Create New Location**.

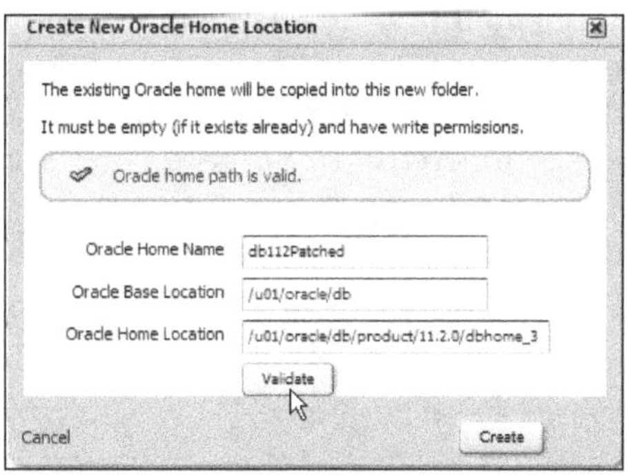

Type in the name and location of the new Oracle home, and click on the **Validate** button. This checks the Oracle home path on the Target server. After this is done, click on the **Create** button.

The deployment options of the patch plan are successfully updated, and the new home appears on the **Step 3** page.

Click on the **Credentials** tab. Here you need to select or enter the normal and privileged credentials for the Oracle home.

Click on the **Next** button. This moves us to step 4, the **Validation** step.

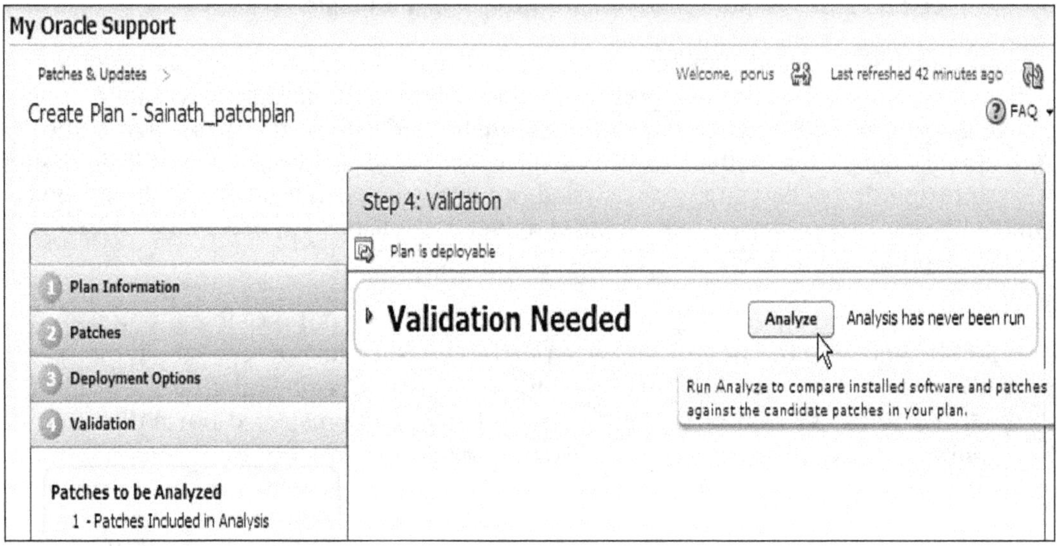


# Pre-patching analysis

Click on the **Analyze** button. A job to perform prepatching analysis is started in the background. This will compare the installed software and patches on the targets with the new patches you have selected in your plan, and attempt to validate them. This validation may take a few minutes to complete, since it also checks the Oracle home for readiness, computes the space requirements for the home, and conducts other checks such as cluster node connectivity (if you are patching a RAC database).

If you drill down to the analysis job itself by clicking on **Show Detailed Progress here**, you can see that it does a number of checks to validate if the targets are supported for patching, verifies the normal and super user credentials of the Oracle home, verifies the target tools, commands, and permissions, upgrades `OPATCH` to the latest version, stages the selected patches to Oracle homes, and then runs the prerequisite checks including those for cloning an Oracle home. If the prerequisite checks succeed, the analysis job skips the remaining steps and stops at this point with a successful status. The patch is seen as **Ready for Deployment**.

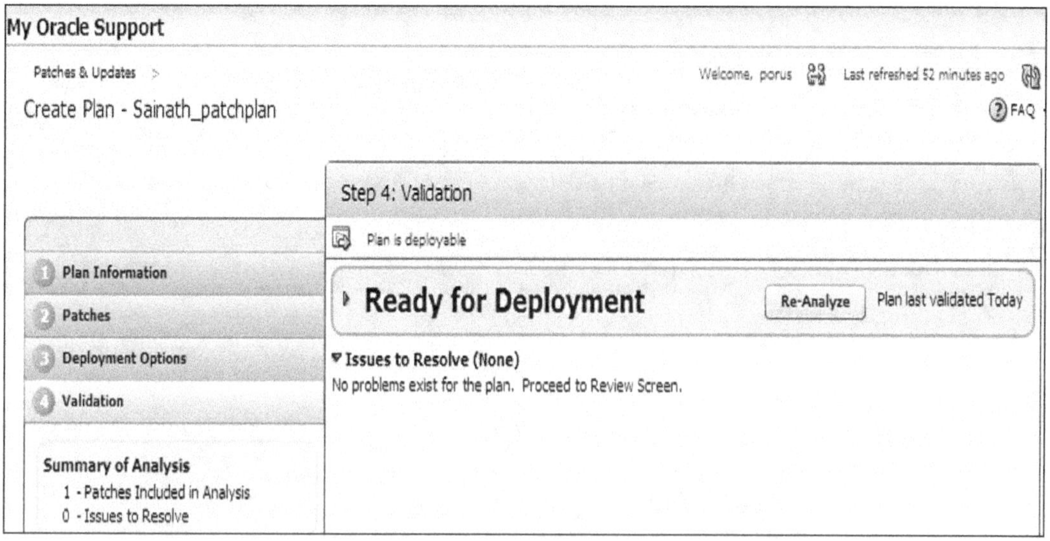


If there are any issues, they will show up at this point. For example, if there is a conflict with any of the patches, a replacement patch or a merge patch may be suggested. If there is no replacement or merge patch and you want to request such a patch, it will allow you to make the request directly from the screen.

If you are applying a PSU and the CPU for that same release is already applied to the Oracle home, for example, `July 2011 CPU`, then because the PSU is a superset of the CPU, the MOS analysis will stop and mention that the existing patch fixes the issues. Such a message can be seen in the **Informational Messages** section of the **Validation** page.

# Deployment

In our case, the patch is **Ready for Deployment**. At this point, you can move directly to step 5, **Review & Deploy**, by clicking on it in the left-hand side pane.

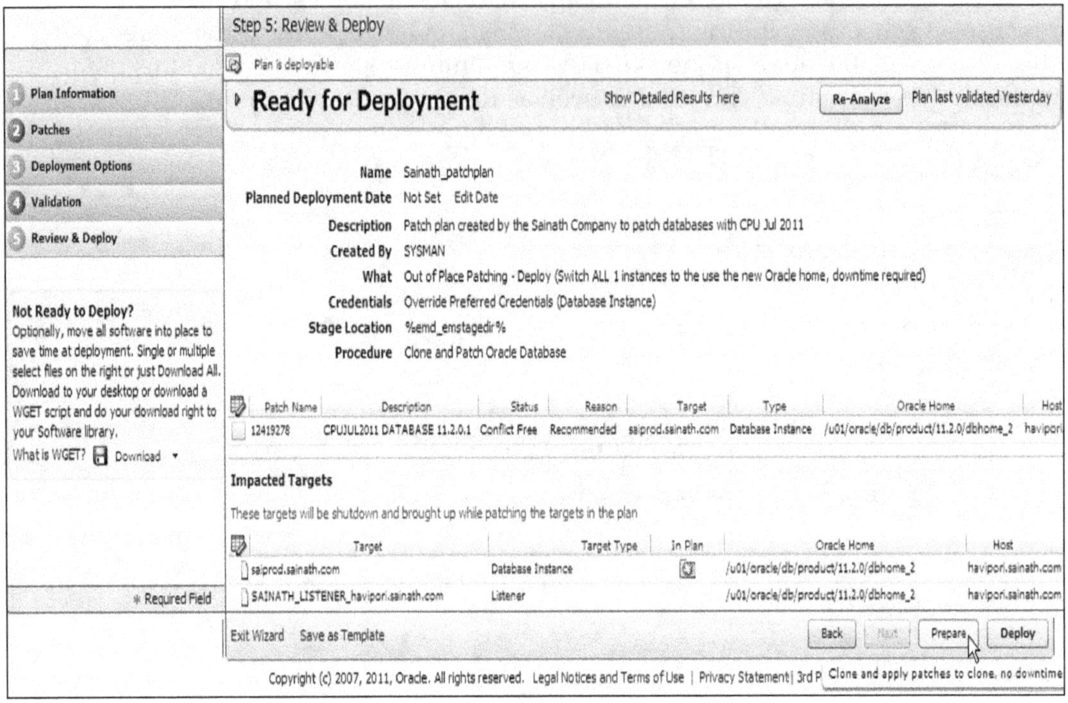

On the **Review & Deploy** page, the patch plan is described in detail along with **Impacted Targets**. Along with the database that is in the patch plan, a new impacted target has been found by the analysis process and added to the list of impacted targets. This is the listener that is running from the home that is to be cloned and patched.

The patches that are to be applied are also listed on this review page, in our case the **CPUJUL2011** patch is shown with the status **Conflict Free**.

The deployment procedure that will be used is **Clone and Patch Oracle Database**, since out-of-place patching is being used, and all instances and listeners running in the previous Oracle home are being switched to the new home.

Click on the **Prepare** button. The status on the screen changes to **Preparation in Progress**. A job for preparation of the out-of-place patching starts, including cloning of the original Oracle home and applying the patches to the cloned home. No downtime is required while this job is running; it can happen in the background.

This preparation phase is like a pre-deploy and is only possible in the case of out-of-place patching, whereas in the case of in-place patching, there is no **Prepare** button and you deploy straightaway.

Clicking on **Show Detailed Progress here** opens a new window showing the job details.

When the preparation job has successfully completed (after about two hours in our virtual machine), we can see that it performs the cloning of the Oracle home, applies the patches on the new home, validates the patches, runs the post patch scripts, and then skips all the remaining steps. It also collects target properties for the Oracle home in order to refresh the configurations in Enterprise Manager.

The **Review & Deploy** page now shows **Preparation Successful!**. The plan is now ready to be deployed.

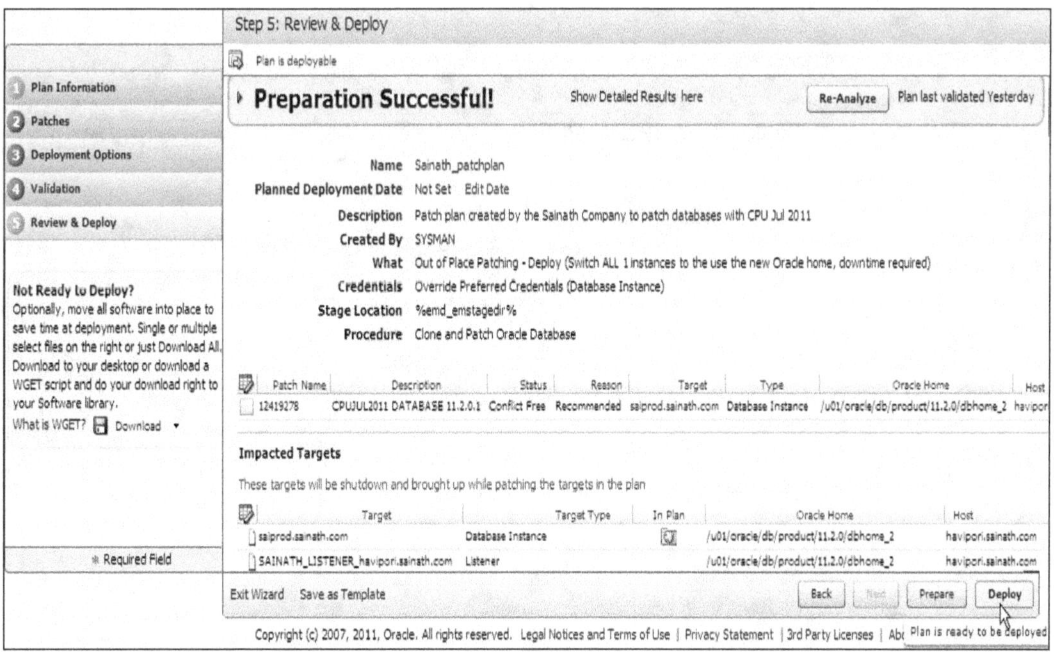

Click on the **Deploy** button. The status on the screen changes to **Deployment in Progress**. A job for deployment of the out-of-place patching starts.

At this time, downtime will be required since the database instances using the previous Oracle home will be shut down and switched across.

The deploy job successfully completes (after about 21 minutes in our virtual machine); we can see that it works iteratively over the list of hosts and Oracle homes in the patch plan. It starts a blackout for the database instances in the Oracle home (so that no alerts are raised), stops the instances, migrates them to the cloned Oracle home, starts them in upgrade mode, applies SQL scripts to patch the instance, applies post-SQL scripts, and then restarts the database in normal mode.

The deploy job applies other SQL scripts and recompiles invalid objects (except in the case of patch sets). It then migrates the listener from the previous Oracle home using the **Network Configuration Assistant** (**NetCA**), updates the **Target** properties, stops the blackout, and detaches the previous Oracle home. Finally, the configuration information of the cloned Oracle home is refreshed.

The **Review & Deploy** page of the patch plan now shows the status of **Deployment Successful!**, as can be seen in the following screenshot:

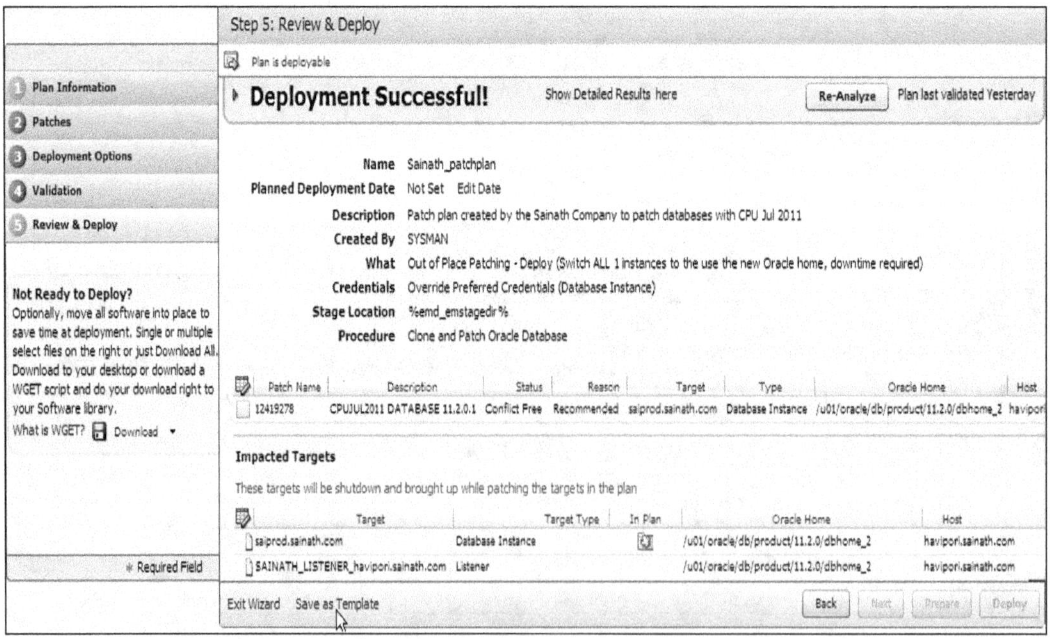

# Plan template

On the **Deployment Successful** page, it is possible to click on **Save as Template** at the bottom of the screen in order to save a patch plan as a **plan template**. The patch plan should be successfully analyzed and deployable, or successfully deployed, before it can be saved as a template.

The plan template, when thus created, will not have any targets included, and such a template can then be used to apply the successful patch plan to multiple other targets. Inside the plan template, the **Create Plan** button is used to create a new plan based on this template, and this can be done repeatedly for multiple targets.

Go to **Enterprise** | **Provisioning and Patching** | **Patches & Updates**; this screen displays a list of all the patch plans and plan templates that have been created. The successfully deployed `Sainath_patchplan` and the new patch plan template also shows up here.

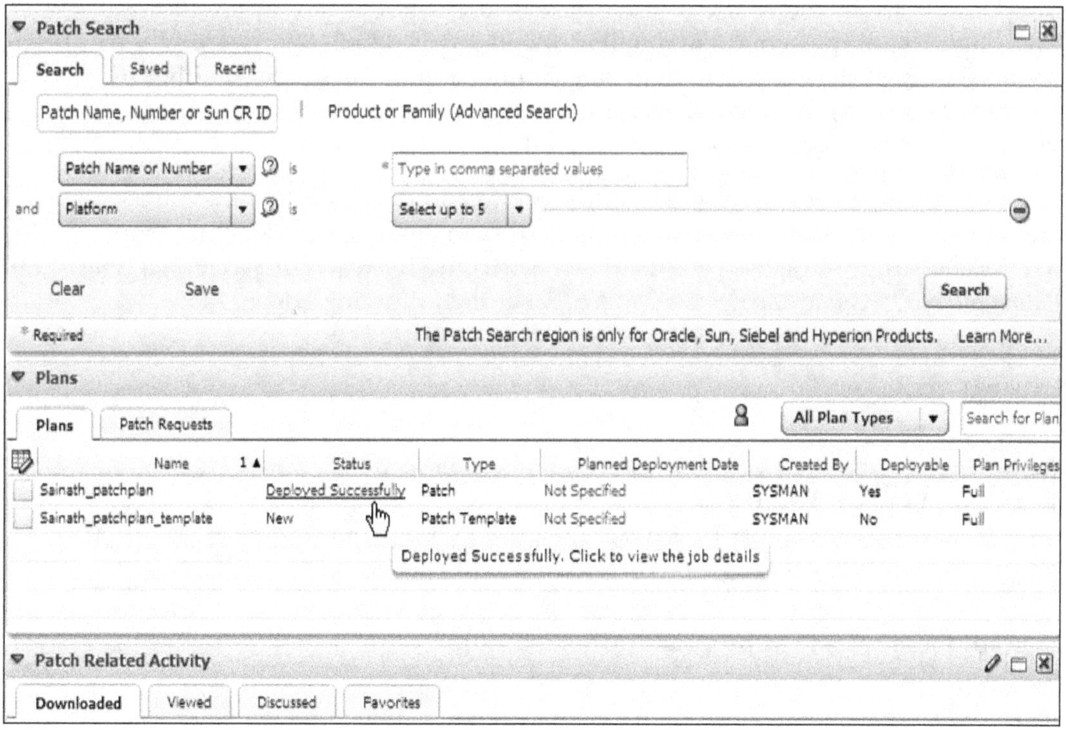

To see a list of the saved patches in the Software Library, go to **Enterprise | Provisioning and Patching | Saved Patches**. This brings up the following screen:

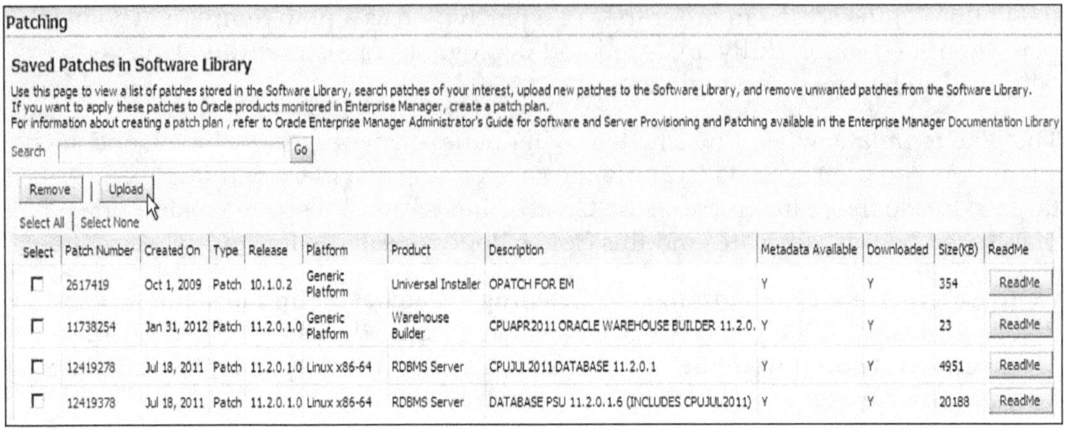


This page also allows you to manually upload patches to the Software Library. This scenario is mostly used when there is no connection to the Internet (either direct or via a proxy server) from the Enterprise Manager OMS servers, and consequently you need to download the patches manually.

For more details on setting up the offline mode and downloading the patch recommendations and latest patch information in the form of XML files from My Oracle Support, please refer to *Oracle Enterprise Manager Lifecycle Management Administrator's Guide 12c Release 2 (12.1.0.2)* at the following URL:

`http://docs.oracle.com/cd/E24628_01/em.121/e27046/pat_mosem_new.htm#BABBIEAI`

# Patching roles

The new version of Enterprise Manager Cloud Control 12*c* supplies out of the box administrator roles specifically for patching. These roles are `EM_PATCH_ADMINISTRATOR`, `EM_PATCH_DESIGNER`, and `EM_PATCH_OPERATOR`. You need to grant these roles to appropriate administrators.

Move to **Setup** | **Security** | **Roles**. On this page, search for the roles specifically meant for patching. The three roles appear as follows:

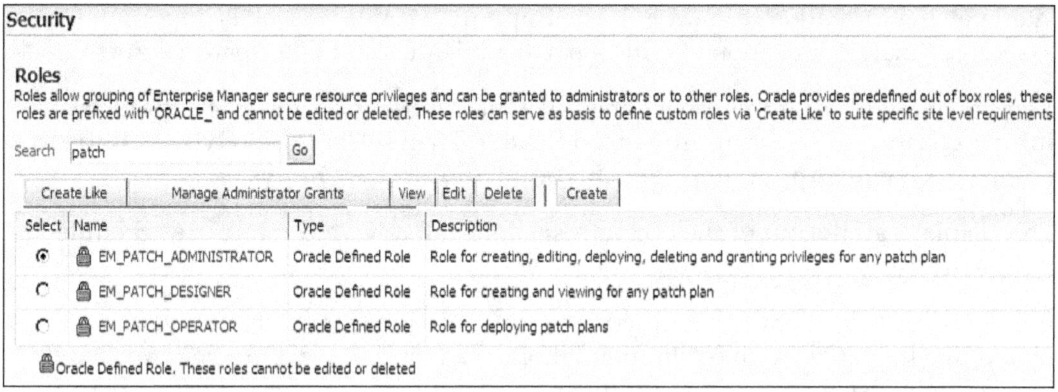


The **EM_PATCH_ADMINISTRATOR** role can create, edit, deploy, or delete any patch plan and can also grant privileges to other administrators after creating them. This role has full privileges on any patch plan or patch template in the Enterprise Manager system and maintains the patching infrastructure.

The **EM_PATCH_DESIGNER** role normally identifies patches to be used in the patching cycle across development, testing, and production. This role would be the one of the senior DBA in real life. The patch designer creates patch plans and plan templates, and grants privileges for these plan templates to the **EM_PATCH_OPERATOR** role.

As an example, the patch designer will select a set of recommended and other manually selected patches for an Oracle 11*g* database and create a patch plan. This role will then test the patching process in a development environment, and save the successfully analyzed or deployed patch plan as a plan template. The patch designer will then publish the Oracle 11*g* database patching plan template to the patch operator—probably the junior DBA or application DBA in real life.

Next, the patch operator creates new patch plans using the template (but cannot create a template), and adds a different list of targets, such as other Oracle 11*g* databases in the test, staging, or production environment. This role then schedules the deployment of the patches to all these environments—using the same template again and again.

# Refreshes

There is an out of the box Enterprise Manager job that runs every day and gets the latest patch information from **My Oracle Support (MOS)**. This job is important for you to receive timely notification of critical patch advisories and other patches from Oracle.

You can check to see if this job is scheduled and running by going to **Enterprise | Job | Activity** and selecting **Advanced Search**. Then select the job type as **Refresh From My Oracle Support** and set **Scheduled Start** to **Last 7 days**.

This displays all the out of the box refreshed jobs that have run and are scheduled for the future.

If there is a requirement to set up your own refresh job (for example if you would like the MOS patch recommendations for your databases to be refreshed immediately instead of waiting for the next scheduled running of the job), perform the following steps:

1. Go to **Enterprise | Job | Library**. On this page, select **Refresh from My Oracle Support** from the drop-down box of **Create Library Job**, and click on **Go**.
2. Give a new name to the job, such as `Sainath Refresh from MOS`. On the **Schedule** tab, set it to run as **One Time (Immediately)**. Click on **Save to Library**.
3. Search for the job in the job library, and click on **Submit**. The refresh job executes and completes in a few minutes. You now have up-to-date My Oracle Support patch recommendations for your Enterprise Manager targets.

My Oracle Support obviously needs to know about the configuration information of all your targets, in order to make the right recommendations. For example, it needs to know if your database is already patched up to a certain CPU and PSU, if not, it can recommend that CPU/PSU.

There is another recurring cycle of refresh that occurs overnight and performs the configuration inventory collection for all the targets managed and monitored by Enterprise Manager. If you wish, this collection can be forced manually in two ways.

Move to the appropriate Oracle home's target home page (after finding it in **Targets | All Targets** and sorting by **Target Type**). Go to **Oracle Home | Configuration | Last Collected**. On that page, go to **Actions | Refresh**. This submits a request to the Agent to re-collect the configuration inventory for that Oracle home.

The other method to force the collection is by using the `emctl` command in the Agent home on the actual Target host. First find the Oracle home Target name given by Enterprise Manager to our Oracle homes, and then use the Target name in the `runCollection` command as seen in the following code:

```
cd /u01/oracle/middleware/agent/agent_inst/bin
[oracle@havipori bin]$ ./emctl config agent listtargets

Oracle Enterprise Manager 12c Cloud Control 12.1.0.1.0
Copyright (c) 1996, 2011 Oracle Corporation.  All rights reserved.
[/EMGC_GCDomain/GCDomain/EMGC_OMS1/OCMRepeater, j2ee_application]
[/EMGC_GCDomain/GCDomain/EMGC_OMS1/emgc, j2ee_application]
[/EMGC_GCDomain/GCDomain/EMGC_OMS1/empbs, j2ee_application]
[/EMGC_GCDomain/GCDomain/EMGC_ADMINSERVER/mds-owsm, metadata_repository]
[/EMGC_GCDomain/GCDomain/EMGC_ADMINSERVER/mds-sysman_mds, metadata_
repository]
[/EMGC_GCDomain/instance1/ohs1, oracle_apache]
[/EMGC_GCDomain/GCDomain/EMGC_OMS1/oracle.security.apm(11.1.1.3.0),
oracle_apm]
[EM Management Beacon, oracle_beacon]
[emrepos.sainath.com, oracle_database]
[orcl, oracle_database]
[havipori.sainath.com:3872, oracle_emd]
[Management Services and Repository, oracle_emrep]
[OraDb11g_home1_1_havipori, oracle_home]
[WebLogicServer10_3_5_0_0_havipori, oracle_home]
[agent12g1_13_havipori, oracle_home]
[common12g1_24_havipori, oracle_home]
[jdk1_2_havipori, oracle_home]
[oms12g1_3_havipori, oracle_home]
[sbin12g1_14_havipori, oracle_home]
[webtier12g1_25_havipori, oracle_home]
[EMGC_GCDomain, oracle_ias_farm]
[LISTENER_havipori.sainath.com, oracle_listener]
[havipori.sainath.com:4889_Management_Service, oracle_oms]
```

```
[havipori.sainath.com:4889_Management_Service_CONSOLE, oracle_oms_
console]
[havipori.sainath.com:4889_Management_Service_PBS, oracle_oms_pbs]
[/EMGC_GCDomain/GCDomain, weblogic_domain]
[/EMGC_GCDomain/GCDomain/EMGC_ADMINSERVER, weblogic_j2eeserver]
[/EMGC_GCDomain/GCDomain/EMGC_OMS1, weblogic_j2eeserver]
[havipori.sainath.com_csa, oracle_csa_collector]
[havipori.sainath.com, host]
[SAINATH_LISTENER_havipori.sainath.com_1522, oracle_listener]
[saiprod.sainath.com, oracle_database]
[Orasidb11g_home1_2012_02_05_05_15_29_havipori, oracle_home]


[oracle@havipori bin]$ ./emctl control agent runCollection OraDb11g_
home1_1_havipori:oracle_home oracle_home_config

Oracle Enterprise Manager 12c Cloud Control 12.1.0.1.0
Copyright (c) 1996, 2011 Oracle Corporation.  All rights reserved.
---------------------------------------------------------------
EMD runCollection completed successfully

[oracle@havipori bin]$ ./emctl control agent runCollection Orasidb11g_
home1_2012_02_05_05_15_29_havipori:oracle_home oracle_home_config

Oracle Enterprise Manager 12c Cloud Control 12.1.0.1.0
Copyright (c) 1996, 2011 Oracle Corporation.  All rights reserved.
---------------------------------------------------------------
EMD runCollection completed successfully
```

# Other patching procedures

There are a number of other deployment procedures available for patching. Go to **Enterprise** | **Provisioning and Patching** | **Procedure Library** and search for `patch` in the text fields. This brings up the list of procedures as seen in the following screenshot:

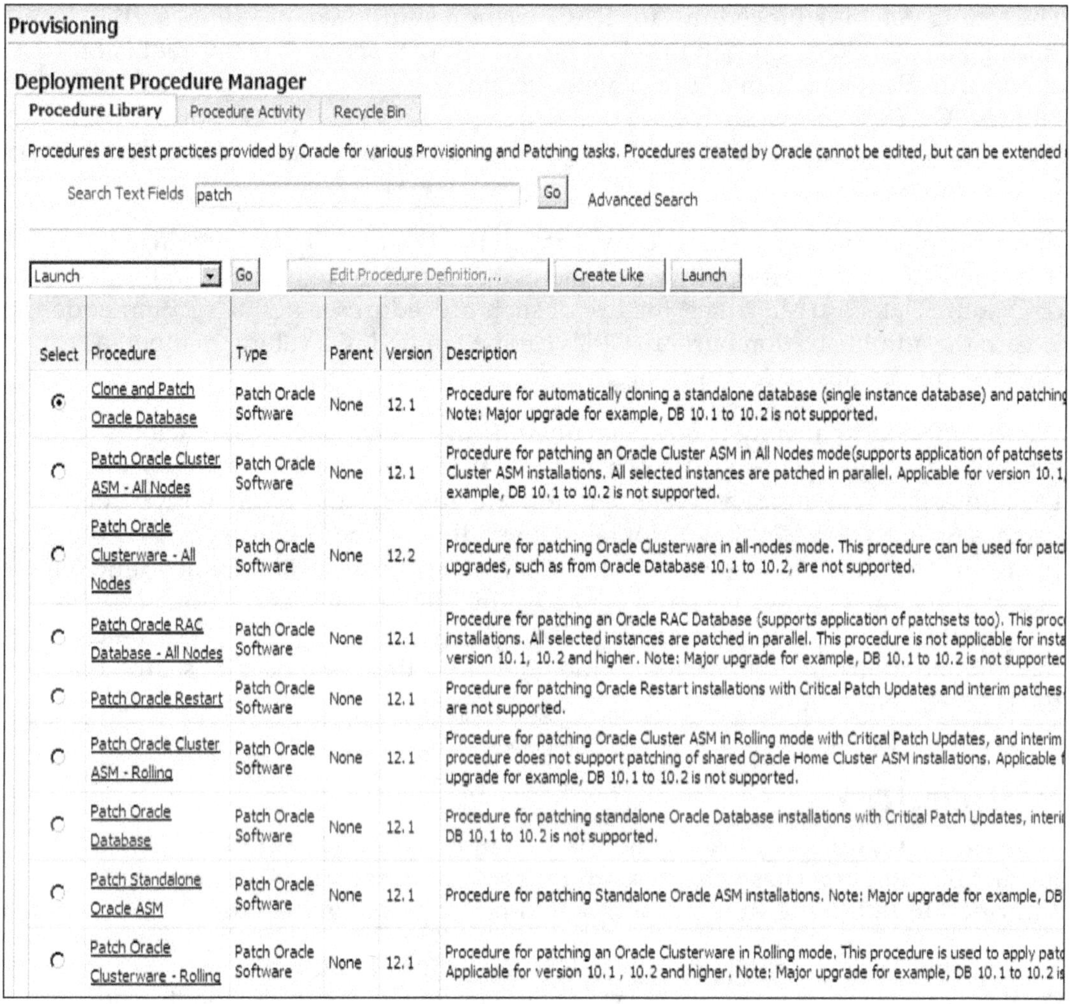


In the case of out-of-place patching, the **Clone and Patch Oracle Database** procedure will be used. There are other procedures available to perform actions, such as **Patch Oracle Database** or **Patch Oracle Home** (in place without cloning the home), **Patch Standalone Oracle ASM**, Patch Oracle Clusterware in either a rolling fashion (one node at a time) or all nodes at once, Patch Oracle Cluster ASM or Oracle RAC Database in a likewise manner, and Patch Application Server.

The rolling patching procedures for RAC perform shutdown, patching, and startup across all the nodes in the cluster in a rolling manner. The pre-requisite checks include detailed checks for cluster health, so as to avoid unexpected failures. The SQL scripts such as `catbundle.sql` (the patching SQL) or `utlrp.sql` (the recompile invalid objects in SQL) are executed on one node at the end of the patching procedure.

This rolling patching procedure is very useful for automating the patching of multiple RAC nodes, especially when there are more than two nodes. In the case of Exadata Database Machines, the use of such procedures is highly recommended to ease the administration burden. CPUs can be applied in a rolling manner, as can clusterware patches or ASM patches.

WebLogic Server patching is now also possible in Enterprise Manager Cloud Control 12*c*. This requires a different license—the WebLogic Server Management Pack Enterprise Edition. The WebLogic administrator needs to search MOS for patches to apply to a WebLogic domain, depending on the WLS version and the platform. The patching wizard in Enterprise Manager checks for conflicts, and allows you to apply the patches in a parallel or a rolling manner across the domain. This can greatly automate the patching of WebLogic domains. However, WLS patch recommendations are not possible at the time of writing. You need to search for the WLS patches yourself.

# Reporting

A rich set of reports is available, such as an Applied Patches Report, and a Target Patchability Report. These are accessed by going to **Enterprise** | **Reports** | **Information Publisher Reports**, and searching for `patch` in the title.

BI Publisher Enterprise Reports can also be used, but BI Publisher needs to be configured for use with Enterprise Manager. For more information on the setup required, refer to the *Oracle Enterprise Manager Cloud Control Advanced Installation and Configuration Guide 12c Release 2 (12.1.0.2)* at the following URL:

`http://docs.oracle.com/cd/E24628_01/install.121/e24089/install_em_bip.htm`

# Summary

Enterprise Manager Cloud Control 12*c* allows automation of the tedious patching procedure used in many organizations today, to patch their Oracle databases and servers. This is achieved via the Database Lifecycle Management Pack, which is one of the main licensable packs of Enterprise Manager.

Sophisticated Deployment Procedures are provided out of the box to fulfill many different types of patching tasks, and this helps you to achieve mass patching of multiple targets with multiple patches in a fully automated manner, thus making tremendous savings in administrative time and effort. Some companies have estimated savings of up to 98 percent in patching tasks in their data centers. Different types of patches can be applied in this manner, including CPUs, PSUs, Patch sets and other one-off patches. Different versions of databases are supported, such as 9*i*, 10*g* and 11*g*. For the first time, the upgrade of single-instance databases is also possible via Enterprise Manager Cloud Control 12*c*.

There is full integration of the patching capabilities of Enterprise Manager with My Oracle Support (MOS). The support site retains the configuration of all the components managed by Enterprise Manager inside the company. Since the current version and patch information of the components is known, My Oracle Support is able to provide appropriate patch recommendations for many targets, including the latest security fixes. This ensures that the company is up to date with regards to security protection.

A full division of roles is available, such as Patch Administrator, Designer, and Operator. It is possible to take the My Oracle Support recommendations, select patches for targets, put them into a patch plan, deploy the patch plan and then create a plan template from it. The template can then be published to any operator who can then create their own patch plans for other targets. In this way patching can be tested, verified, and then pushed to production.

In all, Enterprise Manager Cloud Control 12*c* offers valuable automation methods for Mass Patching, allowing Administrators to ensure that their systems have the latest security patches, and enabling them to control the application of patches on development, test, and production servers from the centralized location of the Software Library.

In the next chapter, we will take a look at the Database Change Management capabilities of Enterprise Manager Cloud Control 12*c* that enable you to create Baselines of your database Metadata, compare Schemas and databases, and perform Schema Synchronizations.

# 7

# Ease the Chaos with Change Management

In a typical data center, there may be many hundreds or even thousands of applications and projects, each with its own database schema and its own development lifecycle. A project's application is typically developed over a set period of time on a development database and application servers that may even be outside the data center, if the development is outsourced. The developers complete the coding of the application and the associated database schema, and send over the scripts to create the schema and all the schema objects. This also includes creating the application's users in the database and the granting of database roles and privileges to these users, as well as object-level privileges on every application object in the database.

The data center's DBA receives the database scripts and is responsible for reviewing the scripts to ensure that they comply with the internal database's standards, for example not granting excessive database privileges. If the scripts pass the review, the DBA may then apply the scripts to a development instance to ensure that they execute as designed. If changes are required, the DBA sends the scripts back to the development team to make changes.

Now the scripts can be applied on a test database, the results verified by the DBA, and the application team will then be asked to perform their testing against the test system. Once application testing has been completed and signed off, the project team will schedule a change for the DBA to implement these changes in the production environment.

So far so good. But now things may not work right. The same application that was tested successfully a few days ago seems to have serious issues in production. The application team has no idea what has happened, and falls back on the DBA to fix the issue. Since the application is now in production, any downtime is a loss in revenue and the pressure is on the DBA, who first of all needs to compare the changes across the development lifecycle. What is the difference between production and test databases? What tables, columns, or other database objects are different? Which users, roles, and privileges are different?

To find out about these things, the DBA needs to query the data dictionary of the different databases, get a listing of the schema structure and security setup, and then make a visual comparison to find the differences. This can quickly become a nightmare, especially if there are hundreds or thousands of application schemas, and the development teams keep coming up with new application versions along with schema changes every few months. The DBA has no choice but to track these changes manually, and this is normally done by placing the application database scripts in subdirectories on the DBA's PC, which only the DBA can access.

In such a situation, database changes can no longer be controlled and all changes deteriorate to an ad hoc manner where changes are applied on the fly, and no history is maintained. At this point in time, if the company's auditors request the past history of all database schema changes, the DBA management will find it impossible to give the company's auditors the information they require.

# Change management

The **Database Lifecycle Management** (**DBLM**) Pack of Oracle Enterprise Manager Cloud Control 12*c* gives you a powerful change management capability, in addition to the Configuration Management, Security Compliance, Provisioning and Patch Automation capabilities we have seen so far.

Using Enterprise Manager, the DBA can easily compare different databases or schemas in the same database. Users, roles, and privileges can be compared. Dictionary definitions can be captured and stored in the Enterprise Manager repository as baselines, and these can also be used in comparisons. For example, you can compare a stored baseline of a production database as it existed a week ago with the actual current database. The baselines can also be versioned to retain the history of changes. Baselines can also be exported from one Enterprise Manager environment to another, beginning from Version 11*g* of Enterprise Manager.

Differences discovered between two database schemas can then be propagated between the schemas—such as comparing a test and production database, finding the latest schema changes that were applied on the test, and propagating these changes to production. Scripts are generated automatically by the change management capability and applied by the Enterprise Manager job system.

Besides the Enterprise Manager interface, it is also possible to use **Oracle SQL Developer** (a free product from Oracle for developers), to access some of the change management capabilities such as Database Diff from Version 3.1 onwards. However, note that Oracle SQL Developer can only compare two schemas at a time, and that only in real time. It does not have the ability to save prior schema definition captures in a baseline, or a multi-schema comparison. For the advanced capabilities of change management, you need to use Enterprise Manager Cloud Control 12*c* and the Database Lifecycle Management Pack license. If you just want the basic Diff capability, you can use it for free in Oracle SQL Developer 3.1 onwards.

Developers can use change plans to capture the development changes and send them to the DBA for approval and propagation to test and production, and this is a further automation of change management seen in the new version of Enterprise Manager Cloud Control 12*c*.

Finally, another great new feature is that data comparisons can now be done and this is specifically meant for smaller-sized reference tables or seed data.

We will now have a look at these useful features.

# Schema comparison

Our scenario is that we have a development database that is named `saidev.sainath.com`. The development team works on this database and creates new applications. They have recently created a human resources application and have placed the required database objects for this application in the HR schema.

In the next phase of the development lifecycle, functional and load testing of the application needs to be performed by the application team, normally in conjunction with the test team. For this purpose, a test database has been created, which is `saitest.sainath.com`. The development schema and all its objects (only the structure or metadata) will need to be transferred over to the test database. We will now see the steps required to achieve this:

First, move to the `saidev` database in Enterprise Manager Cloud Control 12*c*. From the database menu, select **Schema** | **Change Management** | **Schema Comparisons**.

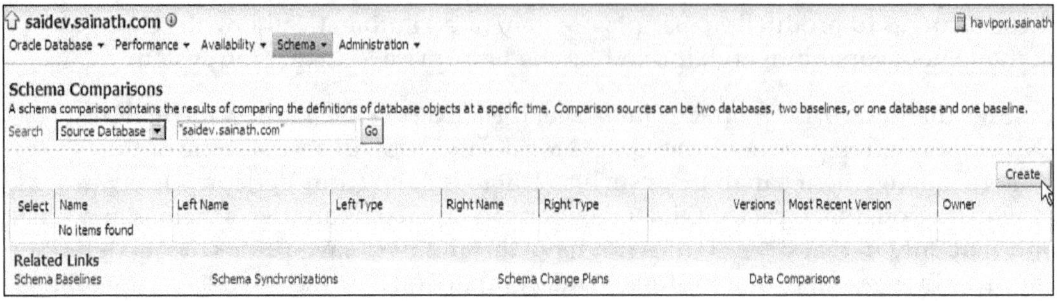

In the **Schema Comparisons** page that appears, there are no saved **Comparisons**. Click on **Create** in order to create a new **Comparison**.

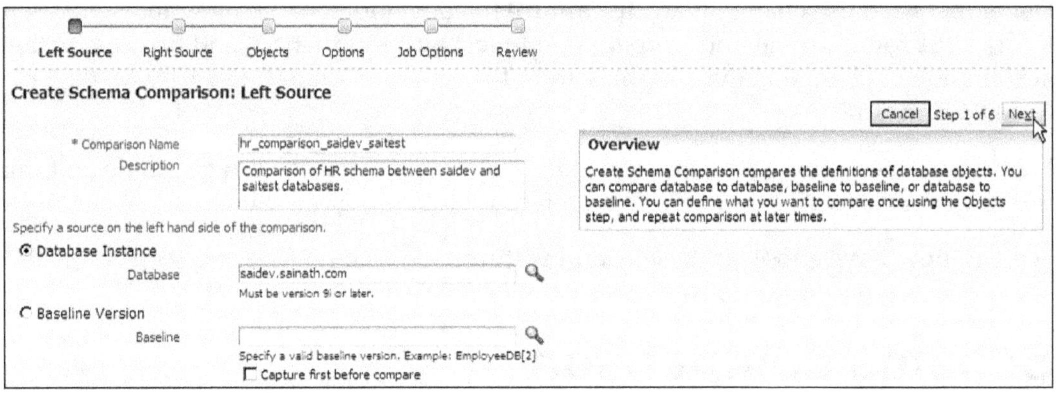

Give a name to the **Comparison** object. We are going to compare the HR schema in the **saidev** and **saitest** databases.

First specify the source for the left side of the comparison. The source can be of a **Database Instance** (9*i* or higher) type or a **Baseline Version** type. A baseline is simply a captured schema definition. If you want, you can capture the baseline first before the comparison by ticking the box provided. (Note that alternatively, you can create a schema baseline by selecting **Schema** | **Change Management** | **Schema Baselines**).

We specify the `saidev` database. Click on **Next** to continue.

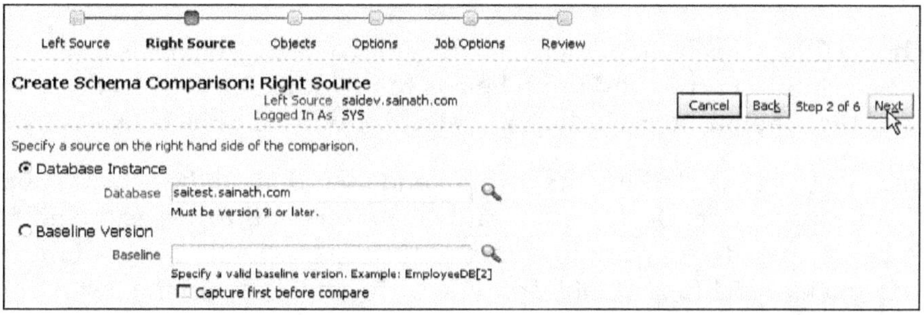

In the same way, specify the source for the right side of the comparison. Either a database instance or a baseline version can be specified as before.

We specify the `saitest` database to be used for the comparison, and then click on **Next**.

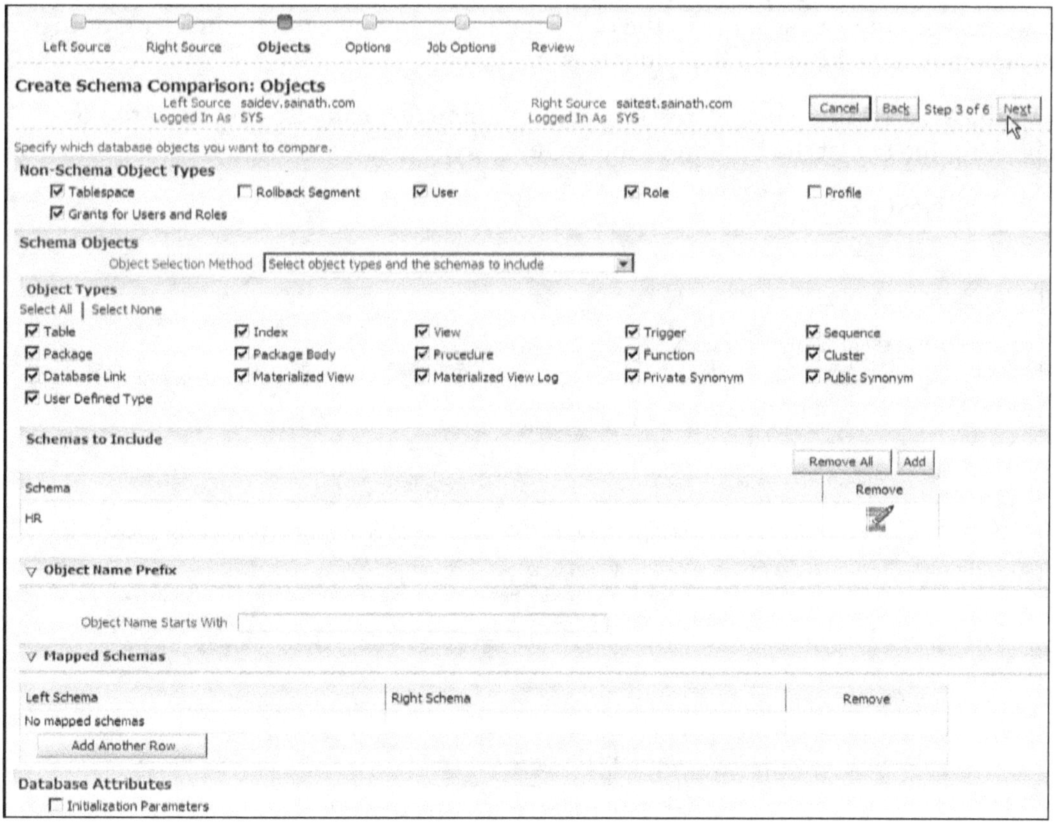

On the **Objects** page that appears, select the **Non-Schema Objects** option and the **Schema Objects** option that you wish to include in the comparison.

In the **Schema Objects** selection, there is a drop-down box, which has three options—**Select object types and the schemas to include**, **Select object types to include and the schemas to exclude**, and **Select individual objects from any schema**.

In our case, we have selected the first option and included all the schema objects, and selected **Tablespace**, **User**, **Role**, and **Grants for Users and Roles** as the non-schema objects to be compared. We want to compare tablespaces so that we can find out if the HR schema uses a different tablespace, which is not there in the test database.

The **HR** schema is selected as a schema to include in the comparison.

It is also possible to select an **Object Name Prefix** string to be used in the comparison. For example, you can compare all objects beginning with "`sales_`".

You can also use a mapping of schemas in the comparison if the schemas to be compared do not have the same name; for example, if you want to compare the `HR1` schema with the `HR2` schema in the other database. In this way, multiple mappings of schemas can be used in the comparison.

**Database Attributes** such as **Initialization Parameters** can also be compared by checking the box at the bottom of the page.

Click on **Next** to continue.

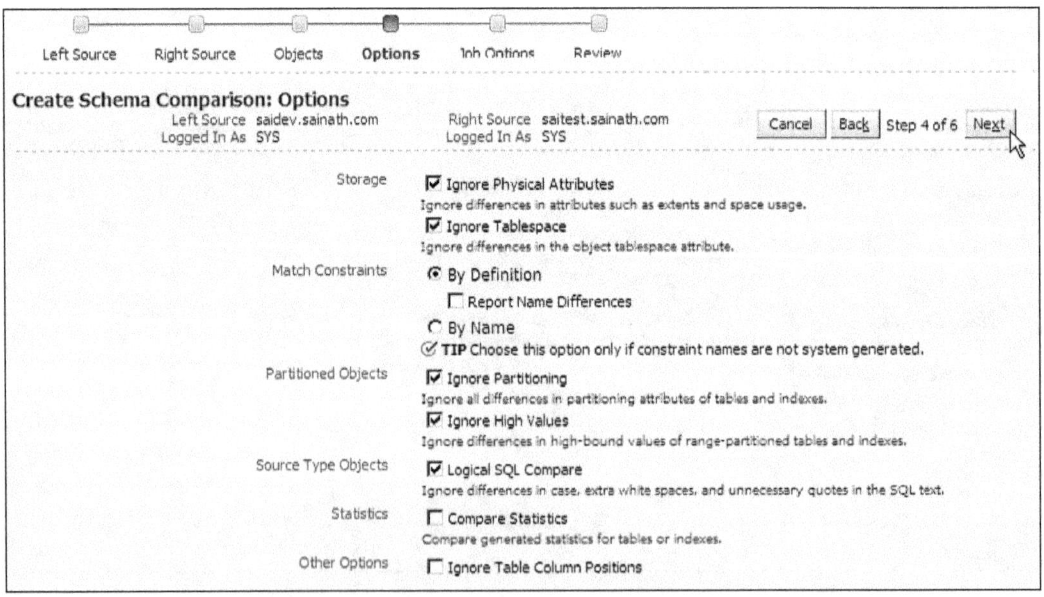

In the **Options** page that appears, you can select several options to control the comparison process. The default options that come up are normally valid; for example, you would normally ignore partitioning in the comparison, and you would not want case differences or whitespaces in the SQL text of an object to interfere with the comparison. Also, you would like to ignore physical attribute differences such as number of extents.

So keep all the defaults on this page and click on the **Next** button.

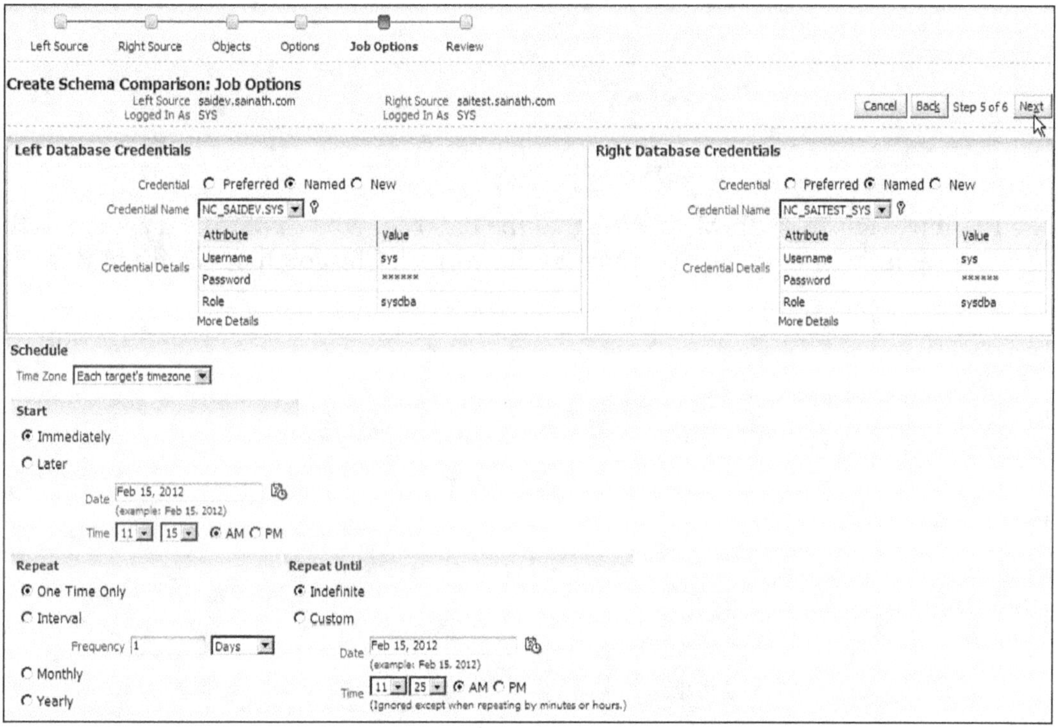


On the **Job Options** page, specify the **Credentials** details for both the databases that are being compared. You can then specify the **Schedule** details for the job, either immediately or at a future time, or put it on a recurring schedule. This makes it possible to perform scheduled comparisons and find out what is different between the two databases or schemas.

Click on the **Next** button to continue.

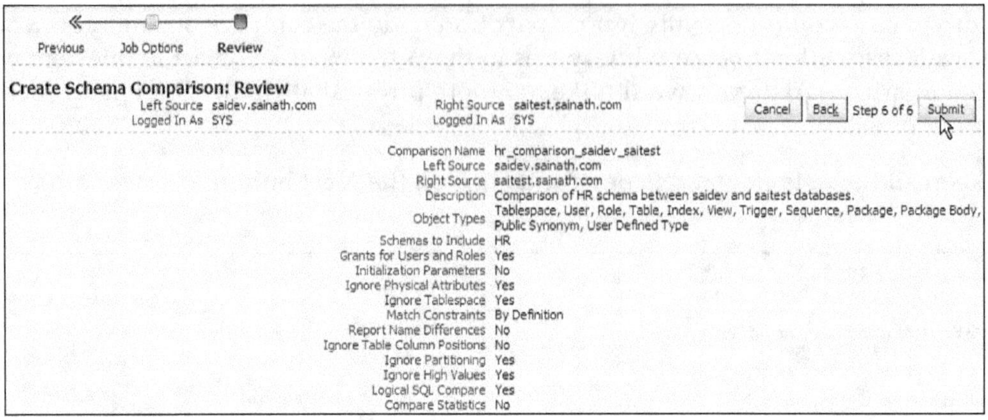


The **Review** page appears. Make sure that the databases to be compared are correctly specified, and the comparison parameters are correct. Click on the **Submit** button.

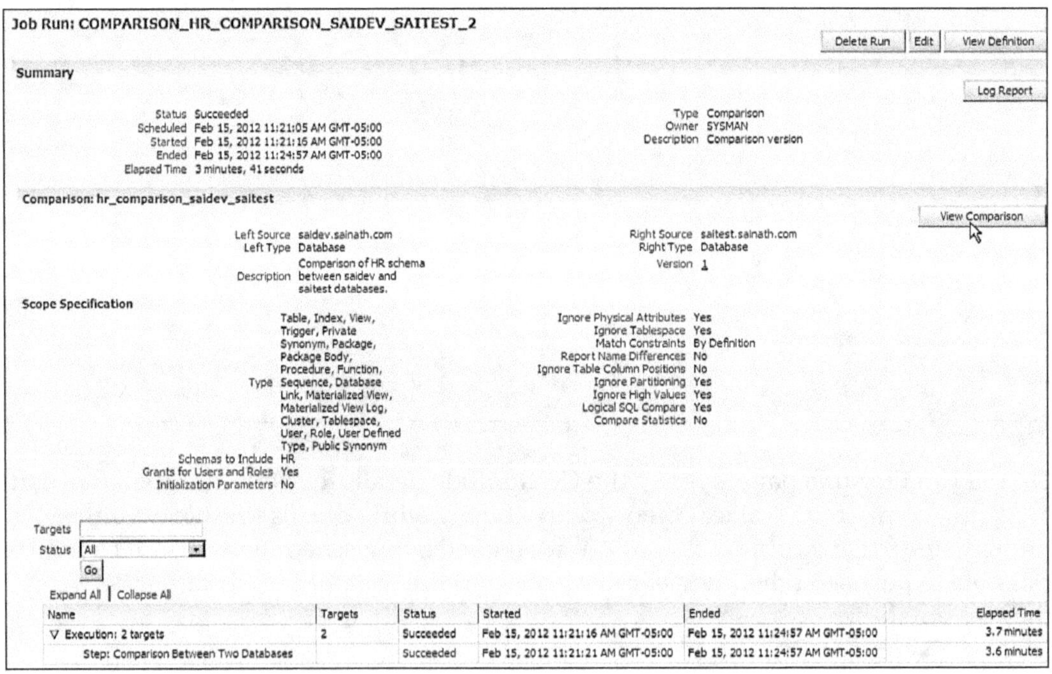

The comparison job starts and completes within a few minutes. You can click on **View Comparison** to view the results at this stage.

Alternatively, you can select **Schema** | **Change Management** | **Schema Comparisons**. The comparison you have just completed appears in the list. Click on the **View** button.

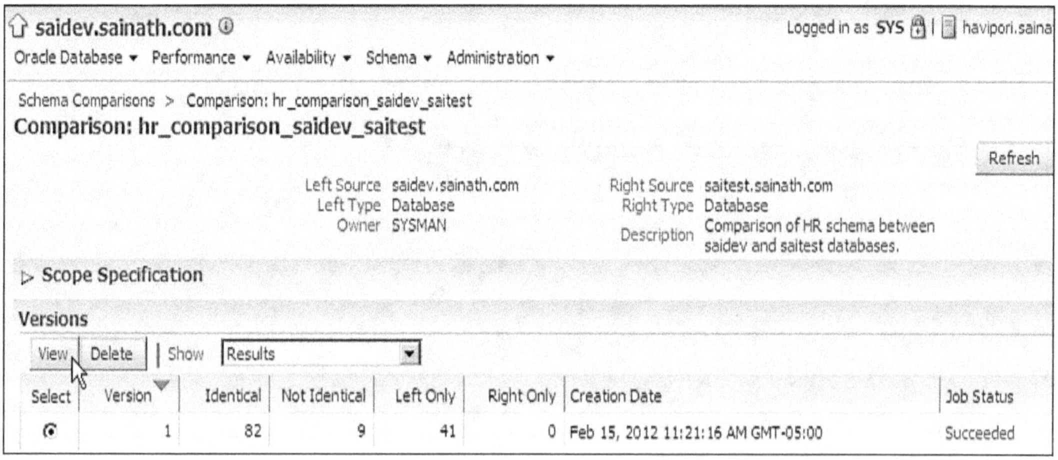


A summary of the comparison results is seen. There are **82 Identical** objects, **9 Not Identical** (different) objects, and **41** objects that are only found in the `saidev` database.

There are no objects that are found only in the `saitest` database. This gives a summary of how different the databases are with respect to the HR schema and the other non-schema objects you selected for the comparison.

The **Show** drop-down box can be changed to include ignored results. By default, ignored results will not be seen. Click on the **View** button.

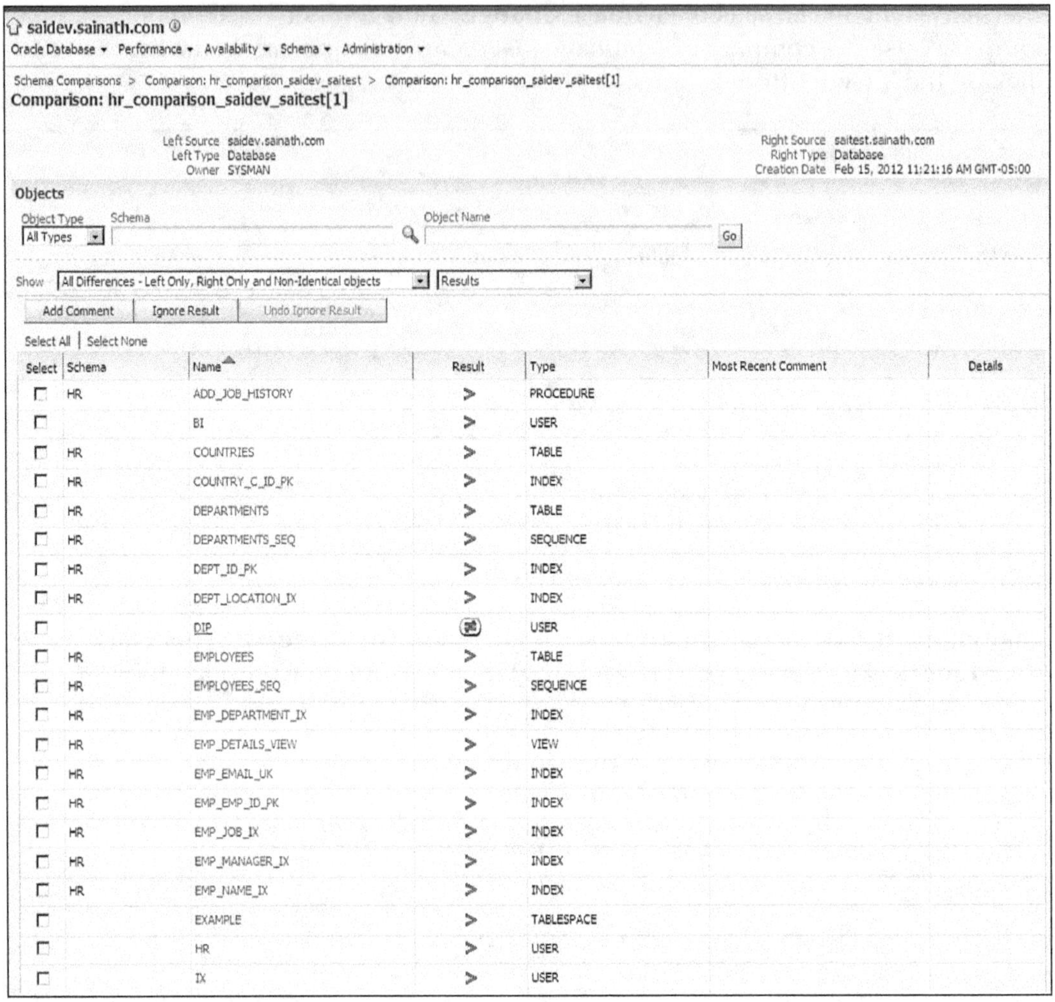

The detailed comparison page now appears. You can choose from the drop-down box to show all the objects within the comparison scope, or non-identical objects that are present in both sources but with attributes that are not identical. You can also select to view **Left Only Objects** that are present only in the left source, or **Right Only Objects** that are present only in the right source, or identical objects that are present in both sources and have identical attributes. By default, all different objects are displayed, including left only and right only objects and non-identical objects.

We can see from this that there are a number of HR schema objects that have been created in the `saidev` database but are not present in the `saitest` database. Even the **USER** type called **HR** and **TABLESPACE** called **EXAMPLE** are not present in the latter.

# Schema Change Plan

Now that we know the differences between the two databases, the next step is to create a schema Change Plan. This is a new feature in Enterprise Manager Cloud Control 12*c*.

Using change plans, the developers can group together some or all of their database object changes, and package them for the DBA. Change plans can be created from comparisons that have found differences. They can also be created from ad hoc changes, or from development tools such as Oracle SQL Developer.

In a normal workflow process, the developer creates a Change Plan and submits it to the DBA, who is then able to review the Change Plan and apply it if the changes are acceptable. This can be done to multiple targets such as the test database, staging database, or production.

Internally, a Change Plan consists of change requests for single or multiple database objects. The change requests are for changes to the **metadata**, the dictionary definition of the objects. The change requests can specify the addition or deletion of columns, or the modification of other attributes. They may also include the creation of new database objects (for example, tables or indexes), or the deletion of database objects.

At the time of deployment of a Change Plan, an analysis is performed on the change with respect to the database it is being deployed to. Based on this analysis, a PL/SQL script is generated, which will perform the actual change.

Let us now see how to create a schema Change Plan. Go to **Schema** | **Change Management** | **Schema Change Plans**. Click on the **Create** button.

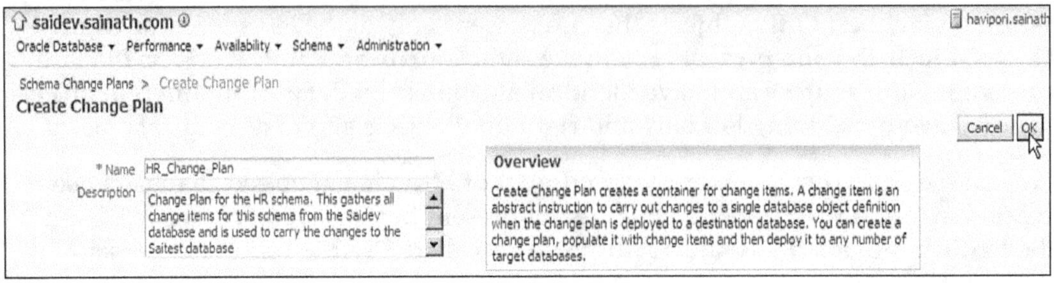


Name the Change Plan on this page. This gathers all change items for this HR schema from the `saidev` database and is used to carry the changes to the `saitest` database.

Click on **OK**. On the next page, select **Create from Comparison**.

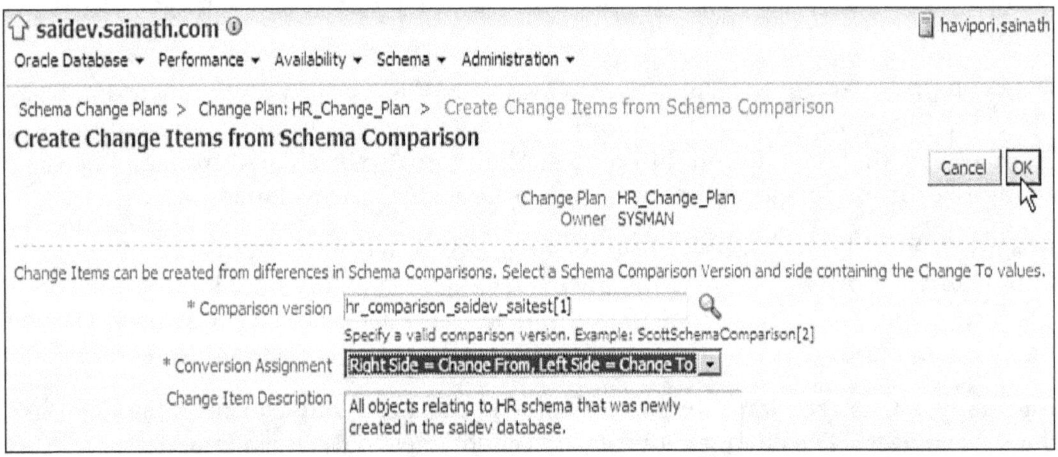


On the **Create Change Items from Schema Comparison** page, first select the **Comparison version** instance to be used. We selected the comparison that was recently created between the HR schema of the `saidev` and `saitest` databases.

Next, you need to select the correct **Conversion Assignment** option. If you select the default option, which is **Left Side = Change From, Right Side = Change To**, then all the HR objects in the `saidev` database will be dropped since there are no such objects in the `saitest` database.

This is not what we want, so select **Right Side = Change From, Left Side = Change To** from the drop-down box. This is the right choice if you want to create the HR objects in the `saitest` database. Click on the **OK** button to continue.

It creates the change items from the comparison in a few seconds. When the creation succeeds, the **Change Items** list is displayed.

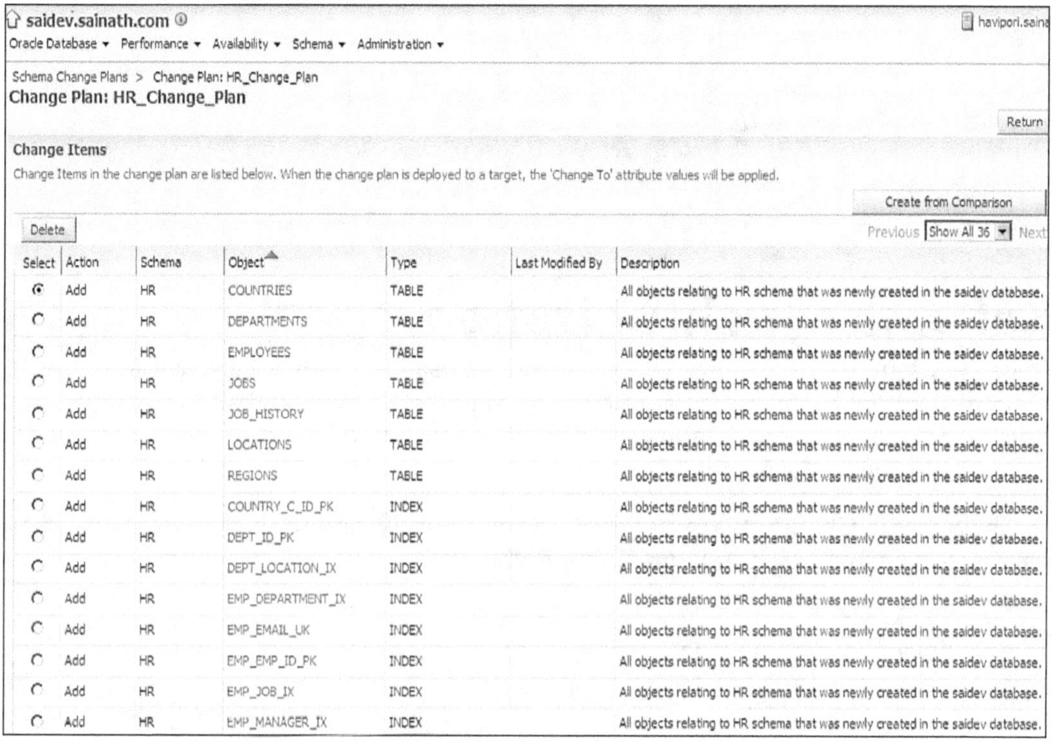

The list that comes up initially includes a number of change items, which we decide not to implement, so they have been deleted by us from the list. This is done one at a time by using the **Delete** button.

The deleted change items include additions of the other missing schemas such as **OE**, **PM**, and **BI** among others (these appear in the list because we initially compared all the schemas).

The deleted items also include modifications to other tablespaces, which are different across the two databases. We are only interested in the **EXAMPLE** tablespace, the **HR** user, and all the **HR** objects. These are the change items we will use for the script generation.

Select **Return**; this brings you back to the **Schema Change Plans** page as shown in the following screenshot:

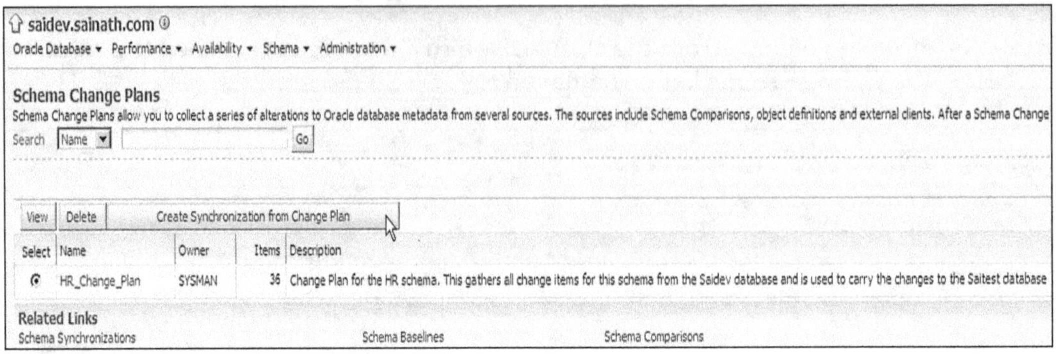


# Schema synchronization

Once the Change Plan has been created, we can use it to perform a schema synchronization. In this process, Enterprise Manager Cloud Control 12*c* will synchronize a source and destination schema so that all the changes in the source will be reflected in the destination.

On the **Schema Change Plans** page, select the Change Plan we just created and click on **Create Synchronization from Change Plan**.

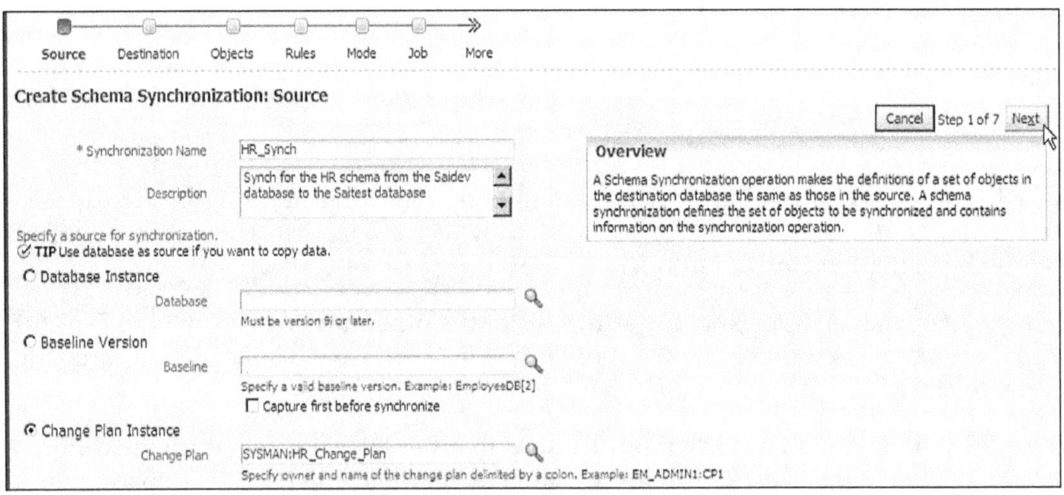

The wizard to perform schema synchronization now starts.

In the first step, give a name to the synchronization and then select the **Source** instance, which can be either a database instance, a baseline version, or a Change Plan instance.

In our case we have selected the **HR** Change Plan that was just created.

Click on **Next** to continue.

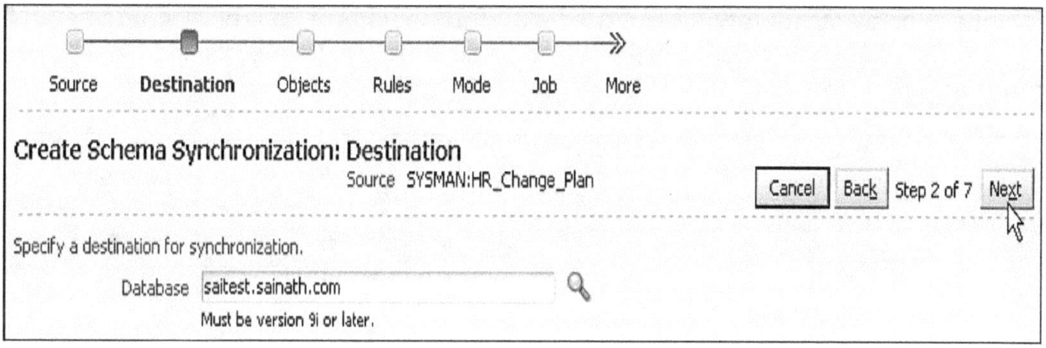


The next step requires you to specify the **Destination** database for the synchronization. This needs to be a database.

Select the **saitest** database and move to the **Next** step.

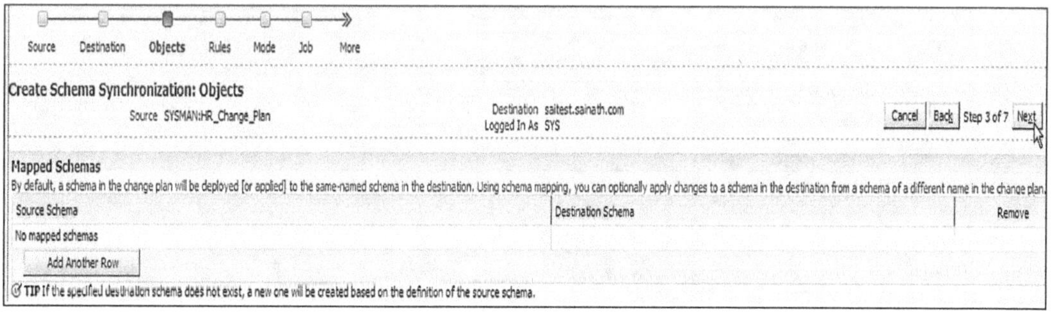

In this step, you can map one or more schemas from one database to the other. This mapping is used if the schema names are not the same in the two databases.

We do not need to specify anything since we want the schema name to be the same. Move to the next step.

# Synchronization rules and mode

On the **Synchronization Rules** page, you need to specify various rules about how the synchronization will be performed. You can choose to ignore storage characteristics such as extents, or the tablespaces used by the objects, or partitioning differences.

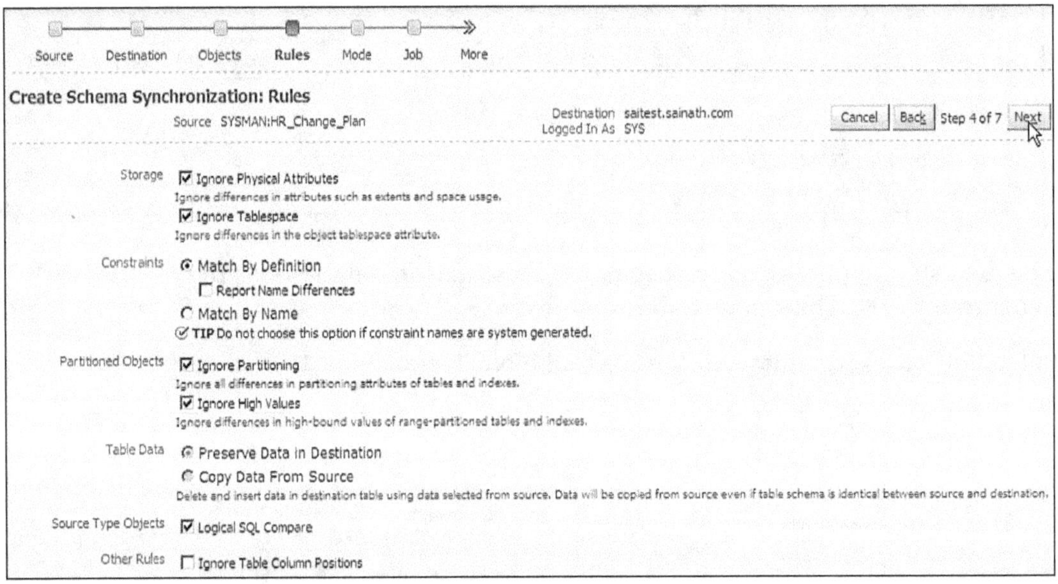

Note that table data will be preserved in the destination in this case. Click on **Next** to continue.

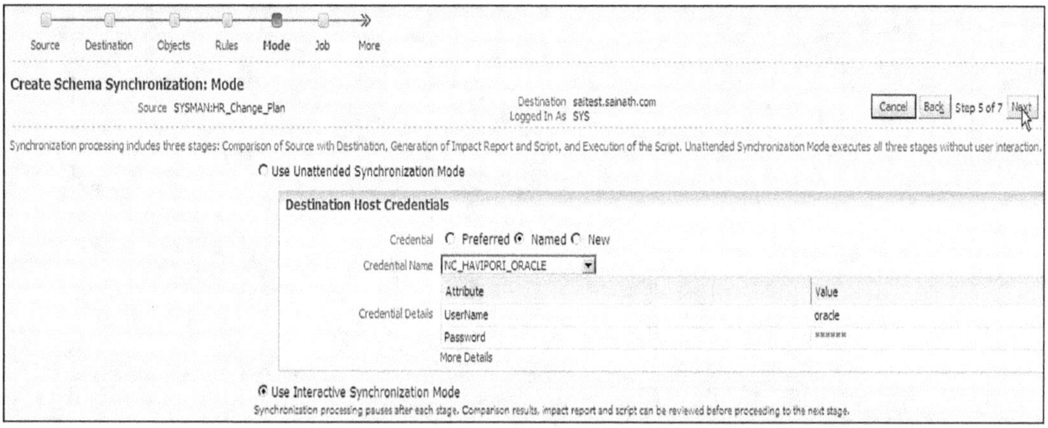


You can now select the synchronization mode to use. This can either be **Unattended Synchronization Mode**, or **Interactive Synchronization Mode**.

In the latter mode, the processing pauses after each stage and you can review the comparison results, impact report, and script.

We select this mode, and proceed to the next step.

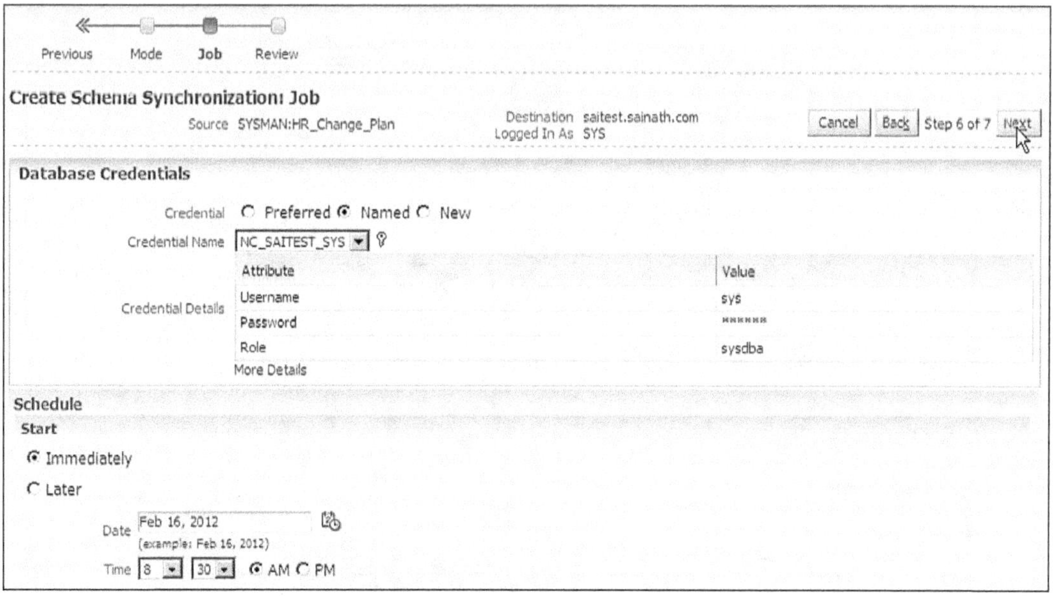

Now, select the credentials for the `saitest` database, and schedule the job to run immediately. Click on the **Next** button to continue.

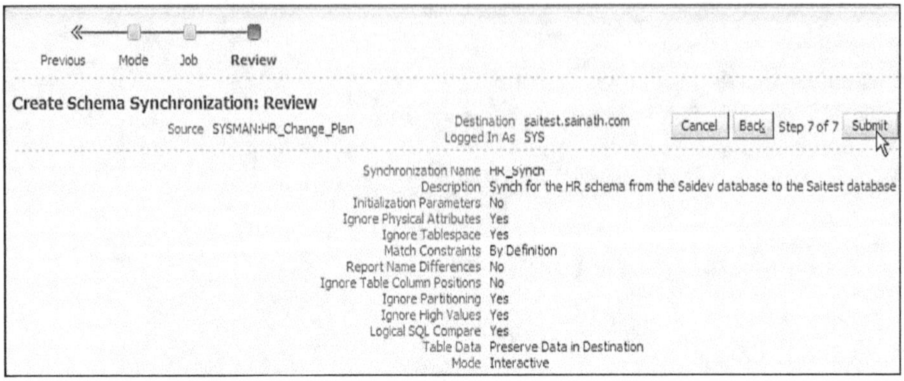

The **Review** screen appears for the synchronization.

Verify that all the details are correct, and click on **Submit**. The job is submitted.

Click on **View Job Details** and watch the progress of the job until it completes successfully.

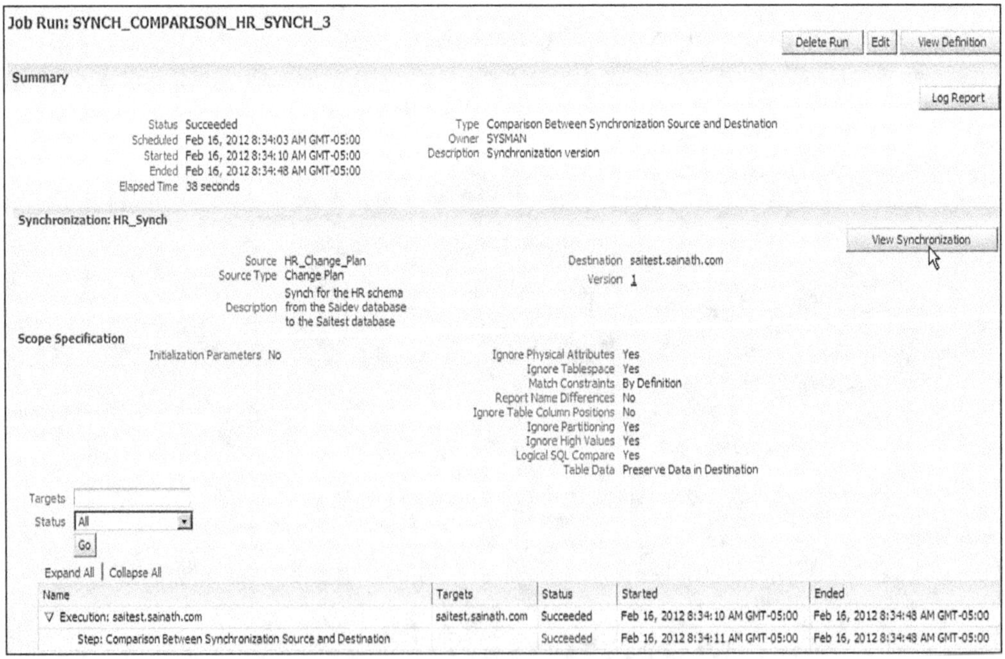

Click on the **View Synchronization** button to see the results.

# Synchronization results

The first thing you notice on the **View Synchronization** page is that there are three tabs—**Objects**, **Impact Report**, and **Script**. These are the three stages of the process.

Right now, the last two stages are grayed out as can be seen in the following screenshot:

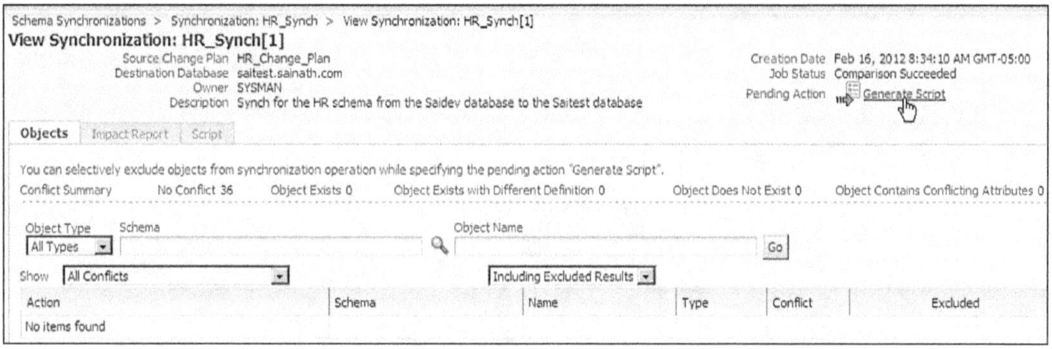


The first tab of **Objects** shows **Conflict Summary**, and tells you if there are any objects with conflicts, such as existing objects, objects with a different definition, or objects with conflicting attributes.

You can exclude any such objects from the synchronization if you wish. In our case, there are **36** objects with a **No Conflict** status so we can safely proceed.

The next thing to do is to click on **Generate Script**.

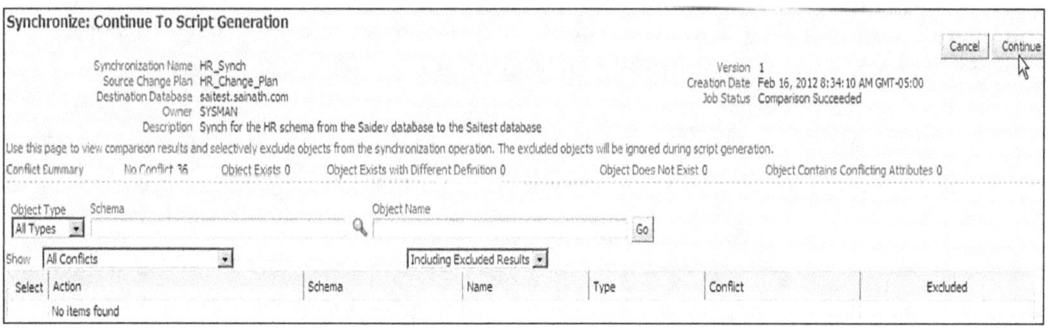


You are given a second look at the conflicting objects to exclude. Click on **Continue**.

On the next page, enter the credentials for the `saitest` database, schedule the job to run immediately, and click on **Submit**. This will start the job for the script generation.

After a few minutes, the job fails. When you drill down on the failed steps, it will ask you to see the **Impact Report** tab. So move back to the **View Synchronization** page, and click on the **Impact Report** tab.

The **Impact Report** tab appears as follows:

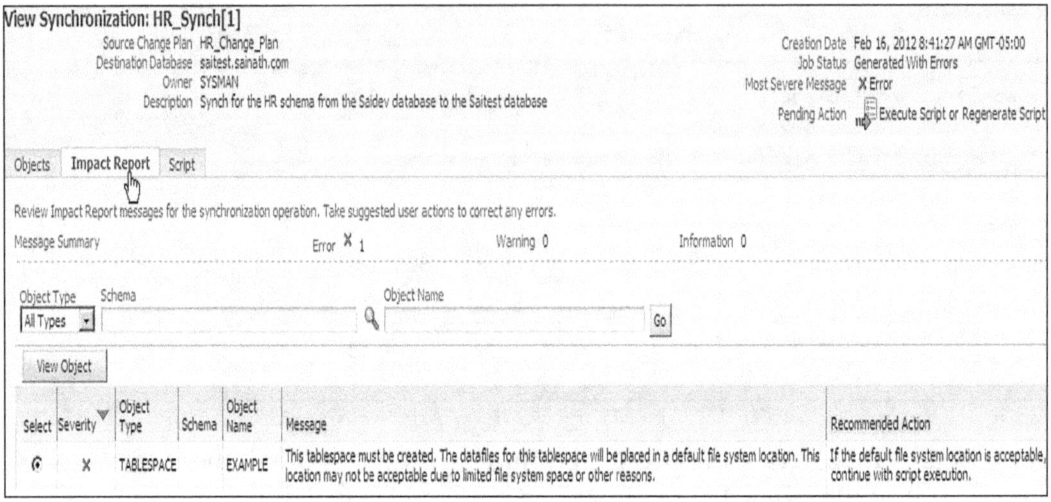

Any possible errors that can happen during the synchronization will be listed along with an explanation message and recommended action.

In our case, an error is shown regarding the **EXAMPLE** tablespace. **Impact Report** warns you that a default file location will be used for the tablespace files (normally this is the `DBS` directory under the Oracle home). To change the file location, you will need to create the tablespace manually using the generated SQL or PL/SQL (in the next tab), or using your own SQL command.

We decide to accept the default location (this is the **Recommended Action** column shown on the screen) and ignore this error, continuing with script execution. Now, move to the **Script** tab.

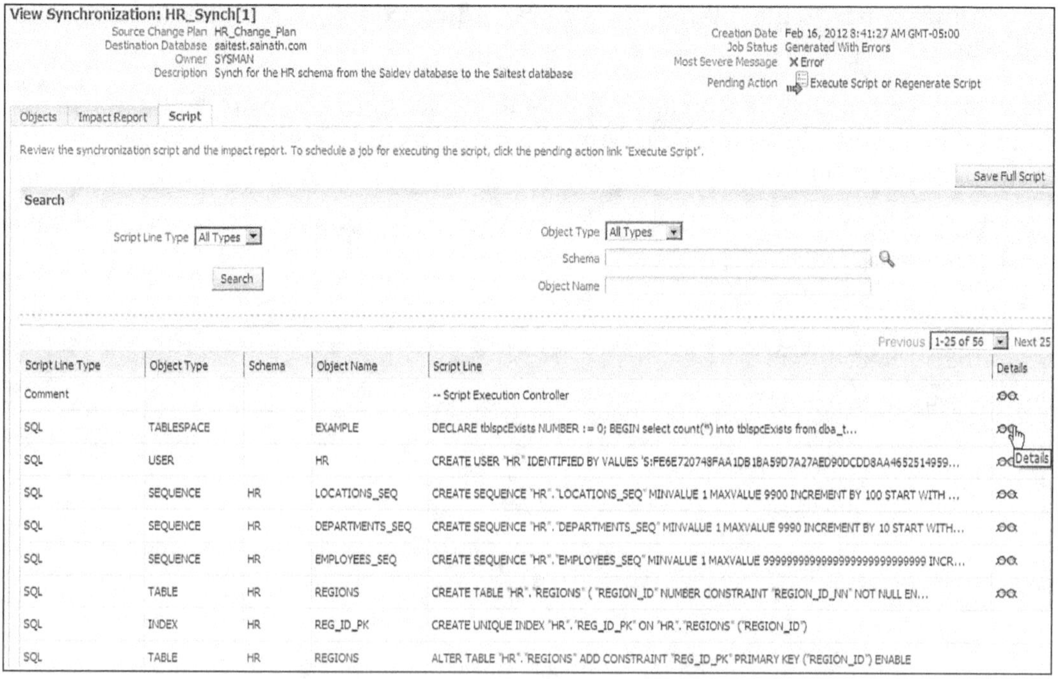

In the **Script** tab, you can examine all the scripts that have been generated to synchronize the objects between the two databases.

You can search for scripts pertaining to certain object types: for example tablespace scripts or table scripts, or you can select **All Types**.

Starting with the **Script Execution Controller** line, we can see that different scripts have been created for objects such as tablespace, user, sequence, table, index, and so on.

The scripts are intelligently ordered—the tablespace will be created first, followed by the **HR** user, followed by creation of all the **HR** objects.

In the case of the **HR** objects, all the sequences will be created first, followed by the tables and indexes. Views, procedures, and triggers (if any) will be created at the end.

You can click on **Save Full Script** if you want to save all the individual scripts as one synchronization SQL file. In this case you can edit and run the script manually in SQL Plus.

Now, click on the **Details** icon against the tablespace object to examine the script that will be used to generate the **EXAMPLE** tablespace. This is shown in the following screenshot:

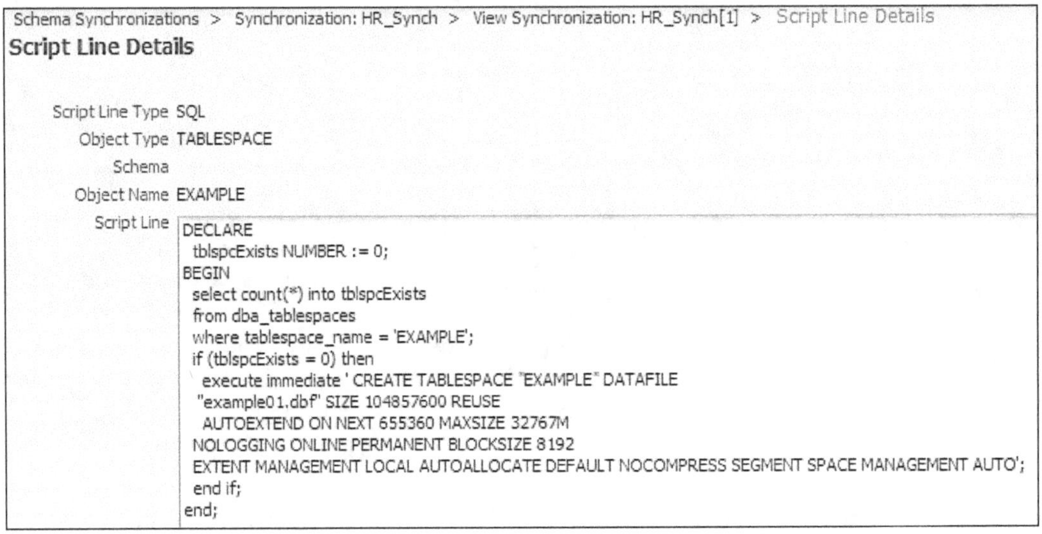


As we can see, the script intelligently attempts the creation of the **EXAMPLE** tablespace only if it does not already exist. This is important, so as to avoid unnecessary creation errors with existing objects.

The directory's location is not specified, so the database file will be created in the default location, which is the `DBS` directory under the Oracle home.

It is not possible to edit the script on the screen in order to make changes. You need to save it as a synchronization SQL file first, before editing it.

## Executing the synchronization

Coming back to the main **View Synchronization** page, click on **Execute Script** at the top corner of the screen.

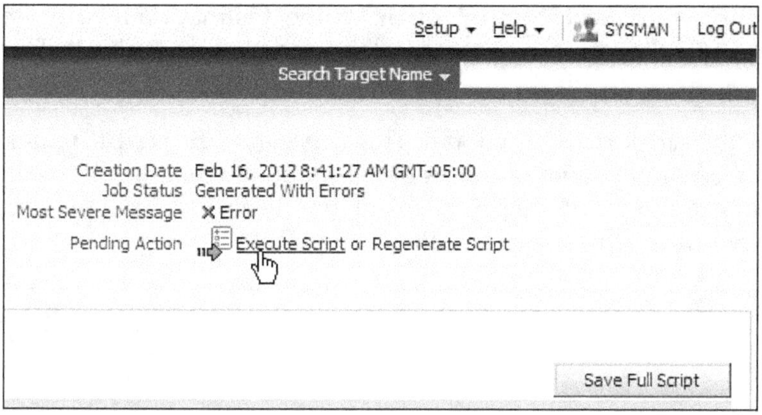


A confirmation appears that you should examine all error severity messages in the impact report and take appropriate action before you attempt to execute the synchronization script. When it asks you if you want to continue, select **Yes**.

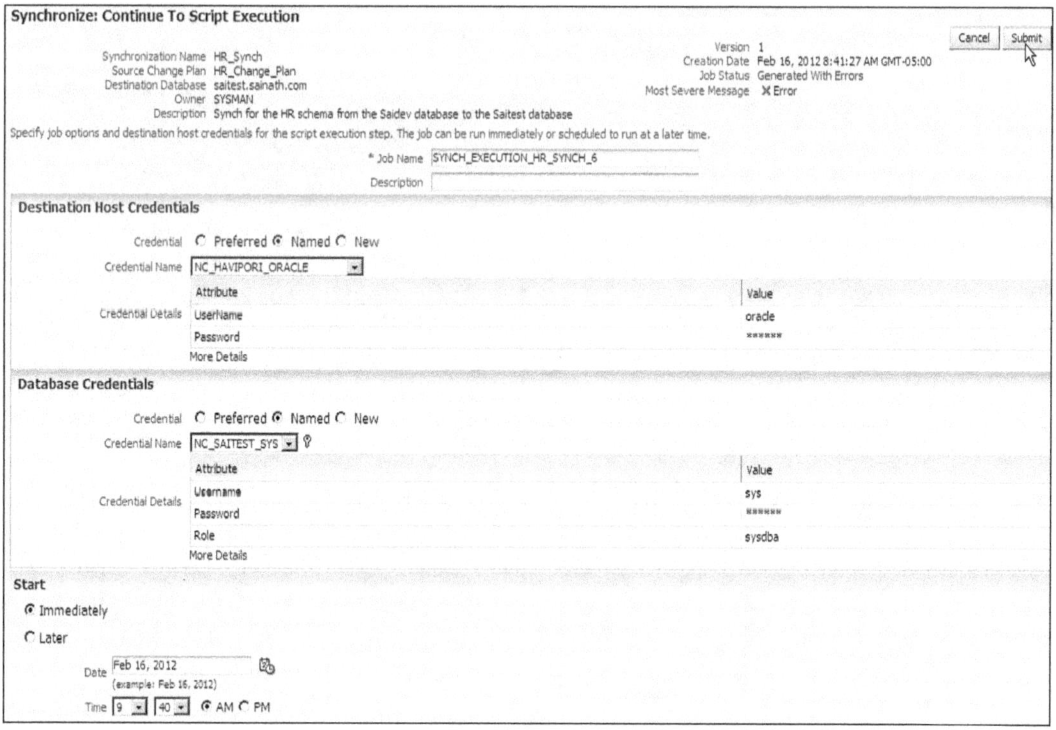

You are now asked to select the credentials for the destination host as well as the database. Schedule the job to run immediately, and click on **Submit**. This will start the job for the script execution.

The first time the script runs, it will fail. This is because the script creates the **HR** user but does not grant any privileges on its default tablespace, or even to connect to the database. You need to grant the privileges manually and execute the script again. This time it should complete successfully.

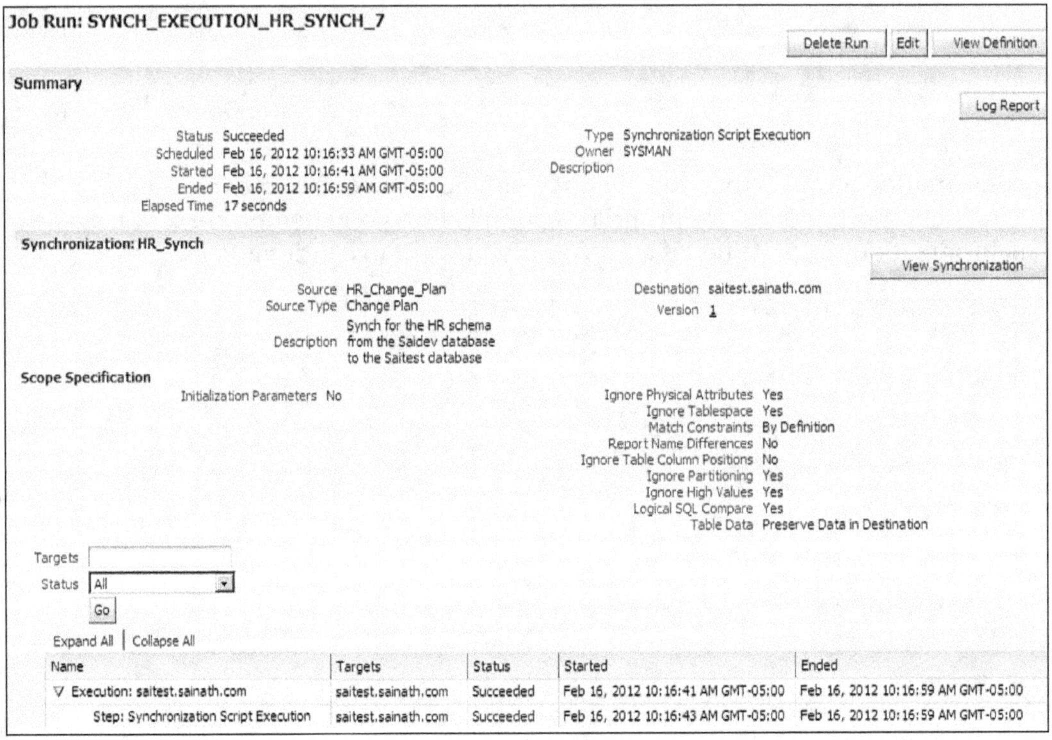

To verify that the objects have been created in the `saitest` database, we can perform a count of the HR objects in each database. The count is **34** objects in each and this is verified in the following screenshot:

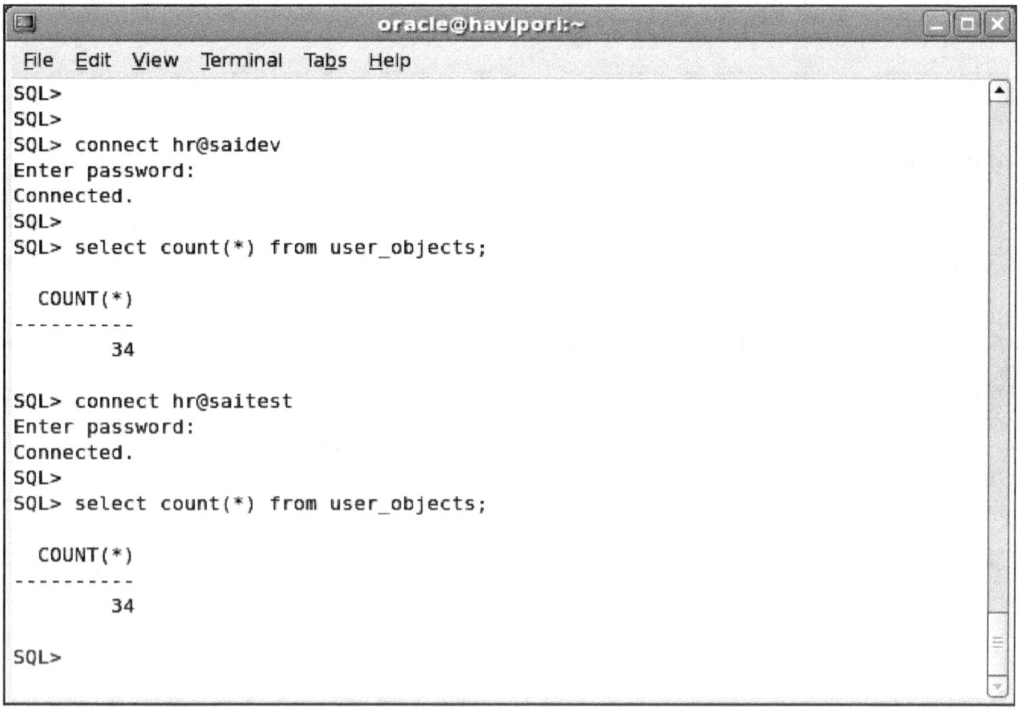


# Synchronization without a Change Plan

Regarding the error about the user privileges not being granted, this happened because a Change Plan was used as the source for the synchronization. Instead, if you had done a direct schema synchronization between the two databases, the user privileges would have been included in the generated script. So if you have a case where the DBA needs to create a missing user in another database as a copy from the original database, direct synchronization is better suited.

Change plans are meant to deliver schema-specific changes to databases: for example, add a missing column, along with related changes such as adding a primary key constraint or foreign key constraint.

On the other hand, direct schema synchronization without a Change Plan will make a set of objects in the second database to look like those in the first database—and this is typically all the objects in one or more schemas. If only the schema is specified, the associated user, roles, and grants will be included by the synchronization process as can be seen in the following screenshot:

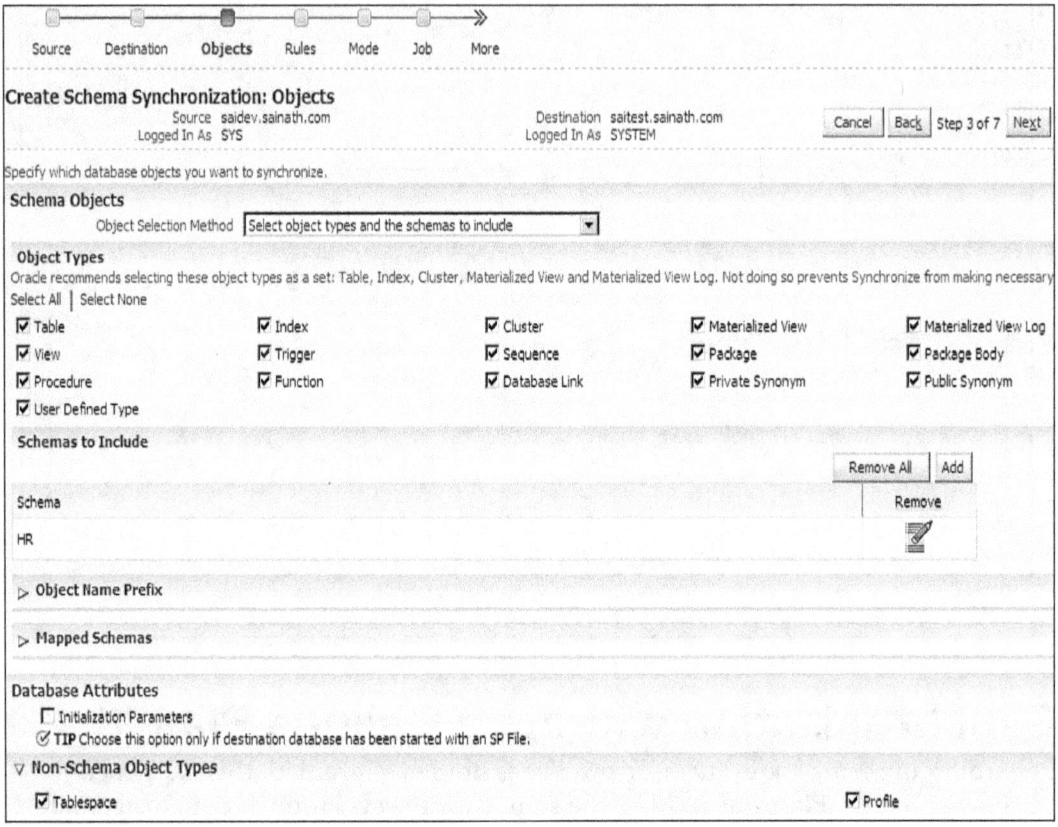


Here, we have created a schema synchronization without specifying a Change Plan. The `saidev` and `saitest` databases are being synchronized, and we have included the **HR** schema and all objects in it. It is recommended to select these **Object Types** as a set—**Table, Index, Cluster, Materialized View**, and **Materialized View Log** so that synchronization can make changes to all related objects. For example, if a **Table** object type has changed in structure and there is a **Materialized View** object type based on that **Table** object type, but the **Materialized View** object type is not selected, then the synchronize process will not be able to change **Materialized View**.

Regarding the non-schema object types, only tablespaces and profiles can be selected as shown in the previous screenshot. You cannot select users, roles, and grants in this scenario since they will be automatically included in the synchronization as per the schemas you have selected. It is recommended to provide a complete scope specification in which all your application schemas are included. Move to the next screen.

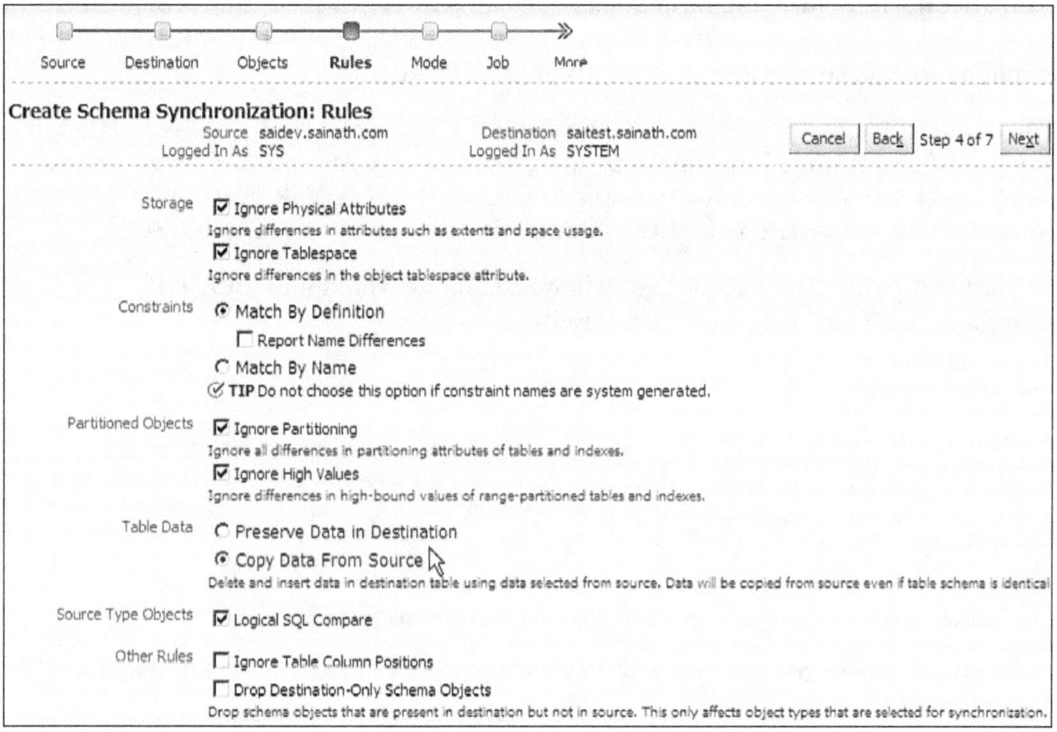


On the **Rules** page, you are allowed to choose whether to preserve data in the destination, or copy data from the source. You can only choose the latter option when doing the direct schema synchronization without any change plans. (If a Change Plan had been used, then this option is grayed out and you are only allowed to preserve data in the destination.)

The direct schema synchronization will then proceed, and generate a script that creates the user as well as assigns the appropriate roles and grants to it.

As we have seen, the Change Plan as well as direct schema synchronizations are restartable in the case of failures. If the synchronize job were to fail, it can be resubmitted (after the issue is manually corrected) and the execution will start from the point of the last failure.

# Data comparison

**Data comparison** is a new feature in Enterprise Manager Cloud Control 12*c*. You are now able to compare the data in different schemas or databases using this feature, which is primarily meant for smaller tables such as reference tables, configuration data, or seed data.

Note that the reference database must be of Version 11*g* or later; this is because it uses the `DBMS_COMPARISON` package, which is available from 11*g* onwards. The candidate database however can be of Version 10*g* or later.

The database character sets must be the same for both databases. Tables, single-table views, and materialized views can be used for data comparison. However, certain data types cannot be used; for example LONG, LONG RAW, ROWID, CLOB, BLOB columns, and so on. You need to exclude such columns from the comparison.

To start comparing the data, select **Schema.. Change Management.. Data Comparisons**. This brings up the following screen:

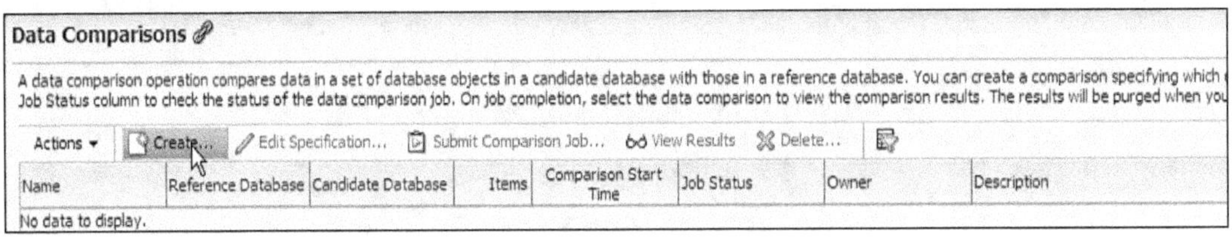


Click on **Create....** This will create a new data comparison.

Internally, this feature uses the `DBMS_COMPARISON` package in the 11*g* database version.

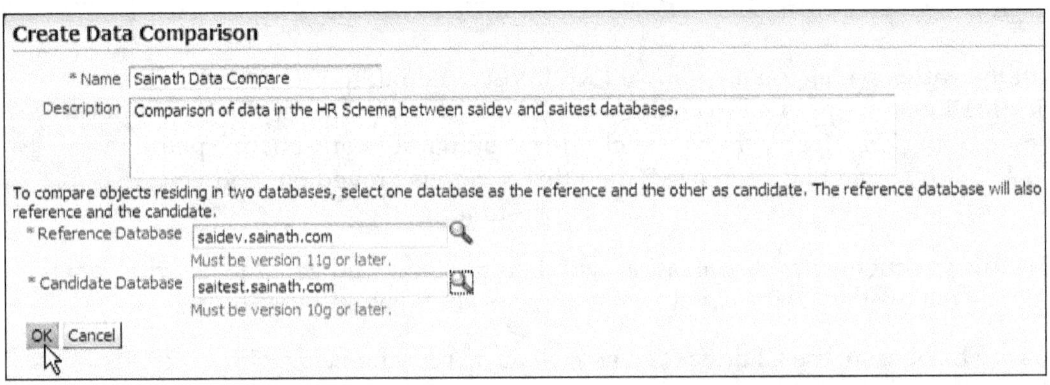

Name the comparison appropriately, and specify the **Reference Database** instance and the **Candidate Database** instance. In our case, select the `saidev` database and the `saitest` database respectively.

Select **OK** to continue.

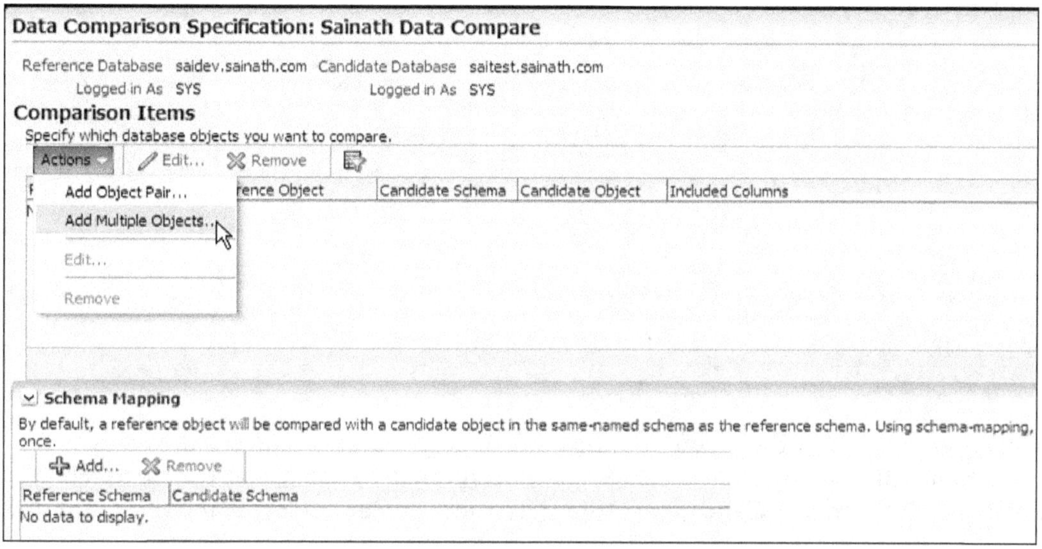


**Comparison Items** can now be specified. You can either add **Multiple Objects**, or individual **Object Pairs**. Specify this from the **Actions** menu.

We choose to add multiple objects. This brings up the following window:

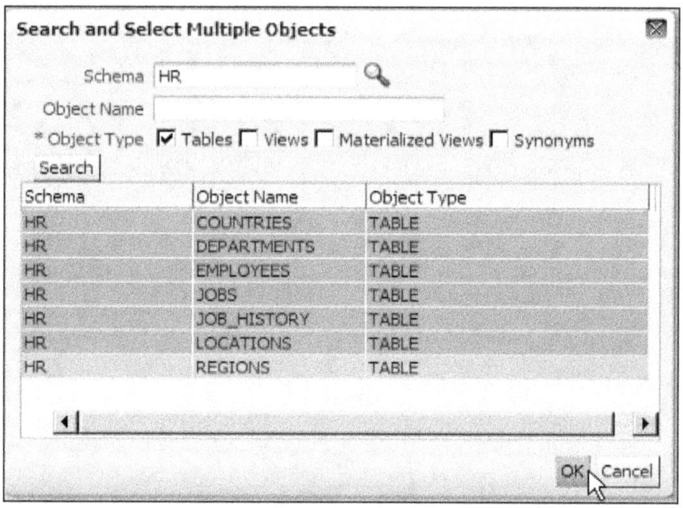

Here we have selected the `HR` schema and searched for all its tables. When the tables are seen, select all of them and click on the **OK** button.

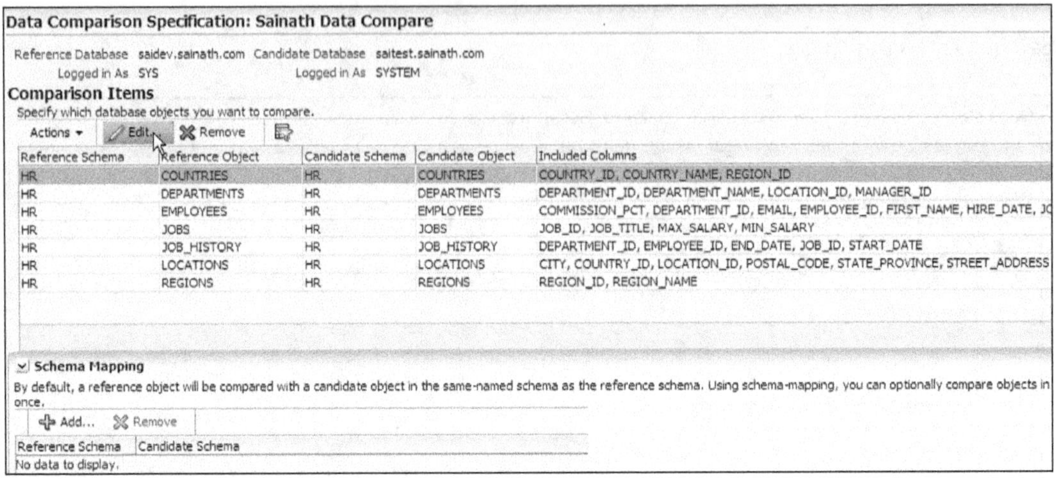

You are now back on the **Comparison Items** page, where you can see the list of items that will be compared—including the **Reference Schema**, **Candidate Schema**, **Reference Object**, and **Candidate Object**. To view an item, select it and click on **Edit...**.

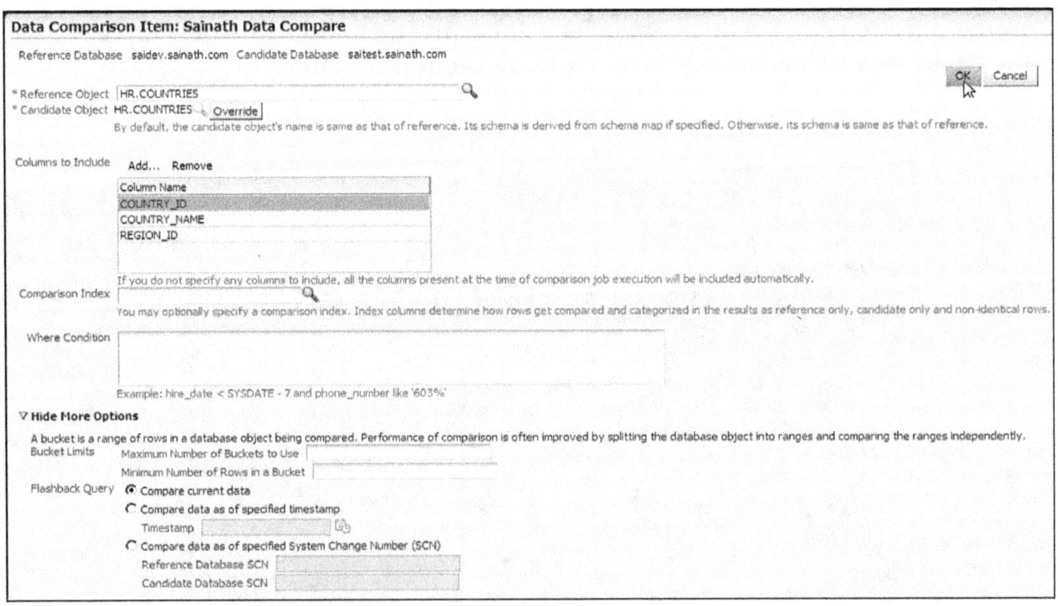

On the **Data Comparison Item** page, the columns that will be compared are displayed. You can **Remove** or **Add...** columns in the list.

You can also override the name of the **Candidate Object** instance and specify a different schema if you wish. In that case, any schema mapping previously specified will be ignored for this item.

On this page, it is also possible to select a **Comparison Index** option, but this is optional. The index must uniquely identify every row you are comparing. **Where Condition** can also be specified.

The performance of the comparison can be improved by specifying buckets of rows with **Minimum Number of Rows in a Bucket**, and **Maximum Number of Buckets to List**. The comparison is done independently for each bucket.

It is also possible to use Flashback Query to compare older data instead of current data. Older data can be specified using either **Timestamp** or **SCN**.

Select **OK** to save your data comparison.

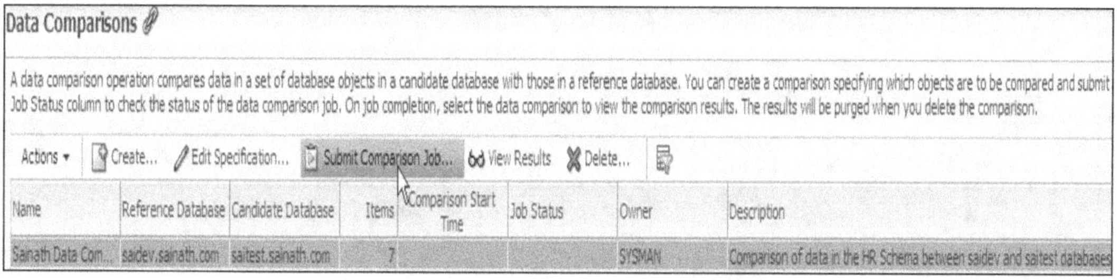

The data comparison you have created is now visible in the list of **Data Comparisons**. Select it and click on **Submit Comparison Job...**.

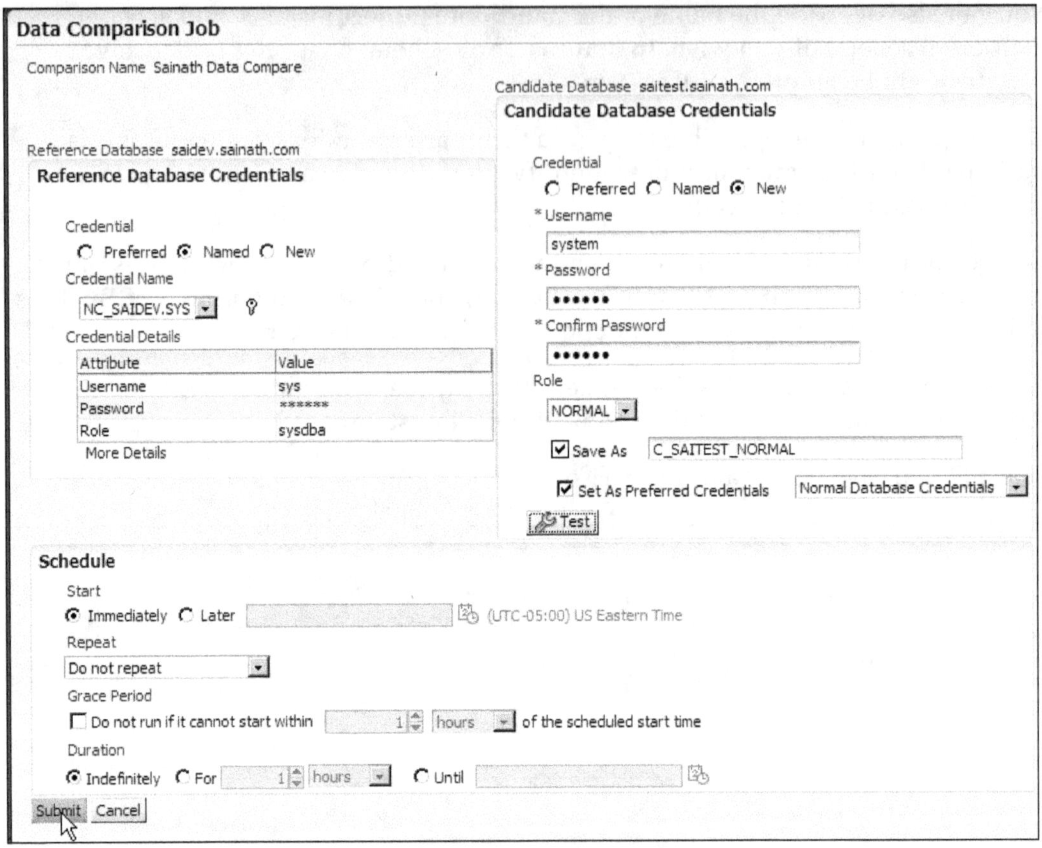


Specify the **Reference Database Credentials** details as well as those for **Candidate Database Credentials**.

Note that you can use the `SYSDBA` credentials for the reference database, but you need to use the **Normal** credentials for the candidate database, since comparisons cannot be done in the remote database as the `SYS` user. If you do not have any normal credentials for the candidate database, create a new set of credentials.

Schedule **Data Comparison** to start immediately. Then click on **Submit**. When the job is submitted, click on the link in the job's **Status** column to view the job status.

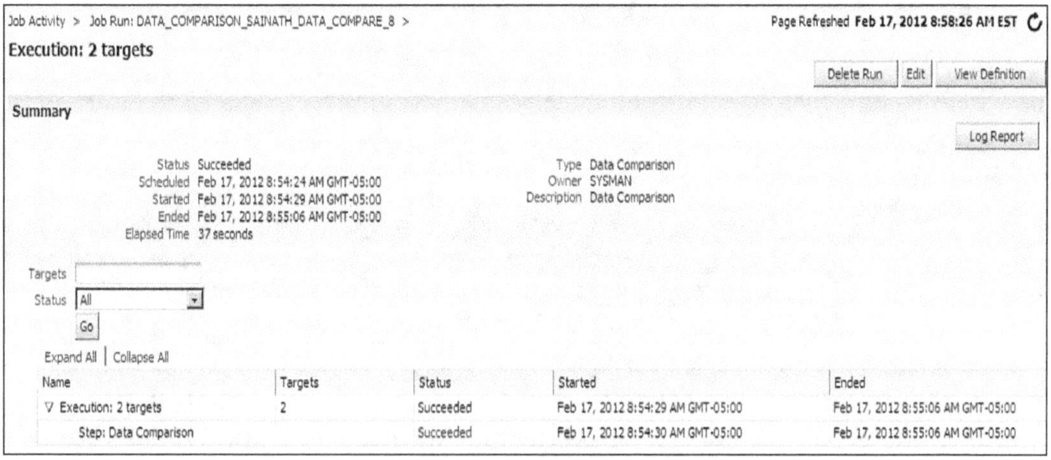


The job completes successfully in less than a minute. Return to the **Data Comparisons** page using the back button on your browser.

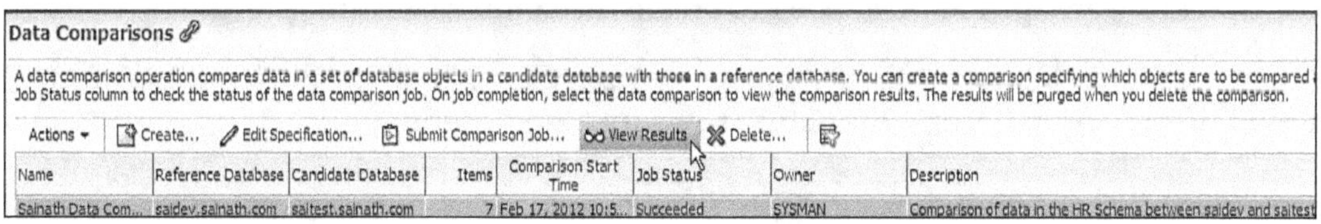

You can now select the data comparison that was just completed and click on **View Results**.

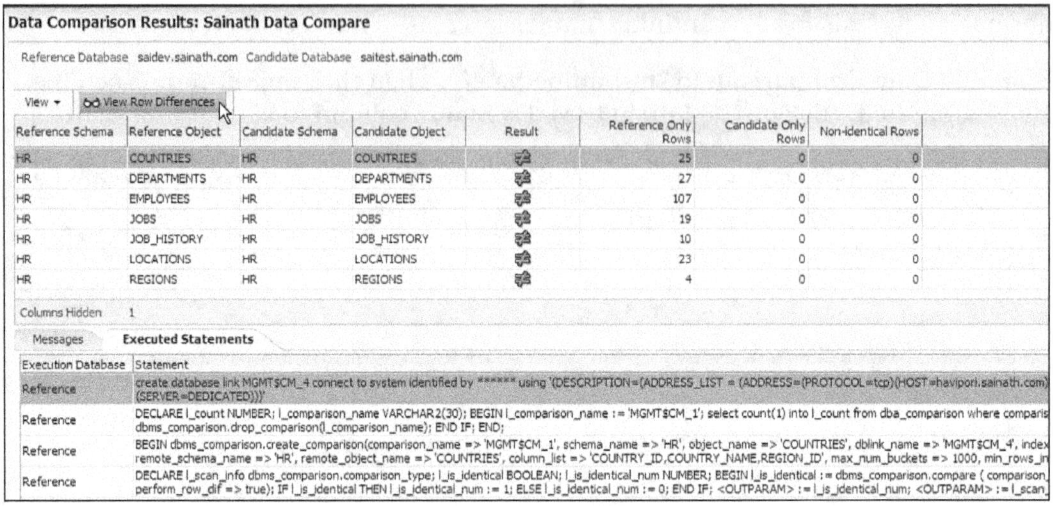


On the main **Results** page for **Data Comparison**, a list of all the objects that have been compared is displayed. We can see that the data is not identical for all the tables. There are zero rows in all the candidate tables.

The executed statements can be examined in one of the tabs in the lower section of the page. You can see that a database link has been created, and the `DBMS_COMPARISON` package has been used to create the comparison and execute it.

Select one of the tables from the list, for example **COUNTRIES**. Click on the **View Row Differences** tab to see the actual rows that are different.

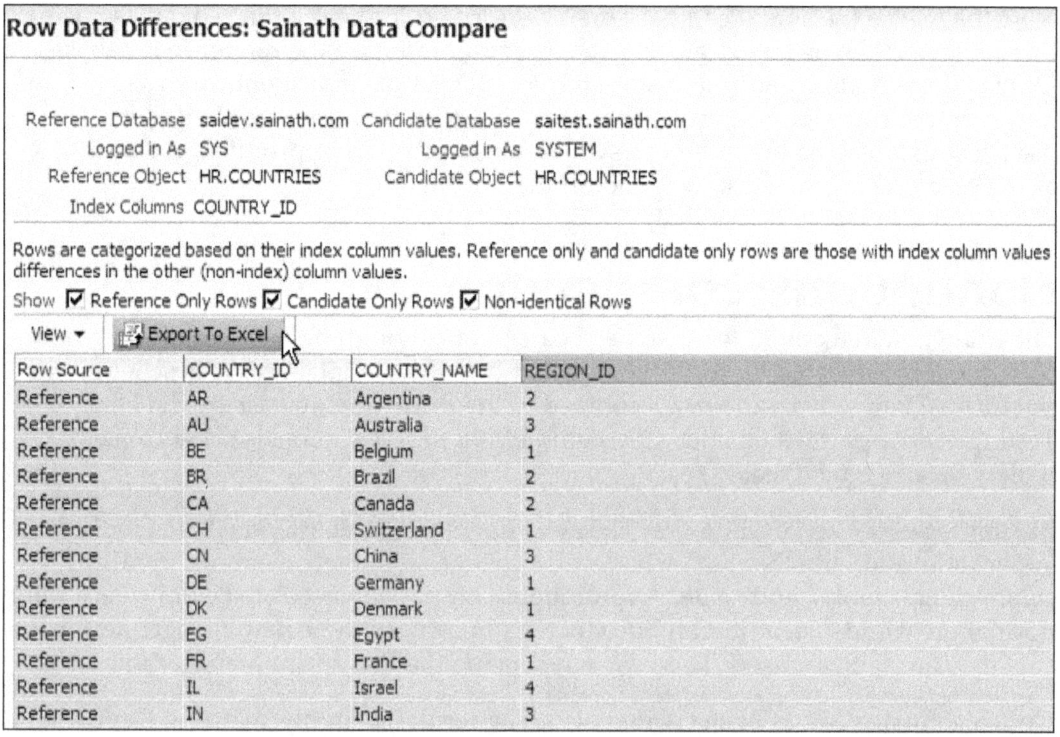

Row Data Differences: Sainath Data Compare

Reference Database saidev.sainath.com Candidate Database saitest.sainath.com
Logged in As SYS Logged in As SYSTEM
Reference Object HR.COUNTRIES Candidate Object HR.COUNTRIES
Index Columns COUNTRY_ID

Rows are categorized based on their index column values. Reference only and candidate only rows are those with index column values
differences in the other (non-index) column values.

Show Reference Only Rows Candidate Only Rows Non-identical Rows

View Export To Excel

| Row Source | COUNTRY_ID | COUNTRY_NAME | REGION_ID |
|---|---|---|---|
| Reference | AR | Argentina | 2 |
| Reference | AU | Australia | 3 |
| Reference | BE | Belgium | 1 |
| Reference | BR | Brazil | 2 |
| Reference | CA | Canada | 2 |
| Reference | CH | Switzerland | 1 |
| Reference | CN | China | 3 |
| Reference | DE | Germany | 1 |
| Reference | DK | Denmark | 1 |
| Reference | EG | Egypt | 4 |
| Reference | FR | France | 1 |
| Reference | IL | Israel | 4 |
| Reference | IN | India | 3 |

This page displays the actual data that is different in the **COUNTRIES** table after comparing the two databases. You can choose to display only the rows from the reference table or only those from the candidate table, or the rows that are present in both the tables and are non-identical.

This data can then be exported to a Microsoft Excel spreadsheet.

At the time of writing, it is not possible to synchronize the data using Enterprise Manager Cloud Control 12*c*, but this can be done using the `DBMS_COMPARISON` package, if you wish.

Note that, since the actual comparison is performed in the reference database using this package, there is an extra performance load placed on the reference database. Extra storage is also required to store the row IDs of the non-identical rows, however, the rows themselves are not stored. It may therefore be a better choice to use a test database as the reference system when comparing production and test, so as to avoid placing an extra overload on the production system.

# Continuous comparison

The change management features can be used on an ongoing basis. Suppose a new `OE` schema was created by the developers in the `saidev` database. This schema was put into a Change Plan and synchronized to the `saitest` database by the DBA. Testing is now performed and, after completion, the `OE` schema is synchronized with the `saiprod` database.

But this is not the end of the story. The developers publish new versions of the application, and with them the schema also changes with new columns, modified columns, new tables, and so on. A continuous comparison needs to be done between development and test, or test and production, to capture these new changes and make sure they are synchronized. This easy when using the Enterprise Manager interface.

Once a comparison has been created, it can be rerun by simply selecting **Repeat Now** from the **Schema Comparisons** page as shown in the following screenshot:

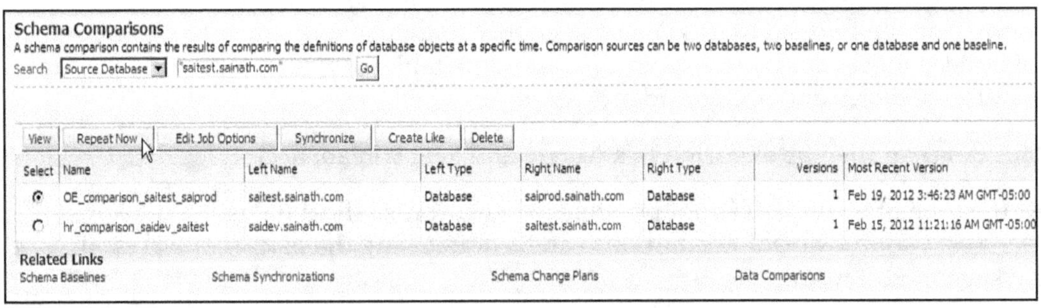


Here we are comparing the OE schema in the `saitest` and `saiprod` databases.

The comparison runs as before and it reveals that the **PROMOTIONS** table has been changed. A new column `PROMO_LOCATION` has been added to the test table, but is missing in production.

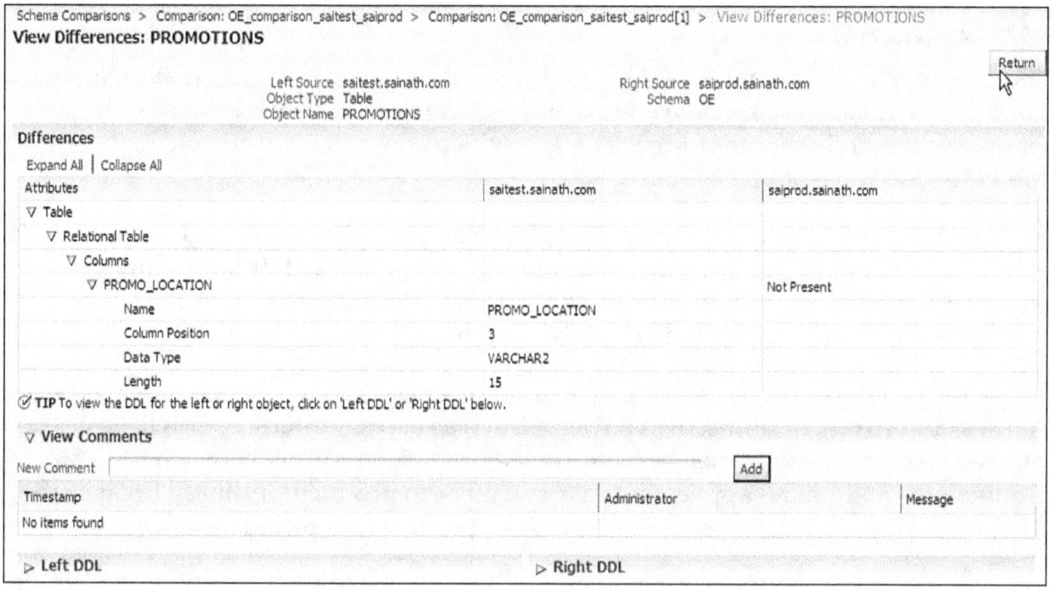


After we progress to the synchronization phase, we can see that the generated script contains an `Alter Table` command to add the missing column.

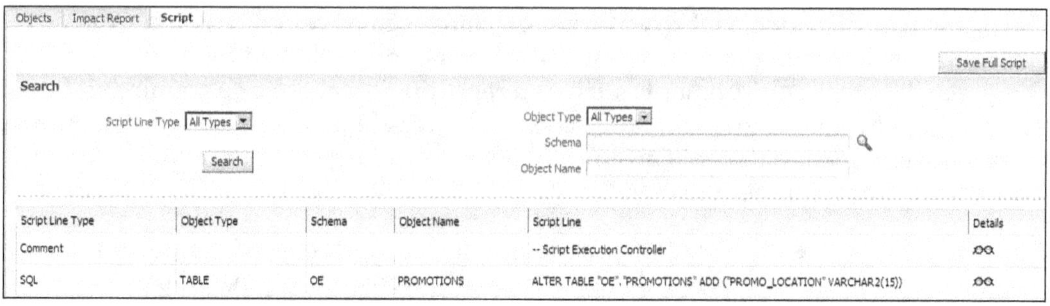


In this way, any changes to any objects in the schema would pass through the various stages of the development lifecycle—from development to test to production. The new concept of the schema Change Plan helps in making sure that the correct changes are passed through to the DBA for their application in controlled databases.

# Use cases

You can use change management for various ends. One example is creating a gold baseline of a database as soon as it goes into production. Every week after that, you set up a scheduled schema comparison job, which compares the current state of the database with the Gold baseline.

Any changes to the production database, for example a developer adding an index, will appear in the weekly comparison report generated. If the changes are unauthorized, you will be able to synchronize production back to the Gold baseline—the unauthorized index will be dropped.

In schema comparisons, the scope can include schemas, schema objects (such as tables, indexes, and so on), or non-schema objects (such as users, profiles, or privileges). The latter can be quite useful when comparing the privileges of users between test and production—at times an application may not work in production simply because the schema had higher privileges in test, but lower privileges in production.

Another use of the change management facilities can be to identify any unauthorized changes in the database application code. Since PL/SQL objects, such as packages, procedures, and functions can also be compared, it is possible to detect any changes to the application code in production by comparing with the Gold baseline.

The prime use, of course, is the capturing of changes in development as a Change Plan, and synchronizing this with test and then staging, followed by production. There may be other environments such as a reporting database or a training database that need to be kept in sync with any schema changes in production, or there may be several development databases around the world in a large multinational company with multiple development teams.

All of these scenarios can benefit from using Enterprise Manager Cloud Control 12*c*, rather than performing schema changes manually across multiple databases.

# Summary

The change management features of the Enterprise Manager DBLM Pack are uniquely useful. From the Enterprise Manager GUI interface, these features allow you to capture metadata (dictionary) definitions from multiple databases, track schema changes in a single database, capture and version dictionary baselines, compare databases and schemas or baselines, and also compare data from various schemas or databases.

You can also compare storage parameters such as tablespaces or the sizes of extents, and so on. Database initialization parameters can also be compared.

Without the change management facility or any other tool, the only way the DBA can compare two databases is by writing scripts to mine the metadata from the dictionary, print out all the schema definitions, and then visually compare the results. This would be the same technique as used by the DBAs of twenty years ago. The DBA of today simply has to use Enterprise Manager Cloud Control 12*c* to capture baselines and perform comparisons, and the results are presented to him.

This increases the DBA productivity considerably. The DBA can now easily identify any schema change that may be impacting performance. Database changes can be managed in an efficient manner and easily promoted across the development lifecycle. Changes can be put in a plan by the developer and approved by the DBA in a seamless workflow, using Enterprise Manager job scheduling and automation across various databases, thus reducing the chances for errors.

In addition to that, because the baselines you capture can be versioned and the full database change history retained, this helps greatly with audit and compliance requirements, since management reports can be easily extracted.

All in one, the change management facility of the Database Lifecycle Management Pack is extremely useful in the day-to-day life of the DBA.

In the next chapter, we will take a look at the new Test Data Management Pack in Oracle Enterprise Manager Cloud Control 12*c*, which allows the data subsetting of large production databases into smaller development or test databases.

# 8
# Ease the Chaos with Test Data Management

There are many instances in production where databases have increased drastically in size, due to application growth and increased usage. These databases must nevertheless be used for testing purposes, and at such times the DBA would be called upon to make an appropriate copy of production for the test team.

The easiest way to make a test copy is to clone a database, and this is fine for small- to medium-sized databases where there is sufficient space allocated in the test system. However, for large databases it is usually not possible to use a similarly sized database for testing because of space issues in the test environment. In this case, the DBA is forced to use a reduced set of data in the test database, in order to meet the space requirements and reduce the storage costs.

But even this is not easy, because it requires an understanding of the data model before the reduced data can be extracted, and manual scripts need to be written for this purpose—painfully extracting data from master tables, child tables, and reference tables. Relational correctness needs to be observed. The scripts need to be tested before they can be used, as they may not be optimized for performance, and this may adversely impact the production system. Errors can happen, as with any manual process or manually written scripts.

Even after all this work on the part of the DBA, any changes to the schema structure of the production database will automatically invalidate the extraction scripts, forcing a rewrite and re-test of the concerned scripts.

Compound this with the large number of huge databases in a data center, and repeated requests for creating test databases from these, and this process would take up an increasing amount of valuable DBA time.

# Test Data Management

Enterprise Manager Cloud Control 12*c* provides a new licensed pack, known as the **Test Data Management Pack**. This is mainly used for the purpose of data subsetting, that is, to create a relationally intact subset of data from production.

For this purpose, an **Application Data Model** (**ADM**) needs to be created and stored in Enterprise Manager. This is a new concept in Cloud Control 12*c*. This model defines the database schema with all its relations. You can then define the subset of the data that is required from the model. At the same time, you can define the data-sensitive columns in the tables, such as a credit card number. This information will then be used to create the subset of data for testing, and also to mask sensitive data using the **Data Masking Pack** (as we will see in the next chapter).

# Creating packages

A prerequisite to using the new facility of Test Data Management is to create special packages in each database that will be used for this scenario. These packages are needed to perform Test Data Management operations. In our case, we will be using the **saitest** and the **saiprod** databases for this purpose. First, select **Enterprise** | **Job** | **Activity**. This brings up the following screen:

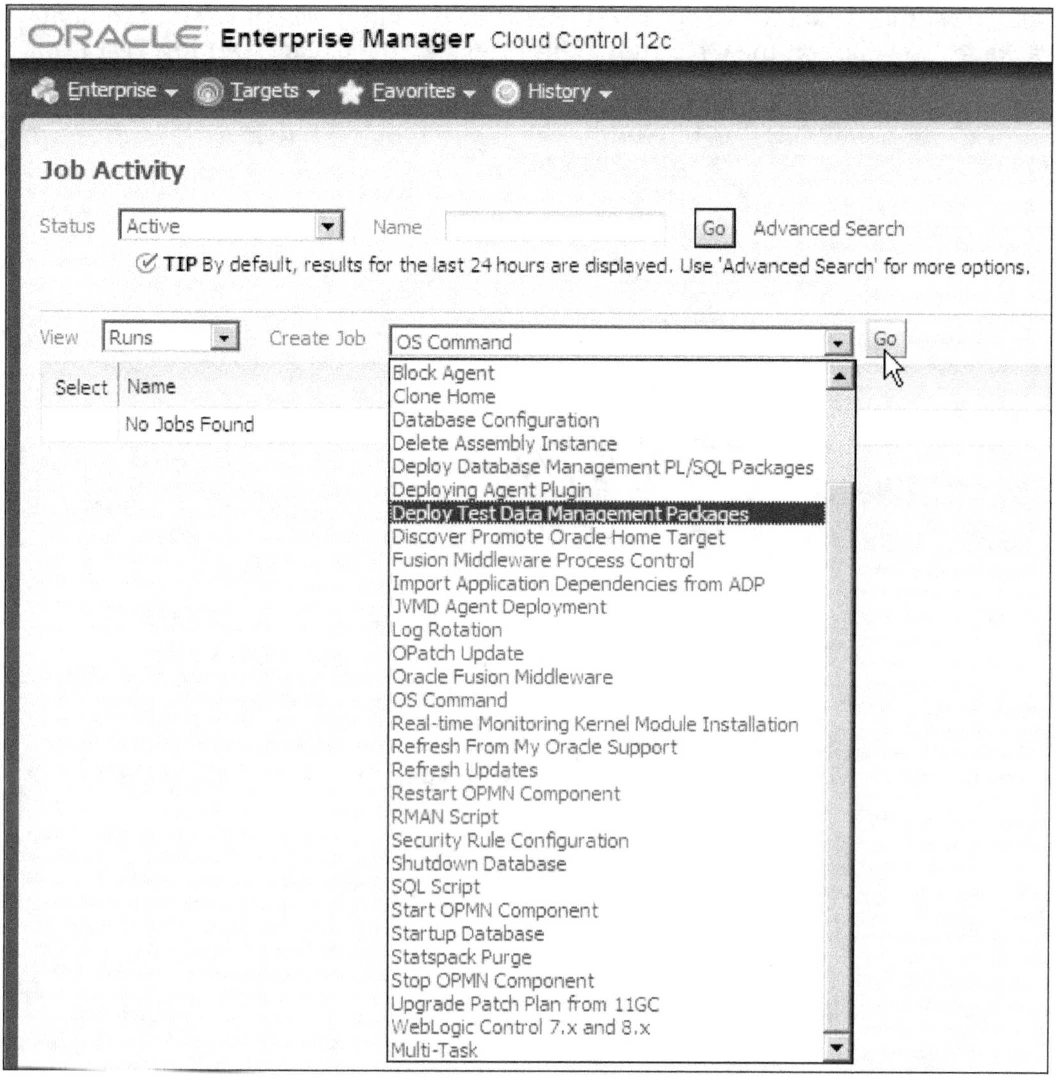
ORACLE Enterprise Manager Cloud Control 12c
Enterprise Targets Favorites History
Job Activity
Status Active Name Go Advanced Search
TIP By default, results for the last 24 hours are displayed. Use 'Advanced Search' for more options.
View Runs Create Job OS Command Go
Select Name
No Jobs Found
Block Agent
Clone Home
Database Configuration
Delete Assembly Instance
Deploy Database Management PL/SQL Packages
Deploying Agent Plugin
Deploy Test Data Management Packages
Discover Promote Oracle Home Target
Fusion Middleware Process Control
Import Application Dependencies from ADP
JVMD Agent Deployment
Log Rotation
OPatch Update
Oracle Fusion Middleware
OS Command
Real-time Monitoring Kernel Module Installation
Refresh From My Oracle Support
Refresh Updates
Restart OPMN Component
RMAN Script
Security Rule Configuration
Shutdown Database
SQL Script
Start OPMN Component
Startup Database
Statspack Purge
Stop OPMN Component
Upgrade Patch Plan from 11GC
WebLogic Control 7.x and 8.x
Multi-Task

Next, from the **Create Job** drop-down box, select **Deploy Test Data Management Packages** and click on the **Go** button. This brings up the **Create 'Deploy Test Data Management Packages' Job** screen, as follows:

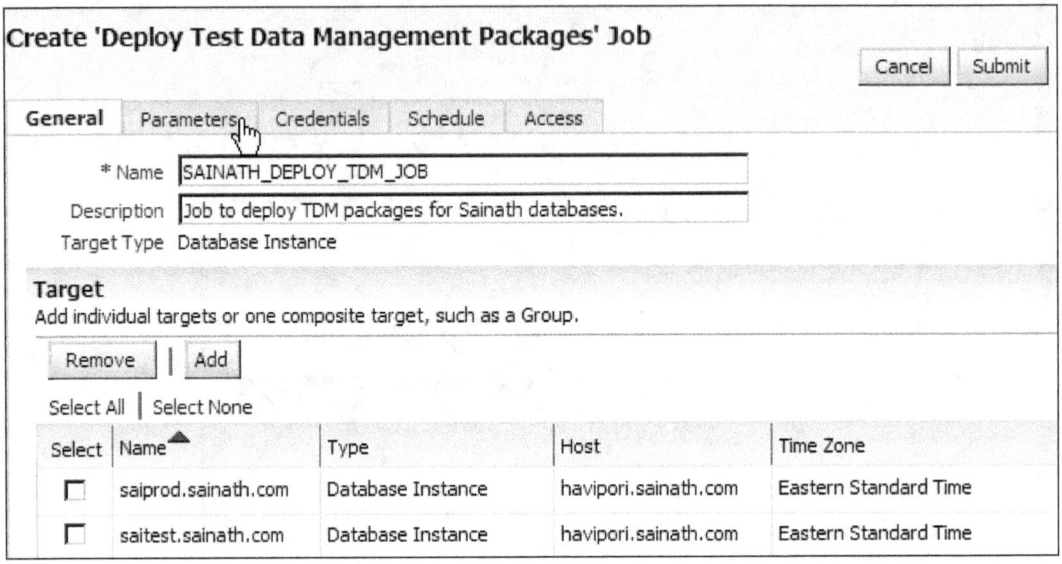


Name the job appropriately, and then select the database instances on which you want **Test Data Management Packages** to be created. In this case, select the **saitest** and **saiprod** databases.

After this is done, click on the **Parameters** tab.

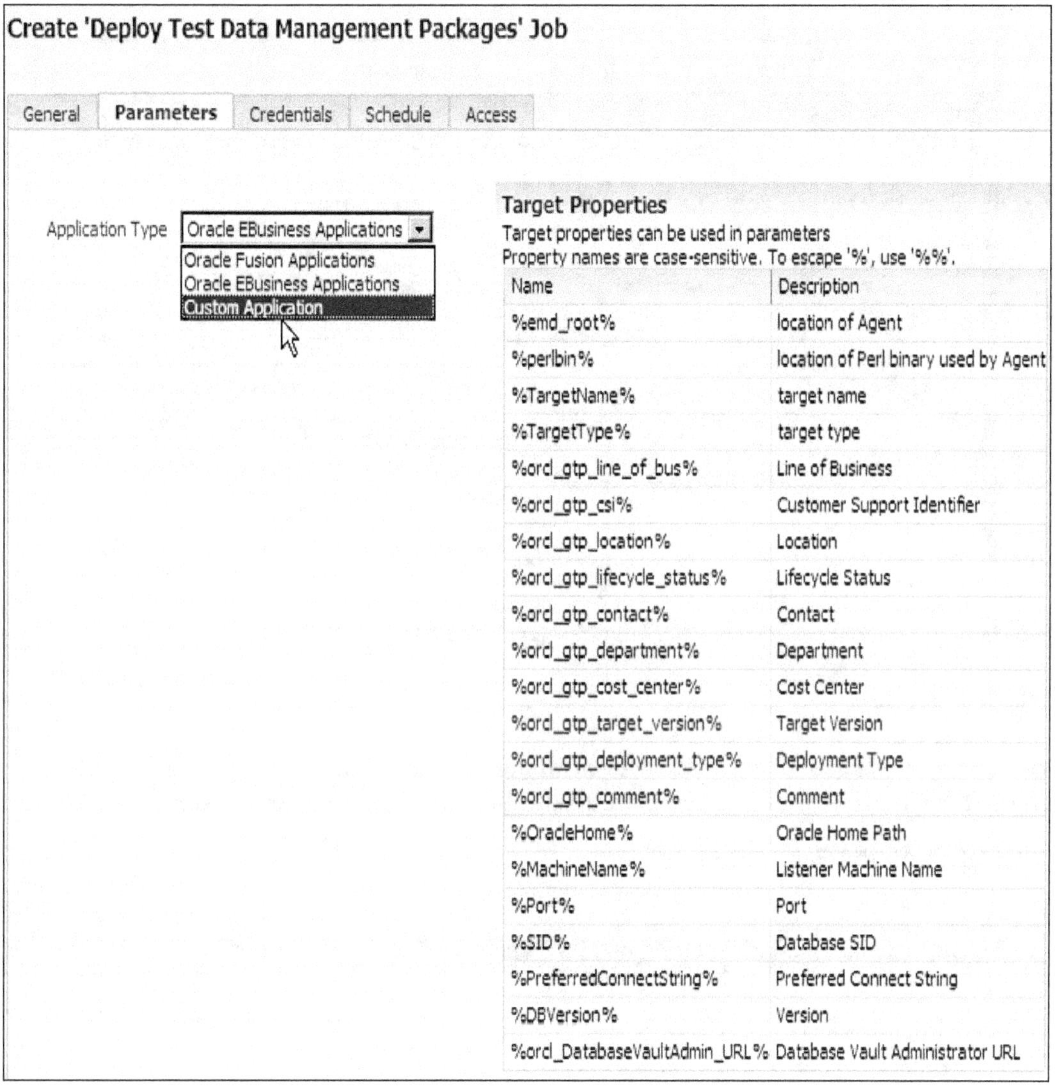

On this page, select **Application Type** as **Custom Application** from the drop-down box. Then click on the **Credentials** tab.

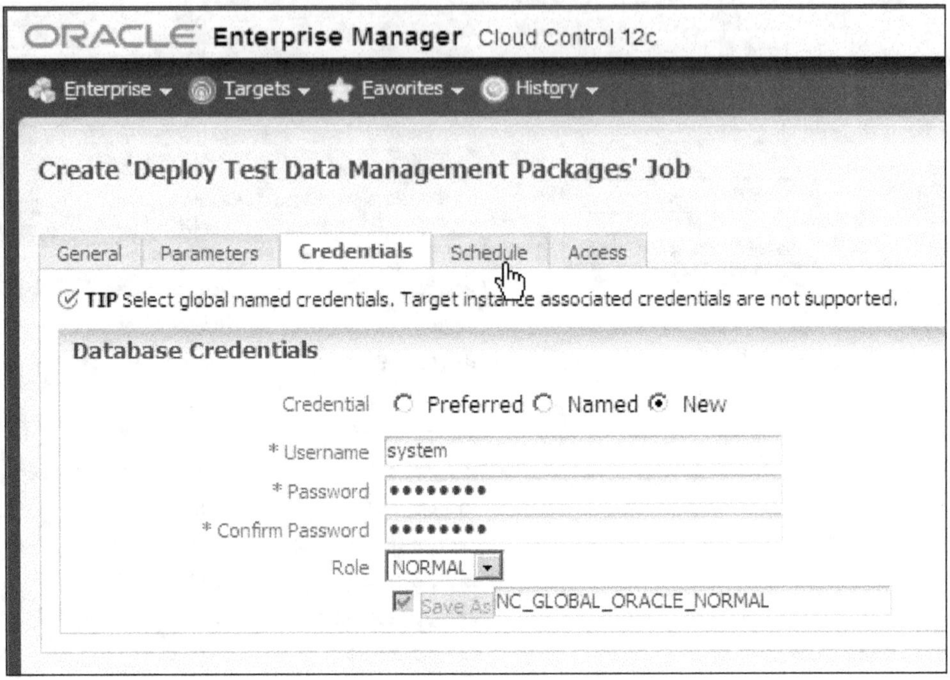


You need to use **global named credentials** for the databases you have selected. Named credentials that are associated with an individual target are not supported.

Next, click on the **Schedule** tab.

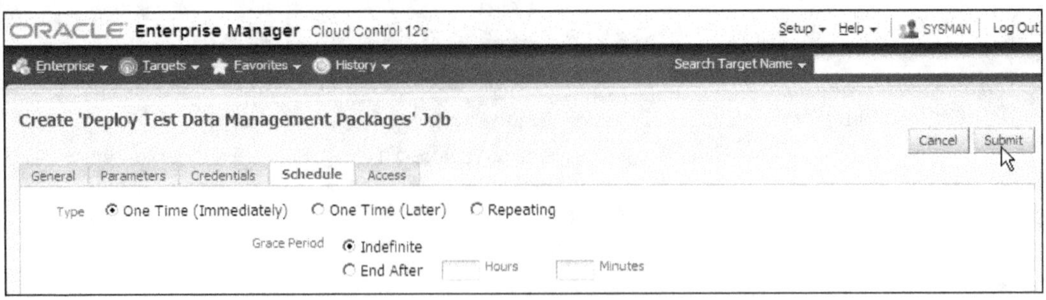

Schedule the job to be run immediately and click on the **Submit** button. The job starts, and is completed in less than a minute.

The packages have now been deployed. We can proceed with the next step, which is the creation of the Application Data Model.

# Creating the Application Data Model

The **Application Data Model** is the basis of the data subsetting as well as the data masking capabilities in Enterprise Manager Cloud Control 12*c*.

Essentially, it is a reverse engineering of the schema definitions from the database dictionary into Enterprise Manager. The schema definition is captured along with the relational constraints (foreign keys). Once the Application Data Model is present in Enterprise Manager Cloud Control 12*c*, you can proceed with either data subsetting or data masking.

Select **Enterprise** | **Quality Management** | **Data Discovery and Modeling**. This brings up the following screen:

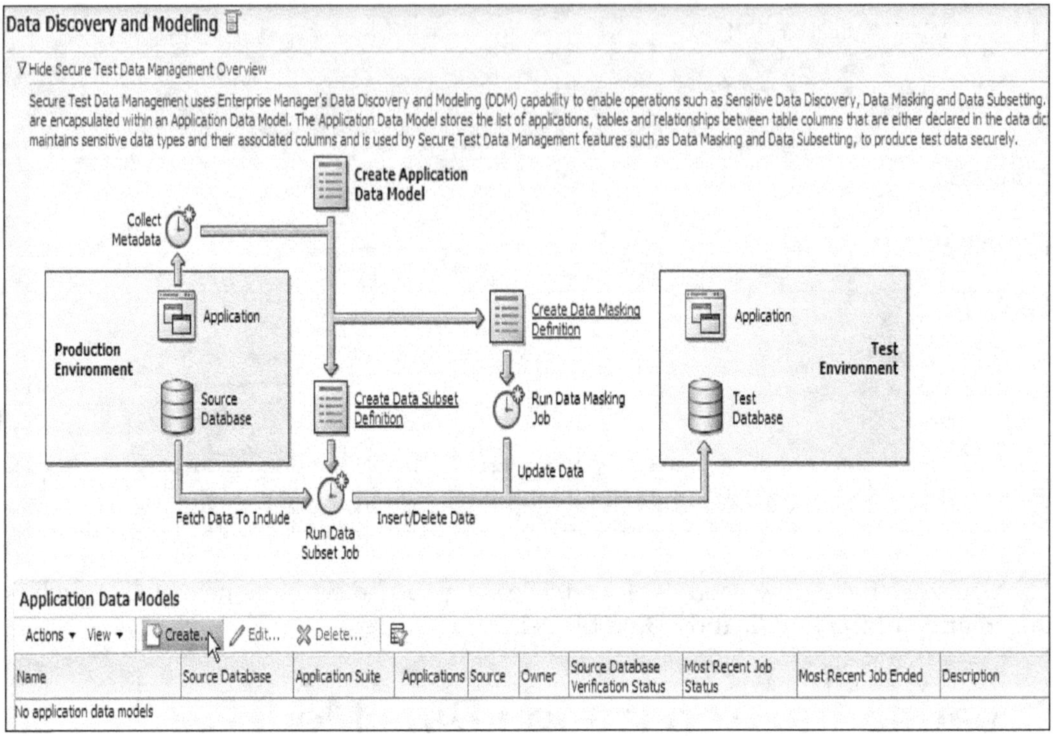


An overview of the Test Data Management Pack is displayed in the form of a workflow diagram. You are at the first step of the process, which is the creation of the Application Data Model. The other steps can be seen on the workflow, such as **Create Data Subset Definition** and **Create Data Masking Definition**. The **Create Data Subset Definition** step will be covered later in this chapter, and the **Create Data Masking Definition** step is explained in detail in the next chapter.

In the lower section of the screen, a list of **Application Data Models** is displayed. Currently there are no models. So as in the first step, we create a model by clicking on the **Create...** button.

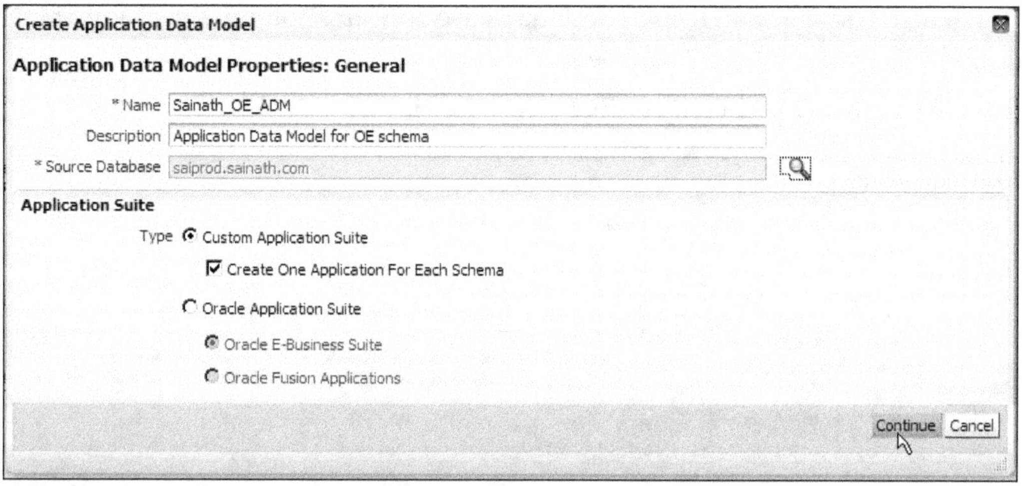


Name the data model and select the `saiprod` database as **Source Database** for the model.

You can keep the default selection for **Create One Application For Each Schema**. Click on **Continue**.

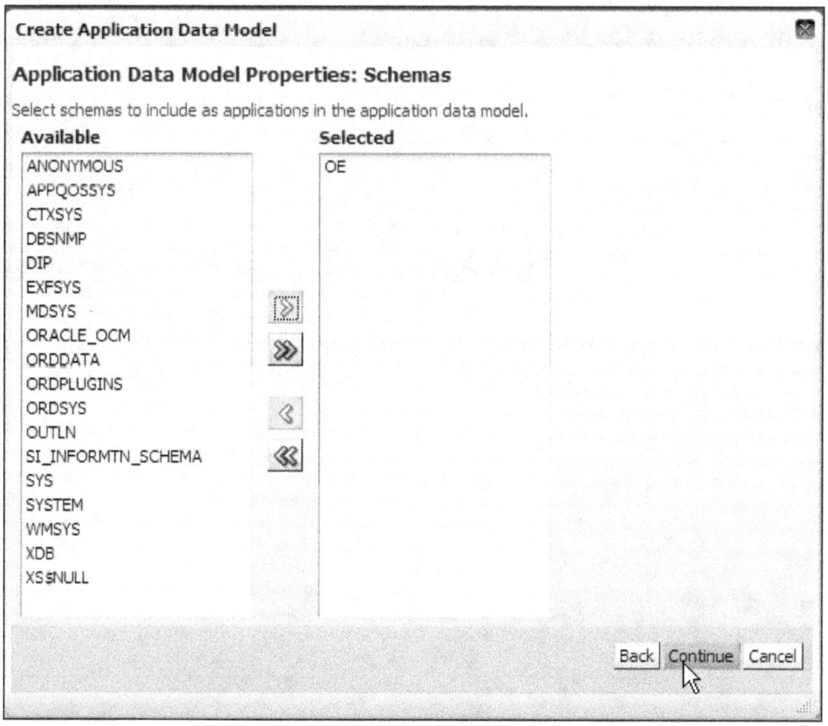

A list of all the schemas in the `saiprod` database appears. You can select any or all of the application schemas from this list.

We will select the **OE** schema only. Click on **Continue**.

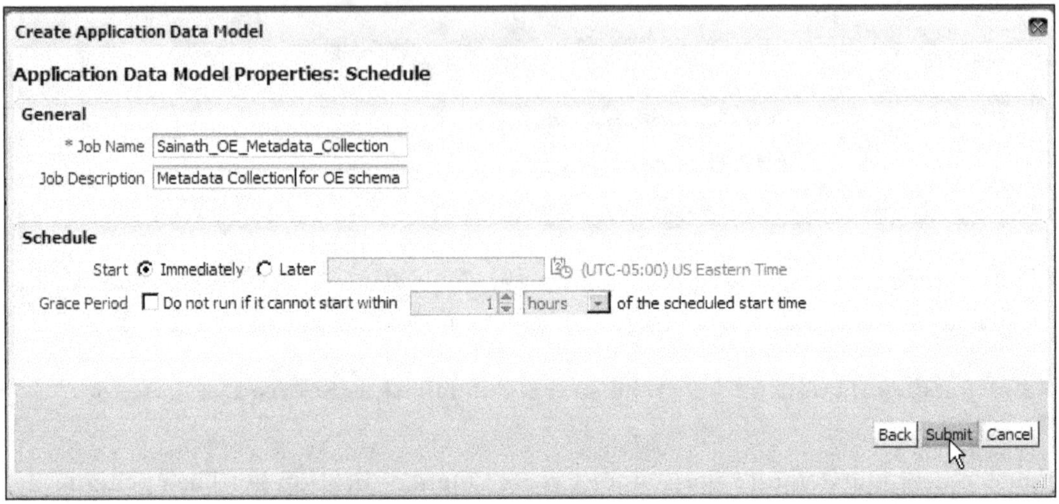


At this point, you can name the job and schedule it to be run **Immediately**. This job will collect the metadata for the **OE** schema.

Click on the **Submit** button.

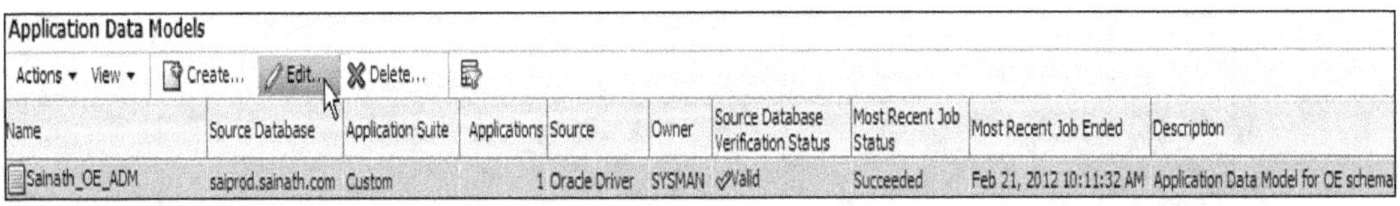


The **Overview** page reappears, and our recently created model can be seen. The status of the job changes to **Succeeded**. Select the model and click on the **Edit** button to see the results.

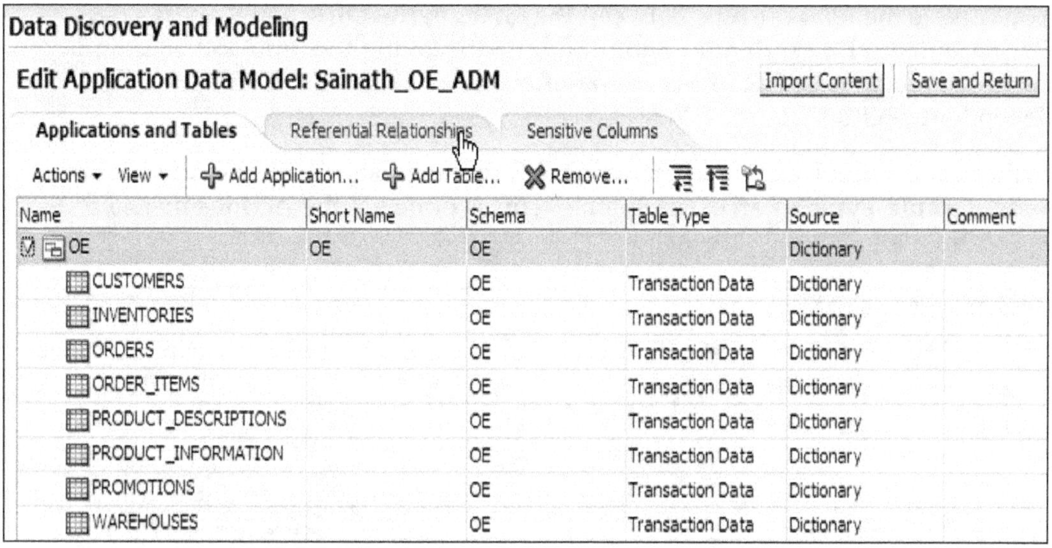


The reverse engineered Application Data Model for the **OE** schema can be seen. On the **Applications and Tables** tab, a list of all the tables belonging to the schema is displayed. It is possible to add tables manually at this point, and also remove tables if required. Click on the **Referential Relationships** tab.

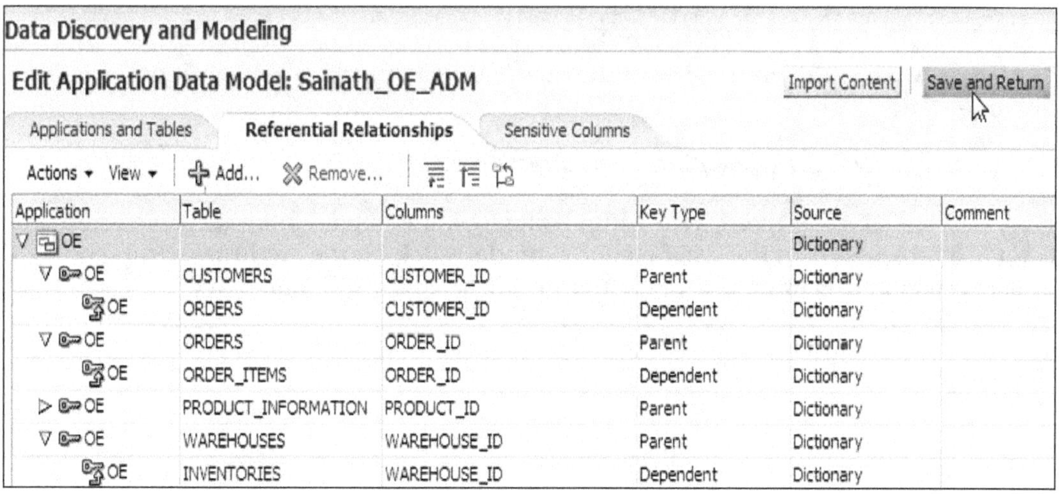

You can see the relationships between the tables in the **OE** schema on this page. The **Parent** and **Dependent** key columns are displaying the type of the foreign keys. As an example, **ORDERS** is a parent table and **ORDER_ITEMS** is a dependent or child table.

In the Application Data Model, it is possible to add a new **Table Type** instance and set **Table Type** for an existing table. This is done via the **Actions** menu, as seen in the following screenshot:

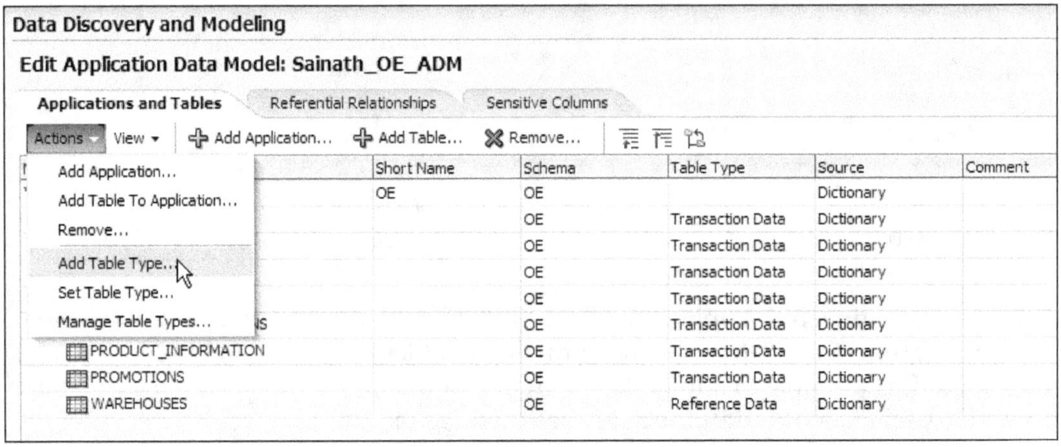


By adding a **Table Type** instance of **Reference Data**, we are able to set the **WAREHOUSES** table in this list to the new **Table Type**. This is useful for documentation purposes.

At this stage our **OE** Application Data Model is ready.

Back on the **Data Discovery and Modeling** page, the newly created Application Data Model appears in the list. Select the model, click on the **Actions** menu, and select **Associated Databases...**, as shown in the following screenshot:

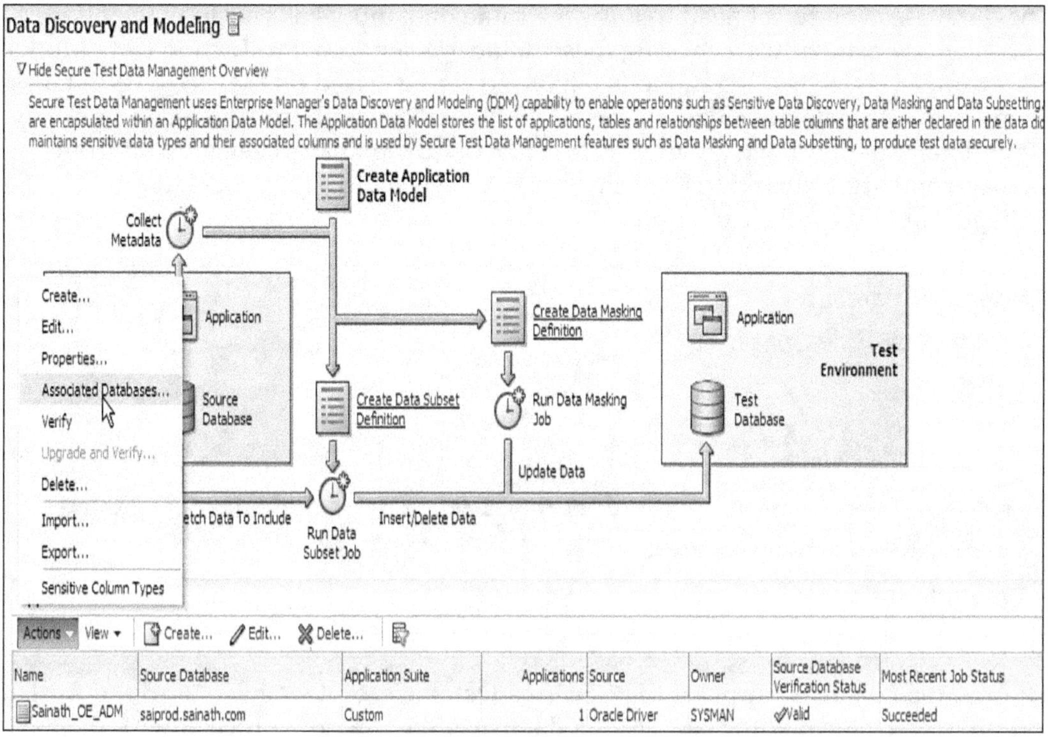


This is an important step and is performed to associate different non-production databases (such as test or development databases) with this model, which was initially created from a production database.

The databases you select need to have the same data model as was in production, since you are manually associating these databases with the Production Data Model. For example, since the data model we have created is based on the `saiprod` database, we need to associate the `saitest` (or `saidev`) database with this model and not any other database—since we know that `saitest` or `saidev` have been created from `saiprod` and are assumed to have the same data structure. The association is displayed in the following figure:

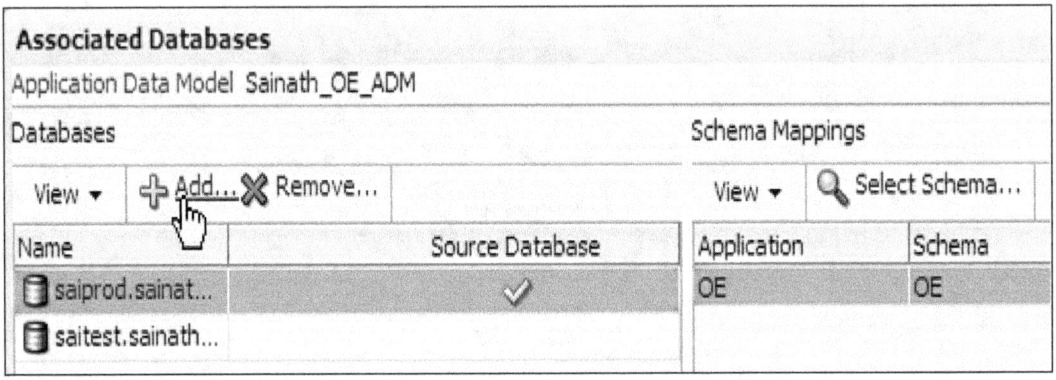


The `saiprod` database appears to be **Source Database**, and we have used the **Add...** button to associate it with the `saitest` database. We can now proceed with the next stage of the workflow, which is data subsetting.

# Data subsetting

The Test Data Management Pack allows the capability of data subsetting. This lets you subset your production databases to create smaller sets of data for test or development databases, based on the Application Data Model. The continual task of refreshing test or development databases is made easier, and storage space is also saved in the process. Let us have a look at how to achieve this. First, select **Enterprise | Quality Management | Data Subset Definitions** to create your **Subset Definition** instance. This brings up the following screen:

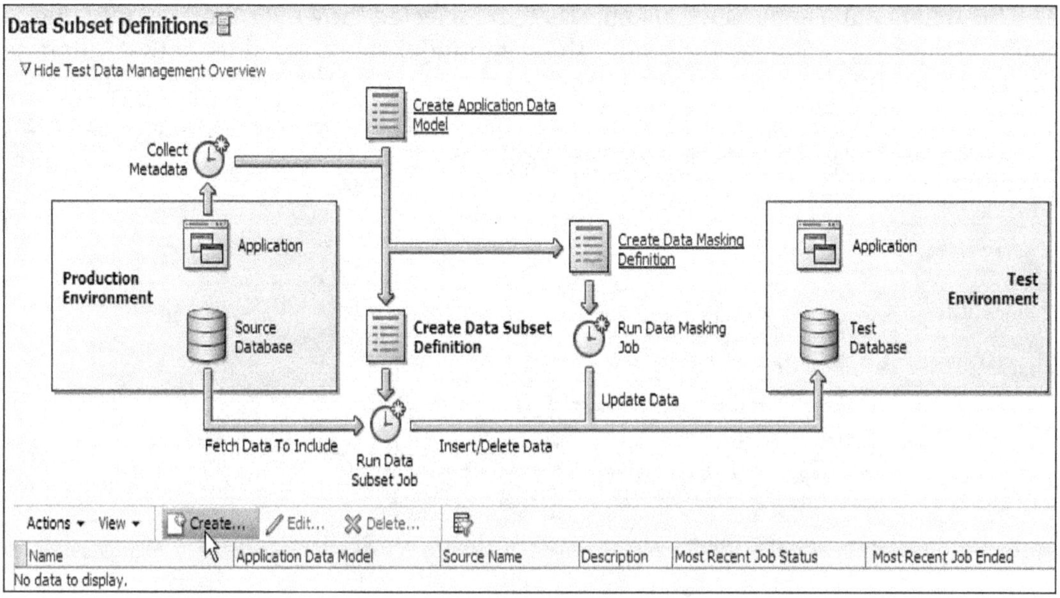


The workflow shown in the preceding screenshot is now at the **Data Subset Definitions** stage, which is the next step in the process. Click on **Create**.

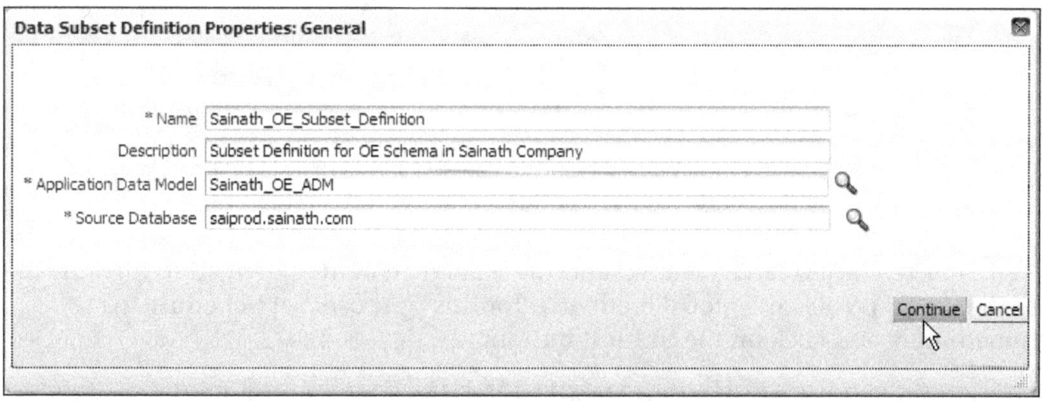


Name the definition appropriately, then select the **Application Data Model** instance to be used.

The **Source Database** instance also needs to be selected, however there is only one choice—the `saiprod` database—since the data model was created from that database. Click on **Continue**.

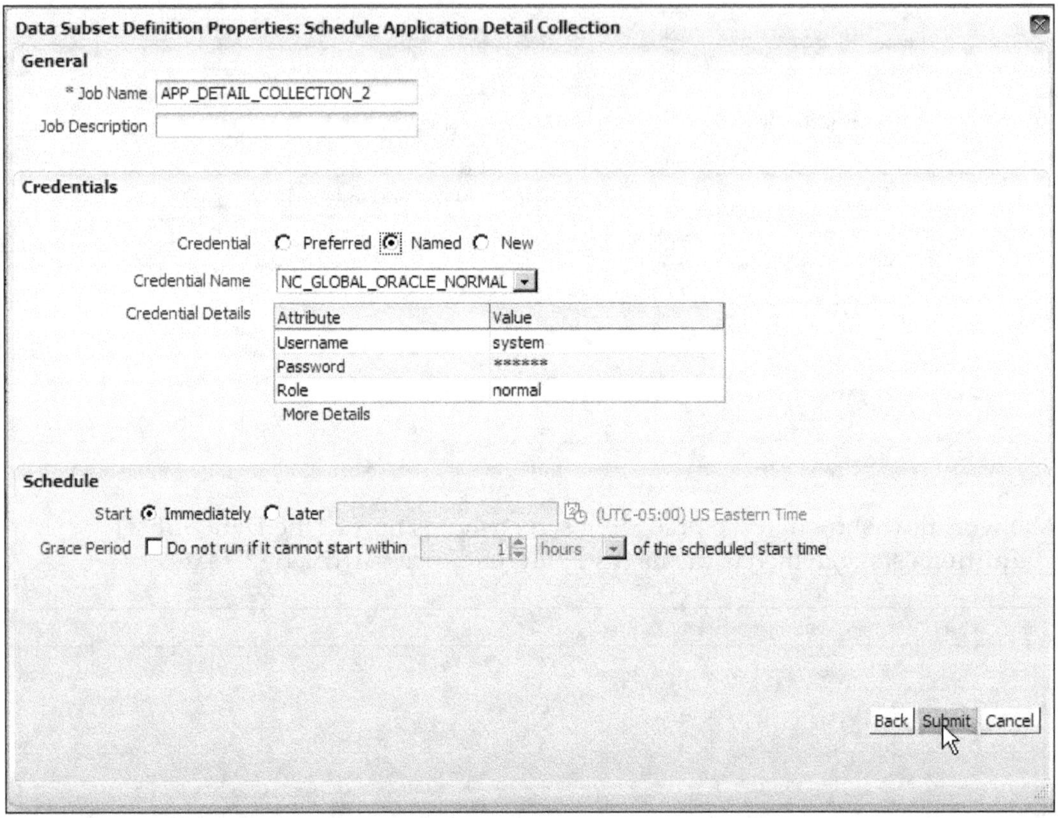


On this page, the job can be named and the named credential defined to log in to the database. We use the global credential for this purpose. Set **Schedule** to start **Immediately** and click on the **Submit** button.

You are told that the **Application Detail Collection** job was submitted successfully. Click on the link in the **Most Recent Job Status** column to view the job details.

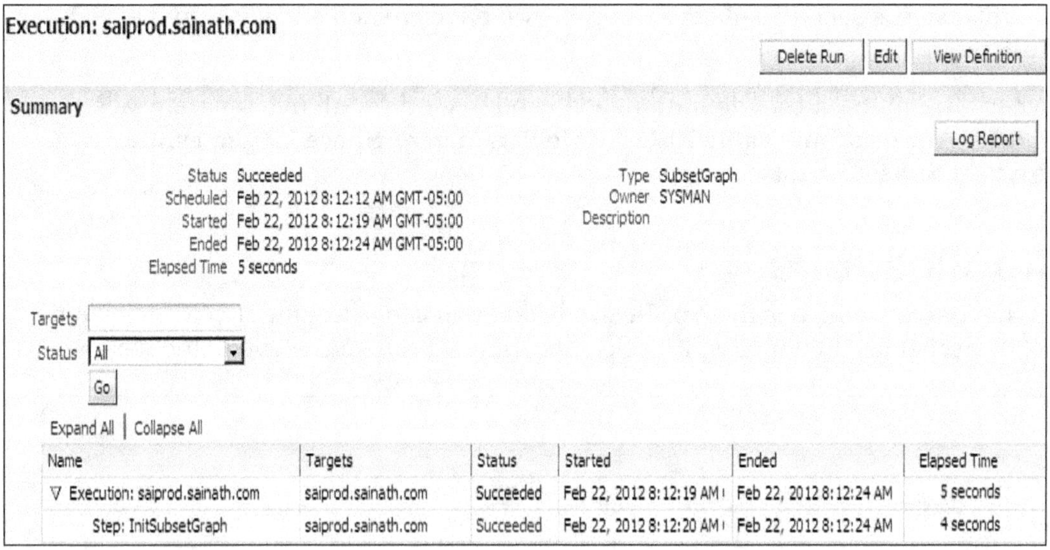


After a few seconds, the job is completed successfully. Return to the **Data Subset Definitions** page by clicking on the backspace button in the browser.

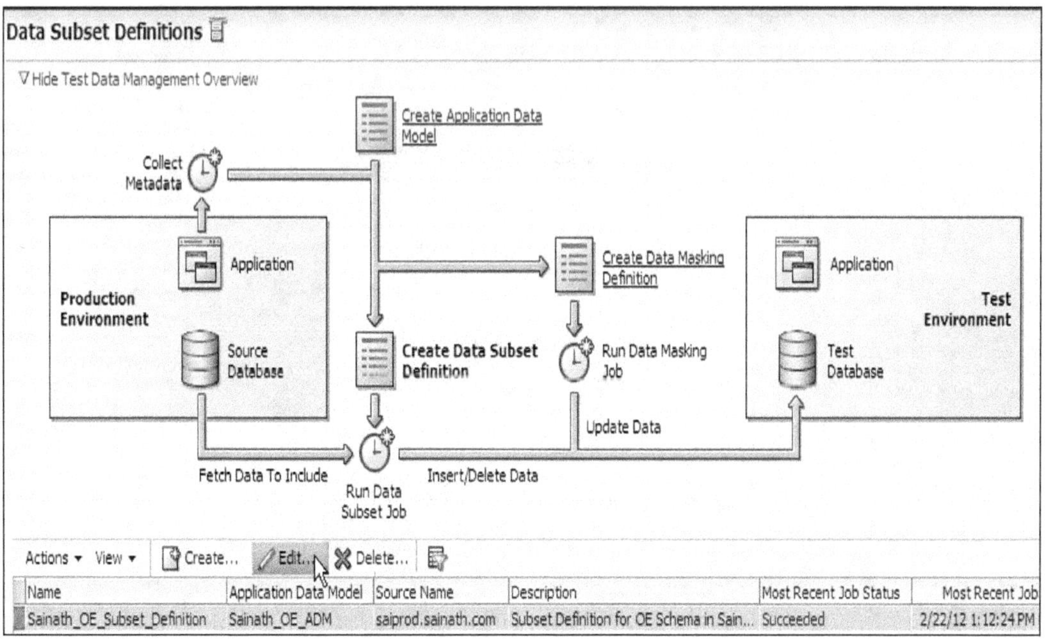

On this page, select the subset definition you have created and click on the **Edit...** button.

When editing the subset definition, you need to go through five separate tabs, namely **Applications, Table Rules, Rule Parameters, Space Estimates,** and **Pre/Post Subset Script**.

# Applications

In the first tab, which is the **Applications** tab, you can select the applications and related schemas. In our case, we select the **OE(OE)** schema. Move to the next tab.

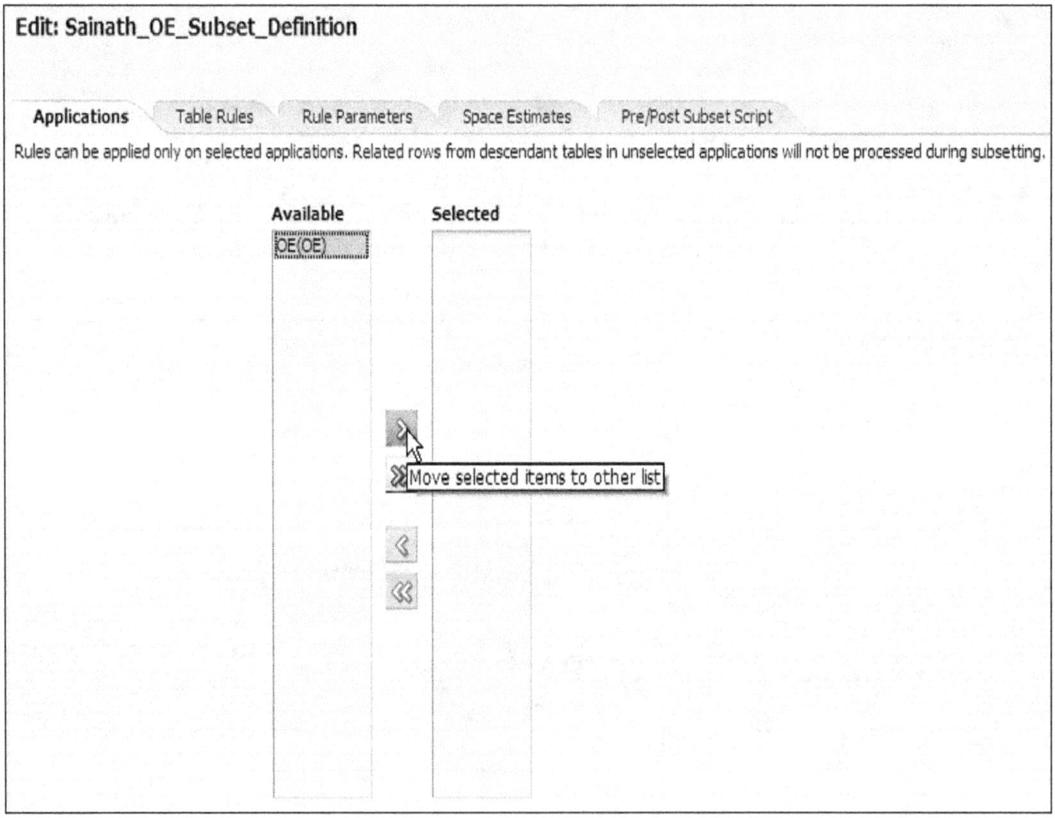

# Table rules

This is the **Table Rules** tab, where we select the tables we want to include in the subset, and the rows we want to include in the tables.

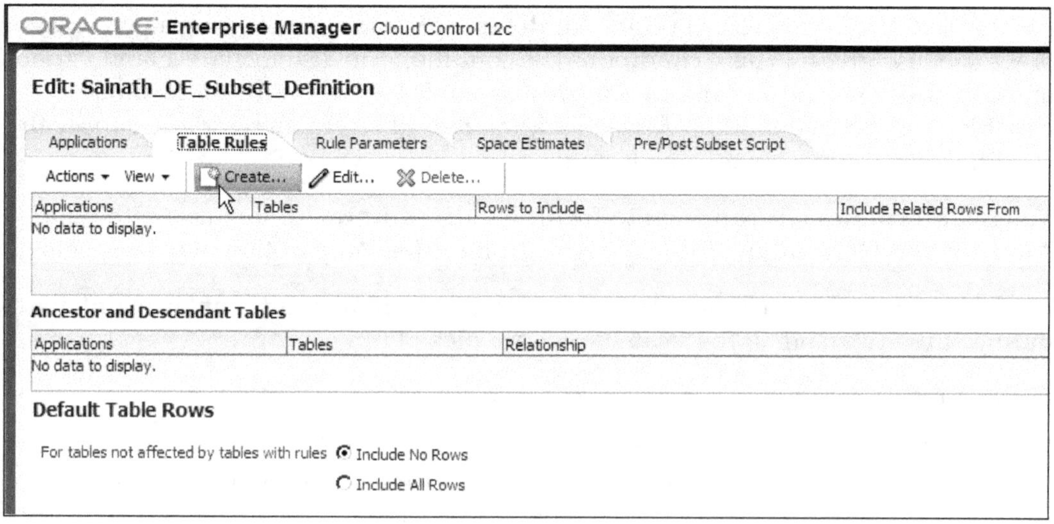


In the next step, click on the **Create...** button to start defining the table rule.

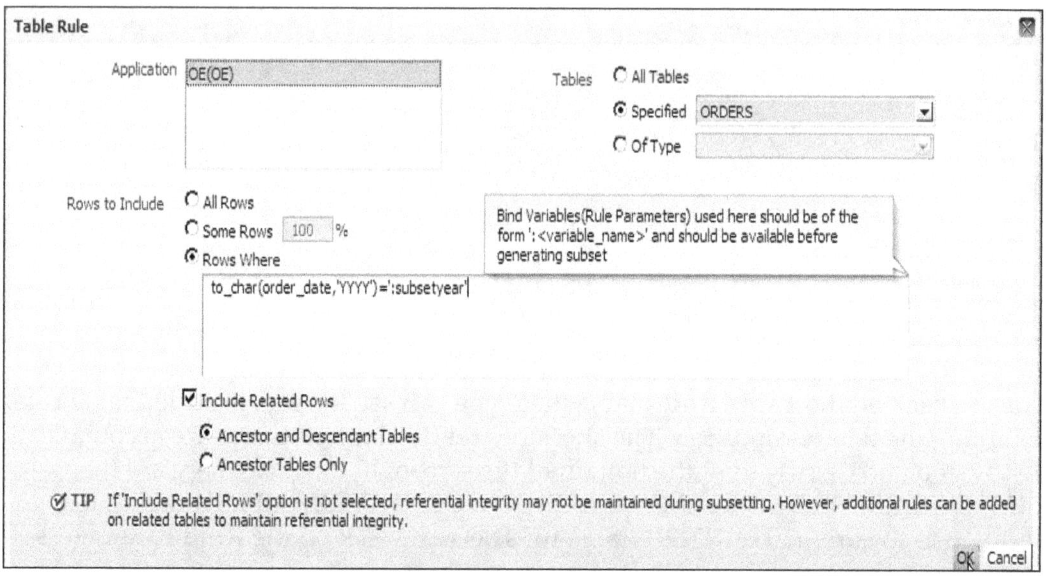

In the pop-up window, you can specify if you want to include **All Tables** from the schema or a **Specified** table that you can select from a list. You can also choose to add tables depending on their type (**Transactional** or **Reference**, or any other type you have defined).

For **Rows to Include**, we can specify **All Rows**, or **Some Rows** (giving a percentage), or we can also give a **Where** condition. The condition can also include a bind variable in the form of <variable name>. The only caveat is that the value of the bind variable needs to be defined before generating the subset. In our case, we supply the condition of `to_char(order_date,'YYYY')=':subsetyear'`.

You can also indicate if you want to **Include Related Rows**. In this case, either the **Ancestor and Descendant Tables** or **Ancestor Tables Only** option may be specified.

It is recommended to include related rows so that referential integrity is maintained during subsetting and all the related rows are picked up.

Click on **OK** to continue.

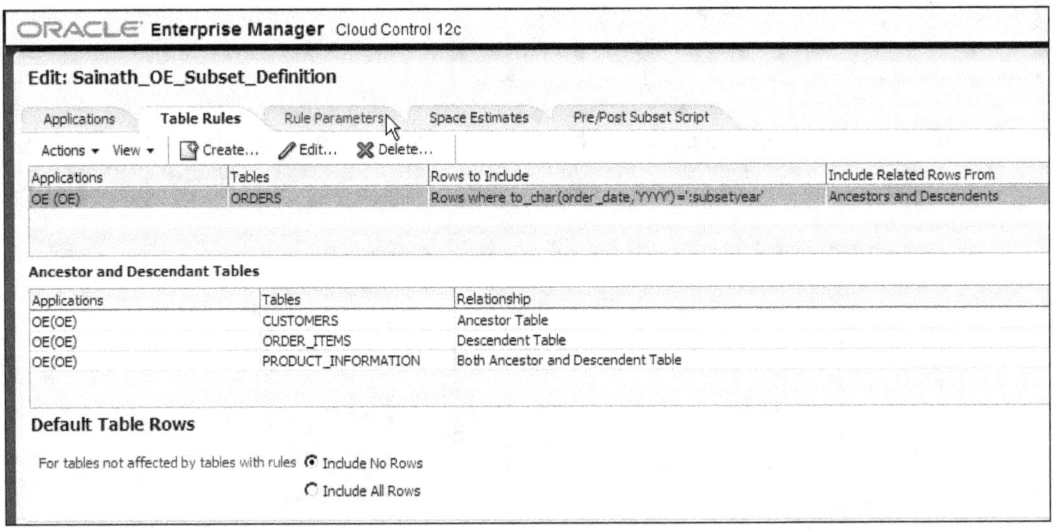


You are back on the **Table Rules** tab, where you can see the newly added table rule, including the **where** condition. The ancestor and descendent tables are automatically discovered and displayed at the bottom of the screen. In our case these are the **CUSTOMERS**, **ORDER_ITEMS**, and **PRODUCT_INFORMATION** tables, in addition to the original **ORDERS** table we selected. Click on the **Rule Parameters** tab to continue.

# Rule parameters

In this tab, you can use the **Create...** button and add a new rule parameter, which is nothing but a bind variable that will be used in the table rule.

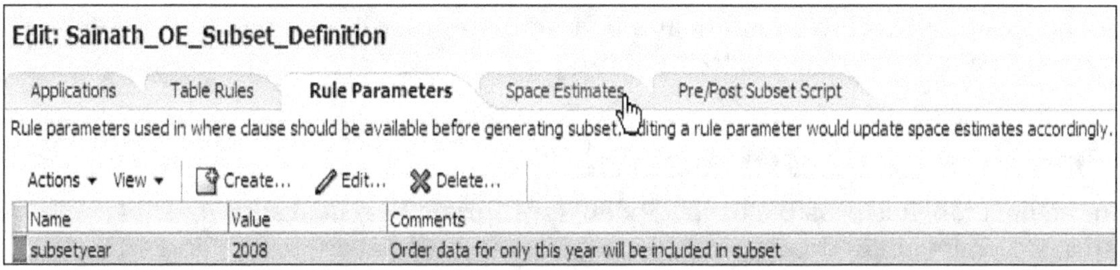


In our case, we create `subsetyear` with the value of `2008`. This variable will be used in the where condition, and only the data for this year will be included. In this way, you can create multiple rule parameters for your table rules.

Now move to the next tab, which is for **Space Estimates**.

# Space estimates

This is an important tab since it tells you the number of rows as well as the size, in MB, of the table that is being added to the subset. Table statistics are analyzed for this purpose.

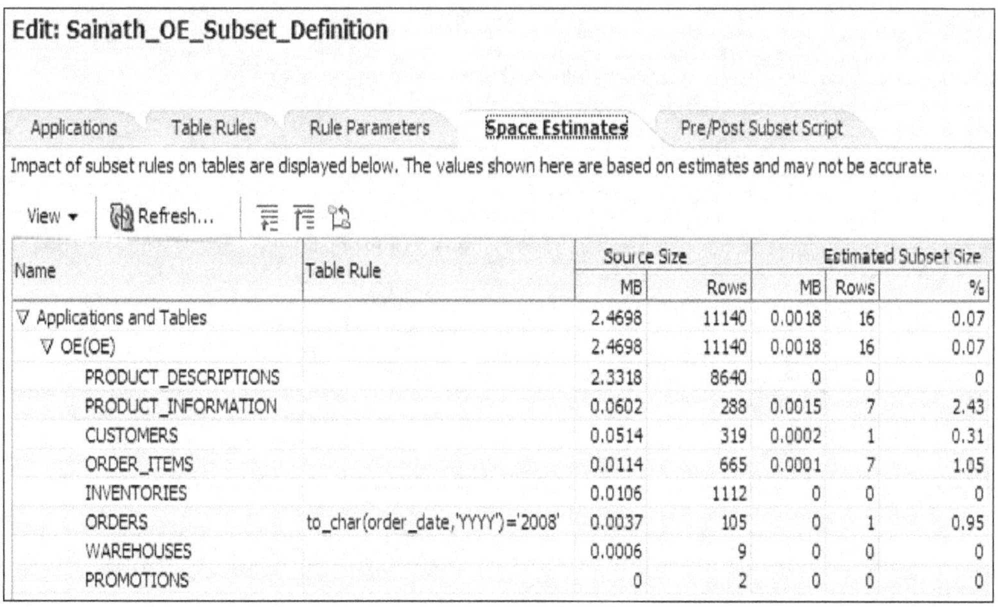

In the preceding example, out of the **288** rows of the **PRODUCT_INFORMATION** table, only **7** rows are being added to the subset. In the same way, only **1** out of **105** rows in the **ORDERS** table and **7** out of **665** rows in **ORDER_ITEMS** will be created in the subset. This is because of the where clause.

So, on this page, you will understand if your where condition is valid, and if enough rows are being carried across to the subset.

# Pre/Post subset script

In the next tab, it is possible to specify an appropriate Pre/Post subset script. This is if you want to do any extra processing on the database before and after extracting the subset. Note that both the pre and post scripts will be executed only on the source database.

There is no requirement to run any such scripts in our case, so we can skip this tab. Click on **Return**.

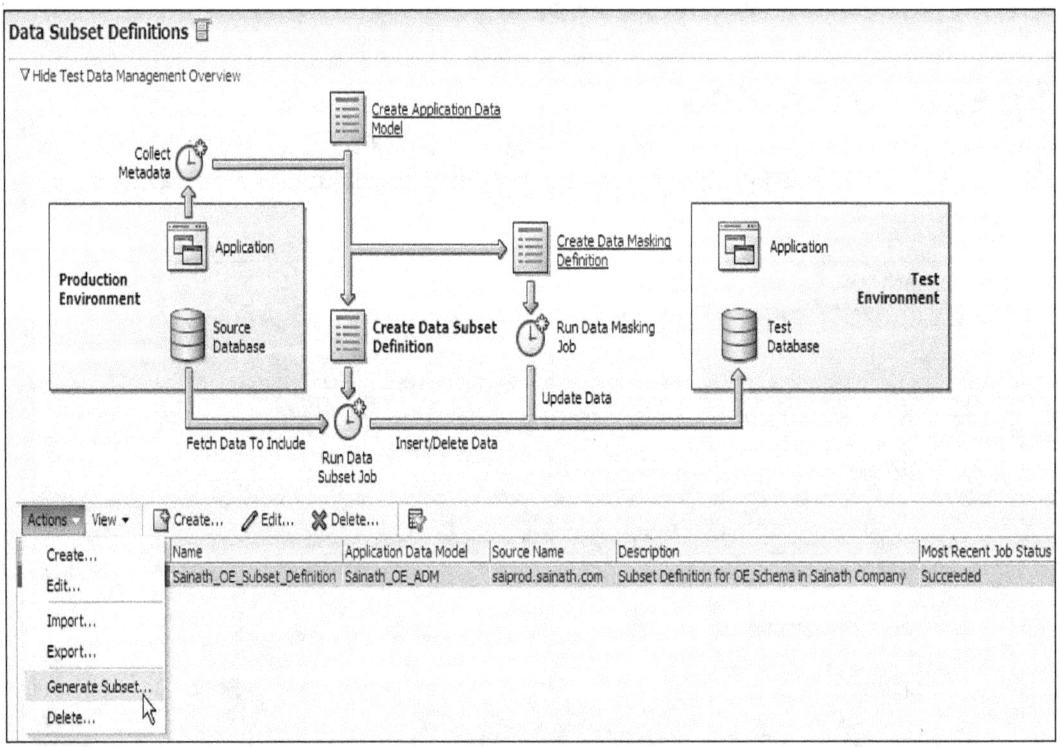


The subset now appears on the **Data Subset Definitions** page.

# Generate subset

From the **Actions** menu, the next step is to select **Generate Subset....**

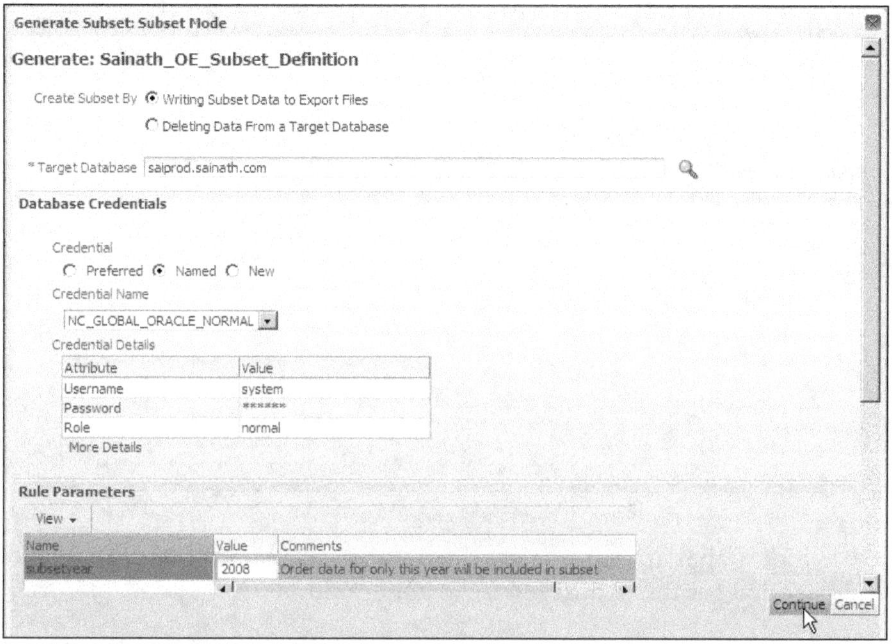


In the **Generate Subset** wizard, you can specify how the subset is to be created. You can either write the subset data to export files (this will use the Oracle Data Pump `expdp` facility), or you can delete the data directly from the target database.

If you select the latter, you will be asked to verify that you are deleting the data from a non-production database. You need to be very careful at this point and make sure you use the glass icon to select the target database. Since we have associated the `saitest` database with this data model, the `saitest` database also appears in the selection list, and you can select it for the data subsetting operation at this point.

However, we decide instead to create the subset by writing the data to export files. Use this option—it is faster and requires the least space. Select the `saiprod` database as the target database, and use **Global Named Credential** as the logon to that database.

The **Rule Parameters** objects, which were defined previously, will be used for creating the subset. These are displayed at the bottom of the page, as shown in the previous screenshot. Click on **Continue**.

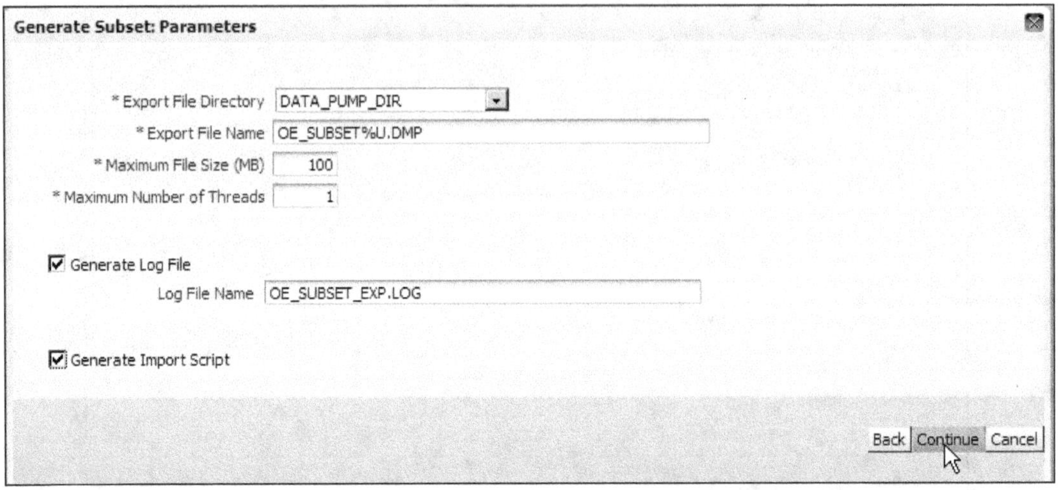


In the next window that appears, select the database directory object that is to be used as the location for the export file to be generated.

You can also name the export file. In our case, we call it `OE_SUBSET%U.DMP`. Note that `%U` means a unique name will be generated.

You can also specify the **Maximum File Size** value in MB (`100` MB by default), and the **Maximum Number of Threads** value when generating the export. This will speed up the data pump export if required.

The export log that will be generated can also be named, and most importantly, you can specify for an Import script to be generated. You can then use this import script to bring the subset data into the different databases as per your needs.

Click on **Continue**.

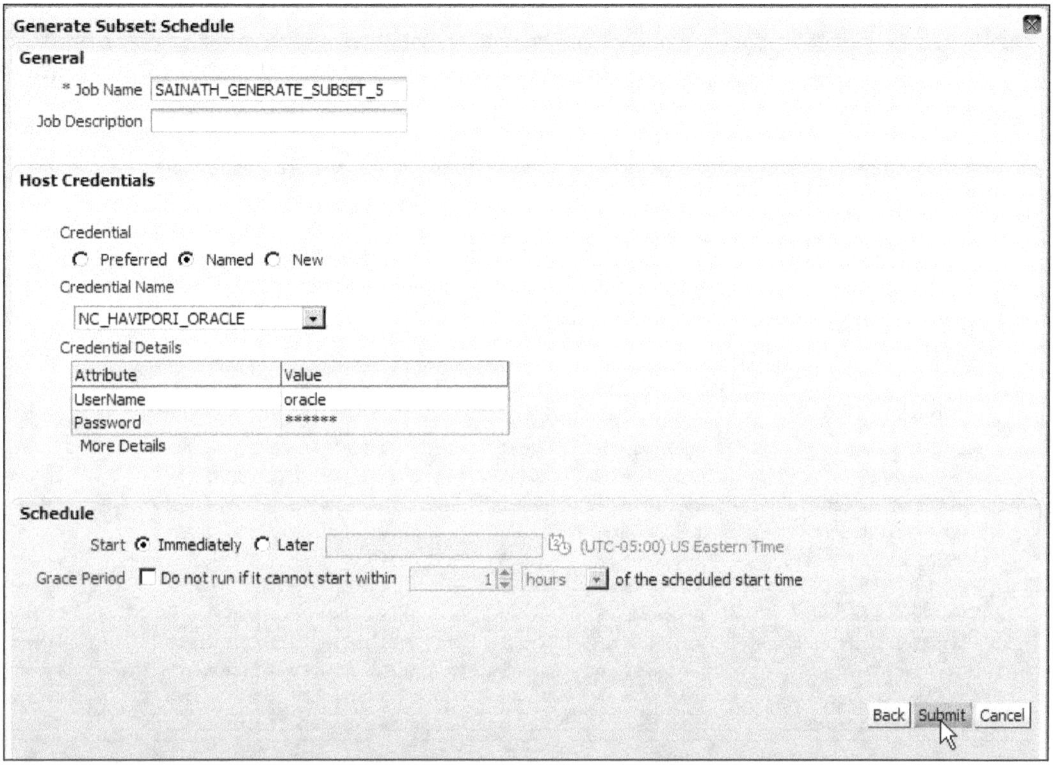


Now you can name the job that will be used to generate the subset. Also, specify **Host Named Credential** for the job to log in at the host level, and specify **Schedule** for the execution (**Immediately** by default).

Click on the **Submit** button. The job is submitted. You can click on the link in the **Most Recent Job Status** column to view the job details.

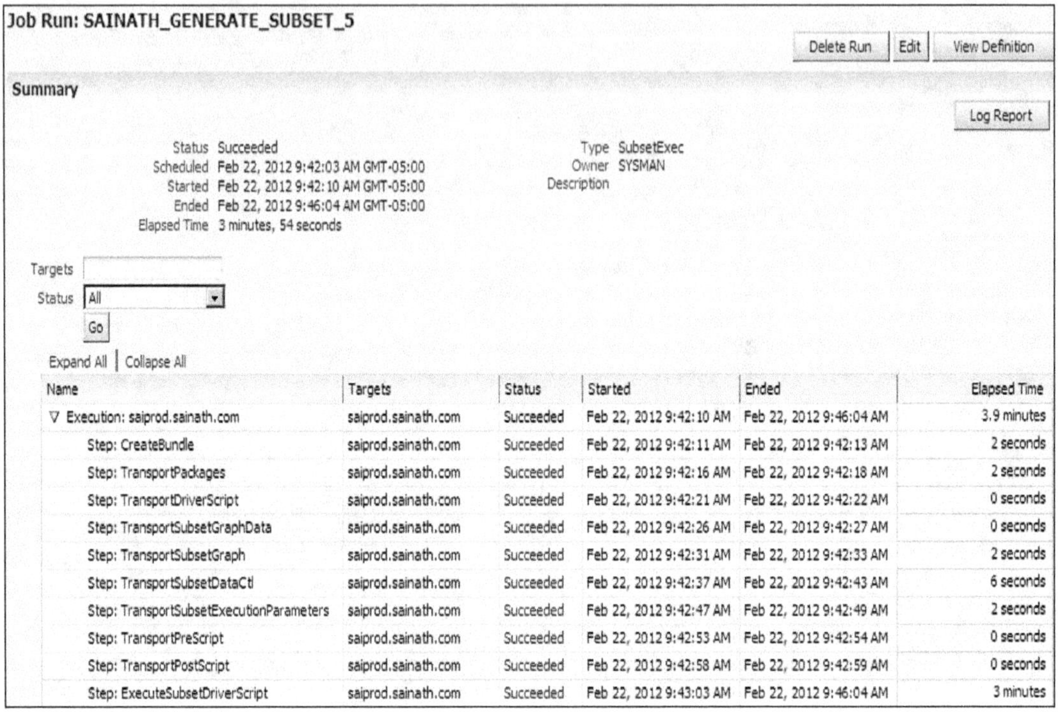


After a few minutes, the job is completed successfully.

Select `DIRECTORY_PATH` from `DBA_DIRECTORIES` in the database to find out the actual directory from where the export files have been generated. In this case, since the directory `DATA_PUMP_DIR` was specified, the location where we can see the export files is `/u01/oracle/db/admin/saiprod/dpdump/`.

```
[oracle@havipori ~]$ cd /u01/oracle/db/admin/saiprod/dpdump/
[oracle@havipori dpdump]$ ls -altr
total 1480
drwxr-x--- 4 oracle oracle    4096 Feb  5 07:34 ..
-rw-r----- 1 oracle oracle     116 Feb  5 10:25 dp.log
-rw-r----- 1 oracle oracle  134480 Feb 22 09:42 dsg_exec_pkg.sql
-rw-r----- 1 oracle oracle    5356 Feb 22 09:42 subset_exec.sql
-rw-r----- 1 oracle oracle    4533 Feb 22 09:42 subset_graph.dmp
-rw-r----- 1 oracle oracle   16030 Feb 22 09:42 graph_tables.sql
```

```
-rw-r----- 1 oracle oracle    1787 Feb 22 09:42 subset_graph.ctl
-rw-r----- 1 oracle oracle     820 Feb 22 09:42 subset_exec_params.lst
-rw-r----- 1 oracle oracle       0 Feb 22 09:42 subset_pre_script.sql
-rw-r----- 1 oracle oracle       0 Feb 22 09:42 subset_post_script.sql
-rw-r----- 1 oracle oracle   11202 Feb 22 09:43 subset_graph.log
-rw-rw-r-- 1 oracle oracle    2968 Feb 22 09:45 OE_SUBSET_EXP.LOG
-rw-rw---- 1 oracle oracle 1290240 Feb 22 09:45 OE_SUBSET01.DMP
drwxr-x--- 2 oracle oracle    4096 Feb 22 09:46 .
-rw-r----- 1 oracle oracle    8712 Feb 22 09:46 subset_import.sql
[oracle@havipori dpdump]$
```

If we examine the generated `subset_import.sql` file, we'll find that it contains instructions to import the data subset (from the `OE_SUBSET01.DMP` file) in three different situations on a target database. Either none of the schemas exist, a part or all of the schemas exist, or the schemas exist with complete metadata but no data. The user is asked to choose between the three situations.

In the second situation, the existing schemas are dropped before the import. In the case of the third situation (existing schema but no data), the constraints are disabled first, and then the triggers. After this, the full import is done, and the constraints and triggers are enabled again.

At the end of the process, the data subset will have been carried over to the development or test database, and the entire process can be repeated again and again.

# Benefits and capabilities

When you create a data subset, you can define subset criteria (such as a where condition), which will limit the amount of data that will be extracted for the subset. As a result, the storage requirements in the target database are reduced. This is one of the most important benefits of data subsetting, since it helps to reduce expensive storage costs.

You can select multiple applications, that is, schemas (in the case of multi-tenanted databases) for the subset. The definition of tables associated with these applications and the relationships between them will be extracted from the Application Data Model into the subset definition, along with additional metadata of the constraints and indexes. You can totally avoid the manual labor normally associated with collecting this information and writing appropriate scripts.

Table rules can be defined with where clauses and bind variables that limit the data that is extracted. Table statistics are then analyzed to get an estimate of the size of the resulting reduced tables. The estimate is very useful to understand the storage benefits of the data subsetting process before the actual process takes place.

In the two methods used for data subsetting, the recommended method would be to generate the data pump export files as we have seen in this chapter. The subset data is directly written to the export file, and it can then be imported into the test database.

This is the faster method and requires the least space. An import script is also generated by the process, and can be used to perform an import of the subset into any test or development database.

The other method is to make a clone of the production database and then run the deletion of the data directly on that, leaving the subset behind. This method will necessarily take more time (because of the cloning and in-place deletion) and also require more space to accommodate the initial clone database.

In the case of certain Oracle-packaged applications, such as Oracle E-Business Suite and Oracle Fusion Applications, the Test Data Management Pack ships with predefined drivers that enable the Application Data Model capability of the pack to be used for the discovery of referential relationships that are defined at the application level. The drivers create the ADM from the metadata of these applications. In the case of Oracle E-Business, the `apps` user can be used to deploy as well as create the Application Data Model.

To generate subsets of these applications, the next step is to create the subset definition that has the actual rules to extract data from the application data tables. At the time of writing, you will need to create this subset definition yourself based on your application-specific expertise, or you can ask Oracle Consulting to assist in creating the subset definition. This suggestion also applies to other Oracle-packaged applications, such as PeopleSoft and Siebel, where there is no out of the box discovery of application-level relationships, neither are there predefined subsetting rules. Only database-level relationships will be discovered in these databases, as with any other Oracle database used for in-house or non-Oracle applications.

An interesting capability is that third-party databases, such as Microsoft SQL Server, Sybase, and IBM DB2, can also be subsetted with the Test Data Management Pack, if Oracle Database Gateway is used for moving data between the non-Oracle database and Oracle, and back again after subsetting. The optimized version of the Oracle Gateway to use for this purpose is `11.2.0.3` onwards.

One other point to note is that it is not recommended or supported to use the Test Data Management Pack for making subsets on production itself, such as for archiving data or separating data in the same database. The Test Data Management Pack should primarily be used to make smaller subsets from production onto other databases. At the time of writing, the Oracle documentation for Test Data Management has been placed as `Part III` in `Oracle Database Real Application Testing User's Guide 11g Release 2 (11.2)`, at the following URL:

`http://docs.oracle.com/cd/E11882_01/server.112/e16540/part3.htm`

# Summary

When we set up test systems, it is often the case that full production copies cannot be used due to the cost of storage, especially for large databases. In such cases, you would need to extract a relationally valid subset of data. Doing this manually is not an easy task, but it has to be done. Consequently, setting up test systems is often a slow, error-prone, manually-scripted process.

A lot of investigation is required to find the relationships in the database across various schemas; the rules for extraction need to be defined (keeping intact all the relationships), and even then you are not sure of the space requirements for the extracted subset.

The Test Data Management Pack allows you to reverse engineer an Application Data Model from your database, which is stored in the Enterprise Manager Cloud Control 12*c* repository. The metadata definition of tables and relationships from a single or multiple schemas can exist in a model, which can then be used to enable test data operations, including data subsetting and data masking. Subsetting requires the Test Data Management Pack license, whereas masking requires the Data Masking Pack license.

The modeling and automation provided by the data subsetting features of the Test Data Management Pack is certainly effective in streamlining the process of creating smaller test or development databases out of much larger production databases. It is bound to be helpful in the day-to-day operations of the data center, especially when a lot of test databases need to be refreshed every now and then.

Once discovered, enhanced, and stored in the Enterprise Manager repository, the Application Data Model can also be used by the data masking capabilities of Enterprise Manager Cloud Control 12*c*. We will examine this in detail in the next chapter.

# 9
# Ease the Chaos with Data Masking

In the day-to-day life of the data center, data is frequently copied from production to non-production databases such as test and development databases, and this is required for volume or functional testing, or for the developers to test out their new programs with realistic data.

However, the copied data may contain confidential information, such as credit card numbers, identification numbers (Social Security Number or passport number), which must be protected as per several regulatory requirements—**Sarbanes Oxley** (**SOX**), **Payment Card Industry Data Security Standards** (**PCI DSS**), **Health Insurance Portability and Accountability Act** (**HIPPA**), and other regulations and laws restricting customer data usage. If the copied data is left as it is in the test or development database, it is possible that external or internal hackers may misuse this data. Therefore, it is incumbent on the database department to somehow de-identify or mask this data before it is copied to development or test.

For this purpose, home grown SQL and PL/SQL scripts written by the DBA are normally used, but these have several disadvantages. The scripts have to be continuously updated when the regulatory policies change, and they soon become difficult to maintain. The scripts have to take into consideration the relationships between the masked table and other tables and have to be rewritten for every database where there is a similar masked column but different relationships. They are not centralized, nor are they scalable enough to handle hundreds of databases. Also, it is difficult for auditors to understand the scripts and make an assessment of the masking processes in use in the company and whether they satisfy the regulatory requirements in full.

What is needed is a centralized, scalable solution for data de-identification, and this is provided by Oracle Enterprise Manager Cloud Control 12*c*'s **Data Masking Pack**. We will examine this pack in detail in this chapter.

# Finding sensitive data

The first step is to discover the sensitive data in your production database. This is done by scanning the database, using out of the box patterns for the discovery.

Select **Enterprise | Quality Management | Data Discovery and Modeling**. The **Secure Test Data Management Overview** page (which we have seen in the previous chapter when the Application Data Model instance was created) appears.

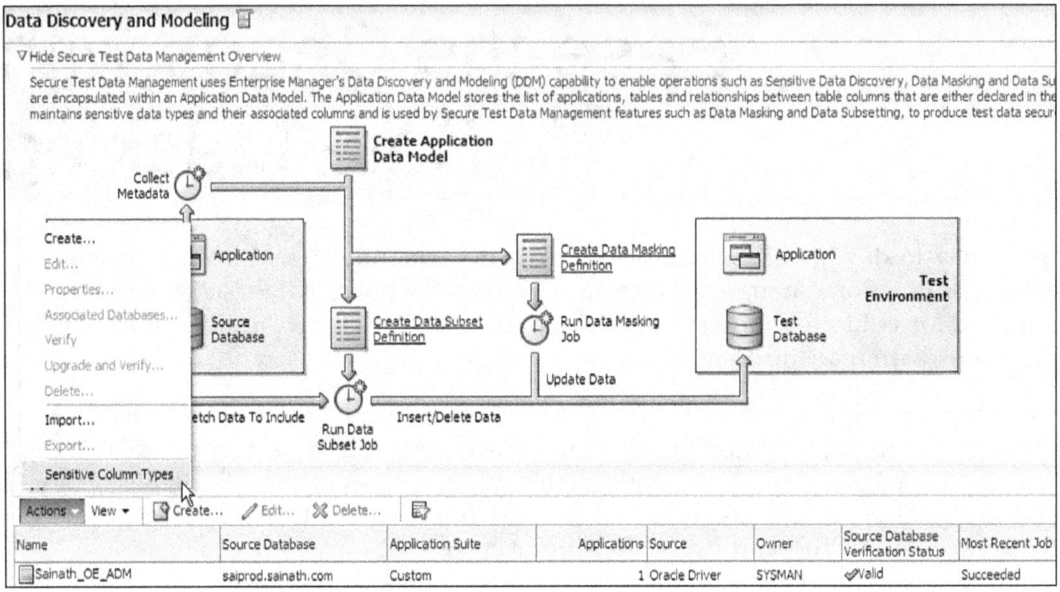


Click on the **Actions** menu and select **Sensitive Column Types**. This displays the following screen:

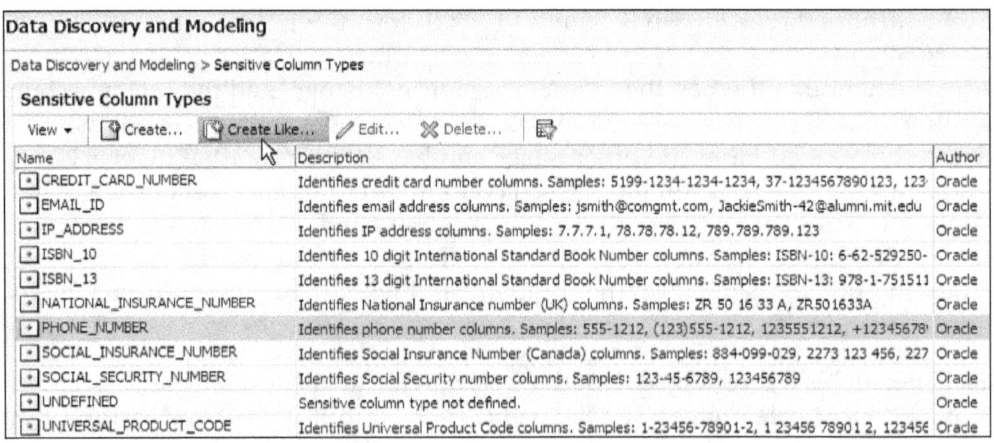

We can see a number of out of the box instances of sensitive column types. These are patterns that help to identify data that would normally be considered confidential, such as credit card number, phone number, email ID, Social Security Number, and others.

Let us create a new sensitive column type. For example, select **PHONE_NUMBER** and click on **Create Like...**.

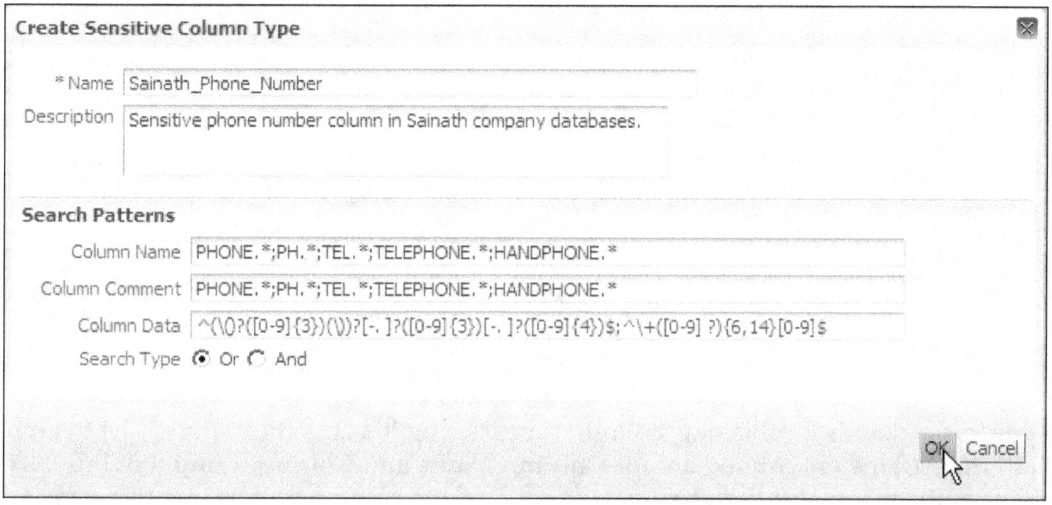


Name the new sensitive column type appropriately. In the **Search Patterns** section, whatever is specified in **Column Name** or **Column Comment** will be used during the search to identify the existence of the sensitive column.

In our case, we have added a few extra values to **Column Name** and **Column Comment**, such as `HANDPHONE.*`. This means that a column or comment containing this word will be treated as a sensitive type.

The pattern of the **Column Data** string can also be changed. This pattern will be used to examine the actual data in the columns in an attempt to identify it as sensitive.

You can force all the conditions to be met during the search by selecting **And** as the **Search Type** option. The default is **Or**, that is, meeting any of the conditions will mark it as a sensitive column.

Click on **OK** to save the new sensitive column type instance. You are back on the **Sensitive Column Types** page. Click on **Create** to create another sensitive column type, this time for any **SALARY** column.

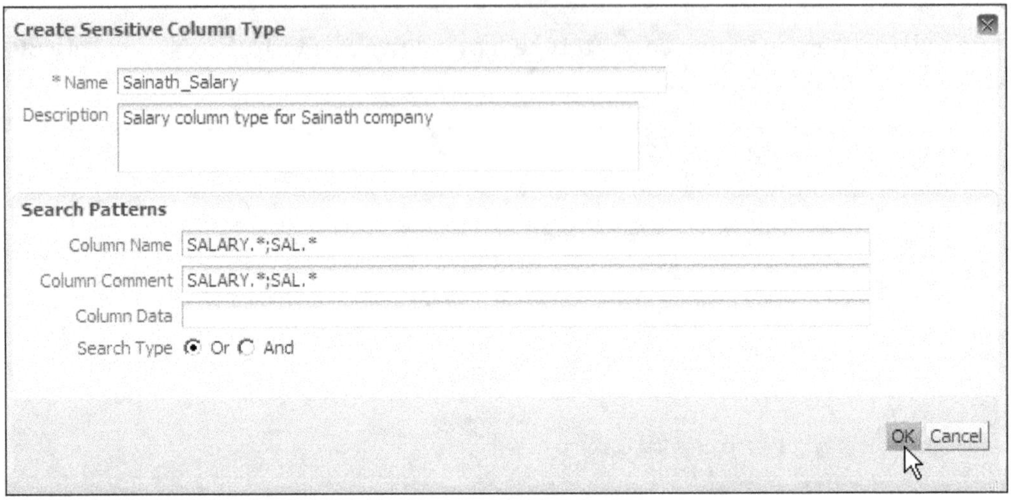


Type in the details for this new column type, calling it `Sainath_Salary`. The **Search Patterns** parameters entered are for **Column Name** and **Column Comment** only. If either of them contains the word `SAL` or `SALARY`, the column will be identified as a potential sensitive column. Click on **OK** to save this column type.

The **Sensitive Column Types** page reappears. Click on the **Data Discovery and Modeling** breadcrumb.

Now, create a new application data model called `Sainath_HR_ADM` from the source database `saiprod`. Select the **HR** schema for this model. After the job is submitted, the Application Data Model will be created successfully.

The new model can be seen in the **Application Data Models** list on the **Data Discovery and Modeling** page.

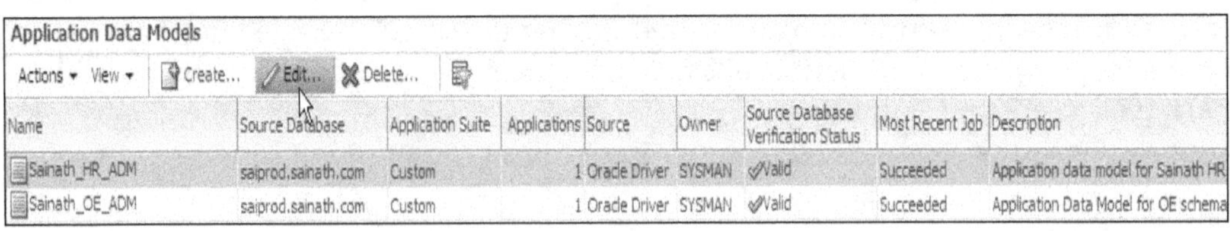

Select the newly created **Sainath_HR_ADM** model and click on **Edit**.

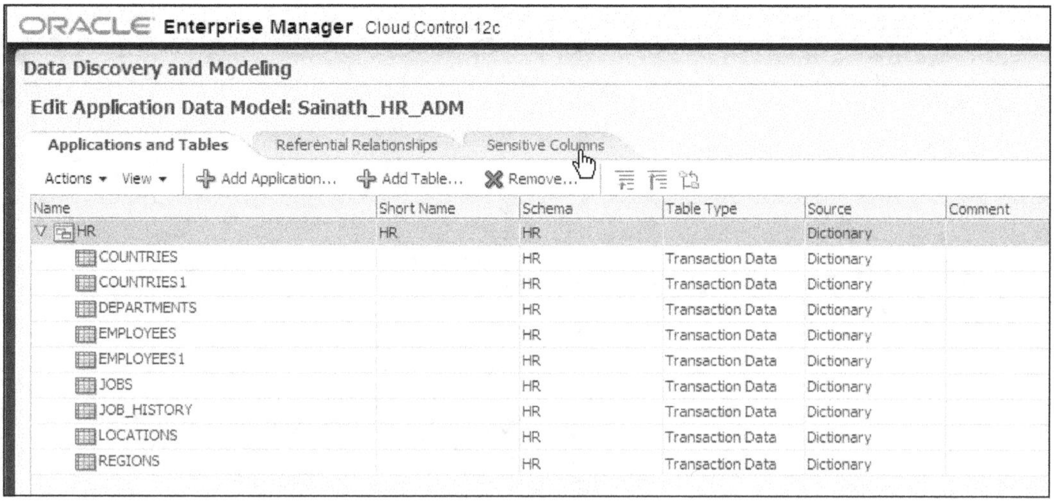

On the **Edit Application Data Model** page, you can see the applications and tables that have been picked up into the model as well as the referential relationships in two separate tabs.

Move to the **Sensitive Columns** tab.

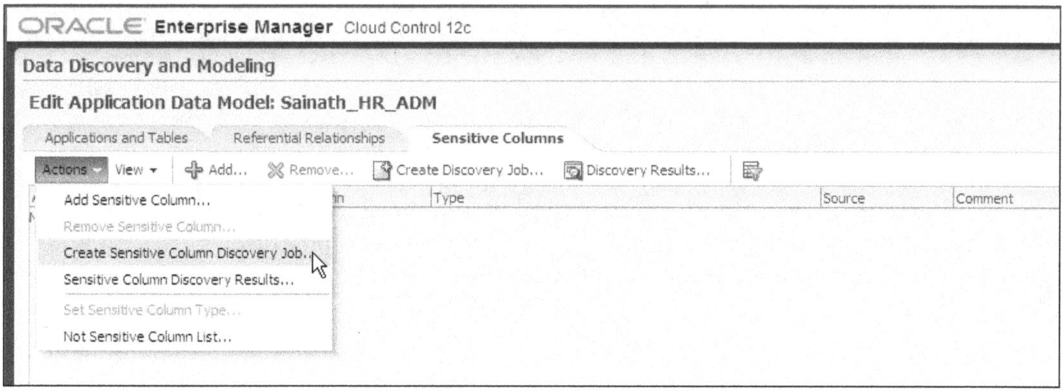

On the **Sensitive Columns** tab, click on the **Actions** menu and select **Create Sensitive Column Discovery Job...**.

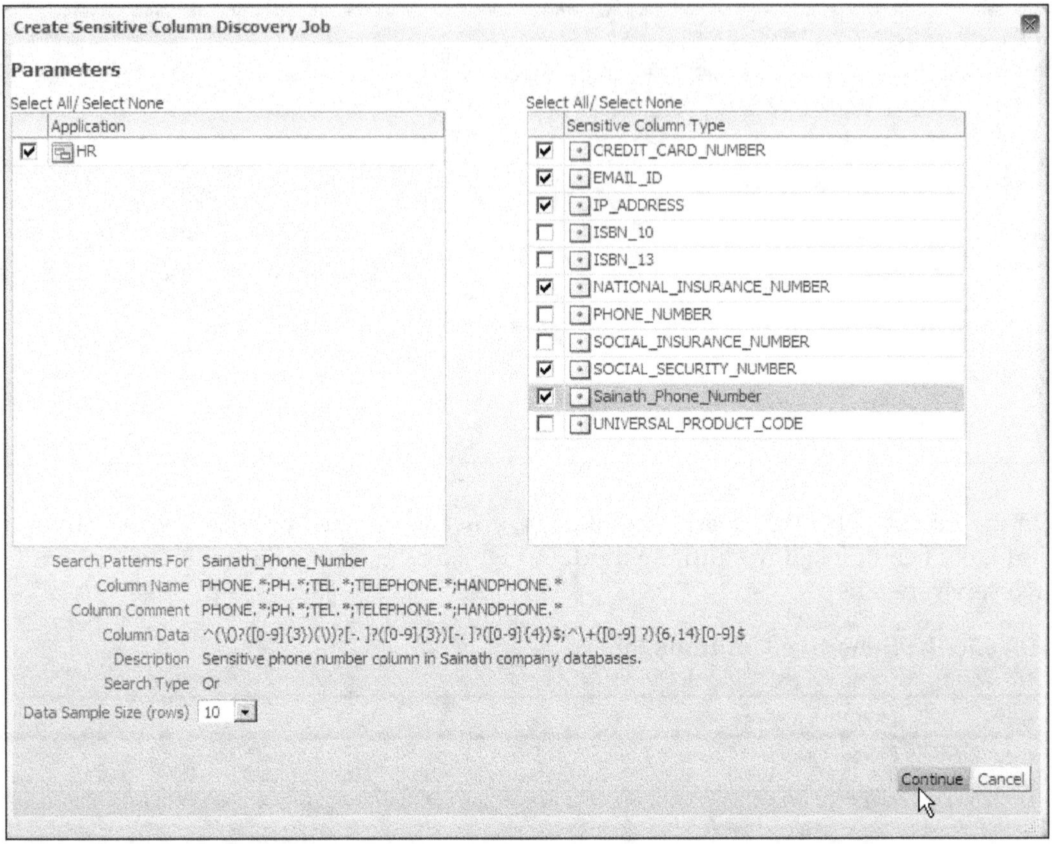


The applications in the data model are displayed as well as the sensitive column types. By default, all are unselected. You must now select the application you want to check and the sensitive column types to use in the checking.

For each sensitive column type that you select, you can change the **Data Sample Size (rows)** to **10**, **50**, or **100** rows. This allows you to avoid scanning the whole table. Click on **Continue**.

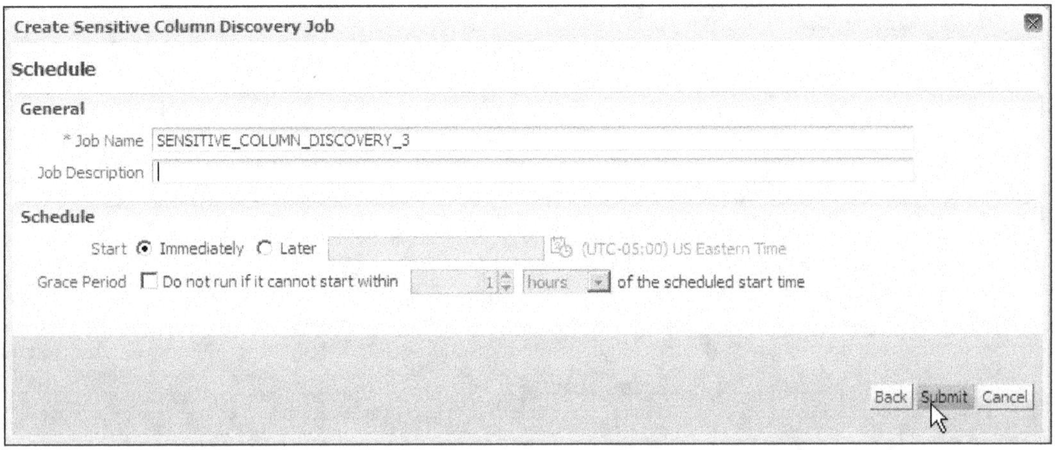


You can change the **Job Name** string if you wish. Schedule the job to run immediately, and click on **Submit**.

The **Sensitive Column Discovery Job** request is submitted successfully. Move back to the **Application Data Models** home page. You can click on the link in the **Most Recent Job Status** column to view the job details. The job is completed successfully.

Select the **Sainath_HR_ADM** model and click on **Edit**.

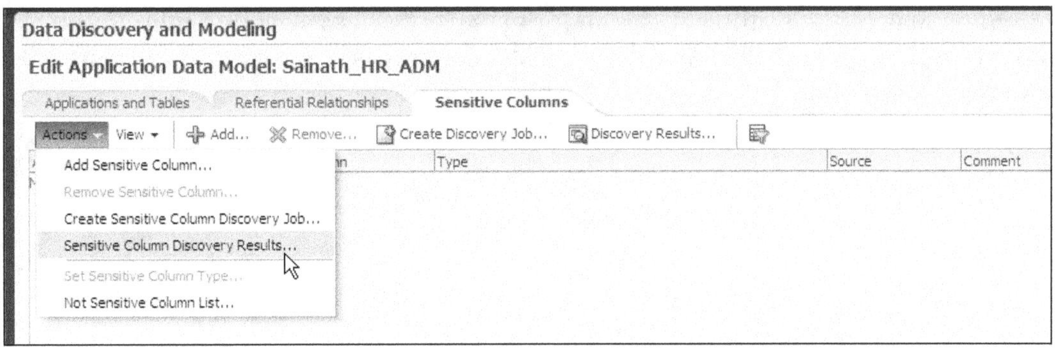

Move to the **Sensitive Columns** tab. Click on the **Actions** menu, and select **Sensitive Column Discovery Results....**

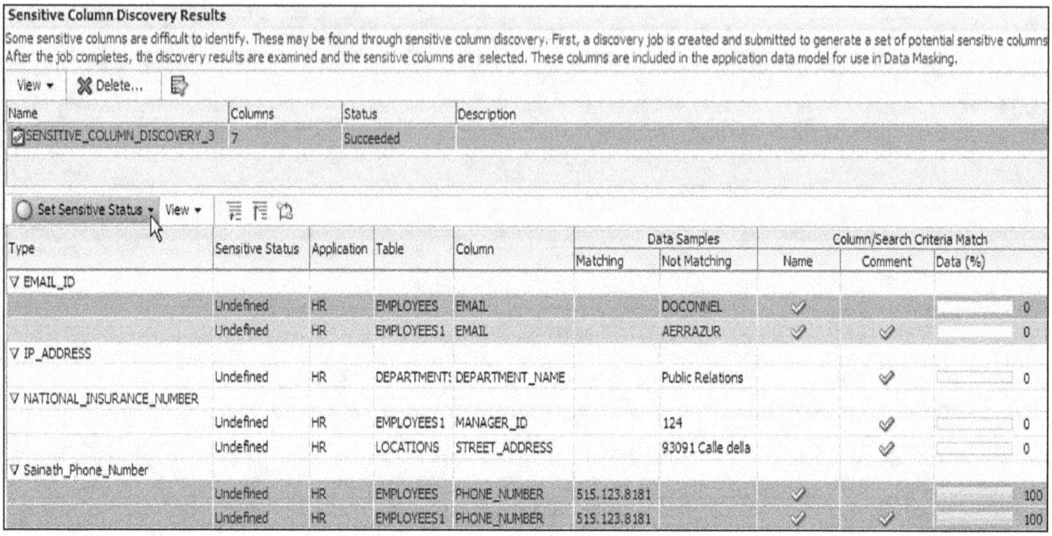


The **Sensitive Column Discovery Results** screen appears. This shows that seven potential sensitive columns have been tentatively identified. The sensitive column types are displayed on the left. The **Sensitive Status** is currently **Undefined** for all the columns.

Whether the name of the column or the comment or the data has matched, is seen on this page. Some columns have had a **100** percent data match. Some have had a wrong comment match (for example, the scan for `IP_ADDRESS` as a sensitive column type has wrongly suggested the `DEPARTMENT_NAME` column as being sensitive because the comment was matched).

You can now judge for yourself and select the columns that really are sensitive, such as the **EMAIL** columns and the **PHONE_NUMBER** columns. Select these 4 columns and click on **Set Sensitive Status**.

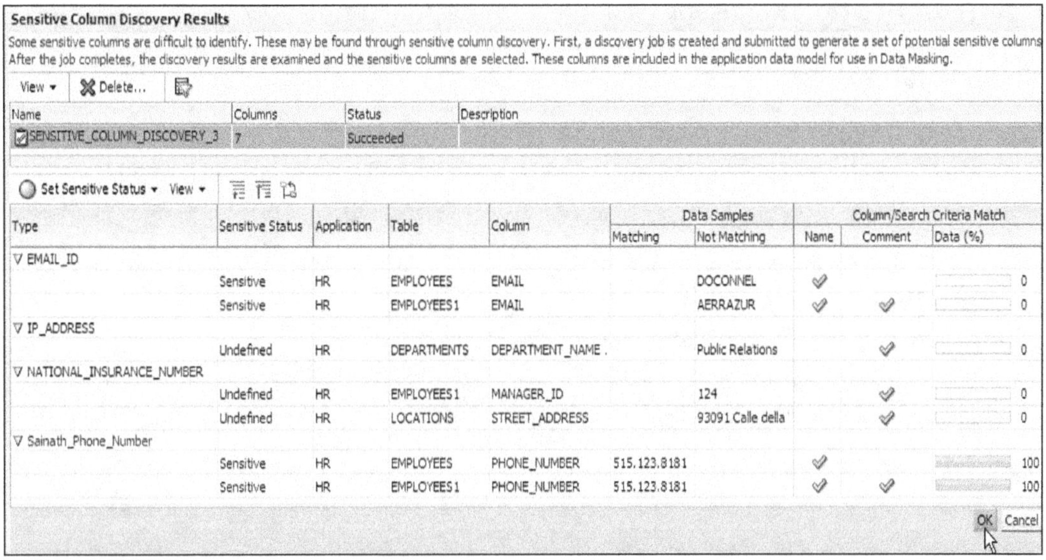

The **Sensitive Status** for these four columns changes to **Sensitive**. Click on **OK**.

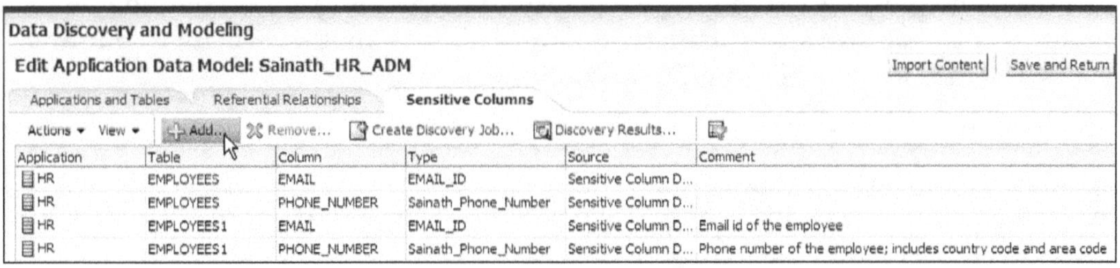

You are placed back on the **Edit Application Data Model** screen. The **Sensitive Columns** tab now shows the four columns that have been marked as sensitive.

In addition to the sensitive column discovery, you can manually add more columns to the **Sensitive Column** list by clicking on the **Add** button.

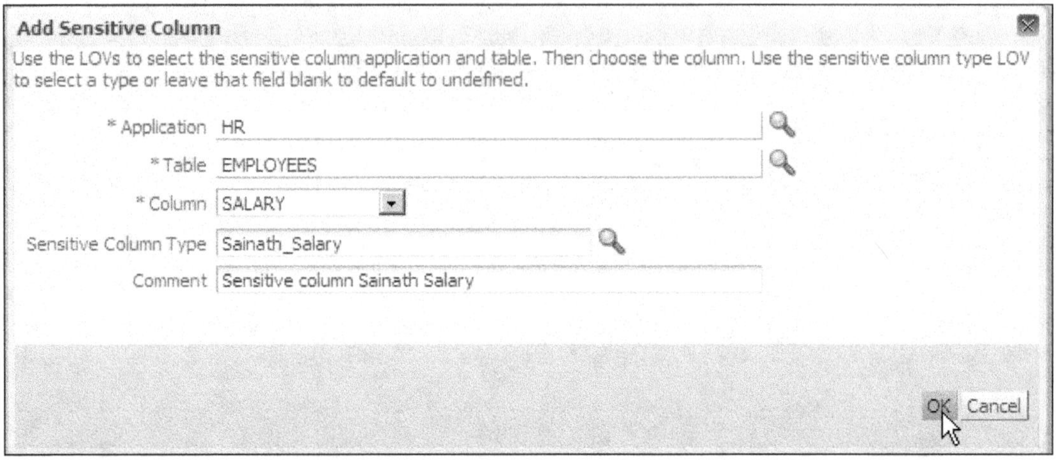


In the **Add Sensitive Column** window, you can select the **Application**, **Table**, and **Column** instances you want to manually add to your **Sensitive Column** list.

Also select the sensitive column type instance corresponding to the column you have chosen. In this case, we select **Sainath_Salary**. This was another sensitive column type we created earlier. Click on **Ok** to continue.

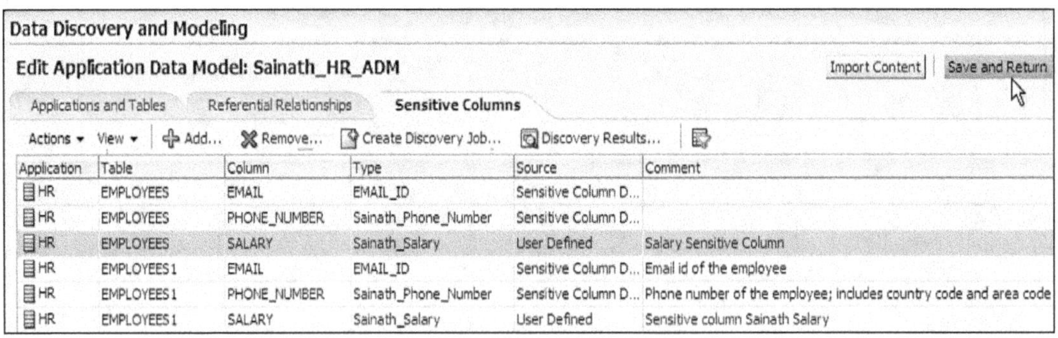

The new column we have added now appears in the **Sensitive Columns** list on the **Edit Application Data Model** page. Click on **Save and Return**.

When you are back on the **Data Discovery and Modeling** page, select the **Sainath_HR_ADM** model from the Application Data Models list.

Open the **Actions** menu and select **Associated Databases**. Use this to associate the `saitest` database with the Application Data Model. Two databases are now associated with the model, the first being the `saiprod` database (which is the source database), and the second, the `saitest` database. This is the database on which the actual masking job will be performed.

# Creating data masking definitions

The next step is to create appropriate data masking definitions. These definitions will be used during the actual masking of your sensitive data.

Select **Enterprise** | **Quality Management** | **Data Masking Definitions**. This displays the **Data Masking Definitions** screen, as shown in the following screenshot:

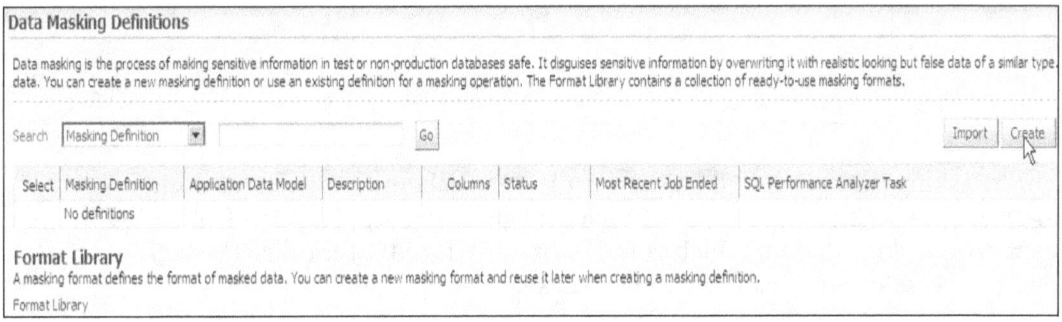

Currently, we can see that there are no masking definitions. A masking definition defines what columns are to be masked and the masking format to be used for those columns. To create the masking definition, click on **Create**.

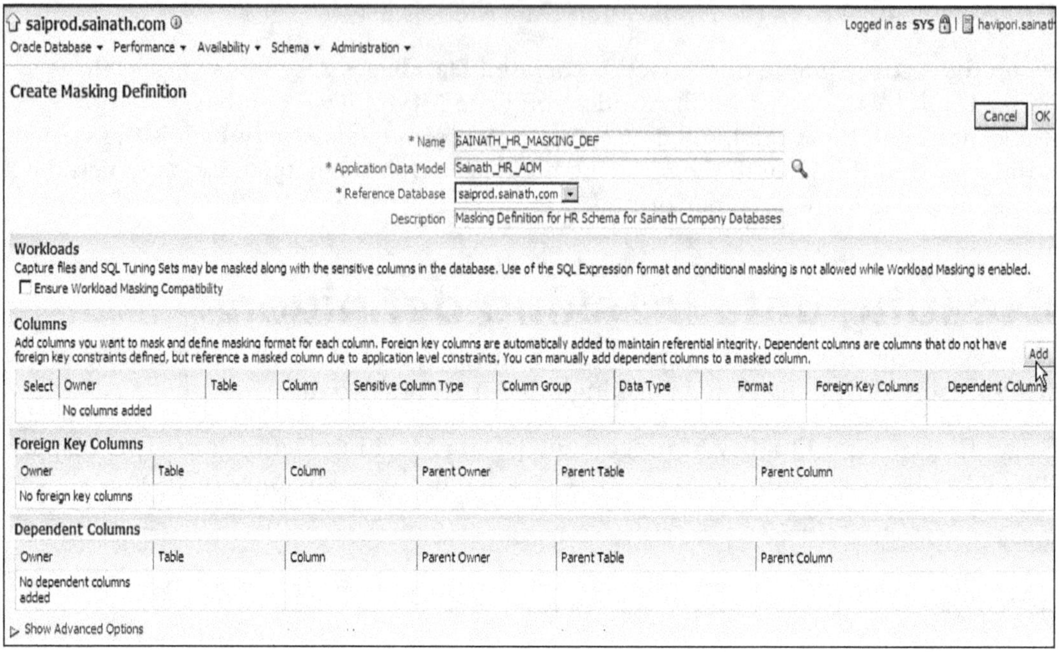

This masking definition will be used for the HR schema, so we have named it `SAINATH_HR_MASKING_DEF`. Select the corresponding **Application Data Model** instance for this schema, which is the **Sainath_HR_ADM** model. The `saiprod` database is selected as **Reference Database.**

# New capabilities

In Enterprise Manager Cloud Control 12*c*, data masking has a new and powerful capability. Along with the sensitive columns in the database, it can also mask sensitive data in the Workload Capture files that are generated and used by the Database Replay feature of the **Real Application Testing** (**RAT**) database option. In addition, it can mask the bind data in the **SQL Tuning Sets** (**STS**) that are used by the **SQL Performance Analyzer** (**SPA**) feature of RAT.

This plugs a loophole that existed in earlier versions. In those versions (Enterprise Manager 10*g*/11*g*), while sensitive data could be masked in the tables themselves, the Workload Capture files and SQL Tuning Sets that were transferred across databases could potentially still contain sensitive data. In Enterprise Manager Cloud Control 12*c*, the sensitive data is also masked in the Capture files and SQL Tuning Sets, and AWR Sensitive Bind Data is purged.

However, workload masking may not be supported by the target database chosen. In this case, an error telling you to apply a patch will be displayed. At the time of writing, the patch is available for the `11.2.0.2` database on Linux x86 and Linux 64-bit. This is patch `12573945: RAT+ DM TRACKING BUG FOR 11.2.0.2.0`. Apply this patch to the staging database where masking will be performed (not on the database where replay is done). Note that this patch may be proven obsolete by future bundle fixes, so please check with **My Oracle Support** (**MOS**).

If workload masking is required, in the **Workloads** section, select **Ensure Workload Masking Compatibility**. Note that, when workload masking is enabled, masking cannot use the SQL expression format, nor can it use conditional masking. The reason for the latter restriction is that, if conditional masking is used, the Database Replay Capture files and SQL Tuning Sets may not contain the entire data set, and also, the conditions may be based on values outside the workload.

Another point to note is that masking of literals is not supported in Workload Capture files and SQL Tuning Sets. Sensitive data should not be stored as literals in the first place.

In our case, we have not selected this checkbox since we do not have any Capture files or SQL Tuning Sets.

# Adding columns to mask

Now you need to add the columns that are to be masked, and a masking format needs to be defined for each column. Click on **Add**.

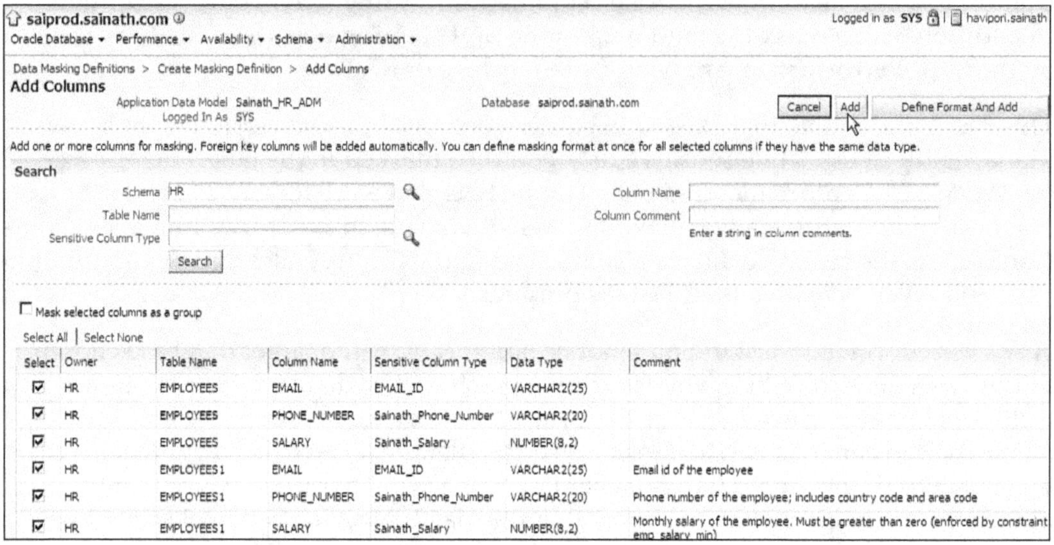

Note that if you are not logged in as SYSDBA, you will get an error message at this stage: **Masking requires execute permissions on package SYS.DBMS_CRYPTO**. Make sure you use SYSDBA credentials to avoid this error.

First search for the columns in the HR schema, using the search fields. This will display either all the sensitive columns, or those of a specific sensitive column type.

Select the columns that appear, such as **PHONE_NUMBER**, **SALARY**, and **EMAIL**.

Note that if you select **Mask selected columns as a group**, the selected columns are associated together for the masking process. This is known as compound masking and is best used for columns that are logically related together, such as **LAST_NAME** and **FIRST_NAME**, or **CITY** and **COUNTRY**. In our case, we are not using this feature since the columns we have selected are not related in that sense.

Click on **Add**.

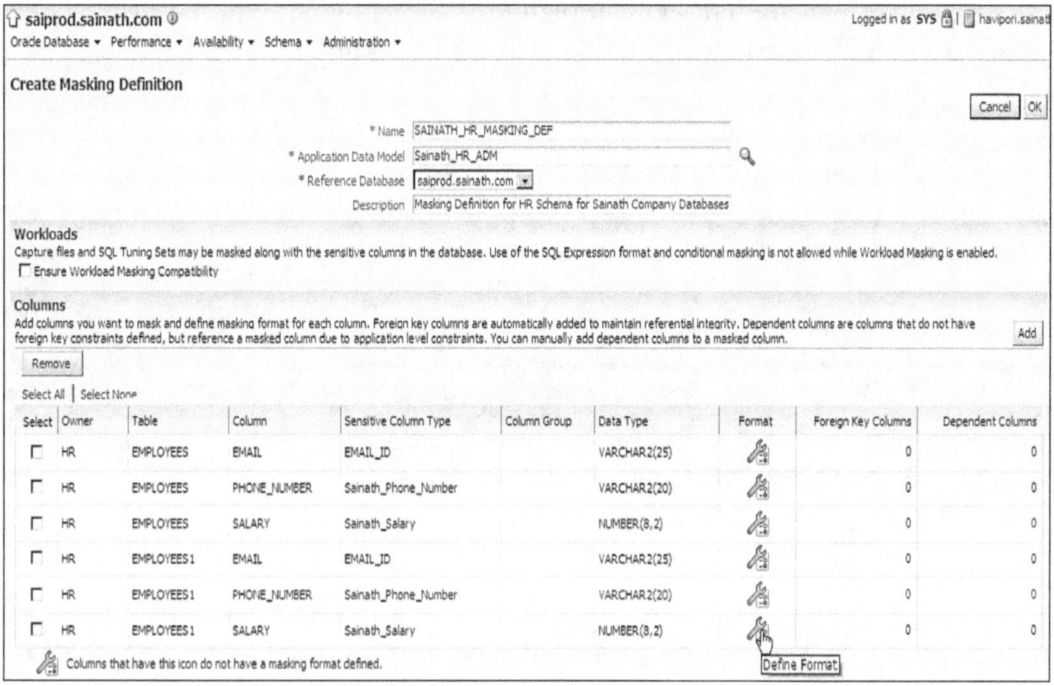


You are placed back on the **Create Masking Definition** screen. The columns you have added appear in the list.

If there are any foreign key columns referring to the sensitive columns, they are automatically added for referential integrity purposes. If there are dependant columns that do not have database foreign keys defined, but reference the sensitive columns by using application-level constraints, they can be added manually by first adding a referential relationship in the Application Data Model itself. Since the foreign key columns or dependant columns are specified and will also be masked, the integrity of the database or application level will be maintained even after the masking takes place.

# Defining the masking format

The next step is to define a masking format for each column. Do this by clicking on the wrench icon. First, we do this for the **SALARY** column.

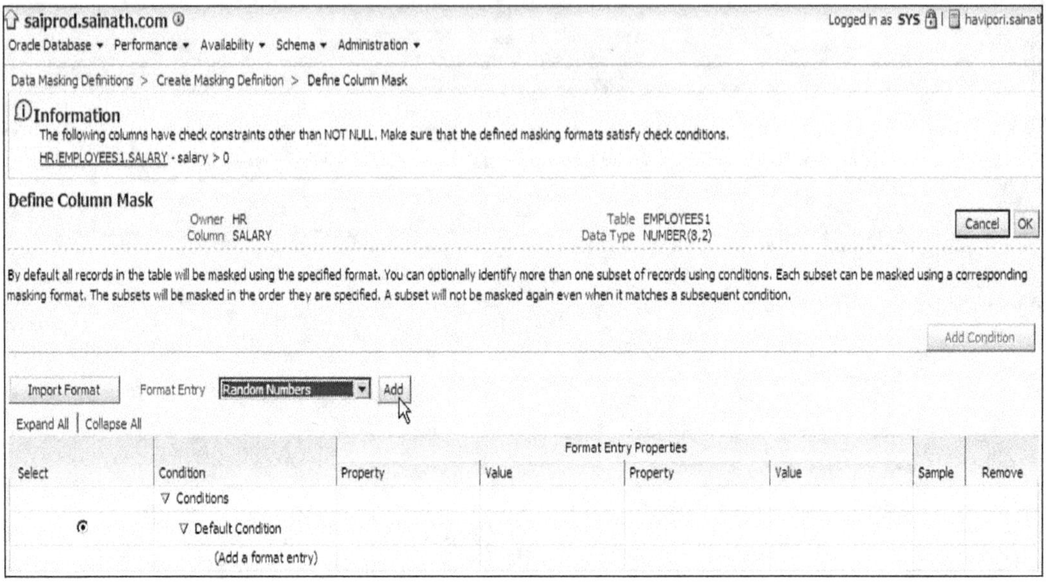

On the **Define Column Mask** screen, an informational message appears making you aware of an existing check constraint on the column. You must make sure that the check constraint is satisfied by the masking format you defined. This means that the value generated for the **SALARY** column should be greater than zero.

The actual process of defining the format is done by adding one or more format entries. In our case, we have selected **Random Numbers** from the drop-down box. Click on **Add**.

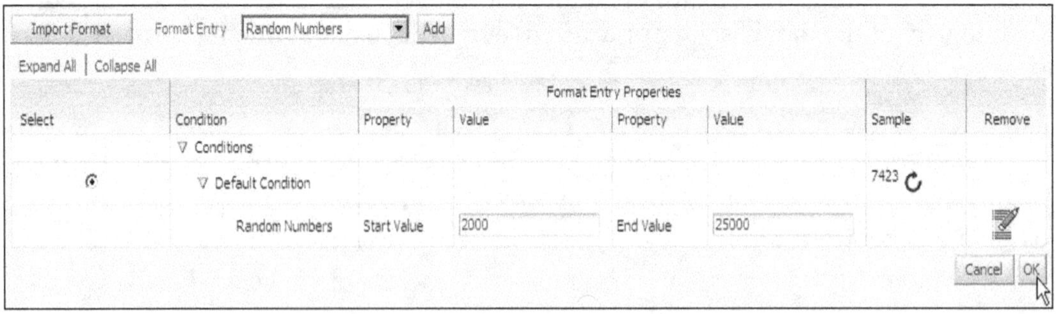

Specify the **Start Value** and **End Value** amounts for the random number generated for this column. Enter reasonable values, after checking the actual data to find the minimum and maximum salary amounts. Uniqueness is guaranteed for the random formats, provided that a large enough range (more than the total number of distinct data values) is used.

Note that it is possible to achieve conditional masking by clicking on **Add Condition** and entering a separate condition for which you can then add a different format entry. As an example, the condition can be as follows:

```
last_name like upper('%GOLD%')
```

In this way, the same column can be masked differently depending on the condition you specify.

Click on the refresh icon in the **Sample** column, this generates a sample value for you to examine. When satisfied, click on **OK**.

You are placed back on the **Create Masking Definition** screen. Next, define the format for the **PHONE_NUMBER** column by clicking on the wrench icon.

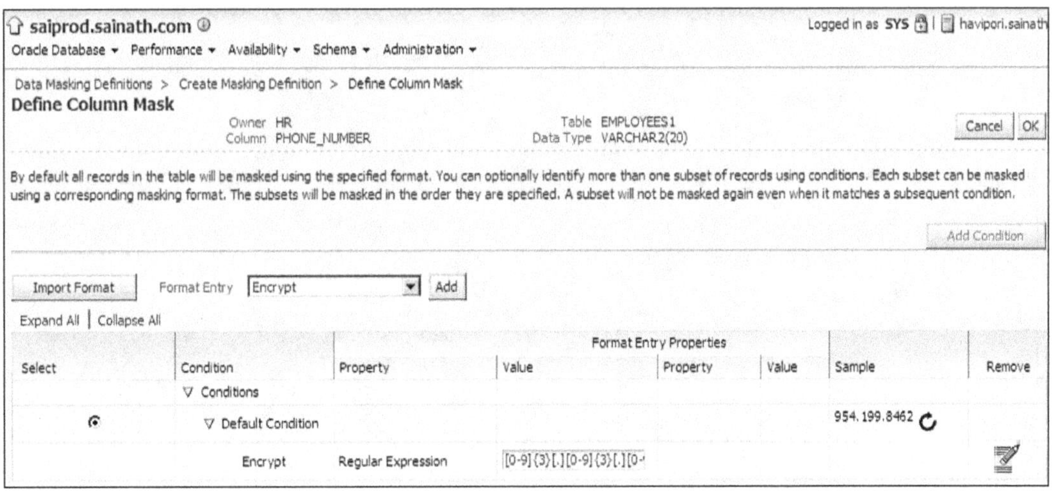


For the **PHONE_NUMBER** column, we choose **Encrypt** as the **Format Entry** option from the drop-down box. Add this entry to the column mask.

In the **Regular Expression** text field, enter the value `[0-9]{3}[.][0-9]{3}[.][0-9]{4}`. This defines the format for **PHONE_NUMBER**. It means three numeric digits from 0 to 9, followed by a decimal point, another three digits, a decimal point, and finally, four digits.

The **Encrypt** type will use this format and change **PHONE_NUMBER** to reversible masked values, based on an encryption seed that will be entered at the time of masking. The data format is preserved with the ability to mask numeric, alphanumeric, or mixed fields of any pattern and any length.

One of the new capabilities in Enterprise Manager Cloud Control 12*c* is key-based reversible masking, which is achieved by using the encrypt format. This is useful when sensitive data is to be sent to an outside party for a business purpose, such as market analysis or reporting. When the encrypt format is used, the data is masked using a reversible masking function based on a secure key. It can then be sent outside the company and used for the required business purpose. When the same data is in turn received by the company, the masking can be reversed using the same key, and the original data is recovered.

Click on the refresh icon in the **Sample** column to generate a sample masked entry in this format. After verifying, click on **OK**.

This brings you back to the **Create Masking Definition** screen. Now define the format for the **EMAIL** column by clicking on the wrench icon.

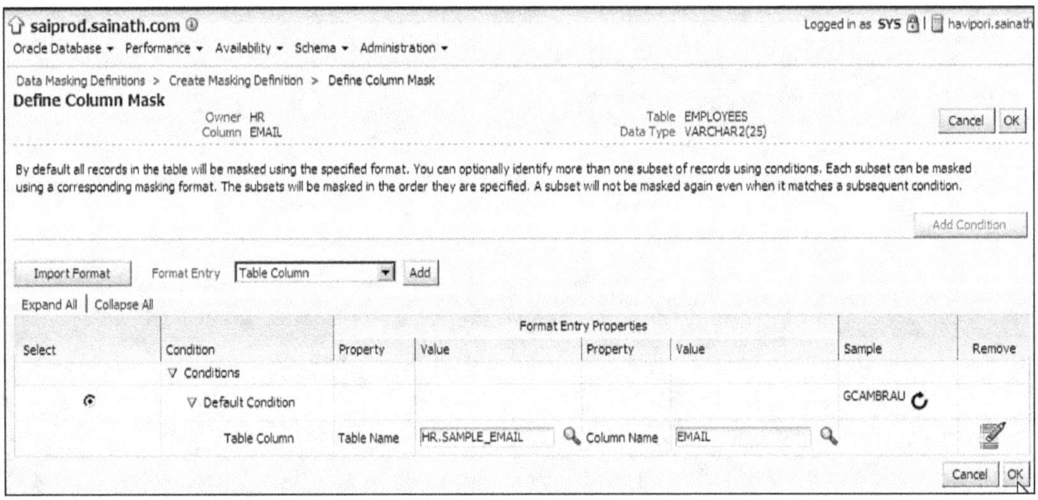


Select **Table Column** from the **Format Entry** drop-down box, and add that to the column mask. This kind of format entry lets you select a table with sample data in the database as the source for the masked value.

In this case, we have created a table, **HR.SAMPLE_EMAIL**, that contains email addresses selected from the production `EMPLOYEES` table, but you can use dummy email addresses. Remember to create this sample table in the `saitest` database as well, since this is where the actual masking will run.

Select the **Table Name** instance and the **Column Name** instance, examine a sample, and then click on **OK**.

In this way, define the formats for the remaining sensitive columns, on the **Create Masking Definition** screen.

# Advanced options

Click on **Show Advanced Options** to view the options as shown in the following screenshot:

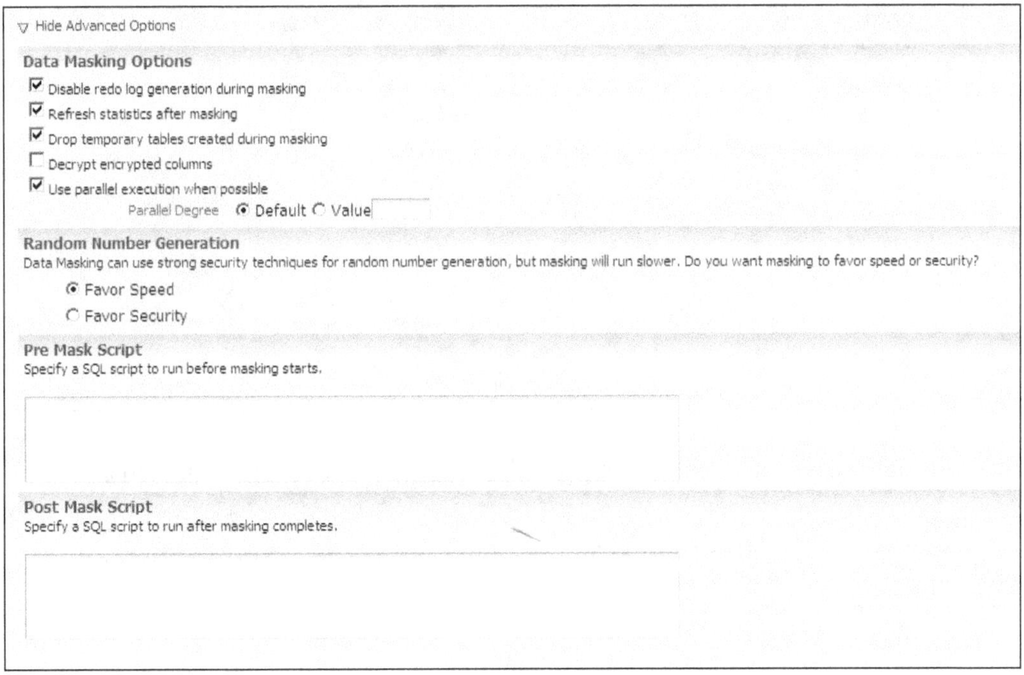


In the **Advanced Options** section, you have options such as **Disable redo log generation during masking, Refresh statistics after masking, Use parallel execution when possible**, and others. The main purpose of these options is to allow you to optimize the data masking process.

You are also able to specify a **Pre/Post Mask Script**. This is to perform operations on the database before or after the masking process, as required.

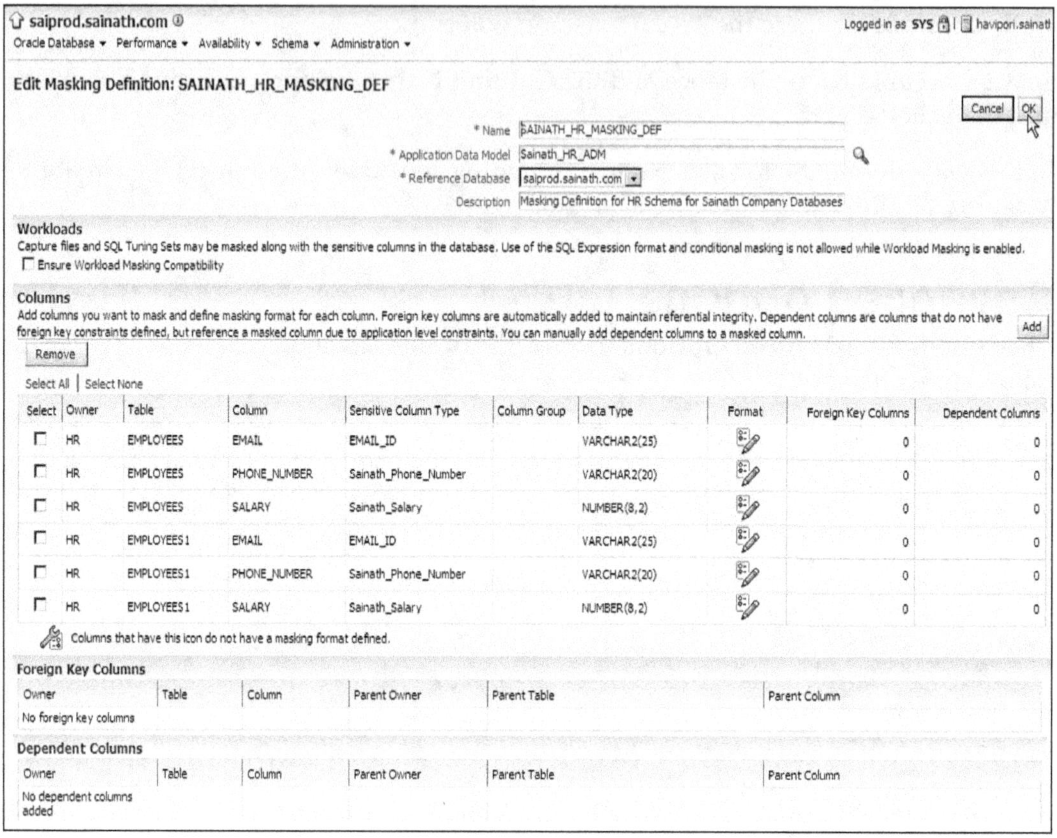


When all the formats are defined and you have specified advanced options, click on **OK**.

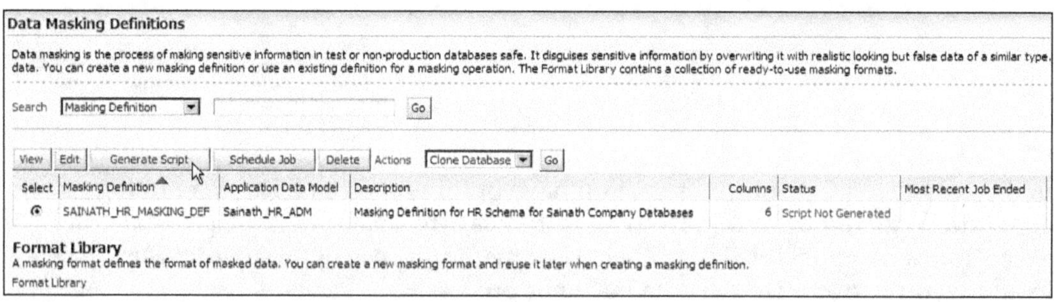

The data masking definition instance that we have created now appears on the **Data Masking Definitions** page. The status is seen as **Script Not Generated**.

Click on the **Generate Script** button.

# Generated Script

The data masking script is generated successfully after a few seconds and is displayed on the page. You can either see the script summary or the full PL/SQL script version.

The PL/SQL code that is generated is highly optimized—bulk operations are used to replace the sensitive column data with a copy of the table containing the masked data. At the same time, original constraints and indexes, and partitions and grants are all retained perfectly. Advanced database features, such as parallel execution along with disabling of redo log generation, speed up the masking process. Finally, the original table with the sensitive data is dropped, with the new masked table taking the place of the original.

Note that there will still be a performance impact after masking of large tables. For a large table, more space will be required to create a copy of the table for masking purposes, also more `TEMP` space is used for the **Create-Table-As-Select** (**CTAS**) process. To attain maximum performance, it is recommended to have free space equal to the sum of the sizes of all sensitive data tables as well as additional free tablespace storage equal to the largest such table.

In the case of large tables, more time will be required to perform the actual masking. However, due to the optimizations in the generated masking script, the Enterprise Manager process of masking large tables will normally outperform home-grown scripts used for the same purpose. On a recent benchmark performed for Exadata X2-2 Full Rack Database Machine, the Enterprise Manager Cloud Control 12*c* Data Masking Pack was able to mask a 72-TB table in 8.2 hrs,. approximately 8.78 TB per hour.

You can schedule the data masking job right from this page by using the **Schedule Job** button, or optionally clicking on the **Clone And Mask** button, which will use a script to first clone and then mask the database.

The **Script Generation Information** section at the lower part of the screen displays findings about all the objects and resources examined during script generation. Any warnings about space or quota will be seen here.

Click on **Return**.

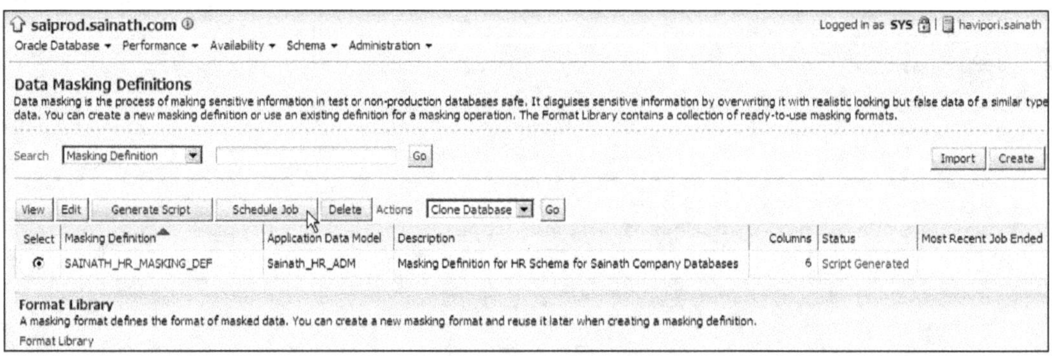

The **Data Masking Definition** page shows the masking definition with the status **Script Generated**. At this point, click on **Schedule Job**.

# Scheduling the job

We can now schedule the data masking job. We have selected the `saitest` database as the **Reference Database** instance for the job. Note that this can only be selected if it has been associated with the data model, which we have done before. The `saitest` database will be the actual database on which the data masking job is executed.

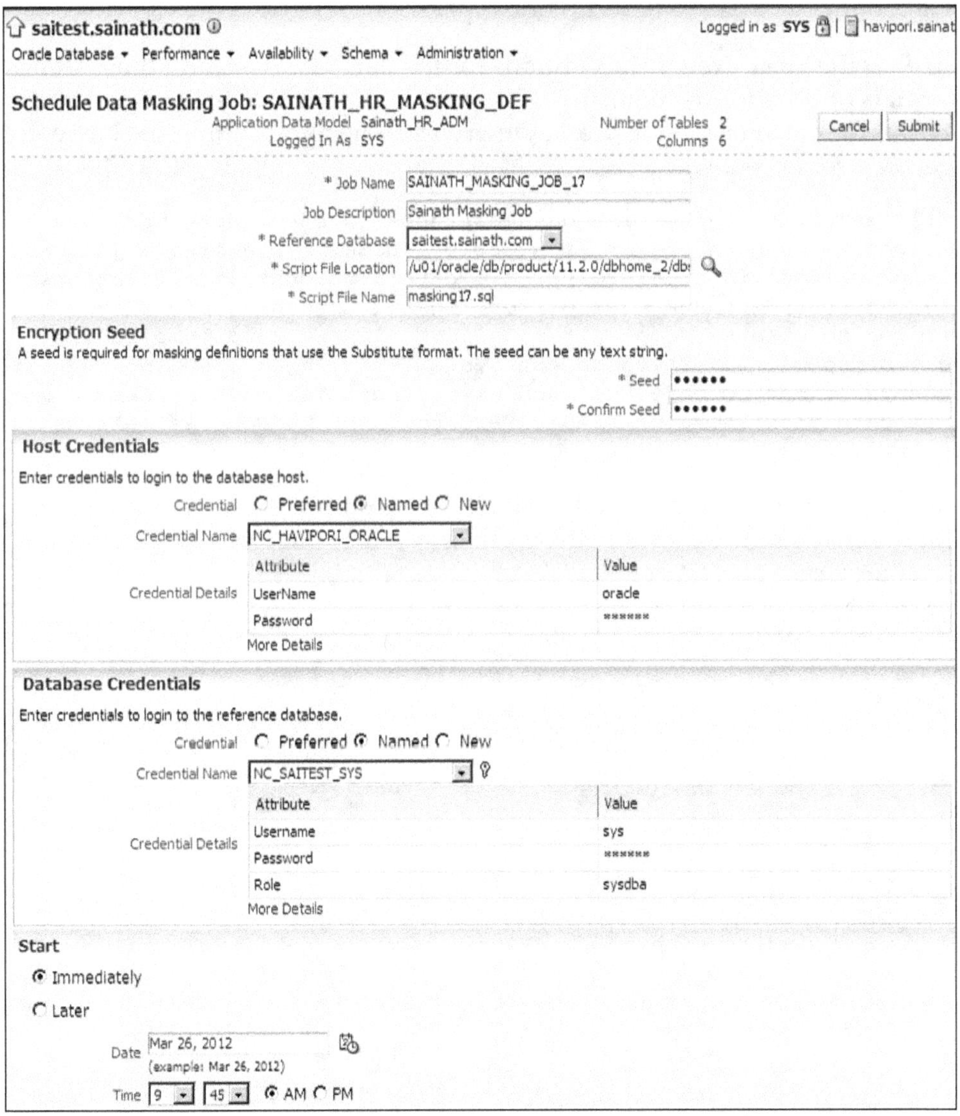

The **Script File Location** value, by default, is the `$ORACLE_HOME/dbs` directory. Enter the **Encryption Seed** string if you have used the encrypt or the substitute format in your masking definitions.

If you had selected **Ensure Workload Masking Compatibility** earlier on, the **Workloads** section (where you can choose to mask SQL Tuning Sets and/or Capture files) would have appeared on this page. You can also select the directory of the Capture files. You can choose to run **SQL Performance Analyzer** (**SPA**) to compare SQL Execution Plans before and after masking, so that any SQL Plan changes can be detected. This of course requires the license for Oracle **Real Application Testing** (**RAT**). In our case, these options do not appear.

Then, select the **Host Credentials** options for the database host, and the **Database Credentials** options for the database. Note that it is important to select `SYSDBA` credentials for data masking to work. Otherwise, when you submit the job, you will get an error as follows:

```
Insufficient Privileges - The database user (system) does not have enough
privileges to execute the masking script. Masking requires object and
system privileges in order to perform data dictionary modifications.
Ensure that the database user performing the mask has object/system
privileges to create, drop, alter, select, insert, and compile the
objects being masked. These object/system privileges are also required on
dependents of masked objects, such as indexes. The masking user also must
have execute privileges on DBMS_CRYPTO and DBMS_RANDOM, as well as alter
system privilege.
```

Schedule the job to run immediately and click on **Submit**. A message appears that the job is submitted successfully. Click on **View Job Details** and wait until the job completes.

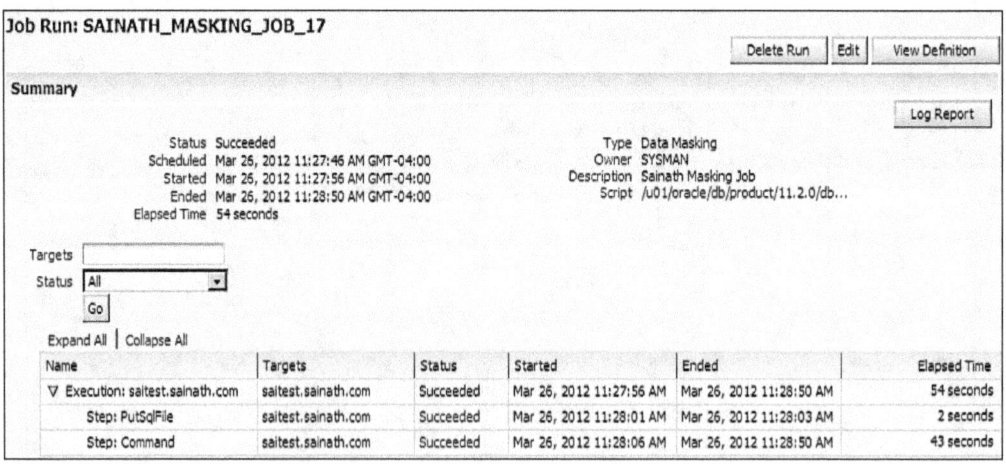

Within a minute, the data masking job is completed.

# Testing the results

You can examine the results of the masking by opening two SQL*Plus sessions, as shown in the following figure:

```
SQL> connect / as sysdba
Connected.
SQL> select name from v$database;

NAME
---------
SAIPROD

SQL> select employee_id, first_name, last_name, salary, phone_number, email
  2   from hr.employees1 where rownum <=7 order by last_name;

EMPLOYEE_ID FIRST_NAME  LAST_NAME     SALARY PHONE_NUMBER         EMAIL
----------- ----------- ---------- --------- -------------------- --------
        174 Ellen       Abel           11000 011.44.1644.429267   EABEL
        166 Sundar      Ande            6400 011.44.1346.629268   SANDE
        130 Mozhe       Atkinson        2800 650.124.6234         MATKINSO
        105 David       Austin          4800 590.423.4569         DAUSTIN
        204 Hermann     Baer           10000 515.123.8888         HBAER
        116 Shelli      Baida           2900 515.127.4563         SBAIDA
        167 Amit        Banda           6200 011.44.1346.729268   ABANDA

7 rows selected.
```

```
SQL> connect / as sysdba
Connected.
SQL> select name from v$database;

NAME
---------
SAITEST

SQL> select employee_id, first_name, last_name, salary, phone_number, email
  2  from hr.employees1 where rownum <=7 order by last_name;

EMPLOYEE_ID FIRST_NAME  LAST_NAME     SALARY PHONE_NUMBER         EMAIL
----------- ----------- ---------- --------- -------------------- --------
        174 Ellen       Abel            4332 987.254.1683         MATKINSO
        166 Sundar      Ande            6216 987.254.1683         SBAIDA
        130 Mozhe       Atkinson        7121 599.442.3144         CJOHNSON
        105 David       Austin         14945 541.212.6392         EBATES
        204 Hermann     Baer           24205 210.444.5866         CDAVIES
        116 Shelli      Baida          10600 170.107.2360         KCHUNG
        167 Amit        Banda           3510 987.254.1683         RMATOS

7 rows selected.
```

We have connected to the `saiprod` and `saitest` database in the two sessions.

We then issue a `select` statement that displays confidential data such as **salary**, **phone_number**, and **email** from the production system. The same `select` statement is also executed in the `saitest` database.

We see that **salary**, **phone_number**, and **email** have been appropriately masked in the test database as per the masking formats that were specified. The masking process has obviously achieved the expected results.

# Format library

We have seen how masking definitions can be created pertaining to an Application Data Model and referring to a particular database, such as the `saiprod` database.

In the masking definition, masking formats can be defined for the sensitive columns in the data model. However, masking formats defined in this way cannot be reused for other Application Data Models or other databases, or even for different columns in the same masking definition. They have to be manually recreated in the same manner each time.

Instead, if masking formats were to be defined in a centralized format library, they would be accessible by all database targets in Enterprise Manager Cloud Control 12*c*, and this is a great advantage.

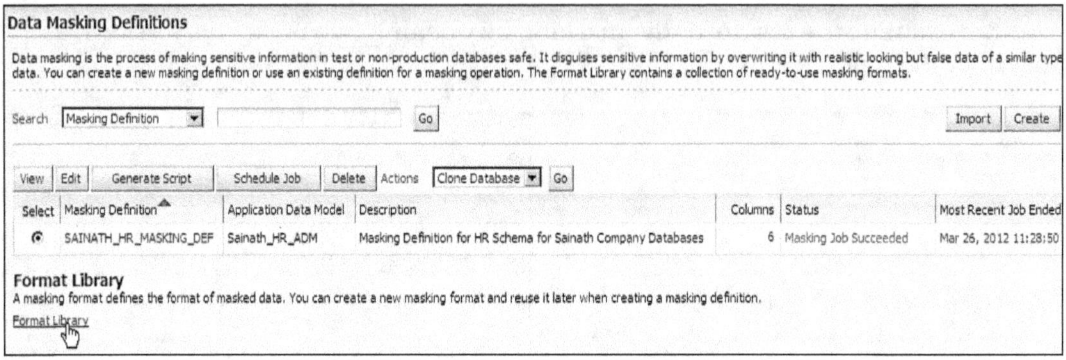


On the **Data Masking Definitions** page, click on **Format Library**. The following screen appears. This is also accessible via **Enterprise | Quality Management | Data Masking Formats**.

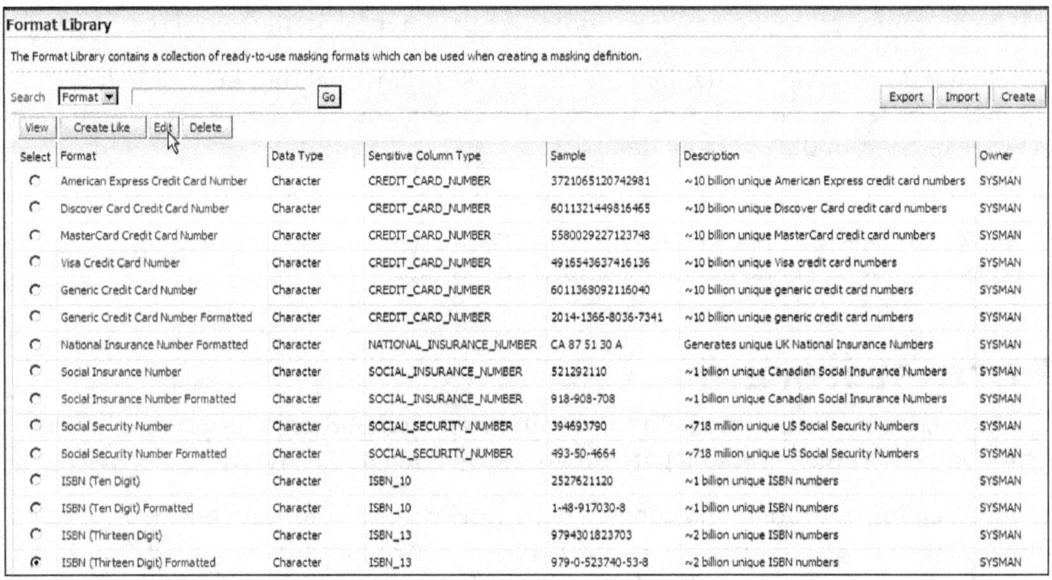

Out of the box, the **Format Library** list contains a number of masking formats that can be used when creating a masking definition. There are masking formats for credit card numbers, Social Security Numbers, ISBN numbers, and so on.

To examine any one of these masking formats, select it and click on **Edit**. We have selected **ISBN (Thirteen Digit) Formatted**.

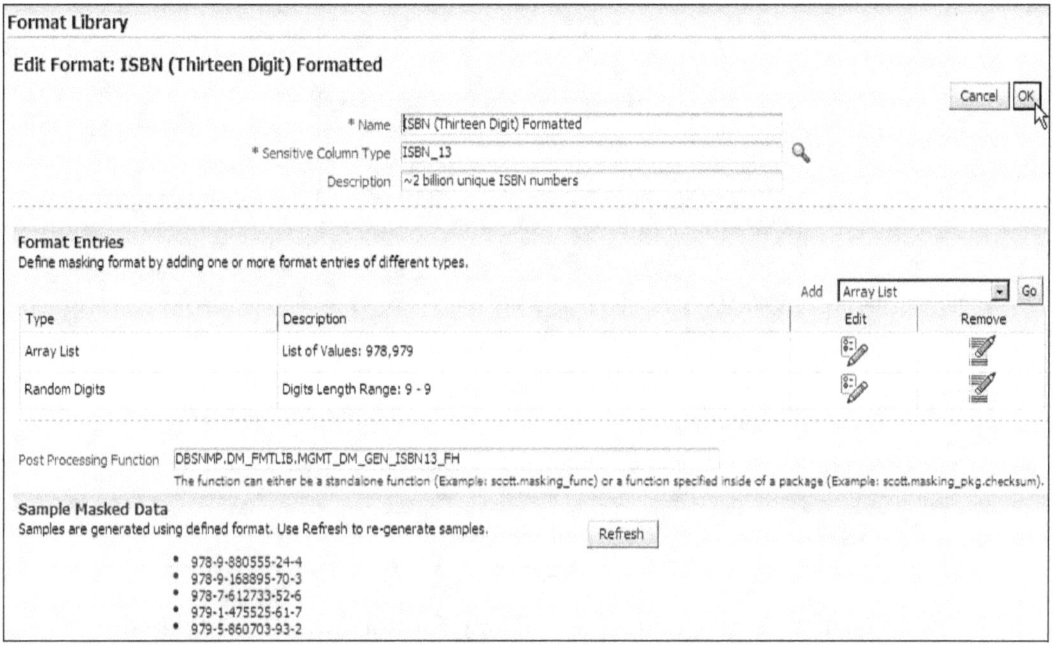


We can see that there are two format entries in this previously supplied masking format. The first is an **Array List** with only two possible values—`978` and `979`.

The second format entry is a range of random digits. There is also a **Post Processing Function** parameter specified, which works on the resulting masked value and modifies it appropriately so that it appears as close as possible to a real value—an ISBN number in this case. **Post Processing Function** can be used to check the validity of the masked value and perform some additional formatting functions, such as inserting spaces between the values that have been generated or adding commas or dollar signs.

Click on **OK**. You are back at the **Format Library** screen.

We will now create a customized masking format for Sainath Company. Click on **Create**. The following screen appears:

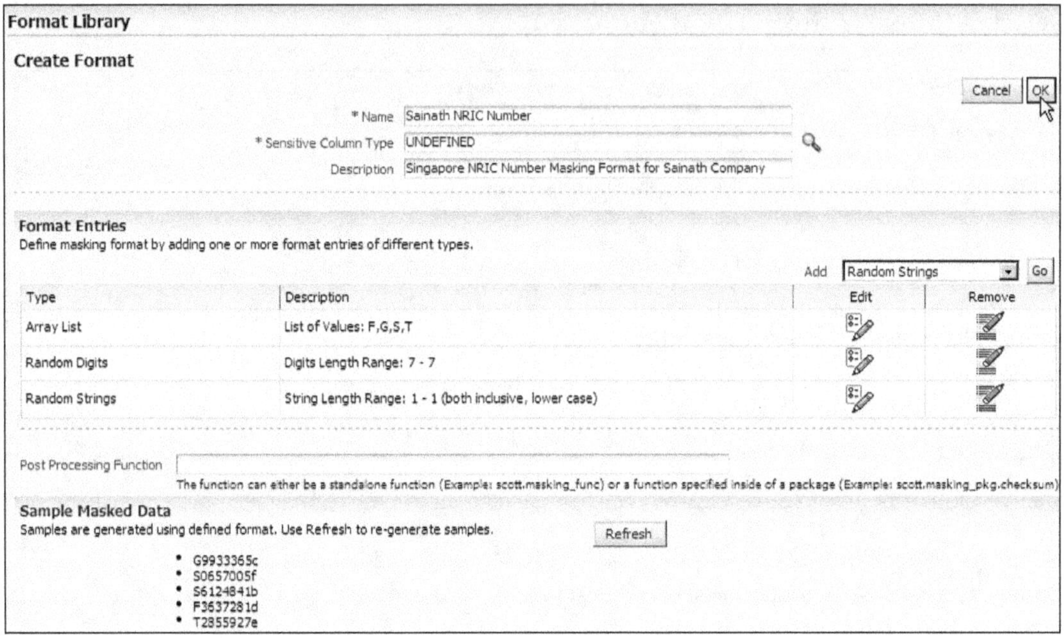


On the **Create Format** screen, name the masking format appropriately. In our case, we are creating a masking format for `Singapore NRIC Number`, which is a Government Identification Number.

For **Sensitive Column Type** we have selected **UNDEFINED** from the list because we currently do not have the NRIC number defined as a sensitive column type in the database.

Now, we can add the format entries to create the masking format for the NRIC number. We need to add appropriate format entries, as per the published format of the NRIC number from official documentation.

First add an **Array List** instance. Allow a list of values, **F**, **G**, **S**, and **T**, for the array. Then, add a format entry of **Random Digits**. **Digits Length Range** is specified with a start and end length of **7**— this means seven random digits will be generated each time. Finally, add **Random Strings** as a format entry. **String Length Range** is specified with a start and end length of **1**.

There is no **Post Processing Function** used for this masking format, however you could specify a function to convert the masked value to uppercase, if required.

In the **Sample Masked Data** section, click on **Refresh**. This displays a few generated masked values. Verify that they look similar to an authentic NRIC number.

Click on **OK** to save this masking format. It will now appear in the **Format Library** list, and can be used to mask any NRIC column in any database that is managed by Enterprise Manager Cloud Control 12*c*.

In the process of creating a masking definition, the **Define Column Mask** screen is used to define a format for each column included in the definition. Instead of adding format entries manually, one by one, you can click on the **Import Format** button on this screen. This allows you to select a previously defined masking format from the format library. In this way, the format can be used repeatedly. Consistent enforcement of masking policies can therefore be ensured throughout the enterprise.

# Benefits and capabilities

We have seen different types of format entries that can be used when creating the masking format. The examples we used were **Random Numbers, Encrypt** (key-based reversible masking), **Table Column**, **Array List**, **Random Digits**, and **Random Strings**. Another format entry is **Shuffle**, which is used to randomly shuffle the values in a column across different rows. You can use this when the format of the column is unknown, making it impossible to generate realistic values. A user-defined function can also be used as the format entry to generate the masked value, for example, if an algorithm is required to derive a value such as an account number.

Alternatively, use **Substitute** as the format entry for deterministic masking. A table and column need to be specified, and the values in the specified column will be selected using a hash value to deterministically mask the original column. This can be used to mask a similar original column in the same way, in multiple tables and even in multiple databases. An example would be an employee number.

There are other format entries such as **Delete**, which deletes specified rows as per specified conditions, **Null Value**, which masks a nullable column using a value of NULL, **Preserve Original Data**, which retains original values for certain rows that match a specified condition, **SQL Expression** (for example, using built-in functions such as `UPPER`, `SUBSTR`, and `TO_CHAR`) to generate a masked value, **Truncate**, which will truncate all the rows in a table, and a user-defined function, which is a PL/SQL function that accepts the original value and returns a masked value.

In the case of compound masking, when two or more columns are masked as a group, you are asked to define a group mask. In this case, the format entries you can choose are limited to **Shuffle**, **Substitute**, **Table Column**, or **User-Defined Function**.

Note that the data masking and Test Data Management (data subsetting) capabilities of Enterprise Manager Cloud Control 12*c* can be used with any database application, including packaged Oracle applications (E-Business, Siebel, PeopleSoft, and JD Edwards), Fusion applications, or any non-Oracle application using the Oracle database.

As a plus point, there are predefined Application Data Models, data masking templates, and data subsetting templates available for some of the packaged Oracle applications, such as Fusion applications. As an example, using the **Import** button on the **Data Masking Definitions** screen, it is possible to import a masking definition from the previously built data masking templates.

The E-Business Suite Release 12.1.3 template for data masking was made available at the end of May 2012. Models and templates will also be available for PeopleSoft in the future, but not for Siebel. In the case of the latter, in-house DBAs can use their Siebel knowledge to create the Application Data Model and perform data masking and data subsetting, or Oracle Consulting can be used for this purpose.

Note that the E-Business-native Scrambling capability has been removed from the Enterprise Manager 12*c* release. Starting from Enterprise Manager Cloud Control 12*c* and going forward, the Data Masking Pack and the E-Business suite template for data masking needs to be used with Oracle E-Business for data masking purposes.

Data masking in Enterprise Manager is also integrated with the Database Cloning process (a capability of the Database Lifecycle Management Pack). When a database is cloned using Enterprise Manager, at the very end of the cloning, the masking of the sensitive columns can take place before the database is opened for read-write access. The cloning process can be accessed directly from the **Data Masking Definitions** screen, where you can choose **Clone Database** from the **Actions** menu and click on **Go**.

So, if you have already purchased the Database Lifecycle Management Pack license, you can clone directly to your test server since the last step of the clone process will involve the masking. Otherwise, if you are performing the masking process separately, it is recommended that you use a staging server in the production network for the purpose of masking. As a rule of thumb, the staging server should be at least 50 percent of the CPU capacity of the production server. Copy the production database to this staging server, and perform the masking process. Then copy the masked database to the actual test server. The staging database can then be removed.

Non-Oracle databases such as Microsoft SQL Server, IBM DB2, Informix, and Sybase can also be masked via the Oracle Database gateway. In this case, a staging Oracle database needs to be used where the data is copied for the masking process. An **ETL** (**Extract-Transform-Load**) method is used with the help of the appropriate gateway. The optimized version of the Oracle gateway to use for this purpose is 11.2.0.3 onwards, which makes the copy process a high performer in both directions.

In this case, sensitive column discovery is not supported on the non-Oracle database, because the Enterprise Manager Cloud Control 12*c* Discovery method internally uses PL/SQL as well as regular expression pattern matching. Also, when masking non-Oracle databases, the Pre and Post Mask scripts will be used to perform the pull of the data from the non-Oracle database and the push back to it after masking is completed.

# Summary

The Data Masking Pack is a highly scalable way to provide fast and optimized data de-identification for Oracle databases, using SQL parallelism where possible. The masking performed is as in-place on the Oracle database and as such is more secure since the sensitive data is masked without being copied to a staging location.

Referential data integrity is automatically maintained. An out of the box format library is supplied; it has the ability to mask many common types of sensitive data, such as credit card numbers, Social Security Numbers, and ISBN numbers, among others. This library can be expanded with your own custom masking formats, and all of this can be used on any appropriate column, on any schema, and on any database.

Thus, in Enterprise Manager Cloud Control 12*c*, we have seen the close integration of the Application Data Model, data subsetting, and data masking processes. Combined together, these capabilities offer a powerful workflow for Secure Test Data Management, making sure your test data is properly defined, subsetted, and suitably masked.

The end result is considerable reduction in storage costs, more robust security, and greater ease in the creation of secure and subsetted test data.

In the next chapter, we will take a look at the discovery, monitoring, and management of the powerful Exadata Database Machine, using Enterprise Manager Cloud Control 12*c*.

# 10 Ease the Chaos with Exadata Management

Many people know about **Exadata**, the extreme performance machine from Oracle for OLTP as well as data warehousing applications. The Exadata Database Machine combines Sun Hardware with Oracle database and storage software, and is installed as a highly optimized and fully engineered system of servers, storage, and software.

One of the open secrets of Exadata is its massively parallel grid architecture, that uses multiple Exadata compute nodes with Oracle **Real Application Cluster** (**RAC**) active-active databases, and multiple Exadata storage cells. This results in fast, predictable performance.

The Oracle technologies used in Exadata are complex and manifold, and these technologies must be managed efficiently. One example is controlling the I/O across all the storage cells in an Exadata Database Machine rack. How do you know what database consumes the most I/O across all the cells? Can you control it efficiently?

How do you apply database patches to all the multiple RAC nodes? How do you know if one Exadata Storage Cell has a different configuration from another? How would you know if a **Power Distribution Unit** (**PDU**) fan has failed, and what service and service level it has affected? How do you find out which Infiniband Switch ports are connected to which compute nodes and storage cells, and if any port has errors or is degraded?

Can you do all this manually, and how much time and effort would it take? All these complex requirements can be satisfied by the use of Oracle Enterprise Manager Cloud Control 12*c*.

Managing such a complex machine without the use of advanced monitoring and management tools, such as Enterprise Manager, would be akin to driving a Ferrari car minus the onboard computer. The result would be an increase in the maintenance costs, while reducing the real benefits and **return of investment** (**ROI**) for Exadata. So what is needed is the full use of Oracle Enterprise Manager Cloud Control 12*c* to monitor and manage the total Exadata system, which we will explore in this chapter.

# Meeting the challenges

There are many challenges in the Exadata world. When deploying such a complicated machine, it is very important to reduce deployment costs and minimize errors. First, you need to identify the databases that will be moved to Exadata, that is, plan your consolidation. You need to make sure the applications that are migrated will continue to work as efficiently as before, or even better, on Exadata. Once you have completed the migration, there needs to be a continuous monitoring of all the hardware and software components of this machine, and you also need to ensure that there is no configuration drift.

Oracle Enterprise Manager Cloud Control 12*c* is very advanced in its management of the Exadata machine. There is an integrated view of the hardware and software, with the ability to monitor storage cells, compute nodes (database servers), as well as the all-important Infiniband network. The **ILOM** (**Integrated Lights Out Manager**), Cisco switches, **KVM** (**Keyboard**, **Video**, **Mouse**) switches, and the **PDU** (**Power Distribution Unit**) can also be monitored.

The entire lifecycle of the Oracle database on Exadata can be managed, from the deployment phase to the maintenance of the production databases. The provisioning and patching of new single instance or RAC databases can be automated. This leads to a vast increase in administrator productivity, and invariably reduces maintenance costs. Out-of-place database patching is possible for both single instance and RAC databases on Exadata, thus reducing the downtime considerably.

Even before you go live on Exadata, you can perform full database testing via the database replay functionality of **Real Application Testing** (**RAT**), which lets you capture production database workloads from existing production databases (that could be as old as the 9i version), and replay these captured workloads on the Test 11.2 RAC databases on Exadata. When you are satisfied that there is no regression of SQL statements in the workload, your new Exadata Database Machine can be used in production.

Note that there is an Exadata simulation capability in the **SQL Performance Analyzer** (**SPA**) functionality of RAT. This simulation can be used to test out the benefits of moving single SQL statements to Exadata even before you actually have a physical Exadata Database Machine. The simulation takes into account the cell offload capability of Exadata.

Once the Exadata system is live, it can continuously be monitored by Enterprise Manager Cloud Control 12*c*, including all of its hardware and software components. Failures can be reported immediately. Exadata services can be monitored on a dashboard, and Root Cause Analysis can be performed on any disruptions to the service levels. Database performance can also be maximized by diagnosis and tuning.

And finally, Enterprise Manager Cloud Control 12*c* can turn the Exadata Database Machine into a powerful database cloud machine, using the **Database as a Service** (**DbaaS**) functionality of the Cloud Management.

Please note that the Enterprise Manager Cloud Control 12c system should ideally be installed on a separate server or servers (as per the architecture we discussed in an earlier chapter), and not on the Exadata Database Machine itself. This is because it is not considered to be the best practice to combine the monitoring software with the monitored environment itself, since first of all there is an overhead of the Enterprise Manager OMS and repository database that can impact your production databases on Exadata. Secondly, if there is any issue with the Exadata machine, the Enterprise Manager system will also be affected and will not be able to warn you that your Exadata Database Machine is down. Therefore, it is always considered the best practice to install Enterprise Manager on a separate server and not on the Exadata Database Machine itself.

# Discovering Exadata

The discovery of Exadata Database Machines in Enterprise Manager Cloud Control 12*c* is wizard-driven, and is considerably faster than the previous version. Components, such as storage cells and Infiniband switches, are now discovered in an out of the box fashion and do not require a separate plugin to be installed for each of these components. Other Exadata components, such as the Cisco switches, KVM switches, and the PDU are also discovered during the guided discovery process, which automatically deploys the Oracle Exadata plugin—a collection of JAR files used to monitor all the Exadata components.

The actual Enterprise Manager agents are installed on the compute nodes, and can be set up during the discovery process to also monitor and manage the storage cells (without physically installing the agent on these cells).

There is a new option in Enterprise Manager Cloud Control 12*c* to discover a new Exadata Database Machine, or to rediscover it. The latter can be useful in scenarios where you upgrade from a half-rack database machine to a full-rack database machine.

The Enterprise Manager Cloud Control 12*c* installation is recommended to be on **Bundle Patch 1** (**BP1**) if it is not already on that patch level. Note that applying the BP1 will not change the EM12*c* version, since it is not a new release or even a patch set of Enterprise Manager. The method to verify that the bundle patch has been applied is to use the `opatch` utility in the OMS home. In the `opatch` output, you should see that the BP1 patch has been applied, which is patch `13242773`.

Please refer to the **My Oracle Support** (**MOS**) reference document for applying the BP1 patch. The document ID is 1393173.1, and it is titled *Enterprise Manager Cloud Control Workbook for Applying Bundle Patch 1 (February 2012) and 12.1.0.2 Plugins*.

For Exadata discovery, the Enterprise Manager Cloud Control 12[italics]c[/italics] installation is recommended to be on Release 2, covered in an earlier chapter. Overall, the Exadata discovery steps are as follows. First, the agent is installed on the compute nodes and a guided discovery of the Exadata Database Machine is then launched. The guided discovery process also automatically deploys the Oracle Exadata plugin and the Oracle database plugin onto the compute nodes.

When performing the steps for this wizard, monitoring agents are assigned to the Exadata components. Next, you enter the agent credentials, the monitoring credentials, SNMP subscription details, and the component properties. We will look at these steps in detail in the course of this chapter.

First, before starting the entire process, you need to go through the prerequisites, including the creation of ILOM service processor users, and checking connectivity to the various components of Exadata from the compute nodes. These steps are documented in *Oracle Enterprise Manager Exadata Management Getting Started Guide* at the following URL:

`http://docs.oracle.com/cd/E24628_01/doc.121/e27442/ch1_deployment_overview.htm#sthref7`

The prerequisite steps are also documented in the **My Oracle Support** (**MOS**) support note Note ID 1437434.1: *Prerequisite steps before discovering Exadata DB machine within Oracle Enterprise Manager 12c.*

After the prerequisite steps are completed, let us have a look at the Oracle Exadata plugin. Select **Setup** | **Extensibility** | **Plug-ins** from the **Enterprise Manager** menu. This will take you to the **Plug-ins** page, as shown in the following screenshot:

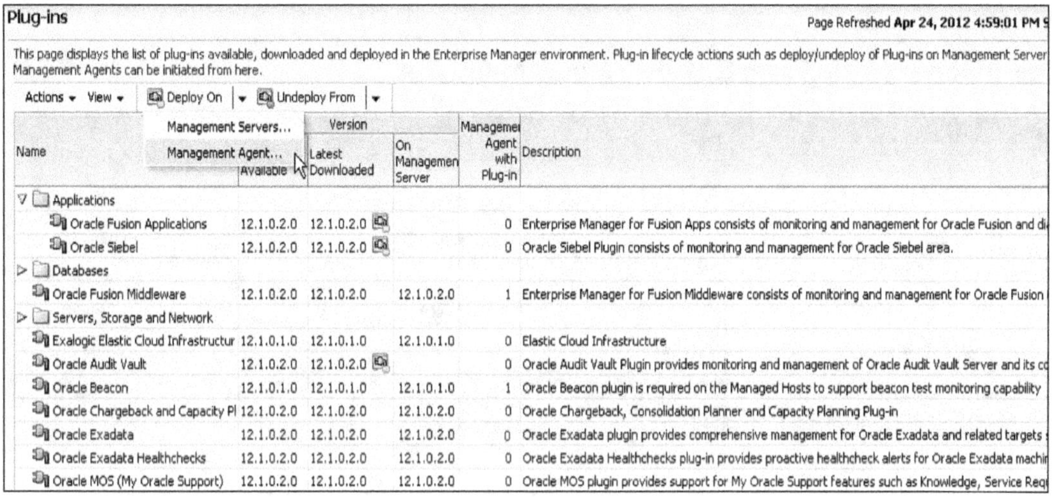


Various plugins are visible on this page, including database plugins, such as the **Oracle Fusion Middleware** plugin and the **Oracle Exadata** plugin. Also note the **Oracle Exadata Healthchecks** plugin, which we will discuss later.

We see that the **Oracle Exadata** plugin has been downloaded and deployed on the management server, but no management agents have been deployed with this plugin.

Before the release of the Bundle Patch 1 (BP1) for Enterprise Manager Cloud Control 12*c* (this was the patch before Release 2), you would have to select **Deploy On** | **Management Agent...** from the menu and choose the management agents on which you want to deploy this monitoring plugin, such as the compute nodes. You would also have to deploy the **Oracle Database** plugin. This would have been after the agent had been deployed to the compute nodes.

However, in the case of an Enterprise Manager Cloud Control 12*c* installation with BP1 or Release 2 that came later, the procedure is different. A separate manual deployment of these plugins is no longer necessary (although it can still be done). Instead, the plugins will automatically be deployed at the time of the Exadata Machine guided discovery.

# Adding the hosts

We will now go through the entire procedure of discovering the Exadata Database Machine. The first step is to add the host targets. These are the compute nodes of the machine.

Select **Setup** | **Add Target** | **Add Targets Manually**.

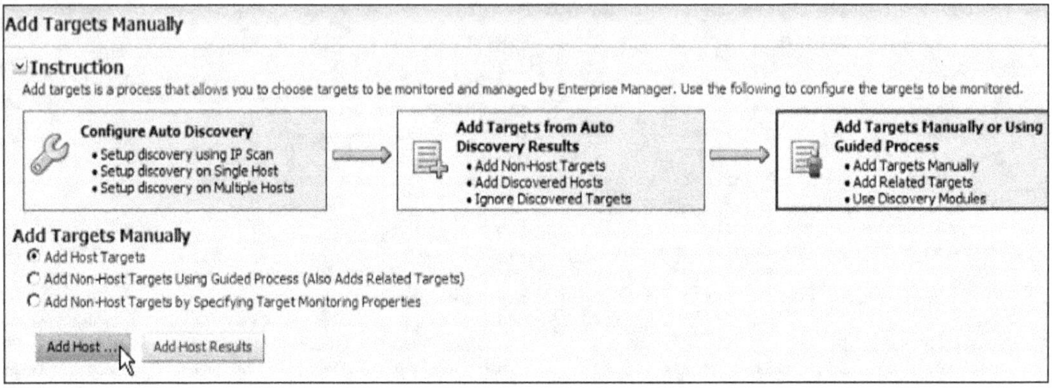


On this screen, select the radio button **Add Host Targets** and click on the **Add Host...** button.

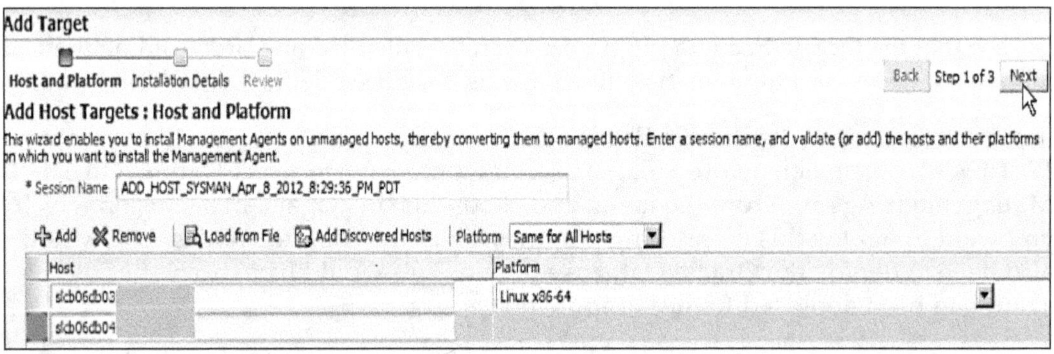


Before adding any hosts, change the drop-down box for **Platform** to **Same for All Hosts**. Then proceed to add the hosts using the **Add** button.

Select the appropriate **Platform** (**Linux x86-64** in this case) and add the two compute nodes. Click on **Next** to continue.

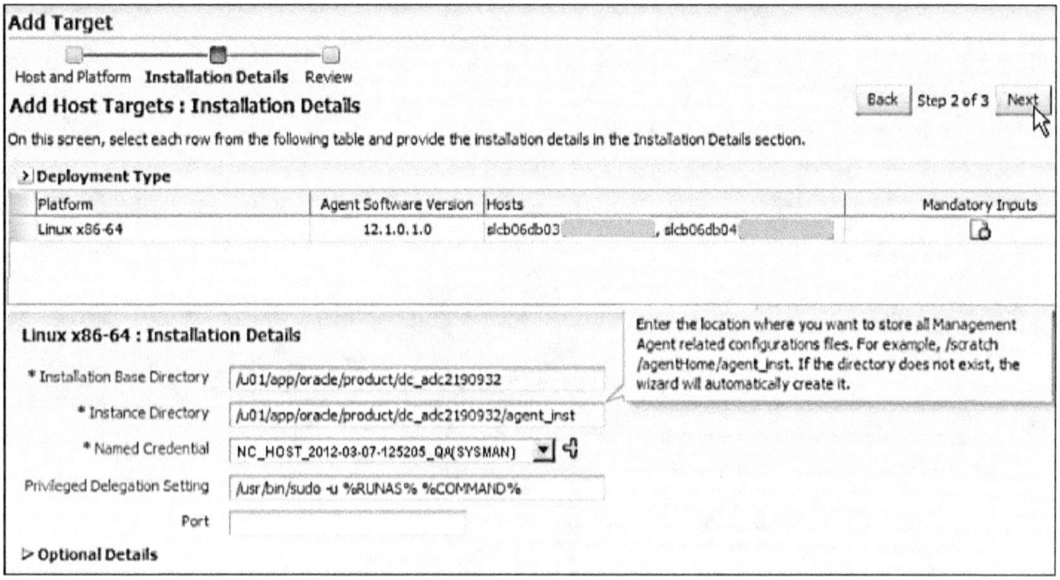

In the **Installation Details** section, first specify the **Installation Base Directory** path and then the actual agent **Instance Directory**. This is where all the agent-related configuration files will be stored.

Select a **Named Credential** instance. This will be used for an SSH connection to the remote hosts to install the agent.

Keep the default **Privileged Delegation Setting** option, that is, the `sudo` command, but blank out the **Port** field (the default value is `3872`). This is the port on which the agent communicates with the OMS. If a port is not entered, the wizard will use the first free port that is available within the range of `1830` to `1849`.

Click on **Next** to continue.

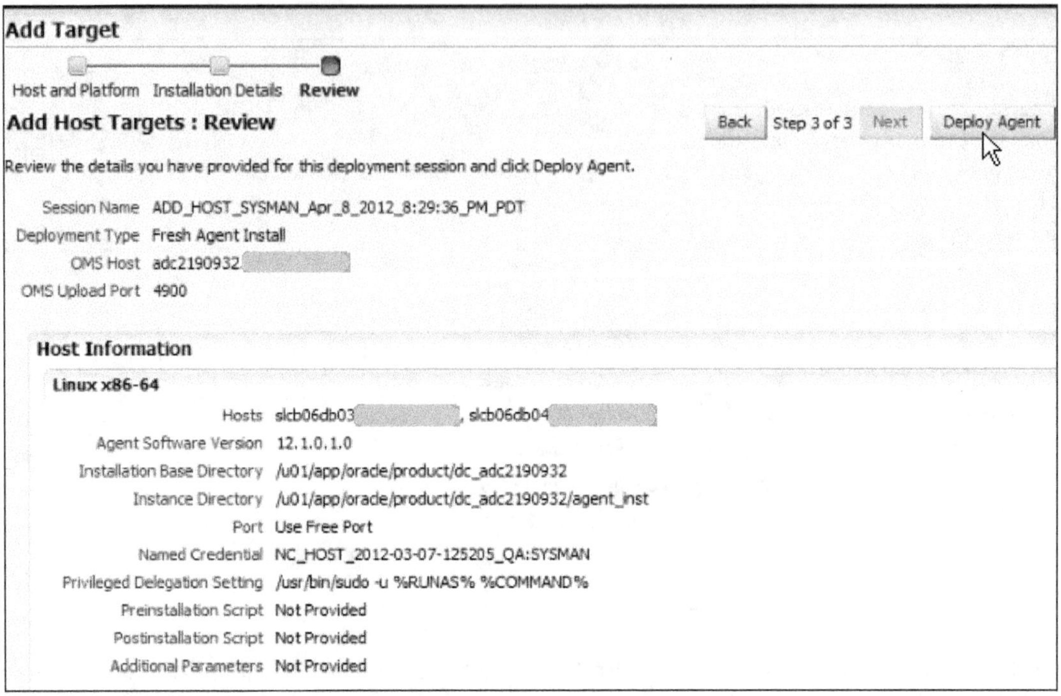

On the **Add Host Targets: Review** screen, check the details and then click on **Deploy Agent**. This starts the installation of the agent on the hosts.

First, initialization takes place. Then, **Remote Prerequisite Checks** are performed. If there is an existing agent home on the host, the prerequisite check will fail, as can be seen in the following screenshot:

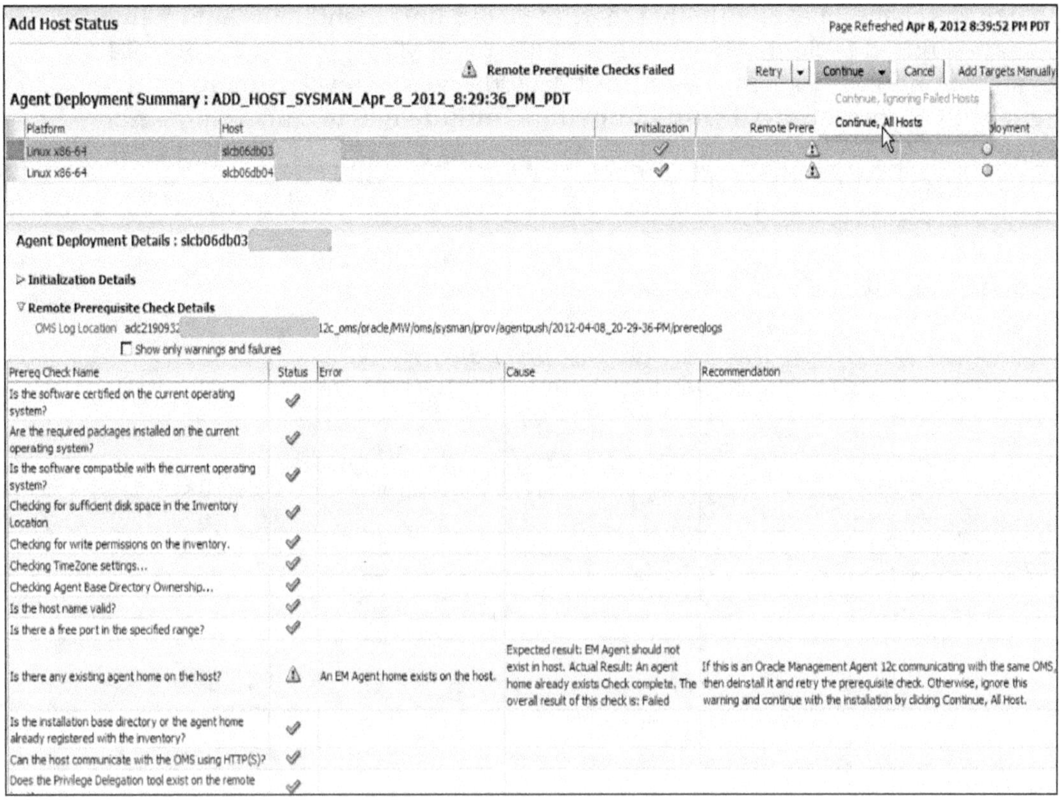


As we can see, the prerequisite checks are very detailed, with checks for certification, write permissions, free ports, and so on.

One of the checks makes sure that there is no existing agent home, and if there is, you are advised to de-install it if it is an Enterprise Manager Cloud Control 12*c* agent communicating with the same OMS. Otherwise, you can ignore this check by selecting **Continue, All Hosts** from the **Continue** menu.

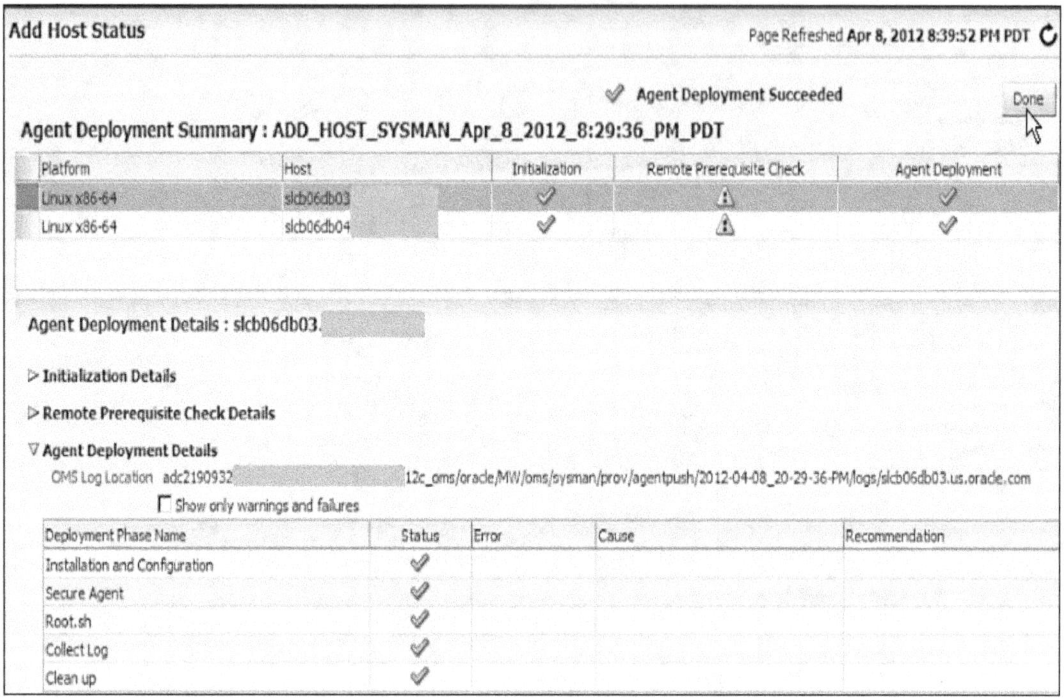

Finally, the agent deployment succeeds on the two hosts. You can check **Agent Deployment Details** with the various steps and status shown, and investigate further, if required, for any step of the process. Click on **Done**.

# Adding non-host targets

As the next step of the Exadata discovery process, you need to do a guided discovery of the Exadata Database Machine. This will include the non-host targets, that is, the Exadata Database Machine components, such as the storage servers, Infiniband switches, Ethernet switches, KVM switches, PDU, and compute node ILOM.

The guided discovery reads information from the following Exadata-specific configuration file on the compute nodes, so you need to first ensure that the hostnames and IP addresses in the file `/opt/oracle.SupportTools/onecommand/databasemachine.xml` are correct.

Note that the version of the `databasemachine.xml` file used should be `503` or higher. Also, the file should have the read (r) permission for the Unix user who installed the Enterprise Manager agent—otherwise the discovery will not be successful.

To start the guided discovery, select **Setup** | **Add Target** | **Add Targets Manually**.

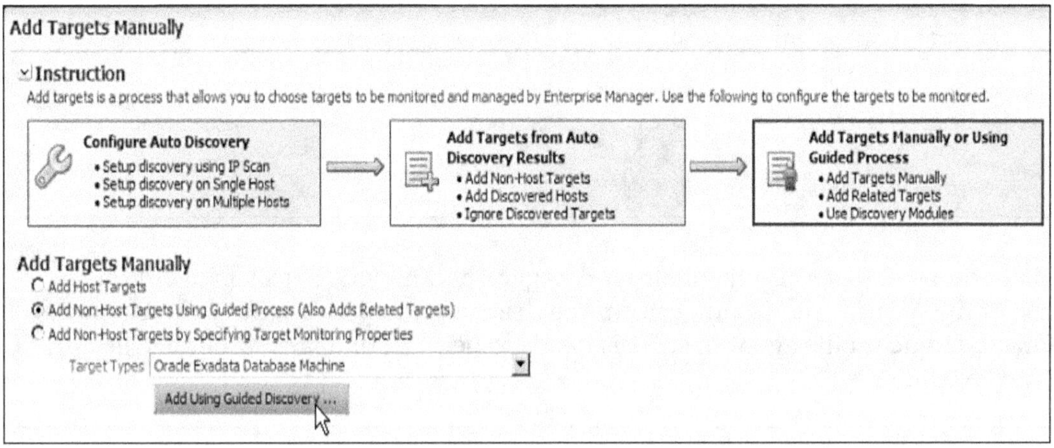


Select the radio button **Add Non-Host Targets Using Guided Process (Also Adds Related Targets)**, and select **Oracle Exadata Database Machine** from the **Target Types** drop-down box. Click on **Add Using Guided Discovery...**.

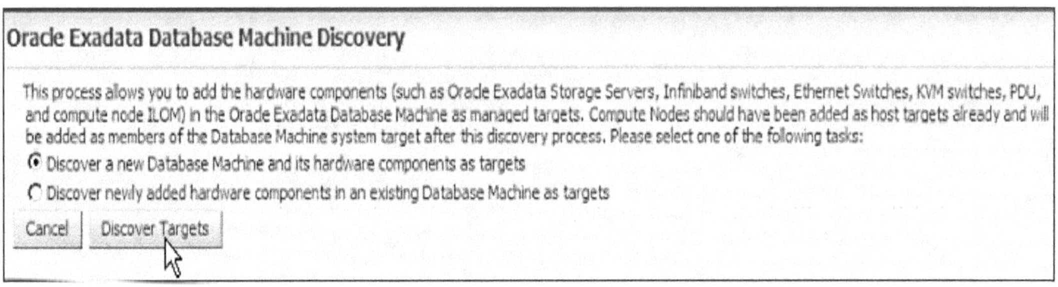


Using this process, you can add the storage servers, Infiniband switches, Ethernet switches, KVM switches, PDU, and compute node ILOM as managed targets.

Select the radio button **Discover a new Database Machine and its hardware components as targets**. Click on **Discover Targets**.

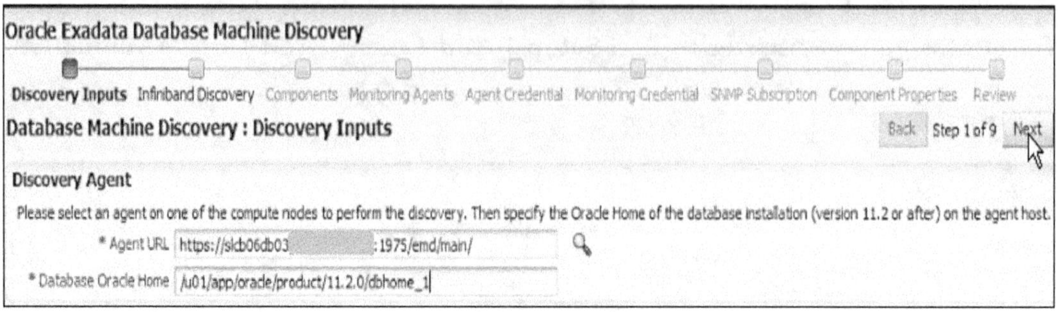

First you need to specify the **Discovery Agent** parameters. Select an agent on one of the compute nodes to perform the discovery, and also specify the **Database Oracle Home** on the agent host. This needs to be `11.2` or a later version. Click on **Next** to continue.

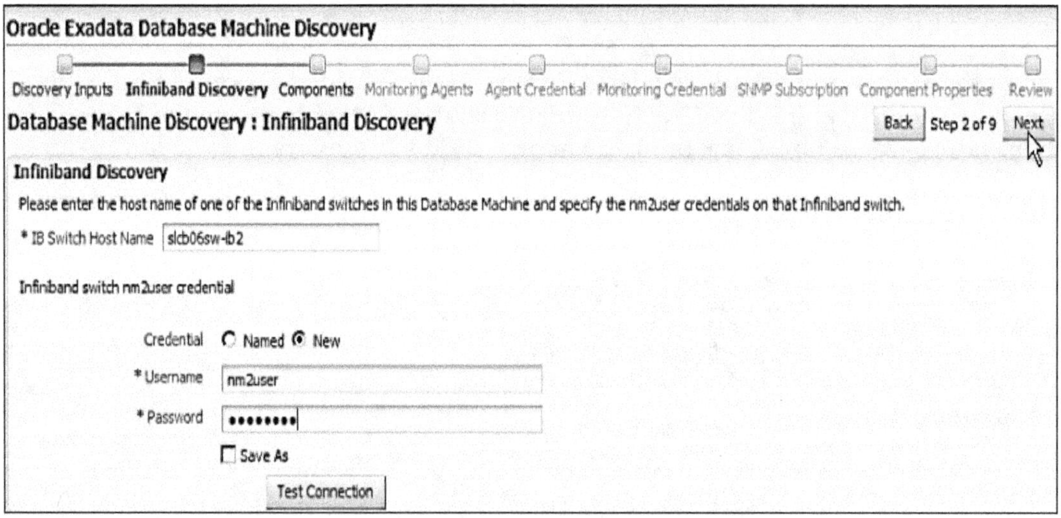

For **Infiniband Discovery**, you need to specify the hostname of one of the Infiniband switches, along with **Username** and **Password** of `nm2user` on the switch. You can also test the connection.

Click on **Next** to continue.

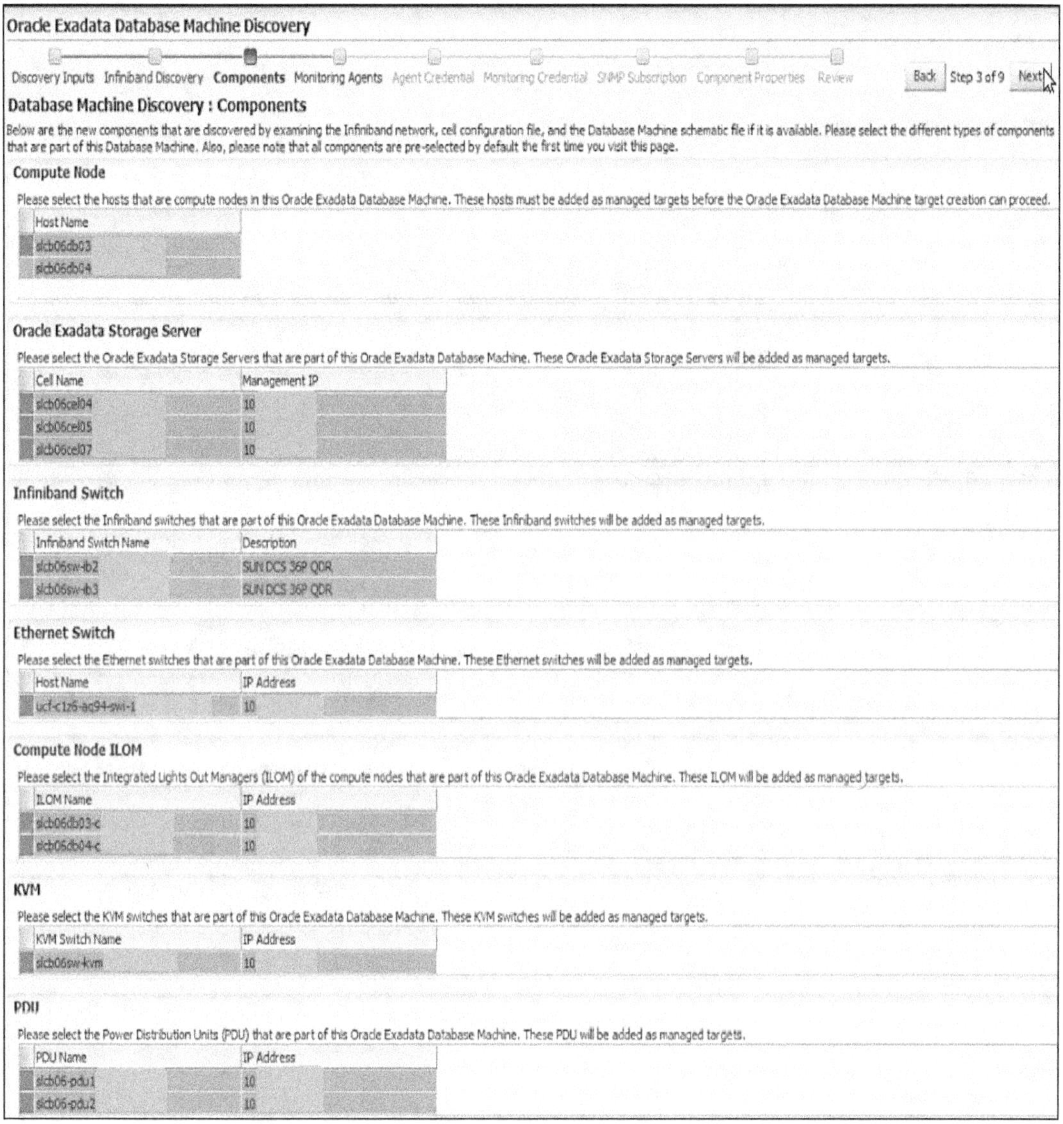

In the second step of the process, new **Components** are displayed. These have been discovered by examining the Infiniband network, the cell configuration file, and the database machine schematic file, if available.

You need to select the components you wish to add. Click on **Next**.

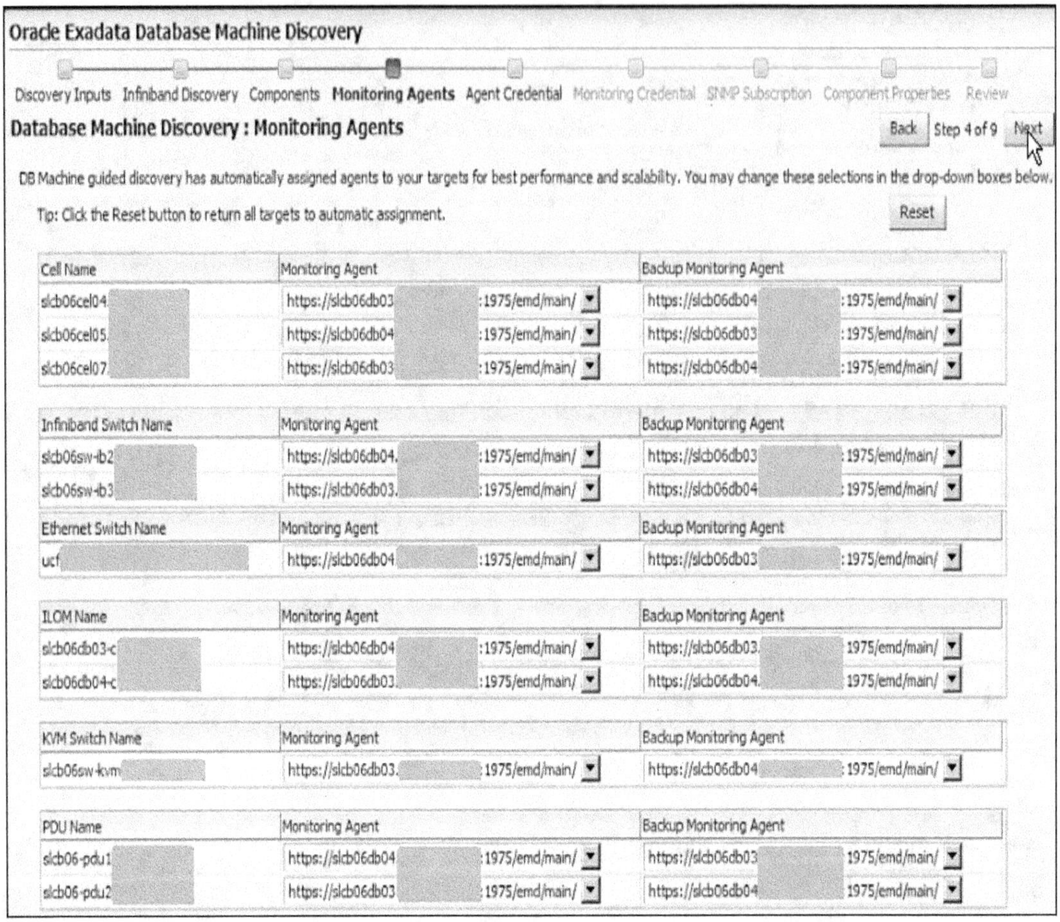

The wizard automatically assigns a **Monitoring Agent** instance as well as a **Backup Monitoring Agent** instance to each target, for best performance and scalability. The selections can be changed if you want. Click on **Next**.

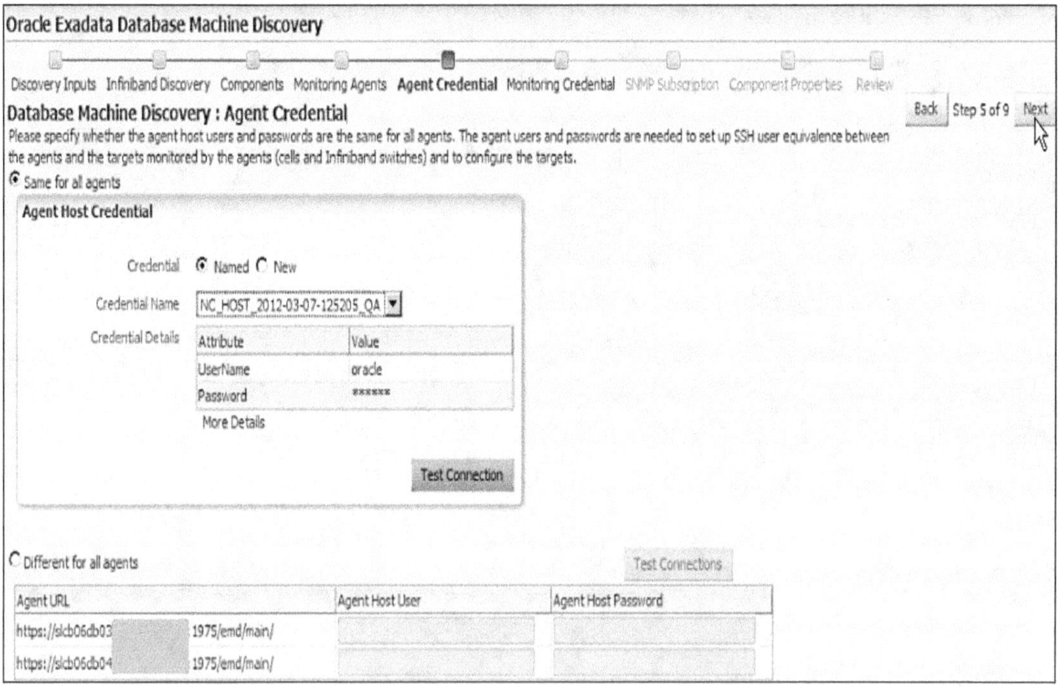

Enter the **Agent Credential** details. These can be specified as the same for every agent or different for each agent. SSH User Equivalence will be set up between the agents and their monitored targets (cells and Infiniband switches). Click on **Next**.

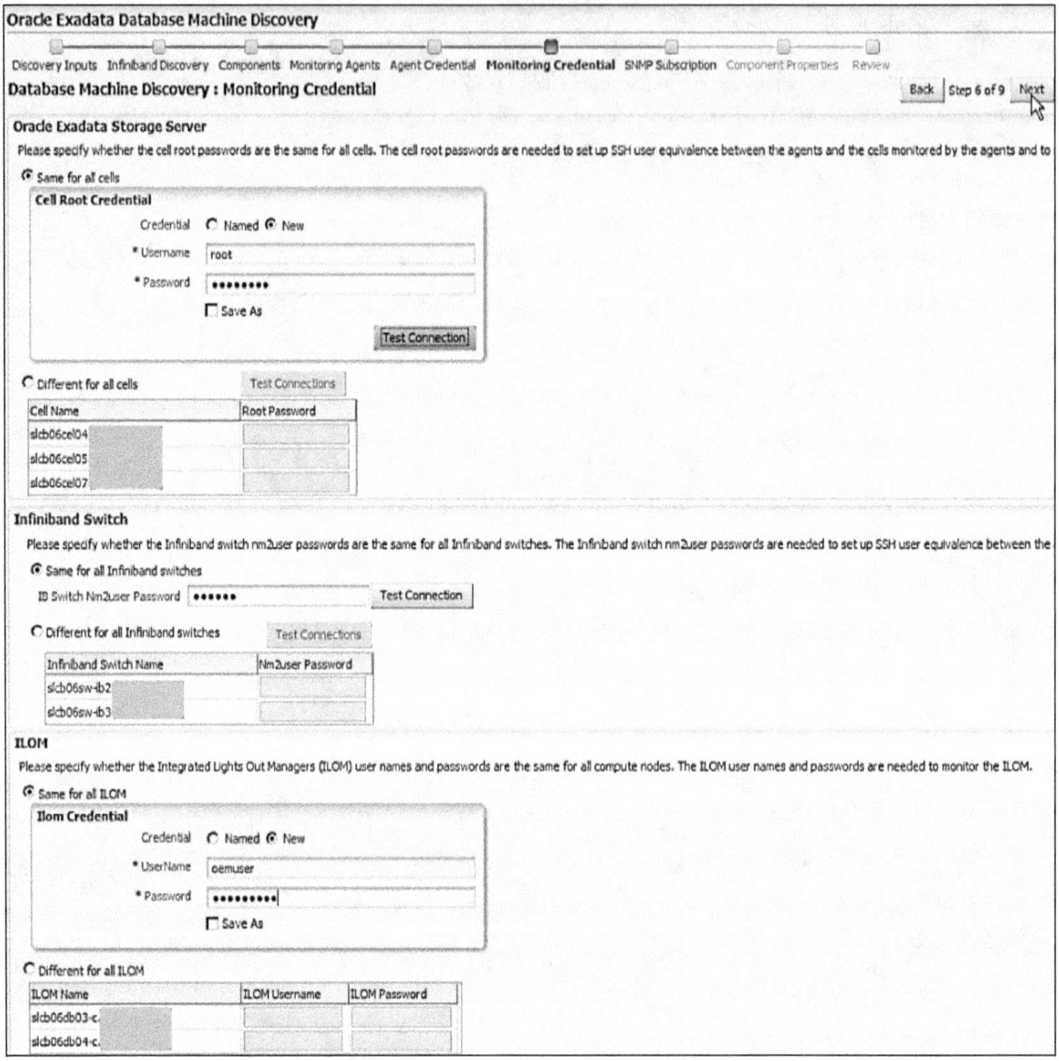

In the same way, on the **Monitoring Credential** page, enter the credentials for **Oracle Exadata Storage Server**, the password for the `nm2user` login at the **Infiniband Switch**, and the **UserName** and **Password** values for **ILOM**. You can specify either the same password or use a different password for each of them. Click on **Next**.

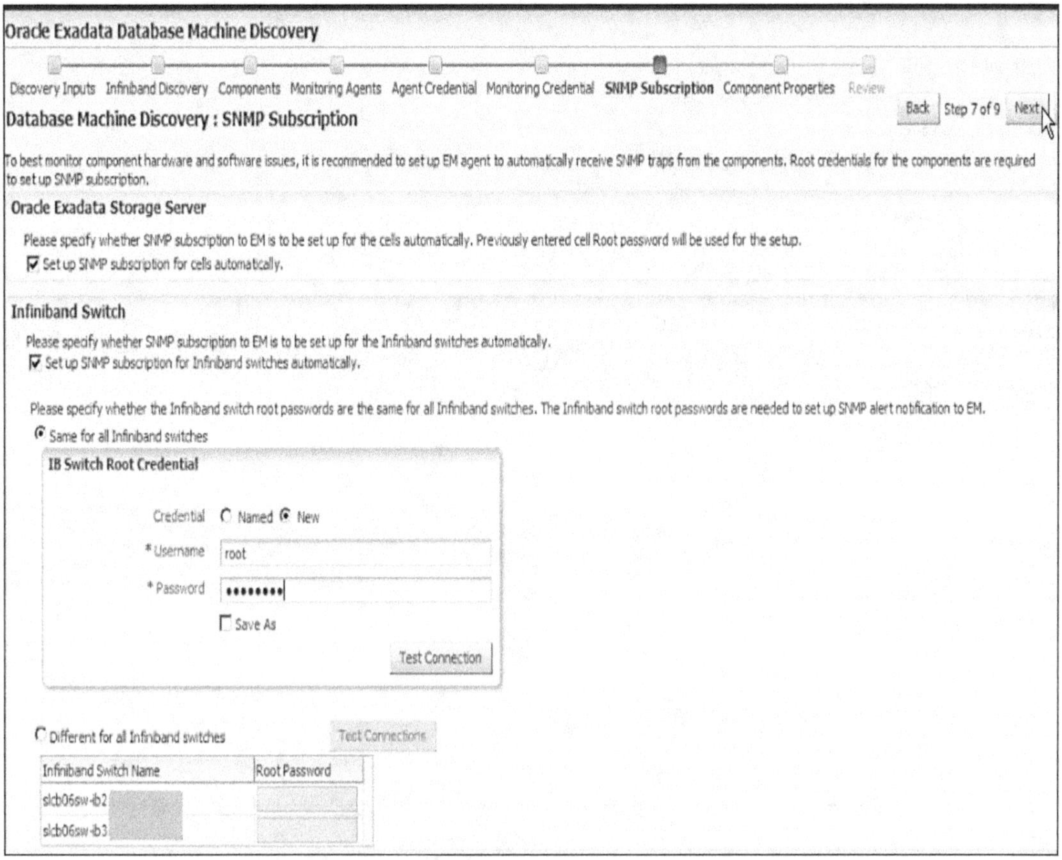


On the **SNMP Subscription** page, you can set up the EM agent to automatically receive SNMP traps from Exadata components. This is recommended for best monitoring of hardware and software issues. Root credentials are required.

This can be done for the Exadata storage servers and the Infiniband switches. Click on **Next** to continue.

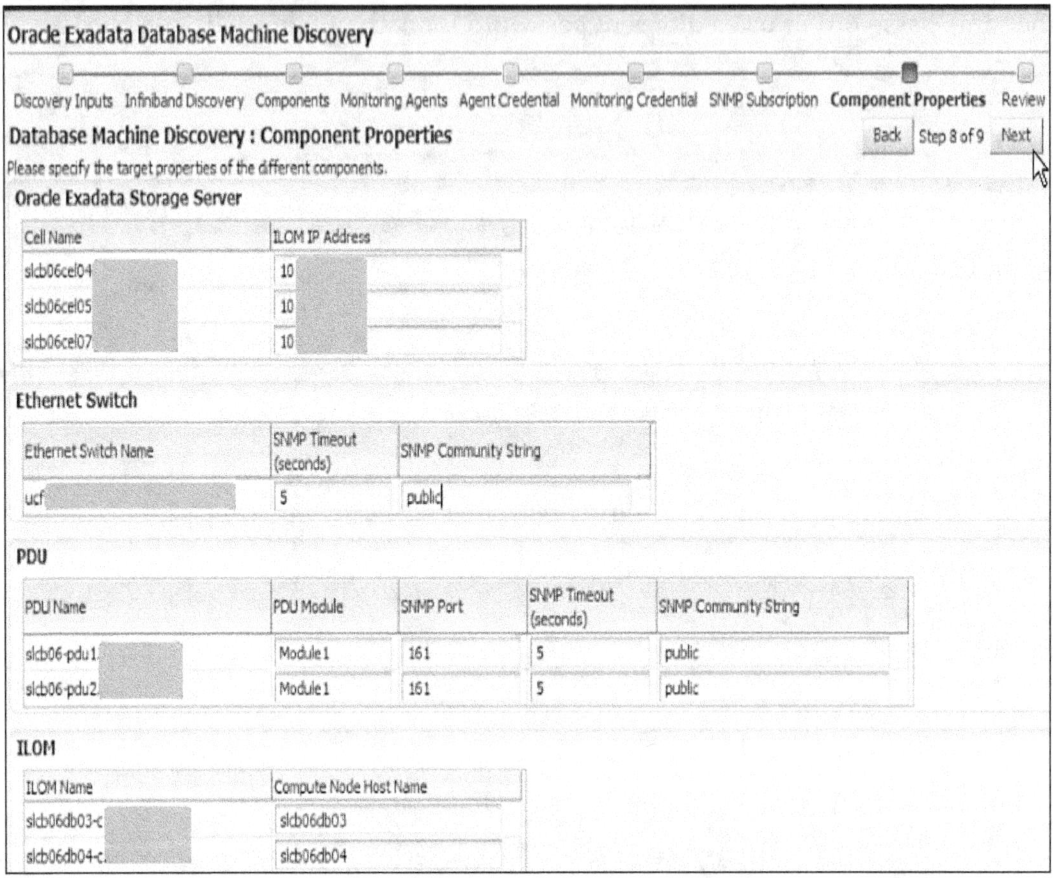


In the **Component Properties** page, verify the **ILOM IP Address** string for each of the **Oracle Exadata Storage Server** instances. Type in `public` in the **SNMP Community String** column for **Ethernet Switch** as well as **PDU**. Verify the **ILOM Name** strings for the compute nodes as well.

Click on the **Next** button.

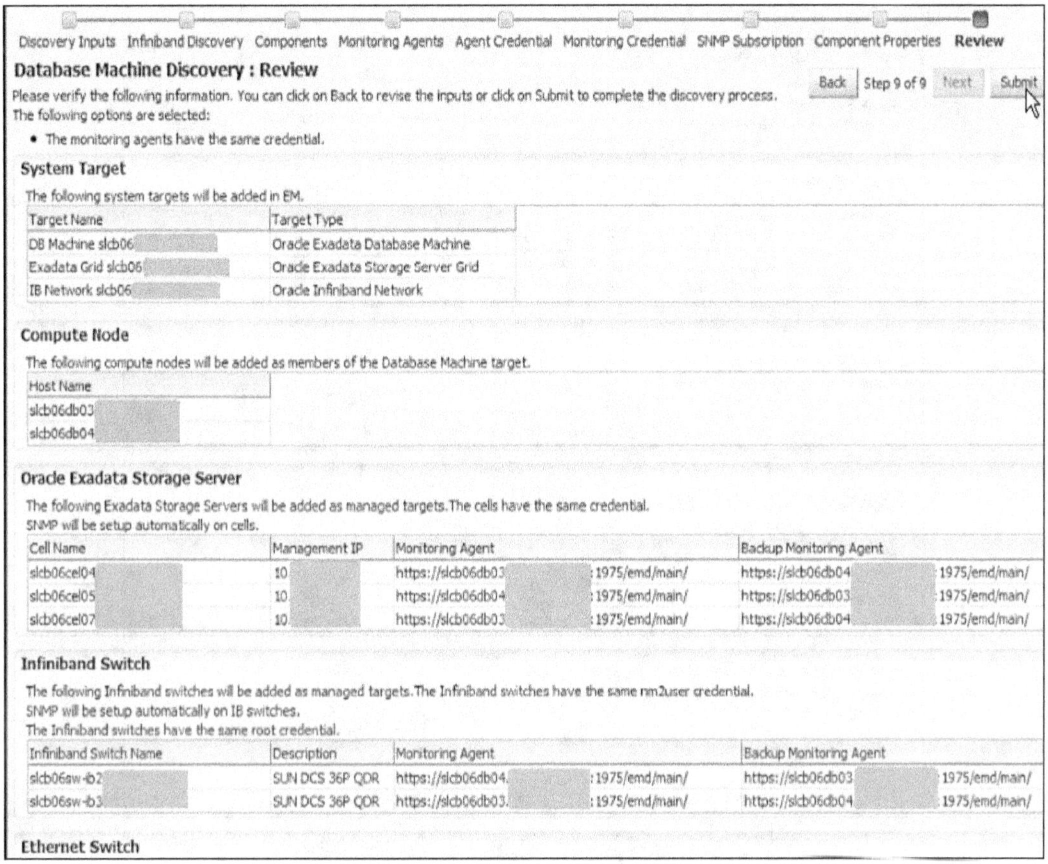


You can verify the information on the **Review** screen. Once you are satisfied, click on **Submit**.

The promotion of the targets starts at this point. When completed, the following screen appears:

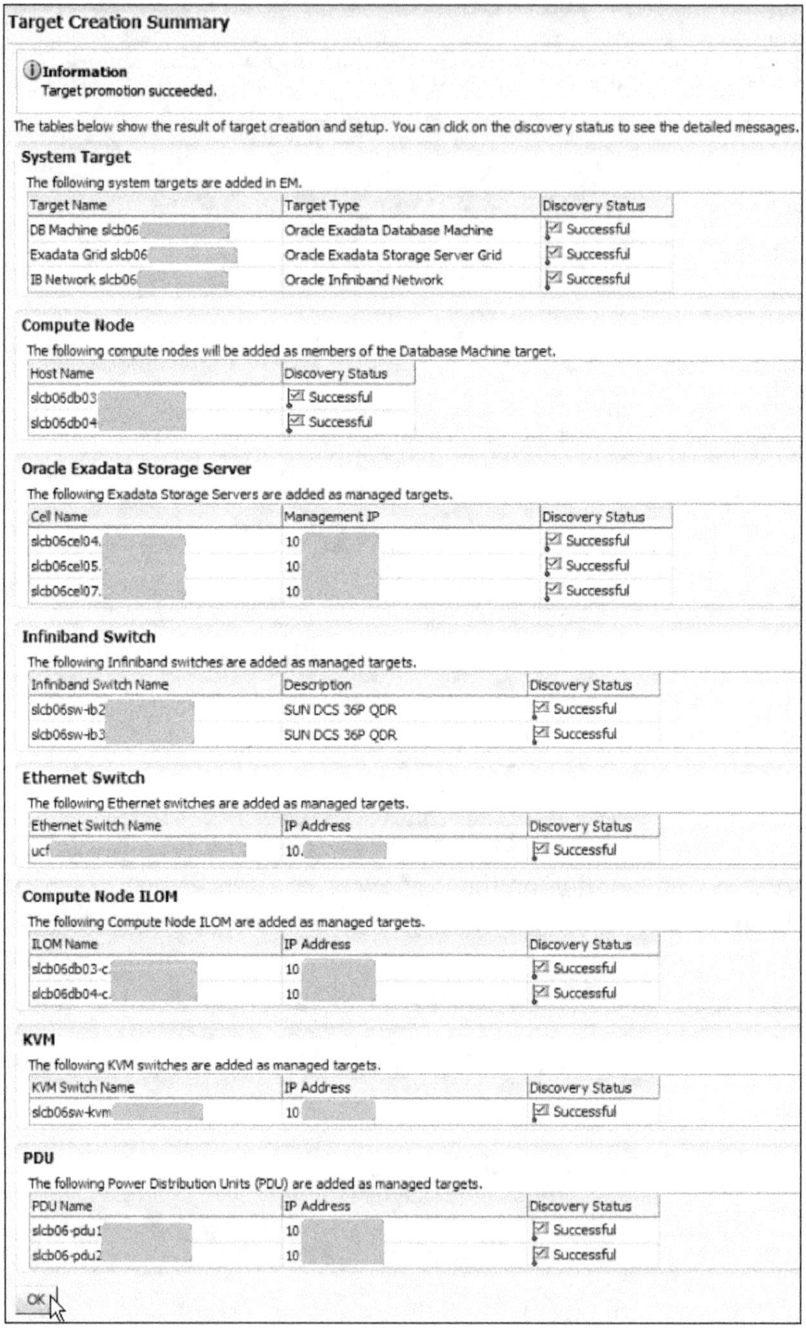

The **Target promotion** has succeeded. **System Targets** for the database machine, storage server grid, and Infiniband network have been added to Enterprise Manager.

The compute nodes, storage servers, Infiniband switches, Ethernet switches, compute node ILOMs, KVMs, and PDUs are also added as managed targets to Enterprise Manager.

Click on **OK**.

Now, log in to Enterprise Manager Cloud Control 12*c* again. Select **Targets** | **Exadata** from the menu.

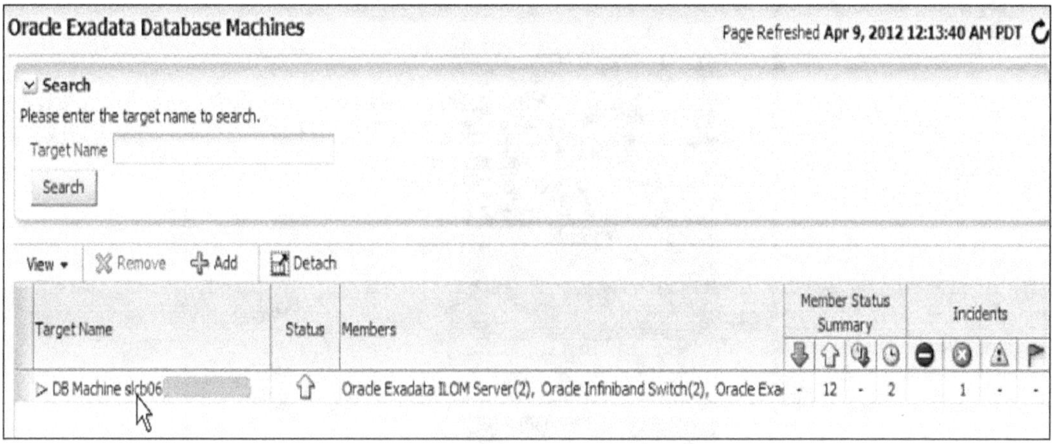

A target list of all **Oracle Exadata Database Machines** managed by Enterprise Manager Cloud Control 12*c* appears on this page. At a glance, you can see the status of the members and any **Incidents** that have occurred. To drill down further, click on the **Database Machine** instance.

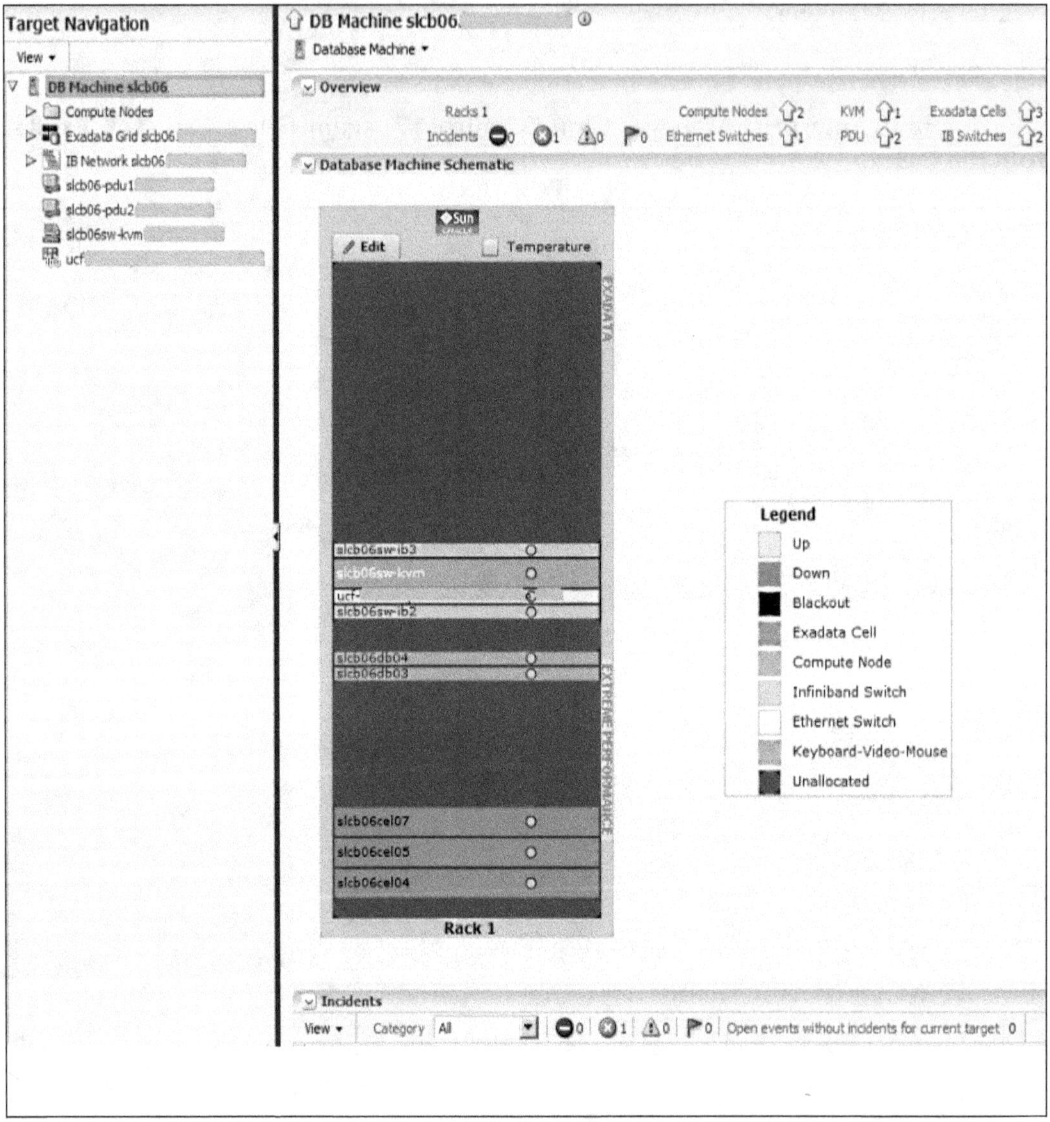

We can see that **Database Machine Schematic** appears on the **Database Machine** home page. In the left panel, the hierarchy of components can be seen. The machine is made up of compute nodes, storage servers, an IB network, PDUs, KVM, and the Ethernet switch. So it means that all these components are now managed targets.

If components such as the PDUs, KVM, Ethernet switch, or storage cells are not discovered, or show as down when they are actually up, or there are other evident issues, you will need to follow the troubleshooting steps that are documented in *Oracle Enterprise Manager Exadata Management Getting Started Guide* at the following URL:

```
http://docs.oracle.com/cd/E24628_01/doc.121/e27442/ch5_
troubleshooting.htm#autoId0
```

It is also possible to click **Edit** in the schematic diagram on the **Database Machine** home page. Right-click on any component, and from the menu that appears, select **Delete Component**. Then, right click on the same spot and select **Add Component**. At this point, you can choose the target to be positioned in that place.

# Adding the cluster and databases

The next step in the Exadata database machine discovery is to discover the cluster, databases, listeners, and ASM.

From the menu, select **Setup** | **Add Target** | **Add Targets Manually**.

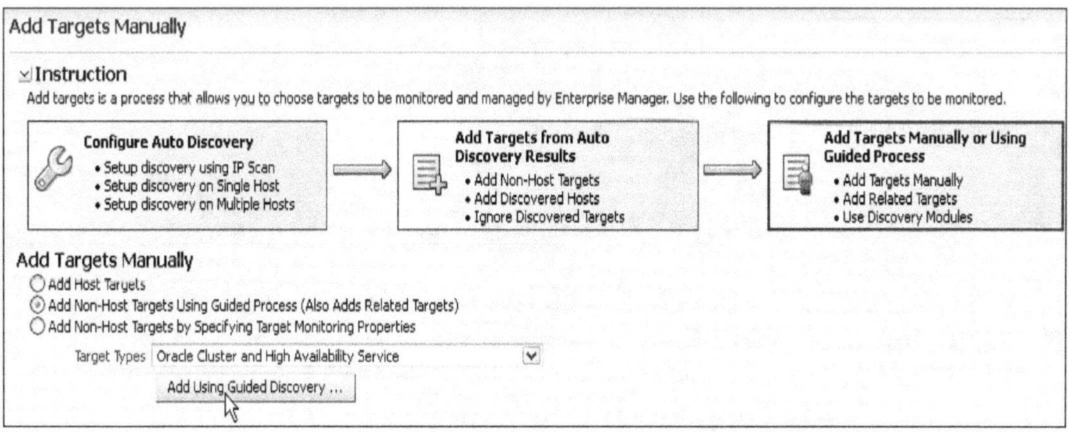

Select the radio button **Add Non-Host Targets Using Guided Process (Also Adds Related Targets)**, and select **Oracle Cluster and High Availability Service** from the **Target Types** drop-down box. Click on **Add Using Guided Discovery...**.

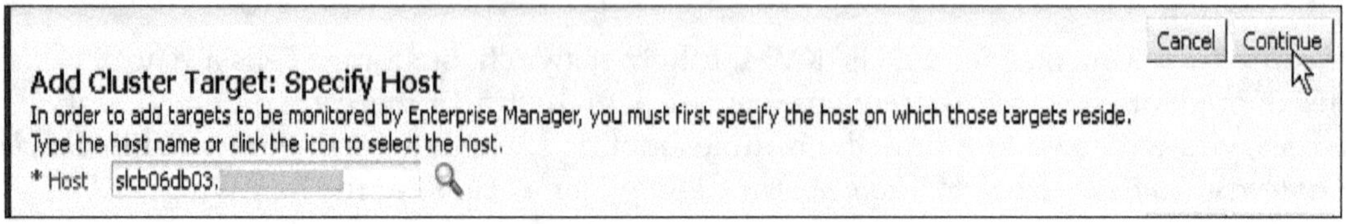


To add the cluster target, you need to specify one of the hosts on which the cluster resides. Select the host by using the icon. Click on **Continue**.

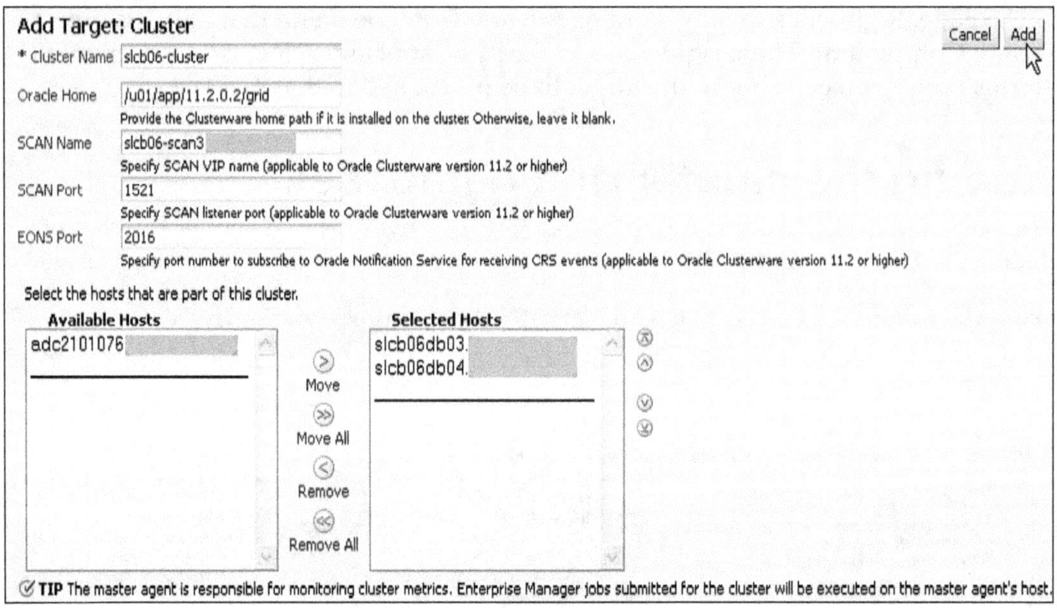


Enter the details of the **Cluster** instance, such as **Cluster Name, Oracle Home** (Grid Infrastructure Home), **SCAN Name** (Scan VIP Name), and **SCAN Port** (Scan Listener Port), as well as **EONS Port** (to subscribe to Oracle Notification Service).

From the list of available hosts, select the hosts that are part of this cluster. Click on **Add**.

The target addition is started. The cluster targets are saved. The two hosts are now part of the cluster.

From the menu, select **Setup** | **Add Target** | **Add Targets Manually**.

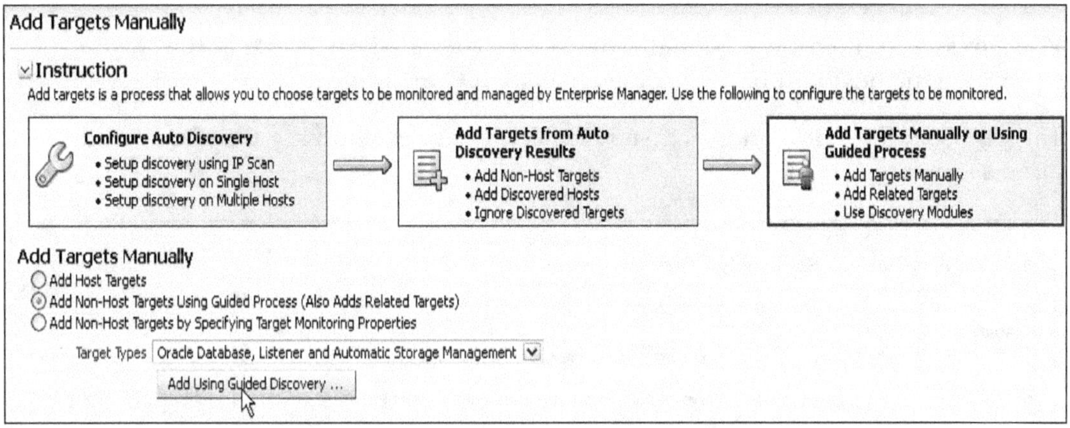


Select the radio button **Add Non-Host Targets Using Guided Process (Also Adds Related Targets)**, and select **Oracle Database, Listener and Automatic Storage Management** from the **Target Types** drop-down box. Click on **Add Using Guided Discovery...**.

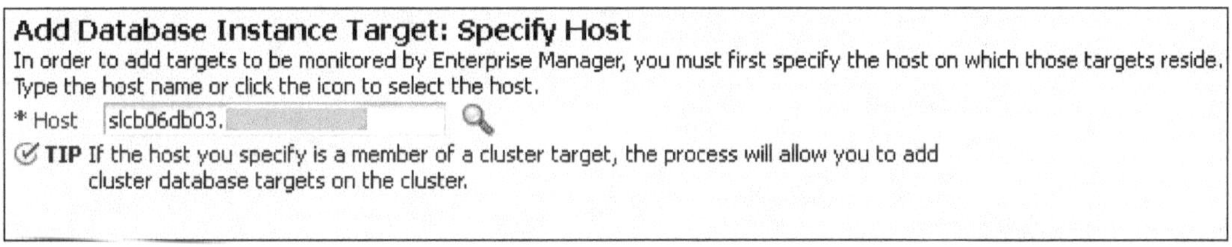


Select the host on which the database instance resides. Click on **Continue**.

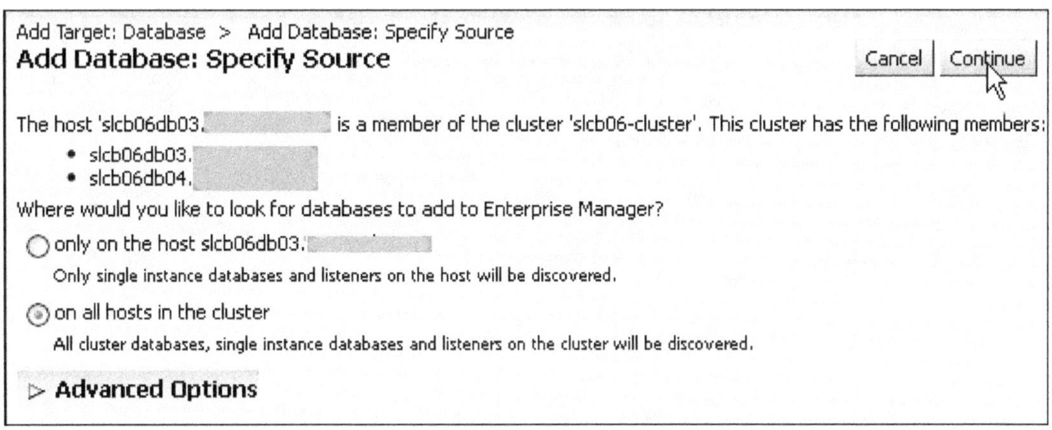

The **Add Database** wizard has discovered that the host you have specified is a member of a cluster.

You can specify if you want the discovery to work on all the hosts in the cluster, or only on the host you have specified. Click on **Continue**.

Target discovery starts on the cluster. Finally, the page showing the discovered targets appears.

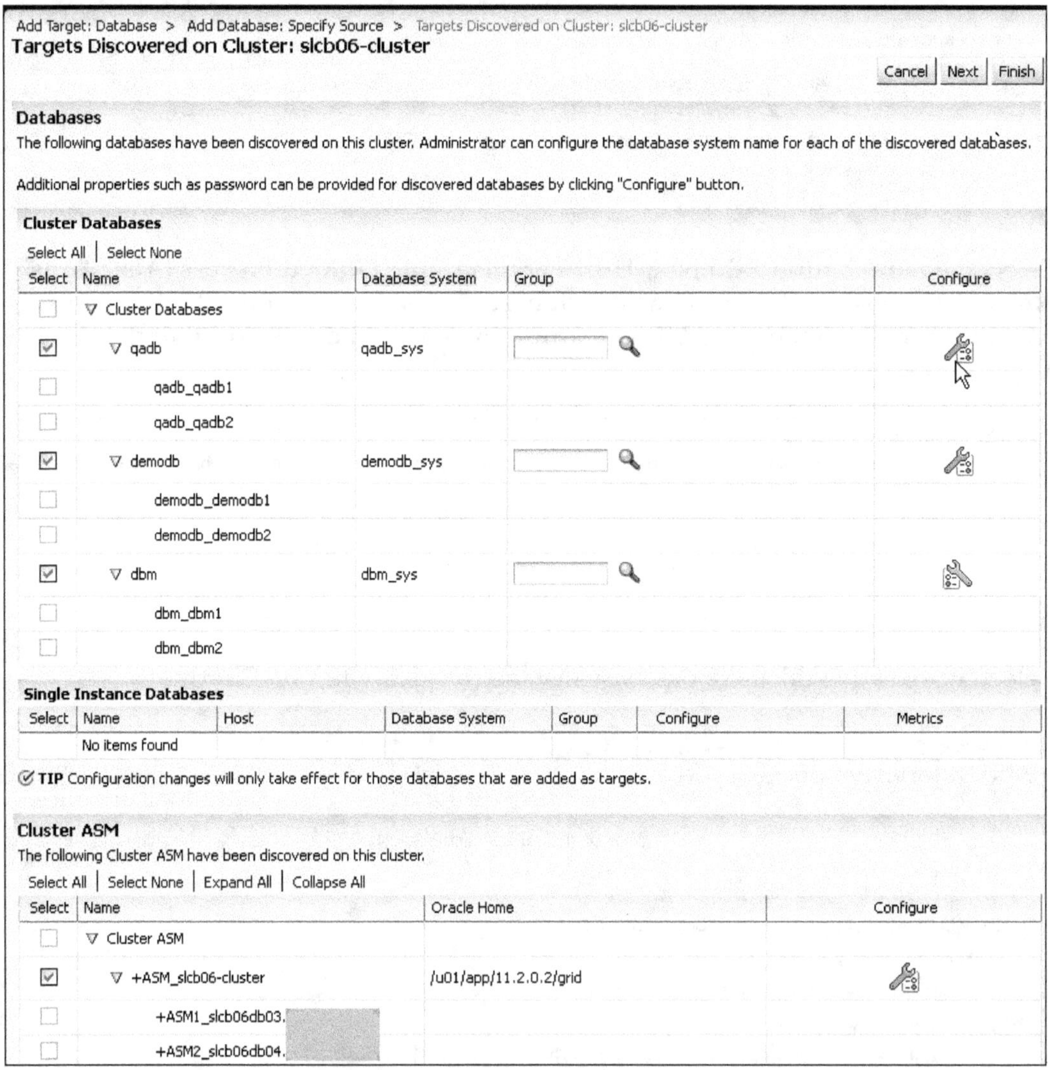

As we can see, **Cluster Databases** along with their instances have been discovered, and corresponding **Database Systems** have also been created.

There are no **Single Instance Databases**. **Cluster ASM** instances, and listeners if any are present, are also discovered. Click on the spanner icon to configure the cluster database.

On the **Configure Cluster Database** screen, type in **Monitor Username** and **Monitor Password**, and specify the **SYSDBA** role. Click on **Test Connection**. When the connection test is successful, click on **Next** to continue.

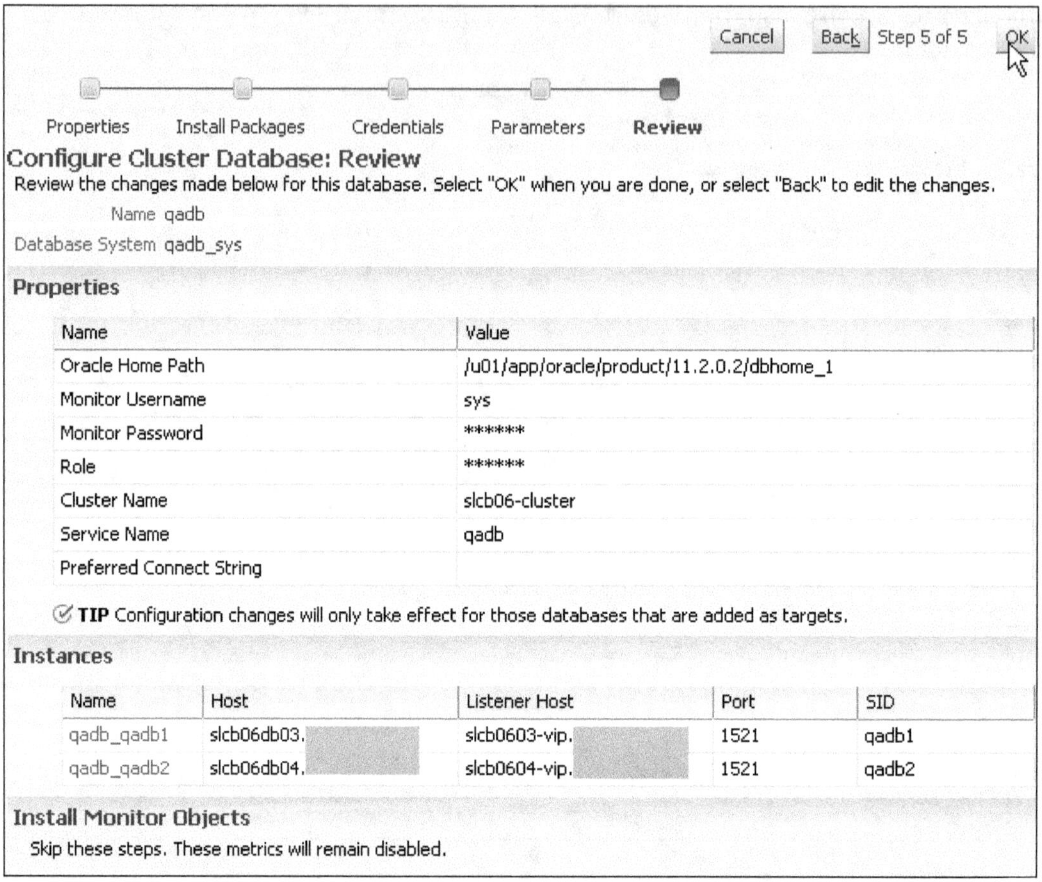


The **Review** screen appears. Check the details of the cluster database and **Instances**, and click on **OK**.

You are placed back on the **Targets Discovered** page. You can now configure the other cluster databases in a similar manner by using the spanner icon.

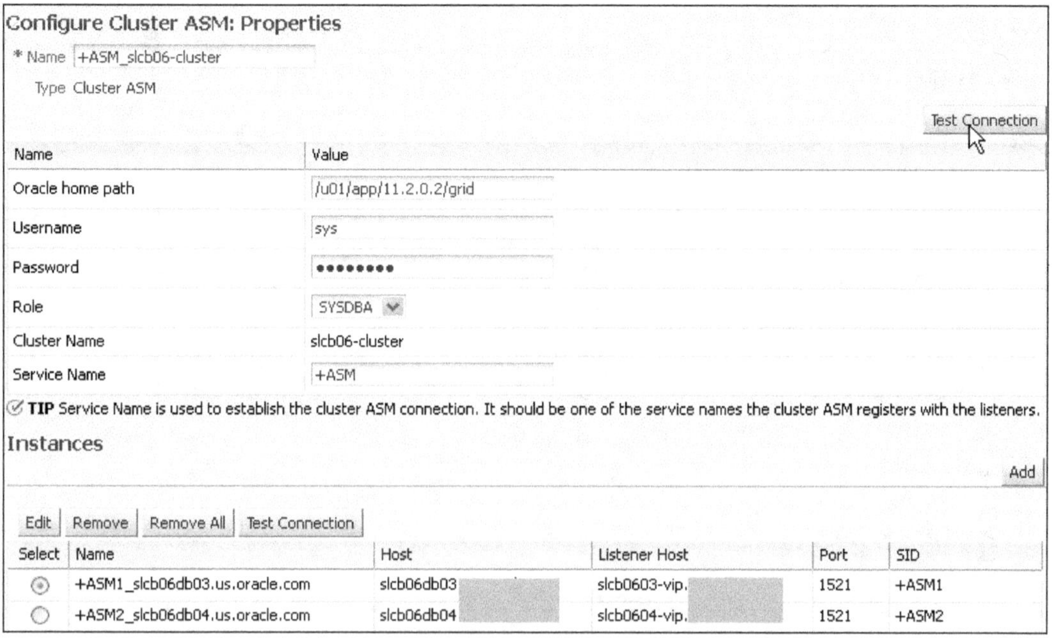


On the **Configure Cluster ASM** page, type in **Username** and **Password**, specify the **SYSDBA** role, and click on **Test Connection**.

When the connection test is successful, click on **OK**.

You are placed back on the **Targets Discovered** page. Click on the **Finish** button.

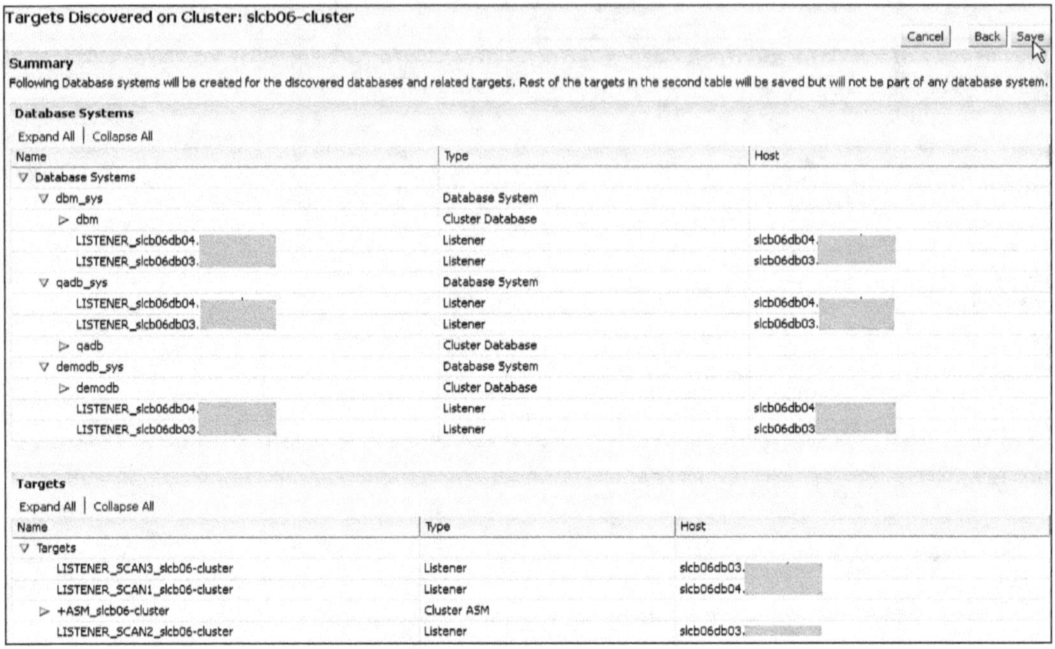


On the **Summary** screen, the **Database Systems** instances that will be created are displayed. The **Cluster Database** and the **Listeners** instances on each node are automatically placed in each **Database System**.

The other **Targets** listed in the lower part of the screen, such as the scan listeners and the ASM cluster, will be saved but will not be included in any database system. Click on the **Save** button.

Select **Targets** | **Databases** to verify that the databases have been added.

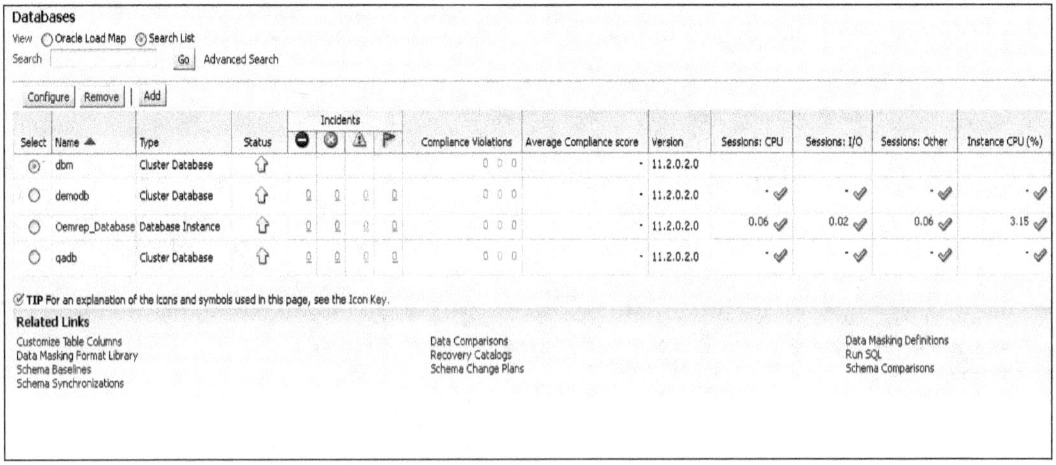


Several **Cluster Databases** can be seen in the **Targets** list, including the ones we have added. This confirms that the target discovery has been successful.

Select **Setup** | **Extensibility** | **Plug-ins** from the Enterprise Manager menu. This takes you to the **Plug-ins** page. We can see that the **Oracle Exadata** plugin has been deployed.

There is also a new plugin, seen in the following screenshot, known as the **Oracle Exadata Healthchecks** plugin. This is not mandatory for monitoring. However, this plugin provides proactive health check alerts for your Exadata system based on the configuration data.

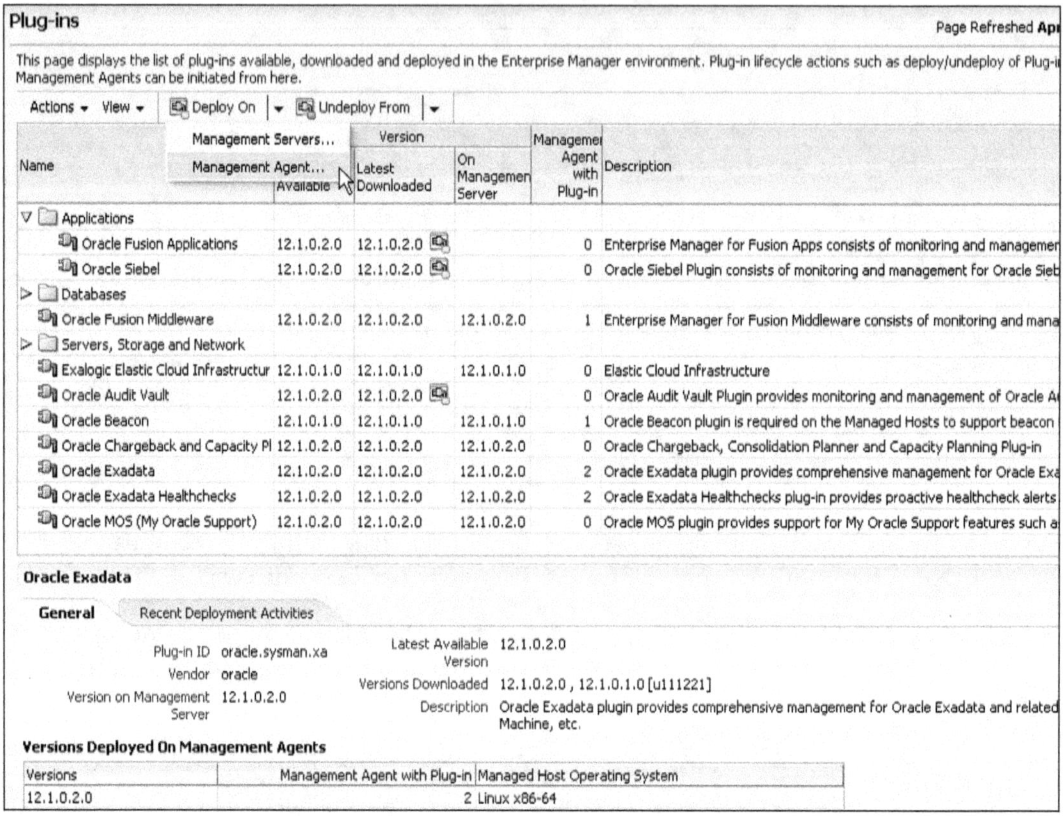

The **Exadata Healthchecks** plugin will not be deployed automatically. The deployment has to be done manually. select **Deploy On | Management Agent** from the menu and choose the **Management Agents** instances on which you want to deploy this plugin, namely the compute nodes.

You can add an Exadata Healthcheck target manually if `exachk` results are available—these results are generated by executing the out of the box `exachk` utility on the Exadata Database Machine. This utility needs to be configured to run on a periodic basis.

Go to **Setup | Add Target | Add Targets Manually**, select the radio button **Add Non-Host Targets by Specifying Target Monitoring Properties**, and then choose **Exadata Health checks** in the drop-down box. Select the agent of the host on which the `exachk` results are available. Then click on **Add Manually**. In the next page, name the new Target appropriately and enter the full directory path of the `exachk` results. Finally, click on the **OK** button.

The `exachk` target will be added in Enterprise Manager. This target will contain all the results and reports of the `exachk` execution. Any failures will be reported, and there is a report to show the `exachk` violations.

# Monitoring and managing Exadata

**Exadata monitoring** covers the databases, compute nodes (database servers), storage servers, the Infiniband network and switches, KVM switches, Cisco switches, ILOM, and PDU. We will have a look at how Exadata appears in Enterprise Manager Cloud Control 12*c*.

Move to **Targets** | **Exadata** and drill down to the **Database Machine**. The **Database Machine** home page appears with the following schematic:

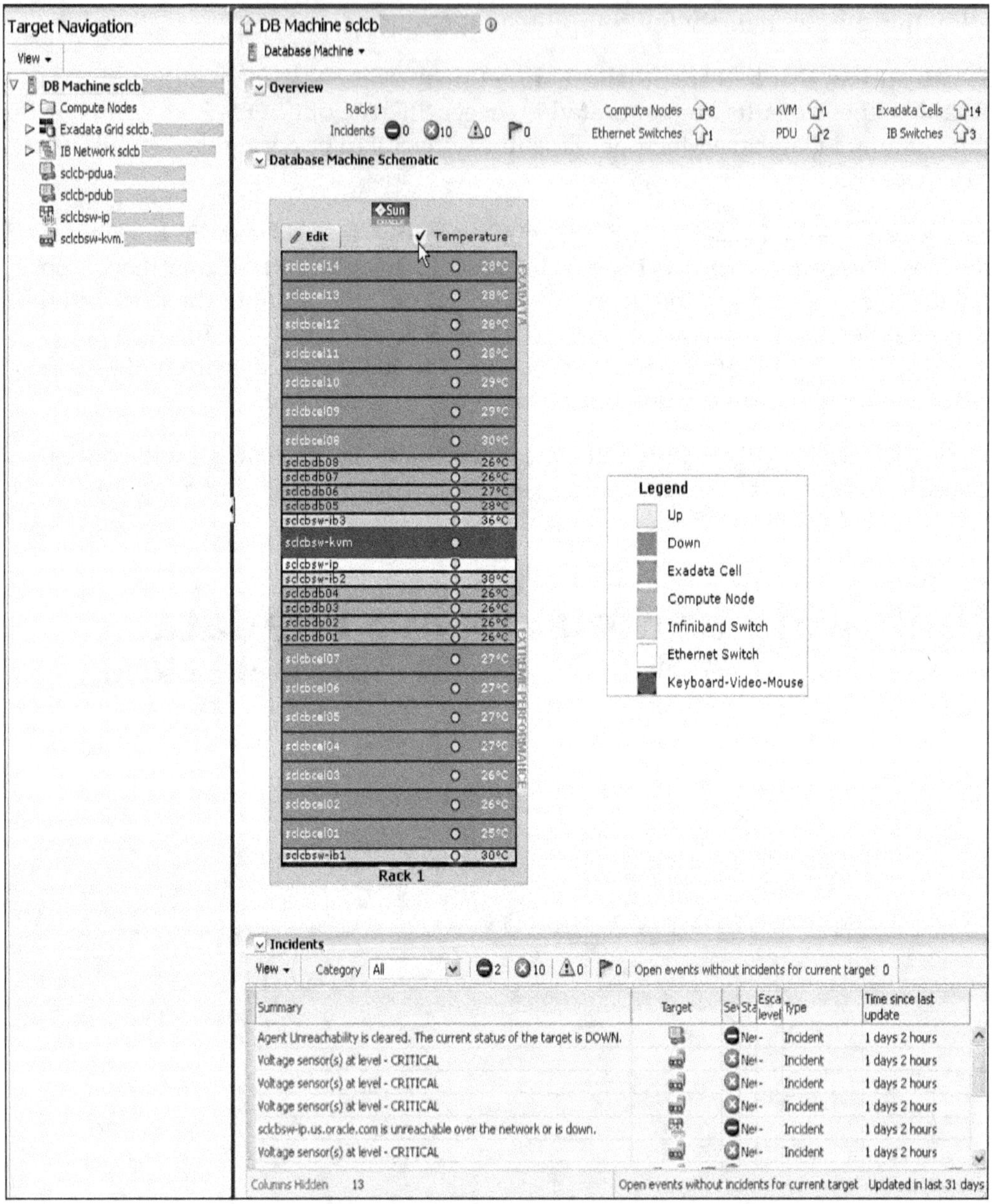

This shows, at a glance, an integrated view of the entire Exadata system in an illustrative, schematic diagram. The **Compute Nodes** and **Storage Cells** are seen in a full Exadata Database Machine rack, along with the **KVM, Ethernet switch**, and **Infiniband Switches**.

Note that the temperature of the components is also monitored—you can show the temperature on the diagram by selecting the **Temperature** checkbox. The temperature is considered to be very important in an Exadata system. It should ideally be between `15` and `35` degrees since overheating can affect performance.

The left panel outlines the Exadata component hierarchy with a list of **Compute Nodes, Storage Cells (Exadata Grid)**, the **Infiniband Network, PDUs, KVM,** and so on. You can drill down into any of these from this panel.

The upper section of the screen shows the status overview of all the components—whether they are **UP** or **DOWN**. Any related **Incidents** are also shown.

Further detail on the incidents is shown at the bottom of the screen. For example, we can see that a **Voltage Sensor** incident of a critical severity level has been raised a number of times. Similar incidents for hardware component issues will be seen in this section.

# Database machine resource utilization

From the **Database Machine** home page, select **Database Machine** | **Resource Utilization** | **Compute Resources**. The following screen appears:

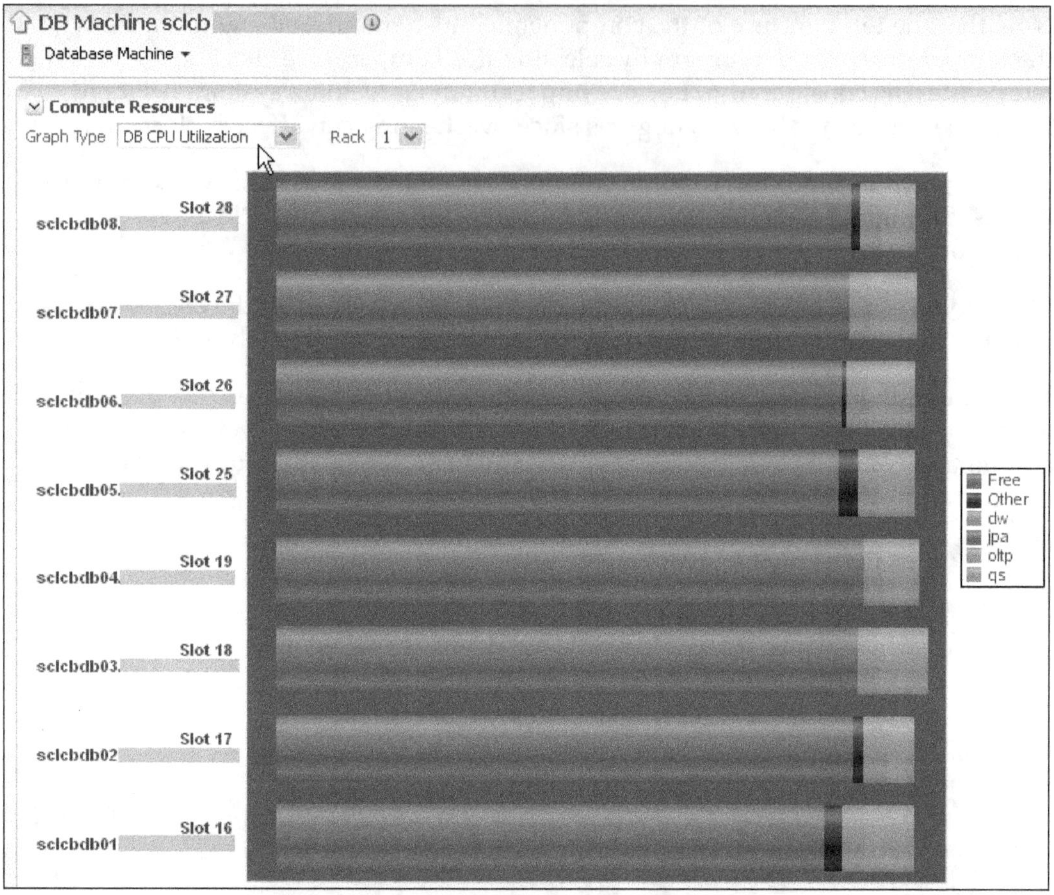


A bar graph appears, showing **DB CPU Utilization** of all the databases across the compute nodes. The green color signifies that the **CPU** is mostly under-utilized across all the nodes. The other databases are seen in different colors. This graph shows, at a glance, if you have enough CPU capacity in your Exadata Database Machine rack. If not, you need to buy another Exadata rack.

Click on the **Graph Type** drop-down box; you can see that there are two other options, namely **Database Placement** and **Cluster Placement**. Select **Database Placement** from the list.

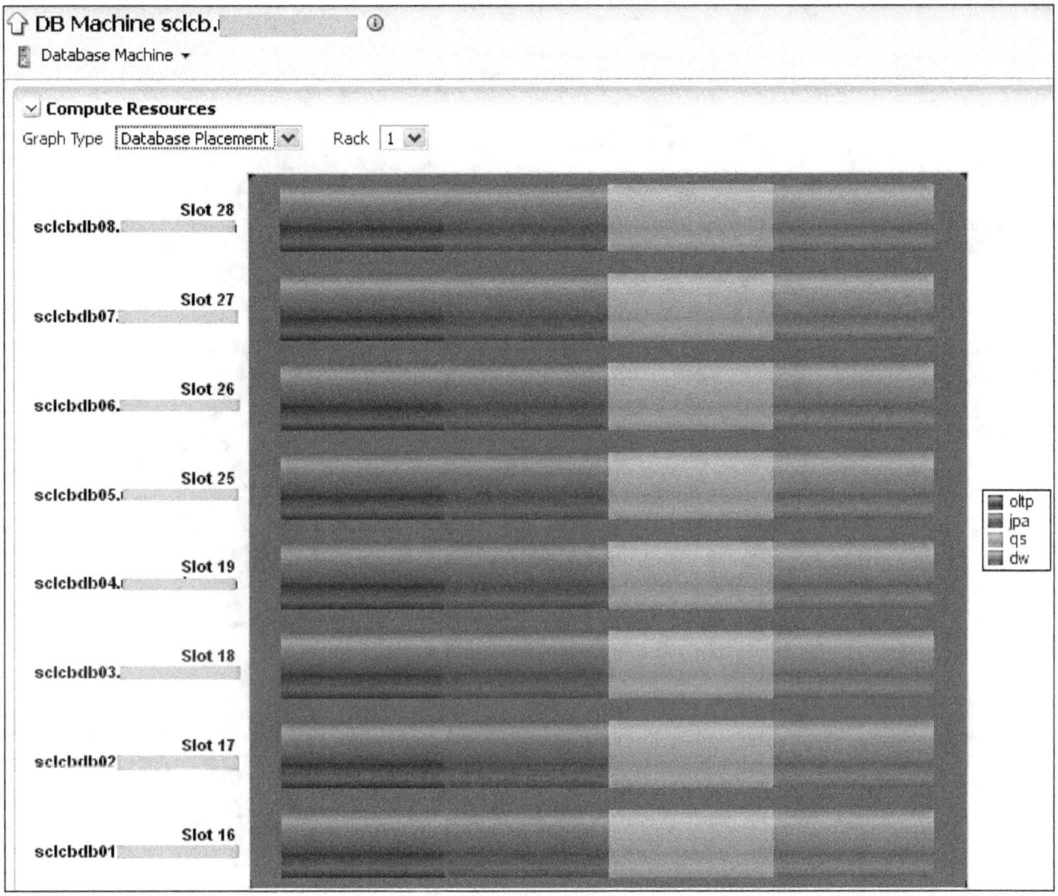


In the **Database Placement** graph, we can see that the four databases in our case are placed on all the eight compute nodes.

Now, select **Database Machine** | **Resource Utilization** | **Storage Resources** from the menu.

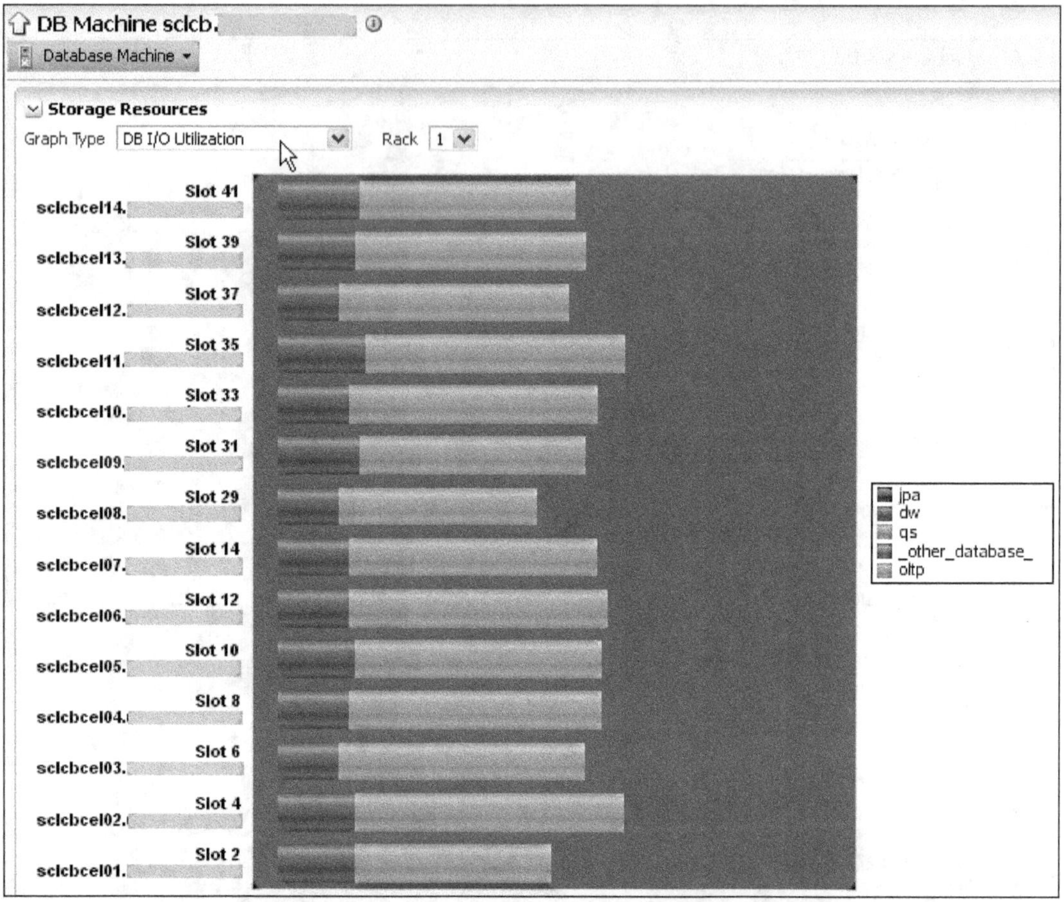


The initial graph that appears is **DB I/O Utilization**. This shows the I/O utilization of the databases across all of the `14` storage servers in the full Exadata Database Machine rack. We can see that the **OLTP** database is using the most I/O across all the storage servers. There is a way to control the I/O resource available to each database. This is via the **I/O Resource Manager** (**IORM**) that we will see soon.

From the **Graph Type** drop-down box, select **Disk Group Space Allocation**.

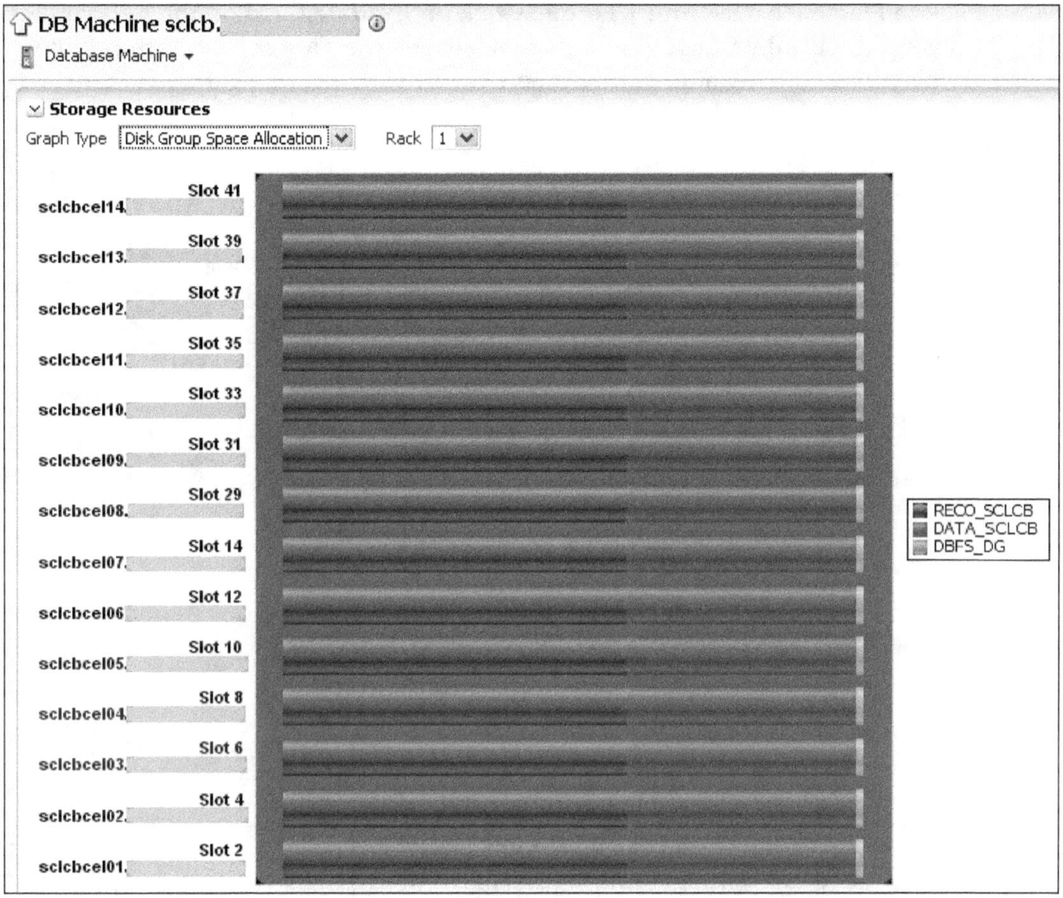


This graph shows us the distribution of the **ASM Disk Group** across all of the storage servers in the full Exadata Database Machine rack. Here we can see that three disk groups have been set up.

# Exadata grid

Move back to **Database Machine | Home**. Click on **Exadata Grid** on the left panel. This brings up the **Exadata Grid** home page. Collapse the **Target Navigation** panel that is displayed on the left side of the screen.

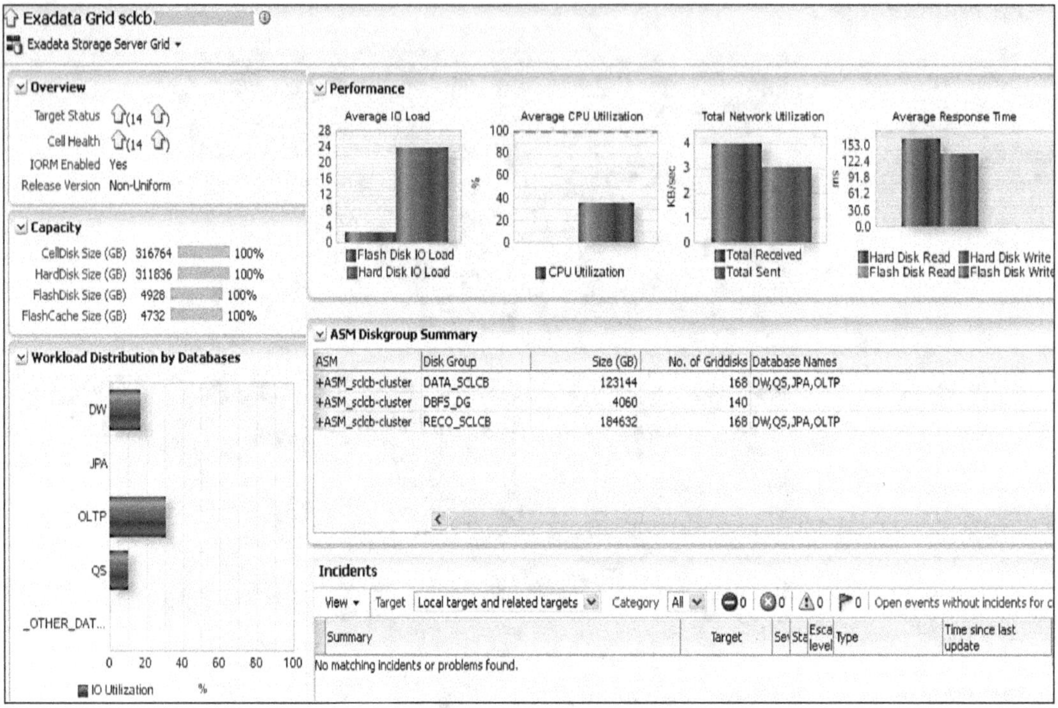


On the **Exadata Storage Server Grid** home page, you can see an overview of the storage cell's status and performance. An up or down status is displayed for all the 14 cells, along with **Cell Health**, whether **IORM** is enabled, **Cell Disk capacity**, and **Flash Disk** and **Flash Cache size** in GB.

A graph on **Database Workload Distribution** shows that the `OLTP` database is taking up 30 percent of the workload. The other graphs displayed are performance-related, such as **Average IO Load, Average CPU Utilization, Total Network Utilization,** and **Average Response Time**—including **Flash Disk Read** and **Write** information. **Average IO Load** has been introduced in Enterprise Manager Cloud Control 12*c* as a new metric specifically for Exadata storage cells.

**ASM Diskgroup Summary** is displayed in a tabular format, showing **ASM Disk Groups**, their **Sizes** in GB, and the databases that are using these disk groups.

**Incidents**, if they have occurred, are also seen at the bottom of the screen. Now select **Exadata Storage Server Grid | Performance** from the menu.

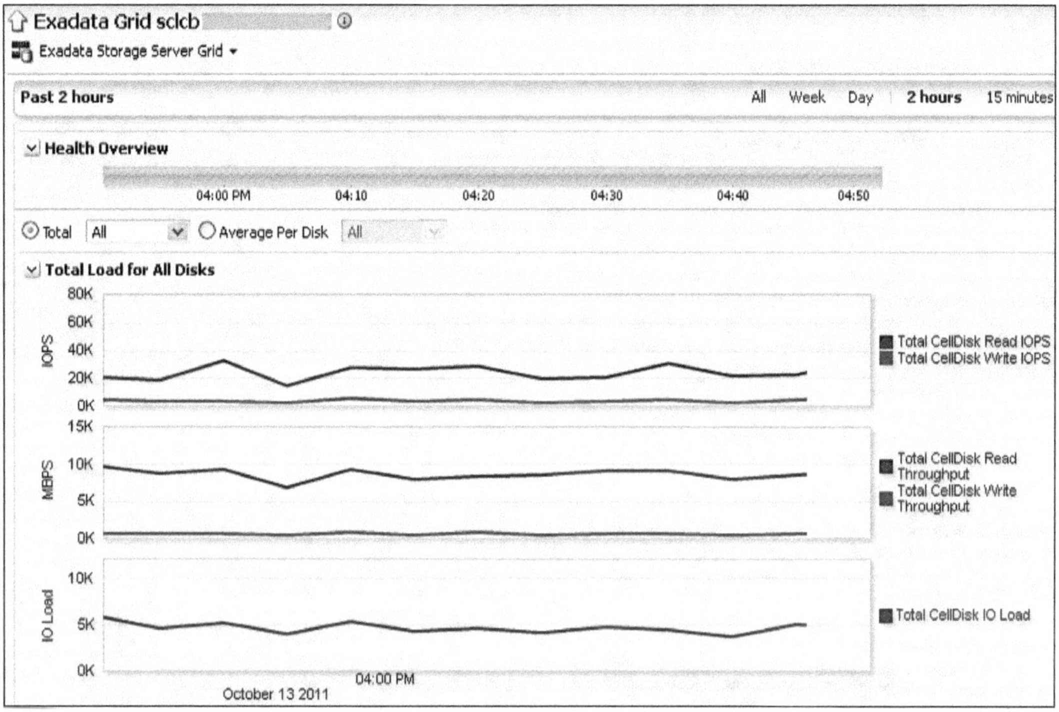


This is the **Storage Server Grid Performance** page. By default, the information for the **Past 2 hours** is shown. This can be changed to the past **15 minutes** or the past **Day**, **Week**, or **Month**.

The **Health Overview** bar results for the specified period of time are displayed. Underneath that, the **Total Load for All Disks** information can be seen, with separate graphs for total **IOPS** (read/write), throughput (read/write), and **IO Load**. You can choose either hard disks or flash disks, and show either the total or the average values on these graphs.

In the next section, shown in the following screenshot, the **Average Response Time** graph for **Hard Disks** or **Flash Disks** is displayed, followed by graphs that show **CPU**, **Memory**, and **Network** utilization, and also the **Flash Cache Usage**, **Throughput**, and **IOPS** graphs. Finally, there is **Workload Distribution by Databases** over time.

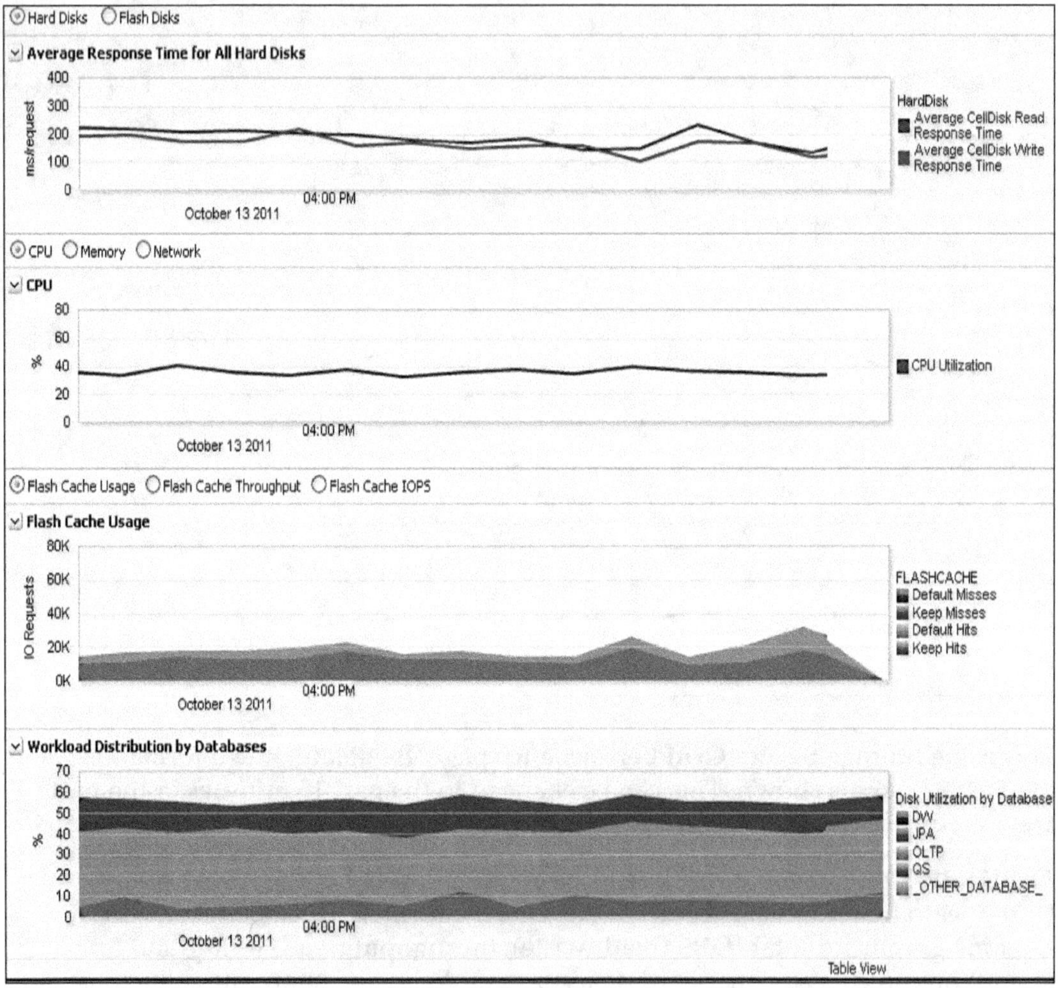

Move back to the **Exadata Grid** home page and select **Exadata Storage Server Grid | Administration | Manage IO Resource**.

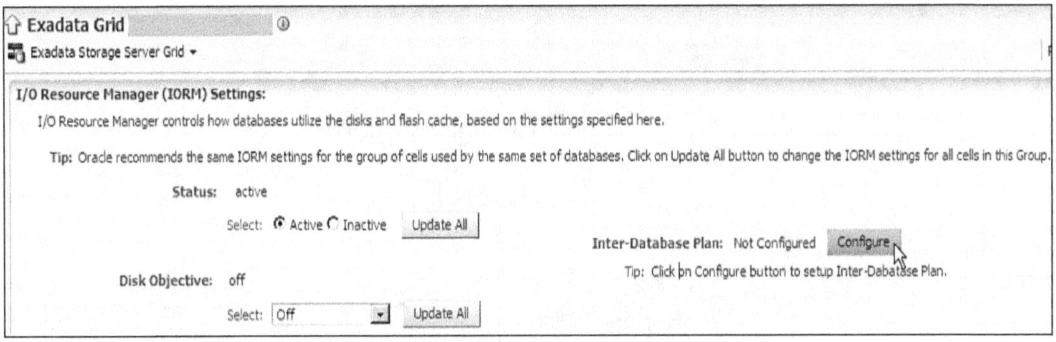


On the **I/O Resource Manager (IORM) Settings** page, you can control how the databases will utilize the disks and flash cache. **Disk Objective** can be set to **Auto**, **Low Latency**, **Balanced**, or **High Throughput**. This is the **IORM** objective.

Note that all storage cells used by a database are automatically placed in a group. The **Update All** button will modify the **IORM** settings for all the cells in a group used by the same set of databases.

You can define a new **Inter-Database Plan** instance by clicking on the **Configure** button. In the plan, you can enter the **Database Name** and the **Disk Utilization** limit, or the **Disk I/O Allocations** as a percentage. In this way, the I/O of any database can be controlled across the storage cells. For example, you can allocate 15 percent of **Disk I/O** to the `saitest` database and 70 percent to all the other databases placed on the same storage cell group.

Administration of storage cells is also possible via Enterprise Manager Cloud Control 12*c*. This can be done at the cell group level. It is possible to issue **Cell Control Command-Line Interface** (**CellCLI**) commands to a group of cells from within Enterprise Manager itself. This is done by selecting **Exadata Storage Server Grid | Administration | Execute Cell Command**.

# Infiniband network

Move back to the **Exadata Grid** home page and reopen the **Target Navigation** panel. Select the **IB Network** component from the hierarchy.

This brings up the **Infiniband Network** home page.

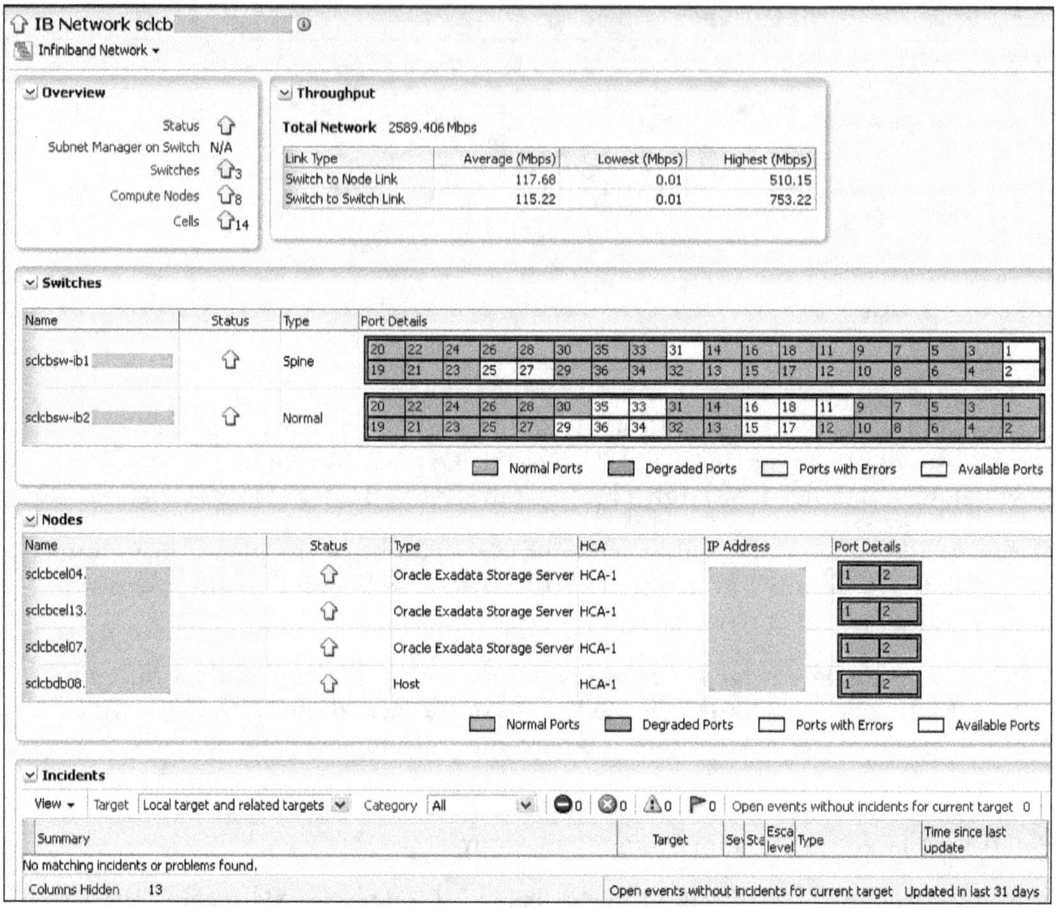


Infiniband is used by the Exadata Database Machine for communication between the database servers and the storage servers, as well as for RAC Interconnect communications.

On the **IB Network** home page, the status as well as the performance of the Infiniband network can be seen. The total number of switches, compute nodes, and storage cells connected to the IB network are displayed in the overview.

The **Throughput** section gives a glimpse of its high performance, showing the MBPS speed for the switch to node link and the switch to switch link.

In the **Switches** section, the port details are tabled graphically for each switch, including normal, degraded, or available ports, or those with errors.

Next, the **Nodes** section shows the storage servers with their IP addresses, port details, and **HCA** (**Host Channel Adapter**) details. You can scroll down to see the full list of the storage cells. At a glance, you can see which of these ports are normal, degraded, have errors, and so on. Placing your cursor on any of the ports, either in the **Nodes** section or the **Switches** section, displays a pop-up box showing the peer port, the errors, and the throughput.

Any **Incidents** associated with the IB network can be seen at the bottom of the screen.

Having all this information at your fingertips helps a lot in real, day-to-day administration activities, especially in troubleshooting.

Now, select **Infiniband Network** | **Performance** from the menu.

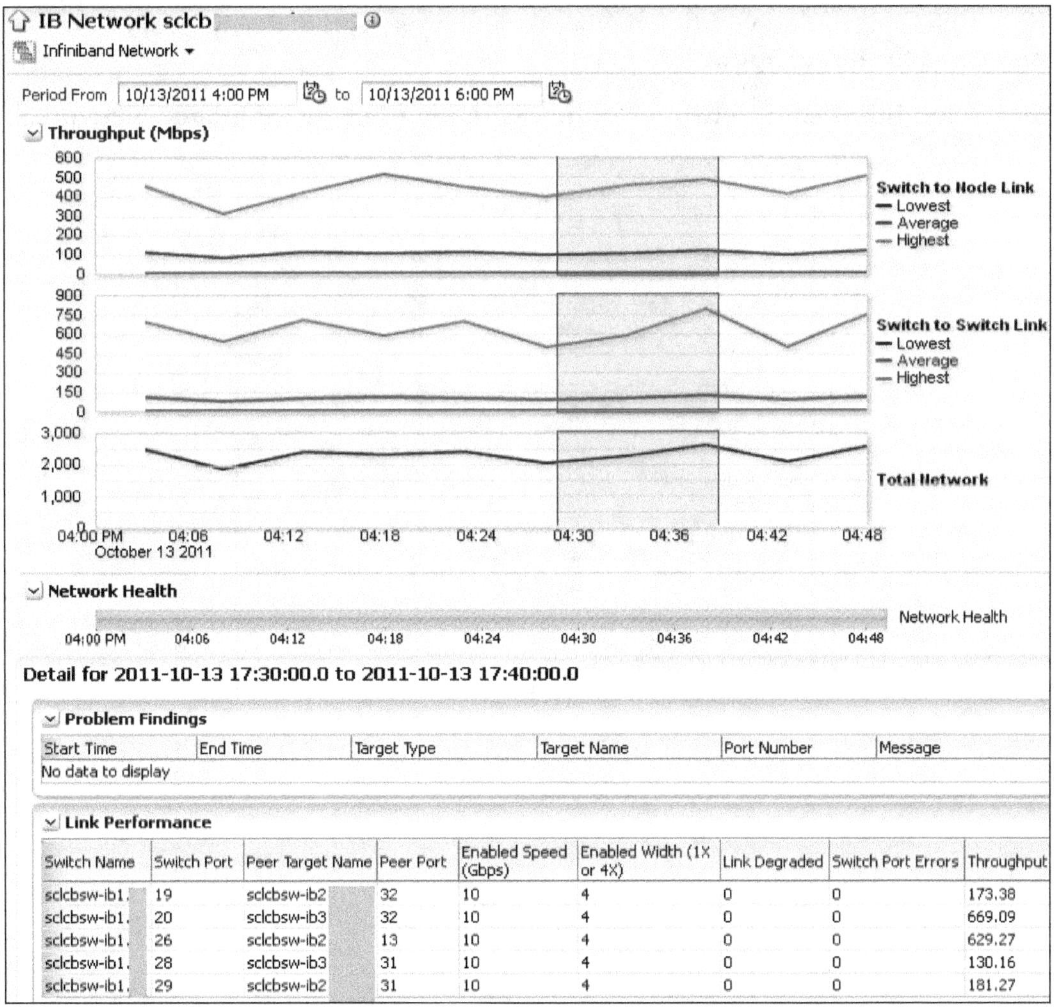

The **Infiniband Network Performance** page allows you to inspect the performance of the network over a time period you specify.

The **Throughput (Mbps)** information is seen in a graphical format for **Switch to Node Link**, **Switch to Switch Link**, as well as for **Total Network**. Three graph lines are visible, which correspond to the **Lowest**, **Average**, and **Highest** speeds. You can move the slider along the graph, and the details for that period of time are displayed in the **Detail** section in the lower part of the screenshot.

We can also see a **Network Health** timeline showing the overall health of the network over a certain period of time.

In the **Detail** section, there is a list of problem findings pertaining to targets and port numbers. Another table shows **Link Performance**, including the switch names and the enabled speeds and widths, whether the link was degraded, any errors were found, and the throughput.

Now, select **Infiniband Network | Administration** from the **Infiniband Network** home page's menu.

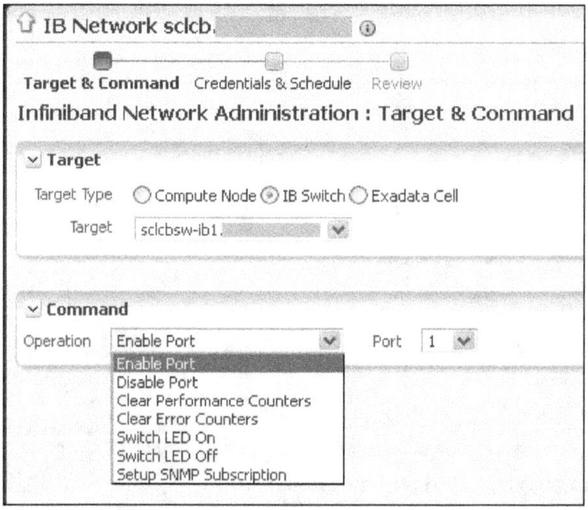

Select **IB Switch** as **Target Type**, and then choose the actual IB switch name from the **Target** drop-down box.

In the **Command** section, it is possible to choose operations, such as **Enable Port**, **Disable Port**, **Clear Performance Counters**, **Clear Error Counters**, **Switch LED On**, **Switch LED Off**, and **Setup SNMP Subscription**. These administration commands can then be scheduled to be executed after specifying the credentials.

A topological view of the Infiniband network is also available by selecting **Infiniband Network** | **Topology**. This view includes switch and port-level details.

Other Exadata components, such as the ILOM (Integrated Lights Out Manager), Cisco switch, KVM (Keyboard, Video, Mouse), and PDU (Power Distribution Unit), also appear in the left panel of the Exadata Database Machine. There are certain common metrics that are monitored for these components, such as fan failure, temperature out of range, and power supply failure.

Other specific metrics include unauthorized SNMP access and configuration change tracking for the Cisco switch. For the KVM, you can also monitor if it is powered on/off, and whether the server that is connected to KVM has been added or removed.

In the case of the PDU, power consumption by Exadata components is monitored. Early warning is provided for any failure due to an impending threshold. The electric current being used by Exadata equipment in the rack is also monitored.

> For most of the performance metrics of the Exadata components, such as the Infiniband switches, the `/opt/oracle.SupportTools/em/` directory on every compute node should be readable by all Unix users. If not, you need to change the permissions by issuing the following command as root:
>
> ```
> chmod u+r /opt/oracle.SupportTools/em/
> ```
>
> After this command is issued, the Enterprise Manager Cloud Control 12*c* agent needs to be bounced on each compute node.

# Database performance pages

Next, move to the **Performance** home page of one of the databases on the Exadata machine. On the **Performance** home page, click on the **I/O** tab. This section is shown in the following screenshot:

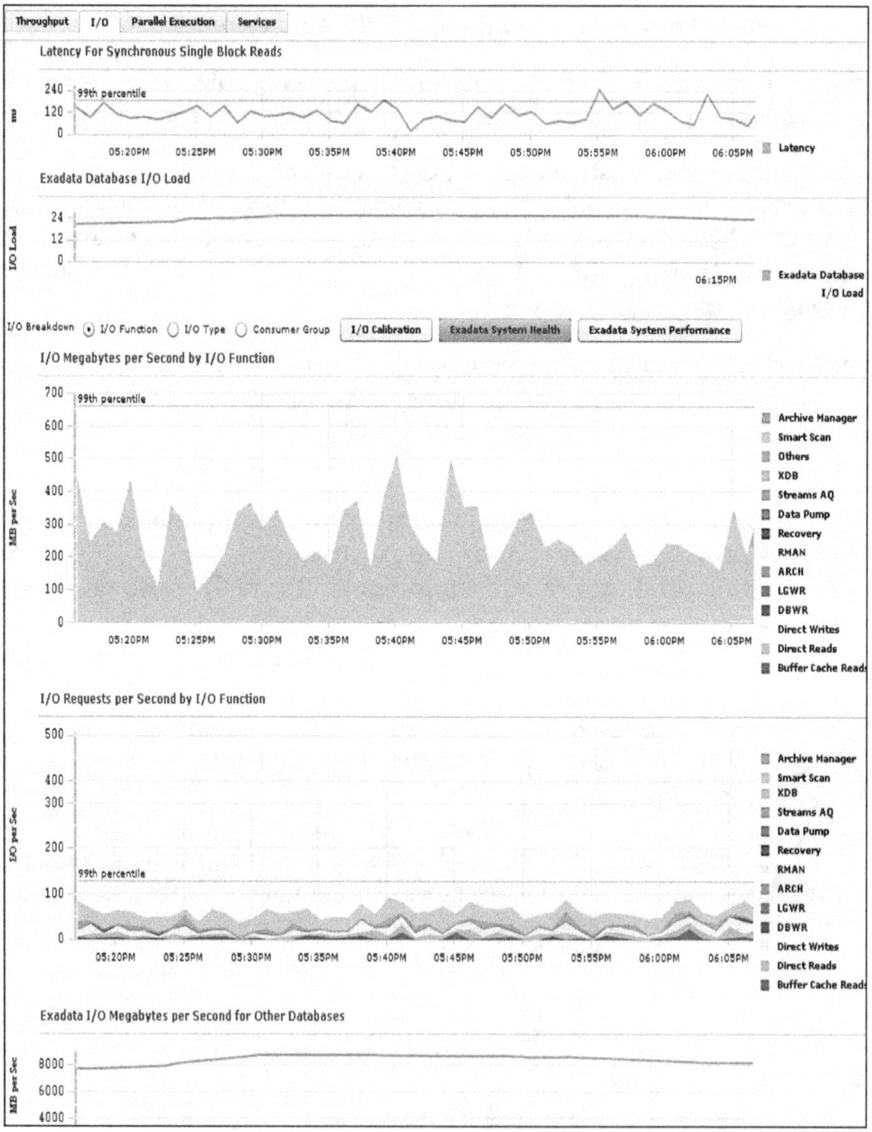

Exadata-specific information will be seen if the database is placed on an Exadata machine. For example, there is a graph showing **Exadata Database I/O Load** information over a period of time. Two Exadata-related buttons are also visible—**Exadata System Health** and **Exadata System Performance**.

Exadata information regarding cell smart scans can also be seen in the two I/O performance graphs (**I/O Megabytes per Second** and **I/O Requests per Second**). This is seen as the I/O function **Smart Scan**.

Since the **Exadata System Health** button is displayed in red (it is normally green), it means there is a problem that needs to be examined further. Click on the **Exadata System Health** button.

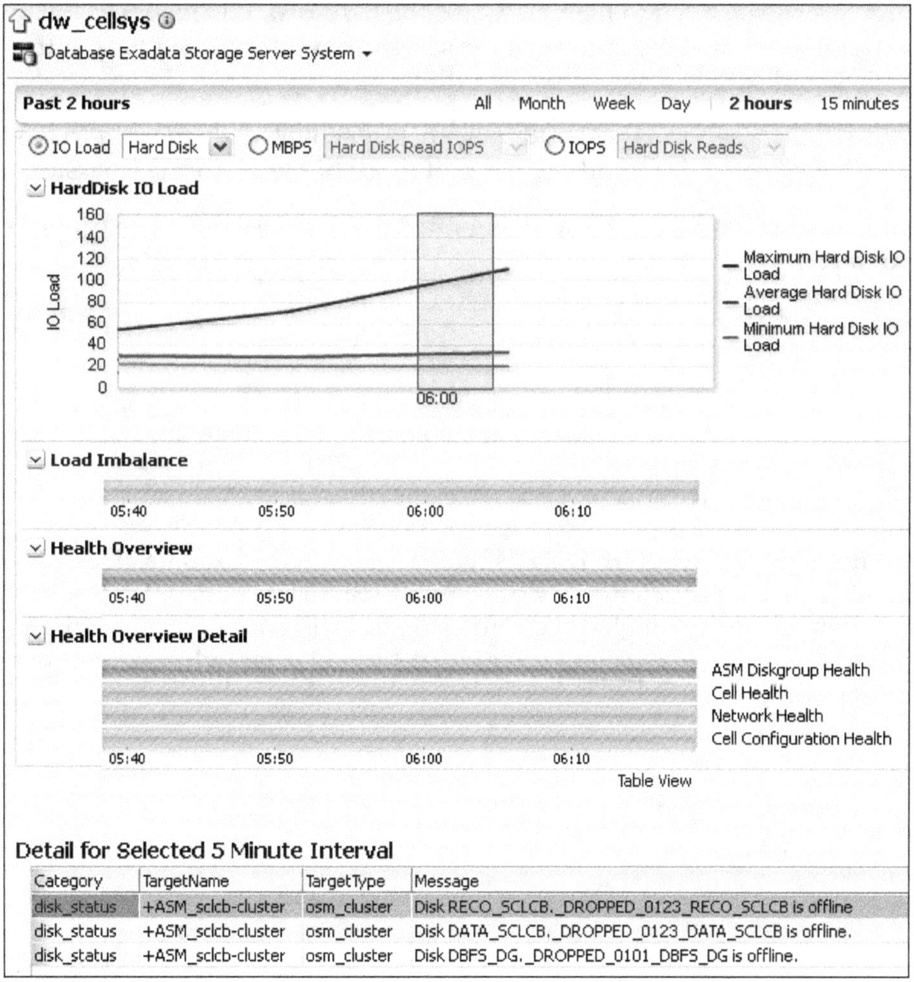

The **Exadata Health** page shows the **Hard Disk I/O Load** information for over a period of time in a line graph showing the minimum, average, and maximum loads. The slider can be moved across the graph to show the details for the selected five-minute interval, which is displayed at the bottom of the screen.

The most important bar graphs on this page are **Load Imbalance**, **Health Overview**, and **Health Overview Detail**. The **Health Overview Detail** graph shows the **ASM Diskgroup Health**, **Cell Health**, **Network Health**, and **Cell Configuration Health** parameters.

It is observed from the **Health Overview Detail** graph that **ASM Diskgroup Health** has an issue, and this has also affected the overall Exadata health.

The slider has been moved to the time when the hard disk I/O load was the highest, and the **Detail** section at the bottom of the screen shows the main cause of the issue—some of the ASM diskgroups are offline.

So we can see that the **Exadata Health** page has effectively helped us in triage, that is, we have been able to find out the root cause of the performance issue.

Move to **Performance** | **SQL Monitoring** from the database menu. Select one of the SQL statements in the list.

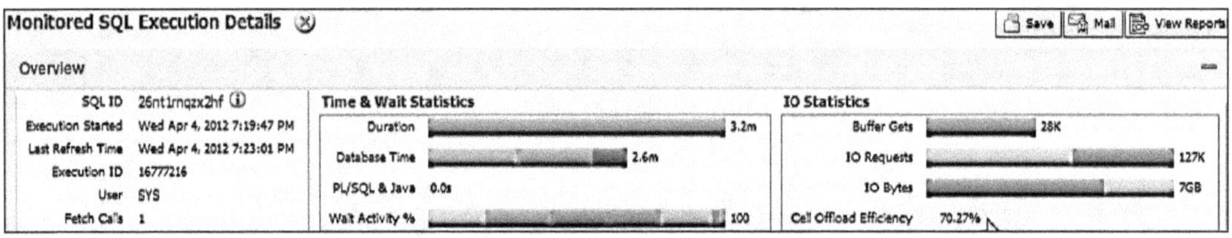


The **Monitored SQL Execution Details** screen is seen to be Exadata aware. It displays **Cell Offload Efficiency** as one of the **IO Statistics** parameters for this SQL statement. Obviously, the higher the **Cell Offload Efficiency** percentage the better, because it means that the database has offloaded the data search and processing to the Exadata storage server.

## Total capabilities

We have seen that Enterprise Manager Cloud Control 12*c* offers an integrated hardware and software view of the Exadata Database Machine. The hardware view on the database machine home page displays a schematic diagram of the compute nodes, storage servers, and the Infiniband/Ethernet switches. It also displays incidents for the hardware components.

Besides the hardware view, Enterprise Manager Cloud Control 12*c* also offers a software or system view of Exadata, showing the availability and performance of the databases and services, and the manner in which the databases are consuming CPU and IO bandwidth. Incidents are also raised for the software, including the database, ASM, and cluster.

There is a dashboard available at **Database Machine** | **Members** | **Dashboard**. The related incidents can be seen on this page. There is also a topological view, where you can see the entire database machine topology. This is accessed via **Database Machine** | **Members** | **Topology**.

There is also a configuration view available for Exadata. If you move to **Database Machine** | **Configuration** | **Last Collected**, you can see the configuration details of all the Exadata components, including all the compute nodes, the Exadata grid (storage servers), the Infiniband network, the configuration of the databases, and so on.

All the Exadata components can be monitored separately, but it is much easier and more effective to monitor the Exadata Database Machine as one. This is done by setting up an Exadata service so that you can have an overall view of the Exadata components. Expected service levels can be set up based on both availability and performance, and **Service Level Agreements** (**SLAs**) can be tracked. There is also an executive service dashboard available that shows all the Exadata services on one page, and allows the business owners to monitor the availability and performance of the Exadata system. You can set up this dashboard by following the My Oracle Support (MOS) support Note ID 1458346.1: *Guide to a create a performance monitoring dashboard report for DB Machine targets discovered by Enterprise Manager Cloud Control 12c.*

Synthetic tests can be set up to run from Beacons in Enterprise Manager Cloud Control 12*c*, which could be endpoints, such as a branch office or a user's workstation. You can set up a topology showing the service, its components, and their relationships. Once this is done, root cause analysis by Enterprise Manager Cloud Control 12*c* can be used to quickly find out the cause of a service issue. For example, a fan failure may have caused a KVM component failure, which in turn caused a KVM system failure, and this in turn caused the KVM service and the Exadata aggregate service to fail.

The new consolidation planner in Enterprise Manager Cloud Control 12*c* can be used to plan for migrations to Exadata. Suitable applications in use by the company can be identified for consolidation to the Exadata Database Machine.

Once identified, the applications need to be thoroughly tested on the Exadata platform before being moved over to production in Exadata. This testing is necessary, since moving to Exadata is a major infrastructure change; it involves a different platform, a different storage system, and also a new version of the database (Oracle 11.2), besides being an RAC database. These changes will be new, especially for those moving from an older version of a database that may have been a single-instance database.

When creating a test database on Exadata, it is possible to mask confidential data using the **Enterprise Manager Data Masking Pack**. The application can then be fully tested at the database layer by using the database replay feature of the Real Application Testing (RAT) option, whereby the entire database workload is captured from production, brought over as Capture Files to the test Exadata system, and then replayed concurrently. This enables any regressed SQL statements to be identified, and its performance to be fixed, before moving to production.

Once in production, for day-to-day diagnosis and tuning of the Oracle databases on Exadata, all the benefits are available, including the AWR, ADDM, ASH, and the tuning advisor and access advisor. SQL profiles offer extra advice to the optimizer and are therefore able to improve the performance of even packaged SQL. SQL parallelization advice is also given, and as a result you are able to use SQL parallelization effectively on Exadata—thereby unlocking the full value of a massively parallel machine. This is done via the **Database Diagnostics and Tuning Pack**.

The DBLM Pack allows deep configuration management of the Exadata machine. You can store the entire Exadata Database Machine configuration as a gold standard, and perform comparisons between whole database machines, individual compute nodes, storage cells, or databases. You can check the history of the configuration changes that were made. Configuration standards and security standards can also be set and enforced for the Exadata database machine.

Using the same DBLM Pack, you are also able to get patch recommendations from My Oracle Support for the databases on Exadata, create patch plans, and apply one or more patches on multiple databases, using either in-place patching or the new out-of-place patching (using a new Oracle home). This applies to both single and RAC databases that have been set up on Exadata. This automation of the patching process increases administrator productivity and also decreases downtime considerably, by using the new, automated out-of-place method.

The Cloud Management Pack for database builds on the functionality of the DBLM Pack, and allows your Exadata Database Machine to be used as a Database as a Service (DBaaS) cloud machine, with the complete cloud features of self-service, metering, and chargeback.

# Summary

In this chapter, we have examined the use of Enterprise Manager Cloud Control 12c in detail, for monitoring and managing the Exadata Database Machine. Discovery is done with greater ease, and the entire Exadata system can be monitored (both the hardware and software). SLAs can be set up for Exadata systems. The management of a number of Exadata components is possible via the Enterprise Manager interface, including, but not limited to, the RAC databases and storage servers.

Partitioned Exadata Database Machine Racks can also be monitored and managed by Enterprise Manager Cloud Control 12*c* using the Exadata plugin. At the time of writing, there is no unified topology view in the case of multirack Exadata Database Machines. However, each rack can be discovered, monitored, and managed individually. Expansion racks or SPARC SuperClusters are currently not supported by the Exadata plugin.

In conclusion, Enterprise Manager Cloud Control 12*c* has vastly improved in the areas of discovery, monitoring, and the complete management of the Oracle Exadata Database Machines in your enterprise. In addition to what we have seen in this chapter, deeper hardware monitoring of the Exadata Database Machine can be achieved—if required—via Enterprise Manager Ops Center 12*c*. This goes down to the **Field Replacement Unit** (**FRU**) level of all the components with the serial numbers and part numbers, and also the energy information, such as the electricity usage levels and trends, firmware levels, and updates of hardware components, among others.

The **Auto Service Requests** (**ASR**) phone-home capabilities (for My Oracle Support purposes) can also be achieved via Enterprise Manager Ops Center 12*c*. An Internet connection would be required for the ASR facility, since it would notify Oracle Support in case of any hardware failure in any component in Exadata, allowing Oracle Support to dispatch an engineer along with the **Field Replacement Unit** (**FRU**). This is provided you have Oracle Premier Support for the Exadata Database Machines. The ASR Manager (or Enterprise Manager Ops Center 12*c*, if it is used, since it has ASR capabilities) is placed on a server that has a direct Internet connection, or via a proxy with a username and password.

In the next chapter, we will have a look at various real-life examples and case studies of actual Oracle customers to show how they have benefited from using Oracle Enterprise Manager Cloud Control 12*c*.

# 11

# Real-life Examples and Case Studies, and It's a Wrap: The Future is the Cloud

Oracle Enterprise Manager has a number of business benefits. First of all, it offers a centralized view of the entire hardware and software stack in a company, including the detailed configuration. It enables you to automatically discover internal IT assets, manage them, monitor their resource utilization, and as a result, helps to reduce underutilization of assets. A consolidation planner is also provided in this version, to plan a move to consolidated physical or virtual machines, and full testing of the database workload can be performed on the target systems to find out if there is any SQL regression that could impact your application's performance.

Oracle Enterprise Manager improves manageability of many complex systems and allows automation of several processes such as provisioning, patching, diagnosis, tuning, configuration management, and change management via the Database Lifecycle Management Pack. It therefore considerably increases administrator productivity. Software can be deployed from standardized configurations, such as gold copies that are set up as per company standards, therefore reducing risk.

Security and configuration compliance rules, standards, and frameworks are provided in an out of the box fashion, and help you understand how security-compliant your databases, middleware, and hosts are.

Through Enterprise Manager tools such as RUEI, real user experience is captured from network traffic and can be analyzed in terms of the business benefits, such as improving a website's conversion rate, decreasing the bounce rate, and increasing customer satisfaction.

We will now look at some customer case studies to understand how Oracle Enterprise Manager has benefited these customers.

# Case study – telecom

In the normal course of business, a large telecommunications company in Australia initiates numerous projects each year to create new services and applications for its clients. Each project needs database servers to be provisioned, so the Unix and database teams are engaged in building servers, installing database software, and creating the required application databases. The Project Managers normally book their time in advance.

The database team waits for the server to be built and allocated to them (that is, the login details) by the Unix team, and then they scp (secure copy) the Oracle software to the box, and install the Enterprise Edition of the Oracle database in a new Oracle home, making sure only the licensed database options were installed—using the Oracle Universal Installer.

This would be followed by the creation of the actual database using the Oracle **Database Configuration Assistant** (**DBCA**) utility. The database would need to be configured as per the company database standards, such as the names of tablespaces, standard extent sizes for small, medium, and large tables, use of **Automatic Storage Management** (**ASM**), and a **Flash Recovery Area**.

The same installation procedure needs to be followed on development, test, staging, and production servers. If a **Real Application Cluster** (**RAC**), multiple-instance database was required by the project, the installation procedure would necessarily be more complex and time consuming—since it would involve the installation of **Oracle Clusterware**, ASM, as well as the database software on hardware that has been set up with shared storage and an interconnect.

After the database installation, the project team would request database backups to be set up using **Recovery Manager** (**RMAN**) for both single instance and multiple instance databases. If **Disaster Recovery** (**DR**) was required by the project, a standby database using Oracle Data Guard would need to be created using a complex manual process. And to complete this process, all this would need to be tested—the backup as well as the disaster recovery.

In all, the work of the database team would consist of long hours installing the database software and creating a database for many different application projects, in a monotonous routine prone to human error due to its manual and repetitive nature.

In a major futuristic project of transformation of the IT infrastructure, 3000 databases, both single instance and RAC, were to be built over two years on over a thousand Solaris servers. There were also multiple database teams in the company over various locations in the country, as well as several partners to whom some of the DBA management tasks had been outsourced, adding to the complexity of the task.

Impressed by the capabilities of the Oracle Enterprise Manager product for database provisioning, the Central Database Team Manager decided that the right solution approach was to create prepatched gold images of the database software and database, and use the provisioning mechanisms to install the gold images on new targets. This would apply both to single instance and RAC databases. These provisioning capabilities are currently part of the Enterprise Manager's **Database Lifecycle Management** Pack (**DBLM**).

A centralized Enterprise Manager installation was architectured with multiple OMS servers, a separate repository server, and a load balancer. Separate administrator accounts for each DBA team were created. A centralized Software Library was set up and the necessary gold images were put into effect. All the DBA teams in the company were requested to use Oracle Enterprise Manager whenever they wanted to deploy Oracle database software or create an Oracle database.

With Enterprise Manager now used for this purpose, the time to deploy was reduced from approximately four hours to under one hour. This resulted in considerable savings in **Operational Expenditure** (**OPEX**) budgets.

Besides the obvious advantages of time saving, it was seen that controlling the gold images assisted the central database department in enforcing company-wide database standards. The Senior DBAs in each team could now hand over the repetitive task of deployment to the junior DBAs and remain assured that the chances for error were low, no standards would be missed out and a consistent build would result every time. The process of provisioning was now reliable, repeatable, skill agnostic (lack of RAC skills did not matter), and adhered fully to standards.

An independent consulting firm conducted an assessment of the use of Oracle Enterprise Manager by the company, and found that this management tool helped the company to achieve considerable financial benefits. The total benefit from the deployment was estimated to be around 1.9 million in US dollars.

This benefit was increased by the proactive management capability of Oracle Enterprise Manager. Administrators were alerted to issues before the critical stage was reached, and they could take proactive measures to avoid further deterioration of the situation.

The other great benefit was that Enterprise Manager monitored the database disk space utilization and alerted management (through reports) if the space utilization was too low as opposed to the allocated space for that project. Since several databases used SAN systems, which were quite expensive, and tended to over-allocate database storage at the time of project creation, this meant that the company could pinpoint those projects and ask for the space to be reallocated to other uses such as backup, therefore reducing the overall storage cost.

Due to the automation provided by Oracle Enterprise Manager, the development and maintenance of in-house scripts was vastly reduced, thus increasing administrative productivity in yet another way. This allowed the company to increase the number of databases managed, without increasing the DBA headcount.

Expensive DBA time no longer needed to be spent in manually creating, setting up, and testing RMAN scripts for each new database, since this could be done easily by the Enterprise Manager RMAN wizard for any version of the Oracle database currently being used in the company. The Enterprise Manager's internal job scheduler was used instead of setting up `crontab` in UNIX. Backup and recovery could now be performed in a similar manner across databases.

Similar benefits also applied to Oracle Data Guard, where the setup could be done using the Enterprise Manager Data Guard wizard instead of the manual method, reducing the time taken to create a standby database, and preventing manual errors. Furthermore, the transport and application of production database logs to the standby database could now be monitored using Oracle Enterprise Manager, removing the need for the older generation monitoring scripts. Using the Enterprise Manager plugins, third-party hardware such as load balancers, storage such as Netapp Filers and EMC, and third-party databases such as Microsoft SQL Server could also be monitored.

# Case study – pharmaceutical

In the case of this large pharmaceutical company, they have an installation of 2000 Oracle databases of different versions, on 500 hosts having multiple platforms. The company decided to apply quarterly **CPUs** (**Critical Patch Updates**) recommended by Oracle, as soon as they were released by Oracle Support.

Applying patches manually to databases is a labor-intensive task, and takes up a lot of the DBA time, especially when there are so many databases, and a limited number of DBAs. Even if counting only around one hour per patch application, applying the patch quarterly to 2000 databases adds up to a lot of man-hours per year, and becomes prohibitively expensive.

The company decided to use the Patch Automation facility of Oracle Enterprise Manager, which is part of the DBLM Pack. This was used to apply CPUs, one-off patches, and patchsets to the 2000 databases.

For any new server deployment, gold images with previously patched database software were used in the cloning process, further reducing the need for patching (until the next CPU came along).

The patches were selected by the DBAs, placed in a patch plan, and validated before deployment. This reduced the failure rate per operation. The patches were then deployed on multiple database homes at a convenient schedule. The one hour (approximately) for manual patch application was reduced to just one minute.

The entire quarterly patching process was automated in this manner, and this resulted in significant savings in time and money for the company.

# Case study – computer manufacturer

This large computer manufacturer wanted to maintain high levels of availability of their IT infrastructure. As a result, they started to use Oracle Enterprise Manager to carry out proactive monitoring of more than 700 production databases, including single instance as well as RAC databases.

The Diagnostics Pack of Enterprise Manager is used to identify the worst-performing SQL statements in each database so that the DBAs can focus on them for tuning purposes. Configuration management (a part of the DBLM Pack) is also used, enabling detailed configuration capture of Oracle software, the operating system, the host, as well as third-party software. Configurations can be compared, and a history of changes is also available.

Using Oracle Enterprise Manager increased the administrator's productivity by 20 percent in the case of this company, and database issues could be diagnosed a lot faster and proactively. As a result, continuous uptime could be delivered for the critical online applications in use.

Enterprise Manager was found to be extremely stable, and the company achieved immediate business benefits by the faster deployment of this technology across all their systems.

Due to the configuration management feature of Oracle Enterprise Manager, the administrators were able to pinpoint any configuration changes in the hardware, OS, or database software that were causing any issues. This was complemented by the database diagnostics features.

As a result, the company achieved 100 percent uptime at the infrastructure level, which was an amazing feat. There was zero downtime.

# Case study – online store

A large online store implemented Oracle Enterprise Manager **Real User Experience Insight** (**RUEI**), in an effort to understand what the users were experiencing. They set up RUEI to capture and analyze all user traffic coming from their internet website, selling a variety of specialized products.

In the Christmas holiday period, one particular product proved to be a bestseller. However, the marketing department of the company had decided to remove the printed manual from the product, and replace it with an online manual. They did this without informing the IT department that managed the website.

Since the product was a big hit, there were many users who received the delivery of the product and wanted to download the online manual. The manual had been placed on the same web server as the online store, and as a result the multiple concurrent downloads that were happening started to degrade the performance of the online store.

The customers who were browsing the store at that time had selected an item in their shopping cart and were about to check out, when they found the website had become unresponsive. As a result, 27 percent of the online customers cancelled their transaction and left the website.

Since the company had RUEI up and running, a user flow or transaction funnel had been set up in RUEI, which included the checkout process and the final order confirmation. The conversion rate was being monitored continuously. As soon as the users started to drop out, the conversion rate decreased and the funnel started to shrink. This alerted the IT department, who immediately investigated the cause of the funnel shrink. The user session analysis in RUEI pinpointed the slow speed of the final transaction pages as the main cause for customer dissatisfaction and drop out.

The web administrators immediately swung into action, and found that the concurrent downloads of the online manual were causing the issue. So they stopped the downloads by removing the manual. The website performance improved immediately, and the rest of the customers were now able to complete their transactions. The transaction funnel increased in width again, and the 27 percent loss was curtailed before it got any larger.

As the next step, the IT department located the email addresses of the 27 percent of customers who could not complete the transactions. An apologetic email was sent by the marketing department to all those customers, along with a discount code so as to attract those customers to place their orders again. Consequently, the company regained most of the 27 percent loss it had incurred.

The real user monitoring provided by RUEI therefore helped the company in two ways—firstly by alerting the IT department immediately, and stopping a loss from getting worse, and secondly by capturing all real user information, so that the dissatisfied customers could be identified and then cajoled to shop again.

# Case study – financial institution

A large bank decided to design their future infrastructure by using modern platform architecture. A mixed applications stack was selected with Oracle comprising a major part of the stack. It was decided right at the start to focus on ease of management and automation, in order to reduce operational cost, and increase the business advantage for the bank.

Oracle Enterprise Manager was chosen to be the main management tool for the new Oracle infrastructure. This included diagnostics, tuning, configuration management, provisioning, and service-level monitoring. The extensible monitoring framework of Enterprise Manager would be used to include monitoring and configuration collection of infrastructure as well as business applications, as much as possible.

The intention was to use enterprise-level monitoring so as to respond quickly to any possible threat to uptime, using the warning thresholds to alert administrators before a critical threshold was reached.

Enterprise Manager Provisioning would help in implementation, and Enterprise Manager configuration and change management would enable standardization and compliance throughout the bank. Also, service-level monitoring would ensure that the service-level agreements for key customers were being met to their satisfaction.

The bank also wanted to ensure that their data center was in compliance with security best practices. Configuration management was required to ensure that all databases created and in operation were consistent with their gold configuration.

The ability to search configurations for compliance with best practices was also important. As an example, the configuration management capabilities could be used to identify those databases that did not have the latest CPU patch installed.

Configurations could be compared easily, a full change history of all configuration settings could be examined, and security policies enforced to make sure that the installations met with the best practices of the company. The bank was therefore able to adhere to regulatory standards, and manage complex compliance requirements with the help of Oracle Enterprise Manager.

In the provisioning space, Enterprise Manager was used for the automated provisioning of standard Linux operating system images on Bare Metal servers, as well as the provisioning of RAC clusters from gold images, thus ensuring compliance to standards.

The patching automation of Oracle Enterprise Manager was used to patch cluster databases and the OS with minimum downtime. Routine administrator tasks of provisioning and patching were greatly reduced in terms of time and effort, thus enabling administrators to concentrate on more important activities.

Manual errors were reduced, and the provisioning of Linux and RAC clusters became skill-agnostic and could be performed even by junior administrators. The provisioning on Bare Metal boxes from the OS level right up to the RAC cluster stage could happen unattended, and took just two hours to complete as opposed to the many days it took earlier.

# Case study – university

A well-known university wanted to centrally monitor and manage their different versions of application servers, databases, and custom targets on different platforms in their multiple data centers, as well as packaged applications such as PeopleSoft.

The main challenge in their case was the patching and updating of critical systems, which had to be done with a minimum of downtime. The University wanted to reduce effort and minimize the resources required, however, at the same time, security standards and compliance had to be observed.

Standard configurations needed to be maintained, and used for unattended deployment of new software. Once in production, any configuration drifts were to be detected and rectified. There was a strong requirement for standardized and automated procedures, for provisioning as well as patching.

Using Oracle Enterprise Manager, the university centralized the monitoring and management of its multiple data centers, which had a heterogeneous mix of hardware and software. A single Oracle Enterprise Manager console now had visibility of all the data centers.

Using gold images stored in the Software Library, and the deployment procedures of Enterprise Manager, the Oracle stack was able to be provisioned and patched in an automated manner. Enterprise Manager's configuration management capabilities were used for compliance with configuration/security standards, as well as the tracking of configuration changes.

As a result, the university became much more flexible and was able to meet burgeoning customer demands faster. It was able to deploy numerous new services in a single change window. A huge amount of administrator time was saved, due to the automation of provisioning, patching, and the assurance of compliance. Since the routine tasks were reduced or eliminated, the administrators could be reallocated to more important proactive and strategic tasks.

The use of Oracle Enterprise Manager and its threshold-driven monitoring was used to alert the administrators at the point of a warning threshold, enabling them to fix the issue before it became a serious problem. This resulted in vastly improved levels of availability for the data center infrastructure, and the critical applications that were so important to the university.

# Future of cloud computing

Cloud computing is a new paradigm that enables organizations to streamline their IT services, to internal as well as external customers. What is the prime reason it is so popular and sought after by businesses today? We feel this is because it drastically reduces the need for the IT middleman when a new deployment is required, enabling the end user or project team to use a self-service console and make a click-through request for the instant deployment of virtual machines, databases, schemas, or fully built applications.

Thus, the company increases its agility by empowering its project teams with the almost instantaneous creation of their required platforms. Projects can proceed faster without having to wait for the traditional provisioning of hardware and software by the IT department. Developers and QA staff can also instantly get the environments they need. Of course, the initial set up of the cloud infrastructure, and its ongoing maintenance is performed behind the scenes by the IT department. This is all actioned by Oracle Enterprise Manager.

The internal cloud that is set up in this manner can immediately justify its costs and prove the value of IT to the business by using the techniques of metering and chargeback. The end user gets things done via self-service, however all usage is metered and charged at established prices. Chargeback plans can be set up that charge for the initial deployment service, the type of deployment (amount of memory, disk, or CPUs) as well as the ongoing resource usage, and this may be up to granular levels such as the application service and the resources it uses.

Thus, it is possible for the IT department to firmly establish, in the eyes of the business users, the value of the infrastructure it provides. The business can no longer take the IT department for granted—since the business is now paying for the infrastructure and the services.

The actual foundation of the cloud is considered to be the grid, as envisioned by Oracle many years ago in the days of Oracle Database Server 10*g*. As a result of this, Oracle Enterprise Manager has a very strong foundation in the grid capabilities of provisioning, patching, compliance, as well as configuration and performance management. Oracle obviously has a good background in the cloud game, and its standing is now strengthened by the new Enterprise Manager Cloud Control 12*c*.

This product, in truth, is probably the most complete solution in the industry for cloud management. A single console can be used for the entire lifecycle of the cloud, including planning, testing, set up of the cloud infrastructure, deployment using self-service, metering and chargeback, and day-to-day monitoring and management of the cloud infrastructure.

Enterprise Manager Cloud Control 12*c* can be used for different kinds of cloud services, such as **Infrastructure as a Service** (**IaaS**) where Oracle **Virtual Machines** (**VMs**) containing databases or WebLogic servers, or entire assemblies, can be offered for deployment using a self-service console.

**Database as a Service** (**DBaaS**) clouds can be used to self-deploy databases, whereas **Platform as a Service** (**PaaS**) can be used to deploy Java applications, for Java as a service or middleware as a service. The deployment of all these clouds can be on either physical or virtual environments depending on the type of cloud service. It can be on Exadata or Exalogic, or non-Exadata or non-Exalogic.

The Oracle Cloud services offer abstraction, which may be the key to identifying a real cloud, rather than self-service or chargeback. This means replacing forty or fifty questions with just two or three questions. One example is the creation of an Oracle 11*g* database in DBaaS without going through the **DBCA** (**Database Configuration Assistant**) inputs, which are abstracted and hidden in the Enterprise Manager deployment procedures behind the scenes. This is where the real value lies.

The application to disk management capabilities means that Oracle Enterprise Manager can manage the entire stack, including the Oracle VM, operating system, database, application server, and packaged application. This is useful to enable Enterprise Manager to manage all aspects of the cloud infrastructure. It is also possible for the product to connect to non-Oracle systems via connectors and plugins, in order to monitor these systems, perform configuration management or exchange alert information with them, as in the case of helpdesk connectors.

In a heterogeneous cloud environment, where an external orchestration framework is being used to provide cloud services for a variety of different VMs, it is possible to use the RESTful APIs provided by Oracle Enterprise Manager for IaaS and DbaaS. The external framework can easily invoke the Enterprise Manager Cloud Management APIs.

Another important and distinguishing feature of the Oracle Cloud is the ability of Enterprise Manager to perform business-driven application management, via real user experience management and business transaction monitoring of the applications deployed on the cloud. Thus, there are many features that distinguish the Oracle Cloud services from the other cloud providers, and these features are provided by the powerful capabilities of Enterprise Manager Cloud Control 12*c*.

Carrying the Cloud paradigm further, driven by the goals of business agility, self-service, abstraction, automation, and accountability (pay for what you use), it is obvious that the future of IT computing is the Cloud—whether internal or external. That is why Enterprise Manager Grid Control was renamed as Enterprise Manager Cloud Control 12*c*.

# Summary

In this book, we have discussed the powerful capabilities of the new Enterprise Manager Cloud Control 12*c* to resolve data center chaos.

Cloud Control 12*c* aids in database performance management by guaranteeing performance levels proactively, using various innovative techniques for diagnosis and tuning.

It performs configuration management by automatically discovering components, collecting deep configuration data and allowing configuration comparisons, and searches of historical changes. Configuration and security compliance rules, and standards and frameworks are also provided in an out of the box fashion. Real-time change detection can be set up, if needed.

Cloud Control 12*c* performs automated provisioning of Oracle databases and software, enabling provisioning designers to use the new facility of profiles and locked-down procedures that make it easier to provision a fully configured gold copy of the Oracle software and database, and at the same time prevent provisioning operators from deviating from corporate standards. Middleware provisioning is available, as is the provisioning of entire operating systems.

The product allows automated patching of Oracle databases in the data center, thus making it possible to easily apply quarterly Critical Patch Updates (CPUs) or Patch Set Updates (PSUs). The patching designer selects from a list of recommended patches, creates a patch plan template, and publishes it to the patching operator, who then creates a patch plan to apply the patch on target databases. After the initial selection, the download, validation, and deployment of the patch (single or multiple) is fully automated, thus enabling mass deployment of patches to multiple database homes at prescheduled times. The new feature of out-of-place patching is included, as is the patch plan templates.

Cloud Control 12*c* allows capture of all database schema changes, and comparison of databases or schemas, to aid in propagation of changes across the development life cycle, and greatly assists in the auditing process as a result. The new change plans and capability of data comparisons for seed or configuration data are also included. It simplifies test data management by allowing subsetting of data, so smaller test databases can be created from a larger production database, thus saving on storage cost. A centralized masking template library can be set up, which aids in de-identification of any confidential data when copying data from production to test databases.

The product provides the new consolidation planner to plan for migration to the cloud, either with **P2V** (**Physical to Virtual**) or **P2P** (**Physical to Physical**) scenarios. It is used to manage the cloud with self-service, metering, and chargeback facilities built on top of the provisioning capabilities, for Oracle VM clouds in IaaS cloud scenarios as well as Oracle Database clouds in DBaaS cloud scenarios.

Cloud Control 12*c* aids in monitoring and managing the powerful Exadata system as a whole, both hardware and software components as well as the network infrastructure. It allows monitoring and management of sophisticated Oracle applications such as Oracle E-Business, Siebel, PeopleSoft, and Fusion applications, aiding in many administrative activities of these complex applications, besides allowing real user experience and configuration management of the applications. Cloud Control 12*c* also allows real user monitoring of any web application, pinpointing problematic pages or problematic Java modules, with integration to database diagnostics or Java diagnostics to perform a deeper diagnosis of the issue.

Various real-life examples and case studies of actual Oracle customers were discussed in this book, to show how these customers have benefited from using Oracle Enterprise Manager. Finally, we explored the future of cloud computing and Oracle's strong standing in the cloud game.

I hope you enjoyed reading this book as much as I enjoyed writing it.

# Index

## A



## B



## C

## D



## E

# F



# G



# H



# I



# J



# K



# L



# M

## R



## S

## T



## U



## V



## W



## Z

[PACKT] enterprise
PUBLISHING
professional expertise distilled

**Thank you for buying**

# Oracle Enterprise Manager Cloud Control 12*c*: Managing Data Center Chaos

## About Packt Publishing

Packt, pronounced 'packed', published its first book "Mastering phpMyAdmin for Effective MySQL Management" in April 2004 and subsequently continued to specialize in publishing highly focused books on specific technologies and solutions.

Our books and publications share the experiences of your fellow IT professionals in adapting and customizing today's systems, applications, and frameworks. Our solution based books give you the knowledge and power to customize the software and technologies you're using to get the job done. Packt books are more specific and less general than the IT books you have seen in the past. Our unique business model allows us to bring you more focused information, giving you more of what you need to know, and less of what you don't.

Packt is a modern, yet unique publishing company, which focuses on producing quality, cutting-edge books for communities of developers, administrators, and newbies alike. For more information, please visit our website: `www.packtpub.com`.

## About Packt Enterprise

In 2010, Packt launched two new brands, Packt Enterprise and Packt Open Source, in order to continue its focus on specialization. This book is part of the Packt Enterprise brand, home to books published on enterprise software – software created by major vendors, including (but not limited to) IBM, Microsoft and Oracle, often for use in other corporations. Its titles will offer information relevant to a range of users of this software, including administrators, developers, architects, and end users.

## Writing for Packt

We welcome all inquiries from people who are interested in authoring. Book proposals should be sent to author@packtpub.com. If your book idea is still at an early stage and you would like to discuss it first before writing a formal book proposal, contact us; one of our commissioning editors will get in touch with you.

We're not just looking for published authors; if you have strong technical skills but no writing experience, our experienced editors can help you develop a writing career, or simply get some additional reward for your expertise.

www.ingramcontent.com/pod-product-compliance
Lightning Source LLC
LaVergne TN
LVHW080014210926
848481LV00011B/3021

* 9 7 8 1 8 4 9 6 8 4 7 8 1 *